Hellenic Studies 92

The Purpled World

Recent Titles in the Hellenic Studies Series

http://chs.harvard.edu/chs/publications

THE PURPLED WORLD

MARKETING HAUTE COUTURE IN THE AEGEAN BRONZE AGE

by
Morris Silver

CENTER FOR HELLENIC STUDIES
Trustees for Harvard University
Washington, DC
Distributed by Harvard University Press
Cambridge, Massachusetts, and London, England
2023

The Purpled World: Marketing Haute Couture in the Aegean Bronze Age
By Morris Silver
Copyright © 2023 Center for Hellenic Studies, Trustees for Harvard University
All Rights Reserved.
Published by The Center for Hellenic Studies, Trustees for Harvard University,
   Washington, DC
Distributed by Harvard University Press, Cambridge, Massachusetts and London,
   England
Printed by Gasch Printing, Odenton, MD
Cover Design: Joni Godlove
Production: Jill Curry Robbins

ISBN: 978-0-674-27256-9
Library of Congress Control Number (LCCN): 2022940330

In memory of my wife Sondra
and in gratitude to my sons Ron and Gerry,
who every day have sought to find ways to raise my spirit
and restore my interest in exploring new ideas

Table of Contents

Part II. Luxury Textiles in the Bronze Age Aegean: Economic Aspects

Part III. Achaeans, Ahhiyawans, and Mycenaean Textile Trade in Anatolia

Part V. Questions of Aegean Textile Trade before the Trojan War and after the Mycenaean Palaces

List of Illustrations

Figures

Plates *(located after page 407)*

Image Credits

Cover Image: After Brecoulaki 2018, p. 403, fig. 14. Courtesy of the Department of Classics, University of Cincinnati.

Figures 1–2, 4–12, 14–16, 18, 21–38 and 40–41: Courtesy of the Corpus of Minoan and Mycenaean Seals.

Figure 3: After Mersereau 1993, fig. 26. Courtesy of the Archaeological Institute of America and the *American Journal of Archaeology*.

Figure 13: Drawing after after Evans 1921, fig. 310d.

Figure 17: After Marinatos 1988, fig. 3. Drawing by L. Papageorgiou. Courtesy of Nanno Marinatos.

Figure 19: After G. Maraghiannis et al, *Antiquités crétoises* (1911), vol. 2, pl. 21.

Figure 20: After Davis and Stocker 2016, p. 641, fig. 10a. Drawing of impression by T. Ross. Courtesy of the Department of Classics, University of Cincinnati.

Figure 39: After Kontorli-Papadopolou, L., Th. Papadopoulos, and G. Owens 2005, fig. 2. Courtesy of Professor Emeritus Thanasis J. Papadopoulos, University of Ioannina.

Figure 42: Betancourt 2007, p. 17. Courtesy of Costis Davaras and INSTAP Academic Press, Philadelphia, PA.

Plate 1: Bridgeman Images, DGA508880. © NPL - DeA Picture Library / G. Nimatallah / Bridgeman Images.

Plate 2: After Rodenwaldt 1912, pl. VIII.

Plate 3: Bridgeman Images, DGA593331. Photo, G. Dagli Orti /© NPL - DeA Picture Library / Bridgeman Images.

Plate 4: Heraklion Museum, inv. no. Y58. Courtesy of the Heraklion Archaeological Museum, the Hellenic Ministry of Culture and Sports, and the Hellenic Organization of Cultural Resources Development (HOCRED).

Plate 5: Bridgeman Images, DGA506056. Photo, G. Dagli Orti /© NPL - DeA Picture Library / Bridgeman Images.

Plate 6: Heraklion Museum, inv. no. T7. Courtesy of the Heraklion Archaeological Museum, the Hellenic Ministry of Culture and Sports, and the Hellenic Organization of Cultural Resources Development (HOCRED).

Plate 7: After Bosanquet and Dawkins 1923, pl. XXa.

Preface

THE introduction and spread of woolen textiles and the application to them of high-quality dyes—primarily murex and saffron dyes—triggered an economic and cultural revolution during the Aegean Bronze Age. Murex-dye penetrated the economy and ideology of Minoans and Mycenaeans to the point that one might rightly say that they worshipped the murex-dyeing process, which was the source of their wealth.

With their demonstration that the art of the palaces is a religious art devoted to the sale of luxury textiles, Chapters 1-2 are the solid ground upon which the bulk of this study is built. They firmly establish the reality of commercial motivation in the Bronze Age Aegean society. It is not otherwise possible to explain the fixation on realistic luxury garments that are depicted in a deliberately unrealistic manner and surrounded with abstract textile patterns, symbols of navigation, references to murex and saffron dye, and to floral-based perfumes.

In what follows, commercial interpretations, primarily of glyptic iconography, are advanced that might be regarded as conjectural or speculative: for example, hybrid creatures, including men with dog's heads who wear the figure-eight shield on their backs, represent traders; and fantastic creatures, combining the heads of eagles with lion's bodies, represent security personnel who escort overseas textile buyers to the showrooms and spread for them the campstools of the *lectisternium* festival. However, the iconographic hypotheses, like some others put forward in this study, need to be evaluated in the context of the base demonstration of the primacy of commercial fashion in the "purpled world" of the Minoans and Mycenaeans. When taken in this context, I think that much of what is "conjectural" becomes "credible," and much that is "credible" becomes "reasonable," and so on. Probabilistic advances of this kind may seem modest, but, even so, they have often been unavailable in specialist studies. Scholars who choose not to deal with the first two chapters cannot reap the full benefits provided in this study as outlined and summarized below.

Outward manifestations of the transformation in economy and worldview include but are not limited to: (1) the construction of innovative architectural "palatial" structures ("megara"/"s"), each adapted to control the production, tempting exhibit, and sale of luxury textiles; (2) the decoration of the walls of the palaces with magnificently colorful, religiously-themed frescoes, mostly processions, whose central elements are garments[1] worn by un-iconic fashion models—both youthful and matronly and typically with elaborate jewelry, hairstyles, and cosmetics; (3) the use of inscribed ceramic plaques and pots to advertise updated or individualized fashions; (4) the quality of palatial textiles attested by means of recognizable iconographic symbols ("trademarks"/"brands"), especially the double-headed axe, running-spiral, and figure-eight shield; (5) the celebration of holidays to welcome foreign textile buyers, including a "festival of flowers," in which foreign merchants were granted safe passage and feasted in the palaces while seated on textile-cushioned thrones; (6) the provision of elaborate, luxurious buildings for housing foreign textile buyers and of *aduta* for storing their valuables; (7) the palaces' employment of *independent contractors* ("collectors") and agents (slaves) to market textiles in the interest of commercial reach, as exemplified in Homer by Odysseus, who sought fine sheep/wool for himself but also as a labor on behalf of Poseidon; (8) the individuals who sold themselves into slavery to the palace or to cults or to individuals in the interests of occupational or geographic mobility; (9) male agents who served female principals depicted with a white skin or wearing items of female clothing, such as a veil (Odysseus); (10) mortal women and goddesses displaying symbols associated with males, including weapons and red skins to demonstrate that they possessed the legal rights of males—that is, that they were potnias; (11) Minoan/Mycenaean palaces' recruitment not only of skilled foreign textile workers but also experienced foreign textile traders, who conducted trading missions and, as the Egyptian tomb scenes demonstrate, even led the traders; (12) the king (*wanax*) and the enterprise (palace) not congruent as shown by the king acting as a "collector" (independent contractor) for the palace; (13) the textile enterprise as the property of the goddess Potnia and the *wanax* who carried out the security and transport functions is her agent; (14) the compaction of population around urban centers, such as Knossos, with a consequent decline in the use of old structures designated as "peak sanctuaries"; (15) Inscriptional (Linear A) evidence pointing to Minoan commercial activity in the Black Sea region, such as the finding of double-headed axes, ceramic evidence, and a Minoan roundel pointing to Minoan/Mycenaean commercial activity on Lemnos and Samothrace, and toponymic evidence suggesting Anatolian commercial activity in Greece; (16) the migration of skilled textile workers from Lemnos and other places in the eastern Aegean to Greece attesting to the growth of the industry; (17) the training of unskilled textile workers and their transfer from the Greek

---

[1] I am reminded of advertisements of the 1940s depicting details of dress, youthful demeanor, and cultural interactions that come together to signal an idealized American way of life, in which the consumption of a "Coke" is the defining element.

periphery to palatial centers; (18) the emergence of the "oared galley," a new type of merchant ship capable of coping with the wind and current problems prevalent at the entrance of the Black Sea while securely carrying and safe-guarding cargoes of valuable textiles and gold.

Homer, who composed his epics prior to the efflorescence of the Mycenaean palaces, testifies that there was a historical Trojan War, in which a commercial motive played a dominant role; (19) Paris/Alexander had ships (oared galleys?) built by Greek craftsmen resident in Troy prior to voyaging with business associates to "mingle" (negotiate deals) with the Greeks at Argos, where he acquired/purchased Helen, a beautiful expert in making beautiful textiles; while the true meaning of the refusal to return Helen remains unclear, the Achaeans illuminate their intention to displace Troy as controller of the Black Sea trade in textiles by building the "Achaean Wall"; (20) the battle in which Agamemnon holds a purple cloth aloft to rally his troops signals the Achaean motive and, at the same time, reveals that the vessels of Odysseus, while fewer in number than those of other heroes, were superior for the carriage of valuable fleeces.

The Mycenaeans waged and won a commercial war (the "Trojan War") with two major historical outcomes: (21a) the economic viability of Mycenaean palaces in mainland Greece and Crete; and (21b) the formation of a new Mycenaean state (Ahhiyawa) centered in the Troad; (22) the mainland and Cretan palatial centers earned vast wealth in gold that, in the absence of an alternative viable source, almost certainly originated in the Black Sea region; (23) Ahhiyawa, the new Mycenaean state, contested with the Hittites in a variety of ways, including a dispute over purple-dyers and over trade with the Assyrians.

Obviously, the above constitutes only a bare-bones summary of some of my least controversial and/or most easily summarized findings, whose content might be useful for a scholar deciding whether to read the book, but which can be validated only by reading it.

Acknowledgments

OVER the course of the past few years, many individuals have been of assistance to me in rendering editorial assistance, providing illustrations, and offering advice and constructive comments. My thanks to Clairy Palyvou, Maria Filomena Guerra. Eric H. Cline, Massimo Cultraro, Gareth Owens, Roger Woodard, Nicoletta Antognelli, Agata Ulanowska, Hariclia Brecoulaki, Katarina Zerzeropoulos, Wolfang Blümel, Monika Matoušková, Thanasis J.Papadopoulos, Lyvia Morgan, Georgia Flouda, Carol Hershenson, Diamantis Panagiotopoulos, Michele Mitrovich, and especially Jill Curry Robbins, Rachele Pierini, Dan Cline, Elizabeth Kresse, and to Carolyn Higbie for her assistance in preparing the index.

Ute Günkel-Maschek provided detailed comments on Part I of the study. Bernice Jones generously read a very early version of the entire manuscript and her observations and corrections were indispensible in its further development. The next vital reading focusing on Parts I and II was provided by Mary-Louise Bech Nosch. The "last" version of the manuscript received a close and generous reading from Tom Palaima, who provided confirmations, corrections, and cautions. The latter led to improvements reflected in the published version. Needless, to add the responsibility for all errors that remain is mine alone.

Finally, I wish to express my gratitude to Leonard Muellner and Gregory Nagy for sponsoring and supporting the publication of my study by the Center for Hellenic Studies and Harvard University. More than anything else, I cherish the confidence in my work by Lenny and Greg.

Abbreviations

Arachne   The central object database of the German Archaeological Institute (DAI) and the Archaeological Institute of the University of Cologne. The object's Arachne number can be entered into the "Search" field to access items cited in the text.
https://arachne.uni-koeln.de/

CAD   Gelb, I. G., et al. 1964-2010. *The Assyrian Dictionary of the Oriental Institute*. Chicago.

CMS I–XIII   Matz, Friedrich, Hagen Biesantz, and Ingo Pini, eds. 1964–. *Corpus der minoischen und mykenischen Siegel*. Berlin.

FGrH   Fragments of Greek History

fr.   fragment

Hesychius   Schmidt, M, ed. 1867. *Hesychii Alexandrini. Lexicon*. Jena.
https://archive.org/details/hesychiialexand00schmgoog
Accessed September 16, 2022.

LCL   Loeb Classical Library

LSJ   Liddell, H. G., R. Scott, and H. S. Jones. 1996. *Greek-English Lexicon*. 9th ed. London.

Perseus Project   The Perseus Digital Library Project is a collection of digital Humanities resources, located in the Department of the Classics, Tufts University.
http://www.perseus.tufts.edu/
Accessed September 16, 2022.

PM   Evans, Arthur J. 1964. *The Palace of Minos: A Comparative Account of the Successive Stages of the Early Cretan Civilization as Illustrated by the Discoveries at Knossos.* 4 vols. New York. Orig. pub. London, 1921–1935.

Pollux *Onomasticon*   Dindorff, W. 1824. *Julii Pollucis. Onomasticon.* 3 vols. Leipzig. https://archive.org/details/onomasticon01polluoft Accessed September 16, 2022.

Suda Online   *Suda On Line: Byzantine Lexicography.* Online database of the Byzantine *Suda* lexicon and related material. Published by the Stoa Consortium (www.stoa.org), hosted by the Department of Computer Science, University of Kentucky. http://www.cs.uky.edu/~raphael/sol/sol-html/ Accessed September 16, 2022.

tr.   translator

Aegean Bronze Age Chronology[1]

Notes

All dates are BCE, and are very approximate.

Chronological periods have abbreviations in two parts:

1. a 2-letter prefix (e.g., EH, MC, LM):
   - the 1st letter signifies the major period: Early, Middle, Late Bronze Age
   - the 2nd letter signifies the place: Helladic (the mainland), Cycladic (the Aegean islands), and Minoan (Crete)

2. and then a Roman numeral, followed sometimes by letters, to denote sub-periods

Examples

The whole Bronze Age is divided into an Early, Middle, and Late phase: for the Early Bronze Age in Crete, the abbreviation would be EM, on the Mainland EH, and in the Aegean islands EC

Each of these major phases is then subdivided: I, II, III. Thus:

- EH II is the middle phase of the Early Bronze Age on the Mainland

- EM IIA = the first half (A) of the second phase (II) of the Early Bronze Age (E) in Crete (M)

- LH III A1 = the first half (1) of the first subphase (A) of the latest phase

---

[1] This is an abridged and modified version of the chronology of John Younger. Available at: http://people.ku.edu/~jyounger/aegeanchron.html (accessed February 12, 2021). This classroom material was last updated by the author on August 3, 2017. For additional discussion of matters of chronology, see *"The Chronology and Terminology of Aegean Prehistory."* Available at: https://www.dartmouth.edu/~prehistory/aegean/?page_id=67. (accessed February 12, 2021).

BRONZE AGE

3000	Early Bronze Age	2800-2600: EBA I (EM I at Debla) 2600-2200: EBA II EM II EH II 2200-2100: EBA
1900	Middle Bronze Age	Middle Helladic (mainland Greece) Middle Minoan (Crete) 1900-1800: MM IA 1800-1700: MM IB-II: "Protopalaces" 1700-1600: MM III: Neopalatial Crete; Linear A
1600	Late Bronze Age	*Mainland:* 1600-1500: LH I, "Shaft Grave Period" *Crete:* 1600-1525: LM IA end. 1525-1470: LM IB 1470-1400: LM II: Greek take-over of Crete (Final Palatial) 1400-1375: LB IIIA: early palaces (Menelaion [SP], Mycenae, Tiryns, Thebes, Pylos) 1375-1325: LB IIIB: 1325-1225: LB IIIC
1200-1100	end of the Aegean Bronze Age	

Introduction

Studying a Purpled World

D URING the Aegean Bronze Age (ca. 3000–1050 BCE), the introduction and spread of textiles made of sheep's (and goat's) wool, in addition to plant fibers, triggered an increased use of colored dyes in order to significantly enhance their quality—that is, the aesthetic appeal of textiles.[1] As succinctly explained by Nosch (2017: I 3), "[C]ellulose fibres do not absorb dyes well, the dyes fade and are not light-fast. However, with the introduction of wool, dyes could be added to textiles and would result in bright, colour-fast and light-fast visual manifestations." Thus, the increased use of wool triggered a revolution in access to color.

The dyes that were utilized included high-quality colorfast dyes made from the labor-intensive processing of crocus flower stamens (saffron dye) and, even more gloriously, costly dyes made from the secretions of certain sea snails (the *muricidae*/Murex). The latter murex-dyes were not only light- and colorfast but yielded an astonishing variety of colors including the color ultimate—famous in much later times as "Tyrian" or "Royal Purple."[2]

The search for this relatively costly purple color became so intense that, as Burke (2010: 79) suggests, cheaper plant dyes "were used for making red, blue, and purple shades imitating the purple color and making textiles more valuable." Purple dyes made with madder roots or woad or from *kermes* (an insect hosted by oak trees) or others are lightfast and colorfast. Even so, they are arguably less colorfast than genuine murex and certainly lack its characteristic vibrancy/luminosity/shininess.[3] Thus, it is most doubtful that pseudo-purple

---

[1]   Andersson Strand and Nosch (2015: 375) explain why "a new name for the Bronze Age might be *Wool Age*." For a valuable survey of textiles, textile tools, and textile technology, see Boertien (2013).

[2]   In this study, terms like "purpled" and sometimes "purple" are used to refer to the *range of colors*—crimson, dark blue, purple—resulting from the application of murex dye to wool textiles rather than always strictly to the specific highly valued *purple* color. Sometimes, however, the specific color is intended and stressed.

[3]   "I should add that, according to a variant reading found in the medieval manuscript tradition of Homeric poetry, the transverse threading [of a purple fabric] at verse 441 of *Iliad* XXII is not

fooled many consumers. Graves (2017: 18) concludes, "It becomes clear that various textiles were dyed using different methods and combinations of dyes depending on the color, quality, and value. More expensive dyes, such as Tyrian purple, allowed for more expensive clothes, while more economical dyes provided for less expensive textiles."

Realistically, textiles dyed with the cheaper plant dyes, such as safflower, must have been popular in the domestic market. However, in the export market, which constitutes the main thrust of the present study, basic economic theory predicts that expensive-to-produce saffron and murex purple-dyed garments would have dominated. The reason for this difference is that the *relative price* of high-quality textiles had to be lower, probably much lower overseas than in the domestic market. Since the transport cost of differently dyed versions of the same textile would be the same, the relative price of the higher-quality dyed version is lower in the export market than in the market of the textile producer.[4] Consequently, all other things equal, the relative share of high-quality cloths purchased would be greater in the export market than in the home market. The "preference" of distant consumers—ancient and contemporary—for higher quality items provides a striking indirect validation of the economist's "law of demand."

The profitable utilization of limited cargo space is a related factor favoring the export of textiles dyed with expensive saffron and murex. Accessing the Black Sea region and its available gold (discussed below) without a costly and risky overland journey required ships to deal with very difficult currents and winds. Traders were invited to use small, fast ships—the Mycenaean oared galleys—which must have substantially raised the implicit cost/rental value of space in their holds. Again, the addition of this cost to the base prices raised the relative price of cheaply dyed textiles and limited the cargo space allocated

---

specifically purple but … simply *marmareē* 'gleaming' in general. As an epithet, *marmareē* refers to the luminosity of a color like purple, not to the color itself" (Nagy 2015s: 2§70). The impact of cloth dyed with genuine purple on the viewer goes far beyond the color of the cloth itself: "To produce the Tyrian hue the wool is soaked in the juice of the pelagiæ while the mixture is in an uncooked and raw state; after which its tint is changed by being dipped in the juice of the buccinum. It is considered of the best quality when it has exactly the colour of clotted blood, and is of a blackish hue to the sight, but of a shining appearance when held up to the light; hence it is that we find Homer speaking of 'purple blood.'" (Pliny the Elder, *Natural History* 9.62.38; tr. Bostock and Riley *Perseus Project*).

[4] In market equilibrium, the absolute price of a garment in the foreign market is the price of the garment in the domestic market + the (given) export cost. The higher quality garment has a higher price than the lower quality garment, but it has the same export cost. Hence, its relative price—the ratio of the two absolute prices—is lower in the foreign market than in the domestic market. It is the relative prices of commodities that, all other things equal, determine the relative quantities purchased. This logic explains why higher quality versions of a commodity would be proportionately more important in the export market than in the home market.

to them. On the other hand, there would be more space for cheaper textiles in larger ships that *perhaps* served, say, the Egyptian market. Serving the Assyrian market required ships to unload their cargoes for a long overland journey. Thus, the increase in transport costs discouraged the carriage of cheaper textiles.

Obviously, the cheaper plant-dyes did not drive the much more expensive murex-dye (and saffron) from the market, as would have been expected had they provided an even vaguely comparable quality—that is, the vividness of color, glow, and permanence (Graves 2017: 18).[5] The important point here is that even the more cheaply colored wool textiles were able to find a lucrative market niche. Consumers unable to afford the real thing could, therefore, still participate in the color revolution.

Other things equal, a related prediction is that the higher quality textiles would be dyed with the higher quality dyes. This prediction is founded on general knowledge rather than on economic theory, however. This general knowledge is embodied in the Scots proverb, "You can't make a silk purse out of a sow's ear." One application of the proverb is that a garment manufactured by selecting a high-quality textile and then dyeing it with a cheap dye costs more to produce than consumers are willing to pay. Consumers will look at the product and say: "It's not worth what you have to pay for it!" The quality dye raises the cost of production without (comparably) raising the value of the product to consumers. Consequently, the product will be found to be unprofitable to produce and will tend to drop out of the market.[6] It must be stressed, however, that this is a prediction based on an understanding of *consumer tastes* and does not have the same scientific status as the law of demand—that is, the quantity of a consumer good demanded will decrease when its price relative to other consumer goods increases.

---

[5]   Thavapalan (2018: 9) explains that in ancient Mesopotamia, murex-dyed wools and alternative methods of dyeing purple with vegetal matter were practiced concurrently and "What is more, the Mesopotamians themselves never distinguish between 'genuine' and 'fake' purples on the level of language." I see three possible interpretations of the failure to distinguish: (1) wools dyed with fake purples were obviously inferior, so there was no need for a label; (2) none of the wools were dyed with fake purple; (3) none of the wools were dyed with genuine purple. Note, with respect to (3), that if there were no difference in the way the wools looked then no one would pay for much more expensive, purple-dyed wool, and the product would simply fall out of the market like "snoogles." Nosch (2017: 23) supports the potential of plant sources of red dyes for wool by noting that Linear B (Mycenaean Greek) employed several terms for red: *po-ni-ki-ja*, *e-ru-ta-ra*, *pu-ru-wa*, and *po-pu-re-ja*. It seems to me possible that the terms might refer to some of the different *shades* of red produced by murex-dye.

[6]   This proposition does not deny that some consumers would choose the expensively dyed "sow's ear" to participate in the prevailing style.

Introduction

In her seminal study of Bronze Age textiles, Barber (1991: 354, 364) explains, "Colours gave the Minoan[7] textiles the possibility of exploring the full scope of patterns, spirals, even figural representations, influencing pottery decorations and creating in the Neo-palatial [Minoan] period, fabrics as complex as Gobelins embroidery in Modern Europe" (cf. Militello 2014: 276). Whittaker (2012: 193) adds,

> Although the remains of wall paintings from the Mycenaean palaces are regrettably sparse and fragmentary, they do show that a love of colour was a prominent feature of Mycenaean culture. The majority of the representations that include people show *men and women* wearing clothes which are characterised by brilliance and polychrome splendour.

Barber then cites numerous examples. The point developed below is that the taste/desire to be clothed in elegant styles featuring brilliant colors was not confined to Minoans and Mycenaeans. Given that this tendency toward rich, colorful clothing seems to be deeply rooted in human nature,[8] it should not be surprising that the taste/desire to be clothed in this fashion was shared internationally and indulged in by those consumers who could afford to indulge. A high fashion[9] industry developed in the Minoan/Mycenaean world to satisfy (and to promote) this demand.

It is postulated here and developed with available evidence below that during the Bronze Age, the heightened desire for dyes increased the demand for dye-making workshops and dyers, especially those skilled in the production and application of murex-dye. The other side of this coin is that the increased production of dyed woolen textiles called forth an increase in the global demand for the services of shepherds, thread-makers, weavers, shipbuilders, seamen, artists,

---

7   The terms "Minoan" and "Mycenaean" are standard terms applied by Bronze Age Aegean scholars to leading participants in the Bronze Age Aegean society. "Minoan" is applied mainly to inhabitants of Crete, Thera, and other Greek islands. "Minoan" is named after the fabulous King Minos of Crete. "Mycenaean," on the other hand, is applied mainly to mainland Greece and, later, to Crete and the other Greek islands. "Mycenaean" is named after the Bronze Age palace at Mycenae in the Peloponnese. The original Minoan language is unknown; the script used to write it, discovered at Knossos in Crete and other places, is called "Linear A." The Mycenaean language is a dialect of Greek; the script used to write it, also discovered at Knossos, is apparently an adaptation of Linear A that is called "Linear B." The terms are discussed further in Chapter 3.

8   Although genetic evidence is unavailable on this point, Part I makes clear this taste for adornment loomed large in the western Aegean Bronze Age.

9   "Fashion" is not used here in a sociological sense but in terms of standard economics. That is, by "fashion industry," I mean the industry that developed to produce and market the desired luxury textile styles during a specific era. Some attention is given to trickle-down effects and changes in styles but not so much to periodic changes in style as essential elements of fashion.

designers, fashion models, traders, commercial agents, and entrepreneurs. These developments, in turn, encouraged growth in other diverse professions, including accountants, occupational trainers, and financiers. The production of expensively dyed woolen textiles drove economic growth and raised living standards not only for natives in the western Aegean but also via migration by Anatolians, especially dyers, to western Aegean centers of textile production. The producers of luxury textiles became very rich in imported gold. Indeed, *gold* was the perfect counterpart to murex-dye in that, unlike other metals, it did not tarnish and lose its luster and richness with the passage of time.

As the means that transformed purple into gold, the sea was reverentially depicted by Mycenaean poets (I include Homer) and fresco artists. In the "Battle Scene" at Pylos (on the cover), as revealed by MA-XRF analysis, the sea is depicted by a technique of superimposed layers: "A layer of Egyptian blue was superimposed to a layer composed of Murex purple mixed with grains of a manganese-based pigment. The addition of a manganese-based pigment served to create darker hues, while the superimposition of a blue colored paint layer created an optical mixture between blue and purple" (Kokiasmenou et al. 2020: 11). Significantly, if I understand correctly, Kokiasmenou et al. (2020: 12) perceives that by this "complex painted stratigraphy" the artist sought not simply a particular aesthetic outcome but also to advance a worldview: Mycenaean warriors are engaging warriors clad in animal skins, thereby suggesting that the murex-purple background signals a global struggle to control the murex-generated wealth in a purpled world.

Despite the limited availability of surviving murex purple, it may be inferred from a variety of behavioral evidence that there emerged during the Aegean Bronze Age a *Purpled Economy* in which dyed woolen textiles were the driving force. Moreover, as will be seen especially in *Part I*, the title "Purpled Economy" *understates* the dimensions of technological, productive resource use, and social transformations. The impact of color on woolens transcended the purely materialistic by forming a new dominant Aegean *ideology* that was appropriate to a *Purpled World*.[10] A world in which purple and gold became deities. This study proposes to reconstruct, in all its richness, this Purpled World and its woolen textile base.

Before moving on to outline this study, I think it is well to offer a defense of the use of iconography—a form of analysis that is not properly appreciated in some scholarly circles. Iconography, by which I mean the analysis of symbols included in images to produce knowledge about the society in which the

---

[10] Perhaps we may find that somewhat equivalent "new ways of life" resulted from innovations such as the automobile, Coca-Cola, and the smartphone with its ubiquitous "selfies."

images were crafted, is sometimes dismissed by scholars as overly *"conjectural."* However, I completely agree with Lyvia Morgan (1985: 19) that, "Iconography, as a notation of a culture, is as expressive and informative as any language. A systematic analysis of the structure of Minoan iconography would reach some way towards the minds of the people." Many of the images should be considered historical or at least anthropological documents. A key is to begin by examining the literature and other textual materials for possible explanations of the iconographic symbols.[11]

Chapters 1 and 2 in Part I are necessary, as they establish the reality of a dominant commercial motivation that is embedded in traditional or newly devised or borrowed religious rituals in Bronze Age Aegean society. They should not be skipped by specialists outside the fields of fashion and merchandising. The remainder of Part I (Chapters 3-6) deals with distinctions among Bronze Age Aegean venues devoted to innovative textile exhibition spaces, including megara and labyrinths—that is, buildings with multiple floors and winding passageways. There follows a discussion of several structural dimensions of the textile enterprise.

Part II focuses on evidence and interpretations of the textile trade. Chapter 7 reviews the archaeological evidence relevant for understanding the production of murex dye and textile dyeing; the evidence uncovered is essential but tends to be inconclusive. Then, attention is largely directed to issues in palatial enterprise and to the analysis of documents written in a script called Linear B (created ca. 1400 BCE) used to record sounds in a form of Greek often referred to as the "Mycenaean dialect." These documents are very helpful, but they are time-and subject-limited because they are accounting documents intended to help Mycenaean palatial authorities keep track of their productive resources—animate and inanimate. Linear A— the script employed earlier by the Minoans—had a broader range of applications on different media,[12] but, unfortunately, this script remains undeciphered. Hittite royal letters and Egyptian annals and tomb art are helpful but limited. Chapter 7 concludes by discussing some helpful iconographic evidence. Next, Chapters 8 and 9 consider some fundamental theoretical issues bearing on the motivation for and practice of palatial trade and then consider significant conventional types of evidence—direct and indirect—for the importance of trade. Chapters 10 and 11 fill important gaps left by the analysis of conventional evidence by studying iconographic evidence.

In Part III (Chapters 12 and 13), we come to the elephant in the room: the role of the Homeric Epics. Are they great works of art in which the details of life

---

[11] Thus, as will be demonstrated, in literature a "young man" is an agent, and a "dog" is a materialistically motivated individual who is typically a businessperson.

[12] Linear A inscriptions are found on jewelry and vases.

are completely fictional or "mythical," or does Homer also convey important truths about history—both generally and especially about economic history? It is shown that Homer's poetry about a Trojan War conveys such historical truths not only because, based on rigorous linguistic evidence, it dates to a time *before* even the Mycenaean palaces (ca. 1425 BCE) but also because Homer wished to convey them. There really was a Trojan War, and this helps to solve a historical mystery: how the Achaeans, as identified with the Ahhiyawans of the Hittite royal letters, obtained their foothold in western Anatolia.[13]

In Part IV, Chapter 14 shows that the Trojan War is not only a historical reality but also that it is best understood as a *trade war*. Then, Chapter 15 views Homeric heroes in their roles as traders themselves and as agents of traders such as the cult of Poseidon.

Part V considers the "before and after" aspects of the Purpled World. Chapter 16 reflects on the myth of Jason and the Golden Fleece. Then, Chapter 17 considers the cause of the demise of the Mycenaean palaces in about 1200 BCE. The "Collapse" is explained as a manifestation of *vertical disintegration* in the Aegean textile industry.

The present study is "*integrated*" because it proposes to make use of all the forms of evidence mentioned above plus interpretative insights from Maslovian psychology and the disciplines of fashion studies, marketing, and economics. Together, the inputs of evidence and analysis serve to recreate a Purpled World that flourished over centuries in the Aegean region.

---

[13]   Many scholars take as a given the existence of a Greek kingdom named Ahhiyawa that operated in the Bronze Age eastern Aegean and attempt (with little success) to deduce its home base in the western Aegean (see Palaima 2011: esp. 54–56). The present study begins by asking how a Greek state formed in Anatolia.

PART I

THE PALATIAL FASHION SHOWROOM AND RUNWAY

1

The Bronze Age Aegean's Color Revolution and Its Revolutionaries

THE Aegean Bronze Age's worldview transformation is reflected in the characteristic use of blue backgrounds for diverse themes in the Minoan world and, later, among the Mycenaeans. Thus, Tournavitou (2017: 26) points out that the blue background "is used continuously on the [Greek] mainland in all the major palatial centers, from early in the 14th century B.C. ... to the very end of the 13th century B.C." and, specifically, "at Mycenae, where the chronological range of extant specimens spans the entire palatial period and beyond." There have been advanced various explanations for the widespread adoption of blue pigment in architectural settings (see Tournavitou 2017: 26–27, 42). However, I propose to see this light and bright blue background as a reference to or, better yet, an exaltation of the special color, sometimes called "biblical blue" (*tekhelet*), made possible by the application of murex dye to cloth.[1]

---

[1]   See the photograph in Smithsonian Magazine, September 21, 2018, Smart News: "Jerusalem Museum Untangles History of the Color Blue, From Biblical Hue to Ancient Royalty." Available at: https://www.smithsonianmag.com/smart-news/jerusalem-museum-untangles-history-color-blue-biblical-hue-ancient-royalty-180970356/ (Found February 16, 2021). It is true that the light and bright blue in the frescoes has nothing in common with the dark and deep one that is also characteristic of murex purple. It is also true that "No chemical evidence has [as of yet] been found for the raw material used to create blue dyes for the blue clothing seen in frescoes from the Minoan period" (Pareja et al. 2016: 26). On the other hand, "Chemical tests of surviving textile fragments dating to the first half of the second millennium BCE from the royal tombs at Qatna in Syria demonstrate that the colors produced include pink, crimson, shades of blue (greenish blue, light blue, indigo blue) and shades of purple ranging from light to deep" (James et al. 2009: 1114–1116; James et al. 2011: 450–460; cf. Sukenik et al. 2015). The analysis reveals that the most likely source of the blue in these luxury textiles is not the indigo plant/woad but rather brominated derivatives of indigo and indirubin from Hexaplex trunculus. It appears that the key factor in determining the shade of blue is the concentration of the indogotins. *However, I am by no means a chemist so I may have missed something in the technical material, but I saw no distinction or exception made for the sources of light or bright blue.* It should be kept in mind that during the murex-dyeing process the fabric is transformed from white to yellow to green, and then to blue and red and purple. See, for example, Pliny the Elder, *Natural History* 9.62.38. 9.65.41). At the same time, murex glands treated with honey and/or urine or subjected to different light exposures

Significantly, while white, gray, and even red backgrounds appear rare, the indiscriminate use of blue seems more regularly interrupted by *yellow* (Tournavitou 2017: 22, 27, 33, 52, 70, 73, 75). I see the latter color primarily as a reference to/exaltation of *gold*—the main payment for luxury textiles—or to *saffron* dye. The latter dye, made from crocus stamens, is a very expensive color-fast dye featured prominently in the frescoes[2] in the large building known as Xeste 3 at Akrotiri in Thera/Santorini and elsewhere (Chap. 4.3 below).

In connection with this prevalent color scheme, Blakolmer (2019a: 273) made a striking discovery:

> While the inner courts and interior rooms and stoai [of western Aegean structures] may have been elaborately painted, there is little archaeological evidence that the outer façades were similarly decorated. Yet, representations of the external architecture hint at decoration. However, there is a high probability that the colours used by Aegean painters for depicting outer architectonic façades and further structural features were not chosen in order to faithfully reproduce actually painted architecture, but for reflecting the heterogeneous materials and the character of their surfaces in an expressive style, in a word: their 'polychromy'.

However, the Aegean "polychromy" is not random or strictly determined by technical considerations; it reflects, I propose, the colors of their main textile dyes or murex dye and gold. As Blakolmer (2019: 257) explains elsewhere: "All these ancient polychrome representations of Aegean architecture share one remarkable feature, namely their brightly painted façades in colours such as yellow, red and blue."

As already noted, saffron dye typically produces yellow (red is also possible), but the results for murex dye are much more varied. Depending on several factors—including the type of snail, use of certain mordants, length of exposure to sunlight, single- or double-dyeing, and heating of the dyed wool—murex dye can produce a wide range of color including the bright sky blue and the deep purple. Madder was used by the Minoans and Mycenaeans with imported alum to produce a lightfast dye for cloth and a lake pigment for architectural painting (Davis and Stocker 2007). Thus, processed madder is capable of producing a range of colors including yellow/orange and red/purple. Thus, conceivably the

---

have an increased range of possible shades of colors: "Orseille and dilute honey (6-carbon sugars of honey act as reducing agents when fermented by micro-organisms) interrupted the oxidation change in shades, and this process yielded green or red or blue at will" (Jensen 1963: 111).

[2] For an overview of the Bronze Age Aegean frescoes, see Chapin (2010).

"polychromy" noted by Blakolmer celebrates the use of the cheaper madder dye for textiles rather than the luxury dyes made from saffron and murex. This suggestion, however, runs counter to the undoubted effort made by Minoans/Mycenaeans to produce murex dye and the emphasis they placed on the tedious collection of crocus stamens depicted in famous frescoes at Akrotiri (see below). *Moreover—and this is for me the most significant aspect of Aegean polychromy—saffron yellow and murex-purple are not only the colors of the main textile dyes but also, long before Roman times, they became the ultimate symbols of wealth itself—gold and (actual) purple.*

Unlike philosophers in later times, the Bronze Age Aegeans did not, so far as we know, dream of unifying the two forms of wealth by applying cinnabar to dye gold from yellow to red (Brecoulaki 2014: 32), but they combined the two symbols in their architecture and, as will be seen, in their textiles. Indeed, even the *sea* from which the murex snail came might be colored with murex-dye as in frescoes found at Mycenaean Pylos (in Messenia on the hill of Epano Englianos).[3]

There is a much more concerning Aegean emphasis on (obsession with) the murex-"purple" and saffron-yellow. For example, in jewelry, the Bronze Aegean seems to prefer the red of carnelian and the yellow of amber (Whittaker 2012: 195). More fundamentally, Whittaker (2012: 196) proposes,

> The fantastic and even surreal use of colour in landscape depictions in palatial wall paintings could suggest that the Mycenaean elites wished to promote themselves as being in control of nature and its resources. Likewise, the cultivation of ideal personal beauty, in which the use of bright and shiny colours in clothing and adornment played a prominent role, may have been intended to express religious identity by conveying the message that they were identifying themselves with the perfection and power of the gods.

Indeed, the ancients especially linked murex dye with gods and the divine sphere because, as was already noted, during the dyeing process (and possibly also with woad), cloth underwent miraculous transformations in color.

In any event, the color red is especially attractive. Barber (1991: 230) supposes,

> [R]ed was one of the most popular colors from very earliest times, found among the first surviving examples of dyed textiles or fibers in every area.... Much of this preference can surely be laid to our physiology,

---

[3] "Murex purple was ... identified as the background colour used to indicate the area of the sea in an unprecedented naval scene recently brought to light, that originally decorated the wall to the right of the doorway between Hall 64 and lobby 66 (fig. 5)" (Brecoulaki 2014: 10).

since we distinguish the electromagnetic waves at the 'red' end of the spectrum most easily and infallibly which is why we still use red for our most urgent symbols. *De gustibus non est disputandum.* All of this sounds reasonable, but it is also true that when the gods gave red and yellow to humans, they enabled them to live like gods—that is, they were made beautiful and *wealthy.*

Dramatic formulations and illustrations tend to make the application of color to textiles seem automatic and inevitable. Was there a new technology in the making of wool cloth or in the making/application of purple dye or in both that served to trigger the color revolution? The simple answer is, "I don't know." As will be seen below, there is evidence for the production of murex-dye in the early second millennium at Crete, the presumed homeland of the Minoan color revolution. In addition, the warp-weighted loom, which certainly played an important role, was known very early in Crete, and there is evidence that this weaving technology spread from Crete to the surrounding Aegean area including the west coast of Anatolia.[4] Indeed, there is evidence, in the form of Cretan-style discoid loom-weights made of non-local clay, that the Cretans (Minoans) not only inspired the use of the warp-weighted loom but introduced it themselves around the Aegean (Cutler 2012: 149–150). Yet, like the fishing of murex snails, the standard use of the warp-weighted loom perhaps came too early—well before about 1700 BCE when the Cretan palaces flourished—to explain the color revolution (Cutler 2012: 148; Ulanowska and Siennicka 2018a: 754). Perhaps the Minoan palaces relied on a modified technology that used spherical loom-weights in addition to the discoid ones. Besides the use of spherical loom-weights, other possible technical changes affecting cost, quality, and variety, include the use of a different type of loom (e.g. a horizontal ground or a vertical two-beam loom) and new weaving techniques (about which Tzachili 1990: 387–388). These will be considered later in discussing the emergence and primacy of the Mycenaean palaces as textile producers.

In any event, the technical ability of textile manufacturers to realize the potentialities of color is only the first essential step in a commercial process. As someone who is professionally an ("Austrian") economist and not an engineer or technologist, and certainly not a weaving practitioner, I find most interesting and important what happens next: individuals—the entrepreneurs—have to comprehend the market potential of the new textiles and they have to be willing to bear the cost of making the textiles known and available to potential

---

[4] "The warp-weighted loom can be used to produce complex patterns, since individual sections of warp threads can easily be lifted independently of each other; it is also well-suited for the production of twills" (Cutler 2012: 151).

consumers. Specifically, they need to arrange for showing their colored textiles to consumers and they need to provide them with a space for negotiating purchases. These individuals—the west Aegean's revolutionaries of color— solved these problems by financing the construction of buildings with chambers for keeping business records, and for the production, storage, and, above all, for display and promotion of the newly available garments.[5] The last listed advertising/ideological objective was in large part realized by covering walls with frescoes "recalling" religious practices that *exalted* their textile designs. Religious feelings, like desires for material gain, are built into human nature and they were harnessed by the entrepreneurs—and I think also truly felt by them—in the interests of selling luxurious textiles. Motives, whether religious or commercial, are invisible to third parties, of course; the religious motive is deduced from the content of the frescoes (processions, deities), while the materialist motive is deduced from the portrayal of the garments in the frescoes (unnatural positioning, attention to details of construction).[6]

In considering the "Crocus Gatherers Fresco" in Akrotiri, Marinatos (1985: 226) explains that the fresco has a dual aspect in which "the combination of two levels of reality, in the divine and human sphere respectively, is an important revelation concerning the mental attitude of the Minoans. It shows that a realistic scène does not conflict with a religious one. It also demonstrates the close association between religion and economy." The decorated structures built by the entrepreneurs were, or became, what scholars today refer to as the Minoan Palaces; Marinatos is certainly not suggesting, and neither am I, that the entrepreneurs were devoid of the sentiments of piety and religious awe.

---

[5] This is the perspective of Maran and Wright (2020: 101–102, 114), although they speak of "legitimacy and authority" as motives, not the display of textiles: "The authors will show in this chapter that there was neither a gradual evolution of architectural forms that developed into what is commonly referred to as the *'palace'* nor did discontinuities in cultural evolution create breaks with the past and lead to revolutionary change. The palace in the form that we understand it is largely an invented plan that elites and their architects self-consciously developed to promote their legitimacy and authority as they expanded their hegemony over much of the Aegean" (see similarly McEnroe 2010: 41). The view that the palatial architecture emerged all at once is challenged by Schoep (2004: 255). I would not subscribe to Schoep's explanation of the changes in palatial architecture in terms of "conspicuous consumption." There remains, however, a real question whether the earlier palaces (in the sense of large complex structures) were intended to serve as centers for the production of "law-and-order," as well as to market luxury textiles as attested by the finding of many loom-weights (see Chap. 2).

[6] Markets already existed and where they did not, they were formed by the entrepreneurs who used them to gain success, including wealth. I would not, however, refer to "*capitalism*." The latter term is popular but also emotionally loaded and is often used to (mis)characterize the "*market system*." Moreover, because of the novelty of their vision, the Minoan/Mycenaean textile entrepreneurs often had to do things for themselves—that is, they had to substitute internal organization (command) for the market.

Of course, to say that textile innovations were carried out by a palace is already skipping several steps. Entrepreneurship springs from an evolved creative instinct and the ability to make connections. Accordingly, entre-preneurial capacity is present in every society and will manifest itself if not suppressed by force or convention. However, it is not a communal exercise—it is an individual exercise: the idea of producing multi-colored textiles for a world market arose in one mind or in a mere handful of minds. The mind may not have even belonged to a "Minoan"—that is to a native of Crete—but to a foreigner who saw the Cretan potential for efficient manufacture and marketing and then created the "Minoan Miracle." "Minoan" is fundamentally a proxy for the name, lost in history, of a figure comparable to Henry Ford or Edmund Cartwright or Asa Griggs Candler or Steve Jobs, to name just a few. The same applies to the later Mycenaean palaces. If we insist on a name, then Daedalus, referenced indi-rectly in the Linear B tablets, will fill the gap nicely.

Two major building blocks would have paved the way for the Cretan palace(s). The first, probably following a few experiments, were complex struc-tures erected to market textiles (during the "Protopalatial period"[7]), and then somewhat later new types of wall plaster (Immerwahr 1990: 22) and/or new painting techniques were invented that facilitated a progression from solid colors to decorative motifs to figural imagery. More specifically, the second building block was a progression from abstract art to frescoes featuring *human imagery* (thus the "Neopalatial period").

However, Gates (2004: 31–32) raises doubt about the need for an artistic progression by pointing out:

> Wall paintings themselves were not new in Neopalatial Crete. The covering of walls in plaster and then painting them, with solid colors or bands, can be traced back to the EM[8] period. Indeed the true fresco technique, painting on wet plaster, may have been already been prac-ticed in Protopalatial times.... The explanation for the appearance of figural imagery in the Knossian wall paintings therefore lies not in a new technical or iconographical inspiration coming from existing neighboring prototypes, but from some newly arising situation on

[7]   Possibly, the builder was an experienced merchant who only later ruled from his place of busi-ness (hence "palace"). For the ancient Near Eastern experience, see Silver (2006a: 7–8). Willms (2010) denies that Greek *(w)anax* could have meant "merchant" favoring a purely military deri-vation. In Pindar (Pythian 4.148 ff.), we see an effort to separate the palace's "law and order" activity from its "business" activity: Jason proposes to King Pelias a division in which he will hold the scepter of rule and Pelias will keep the flocks, cattle, and fields.

[8]   "EM" refers to Early Bronze Age Crete; "EH" refers to the Early Bronze Age on the Greek mainland.

Crete itself that allowed Minoans to refresh their vision and appropriate certain conventions, themes, and techniques from their neighbors, and to integrate them into their own art tradition continuing from the Protopalatial period.

In short, leaving aside possible changes in weaving technology, it appears from Gates' observations that what changed in Crete was not the invention or importation of new artistic technologies but rather the perception of a new market opportunity.

To appreciate the path of innovation, one must understand that the frescoes depicting persons are not art for the sake of art. Neither do the frescoes in the pioneering Knossos palace[9] specialize in images of people (Gates 2004: 28) in response to an emergent interest in the human figure. The frescoes, as will be discussed later, were also uninterested in the figure of the entrepreneur. Given the centrality of garments, it becomes possible to understand why the humans sponsoring the art exhibition (the frescoes) have chosen to remain unseen and unacknowledged (Gates 2004: 33–34), as featuring the mortal sponsors might divert attention from the quality of their product!

Rather, people are featured in the frescoes because they wear the garments made by and offered for sale at the palace. Moreover, as in contemporary fashion, accurate, flattering, or empathetic depictions of the human wearer ("model"!) are regularly subverted to display the garments to their best advantage. This regularity or, better, unifying theme is signaled by Bernice Jones' (2009: 319) notice of an "Aegean convention of rendering lower parts of dresses frontally on profile figures." It may be deduced that the clients viewing the palace's garments are not so much their ultimate wearers or "consumers" but members of "the trade." Most of all, the observed convention signals a proprietary interest in the garments.

Moreover, the frescoes feature themes reminiscent of religion, such as processions, but these have been smoothed out and made stereotypical to focus attention on the garments worn by model processioners or held up for display by a model participating in the role of priestess or deity (the "Graces"?). This is not to say that the models are not priestesses or deities, but only to say that the latter roles were adapted to the needs of the palace.[10]

---

[9]   Frescoes with depictions of people are quite rare at other Minoan centers that have been referred to as "palaces" (Gates 2004: 28).

[10]   Admittedly, anonymity and stereotyping together with detailed depictions of garments are found also in seal devices that presumably are meant to identify the owner. However, for this very reason, the seal image may copy the fresco and serve in a smaller way as a selling instrument. At a more basic level, we see frescoes in which skirts are held between the legs making the wearer look awkward and artificial. To say that this kind of depiction reflects a "convention" does not explain its origin. Certainly, one obvious explanation is to better exhibit the skirt for

To put it bluntly: at some point in time, palace art was applied to the sale of textiles. If we cast our eyes at the Pylos palace, we see that nature has been largely denaturalized. Thus, as Lang (1969: 25–26) explains, the

> Bluebird Frieze (9 F nws) ... uses the birds like beads on a string or like running spirals. The nautilus (1-6 F) is similarly used not for itself but merely as a link in a decorative chain.... With one and perhaps two notable exceptions nature has been very much subordinated to man at Pylos. The only flowers seem to be those in the hands of fair women (51 H nws 53[ad] H nws) except for blooms that have no real context preserved.... The rosettes which appear in spiral friezes or metopes have been so conventionalized that they have nothing to do with nature.

I submit that the nature themes are overwhelmingly props, albeit often with religious overtones, for the palace's promotion of textiles. They reference the modes of delivery of the textiles, festivals celebrating navigation (i.e. trade) season, symbols/trademarks of the textile enterprise, and even textile patterns.

The Minoan/Mycenaean society did also appreciate art for its own sake, in which category I would place *pure* landscapes—that is scenes without humans. These were, however, mainly found in "villas" such as those surrounding the Knossos palace (Gates 2004: 28). Chapin (1997: 23) sees the positioning of land-scape frescoes in expensive non-palatial structures as an "important element in the display of wealth among the elite class of Neopalatial Crete," an elite that she compares to the wealthy art patrons of Renaissance Italy (cf. Immerwahr 1990: 41–62); but, for balance, compare Rehak and Younger 1998:104–106).

Additionally, and importantly, there are *hints* that the pure landscapes enjoyed by affluents in their homes found their way onto expensive garments. I am thinking primarily of the example of three crocus plant-themed faience costume plaques from the "East Temple Repository" at Knossos (Chap. 10.2). There is no greater reason to assume that innovative-pure landscape-decorated textiles of this kind were reserved for goddesses than to assume that pure land-scape-decorated villas were reserved for them (see Chapin 2006: 73–74, 77–78 and below). Under the Mycenaeans, such garments, and perhaps others with pictorial themes, were arguably produced and sold to those who could appre-ciate and afford them (see Chap. 3). Of course, the specific styles of the depicted

---

sale. I cannot think of a different explanation for what we see that is not a stretch. I am willing to listen, however.

garments (open bodice for example) had to fit into the contemporary way of life including its power structure.[11]

Consistently, with Chapin's perspective on the affluent villa, Gates (2004: 40) suggests,

> Even if the origins of the villa may lie earlier, the number of villas increased sharply in LM I. The villas are not identical designs but variants on a theme, and no doubt served a variety of functions that might have ranged from houses of the ruling families, such as those at Knossos itself, to manor houses in the countryside from which regional economic, religious, and social control was exercised.

The rise in the Knossos palace with its human imagery was accompanied by an increase in "urbanization,"[12] judging by an apparent precipitous decline in the number of *peak sanctuaries*—essentially, cult places and textile production centers on/near hilltops (Gates 2004: 33, 40; Chap. 4.2.c)—as well as an increase in affluence attested by the increase in the number of villas.[13]

The evidence of the decrease in peak sanctuaries is substantive but indirect evidence of population compaction. There is also direct evidence in the form of archaeologically attested changes around the palatial centers:

> Using settlement evidence, the really dramatic transformation appears to take place ... in the late Prepalatial period and was sustained at the three major palatial sites [Phaistos, Malia, Knossos] well into or throughout the Protopalatial period. This is hinted at by evidence for large-scale construction activities at each site, but is most clear in the massive settlement expansion which can be documented (with varying degrees of spatial and chronological resolution) at all three

---

[11] To say that the wall paintings of garments are *essentially* pages in a sale catalogue is, I know, extreme. Perhaps part of the problem is the use of the word "essentially." The author is a lover of art-deco posters. Behind me, on the wall, is a rather large poster depicting in the lower right quadrant an elegant woman in a blue dress and gold cloche hat standing in a pose of dreaming/ anticipating. In front of her is a red touring car and above the car, three large one-engine red planes as if landing or taking off or on the way to a destination. In the upper left corner is an idealized skyline of Manhattan. On the bottom is a caption: "Roma—New York—Roma. Crociera Aerea Transatlantica." It is on my wall because I find it thrilling and beautiful but also because it is "essentially" an advertisement for an airline. In the early thirties, the beauty of the depiction labored to sell tickets.

[12] Urbanization tends to be a fuzzy term. It is better to speak of the compaction of the Cretan population around Knossos and other palatial centers.

[13] One study finds that of the twenty-two peak sanctuaries in use in the Protopalatial period only eight remained in the early Neopalatial period and further that this decline reflected changing settlement patterns (Soetens, Sarris, and Topouzi 2001).

emerging palatial centres.... The settlement perspectives explored in this paper mobilize new data to address a long-debated question and help us to define just when the beginning was. A dramatic transformation in the possibilities for social organisation, with widespread implications throughout many aspects of Cretan life, took place late in the Prepalatial period. (Whitelaw 2012: 165; cf. Evans 1928: 566–568).

Whitelaw 2012: 165

Of course, increased affluence facilitated population growth but fundamental changes in residence and social life such as those argued for by Whitelaw do not just happen. Individuals and households needed strong reasons to migrate from rural areas and from overseas to Cretan palatial centers.

The reason, I propose, is the economic opportunity provided by the emergence of an international textile industry in Crete.[14]

The remarkable increase in landscape art in villas is itself evidence of the rising affluence that was made possible by the textile industry.[15] In a Maslovian (Maslow 1970) sense, art depicting nature helps to satisfy higher needs, which emerge as more significant parts of the consumers' budgets once baser, more material needs have been satisfied. Therefore, we can conclude by saying that

---

[14]　The argument is especially strong for Knossos: "Contacts are made on the one hand with the Cyclades, Anatolia, Near East and ultimately Egypt, through the 'gate' of Mochlos and the coastal sites on the eastern part of Crete; on the other hand the 'gate' of Kastri opened the way to the Peloponnese and the West" (Agourides 1997: 19). The importance of the Mochlos "gate" is explored below.

[15]　Comfortable homes with good art on the walls together with monumental tombs are one indicator of Mycenaean wealth. Tsagrakis (2012: 323) shows *especially for Pylos* [relying on the Ta series of tablets], a palatial world with a major need of display and luxury, which employs a great number of skilled craftsmen in order to satisfy this need. Among these craftsmen, specializations may be found, whose existence surprises us and reinforces the image of luxury that we have of the courts of the Mycenaean palaces. A characteristic example is the *ku-wa-nso-wo-ko*, the lapis lazuli craftsmen, a great number of whom are recorded at Mycenae" (emphasis added). Changes in diet are ordinarily good proxies for improvements in living standards but for the eastern Aegean, the consumption of meat and especially fish is the best proxy. "Our first example concerns the individuals from the Mycenae Shaft Graves [Chap. 9.5] whose isotope analysis demonstrates that they regularly consumed marine food—in stark contrast to their contemporaries who all followed a land-based diet. In combination with their more robust bone structure, their better oral health, their greater height, their heavily meat-based diet in comparison to contemporary individuals (Table 6 ...) and the association of their extraordinarily rich graves with the emerging palatial elite of Mycenae, the increased consumption of marine food by several Shaft Grave individuals appears to indicate an intentional and conspicuous consumption activity (Table 4). Given the general lack of fish in Bronze Age peoples' diet and the distance of Mycenae (ca. 15 km) from the coast—sufficiently distant to make regular and ample provision of freshly caught, unspoilt fish doubtful—it is likely that it was the positive, status-enhancing values that were being drawn on by the Shaft Grave individuals" (Berg 2013: 17). There are also references to fish and fishing in fresco (Akrotiri) and glyptic art.

the textile entrepreneurs deployed garment art in their palaces as a tool for acquiring wealth and that the inclusion of landscape art, a higher need, in their mostly urban villas strongly indicates that they succeeded in acquiring this wealth.[16] Evans (1928: viii), the excavator of Knossos, finds "astonishing" the "evidences of culture and well-being among the burgher class in the first half of the sixteenth century B.C."

There are, of course, possible reservations concerning my perspective about showroom art. It is true that some Minoan chambers painted with exquisite visions of nature and women in beautiful and detailed dresses were small and possibly dark as in Agia Triada or Room 1 in the "House of the Ladies" (which includes Papyruses or Sea Lilies[17]) at Akrotiri (see Younger 216b: Plate 129f; discussed in Chap. 4.3). To see the fresco clearly in daylight would arguably have required a lamp/torch, which does not seem to conform well to the idea of a showroom.[18] Neither does viewing by means of a lamp/torch conform very well to any alternative understanding of fresco function. There is neither an *artistic* nor *ritual* need in small chambers lit by torch or lamp for depictions of beautiful landscapes and/ or detailed dresses in glorious color. None, but still the depictions there are real. The space was available, and it was not discarded.[19] *What I can offer is that it was important, certainly more important than in modern times, for garments to look beautiful even in rooms lit by lamp or torch.*[20] If a garment could be attractive in these rooms, then it would be spectacular anywhere else. The colorfully dressed in a fringed mantle "Young Priestess" from Akrotiri (Plate 1) may anticipate my argument as she holds a lamp (or an incense burner). More importantly, not only her lips but also her entire ear is painted a vivid red indicating an innovative use of cosmetics (Dewan 2015: 47; Earle 2012). Note, also, her griffin-like "curl" (see Chap. 11.6).

To conclude, I see no reason at all to believe that the Minoans placed expensive frescoes stressing garments in places where they could not be viewed to advantage. Everyone appreciates beauty but, obviously, beauty presents itself for choice in many forms. The details of garment design and functionality were of no interest to lovers of beauty unless they also happened to be garment buyers and garment specialists.

---

[16]   Assyrian palaces (i.e. public places) featured depictions of the kings brutally subduing their enemies. What was in their private dwellings might have been thematically different. At other times, the distinction between public and private houses was not pronounced.

[17]   See S.P. Murray (2004: 102 n.3) for discussion and references.

[18]   There is a small window on the west wall leading into Room 7 and, according to S. P. Murray (2004: 101), there was possibly another in the north wall to admit light. More certainly, the "House of the Ladies" is constructed with a central light well (see https://www.greece-is.com/ image-gallery-the-highlights-of-santoriniakrotiri-highlights/ (accessed August 8, 2021).

[19]   A reader pointed out to me that many religions have side chapels with special decorations.

[20]   A starry sky has been reconstructed above the women in the "House of the Ladies."

2

The Style Conscious Path to Textile Dominance[1]

S. P. MURRAY (2016: 45 with n. 9) has called attention to "Hints of what must have been a pageant of imagery in the rooms and corridors of the [Knossos] palace [that] can now only be detected in assorted pieces of painted plaster and modern reconstructions." Although the fresco evidence is fragmentary, it still manages to show viewers the "vivid and tantalizing details of fabrics dyed in bold colors and woven with intricate designs." Admiring it, one may well imagine that the palace set the standard for high society and the *haute couture* that signaled elevated status." Furthermore, while women wore most of the high-fashion garments at Knossos, men also were depicted in striking textiles.

Beauty is diverse, and status also has many origins. It is argued that the palaces chose to feature depictions of garments, even unnatural depictions, to sell them and that this objective was served by placing the garments in attractive religion-oriented frameworks. At the very least, this is a viable hypothesis that only gains credibility when considered alongside the palaces' devotion to producing the garments.

The flounced skirt of the "Snake Goddess" (Y65 in Plate 10b, discussed below) and other garments in Minoan and Mycenaean art are skillfully made garments showing the painstaking effort by individual textile specialists (Barber 1994; B. Jones 2001). These are not mass-produced textiles, as we can infer regarding the cloth listed in the Linear B texts and also from later representations of plainer cloth (Burke 2010: 103). Moreover, the emphasis at Knossos on clothing fashion is not of a one-off kind: "Excavations have shown that the palace at Knossos, unlike others at Crete, was redecorated several times during the Neopalatial period with frescoes of women and men in richly colored and

---

[1] I apologize to readers for the use of extended quotations but here, and in some other instances, the reactions of my specialists in art, design, and fashion *are the evidence* and, hence, are best rendered in their own words. They function in the same way as my reproductions of Bronze Age fresco, ceramic and glyptic art.

patterned garments" (S. P. Murray 2016: 55). Indeed, "figurines show us women with painted dresses in Classical Minoan Style lasting down to the beginning of Mycenaean period" (Militello 2014: 267).

Cameron (1971: 43) notes what appears to have been an explosion of interest in elegantly dressed women:

> it is clear that at some point in Middle Minoan III, one group of painters was engaged in decorating different and important parts of the [Knossos] Palace with scenes prominently featuring large-scale pictures of women, gracefully portrayed: there is perhaps a hint here of a thematically coherent yet widespread scheme of decoration in the Palace of this period.

S. P. Murray (2016: 55–56) amplifies this observation:

> The decorative complexities of the garments of the Pseira and Ayia Triada [near Phaistos] ladies, and the emerging iconography of scenes related to female deities, can only make us wonder about the assorted and unconnected fresco fragments of female figures and extravagant costumes that were uncovered at the [Knossos] palace and that suggest pictorial programs prior to the LM IB destruction. Large-scale figures like the Lady in Red (Fig. 3.2) and the Ladies in Blue (Fig. 9.1), as well as miscellaneous fragments thought to show ornate textiles and jewelry (Figs 3.13, 3.14), indicate that the walls of the MM IIIB–LM IB palace would have provided many illustrations of elite figures in prestige garments. One such scene may have formed the early decoration of the west entrance passage into the palace, subsequently to be replaced by the hundreds of figures of the Procession Fresco.

Thus, while it is true that most of the evidence for dress comes from Knossos, the Cretan obsession with high fashion dress is not confined there; there are examples from lesser palatial sites. Even so, it is not only the imaginations of their designers and the skills of the textile workers that elevate Minoan garments to elite status. These dimensions are magnified by the actual use of murex dye or references to it in the garments themselves and their depicted environments.

The "Procession Fresco," from the upper floor Xeste 3 in Akrotiri (on Thera/current Santorini), depicts four distinctively dressed women. On the North Corridor Wall, we see the "Rose Bearer" (#3) and the "Basket Bearer" (#4)—and on the South Corridor Wall, there is the "Lady of the Landscape" (#2) and the "Lady Bearing White Lilies" (#1). As emphasized by Chapin (2008: 49), the women wear garments unlike those common to Cretan procession frescoes. Woman (#1) wears a short-sleeved, net-patterned murex-dyed sleeved purple bodice embroidered (better in-woven patterns) with blue birds on one sleeve.[2] The fragmentary woman #2 also wears a murex purpled bodice, and her costume (probably a bell-shaped skirt) is decorated with a landscape including rocks and birds.[3] "Extremely interesting is her fringed girdle ... which is decorated with purple floral motifs with spirals in added white." (Vlachopoulos 2007: 134). Woman #3 wears a yellow mantle and bodice that is decorated with red flowers and murex-purple bands. Woman #4 wears a red mantle over a yellow bodice decorated with crocus stamens and murex-purple bands; crocus-blossoms, the source of saffron dye decorate her hair (Chapin 2008: 55).

On the upper floor of Xeste 3, the famous "Saffron Gatherers Fresco" depicts finely dressed mortal women gathering crocus stamens to produce saffron dye and makes a variety of fashion references to the crocus. The magnificently attired goddess stands out in this connection:

> The association of this goddess with crocus and saffron ... seems undeniable: she has a crocus blossom painted (or tattooed) on her cheek, and her loose, diaphanous blue blouse is decorated with these flowers.... *The seat of the goddess is not a conventional throne or chair but rather a stack of yellow cushions, which could represent bales of saffron-dyed cloth or even a pile of yellow-dyed garments.*
>
> Rehak 2007: 207–208; emphasis added[4]

However, murex purple dye dominates in the costume of the goddess. Further, the griffin[5] who accompanies her "is shown with blue wings, decorated with spirals,[6] and a white body, tied to the wall with a purple leash. So it would appear

---

[2] Papageorgiou (2014) argues that the woman in the procession carries a bird-catching net.

[3] Landscape designs on garments are unusual but not unprecedented (Chapin 2008: 70–72 and Chap. 3 below).

[4] The theme of dyed textile thrones is discussed in Chapters 7.6 and 11.5, 6 (see also Chap. 4.2 on the Kalavasos krater from Cyprus). For the present, I am inclined to speculate about a festival involving the circuiting of a saffron-dyed cloth/throne such as the one the goddess at Akrotiri is seated upon. Another goddess found in fragmentary condition at Mycenae in the "Southwest House" or "House of the High Priest" is seated similarly: "A tiny triangular area of yellow ocher, behind the crease at the back of the knee on Fragment 12 (see figs. 2, 4), "is the remnant of a yellow ocher seat, parallels for which appear on the stacked cushions on the contemporary ivory plaque from Mycenae" as well as at Akrotiri (Jones 2009: 313).

[5] The griffin (*grups*; Beekes s.v. *grupos*), a fantastic animal (male or female, winged or unwinged) with the beak and talons of an eagle and the body of a lion, is featured in Minoan and Mycenaean palatial iconography. For references to and discussion of the vast literature, see Zouzoula (2007).

[6] I will show that the spiral and the griffin, together with the double-headed axe and "horns of consecration," are major symbols of the textile enterprise that I will call the "*Labyrinth.*"

that only purple was used for the decoration of the so-called goddess and her griffin, indicating a special relation to this colour." (S. Hansen 2015: 123–124; cf. Shank 2012: 563–564).[7]

Descending to the first floor of Xeste 3, the mortal women in the "Adorants Fresco" are linked to saffron dye (Shank 2012 with references). One of the three "Adorants"—the "Necklace Swinger"—is depicted displaying a necklace made of stigmas of crocus flowers distributed along a cord (Shank 2012: 562). In the middle of the scene, the "Wounded Woman" (= "Seated Woman") sits on a rocky outcrop with blood streaming from her foot. Her costume fully uncovers both breasts but she does not wear a flounced skirt: "She wears the usual blue robe (the *heanos*) but below the waist. she is wrapped in a belt from which hang strips of cloth or lappets, a skirt that simultaneously reveals and conceals the lower body" (Younger 2016a: 575). The skirt worn by the "Wounded Woman" reminds me somewhat of the contemporary split skirt.[8]

References to the dyeing of textiles are implicit in "Wounded Woman's" unusual hairpin, about which Verduci and Davis (2015: 64–65 with references) observe is in the form of an olive twig with blue and yellow leaves. The latter colors, I believe, are references to saffron dye (yellow) and murex dye (blue) and also, more obviously, is the woman's (red) blood from her wound; The Elder Pliny (*Natural History* 9.62.38) identifies the color of the best purple-dyed wool with "clotted blood." An additional connection with purple-dyed textiles is that "Wounded Woman" sits close to a "tree-shrine" that is surmounted by an olive tree, which "points to a connection between the built structure and the Seated Woman adorned by the olive branch."[9]

The "Wounded Woman" may illustrate a myth or a ritual or be a complete invention, but the point is the blood, or rather the color of the blood, that also cascades on a fallen/picked crocus flower. It is argued below that the "horns"

---

[7] In the "Griffin Fresco" at Knossos, the individual, spiral-shaped crests of the griffins are *purple* with the body itself colored yellow/gold. The wingless creature is placed against a purple background. Therefore, in both Crete and Thera, as opposed to the mainland, the griffin has a special relationship with colors associated with murex dye. Lang (1969: 110–111) originally concluded from the fresco fragments found in Hall 46 and the adjacent Room 43 of the Pylos palace that the bodies of the (wingless) griffins were painted purple and the lions painted yellow. However, she later recanted the purple color (see B. Jones 2015: 255). A griffin appears to be at least partially painted in light blue (not murex blue) in the West House at Mycenae (Tournavitou 2017: 21 with Fig. 9). On the other hand, Mycenaeans lions are "traditionally rendered with yellow paint" (Tournavitou 2017: 21 with references).

[8] On the "Lappet Skirt" see Chapin (2008: 66; cf. Barber 1991: 255–258).

[9] This connection would be further strengthened by blood dripping from both the "horns" [so-called "horns of consecration"] on the 'shrine' and the foot of the woman" (Günkel-Mashek 2012b: 362 with references). However, Rehak (2004: 87) disputes the presence of blood and accepts that the red color on the shrine is from garlands of saffron stigmas. All of this adds to the uncertainty concerning the symbolism of the "horns."

are an attribute—albeit one whose meaning is disputed—of the goddess Potnia, whose cult in the Minoan Labyrinth, as will be seen, sponsored luxury textile production and marketing. The textile significance of the red-mixed-with-yellow theme is repeated in the costume of "Veiled Woman," who is positioned to the right of "Wounded Woman:" she wears a "white robe with a flounced kilt and a diaphanous saffron yellow veil with red dots over her head and body" (Younger 2016a: 575).

In Room 1 of another multistoried building ("The House of the Ladies") at Akrotiri, three women are depicted in the frescoes, about whom Immerwahr (1990: 54) observes,

> For a discussion of Minoan costume they form excellent examples, since the garments are meticulously rendered down to such details as seams, buttons, and tasseled cords. Further, the scene most likely represents ladies attiring themselves for some festal occasion, and thus gives us a glimpse as to how the garments were put on, enabling us to speculate on their parts.

This is truly remarkable especially when it is considered that Minoan art is not especially realistic in a photography sense. Thus, viewers in a small chamber are shown details of garment construction and wear—details so minute that no "festal occasion" can possibly explain why they are shown to viewers. That is, world art is full of festal occasions that do not inform viewers of details of construction and wear.[10] Akrotiri introduces viewers to other innovatively styled garments that feature the colors provided by murex-purple and saffron dyes. The frescoes would surely have disappointed if the painted colors did not evoke the actual colors of the garments (Brecoulaki 2014: 9).

With respect to the dominance of fashion, S. P. Murray's (2016: 72) summary merits full quotation:

> In many ways this building [Xeste 3], although its primary func-tion may have centered on cult and initiation rites, also represents a showcase of the textile arts, Its frescoes depict a festival dedicated to the collection of saffron (prominently used for dye), a rite for boys with ceremonial display of cloth, a painted replica of a draped wall hanging, and a cavalcade of the finest dresses of sheer linen or silk, fleecy mantles, and showy skirts–the creation of textiles is a current that hums throughout the decoration of this building. Even the highly

---

[10] Details of garment construction are obviously of interest to informed buyers but not to religious participants, including clergy.

ornamental wings of the griffin allude to textile motifs. The splendid costumes of the females in Xeste 3 are not only real markers of their roles in these rituals, but they also serve as a display of Theran skills with the loom and needle.

I would add that in Akrotiri purple pigment paint was employed only on the walls of Xeste 3 (Brecoulaki 2018: 398) and amend Murray's informative statement to say that the demonstration of elegant textiles made with elaborate techniques was the primary function of Xeste 3. Two explanations of the motive are possible (1) the motive was *commercial*—i.e. to "sell" the textiles to foreign visitors; and (2) the motive was *pride* in technical production skills. Both explanations—sale and artisanal pride—seem not to fit the current, standard Aegean Bronze Age palatial perspective. On the other hand, the two motives fit together and build on each other very well and would be difficult to disentangle empirically.

With respect to variations in costume design, there are "curious" models— noted earlier—that depict only the costume (S. P. Murray 2016: 46–47 with Fig. 3.4 and n. 12); their plaques have holes for suspension and display.[11] One such plaque from Knossos (HM 58a = Y 58 in Plate 4) depicts a significant variation on the iconic elaborately-decorated open-bodice Minoan dress worn by such figures as the "Snake Goddess" (see Plate 10b): "Similar bands and stripes adorn the faience dress plaque HM [=Y] 58, and illustrate that the open front can extend to the center to cover the breasts (Fig. 8.15)" (B. Jones 2016a: 109; see Chap. 4.3 below).[12] Surely, this is a feature—or, whether the breasts are covered or uncovered—that would matter to clients. More generally, plaques served to vary and augment styles without repainting the frescoes.

I am wondering whether the open bodice represented high fashion worn only by the models. Today, see-through fabrics dominate contemporary runways, but most women "spoil" the look of the garment they purchase by choosing to wear undergarments of various kinds. More generally, impractical high fashions are modified and then trickle down to the wider market. Such "modified" fashionable outfits are displayed at Xeste 3, in which a woman wears a flounced dress as a foundation garment beneath a transparent dress (Doumas 1992: 144ff; Kyriakidis 1997: 124). On the other hand, as suggested later, the open bodice dress may signal that its wearer has a special status in the society—that she is (or is associated with) a "potnia."

---

[11] Rehak (2004: 95) explains that all the pieces have flat backs and that more complete specimens preserve holes for mounting.

[12] Indeed, the faience "Snake Goddesses" (Chap. 10.2) had holes or perforations permitting them to be hung. Note that despite their prominent breasts and narrow waist, the Snake Goddess figurines depict dresses, not women (B. Alberti 2001).

Boloti (2017: 3–4) also considers the two or three faience plaque-like models of high-fashion Minoan robes and double belts or girdles from the East Temple Repository at Knossos; she notes that the robes are especially elaborate as they are decorated with flowering crocus plants (Plate 4, and see Chap. 4.3 below). Boloti considers the models as offerings to the goddess because in Xeste 3 (Akrotiri) the goddess wears a garment decorated with crocus flowers. The implicit argument is that *only* the goddess could wear such a garment. This, I believe, is incorrect as noted earlier. Indeed, Boloti (2017: 3–4 with n. 6) concedes that the saffron gatherers depicted in Xeste 3 wear dresses similarly decorated to the one worn by the goddess, but this, she says, "simply emphasizes their close relationship with *Potnia.*" There is no rule we know of that would prohibit women generally from wearing this dress (or any other worn by a goddess) and in so doing make herself look as lovely as a goddess does. To dress a goddess in a garment serves to make it more desirable not to make it taboo.

Thus, Whittaker (2012: 196) observes,

> That clothing and jewellery functioned to materialise the relationship between members of the Mycenaean elite and the gods is perhaps particularly evident in the aforementioned fresco fragment from the Southwest Building in the Cult Centre at Mycenae of a woman walking in a procession. The woman is depicted as looking down at a necklace she is holding in front of her in her right hand. This necklace is more or less identical to the one she is wearing. The woman is almost certainly taking part in a ritual procession and the necklace was presumably intended as a votive offering. Accordingly it can be surmised that the act of dedication was intended to assert the existence of close ties between the woman and the deity to whom she was dedicating the necklace.

I agree with Whittaker that it is reasonable to interpret the redundant necklace as a votive offering, which, in this case, means that the deity was to "wear" a mortal's necklace. However, the fresco's focus is not on the exchange but on the woman—that is, on her garment. Similarly, the plaques from Knossos' "Temple Repository" may in some way reflect an original (but unobserved) ritual context (Boloti 2018), but that context had been adapted for marketing the palace's textiles: the hung robe plaque depicts an alternative basic garment available to buyers, and the hung girdles advertise accessories making it possible to vary the robe's appearance. Thus, they represent an important selling point for more economically minded members of the elite.

Egan (2012: 319–320) explains that the depiction of kilts in the frescoes finds

> ... a close parallel ... in the rim of a Palace Style jar, a vessel type that is both contemporary with the kilt paintings, and, on Crete is found almost exclusively at Knossos.... In addition to this practical use ... the jars' large size, elaborate decoration, and discovery in prominent parts of the palace have led scholars to propose that they served also as display objects, harmonizing with contemporary palace wall paintings.

It appears to me then that the Palace Style jars, some of which represent textile designs, played the same kind of role as the just-noted wall-mounted garment models. The display of large jars in open areas or closed chambers provided the palace with an additional relatively low-cost method for updating the styles, patterns, and above all the *quality* of the textiles that was depicted in the more permanent frescoes (compare Egan 2012: 322). No doubt, alternative interpretations are possible.

Moving away from Knossos' frescoes, it seems possible that Mycenaean figurines were used to update and/or demonstrate styles for clients:

> Several types of terracotta figures of deities have been found in sanctuary contexts. The painted decoration on the Type A female figures is suggestive of elaborate clothing and jewellery. In contrast, Type B figures, which have so far been found only at Mycenae, are undecorated and have an unfinished appearance. The most reasonable explanation for this is that they were intended to be covered with garments and adorned with jewellery made of the same materials as those worn by members of the Mycenaean elite.
>
> Whittaker 2012: 196–197

I think the "Type B figures" were decorated with garments and jewelry as needed to accommodate new or revised designs for special clients.[13]

More generally, I see the observed reliance on ceramic design as primarily a device for updating fresco fashions, serving a more diverse clientele, and, above all, accommodating temporary changes and filling gaps between fashion shows. In the case of Minoan palaces, we clearly have garment samples, showrooms for garments, and various measures to keep fashions up-to-date; frescoes are placed for the convenience of patrons. Obviously, we do not have sales data, but it is

---

[13] Marcar (2004: 228) explains the difference between fresco and ceramic designs in terms of independent technical development in different crafts. Clearly, this is a factor, but it does not explain the plaques and figurines and would only partly address the vases in and around the showroom. Note that some vases depicting various designs and symbols had holes in the sides for hanging (Bosanquet and Dawkins 1923: 20–21).

safe to assume that the palace authorities thought the investment in distinct display media would pay for itself.

Turning to some explicitly Mycenaean examples, mention needs to be made of the "Warrior Vase/Krater," recovered on the acropolis of Mycenae and dated to the twelfth century BCE. In Plate 15, we see a file of soldiers wearing uniforms including helmets, studded/beaded tunic, shield, and a thin spear on the shoulder, to which is tied a peculiar small reddish(?) sack or pouch.[14] The discs attached to the uniforms are perhaps beads or perhaps murex *opercula*[15] (Burke 2010: 89 with Figure 50; see below for a discussion of the Knossos Ld tablets).

Brecoulaki (2014: 9–10) observes that the use of murex-purple based paints on Mycenaean wall paintings in mainland Greece is restricted to certain details of figural compositions as in the Akrotiri (Thera) frescoes but:

> Nonetheless, the extraordinary preservation of a variety of purple, mauve and pinkish hues on numerous fragments from the Mycenaean palace at Pylos, never previously recorded, has allowed us to further investigate the use of murex purple in Aegean painting. What is interesting in the case of Pylos is that purple, used either as a background colour or to paint details within figurative compositions, seems to have acquired specific meaning according to the area of the palace or the iconographic program where it was employed.

Thus, in the Pylos wall paintings, purple color on the garments of the "Lyre Player" in the Throne Room and on other figures in the hunting scenes in Rooms 43 and 48 "was perhaps used to underscore the status of the wearers, since the adjective designating purple in Linear B tablets (*po-pu-re-ja*) seems almost always associated with the dyeing of textiles or with sumptuous cloth (L758a, Lc561a, KN X 976)." (Brecoulaki 2014: 10). Alternatively, the purple colors serve to indicate the status/economic value of what is being hunted by the "hunters" and even by the "Lyre Player with Dove" (see Chaps. 10.7 for Calchas and 11.5 for

---

[14]   The "Warrior Vase" and the tied sacks are discussed in Chapter 11.3 (with Plate 15).

[15]   Murex opercula formed a prominent part of the Ulu Burun shipwreck (Chap. 8.6 below). The thousands recovered from the wreck are believed to represent only a fraction of the original cargo (Pulak 2001: 33). We may now be confident that the discs were used to decorate textiles including, of course, purple-dyed textiles. Pulak (2001: 43–44) also explains: "Among the manufactured cargo on the ship one may also include several types of glass and faience beads, many hundreds of which were painstakingly collected individually from the site. Due to complete hydroxylation the slightly flattened spherical and oblong shaped glass beads have lost their original color. Many of the spherical forms were found around and scattered between copper ingots, suggesting that they were carried in perishable containers, such as cloth or leather bags, that have since disintegrated."

Apollo). Another alternative is that the purple designates the high quality of the garments worn by those portrayed in the frescoes.

Questions about trends in fashion leadership are postponed until Chapter 3. For the present, I continue to focus on an important area of commonality in the depictions of Minoan and Mycenaean fashions. Specialists in textiles have shown us not only elaborate and expensive textiles but also, in the clearest possible terms, that ancient artists eschewed realism and that their sponsors used religious traditions and/or religion-like innovations to form a stage for marketing beautiful garments.

The next example may contradict my argument, however. The magnificent Mycenaean "Agia Triada Sarcophagus"[16] is a large, entirely painted chest from a "house tomb" (Tomb 4) in a Minoan hillside cemetery. Presumably, it was made for a funerary purpose, and it contained the remains of several persons. However, this purpose does not preclude the chest from having been a viewing point for subsequent processioners.[17] On each long side, it depicts women and men performing the prescribed ritual libations for the dead. There are two women on one side and six on the other, although only the legs and feet of four are visible due to damage. All the women are beautifully clothed with two wearing blouses together with patterned leather skirts and the other six wearing long striped robes. Each short side depicts two women riding in a chariot wearing long dresses.

In no case are the women's breasts visible; perhaps the open bodice style was frowned upon in a funerary context.[18] On the other hand, as S. P. Murray (2016: 55) explains,

> A curious feature of the dress of the Ayia Triada adorant is the way in which the artist laid out the scale design like wallpaper, maintaining the grid of the pattern regardless of the change in direction warranted by [the?] woman's bent legs. It would appear that maintaining the integrity and clarity of the rapport design was a greater priority than visual naturalism. The fact that the dress has a fancy weave is more important to record than how it fits and moves as clothing. It is as if the artist conceived the fabrics the original bolt straight from the loom. The overall effect is somewhat rigid and monotonous.

---

[16]   The Sarcophagus is on display at the Heraklion Archaeological Museum and may be viewed at: http://odysseus.culture.gr/h/4/eh430.jsp?obj_id=7913 (accessed February 12, 2021).

[17]   Tomb 4 is built aboveground within an enclosure wall and is located near a large megaron (Burke 2005: 410). If the purpose were not to display the Sarcophagus to future visitors why not follow the long-familiar practice of burying the larnax in a pit? (see Preston 2004).

[18]   The dresses worn by the mourners in a Knossos sarcophagus are fragmentary, but it can be said that the bodice is not open (see Morgan 1987: Figures 4, 5, 7).

Since this departure from visual naturalism appears outside the showroom sale context, it may be suggested that the response is to an "*artistic convention.*" However, even if lost to us in the midst of time, conventions have a beginning or origin. My question is why would a convention that required "maintaining the integrity and clarity of the rapport design" at the expense of "visual naturalism" come to be formed? My answer is that the formation of a convention to favor the technical aspects of garment appearance is predictable in an environment of proprietary interest in garments—that is, in an environment stressing garment sale or, very close to the commercial motive, pride in workmanship.[19] At this time, I am not aware of a more credible alternative hypothesis.

In an Akrotiri fresco, the look of the kilt worn by a woman with bent knees who empties a crocus basket could be achieved in the real world either by having the woman tuck the kilt tightly between her legs rendering her immobile or by means of an artistic construct (B. Jones 2005: 710).[20] What mattered was not to accurately display the woman's movement but to display the kilt to the best advantage.

Similar stress on the flattering display of the garment at the expense of a realistic depiction of the wearer is also apparent in the depiction of the men's kilts worn at Knossos in the "Procession and Cupbearer Frescoes" painted in LM II. Egan (2012: 318) points out,

> Rather than depicting the point of the kilt between each figure's knees, the painter (or painters) elected to place it at the front of each figure, creating an overly strict profile that is both unnatural and forced. What is more, this conspicuous break with convention, when combined with the omission of articulated fastenings and cloth layers, makes these kilts appear visually awkward. Rather than having the look of workable garments, they appear unnaturally smooth, snood-like, and, for lack of a better term, 'painted on.' Finally, because it is clear from the presented comparanda that by the time of LM II, artists working on Crete, Thera, and in Egypt understood what an Aegean kilt looked like, how it was worn, and had even developed certain conventions to depict it in art, the question is raised: why were the Procession and Cupbearer examples depicted in this odd manner?

---

[19] Emilio Zegna, the Italian maker of "power suits" for men, has his models stand still at the end of the runway procession so spectators can move up and get a better look at the details of the suits. Now, because of the Coronavirus pandemic, the same result is achieved by photographing the clothes from different angles. (Source: "Fashion Shows Mix Tech and Social Distancing," *The Wall Street Journal*, Thursday, June 4, 2020, A10).

[20] Image available at: https://www.penn.museum/sites/expedition/aegean-dyes/ (accessed February 12, 2021).

The explanation is not that the artists lacked the talent—they certainly had it—but that the task, to which they were set, was to display the decorated kilts to the best advantage. Ritual enactment, for good reason, was vital in ancient cultures. Evidently, the "painted on" appearance of the kilts did not detract from the sense of ritual performance. Indeed, I would suggest that the depiction actually enhanced the ritual. However, it was the eyes of potential buyers that mattered most to the sponsors of the fresco.

Thus, to maximize the information provided to viewers/clients about the kilts the artists employed, Egan (2012: 319) suggests the *technique* known as *Geradvorstelligkeit* is the means by which "three-dimensional objects, landscapes, and human figures are broken down visually into their composite parts, which are then rendered frontally and re-assembled to form new, more visually informative, two-dimensional images." Moreover, the same technique is employed on the "the patterned sleeve borders of the bodices worn by the women in the MM IIIB 'Ladies in Blue' and the LM IA or IB 'Dancing Lady' frescoes ... in order to give maximum exposure to their intricate patterns of snail-shell spirals and zig-zags with dots" (Egan 2012: 319). The snail-shell spirals are likely a direct reference to murex (see e.g. Chap. 4.2.c).

The devotion to the garment rather than to objective reality is apparent even in the glyptic designs employed, presumably, by agents of cult and palace. Thus, Weingarten (2010: 323) explains,

> [Minoan] Seal-carvers emphasized some aspects of the subject while minimizing or omitting others. For example, it has been argued that the aniconic or featureless heads of figures on some LM 1 rings result from the techniques of punching and engraving.... While glyptic style and technique are undoubtedly entwined, technical restraints should apply equally to all parts of the ring, which is simply not the case. The women's flounced skirts on the same rings are almost always so finely detailed that they explicitly 'encourage attention'.... Put another way, whether the women are goddesses, priestesses, or worshippers is not the issue.... These images are statements of what the seal engravers wanted to show, not an objective account of a religious scene ... —in this case that the women's skirts are more important than their heads or limbs.

There is no question that even official seals displayed the depicted garments to the best advantage. Everything else, including the model's faces and bodies, is subordinated to this purpose. The face of the wearer could be left to the viewer's imagination but not the construction of the garment itself. Although sealings might be seen by clients, I would not claim that seals were mainly intended to advertise garments. However, the seal devices were typically taken from frescoes,[21] which means they reflected palatial commercial concerns while making it easier to convey the duties and identity of the sealer. Further, I suspect that participants in the garment trade chose (or were assigned) seal devices highlighting their role (Chap. 10.4).

S. P. Murray (2016: 91) grants, "Some garments in the paintings from Crete, Melos, and Thera seem in their richness and complexity to test our belief in their veracity, but Aegean peoples had the fibers, dyes, and technology to make such textiles, provided they had the luxury of time and the motivation for such extravagant display." The market provided both. Spantidaki and Moulhérat (2012: 188) provide additional insight from the analysis of excavated textile fragments:

> These minute fragments are of great importance not only because they exemplify fine multi-decorated textiles known from the Bronze Age Aegean frescoes, but also because they answer questions concerning the realism of the costume representations depicted. These minute remains demonstrate the fringes which finish the skirts, the sewing which must have existed to adjust the costume on the body, and all the decorative details which until now were known only from the Akrotiri frescoes.

Here and elsewhere in their study, Spantidaki and Moulhérat convince us that while they cared only about the garments, the fresco artists were not unduly glorifying the garments they depicted.[22]

Finally, attention is directed to the fresco processions themselves. We tend to assume they are cultically oriented because they are processions and the participants are carrying "gifts/offerings" (see Weilhartner 2013). However, interpretative caution is recommended by Blakolmer (2008), who points out that while the "gifts" depicted in the processions may express a vestigial cultic

---

[21] Thus, Blakolmer (2012b: 83–84): "Although it has been argued by scholars that seal stones hardly ever copied the iconography of mural paintings, since this would suggest the isolation of a scene from its context on larger wall paintings, this is exactly what we come across in numerous seal images belonging to different narrative cycles. In spite of their small scale, a considerable number of seals and signet rings from LM I Crete present extracts from larger register scenes and frieze-like compositions, as I will try to demonstrate by a few examples. Moreover, it seems reasonable to postulate a distinct art form as delivering the original models of highly narrative relief images, and it will be argued that this art form was the large-scale stucco reliefs concentrated at the palace of Knossos."

[22] Ulanowska (2018b) has expressed some doubts about realism in the garments. For example, she views some of the interlocked patterns beyond the technical possibilities of Bronze Age weavers. Were artists, at least at times, given permission to let their imaginations reign?

(or royal) theme,[23] they do not exhibit the kind of standardization expected in a *ritual*. Thus, Blakolmer (2008: 264) observes, "when putting all procession frescoes together, an amount of ca. 83 objects carried by men or women occurs, but there is hardly any clear pattern beyond a distinction between real commodities on one hand and prestigious and symbolic gifts on the other hand." There is a sense of spontaneity and realism in the objects conveyed to a deity,[24] raising the suspicion that something is happening that is not quite ritual or is a different kind of ritual.[25]

Speaking of realism in ritual, there is a striking resemblance between the fresco processions and the "rituals" of contemporary fashion exhibitions. Although today's runway models do not bear "gifts"—they may walk dogs or carry umbrellas—they do demonstrate the very latest fashions by transgressing a catwalk before a seated audience. As we are reminded by Blakolmer (2008: 261), imagery shows that not every Minoan woman wore a tight bodice and decorated flounced skirt, and not every man wore a breechcloth or decorated kilt. Yet these garments-types are the ones typically worn in processions.[26] Is this difference a matter of "class" and of "elites," as is often assumed, or is it, as I believe, a matter of fashion display? Today's glamorous "supermodels" wear expensive garments and diamonds but are they "elites" or "working women" (*prospoloi*, attendants of the Graces and Horai[27]).

In concluding his especially thoughtful discussion, Blakolmer (2008: 267) is struck by the "strong tendency" in Bronze Age Aegean art "toward a certain 'uniconic' character, namely in that sense, that concreteness had been deliberately avoided by generic, impersonal, anonymous, almost faceless human

[23] Actually, we typically lack evidence that the processions are expressions of "traditional" rituals.

[24] The processions themselves may be rituals although the carried objects are idiosyncratic. This would be the case for processions conveying the varied gifts and payments of visiting traders to the vault (see Chap. 4.3 below on aduta), a well as in the case of other scenarios.

[25] The thought occurs that the fashion-conscious religious processions may have ventured outside the palaces: "While most discussions would seem to envision ritual processions as taking place mainly in the areas of the palaces, there is no reason why they could not have traversed greater distances and perhaps lasted for several days. This would have allowed the participants to be seen by many people along the way" (Whittaker 2012: 197). Such processions may have been organized when "Potnia of the Labyrinth" (Chap. 4.2 below) circuited from one cult center/palace to another (see Whittaker 2012: 198). Indeed, the public exposure helps to explain why the deity circuited in the first place (cf. Chap. 10.8). For additional wise remarks about processions, see Lane (2016: 76–77).

[26] Bietak (2000: 218 with Fig. 9) notes Minoan and Mycenaean processions in which women are represented "with shoulders in frontal view, in order better to show the open *décolletage*. However, only one breast is shown, even when the *décolletage* is wide enough to expose both breasts." I think the reason is to display the pattern and fit on the shoulder and arm of the bodice. Alternatively, or in addition, it may have to do with easing breastfeeding.

[27] The "priestesses" of the Graces and Horai model the palaces' garments and the frescoes gleam from their status as deities of nature's beauty. Was their original function to model garments or to be nature deities? Francis' (1992) discussion is thought-provoking.

figures." Thus, a gold signet ring discovered in Megalo Monastiri in Thessaly (*CMS* V, no. 728 = Arachne 163910) depicts a procession of two women toward a shrine with so-called "horns of consecration" (about which I elaborate on below). However, Rousioti (2016: 237–238 with Figure 6a) observes, "Emphasis is given in the illustration … [to] elaborate skirts, whereas the torsos and the faces are more stylized." Again, in Mycenaean LH IIIB (12th century): "the stylization of the figures and their costumes is distancing them from reality…. But these manne-quins have become stiff and remote." (S. P. Murray 2016: 86). It bears repeating that the extent of stylization raises my suspicion that something is happening that is not quite a ritual of politics or religion. Rather, the evident convention to stress the garment is best explained by a commercial motivation.

Indeed, even the figures understood to be gods appear to be uniconic. However, in placing the highly anonymous visual world depicted in the frescoes, it is well to recall that models in fashion shows are intended to enhance the clothes not the other way around: they are expected to be expressionless and to avoid eye contact with the audience. A textile *showroom* is intended to operate similarly. This is the way the palace does operate.

There is perhaps one major exception to the use of interchangeable fashion models in Minoan/Mycenaean fashion shows. This deviation concerns the fres-coes in Xeste 3 in Akrotiri, which portray fashionably dressed young girls as well as mature women. The age distinction is indicated by apparent differences in breast development and hairstyles. A distinction among models in terms of age may well reflect religious and/or social considerations. Thus, Chapin (2006: 77) observes,

> But despite the high social status suggested by their costuming, the Lady of the Landscape and her processional companions play only supporting roles in the ritual narratives that focus on a younger generation of girls and women. The frescoes seem to suggest that as matrons, these women have ensured the future of Theran society by rearing its next generations and as mature women, they serve their goddess and their community in ceremonial roles intended to support their daughters. Indeed, the entire fresco program of Xeste 3 seems to place an emphasis on *communal*—rather than individual—aspects of ritual performance and deemphasizes the role played by any one figure except, of course, for the Enthroned Goddess.

More concretely, the older women may provide occupational training to their "daughters," including in the production of textiles.

One may accept all of this *interpretation* of the roles and importance of the figures in the frescoes and remain profoundly dissatisfied. *Why do the frescoes place so much stress on the garments themselves?* Could not the objectives outlined by Chapin be just as well achieved without magnificent decorations and references to the use of expensive murex and crocus dyes and, especially, to deliberate technical departures from naturalism? The answer I propose is that the assumed religious/social motivations have largely been repurposed to become a vehicle suitable for a fashion show. We might say that the Mycenaean palaces are built upon epic's primal fashion show, the "Judgment of Paris" (see esp. Chap. 14.5.c).

Now, it is true that in most contemporary fashion shows, the models are young and of a standardized shape. However, there are fashion shows that feature older models and/or big and tall models. "Diversity" on some runways makes economic sense as older or larger women (and men) also wish to purchase stylish garments.

Hägg (1985: 213) is understandably surprised by how apparent goddesses are treated in frescoes:

> But which is their function? For a number of reasons they are unlikely to be cult images, if by cult image we mean an image of a deity with which the priests and adorants interact in some way or other. Cult images are anointed, bathed, dressed, etc.; since most of these acts are difficult to perform with a two-dimensional picture, two-dimensional cult images are very rare in the archaeological record.... If the female figure is not a goddess but a priestess playing the role of the goddess in a cultic performance. This is what I would call enacted or performed epiphany, different from the ecstatic epiphany, i.e. when an individual or a group of worshippers see the deity in a vision. If these representations had been epiphany scenes, I think they would also have included worshippers bringing offerings, like on the Mycenae ring. As far as we can tell, there were no worshippers present in any of these scenes.

In short, the absence of distinctive ministering priests and worshippers makes it difficult to interpret the frescoes as depicting strictly religious themes. More importantly, *the absence of perceived priestly officiants and celebrants makes it difficult—but not impossible—to interpret the richness and glamour of the garments depicted as intended devices to raise the dignity and importance of clergy and, hence, of the religious institution itself.* That is, it is much easier to claim that depicted rituals and participants enhanced the garments than the opposite view that the garments enhanced the (anonymous) rituals and participants.[28] Still, it stands

---

[28] It seems obvious that the men wearing hide skirts in Knossos' "Corridor of the Procession Fresco," wherein they received processions with gifts, are priestly officiants, even though they are not among the richly dressed participants.

to reason that the beautiful garments enhanced both the status of the cult and its commercial prospects. We may take it for granted that both benefits were sought by the management.

Along the same line, scholars sometimes have had difficulty in interpreting the religious reference of observed postures and "gestures of worship" performed by elaborately dressed female subjects in the Aegean Bronze Age. Perhaps this is because, in some instances, there is no religious meaning—that is, the models are simply striking *poses* as in contemporary photo-shoots featuring professional models in which "anything goes."[29] That the models are posing would also help to explain instances in which viewers are unsure whether the model is standing, sitting, dancing, or whatever. This is only a hypothesis, but it cannot be dismissed by simply citing the hypothesis that the religious and secular could not be distinct as long ago as the Aegean Bronze Age.

That the religious actors were also fashion models would also explain why,

All the women depicted in Mycenaean frescoes have long thick black hair which is arranged in elaborate hairstyles, often tied with coloured ribbons or interlaced with beads. The depiction of the eyes would seem to indicate a heavy use of eyeliner, and the white colour of the skin may reflect the use of makeup to achieve a desirable paleness.

Whittaker 2012: 193

Hägg (1985: 209, 214) has noticed the absence from the frescoes of the patron commissioner. There is a very good reason for this: the frescoes are not intended to "sell" the commissioners, but to convince the garment buyer—they are art for the sake of commerce—the textiles produced by the palaces. For this purpose, I think it was successful art.

I am not saying that the Minoans and Mycenaeans cared only about earning profits by selling luxury textiles. I am not suggesting that elaborate and ornate palaces/temples are necessarily selling garments to the public or that the jewelry worn by women in paintings is for sale. I *am* arguing that the commercial aspect is the distinctive ingredient in the palatial evidence available to us. I refer here to the emphasis on the richness of garments and on the technical details of garment construction, which culminated in the counter-naturalistic depiction of garments.

---

[29]   For example, see the pose of a woman wearing a marvelous dress in the "Park Fresco" in Agia Triada. Note also, in support of this interpretation, Rehak's (1997: 167ff. with Fig. 4) discussion of a fresco in which the posing women are embedded in and accompanied by idealized landscapes.

Looming in the background of the argument for commercial motivation is the fact that the palaces were, in fact, devoted to the production of luxury textiles and needed a place to properly display them. An alternative explanation of the evidence of the frescoes might be that the Minoan/Mycenaean elite was composed of artisans and burghers, for whom the quality of their work ranked among the highest values. I think it is possible that the Minoans/Mycenaeans exalted or even worshipped the work of their hands. Perhaps they were not mainly interested in selling for profit. At the same time, however, the religion of workmanship was sustainable because the beautiful depictions and designs brought clients to their places of business.

Another crucial observation made by Blakolmer (2010: 23) is that, unlike contemporary art in Egypt and the Near East, the Minoan/Mycenaean iconography is not only "uniconic" but also "apolitical:"

> Whereas the existence of individual rulers can be denied neither on Minoan Crete nor in Mycenaean Greece, both cultures lack any images of a portrayed ruler. Furthermore, not in a single case might we detect the depiction of an individual event of historical character. Wall paintings, stone relief vessels, seal images and further iconographic media are depicting mainly generic scenes. Political and cosmological ideologies of the elites have rather been transported on a metaphorical level of "hyperindividual" character. Thus, Aegean art appears of a widely "apolitical" and non-historical character.

I will not rehearse the objections to Blakolmer's argument, such as the throne in the megaron. He is certainly on the mark in his remarks about the absence of references to historical rulers and other VIPs from Aegean art. Moreover, Blakolmer (2010a: 266) is surely right in contrasting the "missing ruler" aspect of Aegean Bronze Age iconography with its typically palatial venue (cf. Blakolmer 2017a: 107–109). However, *I would suggest that the relative iconographic invisibility of the political and historical is consistent with my theory that the pictorial program of the palace was to sell textiles.*[30]

Just as contemporary firms often have a spokesperson or brand ambassador, so too does the iconography of the palace understandably not completely ignore the goddess Potnia, because this goddess has to be seen as the essential sponsor and guarantor of the textiles being offered for sale.[31] Typically,

---

[30] As noted in Chapter 1, the architectural features of the palaces became more elaborate over time, but the earliest Minoan palaces had numerous loom-weights: for example, 400 found at Knossos and 100 at Phaistos.

[31] I am old enough to remember the years (1954–1962) in which Ronald Reagan represented GE to the world.

she is an indistinct figure wearing an elaborate dress. However, as will be seen, the commercial role of Potnia is visible in the "genii" (Chap. 11.2) and in the deployment of numerous iconographic attributes—flounced skirt, sacral knot, double-headed axe, figure-eight shield, running spiral, rosette, "horns," and other symbols that persisted in Bronze Age Aegean ceramics, glyptic, and textile showrooms until their demise. The latter symbols, especially when combined, served as virtual trademarks of the textile enterprise.

Blakolmer (2019b: 76) observes,

> While, during the Early Mycenaean period, an independent manifestation of rulership can be defined in the motifs of the warrior in his chariot on the Shaft Grave stelae at Mycenae, by the palatial periods of LH IIIA-B the Mycenaean 'iconography of power' became more strongly orientated towards that of (earlier) Knossos. Therefore, hardly any depiction of a ruler can be recognised. Late Mycenaean iconography points to a palatial élite identity and widely suppressed the identity of the *wanax* himself in both meanings: as the highest office of authority and as an individual person. *Paradoxical as this sounds, the more powerful the rulers at Mycenaean centres became, the more they disappeared from iconography.*[32]

Apparently, the ruler evolved from a newly wealthy participant in the luxury textile business to the position of an anonymous CEO operating under an even more anonymous BOD in an architectural structure mainly intended to market the product.[33]

It probably remained a main function of the *wanax* to preside over ceremonies in the megaron/great hall of the palace (Palaima 1995: 132). However, more important was the *wanax*'s role to defend the palace and its commercial operations with physical force when the need arose.[34] Yet, it is difficult to find frescoes that openly recognize this vital task. At Knossos, it has been observed that the *running spiral* was associated with weapons, ships, and men's clothing

---

[32] Emphasis added.

[33] Palaima (2016: 134) seeks to establish the importance of Mycenaean kings by citing, among other factors, the "survival of Homeric terms" and the "tholos tombs," but both Homer and the tholoi were earlier than the Mycenaean palaces.

[34] Palaima's (2016: 141) comments on the unimpressive military testimony offered by the tablets Vc 73 and Vd 136 from the Room of the Chariot Tablets at Knossos. I think he underestimates the importance of this factor. In addition, he tends to privilege the importance of the Mycenaean king while not mentioning the reported role of the Minoan Minos in suppressing piracy. Palaima (2016: 150) notes that the Mycenaean king was enthroned. I think this is probably true but at the same time the throne at Knossos—the one actually found in place—might reflect an earlier Minoan practice.

that presumably linked them with the king's power in both New and Late Palace (Günkel-Maschek 2020: 563). Egan and Brecoulaki (2015: 298) note that depictions of the Argonaut (a cephalopod relative of the nautilus) "abound at Pylos, and based on their find contexts seem to have decorated rooms of the palace during both its earlier and later phases. Indeed, the Argonaut is so ubiquitous and prominent at the Palace of Nestor that it might even be understood as a royal 'totem,' much like the griffin." The Argonaut design, like the Nautilus design, stands as a proxy for maritime excellence (see Chap. 11.5) and, as Egan and Brecoulaki (2015: 300) observe, the depictions may, therefore, serve to call attention to the vital maritime skills of the *wanax*. The role of the expert sailor and foreign traveler has historically been a major source of entrepreneurial inspiration. The point is that those who understood the iconographic code might possibly recognize the *wanax* in the argonaut symbol. Visitors in later times might also recognize the *wanax* in the iconographic symbols of the griffin (Chap. 11.5) and of the lion (Chap 11.4). My view is that the balance of current evidence suggests that the *wanax* sat in the throne found at Knossos.

Nevertheless, the iconography and ceremonies in the Minoan or Mycenaean palace were constructed primarily to glorify the palace's textiles and only slightly and by reflection—and result—the provider of maritime expertise and physical force. The implication is that the palace is much more like a commercial enterprise than a state. That the iconography in the palace seems not to be fit for a palace serves to confirm the lack of fit of the theoretical models previously applied to it. In the end, Immerwahr (1990: 59, 62) has good reason to wonder whether the Minoan society is a "secular society in which fashion dominated," but she avoids this conclusion by calling attention to frescoes depicting the same garments in which a religious theme is self-evident. However, religion and fashion are not mutually exclusive, and Minoan society, as depicted, is not a secular society in which fashion dominates but rather a religious society in which fashion dominates.

3

Minoans and Mycenaeans

A S NOTED earlier, the terms "Minoan" and "Mycenaean" are standard terms applied by Bronze Age scholars to leading participants in the western Aegean. Their meanings are by no means standard, however. "Minoan" focuses mainly on influences radiating out of Crete (primarily from 1850 to 1375 BCE), and "Mycenaean" applies primarily to influences understood as coming from mainland Greece (1600 TO 1170 BCE). These influences may be broadly conceived as cultural or ethnic, military or economic, or a combination of all of these. Alternatively, these difficult-to-define distinctions can be mitigated by placing them within a temporal context: that is, "Earlier Bronze Age" (Minoans) and "Later Bronze Age" (Mycenaeans); or in terms of institutions: "First and Second Palace Periods" vs. "Third Palace Period," or "Shaft-Grave Period" and "Mycenaean Palatial Period." The entire problem of these meanings is well-discussed by Boyd (2016: 385–387 with references).

The present study adopts an eclectic position: it works mainly within the temporal frame while remaining alert for traces of economically significant differences. *The line between what is Minoan and what is Mycenaean is often difficult to see, and this study sometimes finds itself unable to distinguish between the two.* In particular, changes over time in the frequency and design of glyptic motifs—for example, the double-headed axe—are, with few exceptions, not considered. Although not ideal, I trust that the resulting losses are more than compensated for by gains from an innovative analysis of central problems less sensitive to temporal or other kinds of variations. Fundamental trends are hardly ignored in the present study, however. This chapter, for example, includes an attempt to distinguish between Minoan and Mycenaean garment designs. In addition, Chapter 17 seeks to explore and explain the economic changes that took place after the "collapse" of the Mycenaean palaces.

Chapter 2 focused attention on the numerous and significant commonalities in the Minoan and later Mycenaean garment styles and modes of display. However, in the "Later Bronze Age," the Mycenaeans took over the important Minoan textile center at Knossos in Crete, and, in terms of archaeological visibility, they displaced the Minoans in the eastern Aegean at such centers as Lemnos and Miletus. The question considered next is whether the transition from Minoan to Mycenaean dominance in the textile industry was at its core a reaction to emergent changes in textile fashions and/or manufacturing techniques. Chapter 4 considers whether there is evidence for changes in the management of textile marketing. On matters of textile style and technology, I will rely on the judgments of specialists.

Concerning textile technology, I have not found in Nosch's (2015) thorough analysis evidence signaling a significant change leading to the Mycenaean Era. Furthermore, Trnka (2007: 128) claims there is no significant chronological difference in the types of garments—that is, the Mycenaeans did not introduce new styles: "The typology of Aegean costume types shows a wide chronological span, so that in general, Aegean garment types are not a significant chronological indicator." There are, however, Minoan/Mycenaean differences in the decoration of garments:

> The Minoan textile patterns, especially from the end of the Old Palace Period onward, are marked by the greatest complexity and variety, but also by a kind of refinement concerning color combinations—in contrast to the simplicity of a restricted two-color system of the Mycenaean [presumably palatial] ones. Theran textiles show more simple patterns, either of geometric or floral style, but they are accentuated by a strong light/dark contrast created by different colored border-band combinations.

Trnka's remarks on differences in textile patterns are not clear to me, and my waters are muddied by an additional remark that appears to negate the prior ones: "Distinctions like textile patterns, colors and band decorations within the fabrics might indicate the social rank of the wearer" (Trnka 2007: 128). Does this mean that the Mycenaean patterns differ from the Minoan because the wearers represent distinct social and economic categories?[1]

S. P. Murray's remarks (2016: 44) seem more determinate than Trnka's:

> Dresses and skirts made with intricately patterned fabrics are more characteristic of Minoan and Cycladic island examples, while the garments depicted in frescoes from the mainland (Mycenaean) sites show a tendency toward less elaboration in the garments' main cloth, with more attention being paid to the colors and patterns of their trims.

---

[1] After reviewing the negative or neutral arguments of Trnka and S. P. Murray, I will turn to the research of Bernice Jones (2018), who strongly argues that the Mycenaeans did introduce new types of garments.

Hence, the difference is that the later Mycenaeans placed less emphasis on the main cloth and more on colorful and interesting trims. On the other hand, except at the very end of the Mycenaean period, there was no period when garments became plain and simple:

> In mainland Greece, the strong influence of Minoan culture on Helladic society reverberates through the art and iconography of the LH II periods, and in some subjects, primarily the representations of processions of women in festal attire at Thebes, Tiryns, and Pylos, the iconography of costume is tenacious until the close of the Mycenaean Age. The depiction of exuberant and complex Minoan-style fabric patterns will quickly fade, however, and the interest in decorative textiles will narrow in on the bands that edge bodices and skirts. By mid-LH IIB (13th century BC), most fresco decorations of clothing will show the use of rather plain textiles and simple tunics or a stylized and formulaic ritual dress.
>
> S. P. Murray 2016: 76

Apparently, the intricacy of decorative patterns was reduced in Mycenaean palatial times. However, the practice of displaying the garment to the best advantage continues and is well illustrated in Plate 2, which depicts a participant in a Tiryns procession. Note how the intricacy of the fresco border and the design on the box serve to uplift the status of the garment and garment-wearer.

More concretely, S. P. Murray (2016: 83 with Fig. 3.43) discusses a painting of three female figures in situ in the "Room with the Fresco Complex" at Mycenae.[2] This painting, she suggests, may reveal a confrontation of two textile traditions: "Thus, in this fresco we have three different modes of dress depicted, of which only one expresses the old, familiar signifier for prestige. It seems the Mycenaeans had some ideas of their own about what constituted status garments." It is not clear to me whether the reference is to the introduction of new types of garments or to a change in ideology favoring one style over another.

S. P. Murray (2016: 84–85 with Fig. 3.44) also discusses "The Procession of Women" from Thebes:

> The decorative intricacies of this costume are concentrated on the edgings of the bodice—this is where the artist has focused on the

---

[2] The fresco in Room 31 in the palace at Mycenae is examined from a different perspective in Chap. 10.6.

careful execution of a variety of patterns with differing degrees of complexity.... The display of beautiful and intricate fabrics that was so prominent in the Knossos Procession Fresco is not a priority here, but we can see in the Mycenaean taste for ornamental edgings a practical side: the production of intricate textiles was relegated more efficiently and quickly to the band loom.

In addition, S. P. Murray (2016: 85) finds "reduction and simplification of motifs" in depictions found in dumps at Tiryns and Pylos: "All bodices are red, with borders that are still ornamental but more limited in variety." Similarly at Pylos, Murray (2016: 88–89 with Fig. 3.48) seems to suggest that there are simplifications, although "colorful and highly ornamented edgings remained popular for prestige clothing" (but compare with Fig. 3.46).

Did the (alleged) simplifications (emphasis on decorative trim) in Mycenaean garments make them *less costly* than the earlier Minoan fashions, and was a cost reduction the key factor in causing a Mycenaean boom in textiles? Did the Mycenaeans anticipate Ford's Model T (in 1908, the "first affordable automobile") and produce the first affordable high fashion garments? Nothing in the specialists I have consulted suggests such an outcome. Indeed, in her "Conclusion," S. P. Murray (2016: 90–91) mentions only the Minoan high luxury garments, not the Mycenaean adaptation of the 13th century.

However, there *are* hints of an innovation that scholars have not yet fully accepted. In analyzing the newly discovered "The Pomegranate Bearer" fresco from Tiryns, Papadimitriou, Thaler, and Maran (2015: 190ff.) note first that the pomegranate bearer's dress is in the Cretan style of a flounced skirt with an open-fronted bodice which had been borrowed by the Mycenaeans, but it very much appears that there is a *second* type of flounced skirt that is not borrowed— an asymmetrical skirt, also attested at Mycenae, that

> juxtaposes nonmatching sections of cloth.... The assumption that the change in color served to differentiate both knees is not convincing, particularly if, as now seems likely, the new scene from Tiryns shows standing figures wearing very similar skirts in which sections of yellow cloth with red details alternate with blue and black details as well as with ornamental beads.

This is not yet a textile fashion Model T skirt, however.

One point does seem clear: Mycenaean frescoes in Knossos and on the mainland display the Cretan style garment of a decorated flounced skirt with both open and closed bodice. B. Jones (2018: 177) is explicit on the variations in this basic garment:

At the beginning of the New Palace period on Crete a new Minoan dress design appears that is adopted by the Mycenaeans and continues until the end of the Bronze Age. Images of the garment replicated in this exhibition appear ca. MM IIIb-LM IA on the female figure on the gold repoussé finial of a silver hairpin from Shaft Grave III, Mycenae ... [Plate 3],[3] the Knossos "snake goddesses" HM 63 and HM 65 [Y 63 and Y 65] [Plate 10]; the Agia Triada "goddess and kneeling woman; the Thera crocus basket emptier and the crocus gatherer with blue head, the necklace bearer, the wounded woman and the veiled maiden, and the bending lady and fragmentary maiden; and in LH IIIA1on the two women on the Ivory Triad from Mycenae (fig. 2), the Mykenaia of LH IIIB, from Mycenae (fig. 3), and the ivory statuette from LH III, Prosymna (fig. 4).

The style (partially), adopted from the Minoans by the Mycenaeans, has the V-shaped front and includes both the closed and the famous open-bodice models and, in the case of HM 65, the rows of alternating plain and striped squares (see Chap. 10.2 with Figure 13). These variations are displayed in frescoes from Crete, Akrotiri, and the mainland.

In an innovative study, Konstantinidi-Syvridi (2015) expanded upon the evidence from frescoes and reinforced the conclusion that fashions in the Mycenaean period were not confined to a "traditional" robe that left the breasts uncovered. She studied the uses of numerous clothing ornaments, typically from burial contexts, and found they "indicate that the Mycenaeans had at their disposal a wide choice of costumes, both wrap-around and cut-to-shape (sewn), plain, and embroidered or otherwise decorated." (Konstantinidi-Syvridi 2015: 155). The wide variety of garment ornaments, or accessories, were often made of gold.

B. Jones (2018) has most thoroughly considered the differences between Minoan and Mycenaean garments, including constructing actual—wearable—garments. She (Jones 2018: 181) shows that the Mycenaeans not only displayed variations on a garment of Minoan origin but also introduced a *new* garment. The latter, reconstructed from the previously mentioned Tiryns "Pomegranate Bearers" fresco, is a tunic or *chiton* with sidebands curving into the armpit. This tunic is both elegant and practical with either an open or a closed bodice (see Papadimitriou, Thaler, and Maran 2015: Figures 2–5). Note, in passing, the salesmanship behind depicting the "sidebands" at the front of the dress, so as to better exhibit them to potential clients.

---

[3] For discussion of the iconography of the piece from Shaft Grave III, see Warren (1985: 200–201). The important feature is that the figure grasps and holds a garland of papyrus stems and flowers.

Egyptian tomb scenes of the fifteenth century BCE—from the time of Hatshepsut to Tuthmosis III, a period of fifty to sixty years—depict visiting Aegean traders wearing loincloths with long codpieces. Likely sometime in the reign of Tuthmosis III, the vizier Rekhmire repainted his tomb in an attempt to depict the visiting Aegeans—sixteen in number—wearing pointed kilts (with different designs) instead of loincloths. These "Keftiu" wear the new kilts in the tomb of Menkheperreseneb, the son of Rekhmire. Thus, it very much appears that sometime in roughly the mid-fifteenth century, there was a change in the style of men's garments—from breechcloth to kilt—and that this change may have been of Mycenaean origin. However, Rehak has shown that Minoans and Mycenaeans wore both garments before and after the time of their depiction in the Theban tombs. Thus, even if there was a change in style and even if Mycenaeans inspired the change, it was not as radical as the Egyptians perceived it to be. Matić and Franković (2017: 126) offer the following explanation of the Theban tomb scenes:

> This change [from breechcloth to kilt] cannot be interpreted in ethnic terms either in the Aegean, as already emphasized by Rehak, nor in Egypt. It rather reflects the changes in dress appropriate for processions in the Aegean, reflecting not the composition of the Aegean embassy sent to Egypt, but the change in the way in which the Aegean elite represented itself on such occasions. The local occasions for these processions are not as defined as those in Egypt of the time, because of the lack of written sources. However, the iconography indicates gift-giving as the general idea behind them.

Accordingly, there was no Mycenaean innovation in men's dress.

Having reviewed the Theban tomb evidence and themes on Mycenaean pottery, Barber (2016: 230) has developed a more salient perspective on Mycenaean textile innovation:

> The only sense I can make of all these facts is that the Mycenaeans and the Syrians had been very busy mixing up new textile ideas together during the time between the deaths of Thutmose III [late Minoan/ Cretan-early Mycenaean garments] and Rameses II [mainland or island Mycenaean garments] (certainly the traceable spread of Mycenaean pottery makes this probable), and that in the course of swapping techniques, fashions, motifs, and even people back and forth, they had all by various routes come to the point of making and sometimes wearing friezed and/or paneled kilts, some of which were handsomely decorated in a new Animal Style. To judge from the styles, it would even

seem possible that tapestry technique had finally made its way to the Aegean, alongside the native weft-float methods.

If I understand it correctly, Barber's (2016: 229) new perspective is that the Mycenaeans innovated textiles radically by focusing on pictorial themes:

> Pottery in Bronze Age Europe and the Near East seldom looks so much as though it was copied off of textiles as does the Mycenaean pottery of Rhodes, Cyprus, and the other Mycenaean or 'Mycenaeanized' islands and seaports.... [I]t looks as though some weavers in the Mycenaean world had begun to depict real objects (e.g., birds and animals) and even scenes (e.g., chariot processions), making them quite naturally into friezes and panels; and the potters had followed suit,[4] taking forms directly from the weavers. For remember, too, that a pot-painter is *not* tied to strip-shaped space the way the weaver is, and in fact is normally confronted with complexly curved and nonlinear surfaces that may be covered in any order whatsoever.

Thus, Mycenaean weavers had begun to move from pleasant or striking designs to representational art in "technicolor."

Examples of pictorial-themed Aegean garments are difficult but not impossible to find. The idiosyncratic faience crocus-decorated bell-shaped skirts from Knossos' "East Temple Repositories" (see Plate 4) come immediately to mind, as does the "Lady of the Landscape" with its rocks and blue birds from Xeste 3 (Rehak 2004: 94–96; Chapin 2008). There are many pictorial themes, such as bull leaping, horses with chariots, hunting, and armed battles, painted on the walls (Lang 1969: 26–28). However, if garments with pictorial themes became popular under the Mycenaeans, one wonders why we do not see them depicted in the Mycenaean palaces. For me, this is a complication raised by Barber's theory. *One possible solution is that in the era of the Mycenaean palaces and frescoes, the pictorially decorated textiles had fallen out of fashion.* Is there evidence pointing in this unexpected direction?

Homer testifies to the importance of pictorial themes in *early* Mycenaean times.[5] *Representational art is precisely the dimension of weaving that Homer chooses to stress in the Iliad*: Helen was "in the hall, where she was weaving a great purple web of double fold, and thereon was broidering many battles of the horse-taming Trojans and the brazen-coated Achaeans, that for her sake they had endured at the hands of Arēs." (*Iliad* 3.125–128; tr. Murray *LCL*). A less clear example of

---

[4]   Compare with Marcar (2004: 228–229), who makes ceramic painting the dynamic factor and argues that textile decoration as relatively unchanging.

[5]   It is argued in Chapter 12 that the Epics predate the Mycenaean Linear B tablets.

such a taste is the description of Andromache, wife of Hector as "weaving a web [*peplos* "cloak"] in the innermost part of the lofty house, a purple web of double fold, and therein was broidering flowers of varied hue." (*Iliad* 22.441–442; tr. Murray *LCL*).

There is no reason to assume that pictorially themed textile decoration would have been confined to male garments. In the latter connection, note that when he departed for Troy, Odysseus wore a purple cloak that was *diploos*, meaning double-folded or double-woven—that is, the cloak had two wrap systems (*Odyssey* 19.225–226; Kolonas et al. 2017: 536 n. 22). The passage does not say that the cloak was decorated with pictorial art, but the possibility is hinted at by the revelation: "Verily many women gazed at him in wonder" (*Odyssey* 19.234–235; see Chap. 15.2). Would the "shine" of the garment be sufficient to generate this kind of response?[6]

By working backward from pottery to weaving, Barber has, I think, grasped the nature of the elusive Mycenaean textile innovation that spurred the replacement of the Minoans and simultaneously credited the Mycenaean Argolid with making this innovation (see Chap. 14.6). A new emphasis on pictorial representation in costume may have responded to new cost-reducing technology, or it may have responded to the changed tastes of affluent consumers. I suspect the latter explanation and that Mycenaean entrepreneurs sought and gained control over Cretan skilled labor and showplaces in older Minoan centers such as Knossos, Malia, and Phaistos.[7]

The hypothesis that pictorial themes on garments in frescoes lost out among consumers and were replaced by decorative themes finds support in the fact that Knossos' faience crocus-decorated bell-shaped skirts (depicted in Plate 4) were in fact found buried in cists beneath the palace floors. Hatzaki (2009: 20) presents logical arguments[8] that, under a regular program of "structured deposition," styles/objects were buried/disposed of because they were no longer popular/in use:

> [R]ather than being the leavings of accidental damage during a destruction event, followed by ceremonial disposal, this assemblage [in the

---

6   In the Linear B tablets, cloth is commonly referenced as TELA + PU, which has been interpreted to mean being of "double fold." This kind of cloth is frequently mentioned with color terms such as red and purple. Moreover, in a few tablets from Knossos the TELA + PU is explicitly dyed with murex purple (see Chap. 7.3). I am not aware, however, of evidence that the TELA + PU cloth was, or was not, decorated with pictorial themes.

7   *Odyssey* 19.172–181 testifies that "Achaeans" (mainland Greeks) were present in Crete before the Trojan War.

8   Some of the objects buried were damaged or worn but others were still in new condition. One of the buried objects is a vase with a Linear A inscription.

Temple Repositories] constitutes the remains of a carefully planned ritual in which specific objects were chosen for disposal and were in effect removed from circulation.[9]

Given the high cost of communication, it is reasonable to assume that styles typically changed very slowly in the ancient world, but they did change. The open-bodice may have gone out of style, but it lasted hundreds of years. As noted elsewhere, the information available to clients concerning garment designs provided in frescoes painted on palace walls needed to be augmented by using designs on plaques and ceramics, but eventually the paintings had to be changed as is attested to in the case of Knossos.

In explaining the trends in commercial dominance, it would not be accurate to say that the Minoans were unwilling to innovate or experiment. Minoan variety is visible at Knossos in the "Temple Miniature Fresco" ("Grandstand Fresco")/"Sacred Grove and Dance Fresco," wherein, as Blakolmer (2018: 40) explains,

> A differentiation of female skirts can also be observed ... while the female participants in the foreground as well as the female spectators seated in the front row are clad in the common flounced skirt, the women of smaller scale wearing the horizontally striped skirt with vertical bands are standing beside the multi-storeyed palatial architecture (Fig. 17).

The lack of variety in the fresco—that the women seated in the front row wear, what appears to be, the same dress as the women on the elevated platform—detracts from the variety of garments offered at the Knossos palace. On the other hand, the depiction in the same scene of other women wearing more "practical" garments indicates that *there was, in fact, variety*. Furthermore, while the scene depicts women watching the other women on the platform, "the iconographical language suggests that the women are not only watching but are being watched themselves" (Marinatos 1989: 39).

A grandstand audience of elegant women wearing the latest fashion is also suggested in a fragmentary Minoan fresco (perhaps LM IB) from nearby Tylissos (Rethemiotakis 2020: 119–123, 131). The latter women observe an outdoors procession of fashionably dressed women who model the garments they themselves wear, while at the same time displaying stretched-out fabrics. My source is Rethemiotakis (2020: 128–129), whom I quote at some length:

---

[9] Weingarten (1989a 47) suggests a similar unexplained trend in seal iconography—first to greater naturalism and realism and then to purely decorative.

Specifically in fragment 7, three female figures wearing flounced skirts step leftwards in the procession (Fig. 14). The lower flounce of the first and third figures is also decorated with Λs-and-strokes like those of the seated figures, whereas the second figure's skirt is covered by what seems to be a variant form of the previous pattern, on a larger scale and in a more orderly arrangement, consisting of partly conjoining Λs in zigzag disposition with some additional dots between them. A white material filling the gaps between the three figures, with a wavy blue band along the upper part between the first two, is also embellished with the familiar Λ pattern which according to the evidence provided by the corresponding decoration of the skirts also indicates a textile. In all likelihood this is in fact a large piece of fabric with a tasseled white and blue part, or two superimposed pieces, carried by three women in their hands or, more likely, suspended from a rod resting on their shoulders in the manner portrayed in the procession of gift bearers (Subject 5). In the upper part of another fragment (no. 6) a small part of a blue skirt bearing red tufts is all that survives of another female figure with the same dress decoration (Figs 15–16). Behind her a broad white field with a wavy lower outline, presumably another large piece of cloth, bears faded decoration of a curving series of dots (remains of scale pattern?) and disorderly zigzag lines, probably folds and crinkles of the fabric. There was certainly another now vanished female figure on the right holding the other end of the fabric in the manner described above in fragment 7. It is highly possible, therefore, that all the figures portrayed on both fragments belong to a single file of females carrying fabrics in procession.

In fact, in the Tylissos iconographic corpus, the carrying and presentation of various types of textiles are repeated six times in five fragments. There are different color combinations and, arguably, they are intended to represent the latest fashion creations; some fabrics may have been intended for making garments for males (Rethemiotakis 2020: 131–132).[10]

Rethemiotakis (2020: 140) describes "evidence" that shows that the palaces did not produce the textiles but he grants that the textile work "was probably allocated to workshops in the environment of urban houses and

---

[10] It seems possible to me that the Tylissos miniature wall painting depicts not only garments and fabrics but also references the (purple) dyeing process. I base this surmise on Rethemiotakis' (2020: 132–138) remarks about the carrying of an amphora and the wielding by a man of a "red stick" with a blue and red "hook" at its end.

peripheral centres, elite buildings and 'villas' producing a variety of fabrics under the supervision of the palace." He finds it obvious that "the fabrics being brought in procession were exhibited in the fields to the audience, specifically the elite groups, with the purpose of advertising and attracting attention to the merchandise" (Rethemiotakis 2020: 140). I completely agree. What is also interesting is that the processions intended to advertise (and sell) garments and fabrics to "elites" are depicted on the wall of the palace/labyrinth in Knossos and *on the wall of, what was most likely, the provincial palace/labyrinth at Tylissos.*[11]

Why is the audience depicted in the Knossos (and the Tylissos) fresco? It is no longer always possible to make out facial expressions, but likely the original frescoes depicted looks of delight that would have sharpened the appetites of entering visitors. The image of a large audience on the wall in the hallway multiplied the positive emotions of those proceeding through the hallway to the center where they would become the audience or, in current terminology, it was an "affirmative/enhancing image" (Panagiotopoulos 2012: 72–73).[12]

B. Jones, S. P. Murray, and the other excellent textile specialists have worked diligently to isolate the differences in Minoan and Mycenaean textile technology and fashion. I see clearly that both groups offered garments in striking colors in various styles, including both open and, more practical, closed bodices. In addition, both Minoans and Mycenaeans utilized both art and psychology to make their garments more attractive to clients. On the other hand, except for a possible introduction of pictorial themes, I do not clearly see the importance of the differences mentioned by the experts. The problem is that, in terms of fashion, differences that seem small to outsiders, to which is the group I belong, may be decisive to consumers—which is what matters. I am very much attracted, however, to Elizabeth Barber's proposal that the Mycenaeans emphasized representational art in their garments. Costumes featuring pictorial decoration were previously rare under the Minoans. For me, this constitutes a major innovation

[11] Rethemiotakis (2020: 140) says the murals decorated the walls of a "sumptuous mansion." I find it difficult to believe that the owner of a "sumptuous mansion," who did not also own the advertised textiles and participate in their sale, would advertise them on his wall (compare Rethemiotakis 2020: 141). In other words, the "sumptuous mansion" is a palace or is used by the palace.

[12] The faces of the garment-wearers themselves are purposefully generic to focus the attention of the buyers on the garments; the faces of the audience are delighted to make the buyers feel delighted.

capable of explaining why the Mycenaeans gained dominance in the international market for luxury garments.[13]

***

Turning from textile innovations to maritime technology, it appears to scholars such as Emanuel (2014) that:

> The Mycenaean ascendancy in the 14th and 13th centuries BC was accompanied by the introduction of the Helladic oared galley, a long, narrow, light vessel propelled primarily by rowers and designed specifically for speed.[14] The Helladic oared galley represented a true break with prior ship design, as typified by Minoan sailing vessels and Cycladic craft like those depicted on the famous miniature fresco from the West House at Akrotiri.

The "oared galley," as will be seen below, gave the Mycenaeans special advantages in exploiting the textile market in the rich-in-gold Black Sea region. Perhaps the oared galley was strictly a Mycenaean innovation made in pre-palatial times, together with the brailed rig[15] (Emanuel 2014). This, indeed, would have been a major innovation.

Finally, nothing I have said denies that the Mycenaeans were warlike—indeed, their decisive contribution was probably the willingness to invade the Troad to wrest control of the entrance to the Black Sea. Without this willingness to use force, they could not have fully realized their market ambitions.

---

[13]   If I understand correctly, Petrakis (2012) attributes the Mycenaean's textile success to the introduction of administrative centralization. At this point, I would object, arguing that we know little know about Minoan administrative practices.

[14]   Palaima (1991: 284) cites seven personal names from Knossos and Pylos that attest to the involvement of Mycenaeans in sea trade including *na-u-si-ke-re[-we]* 'Ship-famous' (KN X 214) and *o-ku-na-wo* 'Swift Ship' (KN V(2) 60 + 151.4). "It is interesting to note that most individuals bearing these names are involved in herding-perhaps a mere reflection of the large pool of anthroponyms provided by the numerous and/or lengthy livestock tablets from Knossos and Pylos" (Palaima 1991: 284).

[15]   In the *Iliad*, the oared galleys of the Achaeans at Troy are both "swift" (*thoē*) and "hollow" (*koilos*)—that is, capable of dealing with the prevailing winds and currents and having ample space in their holds for textiles (e.g., 1.11, 1.26). The brailed rig facilitated sailing even into the wind.

4

The Houses of *Haute Couture*
Megaron, Labyrinth, and Xeste 3

A S DRIESSEN (2002: 8) has deduced, the palace—at least the Minoan palace—is a *public facility*:

> The absence of royal iconography and burial and the attention to group activities suggest another hypothesis which is here explored: that the Court Compounds served in the first place as communal, ceremonial centres that were used in both non-elite (outside) and by elite groups (inside) as meeting places for ritual, integrative actions.

While it is true that Driessen does not mention the central courtyard as hosting the rituals of commercial life, his analysis of the palaces as not having "a primary political or residential function" (Driessen 2002: 13) certainly leaves space for this most important and ancient form of communal life.

It is reasonably clear, however, that narrow stoas lined the palace walls of the Minoan courtyards and that the stoas had sheltered balconies accessible from inside the palace. As Palyvou (2002: 173) notes, the balconies were places "to see or to be seen." Given our argument that the palaces were places where textiles were marketed, it is possible to imagine that fashion models and salespersons could have displayed the latest garments on such structure to those gathered below in the courtyard proper.

Maran (2009: 76) has viewed the Mycenaean citadel, including the palace, as a *"performative space:"* "In my opinion, a terminology which derives from performance theory and the theatrical connotation of the term 'staging' is useful to understand not only medieval castles, but also Mycenaean citadels, whose configuration deserves to be interpreted under the viewpoint of performative esthetics." The procession, however, is the central staged element for both Minoans and Mycenaeans.

*More concretely, how did it work—that is, how did Mycenaean and Minoan palaces
structure their interface with visiting textile buyers?*

1. Megaron

The long rectangular central, or great megaron (or tripartite suite)[1], of the
Mycenaean palaces in mainland Greece at Mycenae, Tiryns, and Pylos was an
excellent vantage point for clients to observe both textiles and textile workmanship.[2] It had its own canopied front entrance followed by a vestibule (with
stairs to upper floors) that led into the great hall. The latter term refers to a
long-pillared corridor, provided on each side with points of entry, which also
served to separate the megaron from the other rooms in the palace while rooms
at the very rear were accessible only from the corridors (Hopkins 1968: 45–46,
50). It is important to keep in mind that the entire palace complex, not just the
megaron, played a role in textile marketing.

Generally, "The configuration of images and the built environment in the
palaces were carefully designed to interact with the social practices carried out
on ceremonial occasions. The layout of the architecture preconfigured certain
patterns of movement and guided participants of processions toward the center
of the palace," but, more specifically, "In Pylos ... and Tiryns, procession frescoes flanked the final part of the way toward the throne room and enabled a
convergence between images and actual practices" (Maran and Wright 2020:
114). The configuration of the passageways also makes it clear that only small
groups could have participated in the processions to the center (Maran and
Wright 2020: 115).[3]

There are contemporary remains of the foundations of the megara with
fragments of their superstructures and mural paintings (Hopkins 1968: 46). The
great megaron at Pylos has a libation installation on the floor, whose channels
are near a floor depression, probably for a chair/throne that was flanked by
a griffin, a fantastic eagle-like animal,[4] and a lion. The base for a throne was
also found at Tiryns, and actual stone fragments of the throne were found at

---

[1] The term "megaron" has pronounced ideological overtones in that its basic reference is to a
   specific architectural structure, but the term continues to be used to describe architectural
   structures that may or may not conform to that structure. For discussion of this term, see
   Werner (1993: 3–5). For a recent detailed survey and study of the Pylos megaron, see Egan (2015).
[2] Maran and Stavrianopoulou (2007: 290ff.) consider the religious role of the *wanax* "king," but,
   for me, as stated in Chapters 2 and 3, the religious rituals referenced in the frescoes were not
   ends in themselves but also effective vehicles for selling textiles.
[3] But the wider population must have benefited from the success of the garment industry that
   operated in the palaces.
[4] A winged griffin together with half-rosettes is featured on a seal from a tholos in Pylos (*CMS* I,
   no. 293 = Arachne 157519). About the role of griffins, see at length Chap. 11.5.

Mycenae.[5] (For reasons that will emerge below, I do not believe that conventional thrones were used by goddesses or their priestesses.) There are various indications that visitors in the megaron might be entertained with poetry and music by bards and "wined and dined" (Immerwahr 1990: 133–134; Rehak 1995a: 110; Chap. 11.5).

In small-scale scenes from the "Vestibule Fresco" that leads to the throne room in Pylos, men are wearing elaborate long tunics and various other garments, as well as at least one woman who is

> advancing toward a structure (shrine?). Given the nature of the scene and the movement of the figures toward the actual doorway to the throne room, the representation of high-status members of the court can be assumed. There seems to be an effort here to note, nominally, the more impressive appearance of the tunics worn by elite men for this special occasion: stiff, white fabrics with scatter patterns of dots, ψ-motif (Fig. 3.49), or dotted rosettes.
>
> S. P. Murray 2016: 89

The motif referred to by Murray is the saffron stigma.[6] My view is that these impressive tunics are not (or not only) depicted only to attest what was worn by *anonymous* "high status members of the court" but rather to attest that the garments are available for sale.

A noteworthy feature at Pylos, shared with Xeste 3 (Chap. 4.3 below),

> is the extensive use of purple hues especially in the Throne Room, its Vestibule and Hall 64, where it was primarily used on the backgrounds and accessorily to indicate details. Although purple hues are still

---

5   For a good photograph of the floor depression at Pylos, see Weilhartner 2012: 215, Figure 1. The presence of a throne in the megaron at Pylos (*allegedly*) finds confirmation in the 2014 discovery at Mycenae of a massive stone seat fragment that was "securely identified as belonging to the massive stone throne of the palace at Mycenae—the only Mycenaean throne found so far on mainland Greece" (Maggidis 2019: 165); other specialists strongly doubt that the stone fragment is part of a throne. Maggidis (2019: 169) argues that the length-to-width ratio of the stone throne bases at Mycenae and Tiryns (1.32) is comparable to the throne base at Pylos (1.19) and Knossos (1.24). A number of Linear B tablets at Pylos in the Ta series refer to a wooden throne (*to-no thornos* alphabetic Greek *thronos*). The terminology of "thrones" and "flowers" is fully explored below in Chapters 7.6 and 11.5.
6   Murray refers to "Man with a Long Tunic" Vestibule Fresco (Lang 1969: Plate 120). I thank Marie-Louise Nosch for calling my attention to this interpretation of the design as a saffron stigma. For a much less stylized representation of saffron, see the form of the Linear B sign *33 in Palaima 2020a: 9–10. Sources for Pylos: Hägg 1985: Fig. 2-3; Rehak 1995a: 118; Rasmussen McCallum 1987: 130–132. For analysis of Tiryns' *Frauenprozession* fresco see Maran and Thaler 2017; for the procession of well-dressed women at Thebes, see Reusch 1956.

well preserved on numerous wall painting fragments from the palace (ranging from pink to lavender and red-violet), a large number of burnt plaster fragments exist where purple paint layers now appear grey, with scanty irregular pinkish or purple spots. Such a dramatic alteration of the original colour may be entirely justified, considering that organic dyes and murex purple in particular, when heated to 150°C, turn to grey and decompose entirely in temperatures over 200°C.

Brecoulaki 2018: 399

The fashions worn by the models in the frescoes are complemented by textile themes painted on the floor.[7]

Two final points about the Pylos megaron remain. First, Linear B tablets dealing with textile workers and textiles were found in the megaron (Skelton 2011).[8] Second, Chapter 11.5 shows that the drinking/banqueting "Syrian"-robed men seated on campstools in the Pylos megaron fresco are most probably Syrian textile merchants.

There are reflected several important elements in the reconstruction of the megaron in Homer: when Odysseus enters the Phaeacian's great hall (*megaron*), he finds Queen Arētē, whose skills Athena gave to her, weaving purple cloth—a wonder to behold—while she sat against a pillar (*kiōn*) together with her slaves (*dmōai*) (*Odyssey* 6.304, 306); also leaning against the pillar is the *throne of the king* (*Odyssey* 6.309–310). Thus, there may be two thrones, but only the king's is made explicit.

Who sat on the (alleged) throne in the Mycenaean megaron? Rehak (1995a) points out that seated figures are overwhelmingly female in Minoan and Mycenaean iconography, and he reasons that the figure seated on the throne in the megaron must have been either a queen or a goddess (cf. Maran and Stavrianopoulou 2007: 287–290). In a sealing from Chania (*CMS* VS1A, no. 177 = Arachne 165408), in which an attendant serves the goddess, it is not clear whether the goddess sits on the edge of a chair with a back or upon a stool stacked on other stools.

Homer provides support for Rehak's generalization in that Athena, who has a gift of fine textiles deposited in her lap by the priestess Theanō and the Trojan women, must be seated (*Iliad* 6.297–310).[9] However, as in the case with

---

[7] If I understand correctly, Hirsch (1980) maintains that, if anything, the textile themes were inspired by the natural patterns in the stone floors.

[8] Some scholars believe the tablets were not originally in the megaron but instead fell to this position when the palace was destroyed.

[9] The language in line 6.103 implies that Athena is seated.

the seated Phaeacian Queen Arētē, Homer does disclose what Athena is seated upon, unlike what he reveals about Penelope:

> Then wise Penelope came forth from her chamber like unto Artemis or golden Aphrodite, and for her they set by the fire, where she was wont to sit, a couch/chair without a back (*klisia*) inlaid with spirals of ivory and silver, which of old the craftsman Icmalius had made, and had set beneath it a foot-stool (*thrēnus*) for the feet, that was part of the couch, and upon it a great fleece was wont to be laid. On this then wise Penelope sat down.

Odyssey 19.53–59, tr. Murray *LCL* modified;
tr. Murray *LCL* modified.
For a similar seating apparatus,
see *CMS* II.3, no. 252 = Arachne 159350.

Herodotus (5.72.3) testifies that the Athenian priestess sat on a *thronon*—that is, I submit, on textile cushions (see Chap. 11.5). The explicit "throne" (*thronos*) of King Alcinoos testifies to a male occupant (see further §4.d). There are some seals in which females sit on chairs with backs. Nevertheless, there is reason to believe that the throne in the megaron belonged to the king.

2. Labyrinth

a. Knossos: Structure and Iconography

The "Throne Room" at Knossos may not have played the same role in marketing textiles as the more lineal, axial megaron in Pylos and other Mycenaean palaces did. The Minoan megaron has fragmentary frescoes: positioned next to the throne there are (wingless) griffins decorated with rosettes (shoulder and body), and (Cretan) date-palm trees (colored bright red and reddish-brown); also, present are papyrus reeds with red flowers and lotus. The dominant color of the room is red: the walls, benches, the throne, and part of the floor. Human figures and processions are absent, however (Galanakis, Tsitsa, and Günkel-Maschek 2017).

It is in the palace's—the *labyrinth's*—winding corridors, passageways, and staircases that Minoan textile clients were seduced.[10] The "Corridor of the

---

[10] Let us concede at the outset that it is often/usually difficult to distinguish between specifically Minoan and specifically Mycenaean physical features at Knossos (see Gulizio 2011: Chap. III). About processions, the decision is unanimous. Gulizio (2011: 172) makes an important observation: "What is particularly interesting is the popularity of the procession theme among later Mycenaeans, despite the fact that it is clearly rooted in Minoan religion. The Mycenaeans even maintained the typical Minoan dress. The trend among Mycenaeans to depict monumental,

Procession," for instance, has frescoes depicting life-size figures of women wearing various dress styles and jewelry. Note that the passages were perhaps narrow and needed to be artificially lighted, but the Minoans chose to decorate them with frescoes.

Furumark (1960: 90) anticipates well the impact of the frescoes covering the corridor walls: "There we also find life and movement, extension, a sense of infinity. In the pictures one finds no up or down; the ground is present in both upper and lower margins, and one feels like a spectator in the middle of the scene, present and yet apart." He continues by describing the architectural structure the Minoans employed to activate the sense of incorporation:

> A glance at the plan of a Minoan palace shows that even the architecture has the same expression [of infinity]. There are no façades, no suites of rooms, no direct entrances. By round-about ways, through long corridors, one enters the central courtyard. This is the true heart, for everything else opens on to it.

Morgan (2005: 25–28) adds to this description: "One of the extraordinary features of the original Minoan paintings is their tendency to envelop the spectator in a total environment. In many cases, the paintings covered the entire surfaces of three of four walls, so that the person entering the room was immediately surrounded by the painted world." While paintings in the surrounding town and countryside featured nature, those in the palace emphasized figures: "The different subjects may partly reflect chronological changes (many of the figurative Knossos paintings are later in date than the nature scenes) but also express an essentially palatial programme" (Morgan 2005: 27–28).

Concerning iconography, the Minoan palace arguably had several figure-eight shield frescoes—also fragmentary—the most famous of which is from the "Hall of Colonnades," located very near the "Hall of Double Axes," which, like the (presumed) "Queen's Megaron," had running spirals with central eye rosettes.[11] With respect to the spirals, Günkel-Maschek (2012a: 12) explains:

---

life-sized human figures participating in a religious procession began with the Corridor of the Procession fresco. Perhaps the processional theme was somehow appealing or familiar to the newly-installed Mycenaean administrators at Knossos, that they deemed it appropriate enough for their own religious beliefs and practices to incorporate it into the iconography of the new palace." Whether in Knossos or on the Greek mainland the procession theme was successful in achieving the objective of those who chose it to exalt their religion's luxury garments and/or to exalt the religion of their luxury garments.

[11] For the Minoan connections of the figure-eight shield, see Rehak (1992). It seems to me that when the vertical figure-eight shield is turned sideways, it becomes a stylized double-headed axe symbol. To judge by some of the accompanying pottery the fresco in the "Hall of Colonnades" may date to the Mycenaean period (Immerwahr 1990: 177; M. Shaw and Laxton 2002: 103). For

Formally speaking, the spiral friezes of the Hall of the Double Axes and of the Queen's Megaron at Knossos as well as of the Banqueting Hall at Zakros [in Crete] belong to the category of upper zone decoration. In the Corridor of the Painted Pithos and, most probably, also in the Loggia of the Hall of the Colonnades, the spiral friezes traversed the walls at mid-height and thus accompanied persons moving through the passageways. The spiral provided the halls and passageways with a symbolically charged atmosphere.

For Galanakis, Tsitsa, and Günkel-Maschek (2017: 88), the Throne Room is "part of a broader iconographic 'programme' that includes other important parts of the palace, like the West Porch and Corridor of the Procession Fresco and the polythyron halls in the East Wing." Indeed, the running spiral appears on the kilts of men in the Procession Fresco (Günkel-Maschek 2012a: 123 n. 40 with references).

There is good reason to believe that the operation of the textile showroom occupied several floors in the Minoan palace. Thus, to see a more complete picture of Knossos' textile marketing operation, one must retreat from the Throne Room and accompany a procession of life-size, well-dressed figures down the "Grand Staircase" to the "Room of the Double Axes."[12] However, there is uncertainty here, not least because of later changes in design (Hood 2005: 64). Morgan (2005: 28) stresses the western side of the structure and refers to the depicted procession in the "Procession Fresco" from the "Corridor of the Procession Fresco," negotiating *two* grand staircases: "Real processions of important visitors would have walked between the painted figures who guided the way into the interior of the labyrinthine palace, while focusing attention on the central figure of a 'goddess'."[13] It is possible that the "goddess"—or the priestess acting for her—held a double-headed axe in each hand (discussed by Boloti 2017: 9–10 with Figure 1.14). I find it likely that the processional route included both west and east.

---

the spirals, see Günkel-Maschek (2012a: 119 with Fig. 3). Recall that the griffins are decorated with rosettes.

[12]   Sources: Cameron (1970: 365); Hägg (1985: 210–211 with Fig. 1); Hood (2005: 70). I tread in deep waters here because Cameron's reconstruction of the "Procession Fresco" is very much disputed.

[13]   As yet-unpublished research disputes whether the female figure is a "goddess." A Linear B specialist informs me that in the Knossos Gg tablets, "the context strongly suggests a deity."

b. The Meaning of "Potnia" and of "Potnia of the Labyrinth"

With respect to the Knossos palace as a "labyrinth," note that Knossos' Linear B tablets (e.g., KN Gg[1] 702, KN Oa 745) knew a *da-pu$_2$-ri-to-jo po-ti-ni-ja* 'Potnia of the Labyrinth.'[14]

Potnia is usually translated as "lady, mistress" or even as "goddess," all of which are in themselves rather uninformative with regard to her legal status. It is more helpful to consider that the word "potnia" is the feminine form of Indo-European *posis* 'lord, husband' (Beekes s.vv.). More helpful still is that "potnia" is derived from an Indo-European root **pot* that refers to "power/empowerment" (Nikoloudis 2006: 49–50). What "power" did Potnia possess? A (the?) Potnia is a female who, like males including the *wanax* (see below), possesses the legal right to make contracts and to own property. She is, thus, legally empowered (cf. Chap. 6.3) to control/allocate resources of all kinds.

For example, according to Killen (1983: 74; 2000: 16), Potnia owns a workshop in Thebes in Of 36.2. Sheep designated *po-ti-ni-ja-we-jo* 'Potnian' in Knossos are legally contracted for and controlled for by Potnia (Lupack 2008a: 2–3 with references). Rutherford (2013: 268) observes that "some individuals (smiths, women, a perfumer) are specified as *po-ti-ni-ja-we-jo* = *potniaweios* 'belonging to potnia' or 'potnian', a usage that suggests that religious institutions played a significant social and economic role within the state."

"Potnia of the Labyrinth" may be rendered as "(Female) Owner of the Labyrinth."[15] The references to ownership do not mean, as Ruijgh (1998-1999: 258–260) has suggested, that the specified properties are legally owned/controlled by the priest of Potnia. To say "flocks owned by the priest" would probably mean that although the priest has ownership powers, he remains a priest. The proper meaning of "flocks owned by Potnia" is that the flocks are owned by the legal owner of the Potnia cult. This owner, as explained by Silver

---

[14] Also, there is *da-pu-ri-to* in KN Xd 140, but the tablet is broken off beyond this; cf. Chadwick 1957: 117; Kotsonas 2018a: 370). *Da-pu$_2$-ri-to daburintho* is identified with alphabetic Greek *laburinthos* (Yakubovich 2002: 104ff.).

[15] There are indications that, in some of the above instances, Potnia is playing the contractual role of "collector" with respect to properties owned by the palace, as does the *wanax*. This, if I understand correctly, is the position of Nosch (2000c), who notes sheep-breeding activities in Knossos under Potnia (and Hermes). Thus, in the D1 sheep and wool tablets from Knossos, the adjectival form potniaweios is sometimes found in line A instead of the collector (Gulizio 2011: 239–240). In other words, collectors have legal rights of control, which are ownership rights, but they are not yet free-and-clear ownership (see Chap. 8.4). Chadwick (1957: 119–120) cites the "uncouth form" and notes a variation in Knossos X 7742. As compared to men, women are only rarely linked with property in the Linear B texts, and even less so at Pylos than Knossos. Iconographically, the legal status of Potnia would be revealed by her cross-dressing, or bearing arms, or being colored red instead of white (see especially Chapter 10.6 for discussion).

(1995a: 30–32), might be the state, a private founder (*archēgetēs*), or a family (*genos*).

If I am correct that the title "Potnia" signals the bearer's right to own property, form contracts, and participate in lawsuits—then I see no *logical obstacle* to also calling a number of otherwise distinct deities and mortal women (see below) "Potnia." By "distinct deities," I mean that various Potnias are subject to separate cult managements.[16] In my opinion, any "unmodified Potnia" would refer to "Potnia of the Labyrinth," who, as the deity presiding in the Knossos palace (discussed shortly) and owner of the double-headed axe,[17] is politically, economically, and iconographically the most important of the Potnias. Furthermore, while distinct Potnia cults are possible, my impression, supported mainly by iconography, is that Potnia's functioning in various places, among various groups, or in assorted functionalities is under central management, probably located at Knossos. That is, in practice, there is only one Potnia. I suggest below that this "Potnia" was (and remained) the goddess Athena.[18]

The Linear B tablets reveal the name of several Mycenaean women who, without a doubt, are *qualified*[19] to bear the designation "Potnia." One is the "key bearer" Karpathia at Sphagianes (PY Eb 388), who is being sued by the *dāmos* (PY Ep 704.7–8) for not working two plots of (*ka-ma?*) land assigned to her.[20] Another is the priestess Eritha of Potnia at Sphagianes near the Pylos palace, who also is being sued. Some of the circumstances that reveal her legal qualification are compactly summarized by Palaima (2000: 9; cf. Olsen 2014: 136–138, 217, 223):

> In the principal entry in what we consider the final recension PY Ep 704.7-.8, the 'priestess' *Eritha* is recorded as 'holding' and 'claiming to hold' *e-to-ni-jo* land 'for the deity' (*te-o* interpreted as a dative). This is then disputed by the *damos*[21] in the clause which immediately follows

---

16 Since deities must be regarded scientifically as imaginary, the reference to a deity must be to its real-world sponsors. For Homeric attestations of the title "Potnia," see Cunliffe (1963: s.v.). For Linear B, see Boëlle (2004: 26–81); Blakolmer (2010a); Thomas and Wedde (2001: 4–5). In about 25 or 26 attestations of the name "Potnia," it is modified by what is the name of a place. There is "Potnia of Horses" and perhaps "Potnia of Grain" (at Mycenae MY Oi 701.3), but this is better read as "Potnia's Grain" (Palaima 2000-2001: 478; cf, Potnia's Athēnaiē; Potnia's Mother).

17 The double-headed axe is discussed shortly and is subjected to close analysis in Chapter 10.1.

18 This is not to say that Potnia is the sole goddess with legal property powers. It is to say that for Potnia, this is the central attribute.

19 I do not know why they are never referred to as "potnia."

20 The implication is that the total tax or rent being assessed for this category of land is a fixed quantity with the result that the other landholders must make good to the owner of the land for the shortfall resulting from Karpathia's (alleged) malfeasance. Possible commercial implications of "key-bearing" are discussed below.

21 For the *damos*, as a corporate body, see Lupack (2011: 211–215).

in this entry: "but the *damos* says that she has an *o-na-to* plot of the land category known as *ko-tona-o ke-ke-me-na-o* (partitive gen. plur.)" In the presumably preliminary single entry document corresponding to this entry Eb 297[22], a plural group of 'land-holders', the *ko-to-no-o-ko*, are recorded in the place of the *damos* as the parties disputing the claim of the priestess.

The *dāmos* (represented by the *ko-to-no-o-ko*) asserts that, notwithstanding her legal claim (*eukheto*[23]), Eritha holds the contested plot of land in her own name and, consequently, we may understand, that she is being sued for the payment of rent or taxes due on the (relatively large) plot.[24] Thus, Eritha, who unlike an ordinary woman can be sued, qualifies for the legal status of "Potnia."[25]

Furthermore, Eritha is described as Priestess of Sphagianes—a district in Pylos where, as may be deduced, there is only one priestess and one priest (Nakassis 2013: 11–12). The importance of Sphagianes in Pylos is demonstrated by the fact that the *wanax* "king" is "initiated" (probably meaning "appointed") by a cult in Sphagianes (Chap. 8.4). The unnamed deity to whom Eritha attributes her large plot is likely Potnia, as Potnia is the most important goddess in the Sphagianes district, as measured by the value of gifts from the *wanax* during the navigation season (PY Tn 316).[26] These gifts are directed to "Potnia," not to one or more of the specialized Potnias known to be present at Sphagianes.[27]

---

[22]   That in Eb 297 the name Eritha is omitted, and she is simply referred to as "the Priestesss" (*i-je-re-ja*, *hiereia*) suggests to me that Eritha is the priestess of a monolithic Potnia.

[23]   See Muellner 1976; Nagy 2003: 73–77.

[24]   See Nakassis 2013: 171–172, 253. This formulation of the lawsuit suggests that the payment due to the palace by the *dāmos* or, if they are not different names for the same thing, by the *ktoino-hokhoi* to the *damos* is a *collective payment*—that is, it is a fixed total payment owed by the *damos/ktoinohokhoi* such that if Eritha does not pay her share, the others in the group remain responsible for it.

[25]   Shelmerdine (2016: 619) mentions, "At Knossos, the names of two orchard "owners" can be construed as female:]*ka-wi-ja* (Uf 79) and *pe-ri-je-ja* (Uf 1031). Their holdings are comparable to those of the men recorded in the same series." Kessendra in the Pylos tablets is important (Shelmerdine 2016: 623) but her legal status is insufficiently defined to make a judgment. I do not wish to become involved in a discussion of "ownership" vs. "holding" of land. I have one interesting but unnamed candidate for the designation "potnia." The reference is to a female burial in LH IIIC in Building 1 at Lefkandi Toumba in Euboea: "This individual's jewellery [including two gold discs placed over her breasts] is justifiably celebrated, but she was also interred with a dagger (35 cm), placed beside her head and right shoulder, that is no less remarkable" (Harrell 2014: 99–100; Kosma 2012). It would be easier to find ordinary women with property rights in the correspondence relating to the early second-millennium textile trade between Assur in Assyrian and Kanesh in Anatolia.

[26]   The other deities with Potnia at Sphagianes are Manassa, Posidaeia, Thrice-Hero, and House-Master (Palaima 2004a: 241).

[27]   Texts locate several specialized Potnias in Sphagianes: *u-po-jo* Potnia (Fr 125, 1236) and, Potnia Aswia (Fr 1206).

Thus, it is left to the single/consolidated management (possibly an *archēgetēs* or a *genos*) of an inclusive Potnia cult to allocate resources among its various "Potnia products."[28] There is only one Potnia management at Knossos, and, hence, there is only Potnia;[29] I think the most important name/specialization of the goddess is "Potnia of the Labyrinth."

c. Where Did "Potnia of the Labyrinth" Reside?

The Knossos tablets mentioning "Potnia of the Labyrinth" do not explicitly say where in Knossos the Labyrinth is located (Gulizio 2011: 131). It is essential to place her on the ground, however. To find a placement in Knossos, we may, I think, rely on the archaeologically attested winding corridors, the iconography of processions, and the size/importance of the Knossos Palace.[30] Placement of the Labyrinth in Knossos' Palace of course connects Potnia with—or better, puts in her hands—the *double-headed axe* that is, suffice it to say for the present, the prime symbol of the Minoan palace: labyrinth. At the most basic level, the masons decorated the pillars of the Knossos Palace with double-headed axes.

A linguistic connection of the double-headed axe and the labyrinth can be made by citing the Lycian (southwestern coast of Anatolia) word *labrys* = *laburinthios* = (Greek) *pelekus* 'double-headed axe'.[31] Admittedly, the equation of *labrys* with *laburinthos* is philologically "speculative" (Beekes s.v. *laburinthos*)– that is, it is not supported by a rigorous etymology. Nevertheless, it is possible, and I think plausible.[32]

The main problem with a Knossos location for the Labyrinth is that "labyrinth" is famously identified with "maze." In fact, a square maze-like scheme is depicted on the reverse side of a tablet from Pylos (PY Cn 1287).[33] The text deals with an

---

[28] Here remains the mystery: "Who owned/controlled Potnia?" In this kind of connection, Lupack (2017: 200–201) calls attention to men at Pylos who played important roles in both the religious and secular spheres.

[29] I also believe that this Potnia presided over the entire Mycenaean world. Potnia as a circuiting goddess is considered in Chapter 10.7.

[30] This is not at all to say that Potnia did not retain a Labyrinth presence in other, cult centers (see above and below).

[31] Plutarch, *Greek Questions* 45. Silver 1992: 29; recent discussion Carless Unwin 2017: 16–25. The double-headed axe is typically linked with a female deity. Plutarch has Heracles take it from Hippolyte and give it to Omphale; Homer has Calypso give one to Odysseus; most prominently, Minoan/Mycenaean iconography associates enthroned female figures with the symbol.

[32] If I understand Yakubovich (2002: 106–107) correctly, he sees the adjective *labraundos/laburinthos* as meaning the "place belonging to the ruler." This is agreeable but apparently, the Minoan "ruler" made the double-headed axe the prime symbol of his "place" (see Evans 1901: 106–112). Alternatively, did the Minoan "ruler" occupy the "place" whose prime symbol is the double-headed axe? Were ownership of the labyrinth and of the state legally separable?

[33] The purpose of the maze-drawing is not clear. Some scholars believe it is only a "doodle."

individual who is called a "messenger" (*a-ke-ro* = *angelos/angel*; Beekes *s.v. aggelos*) (Nakassis 2013: 219).[34] I see the maze-symbol not as representing a real maze but as representing a winding path or even a *spiral* path. That is, *in its origin*, the "labyrinth" is, like the Knossos palace, a multi-floored building equipped with winding passages and perhaps with spiral-like stairways. Indeed, the twisted structure of the Knossos palace is referenced by mason's images of the triton shell on its structural pillars.[35] Of course, the winding passages find their echo in the Ariadne's use of a thread to guide Theseus out of the Labyrinth (discussed in Chap. 10.2). In Mycenaean times, it appears that the term labyrinth applies to the entire palace complex, including the tripartite suite known as megaron.

There is some support for an etymological connection between *laburinthos* and *laura* 'narrow street, narrow passage, alley' (Beekes *s.vv.*).[36] The labyrinth's line of interpretation finds support in the *Odyssey* (22.126–140), wherein we find the term *laurē* is used with respect to Odysseus megaron in Ithaca:

> Now there was in the well-built wall a certain postern door, and along the topmost level of the threshold of the well-built hall was a way into a *passage*, and well-fitting folding doors closed it. This postern Odysseus bade the goodly swineherd watch, taking his stand close by, for there was but a single way to reach it. Then Agelaus spoke among the wooers, and declared his word to all: "Friends, will not one mount up by the postern door, and tell the people, that so an alarm may be raised straightway? Then should this fellow soon have shot his last." Then Melanthius, the goatherd, answered him: "It may not be, Agelaus, fostered of Zeus, for terribly near is the fair door of the court, and the mouth of the *passage* is hard. One man could bar the way for all, so he were valiant. But come, let me bring you from the store-room arms to

---

[34] It may well be asked why a scribe in Pylos would sketch a "maze symbol" referring to the palace at Knossos. One answer is that the symbol referred to the *palace* at Pylos (including the relatively linear megaron) as a labyrinth. That is, there were "labyrinths" for marketing textiles in every major Mycenaean center, including in Pylos. The "maze-symbol" applied to all notwithstanding their distinct architectures. Without trying to push the connection too far, it is worth noting that to function efficiently in several places simultaneously a textile-marketing organization would need to employ "messengers/envoys." However, PY Cn 1287 is a long tablet that mentions other occupations and slaves. I hold out the hypothesis that the "agent" (*aggelos*) was recognized in real life and in iconography by a distinctive hairstyle—something like the "topknot" worn by the griffin.

[35] The "triton" may have been identified with a species of murex (see Chap. 7.4).

[36] The earliest mention of the word *laburinthos* in classical Greek literature is in Herodotus 2.148 and refers to a stone structure in Egypt near Lake Moeris: "It has twelve roofed courts with doors facing each other: six face north and six south, in two continuous lines, all within one outer wall. There are also double sets of chambers, three thousand altogether, fifteen hundred above and the same number underground" (2.148.4; tr. Godley *LCL*). It is often added that the *laburinthos* is a mortuary temple (see further Chap. 10.3).

don, for it is within, methinks, and nowhere else that Odysseus and his glorious son have laid the arms."

Odyssey 21.120. Tr. Murray *LCL*; emphasis added

Cunliffe (s.v.) defines *laurē* as, "A passage leading from front to back on the outside of one of the side walls of the *megaron*."[37] Thus, it appears that "Potnia of the Labyrinth" could be at home in structures unlike those at Knossos.

Iconographic support for structures with *spiral paths* is provided by the (probably) gold leaf-covered Minoan "Zakros Rhyton" or "Sanctuary Rhyton" (ca. 1550-1500 BCE) that is said to depict a "peak sanctuary"[38] (see Chap. 1):

> The entire surface of the rhyton is decorated in low relief. Schematic rocks, sparse flowers and shrubs, and wild goats in 'flying gallop' suggest the wildness of the landscape. On the upper part of the vase, the mountain peak, is a tripartite shrine enclosed by a wall. The main entrance to the building is decorated with spirals and topped by a pair of wild goats sitting facing one another [four goats on the roof with two facing one another]. The side rooms are decorated with staffs and banners and have horns of consecration with perching birds on their roofs. In the courtyard of the sanctuary, in front of a flight of stairs, are three altars.[39]

A structure with stairs, running spirals, and "horns" might well be occupied by a Potnia of the Labyrinth.[40]

These are not the only connections with the Labyrinth, however. There are also more direct references to textile production. The landscape surrounding the building is not only "wild" but also "wooly," considering that the Cretan "wild goat" (agrimi), positioned on the roof and galloping among *crocus flowers*, is arguably a source of hair capable of being dyed and made into a high-quality fabric (Frangipane et al. 2009: 20;

---

[37] LSJ (s.v.) adds that in a later source, *laurē* is applied to "an *alley* or *bazaar* at Samos, where women sold delicacies of all kinds."

[38] Noting a baetyl that is flanked by agrimia and surmounting a tripartite shrine within a mountainous setting, Crooks, Tully, and Hitchcock (2016) suggest that this wavy-edged baetyl represents a stylized mountain. However, no tripartite-structured building has so far been found on a Cretan mountain. Apparently, the connection of the tripartite peak sanctuary with mountains is ideological.

[39] The compact description of the "Zakros Rhyton" AE 2764 is from the Heraklion Archaeological Museum and is available at http://odysseus.culture.gr/h/4/eh430.jsp?obj_id=7908 (accessed February 12, 2021). See also J. Shaw 1978: 432–435 with Fig. 8.

[40] Using Linear B values for the transliteration, the term "labyrinth" appears in Linear A "libation formulas" inscribed on two stone vases (PK Za 8 and 15) that were found in eastern Crete (Palaikastro) in or near the Petsofas peak sanctuary (Judson 2017: 58–59).

Del Freo et al. 2010: 340).[41] The meaning of the "Zakros Rhyton" and the agrimi is discussed in greater detail in Chapter 7.5.

Later, but important, support for the view that even a symbolic reference to *winding passageways* can identify a structure as a labyrinth is provided by a monument and inscription of the third or second century BCE from Didyma in Asia Minor. The word "meander" occurs in the monument and the associated inscription, a table of building costs, "identifies the structure as a *Labyrinthos*.... The structure has a ceiling decorated with a swastika-meander and houses two stairways leading up to a roof or terrace from either side of the gate of the great hall of Apollo's temple" (McCabe 1985 Inscriptions *Didyma* 84 and 86; Silver 1992: 234 with n.1 including the omitted references).[42] It is not stated whether the stairways were spiral or decorated with spirals.

As we have noticed earlier, the palace at Knossos featured processions on one or two "Grand Staircases." Pendlebury (1933: 38, 42) states (most doubt-fully) that the staircase had a spiral form that seems to be reflected in the already-noted ubiquitous spiral designs and figure-of-eight shields. Concerning the latter, Rehak (1992: 116 with Fig. 4) has called attention to four MM III B (ca. 1700 BCE) faience plaques from a cist in the South Propylon at Knossos, on which a woman, who holds both hands to her breast, wears a flounced skirt and a necklace of figure-eight shields. These necklaces and the flounced skirts, I suggest, connect the depicted women to service in the Knossos Palace.

Another note with respect to the iconography of what I will, henceforth, call the Labyrinth at Knossos is that the running spiral and figure-eight shield continue to play a central role during the Mycenaean Era. In the throne chamber, this usage is attested to by the presence of as many as twelve stone alabastra and lids decorated with running spirals and figure-eight shields: "The vessels have been considered one possible sign of Mycenaean occupation, since the alabastron shape is nearly identical in mainland and Minoan pottery between LH II and LH/

---

[41] Herodotus (4.189.1–2) refers to the dyeing of goat's hair in the context of Athena's "aegis": "It would seem that the robe and aegis of the images of Athena were copied by the Greeks from the Libyan women; for except that Libyan women dress in leather, and that the tassels of their goatskin cloaks are not snakes but thongs of hide, in everything else their equipment is the same. And in fact, the very name betrays that the attire of the statues of Pallas has come from Libya; for Libyan women wear the hairless tasseled 'aegea' over their dress, colored with madder, and the Greeks have changed the name of these aegeae into their 'aegides'." (tr. Godley *LCL*; cf Chap. 6.2 on Athena as Potnia of the Labyrinth).

[42] At this point, the waters become much deeper! An Etruscan-Corinthian *oinochoe* from Tragliatella (the "*Truia* Vase") dated to the end of the seventh century BCE has a vertical dividing line—argu-ably representing the wall of a building—within which there are two levels (two floors) on each of which is depicted a nude couple lying in bed having sexual relations. Next to the couples, there is the design of a labyrinth that is labeled *truia*: "It may be the Etruscan form of Gr. *Troia*, but more probably, it has the same root as the Latin verb **troare*, which describes the circular movement of dancing Salian priests" (van der Meer 2011: 71–72).

LM III A1" (Rehak 1992: 115–116 with references). Again, with respect to laby-rinths in other locations, the (allegedly) surviving throne bases at Mycenae and Tiryns have relief decorations of a running spiral (Maggidis 2016: 169).

Spirals are clearly central to the identification of a labyrinth. Hesychius[43] gives *laburinthos* the meaning "spiral-shaped place" (*kochlioeidēs topos*), but the literal meaning is *shaped like a certain kind of seashell*. The *Suda* entry includes a reference to the votive offering of the Grotto Nymphs: "You tell me, labyrinth in the sea, who found you as quarry from the grey sea and dedicated you?" The *Suda*'s shell is called *kochlos*, meaning "shell-fish with a spiral-shaped shell, 'sea-snail, land-snail', also 'purple-snail, kohl' " (Beekes s.v.). Beekes also notes the word has the vocalic variation *kochlax/ka-*.

The labyrinth resembles a spiral-shaped shell. Alternatively, the labyrinth is identified as a place involved with spiral-shaped shells or, more specifically, with murex shells. I affirm that the relationship is not purely a geometric one. A prism seal from Palaikastro (*CMS* II.2, no. 262a = Arachne 158903; see Chap. 7.2.5 below) depicts a goat (or agrimi) together with what is obviously a murex snail. The murex snail, I propose, represents the labyrinth, and the seal calls attention to its role in marketing or manufacturing purple wool; recall now the mention of "labyrinth" in two (Linear A) inscriptions from Petsofas.

A relevant Linear B term related to the *kochlos* snail is *ko-ki-re-ja*, which appears in Pylos Ta 711.2.[44] This text records valuable objects presented by the *wanax* to one Augias (*Au-ke-wa*) on the occasion of his appointment/promotion (*te-ke*) to the high office of *damokoro*. A presented object is said to be "decorated with sea-shells" (Kelder and Poelwijk 2016: 572) or, more specifically, with murex shells—*kogchulia*. This seems rather awkward. Is it possible that the object is decorated not with (inlaid) murex shells but with depictions of murex shells or even with murex dye?

Looking back over the discussion, it is possible to suspect that the "place" with the shape of a spiral shell was originally a tholos. In this connection, it is well to recall that the effect of a spiral staircase is attested to in a very large and early underground tholos at Knossos—the so-called Hypogaeum (see Sect. 3 below).

To conclude this already long and winding discussion, there are strong reasons for situating the headquarters of Potnia and her double-headed axe in Minoan Knossos and then in Mycenaean Knossos. However, Potnia, from early on, possessed branch cults housed in winding structures (labyrinths) elsewhere in the Aegean world. This is demonstrated or strongly suggested not only by architectural commonalities

---

[43] *Suda Online*, translated headword "labyrinth;" Available at http://www.cs.uky.edu/~raphael/ sol/sol-html/ Search for "labyrinth" (accessed February 12, 2021).

[44] Pylos Ta 711: .1 *o-wi-de put-ke-qi-ri o-te wa-na-ka te-ke sj-ke-wa da-mo-ko-ro*..2 *qe-ra-na wa-na-se-wi-ja qo-u-ka-ra ko-ki-re-ja qe-ra-na a-mo-te-wi-ja ko-ro-no-we-sa*..3 *qe-ra-na wa-na-se-wi-ja ku-na-ja qo-u-ka-ra to-qi-de-we-sa*.

but even more by the finding of her main symbol—the double-headed axe—carved by masons not only on Knossos' structural pillars but on those of the palaces at Phaistos and Malia and elsewhere.

d. Participation in the Cloth Market

It is very clear that the Minoan/Mycenaean labyrinth/palace at Knossos—and, as will be seen, building Xeste 3 at Akrotiri—like the mainland Mycenaean Palaces, produced and displayed luxury garments for visitors. The finding of two stores of loom-weights testify to the production of textiles at Minoan Knossos. One of the collections of loom weights is

> the collection of over four hundred found with shrine models and other ritual objects in the palace ... and giving the name to the area, the "Loom Weight Basements,"[45] and the second [is] the group of over eighty found fallen with the rhytons and other cult vessels in the Late Minoan I B building on the Knossos Stratigraphical Museum site.
>
> Warren 1988: 21; cf. Boloti 2017: 4 with n. 13; Burke 2010

There is also a famous connection made in a myth of Knossos' labyrinth with textiles: in the version of Pherecydes (148J), Theseus relied on an *agathis* 'ball of thread' to extricate himself.[46] This evidence is admittedly not from a Bronze Age source.

Unlike in the megaron in Pylos (above), no Knossos Labyrinth tablets deal with textiles. However, there is evidence of transactions relating to textile production: a sealing on a nodule of the hanging type (a "*Schnurplombe*") that was excavated on a landing of a Grand Staircase in the Knossos Labyrinth. The sealing (Figure 1, opposite) depicts a number of rams (goats?). The device pertains to the owner of the seal and, in this case, it is reasonable to assume it reflects his/her duties or interests (see Chap. 10.4). That is, the sealing arguably

---

[45] The loom-weights are accompanied by a large jar decorated with palm trees or sometimes a combination of palm tree and lily; the depiction perhaps reveals the textile markets (see Chap. 10.8).

[46] Daidalos built the *Laburiththos* to hold the hybrid Minotaur (Montecchi 2016a: 166 with references). Tablets at Knossos (KN Fp(1) 1) mention a *da-da-re* restored as *da-da-re-[jo-de]* that receives olive oil. Thus, a "place of (the person/deity) Daedalus" or better, I think, a "place of artistic work/ornamentation" (Beekes s.v. *daidallō*). Bull-headed figures with human bodies are depicted on Minoan seals, for example from Chania (*CMS* VS3, no. 154 = Arachne 166462). The connection, if any, of the Minotaur with the Bronze Age labyrinth remains unsettled, however (Kotsonas 2018: 375–376). I think that the Minotaur was an apotropaic device, like snakes or the gorgoneion, intended to protect the vaults of the Labyrinth. One might say that Daedalus built the Minotaur to hold (the wealth of) the Labyrinth.

confirms a transaction in sheep (or goats)–a transaction/transfer, in which, given the findspot, the Labyrinth is implicated as a participant.[47]

Figure 1. String nodule depicting rams and papyrus, from Knossos
(*CMS* II.8, no. 521 = Arachne 169245).

Moreover, the papyrus in the sealing arguably represents Potnia of the Labyrinth (see Chap. 10.8).

A connection between the Labyrinth and textile production and the Protopalatial Petras, there was found in Sector 1 in Sitia, in eastern Crete, thirteen marked loom-weights, one of which is a "partially preserved" double-headed axe (Tsipopoulou 2016: 145). Sitia is a site where there is also early evidence of murex dye production (Chap. 7.2). The wider connections of the Labyrinth are further illustrated by pottery marked with the double-headed axe not only at Knossos itself but also at the palaces in Phaistos and Malia and in the Kamares cave in central Crete (Nikolaidou 2016: 105–106).

A flat packet-type sealing from Zakros (Figure 2, below) depicts a procession of two women. The first wears only a necklace and a long, decorated skirt, while the second wears a long dress and a mantle about her shoulders. On her shoulders, the second woman carries a beam to which is attached a long loom-weight (or distaff); the first woman wields something like a baseball bat, which appears, to me, to be a beater/batten (Greek *spathē*; Latin *spatha*) used for beating-up the weft of cloth. Such swords had tangs at both ends (2017).[48] Obviously, there is a connection with textile production, but beyond an impression about the garments worn by the figures and the processional form, I cannot connect the pair with a labyrinth at either Zakros or Knossos.

---

[47] Processions of rams are depicted in fresco fragments and on an ivory pyxis at Tiryns (New Palace LH IIIB) (Mantzourani 1995: 133 with Fig. 10).

[48] Implements of this kind are attested to in Bronze Age Italy (see Bazzanell et al. 2003: 138–142; cf. Burke 1997: 419).

Figure 2. Packet nodule from Zakros depicting procession of textile workers
(*CMS* II.7, no. 16 = Arachne 169145/160375).

The above discussion only touches the surface of the Labyrinth. Below, it is considered whether it should be regarded as a palace or temple, and whether and how it participated in international trade. The symbolism of the double-headed axe looms large in these discussions. A concluding thought: the Linear B texts refer to a "*Potnia* of the *Laburinthos*" but not to a "*Posis* of the *Laburinthos*." I do not think we should expect to find the latter title because "Labyrinth" refers specifically to the textile-marketing dimension/role of an architectural structure. This dimension was strictly the property of Potnia. The same structure, however, also had a "law and order" dimension that would have been owned by the Posis. Considering King Alcinoos' throne in the Phaeacian *megaron* (§4.1 above), the law-and-order function was headquartered specifically in the *megaron* (cf. *Odyssey* 17.604 and 21.120 for Odysseus' *megaron*).

My theory is that, in ordinary speech, a structure might be referred to as a labyrinth or as a megaron depending on the activity that was of interest to the speaker. Thus, as seen earlier, in *Odyssey* 21, there are references to "passages," but in the context of weaponry, the structure is referred to as megaron. Admittedly, there are no examples, other than the reference to "Potnia of the Labyrinth," in which there is an apparent reference to a structure called "labyrinth." Similarly, the word *megaron* is used by Homer, but in Linear B it appears only once—at Midea, as *me-ka-ro-de*. I will return to this problem in Chapters 6.1 and 15.5 in the further discussion of the division of function between Queen Arētē and King Alcinoos in Phaeacia.

3. Xeste 3 in Akrotiri and the Crocus

Next, I consider Xeste 3, which is not typically seen as a Minoan-styled labyrinth. Nevertheless, there are clear resemblances in the business models of their central economic enterprise. It is true, however, that we do not have a material throne nor, so far as I can tell, a spiral architectural form or spiral staircases in Xeste 3.[49]

On the other hand, if there was not a material throne in Xeste 3, there was a fresco depicting an unusually seated female. As Günkel-Mashek (2016: 259–260) describes,

> This form of staging was not exclusive to the Throne Room at Knossos. In fact, a very similar arrangement was created at about the same time in building Xeste 3 in Akrotiri on Thera. On the northern wall of hall 3 on the first floor, a female figure, flanked by a griffin, was sitting enthroned on a tripartite platform and served by the girls of elite families. Placed behind a pier-and-door partition wall, the female figure was embedded in the midst of a setting composed of rocky and marshy landscapes crowded by saffron gathering girls and by ducks, respectively. When the doors were opened, the whole scene was revealed to the eyes of participants standing in the paved central area of the polythyron hall (Pl. LXXXVa-b). This event certainly constituted an essential moment in the course of any ritual activities performed in this place. In any case, the spatial and visual arrangement in building Xeste 3 confirms the conventions of involving the visual formula of an enthroned female figure into the performance of ritual activities. At both Knossos and Akrotiri, environments were created to experience the appearance of an enthroned figure—an artificial one at Thera, an enacted one at Knossos.

Günkel-Mashek's description of the Xeste 3 "Saffron Gatherer's Fresco" requires a significant amendment: while it is true that the "Saffron Goddess" is depicted seated on a platform, her actual seat is a stack of saffron-dyed textiles. This is a perfectly appropriate "throne" for a goddess of textiles who presides over a showroom for the display and sale of her skilled works. Indeed, it will be seen in Chapters 7.6 and 11.5 that a seat of textiles can be a kind of *thronos*.[50]

---

[49] A small staircase with a spiral intention and effect is in a building called Sector Beta in Akrotiri (Palyvou 2005: 135).

[50] Although the griffin is actually behind the "Saffron Goddess," the important point remains that a griffin accompanies her.

Moreover, as we saw at Knossos, there are in Xeste 3 frescoes featuring processions and other scenes depicting mortals in elegant garments of murex and saffron dyes. In addition, the spiral motif is represented on the girdle of this "Lady of the Landscape Fresco," and on the third floor of Xeste 3, there is an extensive composition of spirals. Most importantly, as in the "Procession Fresco" at Knossos, the kilts of men ascending the staircase in Xeste 4 display the spiral (Doumas 1992: 177 fig. 138; Günkel-Maschek 2012a: 123).

The architectural characteristics of Xeste 3 surely support a showroom interpretation. Xeste 3 is a large (almost 6000 square feet of useable space), well-constructed building (thick stone walls) with three floors and includes up-scale features such as paved stone floors. Palyvou (2005: 54–55, 61) provides a summary of important details and evaluations:

> This was a very large building, indeed, comparable only to the Knossian mansions and large villas. Moreover, it is immediately distinguished for its high quality of construction, the elaborate room arrangement at all three levels (Fig. 66), and the superb wall paintings covering almost every single wall of the main rooms. The building is entered from the east, with a typical entrance system (door, window, and main staircase) occupying the southeast corner (Figs. 67–68). A small forecourt with a built bench is just outside the entrance. A bench is a scarce feature at Akrotiri[51] because Theran houses, as a rule, have no courtyards or inter-mediate zones between private and public domains.... The entrance lobby (i.e., the first landing of the staircase) is larger and certainly much more elaborate than usual.... The desire to create an impressive entrance is further attested by a most unexpected and extreme struc-ture: it seems that the builders spared no effort in order to obtain a large entrance lobby and to ensure a specific round-about access to the interior of the building. So, instead of letting the visitors move inside the building by turning to the right, they made them move straight ahead, through a double door and under the second flight of the main staircase, and then enter Room 4.... From the structural point of view, it differs in the large size and the lavish use of high quality building tech-niques (i.e., dressed stones and timber frames). From the functional point of view, the difference is even more patent in the importance of the part of the ground floor related to the entrance. The remark-able number of pier-and-door partitions, uniting an area of about 80 square meters, offers the possibility to accommodate a large number

---

[51] I am advised by an experienced scholar that benches are common in Akrotiri.

of people when all doors are open, while the wall paintings, with all their symbolical connotations, are a dominant feature. This is surely a building that functioned beyond the everyday needs of a family group. Special functions of communal interest were most probably housed in this building, some of which were clearly related to rituals.

Xeste 3 does not stand complete as *the* palace/labyrinth in Akrotiri. Nevertheless, Xeste 3 does have much in common with Knossos' Labyrinth, whose griffin and presiding Potnia arguably correspond to Akrotiri's "Saffron Goddess." The latter identification finds further support in the fact that the crocus motif was popular in Crete even before the time of the Akrotiri frescoes:

> Though prominent in the fresco program of Xeste 3, crocuses first appear in the Aegean repertoire of design in the Protopalatial period on Crete, in an Early Kamares cup from the Town Drain at Knossos and intriguingly, on a large MC II polychrome vessel recently discovered in excavations at Akrotiri, Thera, *decorated with a landscape of crocus flowers, goats, birds, and a human figure.* Later, crocuses make their appearance in fresco painting in the famous MM III Saffron Gatherer Fresco from Knossos, which depicts a blue monkey in a rocky landscape of wild and potted crocuses.
>
> Chapin in Chapin and M. Shaw 2006: 83–84;
> emphasis added

The reference to the polychrome vessel with crocus plants and goats is especially significant as goats or agrimia, a source of wool (Nosch and Ulanowska 2021: 85-7), flank crocus flowers on a fragmentary fresco from Building Beta in Akrotiri (Chapin and M. Shaw 2006: 80 with n. 78). Day (2011: 354) remarks,

> Many examples come from Akrotiri, all very similar in style. Strainers and kymbai are frequently decorated with crocuses growing from an undulating ground line, with pointed petals and two stigmas visible on either side of the central petal. Often, the flowers are accompanied by agrimia and marine motifs (Table 1:12). It seems that such themes already existed in Middle Cycladic times, for a recently published bathtub from Akrotiri shows identical crocuses alongside goats, although here the flowers do not grow from a ground line but float across the scene.

Add to this evidence, the crocus clumps and agrimia depicted together in the fragmented "Crocus Panel" from Knossos' "House of the Frescoes."[52] Here again it remains possible that agrimia flank the crocus. With respect to the function of Knossos' "House of Frescoes," Chapin and M. Shaw (2006: 88) suggest it had a "ceremonial or ritual character"—perhaps the building was a secondary labyrinth.

The combination, even sometimes heraldic positioning, of goats/agrimia with crocus flowers confirms their relationship and even serves to identify crocus with Potnia and her labyrinth. In support of the relationship or identification, note the faience plaques of elegant crocus-plant decorated garments (Plate 4) found together with the "Snake Goddesses" in Knossos' "Temple Repositories" (Plate 10). In just the same way, the heraldic positioning of agrimi with murex snail in a seal (see §c above) and the combining of agrimi with spirals in the "Zakros Rhyton" (see §c above) serve to identify murex/spiral with the Potnia/labyrinth. If murex and saffron are not identical to Potnia, they are surely sacred to her (see Day 2011: 369). Moreover, the depiction of agrimi in a maritime context—explicitly at Akrotiri and implicitly by means of the running snail spiral in the "Zakros Rhyton"—place the identification of agrimi with Potnia and labyrinth (murex/saffron) in a commercial context.

Finally, there is evidence of administrative and/or commercial links between Minoan Crete and Thera. These links are determined by the presence at various locations in the latter island of about 70 "parcel nodule" (Linear A) documents stamped with a seal identified as Cretan and made of Cretan clay. In particular, the context of the sealing in trench 64 is too telling to be ignored: "a Cretan sealing shut in a wooden box with a balance and weights on the site of Akrotiri" (Karnava 2008: 384). Furthermore, petrographic analysis suggests Knossos at the origin (Karnava 2010: 87).[53] One Linear A ostrakon (THE Zb 5) lists commodities followed by numerals. Three (or two), arguably locally made, Linear A tablets (THE 7-9) have also been found in Akrotiri.

There is, I think, a misunderstanding concerning the meaning of foreign writing on local media. That Linear A is written on local clay, which means that Minoans (Cretans) were physically present in Akrotiri. Alternatively, they had locals on their payroll. Another possibility is that Linear A had become a commercial language, which is, of course, possible but raises the danger of

---

[52] Agrimi and crocus appear together Room 14 of the Royal Villa at Agia Triada and a clay rhyton from Palaikastro decorated with an agrimi protome is painted with crocuses (Chapin and Shaw 2006: 80).

[53] The connections between Akrotiri (Thera) and Crete cast a favorable light on vessels and seamanship of the time as travel between the two involved an open-sea voyage of over 60 nautical miles, implying night voyages (Agourides 1997: 15).

being suspected of advocating for an unfashionable Minoan "Thalassocracy" "Maritime Empire."

An important construction in Xeste 3 has not yet been mentioned: below the "Crocus Gatherers Frescoes," there is a roofed, sunken chamber accessible by a flight of steps. This subterranean structure has sometimes been called a "Lustral Basin," although, as Marinatos (1985a: 224, 229) points out,

> Nothing about it ... suggests that it was connected with lustration or bathing.[54] It is better to call it "adyton."... It is a sacred area, the most sacred area in the building.... It appears that descent into it had definite chthonic associations and, therefore, associations to fertility. Offerings may well have been placed in it because a treasury was found very close to the adyton (fig. 4). Unfortunately, this treasury was found empty. It will be remembered that the girls flanking the wounded figure are carrying gifts, thus part of the ritual offering connected with the adyton was repeated and perpetuated on the fresco.

As far as I am aware, Xeste 3 is the only house in Akrotiri with a structure of this kind.

The Greek word *aduton* has the sense of "forbidden" or "not to be entered," or is a "separated" place that is under the protection of supernatural forces. I completely agree with Marinatos that this *aduton* was the most sacred part of the Xeste 3 and for good reason—I submit that the most cogent interpretation is a *vault*. In this identification, I follow Hollinshead (1985: 438–439) who maintains that the security of valuables was the reason for the presence of similar "cave-like" inner rooms (*aduta*) in classical Greek temples. Given the diligence of "looters" over the centuries, it is understandable that treasure has not been found in such structures (Campbell 2013: 10–12), but Hollinshead's proposal finds support in Athena's advice to Odysseus upon his return to Ithaca that he should set his valuable goods in the innermost recess of the cave of the nymphs (*Odyssey* 13. 360 ff.). The valuables placed in such vaults were centers of cultic activity as the contents were protected not only by physical means but by potent spiritual ones (Silver 2018: 160). Accordingly, I suggest that the "gifts" carried by the women in the fresco above are idiosyncratic because they originate as gifts and payments made to the goddess by visiting traders (see below).[55]

---

[54] There are neither drainage nor water supply facilities.

[55] B. Jones (2016b) sees the Xeste 3 *aduton* as representing Hades' domain and insightfully connects the procession depicted in the fresco with rituals and myths of Demeter and Persephone. Such rituals undoubtedly accompanied the deposit of valuables in the vault: Hades. The rituals made the deposits invulnerable by placing them beyond the grasp of human hands in the netherworld.

It appears that there are three *aduta* (apparently from different ceramic phases) in the Labyrinth at Knossos including one on a side of the throne chamber.[56] Furthermore, under the main entrance (south) porch of the Knossos palace was found a very large, and very impressive, tholos (the "Hypogaeum") peaking in a beehive vault with entrance by means of a winding ("spiral") staircase around the windowed wall (Pendlebury 1933: 17; Palyvou 2018: 41–42).[57] In addition, there are several such structures (sunken areas with stairs) in other Cretan buildings at Knossos and Malia and in palaces at Zakros, and Phaistos (Campbell 2013 and Adams 2017: 55–62).[58] The tholos structures in Crete and the Greek mainland are earlier than the palaces, and it is quite possible that the word *laburinthos* (originally) applies to them as marketplaces under the auspices of Potnia.

4. Textile Showroom as Labyrinth or Megaron

There are clear architectural and artistic differences between the Minoan labyrinth as seen at Knossos and the Mycenaean megaron as seen at Pylos. However, the resemblances are sufficiently fundamental that, hereafter, the textile showroom dimension of the palace will be referred to only as "labyrinth." This choice to omit reference to "megaron" simplifies the discussion and, more importantly,

[56] Thus, two of the *aduta* in the Knossos Labyrinth were located close to entrances (Adams 2017: 55–56).
[57] Yiannouli (2009: 96) considers "problematic" a "monumental building [kouloura] that is entirely subterranean: "Located under the south porch of the later Palace (Fig. 2B), its character still eludes us." There is also a structure of this kind at Phaistos.
[58] I would assume that the subterranean tholos-vault was topped at ground level by an architectural signal to visitors of its presence and availability. Thus, Younger (2009: 44) cites: "One example ... on a sealing, impressed by an amygdaloid seal that was found in the "Room of the Seal Impressions" at Knossos. It depicts a robed male figure with a staff flanked by flowers, two large birds facing each other below him, and, below the bird heads, *a knoblike projection from a ground line*. The scene might reflect the story of the eagles meeting over the center of the earth (the knob as omphalos) with Zeus standing above them" (emphasis added). The symbol, as Younger states, is an *omphalos*. Such "stones" have been found at Mycenaean Phylkakopi (Younger 2009) and near many historical temples (Silver 1992: 67–68 with references). This line of reasoning brings to mind a number of Minoan seals depicting men or women, always naked, embracing boulders that are *omphaloi* (Younger 2009). That the *omphalos*, often rendered as "knob" or "navel," signals a vault for the storage of wealth is clearly conveyed by its beehive-shape (Silver 1992: 67–68). The "huggers" (protectors? employees?) must have some connection to the stored wealth beneath. Having made this connection I was struck by a scene in Euripides *Hecuba* (994–1012) wherein Hecuba inquires of the greedy Polymestor of Thrace about the safety of the gold that Priam's ancestors had deposited in a vault near the *stegē* "temple" of Trojan Athena; the location of Priam's deposited gold is "*marked*" *sēmeion* by a "black rock/stone" *melaina petra* that must be an *omphalos* (Silver 2019: 166–167). Hecuba is linked with "stones" throughout.

acknowledges that Potnia, the controlling deity in both Knossos and Pylos, is textually identified only with the "labyrinth."

With respect to the resemblances, note the dominating use of *frescoes* and the importance of *processions* as depicted on the walls and/or as participated in by visitors traversing the winding corridors leading to the throne chamber. Within the throne chamber, note the presence of the single throne placed on the right-hand wall, the common features of the fresco behind the throne, and the emphasis on the *griffin*. It is easy to understand why scholars have concluded that the Mycenaeans chose to rely on a Minoan conception (see Maran and Stavrianopoulou 2007: 287–289 with references).

5

Provision for Visiting Textile Merchants

IT has been argued that the palaces (including Xeste 3) displayed textiles for sale in showrooms—recall here the reference to "guests" at Pylos possibly wearing "Syrian" robes. Is there also additional evidence that living facilities were available for housing visiting textile buyers? I think so.

An elegant building in Knossos has the following qualifications: it (1) faces a main road leading to the palace; (2) has a basement with a cobbled floor and traces of an animal trough; (3) has freshwater channeled through the basement and, indeed, through the entire building with many access points; (4) has an easily accessible pavilion large enough for a bench with frescoed walls; (5) has a room with at least one frescoed wall with a fresh-water-fed sunken tub long enough to lie down in and deep enough for a hip-bath surrounded by seats; (6) has two additional rooms with terracotta bathtubs and freshwater, even hot water; (6) has polished terrazzo floors and frescoed walls on the remains of the upper floor; (7) and has a sheltered inner court and a roof with a view. Sir Arthur Evans (1928: 102–123) called the building "The Caravanserai." Schofield (1996: 12) sees Evan's point, but for her the building is not a hotel— it is not clear why she thinks it is not—but "more of a club, and a select club at that." This view will do.[1]

Although the dating is uncertain, the luxurious club or hotel may have had attached to it another important amenity for business travelers: a brothel, arguably under cultic auspices.[2] This inference is based on a (LM IIIC-Subminoan) cylindrical house model (Figure 3, below) found in the "Spring Chamber Shrine" attached to the Caravanserai.[3] Through the open doorway of the model, there can be seen a nude-to-the-waist *anasurma*-style figure of a woman:

---

[1]   For caravanserai in the ancient Near East, see Silver (1995a: 84–85).

[2]   The reference to a brothel is not meant to exclude women from among the business travelers arriving in Knossos seeking to purchase luxury textiles.

[3]   For the possible relationship of the Caravanserai and "Spring Chamber Shrine" with the structure known as a "Tripartite Shrine," see J. Shaw (1978: 446–447).

Facing doorway, both arms are raised with open hands, palms forward, reaching just below her ears. Facial features, ears, and small breasts are modeled. Fingers and mouth are indicated by incised lines. She wears a low cap (polos or tiara). Nipples, mouth, eyes, and hands are highlighted with black paint. In addition, her wrists are encircled with paint.[4]

Mersereau 1993: 37–39 with Fig. 26

Evans (1928: 120 with n. 2, 139) points out the dot on the wrist recalls that the wrist-seals worn by the Goddess of the Shrine of the Double Axes, while "The roof bears traces of a spiral ornament." Additionally, in the Caravanserai proper, there is a double-headed axe stand on the upper floor. Evidently, the brothel was under the auspices of Potnia of the Labyrinth.

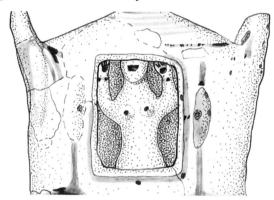

Figure 3. House model with nude woman in doorway, from Knossos.

The thought occurs to me that the raised arms echo the Potnia's so-called "horns of consecration" (see Chaps. 6.3 and 7.5).[5] M. Shaw (1996: 178 n. 35), citing a fresco from the Ramp House at Mycenae, finds it reasonable that raised hands with palms turned away from the face is a "gesture of welcoming or greeting." If so, this gesture, when made by a nude woman standing in the window of her house, is certainly appropriate for a seller of sex.

[4]   For nudity and *anasurma*, see Silver 2019: Chaps. 1–2
[5]   See Platon (2015) for consideration of the "East House" and the connected "House of the Niches" located on the harbor road at Zakros as places for lodging of travelers and sacred prostitution.

6

Structural Problems

1. Labyrinth Textile Showroom
as Palace and/or Temple

THE Labyrinth is a physical structure built, owned, and managed by an organization whose central concern is the production and marketing of fine textiles. In this most obvious sense, the Labyrinth is the showroom of a textile firm.

There are reasons, developed elsewhere, to believe that the king occupied the firm's throne. However, the vital kingly functions of transportation and security of textiles and clients were imbued with a supernatural cover and, therefore, hidden from immediate view. They were fulfilled by griffins and lions who need to be understood as agents of the mostly martial figure: the *wanax* 'king'. Moreover, glyptic indicates that the *wanax* is an agent of Potnia (§3 below), and the king is named/appointed in a temple that houses Potnia (Chap. 8.4). Furthermore, as has already been discussed, the structure called "Labyrinth" is textually linked only to Potnia.

There is a hint, however, that the king's role in the palace was more independent than was allowed for in the ideological terms that were perhaps sponsored by Potnia's management (§3 below). This is well illustrated by an apparent inconsistency in Homer's presentation of Odysseus' struggles in Scheria, which is clearly demonstrated by Whittaker (1999: 140–142):

> In the Phaeacian episode of the *Odyssey*, the figure of the queen is given particular prominence, and in Scherie Arētē seems to enjoy exceptional power and influence. When Nausicaa explains to Odysseus how to reach the palace, she advises Odysseus that when he comes into the main hall, he should first approach the queen, Arētē, in supplication.... Later, when he is going into the town, Odysseus meets Athena disguised as a young Phaeacian girl. She gives him the same advice.... When Odysseus enters the palace and supplicates Arētē as he has been twice advised to do, she remains silent; it is [King] Alcinous who welcomes Odysseus and

provides for his entertainment, and it is he who promises to convey him home.... Later, when Odysseus pauses in the recital of his adventures, Arētē is the first to speak. She praises Odysseus and emphasises that he is her guest, demonstratively, it might seem, asserting her superior authority. She is, however, immediately contradicted, almost reprimanded, by the Phaeacian elder, Echeneus, who explicitly asserts that Alcinous is of the greatest importance, and Alcinous himself, replying to Echeneus, emphatically affirms his position as ruler of Phaeacia.... consequently, the figure of Arētē has often been seen as problematic because Nausicaa's and Athena's presentation of her leads to expectations concerning her importance and the role she will play in the story of Odysseus' stay in Scherie, which are not met. Why Arētē is given any prominence at all is a question to which the answer is not immediately evident.

The facts provided by Homer suggest that Arētē, who sits between the pillars and spins, plays the role of Potnia of the Labyrinth, and the worldly Alcinoos, who sits on a throne, is said to be the (w)anax.

If so, Arētē manages what we might call the *temple*—what is *inside* the textile house, i.e. the labyrinth—and Alcinoos runs what we would call the *palace*, or what is *outside* of the labyrinth, i.e. mainly the sea operations.[1] That is, Arētē produces and displays the textiles for sale, but Alcinoos provides both transportation and security for the textiles and clients. Thus, when Odysseus (7.150ff.) requests of Arētē, "But for me do ye speed my sending, that I may come to my native land, and that quickly; for long time have I been suffering woes far from my friends" (tr. Murray *LCL*), the elder immediately deflects the request to Alcinoos. Had he spoken to Arētē about textiles then, I predict, she would have responded directly and authoritatively.

Consider Kanavou's (2015: 123) understanding of the name Alcinoos:

> The king's name, Ἀλκίνοος, has more than one possible meaning. The element — νοος might allude to Odysseus' journey home, made possible

---

[1]   Frame (2012: @5§24) explains the unusual importance of Arētē among the Phaeacians in terms of an unusual and hidden genealogy, a type of genealogy she shares with the unusually important Athena (see §2 below). Frame's argument seems valid and important to me, but there is a question. I see that Arētē runs the textile operation (the Labyrinth) and wonder whether this role is due to her genealogy or whether her genealogy is due to the importance of her position in the economy. Arētē is not a real person with a predetermined genealogy but rather a fictional person whose genealogy (like her name) can be chosen by the author to meet the needs of the story. In any case, Arētē is important in a very special way.

by the king, who authorises and oversees the relevant preparations.[2] This is where his most important function lies– and in the fact that he provides the audience for Odysseus' narrative of his journey so far. The name's first component could indeed imply the meaning of defending and helping the *nostos* both find poetic expression and reach its desired 'end'; ἀλκή is used in the *Odyssey* to mean 'defence, help' (e. g. 22.305).

Earlier, Frame (2012: @8.§31) saw the meaning in similar terms: "The name Alcinous derives from his relation to Nestor in that –*noos*, the second element of his name, has the same root as Nestor's name, and in the same active meaning, 'bring home': Alcinous is 'he who brings home by his strength'."

Thus, it seems to me that the etymology with the focus on –*noos* can be understood as calling attention to the fact that Alcinoos' duty as *wanax* is to welcome visitors (clients) to the Labyrinth and to make sure they return safely home with their acquired valuables. For Odysseus, the service is to greet him and later to return him to Ithaca from Scheria laden with valuable gifts. In terms of the argument developed in Chapter 11.5, Alcinoos as *wanax* performs the *griffin-role*.[3] Homer is not guilty of inconsistency but is instead sharpening the two roles of a unitarily named but architecturally and functionally varied structure.

Specifically, Arētē may occupy a "(large) chamber" in the "house" of King Alcinoos. Thus, as Wright (1982: 198) has observed,

> [W]e are reminded of the passage in the *Odyssey* (vii 79-81) where Athena leaves Odysseus on Scheria and returns to the stronghold of Erechtheus on the Acropolis, or of Pausanias' report (ix 16.5-7) that the sanctuary of Demeter Thesmophoros at Thebes was located in a building said to have been the house of Kadmos and his descendants.

In other words, the goddess—whether they are Athena, Demeter, or Arētē—is housed in the political seat/palace of a king, whether they are Erechtheus, Kadmos, or Alcinoos.

---

[2] Von Kamptz (1982) in the *Homerische Personennamen* takes the name as from -*noos* and understands it as "strong of mind" which finds support in some of his epithets. On the other hand, Kanavou's interpretation is supported by Alcinoos' treatment of Odysseus and others in Homer.

[3] Alcinoos tells the Phaeacians: "Now that ye have finished your feast, go each of you to his house to rest. But in the morning we will call more of the elders together, and will entertain the stranger in our halls and offer goodly victims to the gods. After that we will take thought also of his sending, that without toil or pain yon stranger may under our sending, come to his native land speedily and with rejoicing, though he come from never so far. Nor shall he meanwhile suffer any evil or harm, until he sets foot upon his own land; but thereafter he shall suffer whatever Fate and the dread Spinners spun with their thread for him at his birth, when his mother bore him" (*Odyssey* 7.186–198; tr. Murray *LCL*).

On the other hand, Alcinoos explicitly recognizes that in respect to his role in transportation and security, he is an agent of Poseidon (Chap. 15.5). Is this recognition only Alcinoos' promotion of *his* house god to a supreme status or, with Wright (1982: 198) and other scholars, should we understand Alcinoos' behavior more generally as reflecting "the replacement of a political seat by a religious cult." These are indeed deep waters that I will avoid.

At the time of the writing of the Linear B tablets, the cult of the *posis* Poseidon probably shared with Potnia the management of the textile enterprise.[4] In Pylos, Potnia and Poseidon were the two main deities at Sphagianes where the *wanax* was initiated (Chap 8.4). In this connection, note the joint management of historical Athens' olive enterprise by Athena and Poseidon (Silver 1992: Chap. 11). This arrangement is portrayed as the result of a *Götterkampf*. Perhaps this was also the case for Potnia (Athena) and Poseidon in the textile industry during Minoan/Mycenaean times.[5]

Is the Labyrinth a temple or a palace? Both, or perhaps neither.

2. Athena as Potnia of the Labyrinth: Supporting Evidence

The name "Potnia" is a name that conveys that the bearer has a legal right to own property and contest lawsuits. It would seem likely that each Potnia was also known by another name, perhaps revealing a specific dimension of her character, role, and/or her geographical sphere of operations. Yet, the Linear B texts reveal only one example in which a Potnia has what *appears* to be a *personal name*: Knossos KN V 521 refers to *a-ta-na-po-ti-ni-ja* 'Athana Potnia'. The name *Athēnē* lacks a Greek etymology: "Like the goddess itself, the name is pre-Greek" (Beekes s.v.). It is argued below, with the help of Homer, that "Athena" is the personal name of "Potnia (owner) of the Labyrinth," who is herself attested to only at Knossos in KN Gg 702.[6]

---

[4]   An expert in Linear B informs me that *posis* in the fossilized vocative *po-se-da-o-ne* and probably once more. It is well to acknowledge an old (now disfavored?) etymology of the name Poseidon. In Linear B Greek, the name is written as *po-se-da-o* in which it is possible to see *posis* "owner" or perhaps in the case of the Labyrinth "co-owner."

[5]   It is possible to wonder whether the emergence or visibility in the Mycenaean palatial period of female versions of main gods, including *di-wi-ja* for Zeus and *po-si-da-e-ja* for Poseidon, reflects their service as agents of goddesses such as Potnia. That is, they are not distinct deities but rather distinct roles played by the male deity (see Chap. 6.3; Duev 2007: 225–227).

[6]   It is possible that *A-ta-na* refers to the place "Athens" where Potnia had a branch of her cult. On the other hand, "*a-ta-na* can be interpreted as the goddess Athena in the dative singular agreeing with *po-ti-ni-ja*" (Gulizio 2011: 125–126). As noted by Chadwick (1957: 116 n. 1), the goddess Potnia is *not* said to be "of Athens" (*Athānās* is not *Athānāōn*). Based on the suffix *-énē*, Nagy (2015b: §6–§7) has argued that "the name *Athénē* refers not only to the goddess 'Athena' but

First, *A-ta-na-je and A-ta-na-te* are mentioned in a Linear A inscription (THE Zb 6, on a Cretan pithos from the "House of the Ladies" at Akrotiri and in two tablets from Zakros (ZA 9.4 and 10.2) (Karnava 2016: 351–352; Montecchi 2016a: 168).[7]

Second, a Pylos tablet (PY Fr 1206) reveals the presence of a Potnia with the epithet *a-si-wi-ja*—that is "Asian (Assuwan) Potnia" (Nikoloudis 2008a: 49; cf. Chaps. 9.6, 10.7, and 11.5). Pausanias (3.24.7) reports that in Laconia, among the ruins of the old town at Las, there is

> a temple of Athena named Asia, made, it is said, by Polydeuces and Castor on their return home from Colchis; for the Colchians had a shrine of Athena Asia. I know that the sons of Tyndareus took part in Jason's expedition. As to the Colchians honoring Athena Asia, I give what I heard from the Lacedaemonians.

Of course, in the Homeric Epics—our oldest source—Athena *Ageleiē* is worshipped by both Greeks and Trojans and has a long-standing relationship with Troy.[8] In *Iliad* 6.297–310, the gates of Athena *Ageleiē* are opened by the *hiereia* (Linear B *i-je-re-ja*) 'priestess' Theanō, and the Trojan women offer Athena valuable textiles to spare the city (Chap. 14.5.c). I think it is significant that Theanō is called the "wife of Antēnor" (*Iliad* 6.299), who previously hosted the delegation of Menelaus and Odysseus in Troy (*Iliad* 3.204–224). To put it in another way, Antēnor interceded with Trojan leaders on behalf of Achaeans, and his partner Theanō interceded with an Achaean goddess on behalf of Trojan women. In their prayer for their city to be spared, the Trojan women refer to Athena as "Potnia" (*Potni Athēnaiē* in *Iliad* 6.305), meaning, as already noted, "owner."[9] As mentioned at several points in this study, Athena's depiction as "Warrior Goddess" is an iconographic testimony to her possession of the legal right to form contracts.

Athena's textile making skills are unparalleled:

> As early as the time of Homer she was recognized as the pre-eminent goddess of spinning and weaving. She was said, for instance, to have woven her (*peplos*) with her own hands, and she was also the goddess responsible for weaving the robe that Hera donned in order to seduce

---

also to everything that belongs to the goddess," which would include not only the acropolis of Athens but also the city of Athens. Thus, if I understand this complex discussion, *A-ta-na* would not be Athens but its owner who may also own many other things (cf. García Ramón 2011: 235).

[7] Anything is *possible* but it seems a stretch that all three refer to "Athens."

[8] In *Iliad* 20.144–146, Athena and the Trojans build a wall to protect Heracles, Troy's defender, from the *kētos* (see Chap. 11.5).

[9] However, in Homer, other goddesses are referred to as "Potnia" including (most often) Hera, Hebe, Calypso, and Circe (see Cunliffe 1963 s.v. *potnia*).

Zeus. Achilles would not marry Agamemnon's daughter even if she challenged Aphrodite for loveliness and handiwork. Similarly, when Athena appears to Odysseus, she is like a "woman handsome and tall, and skilled in glorious handiwork." She is even able to communicate to maidens her skill at spinning and weaving. Most of all, to Odysseus' wife, Penelope.

Luyster 1965: 139–140 with citations

In the *Iliad* 17.543ff., Athena manifests to the Achaeans in a *purple cloud* in a clear reference to purple dye. In the *Odyssey* (6.306, 7.71, 7.111), Athena is credited with having trained Queen Arētē of Scheria, who sits[10] in the great hall weaving fine purpled textiles. However, Arētē is not only queen but also a priestess of Athena. Moreover, the disguised Athena redirects Odysseus' prayer to return home to Arētē (*Odyssey* 7.15, 75–77). One might say that Arētē *is* Athena.[11]

Moreover, Athena circuits between her *alsos* 'grove' in Scheria and her temple in Athens (*Odyssey* 6.291, 7.78–81). At the same time, as L.R. Palmer (1963: 83) points out, in Scheria, the King Alcinoos' landholding is adjacent to the grove of Athena; in Pylos (PY Un 219.7), the landholding of the *wanax* 'king' is adjacent to the land of Potnia Pakijane.[12] Finally, as Frame (2012: @5.24) points out, Arētē shares a type of genealogy with Athena:

The question that Athena raises when she appends Arete to Alcinous's genealogy she also immediately answers when, at the end of her speech, she departs from Scheria and flies to Athens and enters the

---

[10] As in the case of Athena in Troy (*Iliad* 6.297–305) Homer does not reveal what Arētē is sitting upon.

[11] Various etymological derivations have been proposed for Ionic Arētē, but the one that seems most central to me is from 'to prosper, thrive' (LSJ s.v.; Beekes s.v.). This etymology finds support in Bailey's (1959: 93) observation that the Indo-Iranian base *ar-*, meaning both 'get' and 'cause to get,' is reflected in Greek *arnumai* 'win, gain take,' in *mistharnos* 'wage-earner,' and in *aros* 'use, profit' (cf. Chap. 14.2). Note the direct evidence in favor of the connection with prosperity: the Phaeacians are said to be godlike, meaning they are wealthy, as they are described as wondrously wealthy, and the sources of their wealth are expert seamanship and the production of purple cloth. The latter is a specialty of Arētē, herself. However, the *aretaō* etymology is regarded as very questionable. Skempis and Ziogas (2009: 215ff) link Arētē to *araomai* 'pray to' (doubted by Kanavou 2015: 27 n. 151). In *Odyssey* 6.280, she is "the object/subject of many prayers." An etymology in terms of 'being prayed to' returns us, I think, to 'being godlike' and, hence, to wealth as does its base *ar-*. Note, however, that Odysseus wished to address to Arētē his prayer to return home, but the fulfillment of this prayer was outside her jurisdiction and could not be accepted. Instead, the prayer was answered by Alcinoos, who returned Odysseus to Ithaca. This is, I think, what is significant about the prayers.

[12] A Linear B expert cautions me that PY Un 219 is not a landholding text and therefore cannot bear the weight I am putting on it.

palace of Erechtheus. By her action Athena reveals that Arete in relation to Alcinous represents Athena herself as the city goddess of Athens, whose relationship with the Athenian king Erechtheus is the paradigm for the Phaeacian royal couple. This explains the extraordinary honor in which Arete is said to be held by her people, which has no parallel in Greek epic, or in Greek culture generally. Athena Polias as a mother goddess in Athens is likewise a unique figure, or nearly so, and even in Athens she was not destined to last as such beyond the early archaic era.

By parallelism, Athena is Arētē is Potnia.

Homer does not reveal—or rather, hides?—what Athena was seated upon in her Trojan temple when Theanō placed a fine textile in her lap. Similarly, he does not reveal Arētē's seat when she made textiles in her "house" in Scheria. However, Herodotus (5.72.3) mentions that in the later sixth century BCE, the priestess of Athena rose from a *thronon* of "flowers embroidered on cloth" (LSJ s.v.: *Iliad* 22.441)—that is, a cushion decorated with flowers (Chap. 11.5). Thus, the priestess' seat corresponds to the seat of the Akrotiri goddess in the "Saffron Gatherers Fresco" (Chap. 6.2). However, the Museum of Fine Arts in Houston has an "Unknown Greek Statuette" of a woman seated on a backless seat (37.14) and, another of a woman or goddess seated on an armless chair/throne (37.16).[13]

Classical Greek sources famously link Athena with the double-headed axe—the main symbol of Knossos' Labyrinth: Athena was born when Hephaestus opened Zeus' head with a double-headed axe (e.g., Berlin, Antikenmuseen F1704; cf. Silver 2019: 97 with n. 53, 116). In addition, *snakes* are famously one of Athena's main emblems; the aegis (*aigis*), a goatskin worn over her back and shoulders, is sometimes depicted with a border of snakes (Luyster 1965: 145–148; Beekes s.v.).[14] Concerning this connection, we are permitted to reflect on the unique "*Snake Goddess*" (HM (=Y) 63) from the "Temple Repositories" at Knossos, who has snakes wound around both arms and shoulders (see Plate 10). Because of their frightening and repellent attributes, Athena's snake, attested from Archaic times, served her well in her capacity as guardian of subterranean temple vaults, which is a role developed at length in *Odyssey* 13.360ff. (see Chap. 4.3). Her priestess Theanō, who opened Athena's chamber in Troy, has been compared to the "key-bearer" *ka-pa-ti-ja* Karpathia in Pylos (PY Eb 338, Ep 704) (Weilhartner 2013: 161) and, hence, to the smaller "Snake Goddess" (HM (=Y) 65) from the "Temple Repositories" at Knossos (Chap. 10.2 with Plate 10):

[13] Available for download at: https://emuseum.mfah.org/objects/44975/statuette-of-a-seated-woman-or-goddess (accessed September 11, 2021).

[14] Note the "awful" tasseled aegis (*Iliad* 21.400–401) and, in the original text, the gorgoneion on the aegis in *Iliad* 5.733–742 (often removed as interpolated).

The unique checkered dress worn by HM (=Y) 65 finds an echo in an Early Classical Attic white-ground cup ... [British Museum GR 1881.5–28.1] [that] shows Athena wearing a dark red or purple scaly aegis of the 'skin cape' type, which evokes the idea of a monstrous snakeskin or the skin of a snake-bodied monster— in accordance with those myths that explain the origins of the aegis in such a manner.... In Archaic art, snakes often appear with multi-coloured scales, usually in a red/blue scale pattern, and the same kind of scales (blue, red, green) also dominate Athena's aegis in Late Archaic depictions, one particularly striking example being the Athena from the West pediment of the temple of Aphaia on Aigina, a copy of which has recently been restored to its original colour scheme.

Deacy and Villing 2009: 116

I think there is a strong case for identifying the Potnia with the personal name Athena, and with the Potnia who owns the Labyrinth. Whether housed in Athens, or in Olympus, or in Troy or in Knossos and whether called Athena, or Potnia, or Arētē, the manifestations carried out one plan, the plan of the central cultic management. The singularity of purpose is made evident in the treatment of Odysseus at Scheria (see Frame 2020).

3. Warrior as Agent of the *Wanax,* *Wanax* as Potnia's Agent

With respect to agency, note that in classical Greek literature and iconography, "youth" (*kouros*) does not only signify young in years or youthful vigor, as "son" (*uios*) does not only signify a biological relationship.[15] We may easily detect instances in which individuals termed "child"/"youth" are, in fact, adults and agents. Thus, we find gods with "youths" in their keeping" (Hesiod *Theogony* 345-46) and Hermes "in the guise of young man" (*Odyssey* 10.275–306; cf. Silver 1992: 90–92; Golden 1985). Numerous deities—Hermes, Aphrodite, Hecate, Artemis, Ge, Eileithyia, Leto, Demeter, and even Iphigenia (Pala 2010: 204)— bear the epithet *kourotrophos* 'keeper of youths'. The status "youth" (meaning "agent") finds a natural iconographic translation in individuals who will be perceived as *brimming with youthful vigor* and in adult (even aged) persons who are rendered in "*small size and/or as being physically immature.*"[16] Furthermore, in

---

[15]   The difference in meanings of *uios* is not recognized in Beekes (s.v.).

[16]   Full evidence for "youth"/"son" as agent is provided in earlier works: Silver (1992: 93–95; 2019: Part IV.14). I do not know whether the difference between "biological son" and "agent son" finds a reflection in the two spellings of the word "son" attested in both alphabetic Greek and Linear B.

historical Greek law, the agent ("youth"/"son") is a *slave* of his principal.[17] These considerations are not transparently reflected in Linear B, but they are, I will argue, in iconography.[18]

The "Chieftain Cup" from Agia Triada (Plate 5) depicts a young man (B) with a plumed sheath. Figure B raises his long sword to his right shoulder and holds up the plumed sheath in his left hand, as he leans back with a "deferential tilt or nod of his head" as if receiving instructions from a second facing figure (A), who is also youthful but stands authoritatively with head drawn back holding a long staff in his outstretched arm (Koehl 1986: 99–100 with Plate VIIa; Rehak 1999c: 708). "On the back of the cup are three male figures carrying large flattened animal skins that are usually identified as ox-hides or shields" (Koehl 1986: 99).

As a possible reference model for Figure B, an ivory plaque dated from Delos during the Bronze Age depicts a strongly built, not very youthful male figure who wears a helmet of boar's tusks and grasps a long stout staff in his right hand while holding behind him with his left hand a body-sized hide-covered figure-eight shield (Boardman 2014: 27).

I propose that in the "Chieftain Cup," the shorter youth (B), standing at attention with his sword, is the warrior-agent of the figure with the staff (A). There is reason to believe that B's plumed sheath has kingly/godly connections. It is worn by sphinxes (Evans 1928: 417 Fig. 281), by women, including by the "queen" on the "Agia Triada Sarcophagus" (see Chap. 2 above), and by men, including "officials" and perhaps by the king himself (Marinatos 2010: 14–18). My view is that the plumed headgear is an insignia of service to the king/queen or god/goddess.

I have in mind that young man (A) with the plumed helmet leads the "Griffin Corps," whose primary duty is to protect foreign merchants and their goods (see especially Chap. 11.5-6). The figure with the staff arguably is the *wanax*, who, as will be shown next, has multiple links with the sceptron, which, taken most generally, is a symbol of legal authority.

---

[17] Ancient agents were typically slaves/sons empowered by their principals/owners to form contracts with third parties. The details of legal enforcement are not always clear. For discussions of the legalities of agency in the context of ancient Rome, see Kirschenbaum (1987) and Auburt (1994). Today, there is "direct" agency: a third party can make contracts that legally bind the principal to perform certain actions without binding the agent.

[18] There is a rather promising example in Linear B. "[W]e have working women at Pylos who are designated as *ka-ru-ti-je-ja-o* (Pylos Ad 671 genitive plural) = 'women of the man who controls Karustian cloth products vel sim.' They are women to whom older and younger boys are 'attached' in the context of 'headband-makers,' which suggests that the site of *Karustos* was known as a source of specialized cloth production" (Palaima 2011: 72–73). The reference to the "attachment" of "older and younger boys" suggests to me that they are not literally boys but rather agents assigned/owned by the "man" controlling Karustan cloth products.

With respect to legal authority, see especially the fragmentary "Master Impression" sealing from Chania, in which a youthful figure wields a staff as

Figure 4. "Mountain Mother" sealing from Knossos
(*CMS* II.8, no. 256 = Arachne 160886).

he stands above the city/or the palace on a structure atop a mountain (Chania Museum inv. KH 1563: *CMS* V.1A, no. 142 = Arachne 165373; Marinatos 2010: 75 Fig. 5.10).

It is possible to challenge the interpretation of Figure A as an agent by citing Figure B's own youthful status. There is no question that B wields the symbol of legal power. Thus, we must consider the possibility that both A and B are agents. A is the agent of B, whom he salutes, and B is the agent of someone else; that someone else is the one who granted him the sceptron. Who is the granter? In the fragmentary "Mountain Mother/Mistress of the Mountains" sealing from Knossos (Figure 4), it may be understood that a goddess does not wield but rather *bestows/offers* the sceptron of kingship on/to the youthful figure who salutes/entreats her (Moss 2010: 16; Marinatos 2010: 70 Fig. 5.3).

Thus, guided by descriptions of cult matters in Pausanias, Nagy (2020a: esp. §9-§10; 2020b) compares (or identifies) the passage of the police power from the Minoan/Mycenaean "Mountain Mother" to the sceptron wielding figure in the "Master Impression" (noted above) with Athena's deputizing Heracles to guard her sacred space.[19]

Furthermore, on a gold signet ring called the "Epiphany Ring" from Knossos (Figure 5), a miniature male, holding out from himself what appears to be a sceptron, is *depicted in mid-air* before a giant (relatively speaking) female figure wearing a flounced skirt, who is planted on the ground. Nagy (2020c with references) suggests: (1) the descending figure is the *personification* of the sceptron handed over by "Mountain Mother;" (2) the giant female waiting below is a priestess of Mountain Mother; and (3) that when the staff comes to earth,

---

[19]   Once again, we have the identification of Potnia with Athena (see §2 above).

it will be handed over by the priestess to a human who will become the ruler. That is, the transfer of authority originating in heaven is re-enacted between humans. Although I find this analysis convincing, I would underline that both the youthful status of the recipient and his relatively small size attest to his

Figure 5. "Epiphany Ring" from Knossos (*CMS* VI, no. 281 = Arachne 164412).

dependent status: the ruler is understood as the agent (slave) of the goddess/cult (see Chap. 10.6). *Possibly the mortal remains full-sized until he has accepted the sceptron.*

In evaluating this perspective in which legal authority is bestowed by a goddess on a "secular" authority, it is important to recognize that Minoan/Mycenaean cults controlled very significant economic resources (see e.g., Kyriakidis 2001: 127–128; cf. Silver 1995a: 25–32). In part, the wealth of cults is grounded on their international connections that made it possible for them to provide valuable contacts and geographic informwation to local rulers and to the general population (Silver 1995a: 25–27, 32–33).

Much is explained by Palaima (1995: 135–136; cf. Marinatos 2010: Figs. 5.3, 5.7, 5.10), who notes "a close association of the *skêptron* in Homer with the terms and concepts: *wanax* and *wanassein*," and then cites several Minoan-Mycenaean images in which

> figures hold in their outstretched hands a simple shaft or an obvious spear. In all cases, the images have to do either with power or with divine or religious authority. In two cases, the symbolism clearly is that of communication between the divine and mortal realms. This is the Minoan staff of which I speak. This is what I think the Mycenaeans later called *skêptron* or even *doru*. This is what the Mycenaeans brought into their remarkably anonymous and non-represented ritual of kingship. The staff may be borne by the leading male or the leading female.

So, there is really no question that the staff represents royal legal authority. It follows that *if* the goddess bestows the staff on the youth, then she is best understood as Potnia of the Labyrinth. *In ideological terms, the King is the agent of Potnia of the Labyrinth.* This understanding of King as an agent of Potnia is reinforced

Figure 6. King holding staff with Potnia/Priestess, seal from Mycenae
(*CMS* I, no. 101 = Arachne 157322).

by a seal from Mycenae (Figure 6), in which the "enthroned"[20] Potnia/Priestess grants an audience to the young staff-bearing king who is distinctly smaller[21] than the Goddess/Priestess.

That the *wanax* is a cultic agent may also find support in a Linear B tablet from Pylos (Un 03), stating that the *wanax* 'king' is "initiated" (probably meaning "named/appointed") by a cult in the Sphagianes District (Chap. 8.4). The specific cult that selected the *wanax* is not mentioned, but the cult of Potnia in Sphagianes is one of the more important (wealthy) ones. The only designated "Priestess" in Sphagianes is Eritha, who is arguably the Priestess of Potnia (Chap. 4.2.b). The alternative to Potnia is Sphagianes' Poseidon,[22] who, like Potnia, plays a major role in the textile industry (see Chaps. 14.3, 15.4 below).

I turn now to providing evidence for the identification of "Mountain Mother" specifically with Potnia of the Labyrinth. Such evidence is provided in the image of the nearby multistoried structure with so-called "horns of

---

[20]   In this case, the "throne" appears to be a campstool about which see Chap. 11.5.

[21]   Evans 1928: 404 Fig. 324. There are other images in which the figure I have identified as king is taller than the figure of the identified goddess. These may reflect the mortal's pre-*wanax* status (see above).

[22]   Poseidon is explicitly located in Sphagianes in Fr 1219, 1224, and 343 and there are other important overlaps in the Fr tablets and Un 2 and 6 (Bendall 1998–1999: 4–5).

consecration."[23] For Mycenaean times, the "horns" sometimes represent a component or adaptation of the Labyrinth's double-headed axe symbol:

> At the very least, some connection with the double axe has been assumed based on the numerous examples of horns of consecration fitted with a circular socket between the horns. Most scholars presume that these sockets were for the placement of a double axe, a theory that is supported by iconography on seals and sealings.

> Gulizio 2011: 36–37

The adaptation or blending of the symbol of "horns" with the double axe is confirmed by Figure 7, in which the shaft has a knob at the top and palm

Figure 7. "Horns" as blades of the axe (*CMS* II.8, no. 55 = Arachne 160684).

branches at the bottom of the trunk. I think it is possible to see a ship, but this perspective is more evident in Plate 11 ("Pyxis from Aptera").

The remaining problem is, as Gulizio (2011: 37–38) explains, that while evidence for the double-headed axe goes back to Early Minoan times, evidence

---

[23]   The identification of "Horns of Consecration" in the "*Master Impression*" sealing from Chania (*CMS* VS.1A, no. 142 = Arachne 165373), noted above, has been strongly challenged by Pavúk (2002: 576–577): "The architecture on the Master Impression poses a clear parallel to the Keos frescoes (fig. 5), where it is impossible to interpret the projections as 'Horns of Consecration'. The distance between the neighboring projections is much too great and their points are not as sharp.... Other examples of sealings showing the 'Horns of Consecration' simply show two separate projections were impressed by seals that were not cut as carefully as the Master Impression. Moreover, these projections are clearly pointed, which is not the case with the Master Impression. In addition, some of the roofs on the Master Impression or on the Keos fresco have only one cone-like object." "Horns" might represent mountains connected by a ground-level bridge equipped with a socket for inserting objects of interest to Potnia (Marinatos 1984: 117–120; Banou 2008: 40–41). As noted below, I now believe that "horns" are inspired by the raised bow and stern of some ancient ships as attested by models from Mochlus and elsewhere. However, I refer to "horns" or "horns of consecration" in conformity to the overwhelming usage in the literature and the remaining uncertainty.

for identifying "horns" as a component/adaptation of the double-headed axe is for Mycenaean times. However, I would assume continuity and similarity in meaning of the most fundamental symbols—staff, lions, griffins, sacred knot, double-headed axe, and even "horns"—between Minoan and Mycenaean times.

I return now to additional, novel indicators of agent status. Silver (2019: esp. 73–74) argues that not only did Greek iconography portray the agent as a youth or as a miniature adult person but, in addition, when a male served as a woman's agent, this cross-gender service might be signaled by providing the male with elements of female identity. Thus, Dionysus is made effeminate in serving Aphrodite, and Heracles wears women's clothes when he is the slave-agent of Omphale.[24]

This analysis implies that the youthful *wanax* "king" might, in some way, be portrayed as female. This principle has already been illustrated by means of seals from Zakros and Pylos that depict male figures (no breasts) clad in hide skirts, who serve Potnia by participating in processions while carrying the double-headed axe or a garment. That the cross-gender portrayal is not seen in the "Mountain Mother/Mistress of the Mountains" sealing or in "The Epiphany Ring" constitutes a weakness in my analysis leading to the conclusion that the *wanax* is an agent of Potnia.

The cross-gender portrayal may, however, be detected elsewhere in relation to the King. In Minoan *fresco* iconography, including the Agia Triada sarcophagus, sex is indicated by skin color: men have dark red skin, and women have white.[25] In this connection, note the white skin of the "Priest King" (or "Prince with Lilies"). This refers to a restored relief mural[26] in Knossos' "Corridor of Processions" (Plate 6) that depicts a youthful and muscular male figure, presumably the king, who wears a headgear/crown with an attached lily and a codpiece, and who holds something that is no longer visible in his ascendant left hand. It has been suggested that he is leading (controlling) a

---

[24] At the same time, Dionysus and Heracles retained their male identities when acting for themselves or for male principals. For evidence of cross-dressing and effeminacy in classical Greek times, see Surtees 2014. The agency relationships might be cultic or "secular." To speak in these cases of "ambiguous" gender is misleading, as the gender of the service provider is made obvious.

[25] The skin color convention is not followed in sarcophagi generally or in the case of pictorial vases (Eaverly 2013: 86–87). The reason for this apparent distinction is unclear.

[26] The figure is reconstructed from fragments, and it has been argued that the headgear with lily does not belong on a male (Boloti 2014: 255–256). This may be, but, on the other hand, the "Priest-King's" white skin makes him female. As noted by Boloti (2014: 255 n. 76), in a ring impression (*CMS* II.8, no. 248 = Arachne 160878) from Knossos a "male figure" wears a very similar headgear.

griffin (by Tamvaki 1974: 291). This "prince" or "king," if that is his rank, is a man wearing the skin of a woman.[27]

I maintain the hypothesis that the warrior (A) is the agent of the king (B), and that the king is ideologically viewed as the agent of Potnia. Additional examples of female attributes for the king are required for verification.

[27] It has been questioned, however, whether skin color is a useful or at least reliable indicator of gender. M. Shaw (2004: 79) has suggested that in explaining skin color, the determining factor is clearly biological age, or, rephrased in terms of Morgan's [2000: 937–940] view, "a time when one had to front rites of passage." Obviously, we already know that men were rarely depicted in white. Does Shaw mean that based on their age, men also had to be depicted with white skins? Rehak (1996: 41) points out that in the fresco [the "Toreador Fresco"] both the red-skinned and the white-skinned bull jumpers have long hair "which recalls a female characteristic and these adolescent youths and these gender-neutral *paidia* who have not arrived yet at their sexually specific and differentiated adult state." However, all the jumpers are male and all have long hair, so why do some have red skins and others white skin? Perhaps this is explained by *team sports* with red skins representing a male figure/sponsor and the white skins a female sponsor. Note that seals depicting acrobats riding and jumping over bulls are accompanied by "sacral knots" (Evans 1928: 225–227 with Figs. 158, 159), indicating sponsorship of the event.

"The bracelet on the Archer Fragment from Pylos is similar to those worn by the white-skinned toreadors from Knossos.... One fragment of a wall painting from the Kadmeia at Thebes shows a helmeted head with white skin in a window-like opening.... Mycenaean vase paintings depict very feminine figures clad in long dresses and carrying swords" (Brecoulaki et al. 2008: 377–378).

A final point in defense of skin color as an indicator of gender is that in "The Tiryns Boar Hunt," we see pairs of persons standing in chariots with one holding the reigns. The individuals are dressed in sleeved tunics—that is, men's tunics—and have a masculine hairstyle, but they have white skins (Immerwahr 1990: 129–130; Farmer and Lane 2016: 65) The meaning, as indicated elsewhere, is that the cross-dressing figures are women with the legal rights of men (cf. Rodenwaldt 1976 [1912], 96-97).

Janiform Reflections on Part I

THE suggestion that Minoan and Mycenaean palaces featured showrooms for the display of textiles may be doubted by scholars who stress a religious motivation for their frescoes. Some historical perspective may help. The palace at Mari (Tell Hariri), in Bronze Age northern Syria, was a center for the production of textiles that incorporated extensive warehouse facilities. According to Dalley (1984: 15), the palace had a *kār ekallim* "palace market," and "this part of the palace plan closely resembles the plan of a modern bazaar in the Near East." Perhaps this is only a coincidence, but the Mari Palace was decorated with remarkable true fresco paintings. Niemeier (1991) has proposed that this was a task possibly performed by traveling Minoan artists. I must leave this question unsettled because a study of the Mari paintings would take me far beyond the scope of the present study; it would become a study without any possible ending.[1]

I fully accept the religious motivation behind the Minoan/Mycenaean frescoes. At the same time, I suggest that there is no intrinsic conflict between serving one's gods and serving one's material interests. Indeed, gods have been known to openly encourage worshippers to do so as this increases their own "honor" and "fame." Beyond the mutuality of interest, there is the fact that human beings have the innate capacity to create *and* believe in gods that serve their interests. The belief aspect results from the conviction that the god was discovered or manifested itself, not created. The creation aspect is demonstrated by numerous acts of religious creation and adaptation by "priests" and others.[2]

Potnia, sitting in her labyrinths, controlled the production and marketing of textiles. In ideological terms, the king (*wanax*) was Potnia's legal agent, taking care of transportation and matters of security. What is not made clear anywhere is who controlled Potnia—that is, what humans formed and modified the business plan attributed to Potnia? As noted by Roger Woodard in the February

---

[1] Neither is there time to follow the leads in Silver (1992: 228–235), regarding Rahab in Joshua 2, who saved the Israelite spies by helping them escape from her house by means of a (probably scarlet) thread and of Enki, the Sumerian god, who in the third millennium BCE possessed a "house of the sea" whose "interior is a twisted thread" (Kramer and Maier 1985: 49).

[2] See Burkert (1987) and Silver (2011a: 61–67) for examples and discussion.

2021 MASt@CHS Winter seminar (brief notes published in Pierini and Palaima 2021), a reference to the existence of a policy-making group is found in *Homeric Hymn to Apollo* 388–390, wherein "Phoebus Apollo is said 'to ponder' (*phrázomai* [φράζομαι]) what sort of humans he should 'lead to' (*eiságō* [εἰσάγω]) Pytho to be his *orgiónas* (ὀργιόνας; accusative plural)." Apollo chose "men [who] were sailing in their black ship for traffic and for profit [from Knossos] to sandy Pylos and to the men of Pylos" (line 397). The god informed the traders: "Apollo is my name: but you I brought here over the wide gulf of the sea, meaning you no hurt; nay, here you shall keep my rich temple that is greatly honored among men, and you shall know the plans of the deathless gods, and by their will you shall be honored continually for all time" (480–485; tr. Evelyn-White *LCL*). We may entertain the thought that it was the Cretan traders—his *orgiónas*—who chose to install and act for Apollo in Pytho.

Woodard calls attention to Pylos Un 718 dealing with the contributions of four human groups/individuals to a festival of Poseidon. The fourth contributor is "identified by the phrase *wo-ro-ki-jo-ne-jo, ka-ma*. The second term, *ka-ma*, is generally acknowledged to denote some space of *terra firma*." Woodard continues that "the Linear B form *wo-ro-ki-jo-ne-jo*, an adjective, must trace its origin to a nominal **wrogiōn*, from a *zero*-grade root **wr̥g-*." Thus, the *ka-ma* that functions as the fourth benefactor for Poseidon is a "space" controlled by/associated with **wrogiōnes*. Unfortunately, we hear no more about this group from the "sector knowing the mind of the god."[3]

Turning to a more concrete policy issue, I have earlier proposed that the style of the open-bodice baring of the breasts might be specific to the models in labyrinth/palace showrooms. Depictions in the frescoes and elsewhere (e.g. the Agia Triada Sarcophagus) make clear that Minoan/Mycenaean women generally wore styles covering their breasts.[4] Another thought is that some women depicted in the Minoan and Mycenaean frescoes were *mortal nymphs* —that is, single women living in groups under the auspices of a goddess (Potnia of the Labyrinth) and who were dedicated to the production and marketing (including modeling) of textiles (Silver 2018: 154–158). Consider that the nymphs of Homer's Ithaca, into whose vault Odysseus, in heeding the advice of Athena, placed his treasure, were most active in the making of luxury textiles. Even

---

[3]   Some scholars suggest that the phrase is an adjective that defines the land that belongs to a *person* named Wroikiōn (Nikoloudis 2008b: 588–589). I am not sure why they prefer this explanation, as they do not claim the name is common and do not recognize that such a group is attested to in the *Homeric Hymn to Apollo*.

[4]   Based on her study of numerous examples of Mycenaean terracotta female figurines, Steel (2020: 12) notes that clothing mattered a great deal, but also concludes that "women were expected to be fully covered, swaddled in long garments of linen or wool, and the only bare flesh on display was the face."

Helen, a married woman but a goddess, is called a "nymph" in connection with her production of fine textiles.

In Part II, I consider the Minoan/Mycenaean political economy as revealed by material archaeological evidence, plus texts and iconography. Then, Part III argues that Homer can be utilized as a Bronze Age source. This finding opens new research opportunities that are pursued in Part IV. We are only at the beginning of the argument.

PART II

LUXURY TEXTILES IN THE BRONZE AGE AEGEAN
ECONOMIC ASPECTS

7

Wool, Murex, and Purpled Textiles

Bronze Age Potentialities and Procedures

1. Wool Production and Management

IN the Bronze Age Aegean, the first reliable evidence for the use of wool in textile production is provided by the presence of dyeing installations beginning in about 2500-2400 BCE (EM IIB) in eastern Crete at Myrtos. Of course, there are no surviving wool samples; this evidence is inferential for, as is explained by Militello (2014: 266), linen—the main textile-material competitor—is extremely difficult to dye successfully. The wool might have been provided by Crete's wild goats and/or by sheep.

For Mycenaean times, there are records of flocks and wool but not of wild goats. In Crete, Knossos had between 80,000 and 100,000 sheep, mainly castrated wethers. Based on these numbers, it has been estimated that Knossos could have produced between thirty and fifty tons of wool yearly (Killen 1984: 50; Burke 2010: 83). Messenian Pylos had some 10,000 sheep. No systematic flock records are available for other palatial centers, but there are records of wool and textiles (Rougemont 2014: 140–141). At Mycenaean Knossos, the palace employed more than one thousand women and children in the textile industry, and the palace at Pylos employed about 750 women and 750 children (Killen 1999: 115).[1]

Turning to a problem of management, Burke (2010: 82) explains that in the Linear B corpus, there are tablets in which sheep are designated as missing and owed by an *o*. The *o* is "likely an abbreviation for *o-pe-ro*, related to Greek *ophelon* 'deficit, that which is needed' " (transliteration mine; Beekes s.v. *opheilō* 'to owe'). Thus, Halstead (2001: 42–43) calls attention to the relatively small "deficits" in palatial wool flocks, and he suggests that shepherds were making up for the natural deaths of their sheep. Homeric and other literature offers support for Halstead's hypothesis. My understanding is that the missing animals were owed by shepherds and "collectors," who had entered into contracts for deathless/

---

[1]   The estimated total population of Pylos is about 50,000 (Nakassis 2013: 156).

immortal sheep (see Greco 2012: 274–276; Chap. 8.2 on "collectors" and Chap. 15.3 on the sheep of Helios).

Halstead (2001: 41–42) recognizes a more basic problem, pointing out that the number of sheep in the Linear B tablets cannot tell the whole story of wool production. The herds administered by the Knossos Palace were not self-sustaining:

> [R]ecorded breeding stock [rams] were far too few in number to provide the necessary number of replacement wool sheep, consisting primarily of castrated wethers, although this argument could be challenged on the grounds that records of breeding flocks, chanced to be less well preserved than those of wool flocks.

Even so, "chance omission" is not a very convincing or satisfying explanation. Quite possibly, as Halstead (2001) suggests, the replacement wool sheep were provided from *local* herds of privately owned—that is, non-Palace owned—breeding sheep. Such herds would not have been recorded by the palace scribes who concerned themselves with palatial affairs.[2]

An alternative or additional solution to Halstead's problem may be suggested using the Homeric and related literature, wherein gods such as Helios and Poseidon and heroes, such as Odysseus and Theras, are employed in the gathering and raising of sheep in *peripheral regions* (see Chap. 15.2, 4). In real life, agents and independent contractors may have undertaken such duties for the palaces. In any event, the capacity of the palaces to manage herds and produce woolen textiles in substantial quantity cannot be doubted.

2. Archaeological Evidence for Murex Dye Production and Use in the Aegean

This Section surveys archaeological evidence for murex dye production and its use in the dyeing of textiles. Consideration is given not only to the western but also to the eastern Aegean as areas of central concern in the present study. It will be seen that there is much evidence in the western Aegean for the production of murex but very little for its actual application. So glaring is this gap that it becomes viable to hypothesize that murex-dye was converted to powdered form, as for the making of paint in frescoes, and then exported elsewhere for application to textiles. I am referring to the use of *purpurissium*, as the substance was called by Pliny (*Natural History* 35.26), and for which Kanold (2017) has

---

[2] Marie-Louise Nosch cautions me that many Dk and Dl Linear B texts record "reproductive" flocks under the supervision of Potnia and Hermes.

provided an updated recipe that works.[3] More will be said about *purpurissium* shortly and in §3 below.

In addition, concerning the gap between findings of processed murex shells and evidence of the dyeing of textiles, Plutarch reports that murex-dye could itself be stored with no marked deterioration:

> On making himself master of Susa, Alexander came into possession of forty thousand talents of coined money in the palace, and of untold furniture and wealth besides. Among this they say was found five thousand talents' weight of purple from Hermione, which, although it had been stored there for a hundred and ninety years, still kept its colours fresh and lively. The reason for this, they say, is that honey was used in the purple dyes, and white olive oil in the white dyes; for these substances, after the like space of time, are seen to have a brilliancy that is pure and lustrous.
>
> *Life of Alexander* 36; tr. Perrin *LCL*

The implication of Pliny's and Plutarch's testimony is that purple dye in powdered or fresh form might be transported to even distant textile production sites. The practice is confirmed in *Odyssey* 13.95ff., wherein the Nymphs in their "cave" "store purple" and weave "webs of purple dye" (Chap. 15.2).[4]

D'Agata and De Angelis (2014: 349–350, 354–355) believe they have connected honey and murex production in Itanos' Villa of Vai:

---

[3] "A fermentation vat, as mentioned above, needs 7–10 days to mature. A reduced vat is very smelly, precluding transportation by plane or train. Therefore, it was decided for the workshop in Lecce, that purple pigments should be used to make travelling much pleasanter. In his *Natural History*, Pliny called this product *purpurissum*, or the *painter's paint*.... He suggested that *creta argentaria* can be used to absorb the colourant within a vat. Different try-outs led to a simplified version. Fresh glands of *Hexaplex trunculus* were cut out and placed into water in a Petri dish; it turned violet rather quickly. At this stage it was helpful to use a mixer to blend the glands in order to liberate the water-soluble precursors. Various substrates like calcium carbonate, aragonite, and gofun (ground or crushed oyster shells) were added, but only acidic insoluble white pigments such as talcum powder (magnesium silicate) were found suitable. The remains of the fleshy material and other shell debris, which always stick to the separated hypobranchial glands, had to be discarded. Vinegar, or more efficiently, diluted hydrochloric acid, was used for the hydrolysis and separation of the unwanted residues. Continuous heating of the extracts (up to 50°C) helped to accelerate the cleaning process. After that, careful washing with water removed the acids to obtain a neutral product. Once filtered and dried, this purple powder is paint (when used with a binder) or a dye (when reduced with sodium dithionite)." (Kanold 2017). On the extracted crystals and their colors when exposed to light and air, see also Bruin (1970: 80–81).

[4] Perhaps crocus dye is also portable. Note that "Organic residue analysis of ceramics from Pseira and Chryso-kamino has identified isophorone, a compound whose only known natural source is saffron" (Day 2011b: 357 n. 140 with references).

One particular controversy [with respect to beekeeping] has concerned whether or not a Cretan kind of clay basin ... was in fact a beehive. Research on rural areas of Far Eastern Crete, where a certain number of vase fragments belonging to this functional shape were found, prompted us to pursue this question. In the absence of organic residue analysis proving the presence of honey, wax or propolis, these vessels cannot be identified as beehives with absolute certainty. We do believe, however, that there are enough elements to sustain this hypothesis.... In our reconstruction, in the Neopalatial phase the Villa of Vai was involved in the exploitation of murex for the extraction of purple. The intense beekeeping activity carried out in the area may well have been accessory to the production of purple, because honey may have played a significant role in this regard.... The presence of beehives in an area which may have been devoted to the production of purple and cloth dyeing is by no means surprising, but we are still far from being able to reconstruct the relative production system in detail.

Thus, the evidence for murex manufacture using honey in Crete's palm district is tentative. On the other hand, the logogram for "honey"[5] is frequently attested to in the Linear B texts, and, if I understand Varian (2012: 411) correctly, it is often "associated" with garments, skin, and (especially) wool at Pylos and Knossos. *There arises the prospect of a distinct geographic separation between the production of murex-dye and the dyeing of textiles.*

D'Agata and De Angelis (2014) depend on the presence of ceramic beehives to identify sites producing murex. More conventionally, murex production is associated with the finding of murex shells. More than 200 *crushed murex shells* were found in eastern Crete at Petras in Sitia in an MM 1 context (about 2000 BCE). Somewhat later—from 1900 to 1700 BCE—large numbers of murex shells are observed on the islands of Thera/Santorini, Kythera, and Chrysi on the south coast of Crete and, especially, in the port of Kommos in southern Crete. Numerous shells are also observed in eastern Crete at the island Kouphonisi, in Palaikastro at Crete's eastern end, and at Malia on the northern coast of Crete about twenty-one miles east of Knossos.[6]

The surveyed evidence is supportive of murex-dye production because the shells are crushed and fragmentary. Muricid snails are also eaten, but in this case, the shells are kept intact to avoid ruining the meat with shell splinters (Çakirlar and Becks 2009: 97; Kremer 2017 at n. 22). On the other hand, as

---

[5] "Honey" *me-ri* (*meli* or *melit*) is usually expressed logographically rather than syllabically.

[6] Sources: Apostolakou et al. 2016; Gillis 2010: 90; Reese 1987; Militello 2014: 266; for additional sites, see Gillis 2010: 88ff.; M. Alberti 2008).

explained by Marín-Aguilera et al. (2018: 132), "[t]he breaking of the mollusk shell to ensure the rupture of the hypobranchial gland was a crucial phase of the [murex-dye] production process "

Ruscillo (2005a: 808; cf. 2005b) maintains that the excavations at Kommos uncovered not only many crushed murex shells but an installation for extracting the dye:

> The presumed installation was found under the floor of Gallery P5 at its west end. It is characterized by a flat stone slab floor extending under the later walls, and a shallow channel 12 cm in width running east-west.... Both the slab floor, especially at the western edge, and the channel are packed with crushed *Murex*. Both the architecture and debris share the same MM IB/II date and may even predate Building AA's construction. Crushing *Murex* is an odoriferous task; if an industry was established at Kommos, an installation might have been designed to be easily washed down at the end of each session.... It is therefore possible that the architectural finds here represent the earliest *Murex* dye installation found on Crete. A mass of *Murex* would be crushed, and at the end of the session, water would be poured down the paved floor; the channel provided drainage.

Ruscillo's findings and explanations make it credible, I think, that Cretans at Kommos extracted dye from murex as early as 1900 BCE. Did they also use their dye on woolen textiles? Ruscillo makes some interesting observations[7] about this process, but, as far as I can tell, she provides no direct evidence for the dyeing process.

The evidence for the application of murex dye is stronger at Chryssi. Here, there were stone tanks perhaps for storing—and/or breeding—murex snails as well as crushed murex but also other edible and inedible shellfish. The evidence for the application consists of a building with a room (Room 3) including two tripod cooking pots:

> The purple glands would have been boiled or heated indoors, in the cookpots in Room 3, where both light and heat could be controlled. The intensive nature of the work is indicated by the presence of a thick,

---

[7]   Ruscillo (2005a: 963) learned: "To make a sample of Royal Purple took a minimum of four days, not including the airing-out period. We calculated that if a piece of wool 125 cm square required 200 Murex to make a deep purple color, then a whole wool cloak would require at least 5,000 Murex for a nice even color. This estimate is considerably lower than what was originally calculated by scholars: sometimes as many as 20,000 individuals just for the trim of a garment. Procuring 5,000 Murex was no easy task, however."

packed ash layer in this space, which represents the fuel used in the fires. The cups and jug in Room 3 would have served to add liquid to the cookpots and then to remove and sieve the dye. It should, however, be emphasized that none of the objects used in this workshop are specialized tools. They are all, ordinary, domestic objects, which could be put to different uses.

Apostolakou et al. 2016: 203

Thus, the evidence for dye-making is suggestive, but, as archaeologists are careful to remind us, there are other believable explanations for it. Furthermore, there is no evidence of structures for the application of the dye to textiles.

But a recent report from Chrysi provides thought provoking results:[8]

The team found deep beds of thousands of the shells of spiny sea snails called murex [Hexaplex trunculus] ... in several small buildings in the settlement but not in the large building. Instead, the large building was equipped with terraces, work desks, stoves, buckets and a stone staircase, suggesting that it was once inhabited by those who managed the settlement's production of the purple dye, and perhaps its promotion and trade to buyers who visited the island by ship.

Chyrsi Report

Note that the report seems to deal with trade in the dye not in dyed textiles, for which process evidence is not provided. With respect to payment:

Two of the rooms contained 'treasures' with objects made of glass, metal and semi-precious stones. The first one was found in 2018 and is said to have probably been used as a warehouse. It contained a golden ring, 26 golden beads and a golden bracelet, a silver bead, 5 copper ones and a copper ring sling along with a large number of glass beads of various shapes, four of the so-called Egypt blue, 10 from lapis lazuli, one from amethyst and 20 from carnelian, a seal made of agate with the picture of a ship that its stern had the form of an animal's head and a stone amulet with the shape of a monkey.

Chyrsi Report

---

[8] The Chrysi report is available for download at: https://www.foxnews.com/science/gold-and-jewels-found-on-minoan-island-devoted-to-the-color-purple (February 16, 2020). Accessed February 12, 2021.

The evidence is there for a trading station, but not for the dye or for dyed textiles. Moreover, who were the buyers?

Another recently excavated site, Pefka Pacheia Ammos (Alatzomouri-Pefka), on the northern coast of Crete's Ierapetra Isthmus, gives new evidence with one hand and hides old evidence with the other. Industrial installations were found consisting of "nine basins carved directly into the limestone bedrock with channels connecting some of them," and chemical traces of murex dye were detected in a jar, but the quantity of crushed murex was too small for a dye production site (Apostolakou et al. 2016: 204–206). Another important clue is provided by the discovery in the well of a Middle Minoan IIB prism seal that reportedly is similar to examples from a workshop at Quartier Mu at Malia (Apostolakou et al. 2016: 206). Perhaps new excavations will reveal the massive deposits of crushed murex that define a dye production site. Alternatively, perhaps, Pefka Pacheia Ammos dyed textiles but acquired the dye elsewhere. I would note two findings in this connection: first, "Analysis by gas chromatography shows that vessels contained both organic dyes and the natural oil from wool called lanolin. Red from madder, yellow from weld, and purple from murex have been identified by their organic residues" (Betancourt, Brogan, and Apostalakou 2020: 130); and second, numerous transport amphorae were found that might reflect the delivery of dyes to the site or perhaps could have been used to deliver dyes to still other sites.

Near the heart of the palatial center, in the port of Zakros in "Hogarth's House I," there are nine shallow channels with a drainage system which might have been used for dyeing textiles —or the making of wine. "Hogarth's House J" contained numerous loom-weights and a "dye vat," and Room XI had plastered troughs and a drain. Also, in "Hogarth's House A, Room VIII," excavators found numerous sealings, a Linear A tablet and a roundel (Wc 2) used for recording transactions.[9] I can understand why Burke (2010: 37) sees the dyeing of textiles here. However, once again, the problems are that the industrial evidence is ambiguous: deposits of crushed murex (used in constructions) are absent, and there is no chemical evidence for the use of dyes. There is also the practical problem of handling awful odors in an urban center.

At this point in our survey, the evidence demonstrates the extraction of purple dye at various sites in western Aegean. We cannot exclude the possibility that these production sites were exporting their purple dye overseas (Carannante 2011: 11; Gillis 2010: 90) or to other sites in Crete itself (e.g., Pefka

---

[9]   Sources: Burke (2010: 37 with extensive references); Platon (1985). The roundel does not reveal anything specific about the kinds of recorded transactions, although one of the sealings depicts a woman wearing a long dress, who appears to lead a wild goat (see Perna 1994). Thus, we may think of wool and even textile production.

Pacheia Ammos, Kato Zakros). In the latter event, we may theorize that it was less expensive to transport purple dye as a powder (as *purpurissium*) or stored fresh dye in a flask[10] to populous textile production centers elsewhere in Crete than to send workers, wool, grain, and other foodstuffs to isolated seaside locations with living snails suitable for murex extraction.[11]

Lumps of material scientifically identified as murex purple pigment have been excavated in Bronze Age contexts at Akrotiri and in Trianda on Rhodes. The purple dye was adsorbed in the calcium carbonate substrate (Sotiropoulou et al. 2021). To date, no evidence of dying installations has been found in these sites, and neither is there definitive evidence of shell processing. However, there is evidence for the use of purple pigment in frescoes in Akrotiri.

The dyeing of textiles would not have taken place inside the urbanized locales but on nearby mountains so that the prevailing winds would dry the dyed textiles and, more importantly, disperse the odors. There are, in fact, several clues pointing to this kind of location: most obviously, a prism seal from Palaikastro (see §4 below) depicts a goat or agrimi together with what is obviously a murex. The wool of wild goats was used, and it must be significant that the two animals are depicted together. Obviously, live murex does not inhabit hills and mountains the way goats do; their togetherness likely reveals that dye was transported to the hills. A review of the archaeological findings at and *above*[12] the so-called "peak sanctuaries" (Chap. 1) might reveal unsuspected dyeing facilities.

Turning from dyeing with murex to the production of murex, there is evidence that murex production declined in Crete. Burke (2006: 281), discussing

---

[10]   The snail must be alive when the murex gland is removed and then it is mixed with honey (a glucose). This mixing keeps the "dye precursors" in their soluble state with the result that the mixture can be used in a dye-vat much after preparation and far from the sea (Martelli 2016: 116–121). Note that Martelli is reporting on experiments performed by others. But the use of honey is confirmed by Plutarch *Life of Alexander* 36 (above) and in *Odyssey* 13.95ff.).

[11]   It is correct that Kato Zakros is located on a good harbor but also it lacks an extensive agricultural hinterland. The pattern seems to be crushed murex shells in one location but evidence of the dyeing of textiles in another. Thus, note a recent report (July 1, 2019) at Tel Shikmona located south of Haifa: "Tel Shikmona, despite being well documented throughout history, often confused scholars as to why it was established. The shore was too rocky to serve as a harbor, and the land around it was not especially suitable for agriculture. The most notable clues up until this point were the abundance of Phoenician pottery, and large amounts of purple coloring preserved in ceramic vats.... Now, however, an analysis of the findings confirmed that the dye came from sea snails. Findings of purple coloring from this period are exceptionally rare, the researchers stated, and were only found in small amounts in other places. Not only did Tel Shikmona contain an unprecedentedly large amount – indicating production of the dye—but it also contained looms and spindles—indicating manufacturing of textiles as well." (Available at: https://www.jpost.com/israel-news/biblical-era-purple-dye-industry-discovered-in-haifa-594266. Accessed February 12, 2021). There is no accompanying report of crushed murex shells.

[12]   The sanctuaries were not necessarily located at the tops of the mountains.

the evidence of murex-dye production at Petras and other early Cretan sites, observes that during the "formative periods" of the Minoan palaces, there is not only evidence of murex processing at palace-controlled centers but also "After this period there is a noticeable absence of Murex throughout the archaeological record on Crete." Thus, the absence of archaeological evidence suggests that the Minoans may have ceased even to extract murex, at least locally in Crete.

The Minoans continued to make cloth, so perhaps they had it dyed outside Crete—possibly in Lemnos—or, perhaps, they worked with thread that had been dyed elsewhere. The theory that Crete imported purple-dyed thread finds some support in the inferred scarcity within Middle and Late Minoan Cretan palatial centers of spindles for making thread relative to looms for weaving cloth. The number of spindle whorls excavated is reportedly insufficient to supply the thread needed by the number of looms predicted by the excavated number of loom-weights (Burke 2006: 282; Tzachili 1990: 386).[13] Burke (2006: 282) suspects that thread was made in the Cretan countryside surrounding the palaces. This makes economic sense, as rural workers might make thread during their downtime from caring for flocks, obtaining wool, and/or performing other agricultural and domestic activities.

The disparity between whorls and weights at Knossos may have been less pronounced in earlier times.[14] Burke (1997: 416–417) suggests that excavation of the Neolithic strata in the Central Court at Knossos produced evidence of textile specialization *and* ongoing production of both thread and cloth. Pursuing this gap-theme to later times, *it is striking, given the emphasis on textile production in the Linear B tablets, that local weights are rarely found on the Greek mainland* (Burke 1997: 420)—a finding that remains unexplained. Nosch (2014a: 7–8) makes a significant observation:

> Regarding textile tools for weaving, today represented by extant loom-weights, we do not have an uninterrupted use throughout the Bronze Age although it is unlikely that weaving ever stopped. Rather, it suggests that other loom types which do not employ loom-weights, such as the tubular loom, the two-beam loom or the horizontal loom, were used along with the warp weighted loom.

---

[13]   There are "claimed Linear A inscribed 'spindle whorls' from Troy" (Godart, cited by John Younger, AEGEANET, November 29, 1998). Tom Palaima writes: "The Linear A on spindle whorls is pure fantasy. These are spindle whorls with abstract patterns, nothing more" (AEGEANET April 25, 2004).

[14]   The situation is similar in Akrotiri (Santorini). In *Odyssey* 7.103ff., wherein, as Luján (2013: 382) points out, the slave women in Odysseus' palace performed both tasks—making thread and weaving.

Changes from one technology to another and then back to the original are, of course, possible, but there is no evidence, and we run the danger of inventing sinuous explanations to suit unexplained observations.

The evidence for murex-dye extraction and use becomes clearer when we move from the western to the eastern Aegean and the island of Lemnos.[15] Large deposits of *murex brandaris* [i.e. *Bolinus brandaris*] were documented in a Middle Bronze Age context at Poliochni on the east coast of Lemnos opposite Troy (Hisarlik).[16] Thus, the deposits date from much earlier than the Mycenaean palaces, and the deposits seem comparable in date to those mentioned earlier at eastern Crete (cf. Cultraro 2005: 245). Specifically,

> This evidence has been collected by the oldest Italian excavations at Polichni in 1930-36 and a part of the results was updated by L. Bernabò Brea. When I started the general reassessment of the material coming from the strata of MBA I found traces of purple shells coming from some rooms in the Western Area of the settlement. The same information was confirmed by an unpublished study by the Italian bio-zoologist Luigi Cardini in 1936, who examined the faunal and shell remains from Della Seta's excavations. I can tell you that in Poliochni *during the MBA and LBA exploitation* and working of purple shells are well documented.

> Cultraro, February 12, 2019; emphasis added

There is also much crushed murex at Troy/Hisarlik as is reported by Çakırlar and Becks:

> The current evidence indicates a self-sustained, medium-sized industry, but only from a diachronical point of view. In view of the cultural and chronological context of the Late Bronze Age Aegean, what can be concluded from the present evidence is that the 'murex' dye production of the settlements of Troia VIa through Troia VIIa was a flourishing one, probably representing an industry enhancing the growing textile production at the site.[17]... Such instantly recognizable evidence is clearly not represented by the archaeological remains of *H. trunculus* at Troia. Nevertheless, evidence for 'murex' dye produc-

---

[15]   For Lemnos, I rely mainly on a personal communication with Prof. Dr Massimo Cultraro Primo Ricercatore Consiglio Nazionale delle Ricerche, Istituto per i Beni Archeologici e Monumentali, Catania, Italy. The communication is dated February 12, 2019 and is cited and quoted with permission.

[16]   Communication between Poliochni and Troy was facilitated by the prevailing current originating in the Bosporus (Agourides 1997: 8).

[17]   Evidence not comparable to Tyre and Sidon.

tion at Troia represents the most abundant evidence for this industry from the whole *Late Bronze Age Aegean*.[18]... The increased abundance of *H. trunculus* remains in the Late Bronze Age layers at Troia is part of a collective trend we see at contemporary sites elsewhere in the Aegean.

Çakırlar and Becks 2009: 99; emphasis added

Thus, as in Crete, there is evidence for early murex-dye extraction at both Lemnos and Troy. The main species involved is *Hexaplex trunculus* (i.e. murex trunculus).

Çakırlar and Becks (2009: 99) observe, "the earliest evidence of purple-dye production at Troia occurs just at a time when there is a distinct influence from the southern Aegean visible in the archaeological record of the site." That earliest evidence is of a Minoan interest that "is also clearly shown in the findings from the settlements on the nearby islands of Samothrace and Lemnos." We can say then that the Minoan interest in purple dye extracted at Troy, Lemnos, and Samothrace roughly corresponds to a decline in extractive activities in Crete itself. *There is also the sense that the dye-extraction activities increased significantly in Mycenaean times.* Again, there is little archaeological evidence for textile dyeing.

To summarize, there is reasonably strong evidence for the extraction of purple dye in Middle Bronze Age Crete in 1700-1600 BCE and in Lemnos at about the same time; there is also evidence for Samothrace and Troy, but it may date mainly to the period of the Mycenaean Palaces. What is most interesting is that the flourishing of dye-extraction in the eastern Aegean seems to correspond with the archaeological evidence of this activity in Crete and mainland Greece.[19] However, the Mycenaean Linear B documents, especially from Knossos, mention purple-dyed garments. Thus, it seems possible that if the Minoans and Mycenaeans did not import dye from eastern Aegean production sites, then they may have sent their textiles to be dyed there—potentially, by the "Lemnian Women." From there, it would have made its way mainly to the Black Sea region.[20]

---

[18] This statement probably does not take into account the unpublished Lemnos material.

[19] There may be archaeological evidence from Thebes of actual dyeing, but it is disputed. Spyropoulos (1975)—the excavator of a two-room building in Thebes—reports that pits dug into the floor of the building were vats for dyeing cloth. This interpretation is disputed by Shelmerdine (1997: 389). "Room 1" of the building contained numerous records of livestock (probably sheep) imports and also of wool exports to Euboea (discussed below). The building may have served for storing wool (Burke 2010: 101).

[20] An alternative explanation for the absence of strong evidence for murex production is that the cheaper plant-based dyes were more widely employed than I have imagined. However, I know of no direct evidence to support such a theory.

3. Palatial Production of Purple-Dyed Textiles: Textual Evidence

We turn now from Minoan to Mycenaean times. No doubt, the Minoan Linear A texts could tell us much about the purple-dyeing of textiles but, unfortunately, they remain undeciphered. One exception is noted below.

The Linear B-stem *po-pu* which is related to Greek *porphura*[21] "purple-dye," "purple snail," and "purple cloths" occurs only in *four tablets, all from Knossos* (KN Lc(1) 561, KN L(7) 474 + *fr.*, KN X 976 + 8263, and KN L 758). Burke (2010: 78–79) provides important, albeit partially disputed, details:[22]

> Units of cloth are described on three of the four tablets [one in an erasure] attesting the stem *po-pu*. One unit of TELA^1 + *TE*, two units of TELA^2 + PU, and 21 units of TELA^3 + PU are recorded. The fourth tablet refers to professional 'purple' women of *da-*83-ja* making so much of something *wa-na-ka-te-ro*, 'royal'.[23]... No ideogram is on this last tablet to indicate that cloth is being made or dyed but this seems likely ... [because it is found in an area with other cloth related texts].
>
> cf. Palaima 1991; 289–291; 1997

The dispute concerns the significance of *da-*83-ja* and whether there is a reference to "cloth." Burke, if I understand correctly, understands *da-*83-ja* to be an ethnic adjective used as a toponym. However, other scholars regard it only as a toponym, and they see the "purple" but not "professional 'purple' women." Thus, Nosch (2012: 332 n. 136, references omitted) concludes:

> KN X 976 lists something or someone (the logogram is lost) royal (*wa-na-ka-te-ro*) and purple (*po-pu-re-jo*) from or at the place *da-*83-ja*. The term *po-pu-re-jo*[could be an adjective for objects 'of purple colour,' or a noun for a 'purple-dyeing workshop' ... or an occupational designation for the people involved in dyeing, 'the purple dyers.'... The ending in *-jo*, however, excludes that it is purple *pu-ka-ta-ri-ja* cloth."[24]

---

[21] "There are no Indo-European connections; probably a loanword from a Mediterranean language" (Beekes s.v.). Perhaps the word is Minoan or Lemnian, another undeciphered language related to Etruscan.

[22] Note that TELA, a logogram, refers to "cloth." The superscript refers to the number of fringes on the cloth and is not of importance for the present discussion.

[23] The meaning of *wa-na-ka-te-ro* is is discussed in Chapter 8.2.

[24] See further Chap. 8.2 on *wa-na-ka-te-ro*.

Palaima (2020b: 124) has put forward as the "preferable" interpretation of Knossos X 976 that, in the place *da-*83-ja*, there is a *porphureion* (or *porphurēwes*), meaning not "purple dye workers" but rather a "place of purple dye"—i.e. a "purple workshop." Palaima also notes that this "place" is not the one where the dye was extracted from the shells. He puts forward the difficult proposal that the place where the actual marine mollusks were harvested and crushed in the first stage of dyeing was (surprisingly) called *kalkhion* (Palaima 2020b: 127–128; cf. Chap. 14.2). As to terminology, I must leave the matter of the proper understanding of *da-*83-ja* to the Linear B experts to settle.

What kinds of cloth garments are referred to in the Linear B texts? "TELA + the ligature *PU*" (*pu-ka-ta-ri-ja* cloth) is common among the ligatured ideograms, and Burke (2010: 74) reasons that it is related to alphabetic Greek terms meaning "'thick, folded', perhaps meaning cloth that is of double thickness or tightly woven," which, "along with *pa-we-a* cloth ... is often described with color terms, especially red and purple, for example as *po-pu-re-ja* (for example, KN L(7) 474 records 21 pieces, KN L 758 refers to 2 with angular, *o-re-ne-o*, patterns), presumably dyed purple by the murex snail."[25] Thus, the reference must be to a substantial purple-dyed garment, such as the purple double-folded cloak mentioned in Homer (e.g., *Iliad* 10.133–134, 22.441–442; cf. Burke 2010: 74–75). Burke (2010: 74–75) adds: "Large quantities of this type of cloth are recorded in the tablets: Knossos tablet L 5561 + X 5656, for example, lists 980 units, requiring wool from approximately 4,000 sheep," and he cites Nosch's (2000a: 74) estimate that 2,500 pieces of this cloth are attested in the Knossos tablets (cf. Barber 1991, 215–222).

TELA + TE (*te-pa*) is the most common Linear B woolen cloth reference, and the evidence indicates that it is heavy and rectangular and often is described "with red (attachments?)" (see Chap. 7.3). "Female makers of *te-pa*" are mentioned in Thebes Of. 35 (Nosch 2012: 311). Pierini (2018: 111, 115) has recently argued that "*te-pa* refers to a fabric or garment pretty close to Latin *toga*" (Greek *tēbenna*), a rather substantial garment worn over the tunic, and noted that it lacks a parallel in alphabetic Greek. One may wonder whether the garment has a Trojan origin, given the names tēbenna and tebbar and the possible connection with the Etruscans.

An interesting footnote is provided by a *Linear A* inscription, dated to the 17th to early 16th century BCE that is pre-fire-incised on a pithos fragment that was found in the Negev at Tell Haror (Israel). Petrographic analysis establishes that the pithos is from Crete and, more specifically, from Myrtos Prygos on the southern coast. The presence of the inscription is unexplained, but, as far as I am

---

[25] For the possible significance of "double-folded" purple-dyed cloth, see Chapter 3.

aware, it had not been branded as a forgery (see Karnava 2005). What is important for us is that the inscription includes the sign AB 04, interpreted as corresponding to the very heavy textile type TELA + TE (*te-pa*)[26] that is mentioned in
the Linear B texts from Knossos among those that are purple-dyed (Burke 2010:
49, 76). Burke (2010: 76) considers "possible that this heavy cloth was also made
of felt, like the *pukos* variety. Possibly related is Homeric *tapēs* that occurs most
often as thick purple bedding and is often used in epic as a covering for furniture (*Iliad* 9.200, 10.156, 16.224, 24.230, 645 and *Odyssey* 4.124, 298, 7.337, 10.12,
20.150, 24.276) or it may be related to a kind of tapestry" (my transliterations).[27]
The inscription pushes back in time the production of this type of textile and
raises the possibility of export.

It is unclear why the term porphura does not appear in the Linear B texts
of the other Mycenaean palatial centers. Note, however, that the ideogram for
the other main dye—saffron—appears only in Knossos (in 49 tablets; Day 2011a:
371). It is possible to wonder whether these findings indicate a local specialization in Knossos in the application of these dyes or, more likely, their cultivation
and production.

There is reason to conclude that other palatial centers did deal with purple-
dyed cloth. Palaima (1991: 276–277, 291) has noted that in one tablet (MY X 508),
a type of cloth (*pu-ka-ta-ri-ja*) that is explicitly purple-dyed at Knossos was sent
from Mycenae to (Boeotian?) Thebes. There would be no need to bear the cost
of transporting this textile to another textile-making center unless the product
was already valuable due to purpling in Mycenae or was of a quality suitable
for purpling upon arrival in Thebes (see Palaima 1991: 277). In addition, a type
of heavy normally woolen cloth called, *pa-we-a/a₂*, *pharwea* or *pharea* (probably identified with Homeric *pharos*) is attested to at Knossos, Mycenae, and
Pylos. Burke (2010: 75) notes that one text from Knossos (KN Ld(1) 587) lists 453
pieces of this valuable product. *Furthermore, "like pu-ka-ta-ri-ja [noted above], it is
frequently described with color terms, often red/purple"* (Burke 2010: 75–76; emphasis
added).

It is possible—but I think not typical—that a relatively heavy, labor-intensive cloth suitable for use as a cloak for a man or the dress (*peplos*) of a woman
(Barber 1991: 358 with n. 1) would be made "red/purple" by an inferior plant

---

[26]   The Linear A sign 54 corresponds to Linear B *te*, and 04 corresponds to *pa*. Basing her estimate
on Killen (1964), Nosch (2000a: 16) reports that this type of cloth would have weighed about 21
kg (46 pounds) and would have required wool from 28 sheep!

[27]   On the varieties of *te-pa*, Pierini (2018: 112) summarizes: "Linear B tablets apparently show three
different types of *te-pa*: *pe-ko-to* TELA + TE, *mi-ja-ro* TELA + TE, and 'unqualified' TELA + TE" (Firth
2012: 229).... The word *mi-ja-ro* could denote uncombed woolen fabrics with a rough appearance
(Firth 2012: 232) or dyed clothes (Luján 2010: 381), while *pe-ko-to* seems to refer to textiles with
the external side characterized by a hairy and fine appearance (Luján 1996–1997: 345–346).

substitute for murex purple. My reasoning is that many—most—of those who could already afford this kind of expensive cloth could also afford, and of course prefer, the more lustrous color provided by murex. The rationale is that "You cannot make a silk purse out of a sow's ear."[28] Although there are no global estimates available, the texts show us the production in quantity of valuable textiles. Unfortunately, we have to rely on economically oriented inference for the application of murex purple dye in Mycenaean palatial centers other than Knossos. In many ways, the previously discussed palace frescoes provide the most convincing demonstration of the importance of murex use in luxury textiles.

Crosscurrents are (or seem) visible in the evidence. On the one hand, there is a hint that Pylos exported textiles to be dyed outside its own borders in its connection with Lemnos, as is attested to by the reference to female workers designated as *ra-mi-ni-ja* "Lemnians" (Privitera 2005: 228–229). On the other hand, the presence of the Lemnian women in the territory of Pylos would indicate local dyeing of textiles. Was there a change from mostly outside dyeing to local dyeing? Alternatively, does the presence of the Lemnians (and others from the eastern Aegean) merely signal the growth of the textile industry in Pylos? I favor the first proposal.

The economic importance of textiles production is not in doubt, however. It finds support in references to quantities (of sheep, of garments) in texts. Additionally, as has been well known since Adam Smith's *The Wealth of Nations*, the division of labor/specialization is limited by the extent of the market/total production. Cost per unit produced is lowered, of course, by repetition and continuity of effort and supervision. Nevertheless, specialization is typically economically efficient only when there is enough work to keep each specialist busy most of the working day. Thus, assuming a modicum of economic rationality when we observe, as we do in the Linear B tablets, a large number and a variety of textile specialties and specialists, we may infer significant totals in textile production. To give some examples, there are teams of spinners, weavers, sewers, tailors, decorators of numerous kinds, headband makers, wool combers, and many more. None of this is to say that the specialists never performed other types of textile work or that every palace possessed every kind of specialist, but the point remains valid.[29]

---

[28] See the Introduction.

[29] Obviously, the Mycenaean administrators were aware of the economic benefits of specialization, or else they would not have employed and even trained specialists. The Linear B texts and economic inferences concerning textile production are basic as direct evidence of production is lacking (Tournavitou et al. 2015).

We turn next in §4 to some iconographic evidence that provides additional evidence of an interest in murex purple dye in Minoan/Mycenaean times. In addition, textual evidence possibly bearing on the use of *purpurissium* (powdered murex dye) is presented in §5. There is also mention of the presentation to the *damokoro* of a valuable pot decorated with murex shell (Pylos Ta 711; Chap. 4.2.c).

4. Iconographic Evidence of Palatial Production of Purple-dyed Textiles: Depictions of Murex Shells

It is surprising, I think, that, unlike saffron, there are so few explicit references to murex in Minoan or Mycenaean iconography. There are depictions of triton shells, whose main iconographic attraction is easy enough to understand: as already noted, its characteristic whorls reference the winding/twisted nature of the Labyrinth or recall the meander/spiral symbols (Chap. 4.2.c). [30] It will be seen below that some "tritons" are better understood as murex shells.

On some Minoan pots from Palaikastro in eastern Crete, the "triton" is represented with *spikes/spines* that are not characteristic of that species but are characteristic of the murex snail. Marinatos and Hirmer (1960: 76 with Fig. 86) and Bruin (1970: 74–75 with Figs. 2 and 4) identify these shells as depictions of the *murex trunculus* (*hexaplex trunculus*). This seems to be a reasonable view, and I would note that the spikes around the lip of the operculum aperture are suggestive of the muricidae family. In addition, the *murex trunculus* does have shell whorls, although these not as prominent as the triton's. Perhaps one might think of the depicted shells as *murex trunculus* on top and triton below (Bosanquet 1904: 321).[31] The Elder Pliny seems to hybridize the triton or conch with *murex trunculus*.[32] *Thus, it is possible to see this image as connecting the murex (via the triton's whorls) with the Labyrinth.*

---

[30] Four stylized triton/murex combination shells seem to be planted on the dock between two ships on an Enkomi (Cyprus) Tomb 3 amphoroid crater dated to LH IIIB (see Petrakis 2011: 193 Fig. 2b).

[31] Minoan artists were prone to hybridizing natural objects. Thus, Warren (1985: 191–192) observes: "Identification is at once made problematical by a common aspect of Minoan flower- and plant-painting: artists convey a spirit of naturalism while eschewing exact, botanical representation. They seem on occasion to have one or more plants in mind and convey the idea rather than the exactitude of them. Thus, they may suggest knowledge of two plants in a single rendering, or produce an artistic hybrid like papyrus heads on reed stems or the ivy-papyrus head combination ... or, here in garland 2, for example, the papyrus-lily combination. What is frequently offered then is a subtle combination of nature and abstraction." Perhaps we should add to the Minoan combinations, men with the heads of bulls or women with the heads of birds.

[32] "There are two kinds of fish that produce the purple colour; the elements in both are the same, the combinations only are different; the smaller fish is that which is called the "buccinum," from its resemblance to the conch by which the sound of the buccinus or trumpet is produced, and to this circumstance it owes its name: the opening in it is round, with an incision in the margin" (Pliny the Elder, *Natural History* 9.61.36; tr. Bostock and Riley *Perseus Project*). Four stylized triton/

Gill (1965: 79 n. 70) objects that the spikes on the depicted triton shells (and on painted Argonauts) refer not to the spikes characteristic of the murex shell but nodules on their shells.[33] However, I do not believe that the Minoan artists would have felt a need to depict these nodules as spikes. Still, even if it is murex, the image appears on a marine-themed vase, so any possible connection with the Labyrinth via the whorls would benefit from reinforcement.

There is a Minoan conical rhyton (Plate 7), also from Palaikastro, that depicts the same murex-looking shells together with various symbols, including the prime symbol of the Labyrinth: the double-headed axe. Thus, Minoan iconography arguably links murex with the labyrinth. An additional symbol on this rhyton is a "starfish" that is, I think, a rayed star with a rosette at the center and with rosettes between the "rays."[34] My interpretation is that the spiraled central rosette represents the heart of the Labyrinth, and the rays allude to the numerous passages leading into it. An additional point is that inside the open doorway of the shell in Plate 7, the color is purple.

Bruin (1970: Fig. 3) depicts a Mycenaean pot belonging to the National Museum in Athens, but not otherwise identified, in which a shell, similar to the one in the Palaikastro Rhyton, is held by tongs(?). The Metropolitan Museum (Plate 8) displays what it describes as "Terracotta stemmed cup with murex decoration," dating to LH IIIA (Mycenaean) times. Again, the murex shells resemble the examples in the Palaikastro Rhyton.

A Minoan vase from Katsamba near Knossos with a marine theme but also with a figure-eight shield boss below the pouring spout has numerous non-functional spikes and an appropriate shape leading to the view that the vessel itself represents the murex trunculus. The murex would be linked to the labyrinth by the figure-eight shield.

So, it is confirmed, as would be expected, that the Minoans (and Mycenaeans) had more than a passing interest in purple dye and its application. This ceramic evidence complements the frescoes, the sites with numbers of crushed murex shells, and the direct or inferred textual references.

---

murex combination shells seem to be planted on the dock between two ships on an Enkomi (Cyprus) Tomb 3 amphoroid crater dated to LH IIIB (see Petrakis 2011: 193 Fig. 2b).

[33] A difficulty is that while one species of triton (*Charonia variegata*) has a smooth shell, a second species (*Charonia nodifera*) has knobs/nodes on the shell (Reese 1990: 7).

[34] Such "rayed-stars" appear also (on dry land) on a gold ring from Mycenae (*CMS* I, no. 17= Arachne 157238) that depicts the double-headed axe and a procession to a seated goddess. On a seal recovered in Pylos from the grave of the "Griffin Warrior," a rayed star floats above antithetic genii. In addition, the grave included a gold rayed star that may originally have been attached to the "Griffin Warrior's" armor. I have argued (in Chap. 11.2) that genii represent Potnia's commercial agents. Perhaps the "Griffin Warrior" was a rich "Genius" or "table-dog."

A clear depiction of a murex shell together with an agrimi appears on a prism seal from Palaikastro (*CMS* II.2, no. 262a = Arachne 158903; Nosch and Ulanowska 2021: Figure 5.7c).[35]

Figure 8. Workers at a tripod (Seal *CMS* II.8, no. 275 = Arachne 160905).

A final example raises a question that I am unable to answer. I refer to a seal (Figure 8) whose findspot is unknown. The sealing shows two individuals—perhaps a man and a woman—working over a large tripod. The object in the tripod is not recognizable to me. *CMS* at the University of Heidelberg comments:

> The two figures are engaged in an action of either stirring something with the help of a rod-shaped element or grinding/crushing with the help of a pestle. While it is not possible to say with certainty what action is depicted, the shape of the vessel which is known to have been used in cooking could suggest that the figures are involved in the act of food preparation. The image on this seal could, therefore, be seen like a snapshot of everyday life in the Bronze Age Aegean. Such images are rather rare on Aegean glyptic and, when they appear, they provide an exceptional insight into the way of life in these societies.[36]

Yet, floating above the two workers is an object that to me has the shape of a murex shell (murex/*bolinus brandaris*). Is this just a reference to the next ingredient in a stew, is it smoke or a damaged area, or is it a rare scene of dye preparation or dyeing?[37]

---

[35] I thank the authors for making an advance copy of their paper available to me. The depiction has already been mentioned in Chapter 4.2.c.

[36] February 2019, "Seal of the Month." Available at: https://www.uni-heidelberg.de/fakultaeten/ philosophie/zaw/cms/monthlySeal/monthlySealOlder.html (accessed February 12, 2019).

[37] Evidence for the use of large ceramic tripods for Bronze Age dyeing is provided in Pareja et al. (2016: 22). I am reminded of a miniature painting from Kea in which three individuals work over two tripods on the shore of the sea. Morgan (2005: 35–36 with Fig. 1.18) suggests they are cooking food. In fact, at

5. Palm, *Purpurissium*, and Agrimi

Postponed until now is textual evidence possibly bearing on the use of *purpuris-sium*—that is, of murex dye in a powdered form (§2). The discussion was postponed because it needed some iconographic evidence presented in the present Section.

There is a very close linguistic connection between date palm, the color purple/red, and Phoenician: all are called *phoinikos*. In *Odyssey* 6.163, *phoinikos* clearly has the meaning "date palm." Alphabetic Greek *phoinikos* also has the meaning "*Phoenician*" (LSJ s.v.). In explanation, Beekes (s.v. *phoinix*) speculates that the Near Eastern traders who brought dates to Greece were named after the date-palm—that is "Phoenician" (cf. Farmer and Lane 2016: 54)."[38] Third, in *Iliad* 4.140–148, *phoinikos* refers to a purplish/red color:

> So the arrow grazed the outermost flesh of the warrior, and forthwith the dark blood flowed from the wound. As when a woman staineth ivory with scarlet (*phoiniki*), some woman of Maeonia or Caria, to make a cheek-piece for horses, and it lieth in a treasure-chamber, though many horsemen pray to wear it; but it lieth there as a king's treasure, alike an ornament for his horse and to its driver a glory; even in such wise, Menelaus, were thy thighs stained with blood, thy shapely thighs and thy legs and thy fair ankles beneath.

Similarly, Linear B tablets from Knossos concerning chariot parts use the word *po-ni-ki-jo* (alphabetic Greek *phoinikios*) to refer to a *purplish/crimson color* (see e.g., Murray and Warren 1970: 48).

Coming to the heart of the problem, the term *po-ni-ki-jo* appears in the Knossos Ga tablets dealing with food additives (aromatics), including especially *ko-ri-da-jo-no* 'coriander'. Melena (1975a) thinks the term refers to a palm-product, most likely dates. He (Melena 1975a: 77) supports his suggestion by noting, "All of these commodities, except for *po-ni-ki-jo*, are recorded by dry measure. Therefore, it is obvious that they were handled as grain. On the contrary, the commodity named *po-ni-ki-jo* is weighed." Melena properly takes into account the "date palm" meaning of *phoinikios*. The objection to this identification, as is pointed out by Murray and Warren (1976: 46), is that the local Cretan date is typically inedible—that is, it possesses a relatively low ratio

---

Kea, there is evidence for feasting but, despite its prevalence in the neighborhood, not for murex—there are no shell accumulations and no murex pigment in frescoes. So, perhaps the individuals in my sealing are cooking food. I hesitate to concede this because I recall that many years ago when I (Silver 1991) first suggested that the Lemnian women acquired their smell from working murex, I had no evidence of murex-working on Lemnos. Now, the evidence there for murex is plentiful.

[38] This reasoning may explain the other applications of the ethnikon *phoinix*.

of pulp to seeds and pit (cf. Galanakis, Tsitsa and Günkel-Maschek 2017: 81). Therefore, the question arises why dates would be of interest.[39]

Focusing on the "purplish/red" color connection of *phoinikios* and citing various clues derived from a number of Linear B tablets, Nosch (2004: 35–36) understands *po-ni-ki-jo* in the Ga tablets to refer to a dye, and she suggests that the substance is possibly madder dye. Of course, this identification is possible. The objection is that it is not responsive to the known Phoenician and date palm connections of the term *phoinikios*.

My suggestion is that *po-ni-ki-jo*—the weighed substance in the Ga tablets— is the powdered form of murex dye: *purpurissium*. This identification finds support in the fact that murex and murex dye are attested and important for textiles at Knossos. It also has the advantage of linking the reddish color to the Phoenicians and the date palm. The latter tree—which prevalent in Phoenicia but also, perhaps significantly, in Itanos in eastern Crete[40]—has numerous iconographic links to Potnia of the Labyrinth, including in the double-headed axe. Itanos is significant not only because it is famous for its palm trees but also because D'Agata and De Angelis (2014) have offered (the still unproven) hypothesis that the Villa of Vai-Itanos was involved during the Neopalatial period in the exploitation of murex for the extraction of purple (see §2 above).[41]

However, a disadvantage of the *po-ni-ki-jo = purpurissium* hypothesis, as recorded by scribe 136, is its use for *perfuming* (Nosch 2004: 36)—a use which hardly seems likely for a murex product. One more advantage of my identification is that of the ten places delivering *po-ni-ki-jo* in the tablets, the only one with a known location, Tylissos, is on the coast; all ten places possess flocks of sheep (Nosch 2004: 36). There are several iconographic linkages of palm with symbols of Potnia or directly with the palm.

In Figure 7 (the seal *CMS* II.8, no. 55 = Arachne 160684), the shaft of the double-headed axe, Potnia's prime symbol, appears to be a stylized tree, most likely a palm

---

[39] Recent scientific research indicates that the Egyptian date palm (*Phoenix dactylifera/Phoenix P. sylvestris*) was long ago hybridized with the *Phoenix theophrasti*, the Cretan date palm (see "Researchers Uncover New Insights on Date Palm Evolution Using 2,100-year Old Leaf Found in Ancient Egyptian Temple." Available at: https://nyuad.nyu.edu/en/news/latest-news/science-and-technology/2021/september/date-palm-evolution.html (accessed September 9, 2021).

[40] By alternative or additional explanation, textiles dyed with murex undergo striking changes in color, as do dates. Dates, as they ripen, change in color from brownish to greenish to purplish (Ghnimi et al. 2017: 2).

[41] "*Vai*. This beautiful, extremely popular and still reasonably unspoiled beach on the east coast between the ancient sites of Itanos and Palaikastro possesses a palm grove, unique for Greece. Legend tells us how this grove had pushed up accidentally from the kernels of dates eaten by Phoenician merchants, who had anchored here. Some Minoan ruins have been located in its vicinity. The area together with the whole peninsula north of Palaikastro belongs to the rich Toplou Monastery" (Davaras 1976: 334).

tree. The shaft has a knob at the top and palm branches at the bottom of the trunk. Consider next a seal (Figure 9) possibly from Crete's Idaean Cave (*CMS* II.3, no. 7 = Arachne 159088) that depicts an individual clad only in a skirt holding/blowing/smelling a large shell near an altar above which are "horns"—arguably representing bow and stern of a ship, see below—and three stylized trees. Evans (1901: 141–142) thought the trees might be cypresses, and he identified the shell as a conch or a triton. However, the trio of trees and, even more, the tree standing on the other side of the scene are identifiable as palms. Following the above iconographic discussion (§4) of triton/murex blending, the shell is identifiable as the *murex trunculus* (*hexaplex*

Figure 9. Shell carried to palm on incurved altar
(Seal *CMS* II.3, no. 7 = Arachne 159088).

trunculus). If my identifications are accurate, the scene plays on the nominal identification of palm tree = *po-ni-ki-jo* with murex = *po-ni-ki-jo* (cf. Chap. 10.8). Might this identity form the basis of a new interpretation of a multivalued(?) iconographic symbol?

Chapter 4.2.c includes a discussion of the "Zakros Rhyton," which depicts a "tripartite" structure in a (real or ideal) mountainous landscape with stairs, "horns" set on roofs, and "snail spirals" in raised relief, with four agrimi on the roof and additional agrimia galloping among crocus plants that are with and without flowers; and with a rosette in relief at the top of the rhyton (Koehl 2006: 103–104 [cat. no. 204] with pl. 16.204; J. Shaw 1978: 432–435 with Fig 8). The structure represents a "peak sanctuary" or more to the point, I think, a *branch* of the Labyrinth.[42]

---

[42] "[I]n terms of spatial transmission, the peak sanctuary is the only type of Cretan cult space that is both found throughout Crete and, in addition, is imitated on the mainland and Aegean islands. Although the topographical characteristics of peak sanctuaries outside Crete correspond fairly closely to those of Cretan sites, there is a very strong correlation in terms of artefact assemblages" (Briault 2007:123). As branch "plants" of a single enterprise a degree of uniformity, but not necessarily identity, would be expected to hold among the various "peak sanctuaries." The general archaeological picture appears to be a loose one of "similarities exceeding differences" (see Briault 2007: 124 with references).

It was pointed out that the hair of agrimia (or goats generally) was capable of providing high-quality, dyed wool fibers (Andersson Strand and Nosch 2015: 375). This capacity is signaled by the rhyton's placing of the agrimia among crocus plants and crocus flowers, which are the source of the expensive saffron dye. As already noted in Chapter 6.2, the *aegis* is a "goatskin" mantle worn over the shoulders and back of Athena that is of sufficient value in itself to justify the attachment of gold tassels (*Iliad* 2.446–449).[43] The role of murex dye is signaled by the snail spiral and more openly by an already mentioned prism seal from Palaikastro (*CMS* II.2, no. 262a = Arachne 158903), depicting a goat or agrimi facing what is obviously a murex.[44] *The snail spiral signifies the highway—the sea—upon which clients were delivered to the labyrinth/the labyrinth's dyed textiles were delivered to clients.*[45] *The snail itself stands for the place of manufacture—the labyrinth.* The gold leaf on the rhyton calls attention/represents the economic reward to the labyrinth.

The linkage of Figure 9 and the Zakros Rhyton to foreign trade in textiles is finds reinforcement in the discovery in the "Zakros Pit Deposit" of a set of three miniature ceramics. Each bears the "sun-disk in moon-crescent symbol" that is familiar in the ancient Near East (Chap. 11.5). In addition, one ceramic bears the Near Eastern symbol and a "rope-like" relief decoration on one side (see Chap. 10.2) and the head of an agrimi on the other side (Platon 2010: 252–253; Chap. 11.5 below).

There is rough evidence beyond *CMS* II.2, no. 262a, to indicate a linkage between the agrimi and the palm: the murex. Karetsou and Koehl provide the added evidence in an important article discussing a painted sarcophagus from Kalochorafitis in Crete near Phaistos:

> Here the agrimi is depicted on two sides. On the long side, it is found in conjunction with a running dog in a natural landscape indicated by a palm tree and other details. However, on the same side, on the upper left, the main theme is bull-leaping; next to it is a scene with two figures— a male worshipper and a dancing figure—probably a cult scene.... On the other long side of the same sarcophagus from Kalochorafitis are

---

[43]   Again, I predict, "You can't make a silk purse from a sow's ear" (see the Introduction). That is, attaching gold to an ugly garment will not make Athena impressive in the eyes of viewers. More generally expressed, the garment manufactured by adding gold to an inferior textile costs more to produce than consumers are willing to pay for it. Some consumers will say, "It's better than nothing."

[44]   In the Linear B tablets, the logogram *146 refers (solely) to sheep wool. However, Perna (2004: 278–280) has argued that the logogram *142 balances the textile fiber picture by referring to goat hair.

[45]   The tower, or door of the central structure, with its snail spirals in relief, reminds me of the scenes in archaic and classical Greek art, wherein the Athenian Theseus drags the Minotaur through doors decorated by an interlocking S-spiral (e.g., National Archaeological Museum of Spain, Madrid 215557). In the latter example, Athena looks on wearing her gorgoneion-decorated aegis.

depictions of a chariot, hunting, and a ship in a marine landscape, while on one narrow side, visually the most coherent of the four sides, *an agrimi is depicted standing under or next to a palm tree* which covers most of the area. This panel also includes a fish, wheel, rayed motifs and other themes, as well as a bird sitting on the palm tree on the same side as the agrimi. The combination of tree and caprid is of course a familiar iconographic motif, commonly found on seals.

Karetsou and Koehl 2011: 215 (emphasis added)

The agrimia became staples of Minoan iconography because their hair was a staple in the textile industry and perhaps also because of their magnificent "horns."[46]

In conclusion, I am struck by the persistence of the relationship between agrimi and palm—together with the injection of the sea and labyrinth—via the inclusion of the snail spiral in an openly commercial theme in the Zakros iconography. Furthermore, to this commercial theme I have come to see the "horns" as a highly stylized version of the upraised bow and stern of an ancient ship.[47] This perspective is reflected, strongly I think, by Plate 11 ("Pyxis from Aptera").

6. Flower Motifs, Flower Lovers, and Festivals Celebrating Dyed Textiles Exports

Given the importance of cloth production for the Minoan and Mycenaean economies, it is not surprising that there are a fair number of references to loom-weights and warp-weighted loom technology in glyptic sources (see e.g. Ulanowska 2017). That residents of Minoan Akrotiri may have participated in the production of the complex textiles exhibited in Xeste 3 is suggested by the discovery of "numerous"/"dozens" of loom-weights in some of the houses

---

[46] The horns might be about three feet long and were used for making bows. Fragments of gold leaf from the Knossos Temple Repositories have been identified as agrimi horns (Karetsou and Koehl 2011: 210–211 with references). Agrimia are depicted on seals being hand-fed by a goddess or priestess (Karetsou and Koehl 2011: 212–213 with references), and agrimia hunting and agrimia sacrifice are, like bulls, staples of Minoan iconography (Eiring 2004).

[47] I was led to the ship-inspired interpretation of "horns" by an informed back-and-forth discussion of the status of an "object of red clay" from a pre-palatial cemetery in Mochlos: Is it a boat or is it horns? (see Soles 2012: 193-195). That the question might be seriously debated suggested to me that boat and horns might be the same. Needless perhaps to add, other interpretations remain viable. The proposition that "horns" reflect the profiles of certain types of ships finds support in Papadato (2012), Soles (2012), Zervos (1956: 151) and especially, I think, in Evans (1928: 240-44 with Figs. 139 and 140). The identification is dismissed by Banou (2008: 32). It is quite true, as I have been reminded, that there are examples of "horns" that do not very much resemble a ship. There are also "horns" that do not very much resemble an animal horn or mountain. Are we then confronted by horn symbols with different meanings? I believe that the application of horns spread from ships into other structures.

(Palyvou 2005: 50, 65, 75, 80, 89). The loom-weights had the potential to produce a variety of textiles, as they supported both thin and thicker warp threads (Tzachili et al. 2015). In addition, there are less obvious clues to the importance of luxury textiles in the economy.

I suggest that the miniature "Ship Fresco" in Room 5 of the "West House" at Akrotiri (Plate 9) refers to the opening of the navigation season (in March-April) and the welcoming of foreigners (see Säflund 1981: 198ff. with references). Some of the ship's prows are decorated with rosettes, and some hulls with the running spiral in blue and a snake (Plate 9), which are symbols that I identify with the textile-marketing dimension of the Labyrinth (Doumas 1992: 76–77 Fig. 37). Strikingly, the flagship is festooned with instances of a stylized three-petaled crocus: the three-lobed designs that are seen hanging from mast to prow and stern resemble the crocus motif on pottery and gold beads and the special garment of an individual in the "Vestibule Fresco" at Pylos (Chap. 4.1). The same motif may appear on the side of a different boat.[48]

Why decorate ships with a crocus motif? Because, it may be answered, it is a sacred plant. The question remains, however, why cultic administrators *decided* it should be sacred. It is not a stretch to suggest that a community that produced saffron dye from crocus stamens chose this motif to celebrate the export of garments it had dyed yellow. In this section, I argue for a linkage between flowers generally and textile exports.

The *rosette*—so ubiquitous in Minoan and Mycenaean iconography and often appearing together with symbols of the Labyrinth, sometimes rendered in purple (Vlachopoulos 2016)—refers to flowers and, hence, as will be argued, to exports of dyed cloth.[49] More speculatively, an elongated ornament on the prow of ships, depicted on the "Ship Cup" from the island of Mochlos[50] in eastern Crete, has been compared to a *fleur-de-lys* (Davaras 2004: 5–6). After rejecting alternatives, such as that the "hooked object" in the "Ship Cup" is a bird, Davaras (2004: 6) suggests, "In any case, we may perhaps postulate a certain association between this *fleur-de-lys* and the Minoan sacred lily (see Marinatos 2007) because of the quite exceptional emphasis given to this special form of the *akrostolion*."[51] Again, I propose to establish a connection between flowers and cloth exports.

---

[48] Sources: Morgan (1988: 30); Day (2011b: 348 with Fig. 7).

[49] In the conical marine rhyton from Palaikastro, depicted in §4, rosettes that form the centers of the two rayed stars have a reddish color like the inside of the suspected murex shells.

[50] Contemporary Mochlos is an island, but in the Bronze Age, it was attached to Crete. There are some thirteen depictions of boats known from the site (Soles 2012: 188).

[51] Davaris (2004: 6 with references) adds that the fleur-de-lys also seems visible on some ships at Akrotiri. Fleur-de-lys formed akrostolia(?) are clearly on a Minoan fluted cup in the Ashmolean Museum, but here scholars see an "arcade" rather than ships. In addition, a Cornelian amygdaloidal seal is engraved with a three-masted ship with a *fleur-de-lys* at the prow. The British

With respect to the navigation season, a tablet from Pylos (PY Tn 316 front) records the giving of rich gifts to the gods, including Potnia and Poseidon, in the month *po-ro-wi-to-jo*—that is, in the month of *Plowistos* ("of navigation"?). There is some uncertainty regarding the meaning of Plowistos (or Phlowistos or Prowistos) because, as Palaima (2004a: 240 n. 120) explains, "Given other occurrences of this word in the 'recipient' slot of oil offering texts, it is most reasonable to interpret it as the name of a deity, linked alternatively with '*sailing*' or '*flowering*' or '*knowing*'." *A solution would be that the month of navigation was deified.*

The deeper meaning of "flowering" takes on special interest given the crocus and *fleur-de-lys* decoration of ships. The month of "flowering" and month of "navigation" both refer to the spring. There are, in fact, many depictions of flowers carried or presented to Potnia of the Labyrinth. For Pylos, Lang (1969) references several processions (e.g., 53 H nws), in which female participants carry bouquets of red and white flowers. Petrakis (2002-2003: 308–309) generalizes that, "[S]imilar representations of human figures (predominantly female) holding flowers or herbs ... occur in Minoan and Mycenaean iconography." This includes at Akrotiri.

Figure 10: Smelling the flowers seal, from Routsi
(*CMS* I no. 279 = Arachne 157504).

In a seal from Tholos Tomb 2 at Routsi in Messenia (Figure 10), a female figure seems to be "smelling" two flowers (lilies) which, as Petrakis (2002–2003: 307) observes and as in Figure 9, seem to have grown out of an altar(?)-like structure stemmed with the so-called "horns of consecration" (*CMS* I, no. 279 =Arachne 157504; Sakellariou et al. 1964: 315, Nr. 279).[52]

Museum says the object may be a bird (British Museum 1884,0628.9 = *CMS* VII, no. 104 = Arachne 164818). For additional examples and discussion, see Betts (1968).

[52] Given the discussion of the "horns" in ¶5, the question arises whether we should speak of the "horns" as forming an "altar-like" structure or *a "ship-like" structure*. For the representation as a

Also of great interest is the scene (Figure 11) depicted on a

> great gold ring from the acropolis of Mycenae (Fig. 9). On this the woman furthest from the seated goddess, who has just received a bunch of poppies, is bringing a bunch of lilies to offer next. Their typical form and recurved petals are entirely clear in magnified photographs, while the seated goddess also has what are apparently lilies in her hair.

Warren 1985: 203

A rosette floats in the center. Beyond this, Marie-Louise Nosch has called my attention to floating flax flowers, each of which would have five purple petals. The scene of delivery of flowers to the goddess includes such prominent symbols of Potnia of the Labyrinth as the double-headed axe and the figure-eight shield (see below). Potnia's love for flowers is sometimes understood as a reflection of the special love for nature felt by the Minoans and Mycenaeans.

Figure 11. Presentation of flowers to Potnia seal, from Mycenae Acropolis
(CMS I, no. 17 = Arachne 157238).

However, an examination of references to flowers in later Greek literature raises the suspicion that love for flowers might not be so innocent and romantic as has been assumed (Starr 1984).[53] To begin with, Pindar (*Nemean Ode* 7.79) speaks of a "delicate flower (*anthemon*) plucked from the sea-dew." Boedeker cites this passage and then explains:

---

ship, see http://www.salimbeti.com/micenei/ships.htm (accessed March 9, 2021).

[53] An ulterior objective is obvious in Akrotiri in the "Crocus Gatherers Fresco" (Chap. 4.3), in which it is the crocus *stamens* that are of interest to the goddess.

On the basis of a suggestion in the scholia, this 'flower' is usually understood to be coral, which was thought to harden only on contact with air. Yet the evidence of archaeology suggests that the use of coral was scarcely known to the Creeks of Pindar's time. The same scholion suggests another referent, *sea-purple dye*; this possibility is taken up and argued in great detail in D. Petegorsky's [1982] ... dissertation. In this interpretation, the Muse's creation is not a diadem of gold, ivory, and coral glued together, but a woven headband of cloth dyed purple and ornamented with gold and ivory.

Boedeker 1984: 93; emphasis added

Although a purple-dyed headband suits a ceremonial connection (see Chap. 11.5 below), it is an overly narrow referent for the "flower."

The "flower" (*anthos* or *aōtos*) means as Buttman (1840: 187) explains, "the downy pile or nap of cloth, that delicate *lakhnē* which constitutes the fineness and beauty of cloth, and which proves its newness" (cf. Borthwick 1976: 1; Raman 1975: 198, 204). Again, the third century BCE historian Phylarchus (fr. 45) describes the dresses worn by Athenian *hetairai* as *anthina* (cited by Petrakis 2002–2003: 299). Thus, it becomes reasonable to maintain that Pindar's "flower" is wool that was dyed purple or at least made colorful. This suggestion is consistent with the report of Clearchus that "Polycrates, the tyrant of luxurious Samos ... wove the widely heralded 'flowers' of the Samians" (Athenaeus at 12.540; tr. Gulick). The reference to the weaving of "flowers" here may be understood to refer to serving the international market for fine dyed cloth.

Flowers are luxury textiles. To what then do the Minoan/Mycenaean "flower rituals" signify? I propose to examine them as symbolic references to festivals celebrating the production of purple/saffron-dyed cloth for export.

Additional insights become possible once one grants an interpretation of flowers as symbolizing wealth in the form of dyed cloth. The Minoan/Mycenaean processions of richly attired bearers of fresh flowers (see above) or of jars of perfume (south part of the east wall of Room 3, Akrotiri) may be understood as bringing to the goddess what already belongs to her. That is, flowers—dyed textiles—were produced either directly under her auspices in the Labyrinth or under a *ta-ra-si-ja* (a kind of "putting-out") contract. The latter explains why the textiles are carried to her in Figure 11. *The contracts specified delivery around a common date, and on this date, a festival of delivery of flowers was celebrated.*

In the case of the seal from Routsi (Figure 10), it seems that Potnia has possession of the "flowers" and is processing them for distribution. The sniffing of flowers finds its place as a reference to the fragrance of cloth treated, for example, with perfumed olive oil (E. Foster 1974; Shelmerdine 1995: 99).[54] In the *Iliad*, both Helen (3.385) and Achilles[55] (18.25) are said to wear fragrant (*nectareos*) garments. In Homer, cloth may be described as *ambrosios* "sweet-smelling" oil is both ambrosial and perfumed in the *Homeric Hymn to Aphrodite* 63–64, as are clothes in the *Homeric Hymn to Apollo* 184 (Shelmerdine 1995: 99 with Table 6.2). Making textiles fragrant with perfumed substances was valuable in itself, but, in addition, it helped to cover the bad odor of the garment due to the fact that it was dyed with murex purple (see Martial *Epigrams* 1.49, 9.62). The clearest glyptic statement that the cult of Potnia participated in the market is for olive oil rather than textiles. In a gold seal ring from Vapheio (*CMS* I, no. 219 = Arachne 157441), a female wearing a flounced skirt looks on as an olive tree is shaken to bring down the fruit. The tree seems to emerge from a transport amphora. The tasseled double-headed axe that floats overhead and the sacred knot resting on boulders that are arranged in a figure-eight configuration signal to me that the amphora is destined for the marketplace.

That the sniffing by the goddess in Figure 10 is a reference to cloth treated with perfumed olive oil finds support in the view that the prominent trees in the seal from Mycenae (Figure 11) are olive trees with "the rounded elements forming its foliage being the goldsmith's method of rendering on a minute scale the rounded forms of the tree seen at greater scale on the frescoes" (Warren 1985: 202 with n. 63).

To this may be added the observation that the woman in the Routsi seal holds an *olive branch* as she smells the *lily flowers* (Warren 1985: 204 with n. 67).[56] It may, therefore, be suggested that plants were used by the Minoans to make an extract for perfuming their olive oil. This would explain the *fleur-de-lys* on the prows of the Mochlos ships and headgear of leading figures (Marinatos 2007),

---

[54] The seals discussed in this Section seem to place cloth making, dyeing, perfuming, and even olive oil production in close proximity. This seems to correspond to archaeological findings at the Bronze Age Pyrgos-Mavrorachi industrial complex in Cyprus, where an olive press is located next to two adjoining workshop rooms (or possibly two firms). In one room (Room 3), textile fibers are dyed and perfumed, and in the other (Room 4), the cloth is woven (Belgiorno 2008).

[55] The name Achilles is mentioned in the Linear B tablets from Knossos (KN Vc 106) and Pylos PY Fn 79.

[56] Günkel-Mashek (2012b: 365 with references) explains: "The images showing branches growing out of or placed between horns of consecration suggest that libation played an important role in the cult and that the spouted jug as well as the triton-shell served as cultic vessels from which the liquids were poured upon the branches. The pouring of the liquid is often performed by Minoan 'genii' who are further known to be connected to hunting and sacrificing." The treatment of cloth with scented murex dye and olive oil approximates a "libation." In Chapter 11.2, I argue that genii, actually dogs, represent commercial agents of the Labyrinth. I have suggested that the "horns," between which the libations are poured, represent the upraised prow and stern of a merchant vessel. Why is a *shell* used in the libation? See above for the representation of a shell with characteristics of both triton and murex.

and elsewhere. The same, of course, holds for papyrus[57] and the poppy plant, although here, of course, the making of opiates is more obvious. The flower sniffing ritual celebrates the production of scented, purple-dyed textiles—textiles of outstanding quality as well as perfumed olive oil.

That the delivery of perfumed and dyed textiles to Potnia was legally/contractually mandated may explain an otherwise peculiar feature in an idyllic scene: in Figure 11, *the floating individual wearing a figure-eight shield holds a short stick in one hand.* The stick is arguably the kind of "nightstick"—*virga* or *fustis*—held by police/*lixae* in the Roman world for various duties, including tax-collection and control of the marketplace (Speidel 1991; Silver 2016a: 19–20). The closest corresponding Greek term is *rabdos* (see Beekes s.v.), an object with the power to control humans when held in the hands of Circe (*Odyssey* 10.238, 319 etc.) or Hermes (*Iliad* 24.343). That perfumed textiles were delivered to Potnia finds support in the absence of industrial installations for perfuming within the corresponding palaces themselves. Thus, it is suggested that some of the "floating" objects (constellations?) in Figure 11 are intrinsic to the theme in the central register (consult and compare Kyriakidis 2005: 149).

Moving along this path, we may understand that a "flower sniffing ritual" has to do not only with perfuming dyed cloth but also with the dyeing process itself. Consider Akrotiri's fresco, including the "Wounded/Seated Woman" in Xeste 3. Verduci and Davis (2015: 54–55 with references) note that this woman wears "unusual hairpins:" one is in the form of a lily, and they accept that the other "imitates an *olive twig with blue and yellow leaves*" (not a myrtle twig; emphasis added). The colors of the leaves suggest saffron dye (yellow) and murex dye (blue). I see the hairpin as symbolizing a cloth that is both perfumed and dyed. Moreover, murex dye is additionally symbolized by the blood (red) from "Wounded Woman's" foot. Blood that falls on—is joined with—a crocus blossom.[58]

Marinatos (1985a: 228) sees that "a connection between blood and flowers is established. This means that there is a link between blood and plant fertility." I agree that the blood/murex dye fertilizes the flower/textile by making it grow in economic value. At the same time, I would like to insist that the commitment of "Wounded Woman" to the cult of the goddess (Potnia of the Labyrinth), depicted directly above her, is so profound that she bleeds saffron or purple dye!

A problem with the above arguments is that the *linguistic* support for the identification of "flower" with "dyed and perfumed woolen textile" comes only

---

[57] Papyrus flowers are featured in the Throne Room at Knossos and in iconography generally. In *CMS* VS.1B, no. 113 (= Arachne 165791), lily and papyrus flowers are brought to a shrine. *CMS* I, no. 131 (= Arachne 157352) may depict the pulling up of papyrus plants from the root.

[58] Note that the "Veiled Woman" near the "Wounded Woman" wears a "red-spotted yellow drapery" (Rehak 1999a: 12).

from late Greek sources. Linguistic support from Linear B or from Homer has not so far been provided. Support from early linguistic sources is available, however.

The Fr tablets from Pylos, dealing with quantities of olive oil, mention a festival that I link to the navigation season.[59] It appears that this festival had two phases, or perhaps variants or sets of participants. First is the *re-ke-e-to-ro-te-ri-jo* (Fr. 343 and Fr 1217), which finds a Latin parallel in the *lectisternium:*[60] "the making/spreading of the bed/couch." Second, the *to-no-e-ke-te-ri-jo* (mentioned only in Fr. 1222), in which the word *to-no* is taken to mean *thorno* 'throne', as elsewhere in the Pylos tablets. This second variant, I will argue, finds a Latin parallel in the *sellisternium:* 'the opening/ spreading of a stool' or better 'the opening/spreading of a stool made into a throne by spreading it with dyed textile cushions'.[61] I theorize below that the textile buyers arriving at Knossos and Pylos were treated as if they were themselves gods seated on campstools spread with luxury textiles.[62] In what follows next, our focus is on the *to-no* festival variant or phase.

Pylian documents (in the Ta set) refer to numbers of "thrones." E. Bennet (1958: 52–53) has understood from the Fr tablets that Pylos celebrated a religious festival involving the ritualized dragging/pulling of a throne seat. An alternative view is that *to-no* should be interpreted not as "throne/throne seat" but as the neuter **thronon*, meaning *"flower patterned woven textile"*—a term that appears once in the plural *throna* in *Iliad* 22.441, wherein Andromache is making

---

59   In the Linear B olive oil tablets from Pylos another key term is *ke-se-ni-wo-jo* (Py 1231 + fr). The relevant tablets do not specify the name of a month.

60   The latter term is rendered in Linear B as *lekhe-stroterion* (*lechestrōtērion*). See Constantinidou 1989: 13; Meißner 2004: 258–262.

61   The Latin word *selles* "seat, settle, chair, stool, portable chair or sedan, portable chair or sedan." Linear B "stool" is *ta-ra-nu* (Knossos 1521 X).

62   Greg Nagy has kindly called my attention to his analysis of the first word of Song 1 of Sappho. The first word is *poikilothronos* (ποικιλόθρον'), which Nagy (2021: §1) interprets as follows: " '[I invoke] you [O goddess wearing your dress that is decorated] with varied-pattern-woven magical flowers.'... The first part, *poikilo-*, which I have translated as 'varied', refers to variety or variability as the essence of Aphrodite: this goddess loves variety. I highlight, for my first example, the love of the goddess for different kinds of flowers in different situations. Her favorites are roses or myrtles or anemones—to name only those variants that I have tracked so far in my essays. And the second part of the compound *poikilothronos*, which survives independently as the noun *throna*, is linked with the same kind of love for flowers, since this noun can refer to flowers used as love-charms deployed to attract lovers. Patterns of flowers could be woven into your dress, so that the pattern-weavings could attract visually your would-be lover. Or, the attraction could be olfactory, since different fragrances exhaled by different flowers could become acculturated as the ingredients of different scented oils that you could deploy as perfume not only for your body but even for that special dress you would want to wear at some specially festive occasion." The *poikilothronos* of the goddess attracts lovers to her. Viewed as a varied-pattern-woven covering for the *couch* of the goddess, it would certainly attract *lovers*, but in my analysis, it serves to attract *traders* to Potnia.

a *throna poikal(a)*, meaning she is weaving flowers into cloth (see Whittaker 2012: 196 n. 25), or, I submit, *she is using flowers to make a throne of cloth.* The identification of *thornos with *thronos* involves a widely accepted metathesis of *r*. It is important to note that in later alphabetic Greek sources, *throna* may have the meaning *"flowers."*

This analysis would imply that Linear B *to-no* means "throne" but also it means "inwoven/pattern-woven garment" and "flower." The meaning "throne" seems not to fit very well into the ritual, but, on the other hand, when Andromache sprinkles "flowers" (*throna*) on luxury garments, she transforms them into thrones (*throna*). The point is that she is making a kind of "throne" used by (female?) deities. More to the point but much later, Herodotus (5.72.3) tells that the priestess of Athena to rise from *thronon*, meaning "flowers embroidered on cloth" (LSJ s.v.)—that is, from a throne made of flower-decorated cushions. At Akrotiri, the "Saffron Gatherers Fresco" on the upper floor of Xeste 3 depicts a magnificently attired goddess whose "Z ... *is not a conventional throne or chair but rather a stack of yellow cushions, which could represent bales of saffron-dyed cloth or even a pile of yellow-dyed garments."* (Rehak 2007: 207–208; emphasis added; Chap. 7.6 below).[63]

There is more. In Nikander's *Theriaka* (438, with commentary; 1st century BCE), *throna* is explained as *anthōdēs* "flowers," and Hesychius (4th century CE) says *throna* means *anthē*. Beekes (s.v.) mentions "many desperate attempts at finding an etymology" for *throna*, but he notes one attempt linking the word to *anthina*. The circle is closing on the proposition that in Minoan/Mycenaean iconography, the "flowers" Potnia of the Labyrinth concerns herself with are perfumed, purple-and/or saffron-dyed luxury textiles. My argument is admittedly somewhat convoluted, but the implication is that the "throne" of the goddess is a dyed textile and, hence, that the festival is, with E. Bennet, one in which dyed textiles—not literal or conventional thrones—are first carried and then placed upon stools and sat upon. This entire theme will be developed iconographically in Chapter 11.5.

---

[63] At Akrotiri, the cushions rest on an architectural platform. The goddess depicted on a damaged ivory pyxis from Mochlos appears to sit directly on a platform, including a tree shrine (available at: http://www.mochlosarchaeologicalproject.org/pyxis/ [accessed March 13, 2021]). See Soles 2016a: 249 and Tully and Crooks 2020: esp. 46–48.

8

Palatial Enterprise
Basic Questions

1. Redistribution vs. Trade: The "Finley Hypothesis"

KOLB (2004: 581) has emphatically denied that Mycenaean palaces traded:

> In Hittite documents trade and merchants play a marginal role, and in the Linear B texts of the Mycenaean world a large number of craftsmen, workers, and administrative staff as well as foreign goods are mentioned, but not a single one of the texts has any words for "trader," "buy" or "sell," nor do they have any term for "money" in the sense of a standard medium of exchange, as it is represented by the silver shekel in the Near East and without which "trade" seems hardly possible. Thus, the evidence supports the conclusion that the goods accumulated within the Mycenaean palace administration were not traded within the realm of Mycenaean states but redistributed as remuneration or gifts, and that even small retail trade was therefore excluded, whereas long distance trade with the Eastern Mediterranean was organized through gift exchange and/or traders from Cyprus and the Levant.

Kolb has provided a good basis for discussion, but the discussion needs to proceed step by step.

First, Kolb suggests that trade terminology is absent from the Linear B texts. This problem will be discussed below (§5), but assume, for the sake of analysis, that Kolb's claim is factual. Then, Kolb concludes that if specific words for trade/trader are absent, then the activity itself must be absent or rare. Silver (2009a) named this seemingly commonsense proposition "Finley's Hypothesis" (Finley 1952: 270, n. 46; cf. 1981: 71), but, to his surprise, Silver found it difficult to either confirm or to disconfirm. Silver's conclusion (Silver 2009a: 253) is:

Finley's linkage of specialized names with frequency of occurrence is, despite the difficulties, a most useful rule of thumb. It helps a great deal in bridging gaps in our knowledge of the ancient economy. On the other hand, the bridge is capable of conveying us to error and misunderstanding. The absence (presence) in the ancient sources of distinctively named economic actors does not necessarily demonstrate the infrequency (frequency) of the corresponding economic transactions in the ancient economy.... Finley's hypothesis must not be applied mechanically or without due consideration of the economics of contracting costs. Specialized location and specialized non-verbal symbols are often viable alternatives to distinctive naming in reducing transaction costs. On the other hand, as an anonymous reader points out, specializations are not equally amenable to alternative modes of representation. I am not able to offer a generalization explaining these differences in amenability and cannot conduct a case-by-case study of specialisms. Most importantly, it has been suggested to me that real estate brokerage services may be less easily identifiable to contractors by non-verbal signals than many other specializations. Perhaps, but in the contemporary United States the signs of real estate brokers feature the image of a house and the symbolism is well understood by all. I have not found examples of such a practice in the Greco-Roman world.

Locational and iconographic signals of willingness to trade were clearly common in the Greek and Roman worlds. So perhaps Kolb is correct about the Mycenaeans, but also perhaps not;[1] there are specialized commercial terms in Linear B.

Obviously, the Aegean palaces allocated significant resources to the production of textiles. What did they do with all the textiles? Kolb's answer is that the they "redistributed" them to "guests/friends" (foreigners) as "gifts." There is evidence for such a practice (discussed in Chap. 9.2), but even if true, such transfers would account for only a fraction of (say) palatial textile production.

Suppose, however, we follow Kolb's model and begin our analysis not by looking at behavioral evidence but instead for Linear B words meaning "gift." Where and what are the words? Luján (2010: 28; my translation) finds

> on this matter, the direct information that we can recover from the Linear B tablets is quite limited. In fact, the most common word for

---

[1]   The Mycenaeans apparently had no specific word for the occupation of "collector" but, as will be shown, the commercial activities of the "collectors" are plain to see in the texts and they are important.

'gift', *dōron*, only occurs on one tablet, PY Tn 316, where it is found several times on both verso and recto as part of what seems to be a formulaic expression used to refer to the invoice of offerings to gods and sanctuaries.

I have not yet found a text in which the palace *received* a "gift" (but see doubtfully Lujan 2010: 29). Relying on "Finley's Hypothesis," we might well conclude that "gifts" were at best marginal to the Mycenaean public economy and, therefore, that the economy *must* have been organized overwhelmingly by means of markets and trade!

One might well recall the tale of the "Emperor's Singing Contest," wherein after listening to the first contestant, the emperor awarded the prize to the (unheard) second contestant. Whether the Mycenaean economy is a "gift economy" or a "market economy" cannot be determined by the arbitrary decision of which words to look up first. However, this characterization is not what is important. The problem that concerns me throughout this study is whether the Minoan/Mycenaean economy knew markets and whether they operated in important economic sectors.

In response to Kolb, it is sufficient to say that those who deny that profit motivations (and the market) lie behind palatial production decisions are left with the hypothesis that palaces collected taxes and kept careful track of the material and labor resources they acquired to afford to give things away. *More importantly, to deny the profit motivation is to leave completely unexplained the findings in Part I. Namely, the palaces bore the cost of covering walls with exquisite frescoes demonstrating to visitors the brilliant fashions they had created. Did the visitors/guests need to be convinced to take the garments as gifts?*[2]

---

[2]   The internal structure of the "palatial economy" is the main concern of the Linear B documents. It is not, however, the main focus of the present study. The palace is a large firm and, hence, "out of the center, into the center" would have to play a major role. Obviously, there is evidence that palaces provided food and raw materials to specialized workers and that the former returned goods and services to the palaces. However, specialization does not mean that the specialist carried out only one activity but rather that he/she spends more time in this activity than he/she would if the palace had not offered employment. The evidence does not demonstrate that specialists did not also produce food and raw materials, and other valued items for themselves. Indeed, the absence of major self-production is counterintuitive. The total evidence does not demonstrate that specialists worked in their specialties *only* for payment by the palace. There is, for example, evidence consistent with private export from Crete of storage containers and olive oil (Chap. 8.2). The Linear B tablets do not demonstrate that the palatial economy is solely a command economy. There is no explicit evidence that specialists and unskilled workers negotiated terms of employment with the palace. Nevertheless, there are indications that market forces helped to determine rewards to labor power. For example, there are indications that payments increased according to skill level with these taking the form of land grants (Gregersen 1997; Shelmerdine 2011; Hruby 2013: 426). As noted by Silver (2007: 261), "It may be doubted that

2. Gifts vs. "Collectors" of Oil

Perhaps gift motivation explains why a few large oil transport jars (SJs) that are inscribed—on the shoulder and the waist—with painted (before firing) references to the *wanax* "king" were produced on Crete; this is verified often by their bearing of a Cretan place-name and by chemical and petrographic analysis. The jars were sent to (or at least found) in mainland Greece.[3] The inscription would perhaps testify to the generosity of the *wanax*. I will return to this problem shortly after dealing with other matters. However, at this point in the discussion, we may be confident that the Mycenaean palatial economy was not an insatiable consumer that kept every last bit of oil produced in the domain for itself (Haskell 2004: 153).

There is much more that needs to be said about exported oil. Numerous *uninscribed* Cretan manufactured transport jars (USJs) are found on the mainland and beyond, including southern Anatolia. In addition, almost 150 inscribed examples (ISJs) have been found in Crete or on the mainland.[4] These are inscribed with the name of a person, not with a reference to the *wanax*. Most often, the name is in the nominative case but there are, at least, four instances in which the name is in the genitive (together with another name in the nominative plus a toponym). The individuals named in the genitive, and perhaps some of the others as well, are understood to be "collectors" (Haskell 2004; 154f.), about which more will be said shortly.

One strong reason why owners inscribed their oil is that they wished to distinguish it from oil left uninscribed—namely, to claim their own oil when unloaded at the destination (compare van Alfen 1996-1997: 254). This kind of preference suggests to me that the inscribed oil was typical of a relatively higher quality. The oil in uninscribed jars—the overwhelming majority of examples— whether sent by the palace or individuals, was somewhat lower quality and,

---

specialized craftsmen had greater daily food needs than unskilled workers. If they did not and markets were absent it is difficult to understand why payments to the skilled were higher than to the unskilled." There is evidence for the availability of alternative (nonpalatial) employers, including cults, for alternative specializations, including nonpalatial occupations, and for the availability of land not owned by the palace. Hence, market-type calculations would have influenced the payments from palaces to specialists. There is evidence for employment of slaves, for *sale* of slaves, or that private individuals (taxpayers) sold themselves into slavery to private individuals /nonpalatial organizations (Chap. 9.8). Hence, we may be sure that palatial "redistribution" and/or "mobilization of resource" activities were conditioned by market forces. The extent of this "conditioning," like the extent of the palatial economy itself, is a matter of evidence, not of *a priori* considerations. For discussion, see Lupack (2011). The present study is concerned with the international marketing of luxury textiles by palaces.

[3]   Sources: van Alfen 1996-1997: 270–271; Haskell 2004: 153; but see Petrakis 2014: 204–205.

[4]   A Cretan ISJ may have been found in Sidon (Judson 2013: 86 n. 69).

hence, not as suitable as gifts (Duhoux 2011: 60, 71).[5] This reasoning favors the marketing of most of the exported oil as opposed to the redistribution model favored by scholars such as Kolb. This "generic" oil was not meant for connoisseurs but instead to be sold/traded at the destination and then resold/retraded in smaller quantities by the new owners.

This argument is very far from ironclad, however. For example, as Judson (2013: 87–88) points out, both in Mycenae and in Thebes, ISJs and USJs were found in the same context. However, found together does not necessarily mean that owners regarded ISJs and USJs to be interchangeable—the inscriptions were permanent and remained visible. Hence, owners would be able to distinguish the lower from the higher quality oil. Also, find spots may be misleading as to the original oil quality. It is likely that empty jars were reused, which is a possibility that reminds us that the place where a jar was found may not be the place where it was originally sent and consumed (Petrakis 2014: 208). One might even suggest, following Judson (2013: 91–92), the possibility that none of the ISJs were originally destined for recipients outside Crete. This would mean that, counter to the predictions of economic analysis, only the lower quality USJs were meant for exportation.[6] Nevertheless, evidence suggesting that (some) ISJs were actually exported is available from Thebes: "[I]t is of some interest to note that the name *a-nu-to* which is common to both Knossos and Thebes is found at Thebes also on three stirrup jars imported from Crete (TH Z 863–865)" (Hiller 2006: 75).

Oil was exported from Mycenaean Crete to mainland Greece and elsewhere. I favor a quality gradient between ISJs and USJs. Nevertheless, assume that the USJs were not of lower quality than the ISJs and, consequently, were equally suitable as gifts. Next, although it does not follow from any evidence, assume that *all* the USJs sent away from Crete were *palatial* gifts. Admittedly, this is a much smaller number, but I see no reason to believe that the individual owners of ISJs were motivated by gift-giving. There is even less reason to assume that those who inscribed their names in the genitive were so motivated. As will be seen shortly, one would have to believe that as "collectors," they indebted themselves to the palace for the purpose of giving gifts. Moving on to the bottom line, we might say that Kolb is correct about oil exports. However, Kolb is correct

---

5   "But it is worthy of mention that the finds from Khania may perhaps be considered supporting evidence for the view that seals in LM I authenticate rather than prove storerooms or containers intact" (Hallager 1987b). Owners needed to be able to identify later valuables that left their control. It is, thus, *conceivable* that some (or even all) of the uninscribed oil transport jars traveled overseas while remaining under the control of their owners. If so, they were not necessarily of lower quality than inscribed ones.

6   In my opinion, Judson's (2013: 89 with n. 85) recitation that "brands" are at home in a "modern market-based economy" but not in "a highly centralized economic system" would have been better left unvoiced.

about the unimportance of trade because we assumed he was. Furthermore, when we take into account that the *wanax* should be seen as one of the "collectors," Kolb's vision of the structure of the Mycenaean economy is undercut.

To repeat: (1) the individuals named on the oil jars in the nominative case are most likely not collectors but "ordinary" private owners—that is, persons not associated with the palace. In this event, the possibilities of gift and administrative transfer are minimal: the oil was exported from Crete and sold by the named individual.[7] However, (2) the *individuals* named in the genitive in the oil jar inscriptions are "collectors"[8]—that is, they are private businesspersons in a contractual relationship with the palace.[9] I propose that a collector is entitled to the difference, hopefully positive, between what he/she receives in the export market for oil that belonged to the Cretan palace and what he was obligated to return to the palace for being given control over the oil. Next, (3) with respect to the *wanax* inscriptions, Haskell (2004: 153) explains, "The *wanax* has a documented direct connection, albeit limited, to the oil industry, to judge from the few inscribed stirrup jar inscriptions that include the adjective *wa-na-ka-te-ro* (TI Z 29 [Tiryns], TH Z 839 [Thebes]; abbreviated to *wa* on EL Z 1 [Eleusis]" (see Petrakis 2014: 202).[10] Stated directly, the handful of *wanax* inscriptions signal that the *wanax* is one of the "collectors." His participation in the oil market in the capacity of "collector" leaves room for gift motivation but makes it rather unlikely.

Let us examine the position of the *wanax* more closely. The inscribed *wa-na-ka-te-ro* is said to mean "royal," but what does "royal" mean? I propose that the meaning is "oil belonging to the palace that is given to/placed under the control of the *wanax*'s house/firm"[11]—that is, *wa-na-ka-te-ro* needs to be understood as

---

7   In such cases, the inscribed personal names might have served as trade-mark labels (doubted with good reasons by van Alfen 1996-1997: 261–262) or served to identify the owner of the jar when it was unloaded from the ship. The latter explanation seems reasonable when the inscription consists of just a personal name

8   There are 26 collectors designated by personal name in the Linear B texts at Knossos and 4 at Pylos (Palaima 1999a: 374).

9   Rougemont (2009), if I understand correctly, has concluded that collectors were utilized by Mycenaean palaces only in animal husbandry and textile production. I find this conclusion difficult to reconcile with instances in which the inscribed formula on the exported oil jars is much like those on the Pylos and Knossos tablets dealing with sheep or textiles.

10   These three are certain examples. There are also a few cases in which the single sign *wa* is inscribed at Knossos without the accompanying formula and, also, the *wanax* (or *wa*) receives oil at Pylos (Haskell 2004: 153; van Alfen 1996–1997: 270–271).

11   For the etymological and logical connection of *wa-na-ka-te-ro* (the adjective *wanakteros*) with *wanaks* (Petrakis 2020: §9–§10), Tzagrakis (2016: 206) maintains, "The adjective normally denoting something relevant to the *wa-na-ka* is *wa-na-ka-te-ro*, which obviously means 'palatial' compared to the rest of the adjectives. For example, there were palatial fields and other property that did not directly belong to the sovereign, as well as craftsmen some of whom were at his

if it were in the genitive. The *wa-na-ka-te-ro* inscription reveals that the *wanax* is a collector of palatial oil,[12] but this designation does not mean that the *wanax* delivered oil to the palace. The point is that the *wanax* exported the oil (whether for gift or sale) and for this use, he owed a payment to the oil's owner—that is, to the palace. The texts are hiding palatial trade in plain sight!

If this interpretation of *wa-na-ka-te-ro* is correct, it reveals a legal separation between the property of the king and the property of the palace. That the *wanax* is not the palace goes far in explaining the finding that the "*wanax* had a direct interest in only a small segment of the palatially directed economy" and also why there are "relatively few references to the *wanax* in the Linear B corpus" (quoting Haskell 2011: 126). The king is a property owner, but he does not own the palace, which he serves as an executive.[13]

My interpretation also highlights the unexpected *depersonalization of offices in the palatial system* (see further below). The *wanax* took oil from the palace as a "benefit" (*o-no*) and later had to "(re)pay" (*o-no*) just as if he were one of the private businesspersons whose personal name is inscribed in the genitive.[14] A doubt arises, however, about the extent of the alleged "depersonalization." Why was the *personal name* of the *wanax* not used instead of his palatial title in the inscription? I do not intend to enter into the discussion concerning whether *e-ke-ra₂-wo* was the personal name of the *wanax* in Pylos (about which problem, see Nakassis 2012 and Petrakis 2016: 87ff.). The point is that the *wanax* had a personal name and the use of one or the other in a palatial document[15] might

---

service, while others were partially independent." I would not equate *wanax* with palace as there was property that belonged to the palace but not to the *wanax*, and property that belonged to the *wanax* but not to the palace. Tzagrakis (2016: 210) notes that there are no herds designated as *wa-na-ka-te-ra* and also that "it seems almost certain that the *wa-na-ka* had personal property, separate from the palatial estate." The *wanax* resided in and administered the palace but he was not the palace.

12 Van Alfen (1996–1997: 271) dismisses the view of *wanax* as a collector, but elsewhere (van Alfen 1996–1997: 261 n. 34) he accepts the general idea of collector as vendor: "[C]ollectors might be seen as competing with one another in trade. However, it must be remembered that in this scenario collector-trade would still be within the overarching context of palatial (i.e., some form of centralized) control and the goods traded would be those 'released' (an *o-no*-type transaction) by the central authority to the collector." This view of the goods traded is surely correct. See below for more on the *o-no* (plural *o-na*) transaction.

13 The designation of an asset as *wa-na-ka-te-ro* "royal" means that this asset is under the jurisdiction of the *wanax* "king" but it does not mean that the palace no longer owned assets of this type (compare the formulation of Palaima 1997: 411). The palace is a much larger enterprise than the king.

14 For *o-no* as a "benefit" to collectors at Knossos, see Killen (1995: 223–224) and Bennet and Halstead (2014: 276).

15 The inscriptions on the oil jars were likely made by agents of the palace to identify the recipients (debtors) of the palace's oil.

have had an administrative significance. In fact, as noted by Nakassis (2012: 18–20):

> [S]cribes regularly refer to the same individual differently in different texts; the same individual can be identified by name, office, or both, depending on what information the scribe felt was relevant to supply.... A scribe's decision to describe an individual by his personal name and/or title is therefore not arbitrary. Indeed, the extreme economy of Mycenaean scribal practice strongly suggests that the type of information included in a text should generally be regarded as significant.

Perhaps the use of *wanax* (or other palatial office) rather than the *wanax*'s personal name recognized that repayment to the palace would be less than in transactions citing his personal name.[16] I prefer the explanation that the debt was owed by the house of the *wanax* meaning that it would be "inherited" by a new *wanax*. This explanation, however, remains in doubt and provisional.

It turns out there were "oil" collectors who were independent commercial entrepreneurs with a contractual relationship with the palace. A king might participate in this palatial market either as king or under his personal name. Palaima (1997: 408–409) adds that the adjective *wanakteros* applies to quantities of TELA cloth and LANA wool on tablets from Knossos (KN Le 525, cf. also Le 654 for a textile delivery association), and the abbreviation *wa* is used to specify a quantity of HORD (= WHEAT) in the first of four entries dealing with WHEAT on tablet F 51 from the Room of the Chariot Tablets at Knossos. Moreover, the contractual relationship of king with palace does not only involve commodities, such as oil or wheat or wool or cloth, but also applies to human and physical capital owned by the palace. Thus, for example, at Pylos, a potter named *pi-ri-ta-wo*, who held a *ko-to-na ki-ti-me-na* (landholding) at *pa-ki-ja-na*, is described as *wa-na-ka-te-ro* (PY En 467; PY En 371 + 1160; Hruby 2013: 423 with references). In addition, a fuller (*ka-na-pe-in*) and an *e-te-to-mo* "armorer"(?) are said to be *wanakteros*. Again, a *wanakteros* in the Theban Of series (TH Of 36.1) is a

---

16   Petrakis (2012: 84) maintains: "Such personal involvement of none less than the ruler himself in this [the textile] industry, implied by occurrences of the adjective *wa-na-ka-te-ro*, should warn us that the significance of this production was not merely economical and aimed at the end result; it was also deeply political and focused on the process." I think I understand what Petrakis is suggesting and I disagree with his interpretation. I suggest that the "otherness" of the *wanax* results from a political choice that has deep economic implications. However, I agree with Petrakis (2014: 203) when he concludes: "[I]t is likely that the ruler, 'other' from the rest of the society, had the potential to act both as the central figure atop the 'palatial' administrative hierarchy, but could also get entangled within realms of economic activity that lay properly outside the confines of the 'palatial' reach."

woman cloth worker known as a "finisher" in a tablet series dealing with wool allocations.

The meaning of *wanakteros* is "potter (or other artisan) owned by the palace who is assigned to the house/firm of the *wanax*."[17] The potter or other artisan was for the *wanax* a "benefit" from the palace for which he had to make payment. Possibly, the benefit was not control over an individual artisan but over a workshop headed by the latter. The payment may have been the performance of his duties as *wanax*. However, there is some reason to believe that the *wanax* took possession of the artisan in his private capacity and had to make payment accordingly. Zeman (2019: 41) explains that the Pylos artisans are listed on a tablet *found in the "Northeast Building"* (see §5 below), which has come to be viewed as a clearinghouse for property collected or disbursed by the palace (cf. Wiener 2007a: 272–274). That is, it is a place where citizens arranged to receive benefits from the palace and to make repayment (*o-no*). In short, a place where collectorship contracts were formed.

The *"wanax* as collector" interpretation of the inscription somewhat clarifies the meaning of the disputed Knossos tablet (KN X 976) (previously cited in Chapter 7.3) dealing with something at the place *da-*83-ja* that is *wa-na-ka-te-ro*. The "something" might be purple-dyed cloth or professional purple women dyers or, according to Palaima (2020b: 124), a purple dyeing workshop. My interpretation is that the "something" (probably a workshop) belongs to the palace and is assigned control of the house/firm of the *wanax* in return for a payment (compare Tzagrakis 2016: 211).[18]

The structure of the Mycenaean economy emerges from the proposed understanding of *wa-na-ka-te-ro* as much more sophisticated and much less monolithic than redistributionist scholars have described. Not only does there exist a "non-palatial" sector but also the "palatial sector" includes within itself islands of private enterprise trading in palatial property. These significant themes are further developed in the following sections.

3. The "Importance" of the Mycenaean Luxury Trade in Textiles

How *important* was this Mycenaean luxury textile trade? This turns out to be a difficult question to answer and even comprehend.

---

[17] This line of understanding undermines any temptation to understand the inscription *wa-na-ka-te-ro* on an oil jar as a brand name of reference to the quality of the contents.

[18] The "collector as vendor" understanding is tested and supported later in the context of collectors vs. non-collectors in the *ta-ra-si-ja* system for textiles.

Kolb has his own approach to the problem. In discussing the more than 700 mile-by-mule train market trade of Assyrian textiles for Cappadocian silver and gold in the earlier second millennium BCE (Veenhof 2010; Larsen 1976: 89; H. Lewy's 1964), Kolb (2004: 586) reflects that the trade amounted to only 2,000 textiles per year. He ignores the value of the textiles, but, in any event, the value of even fine textiles fit for the gods could be minimized by expressing it on an annual basis. There is very little in the ancient world that could not be made to look unimportant in this way. We might as well say that in the ancient world, there was no market trade and no royal gifting, which is even less impressive than trade when expressed on an annual basis! Despite the 25,000 texts found at Kanesh, there is literally nothing for us to write about. Indeed, a similarly oriented economic historian may perhaps look back to the twenty-first century and see unimportant quantities traded.

The economic historian is forced back to first principles. Kolb does not try to explain why the Assyrian traders left their homes in Assur (today's Qal'at Širqāt) to live in Kanesh (today's Kültepe) for years and invested so much effort for such paltry results. Obviously, the 2,000 textiles per year mattered a great deal to them and to their families. Suppose that participation in the textile market raised their wealth by 100% or even more? I fear that Kolb would say that the increase in wealth was small relative to total wealth or that the number of traders was small relative to total population. No matter, the increase in their wealth and the resulting sense of achievement from subduing stubborn environmental and institutional opposition explains why ancient people behaved the way they did, and this explanation is what matters for the economic historian.

Kolb (2004: 586), against his own per annum quantitative test, seeks to rescue the importance of gift trade: "The low volume of Bronze Age [gift] trade, compared to that of later times does not mean that [gift] trade was not important for Bronze Age civilization." Then there is a flash of insight when Kolb (2004: 586) calls upon the incentive value of "conspicuous consumption by elites." In my judgment, Kolb is right to call upon this kind of phenomenon in considering yesterday's trade. Yesterday's numbers are typically small. Economic history is the record of inspiration, effort, and achievement, or failure.

4. Fundamentals of "Collectorship" and of "Kingship"

We have seen non-royal collectors and the *wanax* participate in the oil trade. Now let us move on from the "*wanax* as collector" problem to consider more deeply the fundamentals of "collectorship." Certain individuals were initially called "collectors" by modern scholars because of their occasional association (in PY Cn 655 and Py Cn 453) with the term *a-ko-ra* (*agorā*, cf. ἀγορά), translated as "collection"/"gathering." Kyriakidis (2010: 141 with n. 8) understands the base meaning of *agora* to be the "gathering of a flock/herd," a definition which over time came to refer to a "gathering of people."

In one Pylos tablet, PY Cc 660,[19] individuals listed are designated "with the verb *ageirei* (*a-ke-re*)," rendered by J. Bennet (2007a: 195) as "[he] collects." The conclusion that the individuals are independent contractors is reinforced by the terms related to alphabetic Greek *agora* and *ageirei*. I do not accept that the semantic meaning of these terms is captured by abstractions such as "gathering" or "[he] gathers." In connection with the semantic meaning, I call into play the term *agorazō*, meaning individuals who "occupy the market-place," "buy in the market," and "haunt/gather in the market" (LSJ s.v). I think that the Mycenaean scribes understood *ageirei* in precisely this sense—namely, as individuals who "gather with others for the purpose of doing business" or even, taking into account the etymology offered by Kyriakidis (2010), "who gather with others for the purpose of doing sheep business." The place of gathering is the "*agora*."[20]

When the scribes designated individuals as "gatherers," they meant that they were independent businessmen and should be dealt with accordingly. That the Mycenaean economy was familiar with business persons—that is, with individuals specializing in risk-bearing as opposed to a narrow technological process—is supported by the "notable overlap" at Pylos between the names of "shepherds" in the Cn records and "bronze-smiths" in the Jn records (Kyriakidis 2008: 449). Kyriakidis (2008: 459) concludes that the "shepherds" were not so much shepherds as they were individuals who "at the end of the day" were responsible for looking after the palace's sheep.

The common practice of citing the alphabetic Greek equivalents of Linear B Greek terms makes no sense unless we assume they have, at least, roughly the same meaning. To make an exception in the case of *agora* means that we have surrendered to a preconceived primitivist view of the Mycenaean economy. Is there evidence on the ground of Mycenaean agoras? Although the texts are silent about their function, archaeology shows us "Great Courts" in front of the megara at Tiryns, Mycenae, and Pylos and some "Lesser Courts" (Cavanagh 2001).

An alternative interpretation is that *agora* means "flock" (Kyriakidis 2010: 143). Kyriakidis (2010: 147–148) cites this meaning as corroborating his view that "collectors" are owners of the flocks they manage. He seems to assume that an individual is either an "owner" or a "beneficiary" and that an individual of high status must be an owner. Thus,

---

[19] A second example of *a-ke-re* has been found in PY X 1587 but context is lacking.

[20] There were in fact "gathering places" in Neopalatial Crete": "All of the operating palaces were surrounded by towns, though some towns like Pseira flourished without palaces. The main organizing architectural feature in most towns was the plateia, or town square, which probably served the same centralizing function as the palatial courtyards" (Rehak and Younger 1998: 106).

it is unthinkable that the *wanax* was a mere supervisor of a workshop, or that he was the beneficiary of the workshop which was bestowed on him by someone more powerful. If, indeed, the 'collectors' and the *wanax* are treated in a comparable way, as their identical position in this formula shows, then this would be one of the strongest pieces of evidence in favour of 'collector' ownership.

Kyriakidis 2010: 151

However, the authority above the king might be a god (cult) as indicated in Chap. 6.3, and/or there may be an elective kingship.

Thus, in Plato *Minos* 319b we find that "Minos" or "a Minos" was chosen by Zeus and served a term of eight years: "For Homer, in telling of Crete that there were in it many men and 'ninety cities,' says: 'And amongst them is the mighty city of Cnossos, where Minos was king, having colloquy with mighty Zeus in the ninth year'" (tr. Lamb *LCL*). For Homer (*Odyssey* 19.179–180), the ruler is Minos *Enneöros*.[21] Elective kingship or appointment by the cult would go far in explaining the absence of emphasis on dynastic considerations in Minoan/Mycenaean iconography and Linear B texts. Today an individual is the *wanax* (CEO), but tomorrow someone else occupies the office, and the individual has returned to his status as a member of the elective body (BOD) or of the general public.[22] Generally speaking, the modern corporation does not foster a cult of personality.

There is good reason to believe that Plato and Homer knew whereof they spoke. Lupack (2011: 211) presents documentary evidence—the heading of tablet Un 2—that the *wanax* was chosen by the cult at Sphagianes in Pylos:

For more prestigious sanctuaries like *pa-ki-ja-ne* [*pakijane* "the place of slaughter"], it [the influence of the cult] could have extended to the *wanax* himself. An indication that this was the case can be found in tablet Un 2 of Pylos. PY Un 2 records a list of foodstuffs similar to those found on other tablets (e.g., PY Un 718) that were destined to be

---

[21] For the election/selection of rulers, including merchants, in the ancient Near East, see Silver 2006a: 7 with n. 3. The clearest example is Urukagina whose predecessor continued to live in Lagash and whose wife, a noted trader, said in an inscription that her husband was "chosen by the (god) Ningursu from among 36,000 individuals" (for this and other examples, see Silver 2006a: 6–7). In the myth of the "Gordion Knot," Midas, who arrived in Phrygia in a wagon, was chosen as king. Hittite ritual texts mention the name Mita = Midas meaning "red wool" (Burke 2002). The rich man who arrived in a wagon—the prime vehicle of the merchant—carrying purple-dyed wool became king. In *Odyssey* 11.568–571, the wealthy Minos, son of Zeus, judges the dead in the House of Hades.

[22] In a letter of a Hittite ruler of the first half of the 13th century BCE, there is arguably a reference to an active personage named Tawagalawa who is said to have been the king of the Ahhiyawans (Achaeans) before the current king (his unnamed brother).

consumed at a ceremonial or religious banquet. The heading of PY Un 2 states that the occasion of the banquet was the initiation [*mu-jo-me-no*] of the *wanax*, and the location of the ceremony was *pa-ki-ja-ne* itself. It seems likely that the initiation ceremony conferred a symbolic stamp of divine approval on the *wanax*, an approval that most likely helped him maintain, or at least enhanced, his position as head of state. PY Un 2 shows that this religious sanction was bestowed on the Pylian *wanax* specifically by the religious leaders at *pa-ki-ja-ne*. Thus, the religious personnel of *pa-ki-ja-ne* seem to have had a role to play in legitimizing and supporting the position of the *wanax* in Pylian society.

"Initiation" of an individual as *wanax* likely means that the king was chosen by the cult. That is, cults granted the power to maintain order by force to that individual. Arguably, the choosing cults included Potnia's, the sponsor of luxury textiles, and Poseidon, the other main deity at Sphagianes (Chap. 6.3), whose expertise lay in sea transport (see Chaps 14.3, 15.4). Palaima (1995: 131) adds that the *wanax* is the only figure said to undergo an initiation. In addition, it was a relatively large celebration as would be expected.

With respect to the depersonalization of offices, the "constitution" may have arranged that the king paid taxes on his private income and was permitted to benefit from his tax-exempt (or reduced tax) *temenos* only while he remained king (Silver 1995a: 74–79). Thus, in Linear B tablets of Pylos (PY Na 334 and Na 1356), there are references to flax/ land holdings of the king that are *wa-na-ka e-ke e-re-u-te-ra* (*eleuthera*) "free (of taxes)"/"remitted" (Killen 1985: 248; Tzagrakis 2016: 215–216). It appears then that even the *wanax normally* had to pay taxes to the palace. The king is permitted to benefit from the use of the *temenos*, and he repays (benefits) the community by providing kingly services. In this sense, the king is an independent contractor (see Kyriakidis 2010: 153–157). In another sense, he is the owner of the *temenos*, but he is not the absolute owner; rather he is a contingent owner—that is, his ownership is contingent on performing the contracted services (thus, making payment). Under either line of interpretation, he remains a member of the "ruling class." I also disagree with Kyriakidis' interpretation of the term *e-qe-ta*, which I think means "agent" (see Chap. 9.2).

However, to return to the collectors, J. Bennet (2007a: 195) maintains that the "collectors" were not "independent economic or political entities." We might agree that collectors did *not yet* fully own the resources they currently controlled. "Not yet" because they had not yet fulfilled their obligations to the original (and still) legal owner of the resources.[23] On the other hand, collectors were not salaried employees of the palace either.

Were collectors the "beneficiaries" (*o-na-le-re*) of the palace? I am not sure about the saliency of this term. Salaried workers have the benefit of the wage paid to them by the palace, and collectors have the benefit of using the palace's flock or oil. On the other hand, the palace is the beneficiary of the labor power of the hired workers and of the wool returned by the collectors. Collectors are best viewed as businesspersons who earn profits (or losses!) depending upon their stewardship of palatial resources.[24] To repeat, the collector is neither the full owner of the resources he controls nor the recipient of a fixed/contractually determined income. I wonder if Kolb would agree with me in seeing such arrangements as important elements of a market economy.

Lupack (2008b: 90) objects: "Originally it was proposed that the collectors were palatial agents, who were sent out to collect the sheep, wool and cloth specified on the tablets. But this solution was quickly discarded since it does not make sense to have such agents associated with some flocks but not with all of them." This is a difficult line of argument to maintain as "all or none" is not typical economic behavior. There is no theoretical objection to "all-or-none," but today we observe economic actors who simultaneously rent and own machines and buildings; and others who simultaneously borrow and lend or contract with "gig-workers" and employ full-time help. Businesspersons explore the commercial environment until they find the profitable margins.[25] Most obviously, due to the law of diminishing returns, at some quantity performed, the rising incremental cost of performing an activity yourself will exceed the incremental cost of having others perform additional units of the activity. To put it another way: at some quantity performed, the net revenue from having others do something for you will exceed the net revenue of doing more yourself. The outcome is that you market some of your own wool (oil) and place the remainder in the hands of contractors/collectors.

"The 'collectors' are a heterogeneous group, then, with a wide array of duties. The main reason to lump them into a single category is the fact that as individuals, they do not easily fit into the rigid framework of Mycenaean

---

[23]   We might say that the collector transformed key dimensions of resource ownership (i.e., control over the resources) into full ownership of the resources at the point of fulfillment of the contract.

[24]   I say "stewardship" to emphasize that the collectors are residual income recipients.

[25]   They do so not only because the economic system is "capitalism" (better "market economy") but also because it is in their private interest to do so. I see no reason to believe that "all or none" was a fixed principle governing the palace and cooperating individuals. An "all or none" rule for commercial behavior might emerge if its implementation sufficiently reduced the cost enforcing contracts. However, this is again a matter of private interest in lowering costs.

officialdom" (Nakassis 2013: 18). The "single category" in which "collectors" most easily fit is *"businessperson."* Collectors are, moreover, important business-persons as, according to Rougemont (2014: 346 n. 44), they "appear in c. 30% of sheep flock records; some of them are also associated with textile produc-tion and textile workers." Nosch (2014b: 382) finds that collectors "appear in approximately 30% of the records pertaining to textile workers, sheep, textile production, landholdings, and metallurgy; the 'collectors' exist in all Mycenaean palace administrations."[26] In Chapter 9.3, attention is given to the participation of collectors in the international market for textiles and the mordant alum.[27]

In short, we might say that Kolb in correct is saying there was no special-ized term pertaining to the role of the (scholar's term) "collector." However, the economic role of "collector" was performed and understood by all, and the term is implicit in the way the scribes formulated their tablets (with individuals named in the genitive). Moreover, "collectors" from the *agora* ("the assembled collection") went about their *business* in a good portion of the Mycenaean *palatial* economy. There is no reason to doubt that the same individuals and others did business using their own resources. The question of commercial terminology/behavior is further elucidated in the next section.

5. Commercial Terminology

As already demonstrated, Kolb cannot produce a positive argument concerning the nature of the Mycenaean economy. He has simply *chosen* to structure his line of analysis in a manner eliminating markets and, thus, leaving him free to *assume* the existence of something else.

There are several Linear B texts that refer to *buying/selling* of a slave (*doero, doera*). The most important of these is understood by Olivier (1987) as an extracted record of a full *contract*, presumably written on a perishable mate-rial[28], in which an individual of unstated status purchases a slave. This text is from Knossos (KN B 988 and KN B 822), and the relevant verb is *qi-ri-ja-to*

---

[26] "Collectors" in the wool/textile business are discussed in more detail in §3.

[27] Given the relatively closed nature of ancient capital markets, it is not so surprising that collec-tors would be drawn from the ranks of the relatively rich who could be able to "self-finance." Given the relative importance of "trust" in ancient societies, it would, furthermore, not be surprising for collectors to be members of only a few biological families who would view one and other as trustworthy. On the other hand, I suspect that not only did the rich become even richer but some, if only a few, poor persons became collectors and became rich and founders of rich families.

[28] An inscribed sealing from Thebes (TH Wu 429 = *CMS* VS.3, no. 371 [Arachne 166702]) = Thebes Mus. inv. no. 32723) from the "Room of the Treasure," an administrative area in the palace at Thebes (the Kadmeion) depicts a bull-leaping scene. The inscription refers to *di-pte-ra* (*dipthera*) that, according to Aravantinos (2015: 38 with Fig. 18), is "an entry for animal skins, destined

'he has bought' (= *epriato/priato*; cf. *Odyssey* 1.430). The same verb is found in other Knossos texts concerning slaves (e.g. Ai 1037.2 and Ai 5976.1; cf. Killen 1985: 284, n. 39).

More generally, the transaction term *qe-te-o* (in various alternative versions) meaning "to be paid"[29] appears a total of eighteen times in the tablets from Knossos, Pylos, and Thebes in which it is applied to cloth, olive oil, olives, livestock, wine, and grain. The commodities are transferred to the palace or from the palace to cults and individuals (Burke 2010: 96; Hutton 1990-91; R. Palmer 1994: 95–101). Petrakis (2020: §8) notes, "we may now confidently add the most explicit case of a Mycenaean contrastive pair well known from later Greek: *po-ro-te-ra: -u-te-ra* /proterā: husterā/ 'former: later, next' modifying temporal stages of an *a-pu-do-si* /apudosis/ 'delivery, payment' on MY X 2.1, a document from the Late Helladic IIIA2 Petsas House at Mycenae." The Petsas House is part of a sophisticated industrial complex whose relationship with the palace is unknown (Shelton 2002-2003: 395).

In a tablet from Pylos (Un 1322), a net-maker and a weaver receive wheat from the palace as *o-no*—that is, as a "benefit," but, more accurately, as "payment" since *o-no* is related to Greek *oninēmi* "profit"/"gain" (Beekes s.v.)—in return for (probably) linen fabrics.[30] A tablet from Pylos (PY An 35), for example, shows one *a-ta-ro* (Aithalos?) receiving/being paid (*o-no*) wine, wool, and other goods from the palace in exchange for the imported mineral alum (*tu-ru-pte-ri-ja*), an astringent and mordant used in building, leatherworking, and cloth dyeing.[31] Similarly, in yet another *o-no* transaction from Pylos (PY Un 443), an individual named Kuprios receives cloth and wool from the palace in exchange for alum. Presumably, in these transactions, the palace and Aithalos or Kurprios were acting in their own interests, although the bureaucrats acting on behalf of the palace had their personal interests to consider as well.

---

perhaps for making a type of parchment." Beekes (s.v. *dipsthera*) notes the variant *dipsera* and mentions the meanings "hide, prepared skin" as well as meanings related to "parchment."

[29] There appears to be an added implication of "as a religious penalty." Perhaps this refers to the swearing of oaths by the contractors, calling for the god(s) to punish the one who violated the terms of the agreement (see Silver 1995a: 10–18 and esp. 2011a: 52–57; cf. *Iliad* 19.259–260). In the case of the duel between Menelaus and Paris (*Iliad* 3.103–107, 276–301, 310–311), the oath is intended to settle a dispute over the possession of property. By reducing transaction costs, the "oath" institution permitted ancient societies to enjoy living standards that were high relative to their technological and scientific capabilities. The gods were more feared and heeded than expensive police and judges.

[30] One suspects that the net maker and weaver were "collectors" (Chap. 9.3). See Michailidou 1999: 99; Lujan 2010: 27; compare Gregersen 1997: 398–399; more generally, Killen 1995: 219. *O-no* transactions are attested in 16 Linear B tablets. It has been argued that they necessarily had a short "shelf-life" (Bennet and Halstead 2014: 276–277).

[31] Sources: Baumbach 1987; R. Palmer 1995: 283; Firth 2007.

Regarding the palace's acquisition of alum in trade (above), it is worth noting a circumstantial connection not simply with trade but with Anatolian trade. The possible connection is that the traders Aithalos and Kuprios obtained their alum-stone, used for dyeing wool, by trading in or with Phrygia (Pliny 35.52, 36.36; Firth 2007: 135). Unfortunately, other sources remain possible including Cyprus (*ku-po-ro*) and Melos.

In addition, there is a text from Knossos (KN J 693) in which quantities of "very fine" linen textiles are followed by quantities of bronze. It appears from the use of the term *qe-te-a* 'to be paid' that the palace *receives* the bronze as the price of its cloth.[32] Also attested are payments by the palace at Knossos for labor power—the word *e-mi-to* corresponds to alphabetic Greek *misthos* 'wage' (Lujan 2010: 27).

Finally, and importantly, *agora/ageirei* arguably refers to a place where independent economic actors gathered for the "purpose of doing business" or even "for the purpose of doing sheep business" (§4 above).

One could certainly hope for more terminological evidence of market behavior in Mycenaean times. I will consider other important evidence later. However, what has been presented is sufficient to cast further doubt on any monolithic model of a redistributional economy. Most importantly, the evidence testifies that the palaces sent luxury textiles to the Black Sea for payment in gold, not for gifts.

6. More Controversy: Gift Giving vs. Trade, vs. Gift Giving Leading to Trade

The giving of gifts is often taken as an alternative to trade (e.g. by Kolb 2004). However, the supporting evidence is sometimes skewed as in Kolb's (2004: 584) discussion of the cargo of the late fourteenth century BCE Ulu Burun shipwreck in south-western Turkey:

> In regard to quantity, quality, and composition this multicultural cargo strikingly recalls the above-mentioned lists of gifts exchanged between the courts of Near Eastern rulers, but it also reflects the variety of objects found in the Aegean, and it seems therefore to be a plausible suggestion that at least a great part of this cargo was destined for a ruler of the Aegean world. The metal would have sufficed to equip a Mycenaean army.

---

[32] Sources: Del Freo, Nosch, and Rougemont 2013: 267; Nakassis 2010: 131 with n. 5; Hutton 1993; compare Luján 2010: 30.

Thus, if the cargo includes only those items found in texts concerned with royal gift exchange, then the cargo is a gift for a ruler. On the other hand, if the cargo includes just about anything found in the region, then it is also a gift for a ruler. Is there a ship's cargo that might unequivocally be consigned to ordinary market trade? Kolb's answer is left unclear. Of course, it is true that the Mycenaean palaces had the resources to commission large ships—in one "Rower Text" from Pylos a 30-oared ship. However, this does not mean that ship was loaded with "gifts" as opposed to textiles for sale.

Kolb does not mention that the Ulu Burun ship carried *Hacksilver* for making payments. Indeed, Pulak (2001: 34) adds: "Much of the gold, whether intact or from scrap, was excavated in the same small area of the site, supporting the view that it was kept together and used as bullion when required." The trading interest is confirmed by the presence of four sets of balance weights (Pulak 2001: 45). Evidently, there was an expectation that someone, somewhere along the route would expect payment in precious metal (i.e. money).

However, there is a basic problem in Kolb's view: parties either met across a personal interface, or they met across a market interface; in other words, it was either one way or it was the other. Thus, it may be suggested that Minoan and Mycenaean textiles were not exchanged for other valuables; instead, they were presented to guests/friends. The distinction is real but, historically, the "gift" given "at a port of trade" is only a preamble, albeit an important one, that served to unlock the door to ordinary commercial trade.[33]

Thus, in the *Iliad* (7.467–475) we find Euneos 'Fine Ship-man', the "son" of Jason of the *Argo* and ruler of Lemnos, giving a large quantity of wine to the sons of Atreus, Agamemnon, and Menelaus. This *gift* was by no means the end of the matter. For then Euneos *sold*—that is, the eager Achaeans *bought*—the main part of his cargo of wine. Similarly, when the *Phoenicians* arrived to trade in Lemnos, they first presented King Thoas with a Sidonian silver mixing bowl (*Iliad* 23.744–745). The practice of giving gifts for the privilege of trading rights may indeed apply not only to foreigners but also to natives. For example, in *Iliad* 9.71–72, Nestor admonishes Agamemnon: "Full are thy huts of wine that the ships of the Achaeans bring thee each day from Thrace, over the wide sea; all manner of entertainment hast thou at hand, seeing thou art king over many" (tr. Murray *LCL*). The "Achaeans," whether drawn from among those before Troy or from Greece itself, gifted Agamemnon for the privilege of trading with the Achaean forces at Troy. Outside epic, "first gift then trade" is explicit in trade among officials and rulers at el-Amarna in Egypt (Bachhuber 2003: 47 with sources).

In fact, the "gifts" offered by foreign merchants to rulers served as payments—whether goodwill/conventional or real—for the right to trade

---

[33] The same kind of reasoning might apply to gifts given to "guests," see Chap. 9.3.

in their domains. It might be viewed in contemporary terminology as a tax/payment for a trading concession. In the reign of Egypt's Tuthmosis III, we find foreigners "bearing their gifts on their backs" as they approach the ruler "like dogs" (see Chap. 11.2) to request the "breath of life'; to receive the "breath of life" is to be granted the right to trade within Egypt. Thus, as the tomb drawings make clear, the Egyptian "messengers" in Punt engage in barter exchanges with the citizens of Punt, and then, when the Egyptians are returning home, the rulers of Punt ask for the "breath of life" in Egypt. "Life" without the permission to "earn one's living" is indeed a paltry invitation.

Thus, Panagiotopoulos (2006: 398) explains:

> The commemoration of the trade expeditions to Punt or Lebanon was a more intricate matter than the theme of gift giving, because in this case a simultaneous exchange of goods took place. Egyptian texts and images, though, preferred not to fully conceal the barter but to translate it into a more "acceptable" activity. Their elegant solution was to describe the Egyptian goods offered to foreigners as offerings for the local deities. Hatshepsut's expedition to Punt made thus a sacrificial offering to Hathor of Punt. Sennefri traveled to Lebanon to offer gifts to a goddess, the name of which has not been preserved. But we should not exclude the possibility that in reality the members of the Egyptian expeditions arranged this profane barter exchange as a ritual performance.

Indeed, Egyptian traders themselves "bribed" Nubian rulers for the trading privilege, as is illustrated by the expedition of Harkuf in the third millennium BCE.[34]

In Egyptian tomb art, we see textiles depicted as gifts/tributes from Keftiu (Aegeans) in the tomb of the "Prophet of Amun" Mencheperresonb (second half of the fifteenth century BCE): Bolts of tasseled cloth are carried by three Aegeans and two others (Kantor 1947: 58–59; Wachsmann 1987: 75; cf. Barber 1991: 338–340). We stand on historical precedents when we assume that the Keftiu merchants went on to sell Aegean textiles to Egyptians.[35] An inscrip-

---

[34] See Silver (1995a: 99–103) for numerous examples, including from pharaonic Egypt, of gift as payment for trading concession.

[35] Including, as Barber (2016: 207 with figures 8.3 and 8.4) observes, for covering the amidship cabins (*ikria*) of their boats with Aegean designs: "[T]he creation of such cabins on what seem to be pleasure boats must have entailed a fairly brisk trade in large and elaborately patterned Aegean wool rugs. The alternative is that the cabin sides were wood (making for a hot, less airy cabin), painted to *resemble* Aegean rugs. Either way, Egyptians connected boat cabins with Aegean textiles."

tion in Amenhotep III's mortuary temples attests that Egyptians had a trading interest in Greece; it is manifested in the presence in Mycenae of fragments of several *plaques* (between 8 and 11) bearing the name and title of Amenhotep III. As plaques are made to be seen, I would assume they were hung in a public building probably as votive offerings to a local deity. However, at some point, they may have been sawn up and used as a foundation deposit for a temple/shrine devoted to the ruler himself (see Hankey 1981: 45–48).

In the annals of Egypt's Thutmose III (1490–1436 BCE), some incoming goods are termed *bakew* 'production, trade goods' and others *baat* 'wonders'. The "wonders" typically have their origin outside the donor's native land (Silver 1995a: 48f.). Thus, the textiles delivered by Aegeans to Mencheperresonb must have been trade goods. Moreover, and here we have a preview of the next section, the wonders delivered by Aegean tribute bearers included lapis lazuli, turquoise, and objects made from nonnative gold or even gold itself (Wachsmann 1986: esp. 29, 54, 62, 73).

Let us now briefly return briefly to the cargo of the trading ship wrecked at Ulu Burun. Pulak (2001: 44) reports:

> Sieving the sediment contents of Canaanite jars ... did reveal a number of individual woolen(?) fibers, mostly dyed blue to bluish purple but those dyed red were also encountered.... Although sample fibers of both colors were submitted for analysis, the results were inconclusive. That the blue to bluish purple color of some of the fibers from Ulu Burun came from murex shellfish dye is almost certain.

It is not made clear in what way the tests were "inconclusive" or why the use of murex dye is a near certainty. Nevertheless, it does appear that the Ulu Burun trading ship carried precious textiles. Pulak (2001: 44) goes on to say that "there is no evidence that bulk textiles comprised a significant portion of the original cargo." I am not sure what Pulak means by "*bulk* textiles," but surely, he has presented *some* evidence that *luxury* textiles comprised a significant/valuable part of the original cargo. (Obviously, the dyed fibers are the residue of dyed cloth.) Furthermore, some scholars reason that the ship was headed for the Aegean (Pulak 2001: 13). On the other hand, there are other considerations raised by Pulak (2001: 47–48) that the ship may have been bound for a port on the western shores of the Black Sea. The next chapter is devoted to digging out evidence of all kinds for the textile trade.

9

Palatial Textile Trade and Traders

A Closer Look

1. Direct Evidence for Textile Trade: Transfers to/from Named Places or Persons

THE Linear B tablets at our disposal provide good reason for believing that the Mycenaean palaces produced numerous textiles. Yet the same tablets do not show that most of the textiles were disposed of by trade—that is, across a market interface. Does this silence mean that the market was unimportant as a destination for the palace's textiles? Hardly, as the tablets do not demonstrate that most of the textiles were disposed of by palatial gift-giving.[1] Neither, for that matter, do the tablets demonstrate that the textiles were mostly consumed by the palace itself. Perhaps, then, the palaces, like Marx's capitalists, viewed textile production as a worthwhile endeavor in itself and greedily accumulated textiles. Unfortunately, the tablets do not demonstrate even that the palace's textiles were mostly stored.

Some scholars suspect that the records attesting to the final disposition of the produced textiles were kept on perishable materials, such as leather, or in separate buildings, such as the "Northeast Building" at Pylos, which were devoted to that purpose (Bendall 2003: 224; Shelmerdine 1998: 293). This may well be true, but such explanations are unsatisfying unless we can also explain why the records documenting the disposal of the textiles were treated differently. As far as I am aware, no satisfactory explanation has been offered. There is also the possibility that the Mycenaean palaces did not always keep records disclosing what was done with the palatially owned property once it became free and clear. What follows is a survey of the most obvious indications of palatial trade.

---

[1]   It is true that the palaces turned over some textiles, oil, etc. to gods. These transfers may have fulfilled obligations or generated obligations.

In Thebes, a building served as an allocation center for livestock and livestock products.[2] Most of the 56 Of tablets from Room 1 record administrative transfers, although Palaima (1991: 279) mentions the presence of "economic transactions vocabulary." At least a hint of trade can be found in the fact that several sealings seem to record overseas transfers of livestock (including no doubt sheep) and wool from/to a place identified with the island Euboea to Thebes in Boeotia. A shipment of livestock is recorded as *te-qa-de* (*Thebasde*), 'to Thebes'. On the other hand, there is a record of a shipment of about forty pounds of wool "to Amarynthos." Thus, my understanding is that Thebes was sending wool to Euboea and receiving animals from Euboea (but compare Burke 2010: 101).[3]

The transaction pattern has the feel of market trade based on comparative advantage, but it is not known whether Thebes and Amarynthos were decentralized units of one palatial enterprise. I am reminded not only of the "labors" of Odysseus in acquiring flocks for Poseidon but also that Odysseus' palace in Ithaca had flocks of sheep on the mainland (see Chap. 15.2, 4).

A tablet from Mycenae (MY X 508) from the "House of Shields" records the dispatch of a kind of cloth (called *pu-ka-ta-ri-ja*) cloth *te-qa-de*, 'to Thebes'. "This type of cloth seems to have been of high quality, associated with palatial elites, and was often quite colorful" (Burke 2010: 75). Again, as in TH Of 25, there is a question as to whether the destination is Thebes in Boeotia or Thebes in Egypt. The doubt is understandable because, as just noted, bolts of cloth sent from Mycenaean Greece are depicted in a "tribute" scene of the second half of the fifteenth century BCE in the tomb of Mencheperresonb, "Prophet of Amun" under Thutmose III (Wachsmann 1987: 75).

Trade seems an appropriate designation for MY X 508 because it arguably involves a market interface. The cloth is not transferred to the Theban palace but rather to one *ma-ri-ne-u*, perhaps a deity,[4] who is known to possess a *woikos* 'house/firm' in Knossos (KN As 1519.11) and, in Thebes, employs female textile workers (*ma-ri-ne-we-ja*) in TH Of 25.1. Possibly, Marineus acts as a contractor ("collector")—that is, he owes a payment to the Mycenaean palace for permission

---

[2] A similar kind of function has been proposed for the "House of the Oil Merchant" (= "West House") at Mycenae. Note the inscribed sealing from the palace at Thebes (*CMS* VS.3 no. 373 = Arachne 172763) mentioning *di-pte-ra* which may refer to *dipsthera/dipsera/dipthera*, possibly animal hides used for parchment (Aravantinos 2015: 38 with Fig. 18).

[3] Thebes tablets mention places in Euboea including *a-ma-ru-to* = Amarynnthos (Of 25 and Wu 58.gamma) and also *ka-ru-to* = Karystos (Wu 55.beta). Probably "to Thebes" refers to Thebes in Boeotia not in Egypt as the same word occurs in three nodules (Wu 51, Wu 65, Wu 96) found in Boeotian Thebes. Sources: Palaima 1991: 278–279; Shelmerdine 2007: 43.

[4] L.R. Palmer (1979: 1338–1339) has argued that *ma-ri-ne-u* should be read as Mallineus "God of Woolens."

to use the cloth from Mycenae in his own enterprise in Thebes. There are two other female worker groups—*a-ka-i-je-ja* in TH Of 27 and *ko-ma-we-te-ja* in Of 35 with designations derived from the names of the Cretan collectors *a-ka-i-jo* and *ko-ma-we-ta* (Hiller 2006: 74).

A Pylos tablet (Ad 671) strongly suggests not only a market exchange of cloth between Mycenaean centers but that the participants are private individuals. The text refers to women at Pylos as "women of the man who controls Karustrian cloth products *vel sim*" (Palaima 2011: 72–73). Younger and older "boys" (arguably agents, Chap. 6.3) are attached to the women in connection with "headband makers." The "women" and "boys" constitute a branch of an enterprise directed by the "man" in Karystos.

Also, there is a (disputed) Theban reference (TH Gp 227) to the presence of a *ra-ke-da-mi-ni-jo* "son (*uios*) of the Lakedaimonian"[5]—that is, someone of Spartan ethnicity or, better, given the use of "son," to the presence in Thebes of an *agent* from the region in Mycenae (see Chap. 6.3). Especially in the latter case, we would expect return shipments from Thebes to Mycenae. Thus, there is reason to believe that MY X 508 is not a one-off transfer. This line of interpretation finds some support in the presence in Thebes of a *mi-ra-ti-jo/ja* 'Milesian'(or 'Milesians') from Anatolia in the Fq series.[6]

A nodule (label) from Knossos (KN Wm 8493) seems to refer to a wool transaction between two unknown localities: the wool is to be sent from one place (*se-to-i-ja* on side .a) "to *ki-ri-ta*" (in the allative form, on side .b). "The use of the verb *do-ke* 'he/she/it gave' reminds us of transactions between individuals" (Rougemont 2014: 357–358).[7]

Knossos tablet Od 667 describes wool dyed blue or bluish-green—arguably purple-dyed—by the adjectives "Cypriote" and "Cretan." Palaima (1991: 201) explains, "The dyed wool was either imported from Cyprus and Crete or, more likely, it was to be exported from Knossos to 'Crete' and 'Cyprus' with 'the amount being allocated in a Cypriote market being two times that destined to stay in Crete." I would prefer to say, "two times that destined for the Cretan market." A commodity whose market is described in such broad terms as 'Cypriote' or 'Cretan' is destined to be sold in the anonymous marketplace, not presented to

---

[5]   Sources: Aravantinos 2010: 63, Palaima 2011: 73–74. What remains unexplained is why the "son of the Lakedaimonian" receives wine from the Theban palace. Witczak (2011) says the Theban text refers to *two* sons whom he understands to be the Dioskouroi.

[6]   A commercial or administrative connection between Thebes and Crete is hinted at by two vases found there bearing the disyllabic name *pi-pi* (TH Z 846 and TH Z 854) that, Meißner reports (2019: 38), were made in western Crete.

[7]   The tablet was not authenticated by a seal imprint and there are other questions as well.

a known in advance guest/friend. The same anonymity holds if the dyed wool was imported to Knossos from Cyprus and Crete.[8]

As a final example of the possible textile trade, Burke (2010; 76) explains,

> The ideogram *TELA* + the ligature *KU* is a difficult textile to identify. No term beginning with *KU* has been found on the cloth tablets and this is one of the least common ligatures. The *KU* sign might refer to *ku-do-ni-ja* cloth (i.e., cloth from or for 'Chania') or possibly *ku-pi-ri-jo* ('Cyprus' or even 'Byblos').... Although no other cloth is described by a specific geographic adjective.

None of the textile transactions referenced above are surely mediated by the market, but neither are they obviously mediated by the "visible hand" of palatial administrators. I see little that is recognizable as gift trade.

2. Cloth "For Guests" and "For Followers": More Gift vs. Trade

At Knossos, the cloth *pa-we-a*, wearable as a cloak, is modified by the adjective *ke-se-nu-wi-ja*. The spelling of the adjective is one of several of the stem /xenwos/ in Mycenaean Greek and is attested to at Pylos as well as Knossos. Varias Garcia (2017: 426) explains that the Linear B meaning comes close to the meaning in the first Greek alphabetic texts as 'guest' and 'foreign,' referring to products or people from another state, Mycenaean or not, as in alphabetic Greek.

I focus attention on two of the possible meanings for the designation "for guests/foreigners:" (1) cloth for *gifts* to foreigners or (2) cloth for *sale* by foreigners in foreign markets.

However, in four cases, the same type of cloth is termed *e-qe-si-ja*. This cloth has been understood as destined for *domestic use*—that is, for the internal market. This (internal) destination of the cloth may be understood correctly but the designation means "for followers" or better "*for agents*" (Hooker 1995: 13–14).[9]

Again, I limit the possible meanings to two. The designation might mean (1) cloth for *gifts* to followers/agents, or (2) cloth for *sale* by domestic agents

---

[8]   With respect to the problem of "sending owls to Athena" (Palaima 1991: 276–277, 294) or, more favored by economists, "sending coals to Newcastle," the question is not whether the Cypriotes were capable of producing the product themselves. Of course, they were. The question is whether the Knossos palace expected to make a profit by selling the commodity at the prevailing (positive) market price in Cyprus.

[9]   In Palaima's (2015: 624, 641) view, "the *hek^wetai* are 'agents of making others follow or attend,' i.e. very close in meaning to 'mobilizers' of personnel, often for military service."

(probably) in domestic markets/cloth for use as a *means of payment* by domestic agents.[10]

I will endeavor to show that option (2) is correct or possible for both adjectives. I hope readers will not regard this to be an impossible dream.

To begin this effort, I will more fully consider the meaning of "follower" or "agent." According to Nakassis (2013: 7), "Thirteen men at Pylos are designated as *hek^wetai* (singular *hek^wetās* = *hepetas*), which is universally translated 'follower' (Linear B *e-qe-ta*, cf. *epetēs*)." These men are usually thought to be a band of aristocratic warriors who attend upon the *wanax*. *Epetai* appear to play a role in defending the coast but they also play a cultic role. Nakassis (2013: 7 n. 39) adds that at Knossos, there are textiles classified as *e-qe-si-jo* (in Lc 646, Ld series, L 871) "for the followers." However, these cloths cannot serve as standard compensation to military mercenaries (with Burke 2010: 90) because the cloth "often varies in color and decoration ... [and] is sometimes described as *a-ro$_2$-a* 'of better quality'" (Burke 2010: 90). I suggest that the cloth given to the "followers"/"agents" is intended for further distribution by them, including either by sale domestically (but possibly sale overseas) or to make purchases of needed resources.[11]

In the Pylos Linear B texts, "follower" is a general term for "agent" and does not exclusively refer to agents of the king. Thus, in Pylos, a "collector" ("businessman"/"independent contractor") named Amphimēdēs (*a-pi-me-de*) had three *do-e-ro* 'slaves', who are described as *hek^wesioi* (*e-qe-si-jo*) (Ed 847), literally "of the agents." This Amphimēdēs manages a flock of 190 sheep (Cn 655), but he also is a landholder of a type designated as *etōnion* (Eb 473/Ep 539), meaning perhaps that he did not have to pay taxes (Lejeune 1966; Nakassis 2013: 13 n. 98, 164, n. 29, 171). In Pylos PY An 607, a very difficult text, the palace turns over a number of women who are slaves, but not legally slaves of a god, to the *e-ge-ta* for *te-re-te-we* "for use by them"(?), "in return for their services"(?) (cf. §8).[12]

---

[10] My thanks to Tom Palaima for the "means of payment" suggestion.

[11] In Knossos tablet As 4497, *eqeta* is modified by a word restored as *ereutere* 'inspector' (Hooker 1995: 14; alphabetic Greek *eiromai* 'asker' but also 'petitioner' (LSJ s.v.; Beekes s.v.). The meaning is unclear to me but perhaps the agents authenticated/vouched for the cloth.

[12] See §8 below. With some guidance from Deger-Jalkotzy (1972), my unsteady understanding is as follows: (1) That the palace can legally allocate the services of these women signals that they are its slaves; (2) The implication is that the "parent" not mentioned as being a slave of the god is nevertheless a slave of the palace; (3) Perhaps the daughters have reached an age at which the palace will claim their services; (4) The legal status of the parents is mentioned to demonstrate the legal status of the daughters—that is, their status as slaves of the palace; (5) It is not clear why the palace has precedence over the god with respect to the daughter's services. Deger-Jaklotzy (1972: 151–152) solves problem five by assuming that the (these?) slaves of the god were slaves of the palace.

Now let us return to the problem of cloth "for guests/foreigners." Hypothetically, the anonymous "guests"/"foreigners" for whom provision is being made in the texts are foreign businesspersons who arrive for the navigation season and take up residence near the palace showrooms (see Part I). *Ke-se-nu-wi-ja* "for guests" might signify a general gesture of hospitality by the palace to *all* the visiting foreigners or it might apply only to the subset "(real) guests," who will serve the palace as agents for the *pa-we-a* garments (see Chap. 11.7 on the Syrian who is "chief of the Keftiu").

The argument is that *ke-se-nu-wi-ja* refers to cloth for agents from among foreign businessmen and *e-qe-si-ja* designates cloth for agents from among local businessmen. I see no implication that the foreigners and locals would do business *only* with the palace's *pa-we-a* garments. In addition, the local businessmen/agents might export their palatial cloth, but given their local connections, they would be more likely to deal in local markets. Certainly, they would be much more likely to deal locally than with foreign agents. The use of cloth in the domestic market is much more likely if it is given as a means of payment for acquiring resources.

My reasoning is strengthened by the fact that it offers the same explanation—the use of sales/purchase agents—for both cloth assignments. An obvious weakness is that the palace may have had this type of garment produced specifically as a gift. As far as I am aware, the possibility that "For agents" implies "as a gift" has not been raised. Although it is true that Homer provides instances in which *foreign visitors* are given textiles as gifts (e.g., *Odyssey* 8.387ff., 15.194ff.),[13] it is not unreasonable to give the same standardized gift to both loyal "followers" and foreign guests. However, this objection is not cogent for two reasons.

First, the cloths designated as "for foreigners/guests" represent only about a third of their number: 110 to 130 out of a total of 380 (Varias Garcia 2017: 319). I understand from this that most of the garments of this type were not produced as gifts.[14] Or, at least, there is no evidence to support such an assertion. If 130 textiles can be designated as gifts, 380 may just as easily.

Second, the garments are *not* obviously made suitable for gifts by being standardized. In at least three of four tablets [Ld(1) 573.a, 585.a and 649.a.], the cloth "for foreigners/guests" is further refined by the designation "*e-ru-ta-ra-pi/eruthrāphi/* a form of adjective *e-ru-ta-ra* /eruthrā/," thus "qualifying the cloth with the meaning 'with red (attachments?)'" (Varias Garcia 2017: 419 with references; see Chap. 9.2 on *te-pa* garments). The red attachments may be

---

[13] In the cited examples, the guests are unexpected (gifts to Odysseus from Alcinoos; to Telemachus from Nestor). In our texts, the garments are designated.

[14] At most, 34.2% of one type of textile is to be given as gifts. This hardly constitutes strong evidence for a palatial gift economy in textiles.

designs or images woven into the cloth, as in Homer, or tassels or fringes, or more physical attachments.

Hence, based mainly on the absence of standardization, my assessment is that the designated textiles are for sale, not for gifting. Some pieces are to be sold by foreign agents and some were sold or spent by domestic agents. With respect to the pieces not designated either as "for foreigners/guests" or "for followers/agents," I surmise they were marketed through independent contractors ("collectors") or, more probably, directly by the Knossos palace in the showroom.

If I am correct, all the garments allocated by the palace are destined for the market. If I am completely incorrect, then all the textile transfers are gifts, although the word "gift" is not written.[15] However, in my view, the gifts would be gifts from the palace to visiting textile merchants ("guests") and to domestic agents. As such, they might be regarded as gestures of goodwill that would also have incentivized the recipients and, thereby, served the interests of market trade in most of the textile products produced by the palace.[16]

3. Palatial Employment of Textile Collectors: *Ta-ra-si-ja* and Kuprios

There is stronger evidence than provided in §2 for the palace's use of commercial agents/contractors in the marketing of textiles owned by the palace. Chapter 8.2 shows that businesspersons called "collectors" marketed oil belonging to a Cretan palace to the Greek mainland and elsewhere. In Chapter 8.4, mention was made of the economic importance of "collectors" including in the wool business. The present section deals with the additional details and problems of the marketing of palatial textiles via "collectors."

Some of the palace's textiles were acquired by collectors under the *ta-ra-si-ja* system attested to in the Linear B tablets from Knossos, Pylos, and Mycenae (KN Lc 535.A, 536.A, Le 642.1, X 8211; PY La 1393.1; MY Oe 110.1).[17] *Ta-ra-si-ja* means "wool (or bronze) weighed out for working" and corresponds to alphabetic Greek *talasia* and Latin *pensum* (Beekes s.v. *talasia*). As attested in the Knossos Lc tablets, wool is provided by the palace to textile workers for whom production

---

[15] I see no purpose in considering that I am correct about foreigners/agents but not about agents/ foreigners.

[16] The giving of gifts to temples and cults does not imply that the latter was under the control of the palace any more than the giving of gifts to foreigners had this meaning. Surely, the palaces hoped the gods would look at them favorably and reciprocate in the ways that only gods were able to (*do ut des*).

[17] The palaces probably also employed slave-agents to market textiles. Also, textiles were produced by palaces outside the *ta-ra-si-ja* or "putting-out" system (Nosch 2011; M. Alberti 2007: 245).

targets are set. Sometimes the target is accompanied by an entry designating a collector—this is, a masculine personal name usually written in the genitive. Alternatively, and less transparently, the production targets are accompanied with an entry pertaining to non-collectors—they record only a place, name, and an ethnic or professional designation. In addition, there are tablets of totals of textiles for collectors and non-collectors (Nosch 2000b: 43).

Why are there two types of textile recipient "groups?" The first occuring thought is that different types of textiles are involved. Nosch (2000b: 44) observes, however, that in the total allocated to each group, the same three types of textiles are listed. This finding, together with the collector's personal name in the genitive, convinces me that the textiles allocated to the collectors left the palatial system—that is, they came under the control of the collectors to do with as they chose. Of course, they owed a repayment to the palace.

Reinforcement of this understanding of textile collectors is provided by the finding that collectors were not nobodies—they included leading figures in Mycenaean society, not only locally but internationally as well (Burke 2010: 73–78). Indeed, as in the case with the oil, the collectors included the *wanax* himself. Recall that at Knossos (in tablet KN X 976), something to do with purple is designated as *wa-na-ka-te-ro* 'royal'. The other textiles allocated to non-collectors remained not only under palatial ownership but also under palatial control.

To date, I have not been able to find a receipt/record issued by the palace to a collector for (expected) (re)payment for the collector's business use of the palace's cloth. However, there is relevant evidence provided in *o-no* transactions: at Pylos, the individual named Kuprios (Linear B *ku-pi-ri-jo*) is certainly a smith and a shepherd of two flocks with a total of 110 sheep, all in the northern Hither Province. This smith/shepherd can probably be identified prosopographically with a *Kuprios* who receives cloth and wool from the palace in exchange for alum (PY Un 443), a material that is not native to the Peloponnese and must have been imported (Nakassis 2013: 8, 99, 146, 160, 224). Killen (1995) has argued, moreover, that a man named *Kuprios* is a "collector" at Knossos, and Olivier (2001) includes *Kuprios* in his list of "international collectors," whose names recur in prominent positions at multiple Mycenaean sites.[18] Thus, I hold out the possibility that Kuprios as a collector received "cloth and wool" as "benefits" from

[18]   At Pylos, Kuprios draws rations from Poseidon (or possibly, he is instead offering grain to the god). In the *Iliad* 15.639, we find "Kopreus the father of Periphētes, herald of Eurystheus." Eurystheus, king of Mycenae, is elsewhere known as the principal who sent his agent Heracles of Tiryns on various commissions (*aethloi* 'labors').

the palace and later made "payment" to the palace in the form of alum that he acquired overseas.[19]

The argument that the palace employed collectors to sell some of its textiles on the overseas market is strong, as it is based on the recording of a name in the genitive in some cases but in others not. Given that the palace sold some of its textiles through independent businesspersons, it seems safe to assume it was also willing to sell to them directly.

4. Indirect Evidence for Textile Trade: Adaptations in Ship Design and the (Alleged) Shipping Problem

Tartaron (2013: 61) tells us what we must know about changes in the design of Bronze Age Aegean vessels: images on pottery reveal "a fundamental transformation ... from Minoan oared sailing vessel to Mycenaean rowed galleys.... The Mycenaean galley moved toward a more purpose-built design. Although equipped with a mast and sail it featured a long, narrow hull that emphasized oar-driven speed at the expense of wind power and storage capacity."

From the changes in ship design, we may credibly infer changes in the objectives of their users. Mycenaean shippers had invested in a vessel not well suited to carry bulk cargo such as grain and amphorae filled with wine or oil. This changed what might be left behind at the other end of a journey from Greece. Obviously, findings of Mycenaean ceramics have become less likely than in earlier times and, if found, it is more likely than earlier that they were carried in the holds of vessels belonging to third parties, such as Phoenicians, or even to have been produced by locals at the destination. It might very well appear to observers in later times that the Mycenaeans had, mysteriously, ceased to voyage wherever.

Where, however, was the Mycenaean *wherever*? Somewhere that placed a premium on compact cargoes that were of high enough value to make the voyage economically worthwhile. Somewhere that had something compact and of high value to make the return trip economically worthwhile. Somewhere ships could not depend on wind for sailing and benefited from exceptional speed. Where else than the Black Sea region with its perverse perennial winds and currents?[20]

---

[19] Also, it is known that there were facilities such as the Northeast Building at Pylos which may be understood as a place for "redistribution-type records" (Bendall 2003: 224). Bennet and Halstead (2014; 276–277) have suggested that *o-no* ('benefit'/'payment') transactions typically had a short "shelf-life."

[20] Sailing vessels were often queued up at the western entrance of the Dardanelles, waiting for the strong-prevailing northeast wind to slacken (Korfmann 1986b: 6–7). It's no wonder, as Korfmann (1986b: 8) notes, that Homer often speaks (seven times) of *ēnemoessa* "windy" Ilios (e.g. *Iliad* 3.305). I do not distinguish between Homer's Ilios and his Troy (*Troiē*). It may be that Ilios is

Where else but a Black Sea region that was capable of paying for luxuries with gold? What else was the incoming cargo except the purple- and gold-colored textiles advertised by the frescoes in the palace showrooms? For these products, the question was not "do you love them?" but "can you afford them?"

The Mycenaeans did not adopt the new streamlined oared galley because they wished to give luxury textiles as gifts. They were intent on carrying into the Black Sea small quantities of luxury textiles and returning to Greece with gold. The great speed produced by numerous oarsmen facilitated the daunting passage into the Black Sea. However, the oared galley had not only speed. The numerous hands that gripped the oars propelling the vessel might instead grasp spears that discouraged the greedy intentions of pirates (Tartaron 2013: 63–64). The numerous spears also served to discourage royal tax collectors. Further, on occasion the crew of the galley might themselves become effective pirates when a rich target happened to present itself.

The oared galley represents the kind of risky investment that cautious investors would fear to make: deviating from the older all-purpose design (seems to) involve reducing revenues by throwing away cargo space and simultaneously increasing costs by requiring larger crews. However, it is precisely this kind of counterintuitive innovation that spurred an entrepreneurial decision to specialize in producing purple-dyed textiles for the Black Sea region.[21] It was an element in a radical business plan conceived by Mycenaeans that arguably made *vertically integrated* textile-producing enterprises (palaces) both necessary and successful.[22]

Tartaron (2013: 68), who cites Wedde (2005), is certainly correct about the importance of the oared galley, which entrepreneurs designed to overcome the difficulties they experienced while trading in the Black Sea region:

> Iconographic representations of the Mycenaean galley are virtually absent until the mature palatial phase of LH IIIB, but since the Mycenaean world had experienced tremendous growth economically

---

the capital city and Troy the country (del Valle Munoyerro 1997/1998; and below). There is a strong, prevailing outward current at the western entrance of the Dardanelles (Agourides 1997: 3; Korfmann 1986b: 6–7). Mycenaean ships were shallow-draught ("keelless") vessels, and when it was necessary to find shelter or wait out a delay, they could be beached on sandy bays like the Achaean ships Greek ships besieging Troy.

21 The Bronze Age Greeks were not just swashbucklers. Archaeological evidence points to the existence of, at least partially, paved roads in fifteenth-century Minoan Crete and thirteenth-century Mycenaean Greece (Jansen 1997). Note, for example, the "fine paved road leading directly to the sea [at Kommos in southern Crete] from inland central Crete" (Warren 1989: 3).

22 There will be much more to say about the cycle of vertical integration and vertical disintegration in discussing the "collapse" of the Mycenaean palatial system of producing textiles in Chapter 17.

and politically by LH IIIA2—including the emergence of palaces at Mycenae, Tiryns, Thebes, and Pylos—there is reason to believe that *the galley was part of this transformation....* The rapid development of the galley could be explained in terms of a feedback loop between a dramatic increase in overseas interaction in LH IIIA2-IIIB1 on the one hand and innovations in technology on the other. (emphasis added)

Prior to the oared galley, not many large-sailed ships traversed the Dardanelles and the Sea of Marmara and into the Black Sea, if they even came at all.[23] Instead, for most, if not all, *Troy*/Hisarlik[24] represented a trans-shipment point (Korfman 1986b; Easton, Hawkins, Sheratt and Sheratt 2002: 104). Alternatively, cargoes were sent from Troy overland to the Black Sea region (Şahoğlu 2005: 352). This changed with the oared galley and its cargo of luxury textiles and then gold.[25] In my view, Troy remained even more centrally and profitably positioned under the new trading scenario.[26]

Singer (2008: 27) is on target: "To the growing list of Cretan export items, including itinerant artists, we should now add purple-dyed textiles, typical luxury objects of high value and very low bulk." The question of Greek navigation to the shores of the Black Sea during the Mycenaean period remains an open question for some scholars. However, the proposition also has active supporters, including Hiller (1991) and Lordkipanidze (2001). To this number, I add myself. The dating of this penetration remains open for discussion.

5. Indirect Evidence for Textile Trade: Gold, Gold, and More Gold

Cline (2007: 195–196) remarks on the relatively small number of worked artifacts from Anatolia found in the Late Bronze Age Aegean: "Put succinctly ...

---

[23] Korfmann (1986b) thinks it unlikely that the Ulu Burun ship would have passed on into the Black Sea. I am not sure why.

[24] The reference to the role of "Troy" is explained and justified shortly.

[25] Was the *Argo* just lucky (favored by the gods) or was it the first oared galley? It certainly had an ample crew and only *fleeces* and a *golden fleece* stand out as cargo.

[26] Grethlein (2009: 124) objects: "To begin with, the thesis that Troy was a major trading port not only rests on shaky ground but it also runs the risk of falsely projecting modern notions of trade onto an archaic system based on the exchange of goods.... The interpretation of Troy as an important city and port is supported by the desire to lend significance to the site and to facilitate connecting it to the *Iliad*." "Importance" can be a most difficult concept to define (see Chap. 8.2) but the *market* trade of luxury textiles, tin, and lapis lazuli (from Assur in Assyria) in exchange for precious metals (from Kanesh in Cappadocia) is extremely well documented in the correspondence of independent Assyrian merchants dating from the early second millennium BCE. Call this trade "archaic" or call it "modern" but surely call it "important" to the participants. Certainly, Troy might have been important in the same way as Kanesh was.

there is still no good evidence for trade between the Central Anatolian Hittites and Mycenaeans during the Late Bronze Age." This line of analysis regarding "good evidence" is lacking in several respects. This section moves from Cline's evaluation to a consideration of what findings in the Aegean would constitute good evidence of trade.

First, trade between Mycenaeans/Minoans and Anatolians did not require Anatolians (Mycenaeans) to accompany their traded goods together with their various personal, professional, and cultic artifacts to the shores of their trading partner. That is, the physical transfer may have been the province of third parties who carried along "worked artifacts" not of Anatolian (Mycenaean) making but of their own. Alternatively, Mycenaeans (Anatolians) did accompany their traded goods, but they had little interest in or *valuable space* for Anatolian (Mycenaean) artifacts in their ships.

Second, we do not have reason to believe that the Mycenaeans expected to be compensated for the textiles they brought with them with Anatolian ceramics or their contents. Cline does not explain why he would expect to find numbers of worked artifacts from Anatolia in Mycenaean centers. It is true that anthropologically-oriented archaeologists sometimes misplace ancient men and women in small, face-to-face societies and then assume they were motivated to acquire foreign exotic objects for prestige (discussion S. C. Murray 2017: 11–14). Of course, prestige, now and in the past, is a human value, but there are many ways of earning it.

Granted, there is a reason that Minoan/Mycenaean ceramics, especially figurines, signal Mycenaean trade contacts in Anatolia. Traders brought their figurines to the Black Sea region for purposes of worship, display of garments (see Chap. 1), and the swearing of oaths. Some figures were inevitably left behind there. Furthermore, after an acclimation period, local residents may have been attracted to Minoan/Mycenaean cultural/religious traits, leading them to acquire foreign ceramics (Vetters 2016: 41). Obviously, textiles, unlike ceramics, only very rarely leave an archaeological footprint. Still, a credible vision of textile exports is unlikely to emerge solely from counting ceramics.

Fortunately, there is an obvious candidate for the main Minoan/Mycenaean *import* from Anatolia: *gold*. Gold was not *economically* available in Bronze Age Greece: that is, the existing sources were either unknown or could be exploited only at a prohibitive or relatively high cost compared to other available sources.[27]

---

[27] There is no evidence that "gold sources situated in the Aegean, Siphnos in the Cyclades, or Thasos close to the Thracian shores were exploited before historical times" (Laffineur 2010: 446). It has been suggested that Mycenaeans earned gold by helping the Pharaohs drive out the Hyksos. There is no evidence for such service; this "classic" view is based on an ideological conception of the Mycenaeans. Moreover, Laffineur (2010: 446) notes "the fact that the

Under these circumstances, foreign gold not only qualifies as an exotic object but also is desired because it buys other valued things. Moreover, the possession of gold is measurable. The Mycenaean/Minoan palaces were in actual fact *"rich in gold,"* and the accumulation of gold and other wealth began even before the rise of the palatial system.

During the last phases of Middle Helladic (MH III) to the beginning of LH II A (ca. 1650–1520), much wealth was deposited in graves. Most strikingly, in the Shaft Graves at Mycenae:

> The distinctive feature of the Shaft Graves is the extraordinary quantity and quality of the gifts, especially those in the graves of Circle A, wherein some cases the expense becomes conspicuous waste. Alongside the famous gold ornaments such as headbands, masks and a sceptre, ... there is a profusion of jewels, arms, pots in clay and often precious metals, amber and other exotic items, and ritual objects such as rhytons and sacred knots.
>
> de Fidio 2008: I 88

Swords were ubiquitous in the burial goods of Mycenaean men together with gold signet rings depicting duels. However, some of the swords interred in the Shaft Graves had gold hilts and so were non-functional (Kramer-Hajos 2016: 39 with references).

Previously, a dead body was laid out in a contracted position with few accompanying goods. Now the dead body was featured in an area for display: "in the Shaft Graves bodies are laid out and sometimes literally covered with gold.... Similar finds from elsewhere in the Argolid, Laconia, Messenia, and Central Greece suggest that the Shaft Graves were not an isolated phenomenon (Kramer-Hajos 2016: 39 with references and discussion of the layout of Shaft Graves).[28]

The excavation of gold in tombs continues to the present day. In 2019, excavations in Pylos revealed two large Bronze Age tombs, both previously looted, in

---

enrichment had begun at Mycenae before the Late Helladic I phase, in the late Middle Helladic and traditional grave circle B, though on a more limited scale, and that it consequently predates the end of the Hyksos dynasty in Egypt has been considered as a major obstacle to the Egyptian theory." It may be added that none of these theories about the origin of the Mycenaean gold explain why they produced textiles and why Troy mattered: the Black Sea region provided the cost-effective channel for obtaining gold.

[28] Kramer-Hajos (2016: 39) attributes the change in Mycenaean burial practice with its evident "conspicuous consumption" to contact with another culture (the Minoans). This may be true, but a sufficient explanation is that the practitioners of conspicuous consumption had become very rich in gold. Conspicuous consumption is inherent in human nature, otherwise, we would be unable to explain its first manifestation.

which were discovered thousands of pieces of gold foil from sheets of gold that had originally lined the floors. "Both the [already published] Griffin Warrior and the two tholos tombs belong on a pottery-based time scale to a period known as Late Helladic IIA, which lasted from 1600 to 1500 B.C.E., although the exact dates are disputed."[29]

It very much appears that exotic pieces like the "Golden Bees Pendant" from Malia, which was found in the mostly looted tomb called Chrysolakkos ("Pit of Gold"), were produced by Greek craftsmen (Laffineur 2010: 447ff.). Again, such pieces loudly signal generalized wealth when found in graves even after centuries of tomb looting.[30]

Gold is also plentiful in the Linear B tablets. Numerous Pylos tablets mention gold, including in large amounts.[31] One Pylos tablet (PY Tn 316) records that, in the month *Plowistos* ('of navigation(?)'), the gifts presented to the gods and heroes included [thirteen] gold kylikes (two-handled wide drinking cups) and chalices as well as people (Luján 2010: 28; Lupack 2011: 210–211). The most reasonable interpretation of a tablet from Pylos (PY Ae 303) is that fourteen slaves were purchased for gold. Furthermore, the collection of different quantities of gold as contributions from various relevant characters of the kingdom of Pylos is registered on the (reconstructed) tablet PY Jo 438. The quantities range from, approximately, one kg. to sixty grams, but there does not seem to be a correlation between the [official] rank of the person and the quantity of gold provided. Chadwick (1998: 33) has estimated the total quantity of gold transferred by palace officials to be between five and six kg.—an amount he sees as too large to be repeated with regularity, even in a "wealthy kingdom." Bendall (2003: 212) suspects the transfers represent tax payments. If so, they might well be regular tax payments in a very wealthy kingdom. "*This tablet shows, at least, that gold may have circulated inside the Mycenaean kingdoms*" (Luján 2010: 30; emphasis added).

Moreover, Iolcus in Bronze Age Thessaly, the port that launched the Argonauts to Colchis, possessed gold of *alluvial origin*—an origin that, as will be demonstrated shortly, is in ample supply in the Black Sea region. Finally, while graves and Linear B tablets are our main source for gold riches in Greece, gold objects have recently been found in the small settlement Chrysi in eastern Crete that, significantly, was an early center for the production of murex-dye (Chap. 7.2).

---

[29] Available for download at: https://www.nytimes.com/2019/12/17/science/tombs-archaeology-ancient-greece.html (accessed February 16, 2020).

[30] Sources: Tomkins and Schoep 2010: 75; Laffineur 2010: 444 with Fig. 33.1, 446.

[31] See Nakassis 2013: Appendix Entries 29, 33, 145, 182, 199, 227, 312, 449, 525, 617, 652, 710, 821, and 948.

These findings are most important because although gold is not perishable, it is liquid—that is, it tends to flow from the hands of the first recipients to sometimes distant third parties.[32] That so much gold remained stuck in Minoan and Mycenaean hands is first a tribute to the affluence that permitted them while living and while dead to indulge in the human taste for beautiful golden objects (Whittaker 2006). Just as importantly, I think, it attests to an ongoing trade relationship with the Black Sea region—that is, gold is caught in Mycenaean hands, so to speak, *in mediis rebus*, caught before it can continue its flow into other hands.[33]

The Mycenaeans had much gold, and I am suggesting that they traded for it in Anatolia. What did they give in return? My fifth, long-delayed response to Cline is that there is no reason to assume that Anatolians (primarily those in the Black Sea region) expected to be compensated for *their gold* by exotic Mycenaean objects.

Interestingly, there are a few such finds in the Black Sea region, but, as noted by Kolb (2004: 592), "As for the Caucasus region, the Mycenaean-type swords discovered there seem to belong to the *Early Mycenaean period*, and not to the 15th–13th centuries" (emphasis added). Kolb (2004: 592–593; emphasis added) points to a variety of objects (swords, double-headed axes, spearheads, oxhide copper ingots, pottery, and sandstone anchors) with Mycenaean connections that have been found in the Black Sea region, but then he correctly notes,

> There is, however, no indication that such objects were transported by ship through the Dardanelles and the Bosporus; they may very well have been carried on overland routes. *In sum, at present, not one single object found in the Black Sea region can safely be considered to be the result of Bronze Age sea trade through the Dardanelles and the Bosporus.*

There are problems here. First, the Mycenaeans and Black Sea residents may have traded overland around the Dardanelles (Şahoğlu 2005: 352). An overland transfer would raise transportation costs but would not necessarily be prohibitive. Perhaps the cargoes were transferred in wagons—that is, over real roads. The earliest known three-dimensional evidence for spoked wheels comes from eighteenth-century BCE Anatolia (Littauer and Crouwel 1986). More seriously, Kolb's logic is uncomfortable: why not say that we cannot safely exclude a single

---

[32]   There is already considered evidence (the mysterious little sacks) that the Mycenaeans gifted gold to Egyptian officials and rulers. I would assume that Mycenae paid with gold for the green marble used for the façade of the "Treasury of Atreus."

[33]   Kopcke (2016) cites the findings of Mycenaean-styled made-of-gold swords in Transylvania and theorizes about the movement of Carpathian gold by force from Crete to Mycenae's Shaft Graves.

object found in the Black Sea region from having come through the Dardanelles *and Bosporus?*[34] Is this conclusion in any way inferior to Kolb's formulation? I think not.

Perhaps matters may be improved by looking at *probable origin* instead of at *possible origin*. Mycenaean swords may have arrived "by way of the well-known trade routes connecting the Caucasus with Mesopotamia and the Levant"; Mycenaean objects found on the northern shores of the Black Sea may have arrived by way of "trade routes along the Adriatic coast of Greece and the river valleys of Macedonia and Thrace"; "It is also possible that ships landed on the west coast of Thracian Chersonesus, where at Ainos, on the mouth of the Hebros River, vestiges of a Bronze Age settlement have been discovered, whence merchandise could have been transported by mules or donkeys parallel to the west coast of the Marmara Sea and the Bosporus to the shore of the Black Sea"; the stone anchors "may be local imitations of Mediterranean shapes since Eastern Mediterranean anchors were well known to Balkan traders who were in contact with the Aegean world" (quotations from Kolb 2004: 592–593).

But against Kolb's options, I advance the following propositions: (1) Mycenaeans were positioned in western Anatolia and at Troy itself; (2) the Mycenaean oared galley was capable of expeditiously penetrating through the Dardanelles and returning with a cargo;[35] and (3) the substantial investment in constructing Troy's [Hisarlik's] citadel (Kolb 2004: 599), even in its earliest incarnations,[36] would not have been made without a very good economic reason. Troy was not built and rebuilt by means of gifts. So, what was the good reason?

Kolb (2004: 598–599) is more interested in discussing bad reasons. There is no archaeological evidence that supports the local production of export-quality textiles or transport containers, or attractive ceramics, or even the provision of administrative services.[37] Thus, the question raised by the archaeological evidence is not so much whether Troy "was a city at all" (Kolb 2004: 499–500) but why Troy even existed at all! Kolb, although he insists on evidence, presents none to answer this question. There is evidence suggesting that Kolb vastly underestimates the importance of Troy.

In this respect, Bachhuber's (2009: 7–8) appraisal merits quotation:

---

[34] The evidence for finds of Minoan and Mycenaean objects and inscriptions is taken up in detail in Chapter 9.

[35] For a summary of the weak textual and strong iconographic evidence for Mycenaean use of the oared galley especially in LHIIIB and LHIIIC, see Yasur-Landau 2010: 48–50 with Figures 2.4 and 2.5, 104–106.

[36] Troy I's wall is made of stone like other coastal sites but unlike several inland sites whose walls were of mudbrick (Mac Sweeney 2018: 40).

[37] I am not aware of any archaeological evidence suggesting that Troy exported grain or wine or any other agricultural or marine products.

The surge of monumentality in Troia Iia-f (phase Iic-e) included the construction of the central megaron complex, which remains to this day the largest building in the Early Bronze Age of western and central Anatolia, the construction of the monumentalising Gate FM and an expansion and woolen industry generally and strengthening of the citadel fortifications. These architectural developments correspond with the earliest identification of Syrian forms in western Anatolia.... Clearly the horizons of Troy had expanded, observed most poignantly in the exotic objects and materials that comprise part of the Trojan treasures.

In Troy VI, the area enclosed by the fortification wall more than doubled (Mac Sweeney 2018: 49–51). Even putting aside the problem of whether the lower settlement was protected by a defensive wall (Mac Sweeney 2018: 51), the Trojan structures and treasure make clear that the Trojans had much worth safeguarding.

With respect to the Trojan administration, five (5) Mycenaean seals were found in the cemetery at Besika Bay (see Chap. 14.3.f). Admittedly, not a large number, but then not all/many Mycenaean seal owners would have died while visiting Troy. There is significant evidence of Trojan facilitation of foreign commerce:

> [A]t Troy, from the second half of the third millennium BC, multiple weight systems were in use, which clearly indicate Near Eastern and, more precisely, eastern Mediterranean contacts with the settlement.... [T]he balance weights at Troy were found in public buildings ('palaces' or 'temples'), gates (i.e., public buildings within or by gates) and treasures (found in or in association with public buildings), in contexts with artifacts related to craftsmen and cultic activities, as well as to trade.
>
> Bobokhyan 2009: 44–45

In addition, Bobokhyan (2009: 41) explains that the balance weights are found in the same archaeological context as objects used in textile production, such as whorls and loom-weights.

Various explanations have been offered for the absence of writing in the settled area of Troy.[38] One possible factor is that the Trojan authorities did not

---

[38] "One possibility is that the archives have been lost or destroyed, likely by Schliemann's hasty excavations. Also possible is that the Trojans wrote on a perishable material, which has not been preserved in the archeological record. After all, a letter from a Hittite King in the mid-thirteenth century mentions wooden writing tablets sent to the king of Troy [the Milawata Letter CTH 182 = AhT5]" (Mac Sweeney 2018: 52). Add to Mac Sweeney's argument that fragments of a

centrally control the production of commodities like the Mycenaean/Minoan palaces did. One finds in the Mycenaean centers administrative documents—not letters, not historical inscriptions, and not literature, all of which surely must have flourished there. Troy's economy arguably was mainly oriented towards the provision of *services* for foreigners, such as banking and prostitution (see Silver 2019: Sections VI and VII) and, of course, with the collection of duties and other fees. Accordingly, archaeologists would be more likely to find buried treasure than archives.

The treasures are well-illustrated in the so-called "King Priam's Treasure" (from Troy II 2550–2300) and visually documented in Tolstikov and Treister (1996). Bachhuber (2016: 357) conceptually links the treasures of Troy with the woolen industry generally and with dyed-purple cloth in particular. The city was well-positioned to act as an intermediary (Branigan 1974: 63) by acquiring gold in the Black Sea region and, I argue, offering it for Minoan and Mycenaean textiles.[39] The nearby islands of Lemnos and Lesbos—both centers for the purple dyeing of textiles—also stand out in this connection with the possession of gold (Laffineur 2010: 443–444 with references).

At this point, we are finally close to seeing the light at the end of the tunnel. Much documentation and argument have been brought forward to establish that the Mycenaeans were very rich in gold and that the Troy discovered by the archaeologists was a substantial and expensive-to-build and maintain city. As such, it was a city that could not have existed without strong demand for traders—royal and private—to sail from the Aegean into the Black Sea.[40] It has been proposed that the Mycenaeans obtained their gold by rowing through the Dardanelles in their oared galleys and trading their quality textiles for it in the Black Sea region.[41] It has not yet been established, however, whether it is plausible to trace the Mycenaean (and Trojan) gold to the Black Sea region. Was there, in fact, relatively easy gold beyond the Dardanelles?

---

wooden writing board set were found in the Ulu Burun wreck dated to the fourteenth century BCE (discussed by Payton 1991).

[39] Kirk (1990: 40) suggests, "No signs of booty that might have come from Troy have been found in Greece, for what that is worth." It is not worth much as evidence against a historical Trojan War because Kirk does not reveal how he knows whether the gold found in Greece came there from Troy. Without a test, one might just as easily say, "Much (or even all) of the gold found in Greece came from Troy."

[40] Previously unnoticed elements in the *Iliad* and *Odyssey* offer strong support for this conclusion about the role of Troy and Mycenaean/Black Sea trade relations.

[41] In this context, to insist on Anatolian artifacts as a measure of Bronze Age Greek imports not only falsifies the commodity composition of trade but also trivializes trade itself. The objection is not to the use of "archaeological evidence" (S. C. Murray 2017: 18–21) but to the use of evidence that is not very relevant. Much of this kind of material should be regarded as souvenirs or presents brought home by sailors or other visitors (Pini 2004: 778, 780).

The provenancing of gold is a most difficult problem because, to begin with, it is so often recycled and mixed (Evely 2010: 391). However, the Black Sea region (not Central Anatolia) is rich in gold, most famously alluvial gold as is attested in ancient authors such as Strabo 11.2.19 and Appian *Roman History* 12.103. This testimony about local gold finds support in numerous findings in burials, especially of the first half of the fifth to the third century BCE. These include magnificent diadems and necklaces that are artistically related to gold objects of earlier times, thus suggesting local production.[42]

We may also cite contemporary regional studies—such as Okrostsvaridze, Bluashvili, and Gagnidze (2014), and Okrostsvaridze, Gagnidze, and Akimidze (2016)—that have examined past and present gold-bearing bedrock and placer gold contents of the Svaneti region and found them to be a viable source of the alluvial "gold sands." Okrostsvaridze, Gagnidze, and Akimidze (2016) explain their findings:

> Generally placer gold is widely distributed in almost all alluvial river systems draining important bedrock gold districts of the world. Mobilization and transportation of the erosional products of the weathering of these deposits are the source of alluvial gold. The coarsest gold scales or grains (i.e.> 0.5 mm) accumulate near the mineralization sources while the finer-grained gold particles are carried several kilometers from the source by water flows. During transport and subsequent deposition the gold grains undergo significant changes ... in the shape, size and chemical composition.... As a result of dissolution and reprecipitation after deposition, the gold grains may increase in size and a "cleansing" of contained iron, copper, and other impurities takes place; this leads to an increase in the fineness of the gold grains. Svaneti placer gold is mainly found in alluvial sediments. Goldbearing alluvial sands (gold sands) or gold placers in Svaneti are widespread and the scale of their distribution varies from few to hundreds of meters.

Further:

---

[42] Sources: Chqonia 1981 and Nadiradze 1990. Braund (1994: 21) objects that Colchian (Black Sea region) gold artifacts are "found in any quantity from the fifth century BC before the seventh century there is almost nothing." The first problem is how to decide whether a gold artifact found *outside* Colchis originated in Colchis. The second problem is Braund's implicit assumption that exporters of goods to Colchis wished the gold they earned to be turned into Colchian objects. Certainly, gold has other uses and, moreover, the Mycenaeans and Minoans were capable of making their own gold objects. Basically, even if it is true that very few of the gold objects found in Colchis are earlier than the fifth century BCE, they still testify that the gold had *always* been in the Colchian rivers.

Given the large area of bedrock gold mineralization, and its relation to the headwaters of the primary river system in the region, we think that the Svaneti goldfield should be one of the main suppliers of alluvial gold of the Svaneti region.

The findings of Hauptmann and Klein (2009: 80) are important, but I found them to be rather tentative and somewhat unclear. However, they do confirm gold mining in Georgia: excavations proved that the Svaneti (Sakdrissi) gold mine is the oldest in the world, and gold was available in the Black Sea region from the streams and upstream in the placers and in the bedrock itself.[43] A later study by Stöllner and Gambashidze (2011) supports systematic gold production beginning as early as 3,000 BCE.

Eighteen gold objects from a Mycenaean tholos at Kasanaki (Volos, Greece), a site corresponding to the mythical center of Iolcus, were analyzed by means of ion beam techniques at the Center for Research and Restoration of the Museums of France (C2RMF). Consistently with Strabo's (11.2.19) account of panning gold in Colchian streams, the analysis found that the two gold objects tested had the high level of tin that is a normal characteristic of the exploitation of an alluvial deposit. However, while the findings are supportive of an alluvial origin for the golds, it is not possible to determine their origins. More specifically, it is not possible to determine whether the golds originated in the Volos region or in Colchis (modern Georgia), because no geochemical reference is known for either location (Adrimi-Sismani, Guerra, and Walter: 2009).

Also, in a paper published in 1983, Muhly (1983: 3–4), relying on the research of Hartmann, reported that gold from a grave in Mycenae was free of tin and platinum as was one type of gold ("B gold") from Varna on the Bulgarian coast of the Black Sea. So, these golds would not have been alluvial (or placer gold) as in the study of Adrimi-Sismani et al. (2009). The two golds might have had a common source, but, noting the absence of local gold in Mycenae, the latter gold might have originated in the Black Sea region. The "B gold" amounted to about 20% of the Mycenaean sample. However, Muhly is generally critical of Hartmann's findings citing problems of reuse and alloying.[44]

---

[43] Also worthy of note is the sensational Valchitran Gold Treasure (13 gold vessels with a gold content of about 88% with a combined weight of more than 25 pounds of pure gold) from northwestern Bulgaria that has been dated, for reasons unknown to me, to the second half of the second millennium BCE. Source: http://archaeologyinbulgaria.com/2019/05/08/ancient-thraces-largest-gold-treasure-valchitran-treasure-to-be-shown-in-bulgairas-black-sea-city-burgas-for-the-first-time/ (accessed February 12, 2021).

[44] I have been unable to obtain Hartmann's latest study (Hartmann 1982), so I quote Treister's (1996: 231) summary: "Research has shown that the majority of articles from Poliochni [in Lemnos], including lobed earrings, which have been analyzed were made of gold containing platinum of the group known as RS. A. Hartmann ascertained that the source location of this

Finally, more useful analysis of some items of gold from Early Bronze Age Colonna in the island of Aegina, about 17 miles from Athens, and from Akrotiri in Thera (in the Later Bronze Age) are consistent with the use of alluvial gold (Pantazis et al.: 2003; Reinholdt 2008).

With all due reservations and caveats, a body of evidence ranging from ancient commentators to Colchian burials to contemporary surveys to scientific tests points to the Black Sea area as the ultimate source of Minoan/Mycenaean (and Trojan) gold (Legarra 2019: 107). The postulated textiles-for-gold theme is captured nicely in a reconstructed gold headband from Pylos that bears the image of a Mycenaean oared galley with a long bird-headed stem (Blegen and Rawson 1973: 16 Fig. 108a–f; Kramer-Hajos 2016: 132). I think this Section has accomplished its objective of credibly linking the gold of the Black Sea region with the ample gold possessed by the Mycenaeans. It becomes technically possible and credible that the Mycenaeans and Minoans traded their luxury textiles with the Black Sea Region for gold, *but this is not yet a certainty.*

6. Toward Certainty of Trading Connections: Linear A Inscriptions, Linear B Toponyms, Settlements, and "Incidentals"

Obviously, for Region A to trade with Region B, the two must have contact— whether direct or indirect. There are several indicators of the kinds of contacts that might serve as precursors of trade. As noted in the discussion of findings in Akrotiri (Chap. 4.3), the most important is an *inscription* written in the language of Region A (B) that is found in the territory of Region B (A). Moreover, by examining the media bearing the inscription, clay, bone, stone, or metal, it is often possible to determine whether an inscription in the language of Region A (B) was made in Region A (B) or locally in the region where it was found.

This section first focuses on Minoan inscriptions found in Anatolia with special reference to the Black Sea region. It then moves on to consider references in the Linear B tablets to toponyms in Anatolia. The final task is the examination of ceramic connections among Greece, Lemnos, Troy, and the Black Sea.

Linear A inscriptions are most common in Crete itself, but also in the Troad and even beyond. Specifically, out of nine (9) Linear A "inscriptions" found outside Greece,[45] five (5) were found in or near the Troad, in western Anatolia,

---

group was in the Aegean Basin or surrounding areas. Gold from the same source was also used as analysis has shown in the Mycenaean area (Hartmann 1982, 32, 46–47, tab, 31' pl. 103)."

[45] By Greece, I mean Crete, the Greek islands, and mainland Greece.

or the Black Sea region: Samothrace (SA Wc 1), Troy (TRO Zg 1–2), Miletus (MIL Zb 1), Amisos of Pontus (Bossert 1942: Abb. 6).[46]

What might be the objective of Minoans traveling to Anatolia? Perhaps they were not traders but tourists, or diplomats, or soldiers. Even so, it is difficult to imagine the latter forms of contact in the absence of a previously established trading relationship. The "flag" has often been known to follow the trader.[47] Thus, the finding of a Linear A inscription would credibly signal a direct trade relationship between Crete and Anatolia. This would be the case whether the Minoans brought the inscribed object with them from Greece or inscribed it sometime after they arrived in Anatolia. Suppose, on the other hand, that the Linear A inscription was brought to Anatolia by a third party. The logical candidates for this role would be Syrians/Phoenicians with a strong implication of a mediated trading relationship between Crete and Anatolia.[48] A third possibility is that Linear A was inscribed by native Anatolians. Although Minoan Linear A is presently undeciphered, it, like Mycenaean Linear B, is designed for ease in recording production quantities and keeping track of transfers (Olivier 1986: 379). Hence, the native Anatolians who were familiar with the Aegean scripts would almost surely be local trading agents of the Aegeans. Thus, while not infallible, the presence of Linear A (or Linear B) inscriptions in Anatolia signals the presence there of individuals who were commercially motivated.[49]

Of course, the *content* of the inscription might also be revealing. The very important materials from Samothrace that suggest the presence there of Potnia of the Labyrinth is reserved for extended discussion in Chapter 11.1.[50]

Regarding the Miletus Linear A inscription, Palaima (AEGEANET, July 25, 1996) suggests that Sign no. 1 (L 1/AB 56) occurs infrequently not only in Mycenaean Greek Linear B but in a pattern of alternative spellings that clearly shows that the sign was retained by the Mycenaean scribes to render, in precise

---

[46] I am excluding from consideration the *highly controversial* inscription from Drama, southeastern Bulgaria in the Black Sea region, (DRA Zg 1). See De Boer 2007–2008: 294–295 on the report of Benecke, Fecht, and Lichardus (2000: 159).

[47] See Silver (2015b) on Gallagher and Robinson's "Imperialism of Free Trade" applied to Roman Gaul.

[48] In the false tales of origin told by Odysseus (*Odyssey* 13.256–286, 14.199–359, 19.172–202), he is invariably a Cretan and, in the first two tales, Phoenicians and their ships play key roles. Sherratt (1996: 91) has noted: "For all that Homer avoids any suggestion of permanent Phoenician inhabitants as such, his Crete is clearly an island in which one regularly expects to encounter Phoenicians or find a Phoenician ship without too much trouble."

[49] Finkelberg (1998: 265) reports "many" of the Linear A inscriptions found in mainland Greece and especially the Cyclades were proven to be made locally. This issue has not, however, been subjected to rigorous study.

[50] A scholiast to Apollonius Rhodius *Argonautica* (1.917) tells that those initiated in the Samothrace Mysteries wore purple fillets.

spellings, Minoan anthroponyms, theonyms, and toponyms and also two Minoan loan words for a *special kind of vessel and a particular color used in dyeing textiles*. As such, AB 56 (along with AB 22 and AB 29) is closely connected with the phonological peculiarities of the Minoan language. This makes it nearly certain that the Linear A MIL Zb 1 represents a Minoan word.[51] If I understand correctly, the inscription has to do in some way with dyed textiles, which I have postulated is the Minoan export commodity.

More needs to be said about the Linear A inscription from the Pontus. The inscription is on a statuette of a ram (reportedly) from the Black Sea port of Samsun (ancient Amisos). The circumstances of the find are obscure. It is known that it was acquired by Professor Archibald and that a line drawing was published in 1935 by Evans (1964: 768) and then reproduced by Bossert (1942). The ram statuette was then housed in the Ashmolean Museum, which dated it to the mid-late first millennium CE, which makes the Linear A inscription a fake. Here is the strange part of the story: Evans (1964: 768) says that "a careful examination of the graffiti has assured me that the bulk of the signs represent a recognizable form of the Minoan linear Class A," and he adds in footnote 3, "Obviously the votive figure had been acquired by Professor Sayce in pre-Minoan days [that is, prior to the discovery/recognition of Linear A inscriptions]. In his MS., description it appears as a 'graffito inscription in an unknown script'." Assuming that (1) the inscription is really Linear A as it seems to be and that (2) Sayce would have recognized the inscription as Linear A once that script had been discovered in Knossos, we are left with the conclusion that someone forged a Linear A inscription before Linear A was even known! Am I missing something? If not, then I accept the ram as evidence of a Minoan contact with the Black Sea. Clearly, the fact that the inscription is on a ram from the Black Sea region evokes Jason and the Golden Fleece. It certainly evokes wool and, therefore, textiles. However, "too good to be true" does not constitute evidence of forgery. I have not seen any recent claims that the inscription is a forgery.

Various indications, albeit uncertain, suggest that most of the Linear A inscriptions were made where they were found (Finkelberg 1998: 265–272). Thus, there is evidence of direct connections—the Minoans were physically present in the areas where inscriptions were found, or else their agents, who had sufficient contact with Minoans to master Linear A, were.

In conclusion, Minoans had contact with Anatolia and the Black Sea region, and the contacts are most reasonably based on trade. Given an inscribed ram and a reference to the dyeing of cloth, a Minoan textile trade is credible.

---

[51] Finkelberg (1998: 265–266) reports that the Miletus pot is made from local clay and that the pot was inscribed before it was fired. As noted in Chapter 11.1, this means that Minoan traders or their local agents were present in Anatolia.

Next, mentions in documents from Region A (B) of persons, deities, or places native to Region B (A) indicate contact and potentially trade. As noted shortly, the Linear B tablets attest to the participation of individuals in the Mycenaean textile industry linked by nomenclature to western Anatolia and the islands on the sea lanes to the Troad, for example, "Lemnians." These foreigners may have been forcefully taken by Mycenaean raiders or purchased in slave markets. The alternative modes attest, albeit in different ways, to Greek participation in the Anatolian economy. However, Hittite and Linear B documents help to suggest that skilled foreigners *sold themselves into Mycenaean slavery.*

It might be objected, of course, that the Anatolian nomenclature refers to the type of work characteristically done in Greece by workers of local Greek origin. Even so, knowledge of characteristically Anatolian skills was most likely acquired during and because of trade relations.

Other individuals in Greece with foreign nomenclature—e.g. "the Milesian" or "Smintheus"—have unspecified local economic roles. Perhaps some were tourists, who would also say something about economic connections. Alternatively, they were "guests" from Anatolian centers who hoped to return home with luxury textiles to sell, which would say much more. Niemeier (2005: 12) reports the finding *at Miletus* of two fragments of pottery that seem to have Linear B signs.

I agree completely with Woudhuizen's (2009: 2) conclusion:

> Now, it seems unlikely to assume that the correspondence in the distribution of Linear A inscriptions outside Crete on the one hand and that of reflexes of foreign toponyms in the Linear B tablets on the other hand is due to mere chance. Therefore, we appear to have a pattern here, indicating Minoan and Mycenaean interest in the north-Aegean region, in particular that part giving access to the Black Sea. This interest, then, was no doubt for commercial reasons.

The commercial reason was the exchange of Greek luxury textiles for gold. Let us consider some specifics.

Woudhuizen (2009: 7–8) has collected thirty (30) Linear B forms related to toponyms located outside Crete and the Greek mainland (including Euboea). Of these, I would identify fifteen (15) with Anatolia, including, most importantly, Lemnos, Troy, and, apparently Colchis in the Black Sea region—a land made famous as the destination of Jason's quest for the Golden Fleece. There are also a number of references to Phoenician places. The findspots of Linear B inscriptions and the places referred to in Linear B tablets leave little room for doubt to the reality of Minoan and Mycenaean contacts with Anatolia, including person-to-person contacts, and, specifically, of contacts with the Troad and the Black Sea region. This is only a minimal statement of connections.

The connections were economic in nature, and, indeed, the Linear A inscribed ram from Samsun and the Linear B references to Colchis offer specific support for my hypothesis that Minoans and Mycenaeans traded purple-dyed textiles for gold from the Black Sea region.

The references to Colchis appear in three Linear B tablets: two from Knossos (KN Sd 4403, 4430, KN Fh 5465) and one from Pylos (PY Ea 59). Mention is made of *ko-ki-de-ja* 'Kolkheideos' and of *ko-ki-da* 'Kolkhidas', 'the man from Colchis' (Palaima 2004b: 454 with references).[52] Admittedly, most(?) Bronze Age scholars do not accept the reading "the man from Colchis": Sd 4403 (and 4430) deals with chariot wheel manufacture, and *ko-ki-da* is followed by *o-pa* 'workshop'. Hence, it is reasonable to understand that *ko-ki-da* is the name of the owner of the workshop. I don't think this explanation applies to *Kolkheideos* 'Colchian(?)'. In any event, the *Pylos* text series Ea deals with *landholding* so there is no obvious reason to think of the name of a chariot repairer/maker. Moreover, it is also quite possible that at Knossos, *Kolkhidas* is an ethnic name—that is, the bearer is *both* a chariot repairer and a "man from Colchis." In historical times, the name Kholkhos is often used for Colchian workers—slave and free (Braund and Tsetskhladze 1989: 121–123). Thus, "the man from Colchis" remains a valid and even the preferred reading, but it is not a certain reading.[53] On this basis, it takes a place in the body of evidence attesting Mycenaean trade with the Black Sea region.[54]

As already noted, the remains of a murex industry were discovered on the east coast of Lemnos. This industry is earlier, apparently much earlier, than the Mycenaean palaces and even than Homer's Trojan War. "[T]he existence of imported matt-painted vases, hand-made and usually of closed shapes, indicate [Lemnian] trade with the region of Magnesia and with Aegina, while sherds with a dark-on-light decoration attest to trading with Crete of the Old Palace Period [second half of 18th century BCE]" (Boulotis 2012).

---

[52] Eumelus, (fragment 2A), writing in the eighth century BCE, places Aēetēs among the Colchians in the Black Sea region.

[53] The basic problem remains that the Linear B form of Greek creates uncertainties in transliterations and the spelling of consonant clusters because it omits final consonants.

[54] The connection with the Black Sea and the Argonaut saga cannot be ignored merely because it is too good to be true. "Colchis" is not a late name, as it does appear in texts of the later second millennium BCE from Urartu and Assyria. Add that quite a number of names from the Argonaut story are mentioned in the Linear B tablets from Pylos (Hiller 1991: 214). These include early heroic names ending in *-eus*. Again, some of the names such as "Jason" (*i-wa-so*, PY Cn 655) can be rendered in other ways but not *Aiaia* (Aia).

A Mycenaean presence finds confirmation in the finding of two Mycenaean painted pottery fragments from Poliochni that have been dated from this period (LH IIB) and that also have probable Thessalian connections. I quote Cultraro (2005: 239):

> The first [of the fragments] belongs to the flat base of ES 224 Vapheio Cup.... The cylindrical lower profile suggests a shape in LH IIB. On the basis of the pale orange clay and of the fabric it may represent an import, probably from Mainland Greece. Vapheio Cups are well-documented in the central regions of Greece, namely in Thessaly and Phocis, and also four examples from Torone, in the middle peninsula of Chakidike, must be considered. Two Vapheio Cups from Atsitsa, in the island of Skyros, may also be considered.... The second fragment can be identified as the upper part of the body of a closed shape, probably a squat jug PS 87.... Good examples are from Phthiotis and Thessaly, where the squat jug PS 87 was very popular in LH IIB.... According to the quality of the clay and the decorative system the sherd from Poliochni is a *probable import from eastern Thessaly*. (emphasis added)

In addition, Cultraro (2005: 242) classifies as Late Helladic three fragments from Myrina on the western part of the island that are being held in Vienna [the Schachermeyer collection]. One of these, "a product of high quality" has "orange clay ... very similar to the Mycenaean pottery made in Thessaly and the vase from Myrina could be an import from there."

Also, later Mycenaean pottery of the twelfth and thirteenth centuries has been found on Lemnos (Guzowska and Yasur-Landau 1999: 475), and fragments of figurines (in human and animal form) were discovered on the small islet of Koukonisi: "Since Mycenaean figurines are extremely rare in this period in the islands or in Western Anatolia, their presence, as well as that of other Mycenaean objects, may indicate a different and a more intensive type of interaction than in the other islands at the same time" (Guzowska and Yasur-Landau 1999: 475). Perhaps the abandoning of figurines, used in swearing oaths (Chap. 8.5) and, especially, in syncretistic worship (Vetters 2016: 41) signals a relatively lengthy occupation. The name Koukonisi is opaque, but residents use "Koukos" to describe piles of stones (Boulotis 2012). This description brings to my mind the tholos tombs found on the Mycenaean mainland.[55]

"Mycenaean pottery found in Hephaistia," Boulotis (2012) explains, "and to a lesser degree in other Lemnian sites testifies to a widespread Mycenaean

---

[55] Eleven Mycenaean chamber tombs have been found in the area of Bronze Age Miletus (Niemeier 2005: 13).

presence on the island. Ceramics feature a double-mouthed cup that is found in Anatolia, the islands [Crete] and mainland Greece." On the other hand, "incised linear motifs, designed in horizontal lines—patterns of strips, triangles, and multi-shaped angles—were usually filled in with a white pigment. By their contrast with the red surface of the pots, one gets a strong impression that the decoration of these vessels was influenced by contemporary textiles" (Boulotis 2012). These vases combine with the presence of Minoans and Mycenaeans and a murex industry to reinforce the importance of purple dyeing for Lemnos' economy.

The connections established by ceramics run deep. Most importantly, Cultraro (2005: 243, 244) finds:

> The evidence from Troy, Samothrace and Lemnos calls for a re-evaluation of the Minoan pottery found in the level of *Phase 6 Mitte* at Pevkakia Magoula [later Demetrias about a mile from Volos on the coast of Thessaly], and suggests that Thessaly was involved in the trade relations between the Southern and Northern Aegean.... The evidence from Poliochni and from Koukonisi shows that trade relationships were established between the Northern Aegean and Mainland Greece from the last stage of the Middle Bronze Age. The Mycenaean material from Lemnos firstly confirms that the earliest Mycenaean imports to the Northern Aegean occur during the LH 1 and II, not LH IIIA/2 IIIB1 as previously thought.

That the earliest contact of Greece with Troy may have been from the eastern coast of Thessaly finds additional support in Neutron Activation Analysis of fragments from Troy VI e-f level supporting a possible Thessalian provenance for a fragment of Albastron FS 83 (Cultraro 2005: 244).[56]

Linear A and Linear B inscriptional evidence, connecting Greece with Anatolia and the Black Sea region, has already been considered. Next, having dealt with ceramic evidence connecting mainland Greece—including Thessaly with Crete, with Lemnos, and then with Troy —the next step is to consider Black Sea connections. Mycenaean clay pots are widely scattered along the Anatolian coast from Troy to Tarsus (especially Caria) and in the Black Sea region during the period from LH III A1 to the end of LH III B1 (ca. 1420/10-1250). The quantity of findings in the Black Sea is small (de Boer 2006–2007), but a concentration of Mycenaean pots and double-headed axes comes from Mashat located about eighty-one miles from the southern Black Sea coast. One double-headed axe was found on the western shore of the Black Sea (Harding 1984: 238).

[56] Troy VI is dated middle 15th BCE end 1300–1250; VIIa 1250–1175.

It might be objected that trade between Greece and Anatolia during the Bronze Age could not have been very significant in the absence of settlements of foreigners (discussed by Malkin 1998: 132ff.). However, this kind of perspective underestimates the importance of trading stations inhabited by foreign merchants. Thus, Boulotis (2009: 207) thinks of settled Minoan trading groups on the islet Koufonisi (Lemnos) as comparable to the Assyrian textile traders in Kanesh in Cappadocia in the early second millennium BCE. As mentioned previously at several points, the latter merchants arranged for the production of valuable textiles in Assur and then had them shipped on donkeys to Kanesh. On the other side of the Aegean from Lemnos, in palatial times, a Pylos tablet (PY Fr 1206) reveals the presence of a Potnia with the epithet *a-si-wi-ja*—that is "Asian (Assuwan) Potnia" (Nikoloudis 2008a: 49). We may assume that this epithet is not a complete abstraction—that is, Potnia not only came from Asia but she also had Asian "congregants." As owner of a "House of the Asians," Potnia was tithed by and served emigrant Anatolians who would have been traders (see also Chaps. 6.2 and 11.5).[57]

There is perhaps evidence for the regularized presence of Anatolian traders in mainland Greece at Lerna located in the Argolid very near Tiryns on the Gulf of Argos. The reference is to about 220 sealings[58] (more than seventy distinct seal types) deposited in the substantial "House of the Tiles" (a "Corridor House") in Early Helladic IIB-Lerna III (2700–2200 BCE) long before the time of the Mycenaean palaces (megara). Except perhaps in myth (Hera), there is no evidence for the identity of the local protective deity.

According to Weingarten (1997) and also Weingarten et al. (2011: 156), experts on sealing practices, the Lerna sealings manifest specifically Syrian/ Near Eastern sealing and architectural practices.[59] Weingarten is convinced that "Anatolians" were physically present in Lerna to implement their sealing system and opportunities for international trade must have motivated their presence there. Obviously, it would be difficult to think of a motive other than trade in objects of high value. Most of the seals come from one small room (Room XI) that

---

[57]   Keftiu, that is, Aegean traders in Egypt (Chaps. 3, 8.6. 11.7), had cultic hosts. Thus, a stela (CG 20539) inscribed by a "12th dynasty treasurer of Senwosret I named Montuhotep, links the Minoan Keftiu to Horus Montuhotep [and] refers to himself as 'Ḥm-priest of the secrets of the house of life', 'Overseer of the 'Big Hall/Portal', and 'Ḥm-priest of Horus of the Keftiu" (Judas 2015: 125 with references). See below for "Life" as permission for foreigners to trade in Egypt. Judas (2015: 126) notes that Horus cults were typically found at Egyptian boundaries which, like those elsewhere, were centers for trade (Silver 1995: 19–23).

[58]   *CMS* V, nos. 43–119.

[59]   The details of Weingarten's argument are beyond the scope of the present study. The Lerna sealings have not been widely discussed and, to the best of my knowledge, only Weingarten has deduced the participation of Anatolians. The Lerna center was destroyed by fire and ceased to function beyond the end of the third millennium. Nearby Tiryns remained more or less undisturbed.

could be entered only from the outside of the building. In addition to the sealings found in the "House of the Tiles" (named after its tiled roof), examination of the ceramics revealed, "an unusually large number of individual saucers" [in Room XI with the sealings], suggesting holding of "large-scale feasts" (Peperaki 2004: 216, 223). During roughly the same period, relatively large numbers of sealings are also found in Geraki and Petri, in the mainland of southern Greece. The seals employed in Geraki, in particular, bore some relationship to those in Lerna.

There also exists concrete evidence of Minoan merchant settlements in the Eastern Aegean.[60] The already discussed Linear A inscription from Miletus does not stand alone as evidence of contact with Minoans. Niemeier (2005: 3f., 7–10) notes evidence for the physical presence of Minoans in the form of typical domestic ware and Minoan commercial dealings in the form of two seals and a clay sealing. Somewhat later but still in the first half of the second millennium, there are findings of Minoan-type frescoes and loom-weights and Minoan balance weights, Linear A signs on six fragmentary vessels, one of which appears to have originated in Crete itself. Beginning in the mid-second millennium BCE, there is evidence of a Mycenaean presence, including ample domestic pottery and two possible Linear B inscriptions (Niemeier 2005: 10–16).

We cannot expect to find Minoan/Mycenaean textiles in the Black Sea region. Mostly what we can hope to find there are "incidentals"—that is, objects that had belonged to traders but were not themselves traded goods. *So, assuming that the Mycenaeans were really trading textiles for gold in the Black Sea region, how many of their non-traded "incidentals" should we expect to find there?* There is no formula, and no one can say. Obviously, people are careful with gold—they may bury it but they do not discard it on the shore like fragments of used pots. My view is that enough of the material "incidentals" has been found on the ground to confirm that the Mycenaeans had direct contact with the crucial Black Sea region. It bears repeating, I think, that Anatolians imported luxury textiles from Greece and not exotica, or wine, or oil in durable containers, or even people.

On the other side of the Aegean, there is strong evidence that Anatolia paid for its Mycenaean textile imports with people and, above all, with gold originating in the Black Sea region. I submit that the evidence has taken us beyond a high probability of trade to a "certainty" of contacts, including trade contracts, between Minoans and Mycenaeans on one side and Anatolians and Black Sea dwellers on the other.

---

[60]   Similar to the evidence for the presence of foreign merchants in Crete and the mainland, this evidence is chronologically and geographically scattered. Perhaps there is additional evidence to be found, but at this writing (February 20, 2021), it is complete. The reader will judge the importance of my findings accordingly.

7. Toward Certainty of Trading Connections: Migration of Skilled Workers to Greek Palatial Centers with Consideration of Their Legal Status

As outlined in the previous section, there are numerous Anatolian toponymic, including "man of Colchis" in Linear B tablets from Knossos and Pylos. Next, many of these toponymic are considered in detail and evaluated. Strong evidence is found for the migration of (mostly) women to work in the palatial textile industry. Having accomplished this objective, the remainder of the chapter explores the legal status of the workers from eastern Aegean. Were they slaves or free persons? If they were slaves, were they enslaved by force or by contract (in the market)?

Numerous toponymic ("ethnics") in the Linear B tablets testify to movements among Mycenaean palatial centers and to palatial centers from foreign places (Nikoloudis 2008a: 47 Fig.1). These references reveal previous economic relationships and the movement of labor power to take advantage of differences in economic returns to human capital. Thus, at Pylos, we find, for example, there are men from Zakunthos, who are mentioned in a list of rowers (An 610) and who are referred to as settlers (*ki-ti-ta*). Palaima (2011: 65) observes, "The Pylos texts also contain records of Zakunthian-style chariot wheels, which might imply steady contacts with the island of Zakunthos to acquire products or crafts personnel." This is the "demand" side but also there is a "supply" side—that is, Zakunthians saw an advantage in transferring their products and skills to Pylos.

In Pylos, we note also a "woman of Thebes," "women of Kythera," "men of Olympia," but also a "man from Cyprus" and individuals from numerous places in Western Anatolia. At Knossos, there are men and women from Nauplia, Thebes, and other places in Crete, as well as individuals from Cyprus and Egypt. Mycenae has a "man of Zakynthos" and of "Asia," and Thebes hosts a "son of the Lakedaimonian" and a "Milesian." Mycenaean connections with Anatolia are attested in the Linear B tablets.

As Palaima (2007b: 198–200) points out, citing the earlier research of Hiller (1975), "the list of probable 'Hellenized Anatolian names,' recorded as the names of human beings in the Linear B tablets, is still compelling: *a-pa-si-jo* (Ephesos, cf. Hittite *Apasa*); *di-du-mo* (cf. Didyma); *pa-pa-ra-ko* (cf. Paphlagonia [a region located south of the southwestern shore of the Black Sea]); *ra-pa-sa-ko* (Lampsakos [located at the eastern limit of the southern shore of the Hellespont]); *ru-ki-jo* (cf. Hom. Λυκία, Λύκιοι); and finally, *to-ro*, which Hiller [1975: 389] rightly compares with both Τρώς [Troy] and Τλῶς [in Lycia]." If *to-ro-jo*, who is a *do-e-ra*—the name of a woman in PY Ep 705.6—is identified with

Troy (*Tros* and *Troia*) instead of with Lycia (*Tlos* and *Tloia*), we have discovered a "Trojan Slave-Woman" in Pylos.[61] Palaima (2007b: 199) expresses due caution but concedes, "Minimally, ... such individual names may indicate current or past contacts between regions, either by settlers or by individuals who 'have to do with' other regions."

In addition, many of the referenced individuals who arguably migrated from other locations were currently engaged in textile production. Thus, at Knossos, there is a "woman of Thebes" who so participates (KN Ap 5864), and at Pylos, texts dealing with wool and textiles refer to working women by "ethnics," based on places in the eastern Aegean, such as *a-si-wi-ja* Assuwa (in Lydia? In the Troad? In the Black Sea region?), Knidos (*ki-ni-di-ja*), Halicarnassus (*ze-pu$_2$-ra$_3$*), Chios (*ki-si-wi-ja*), Miletus (*mi-ra-ti-ja*), and Lemnos (*ra-mi-ni-ja*; probably Lamniai) (PY Ab 186.B). The last named is the feminine form; the masculine form is *ra-mi-ni-jo* (PY An 209.2, Cn 328.4), and the man so designated appears with registers of sheep and goats so that he too, like the female Lemnians, is possibly involved in cloth production albeit an earlier stage in the production process (Guzowska and Yasur-Landau 1999: 471 with fn. 3).[62]

8. Legal Status of Workers Designated by "Ethnics"

The remainder of the chapter is devoted to considering the legal status of workers designated as "ethnics." The intention is to provide new insight into the role of market forces in the Bronze Age Aegean labor market. At the same time, this discussion sets the stage for Chapter 10, in which the analysis of glyptic plays the central role.

First, consider a seal (Figure 12, below) depicting a Hermes-like figure or, better, a Theseus-like figure[63] who carries a peculiar staff and wears a headgear. The figure is in the process of binding or lashing together two figures, prob-

---

[61] Palaima (2007b: 202) does not, I think, reject such an identification outright, but he does warn against "Troy-mania." He is right to do so, but I suggest that "Miletus-mania" is also a danger.

[62] Sources: Billigmeier and Turner 91981: 4–50; Nikoloudis 2008a: 46–47; Palaima 2007b: 202; and Smith and Tzachili 2012: 147.

[63] Montecchi (2016a: 168–169) sees "a man with a possible bull's head." I think the man is more likely Theseus than the Minotaur. It was Theseus who delivered the "tax" consisting of young persons from Athens to Minos and extricated himself from the labyrinth with a thread. The name "Theseus" appears in the Linear B tablets from Pylos (En 74) as a "slave of the goddess" with a landholding (Palaima 2004b: 453). In conveying individuals from one (overseas) destination to another, the depicted figure is like Hermes or Theseus or, more generally, like a "herald" (*kērux*; Linear B *ka-ru-ke*; Pylos PY Fn 187, Un 21) or even, in my iconographic discussion, like a "griffin"! Indeed, the symbol on the staff might also be compared to Hermes' "staff with three branches"/"staff with three leaves" (*Homeric Hymn to Mercury* 528–532).

ably women (Younger 2016b: 434–435). The two being led away from a pillar are marked with an upside-down version of the symbol on "Theseus'" staff and head. I see this symbol as either a stylized double-headed axe—the heads of the figures serve as top/bottom of the shaft—and/or, perhaps, a stylized palm referencing Potnia of the Labyrinth.[64] The same symbol also stands elevated in the mid-background. Arguably, the two figures have been purchased for the Labyrinth in the slave market as represented by the pillar. The seal comes from Grave VIII in the Athens Agora.

Figure 12. "Theseus" transports bound women
(*CMS* V no. 173 = Arachne 163313).

The women textile workers grouped by ethnicity are not called slaves, but this is their probable legal status (see above on women called "[textile] decorators").[65] Even so, this does not mean they are *forcible* slaves taken by

---

[64] It will be recalled that the Cretan palm embraces the throne in Knossos' Throne Room (Galanakis, Tsitsa, and Günkel-Maschek 2017).

[65] There are some misconceptions about slavery in the relevant Aegean literature. Thus, in considering the legal status of persons referred to by "possessive adjectives in *-e-jo*," Ruijgh (1998–1999: 269) responds that some individuals addressed in this way "were obviously free men, since many of them had a *do-e-ro* ['slave'] themselves." Similarly, Ruijgh (1998: 258 n. 29) alleges that land leasing by slaves is "hardly conceivable." In fact, slave-owning slaves are well known in the ancient Near East and in Rome. In four Roman legal texts, *ordinarii* are understood as slaves who own other slaves termed *vicarii*: Digest 14.4.5.1 (Ulpian); Digest 15.1.17 (Ulpian); Digest 15.1.19.pr (Ulpian) and Gaius *Institutes* 2.20.17; Silver 2016a. In classical Athens, the slave Midas ran a perfume shop and accumulated substantial debts from borrowed funds (Hypereides *Against Athenogenes*). There is also direct evidence for privileged slaves in the Linear B tablets. Thus, at Pylos the wealthy priestess Eritha (e.g. PY Ep 704), priestess of Pa-ki-ja-na (?), owned slaves (*do-e-ra*), "who in turn are prosperous and landholders. One *do-e-ra* listed on the same tablet, owns nearly as much land as Eritha" (Billigmeier and Turner 1981: 7). The women known as *ki-ri-te-wi-ja* who appear on tablets at Knossos and Pylos administer wealth and have significant land holdings in PY An 607, and are said to be daughters of slaves (*doera, doero*) of the goddess Do-qe-ja (Billigmeier and Turner 1981: 8). More generally, ancient "chattel slaves" may often

raiders or the like. It would not be easy to collect skilled workers by such violent means.[66] The women with eastern Aegean ethnics more likely agreed to sell themselves into slavery/indentured servitude in order to finance their transport to Pylos and then to find a place in the prosperous textile-driven Mycenaean economy (Billigmeier and Turner 1981: 5). To characterize them as "refugees" (Billigmeier and Turner 1981: 4) is probably apt, but this designation fails to distinguish between the motives of the women and their legal status upon arrival at Pylos. Questions about the origin and status of some Mycenaean purple-workers are raised in a Hittite letter analyzed in Excursus 1.[67]

Mention has already been made of the objection that the women designated with east Aegean ethnics were not really immigrants from Asia at all. Rather, the ethnic descriptors acknowledge that the native women are proficient in crafts for which their various "places of origin" were famous (Billigmeier and Turner 1981: 4). However, this argument only begs the question of how these women compensated employers for training them in very marketable skills—that is, in skills a free person could transfer to a different employer and to a different geographic location.

It appears that in Jo 438, there are female workers *designated with ethnics (or place-name adjectives) referencing places in or under the jurisdiction of* Pylos. Olsen (2014: 77), for good reason, finds it

> interesting to note that these ethnically-identified women have not remained at their origin-site within the Pylian state, but have instead been transferred to the palace environs. Both these work-groups, the *ti-nwa-si-ja* and *e-wi-ri-pi-ja*, are transferred to secondary locations where their labor activities are performed: the Hither

---

have been of above-average social and economic status. In Linear B texts the term "daughter" (*tu-ka-te* = *thugatēr*; abbreviation *tu*) here and elsewhere may refer to a slave agent and not to a biological relationship. Obviously, it remained important for the palatial authorities to keep in mind the legal status, slave or free, of those they entrusted with palatial resources or made demands for resources upon.

[66] It is often assumed that in antiquity, it was not necessary for outsiders to train women in weaving because they learned this skill in their households beginning when they were young. As Cutler (2016: 174–175) cautions, "Although the length of time required to become proficient in weaving on the warp-weighted loom is likely to have been reduced if the individuals learning the new skill were already competent in weaving on another type of loom, the need for sustained contact between novice and experienced artisan suggests that either individuals travelled away ... in order to learn the new techniques, or that weavers skilled in the use of the warp-weighted loom spent a significant length of time as visitors or immigrants in these communities." Homer has Odysseus teach textile-making skills to his slave women, who instead of being appreciative betray his household with the suitors.

[67] It is well to keep in mind the report of Herodotus (4.145) that decedents of the Argo's crew moved from Lemnos to Lakeidaimon not so very far from Pylos. Pausanias (3.21.6) reports on the superior quality of murex shells on the Laconian coast.

Province-originating *e-wi-ri-pi-ja* perform their tasks at the Further Province capital of Leuktron, and the *ti-nwa-si-ja*, thought to originate from an island under the aegis of Pylos, do their weaving at the palace site of Pylos itself.[68]

Olsen (2014: 99) goes on: "As it would be easy for the palace to simply leave these two groups in their place of origin, it would appear that an administrative choice has been made to place these workers in a location other than that of their origin." The problem is that free persons cannot simply be "placed" where the employer wishes them to be. Further, the evidence can be read to mean that the women became known by ethnics *after* they were placed in new locations. Possibly, then, the women sold themselves into slavery to finance migration from the margins to the remunerative textile centers at the heart of the Kingdom.

This brings to mind a peculiar finding with respect to "slaves of a god." Duev (2012: 5) has noted: "An interesting difference between the mainland and Crete is that only one *te-o do-e-ro* is mentioned in Knossos on KN Ai 966, while in Pylos more than one hundred *te-o-jo do-e- ro/do-e-ra* are recorded, 45 of which belong to Sphagiana, the cult centre of Potnia near Pylos." The extreme difference between Crete and mainland Greece in the presence of "slaves of a god" is most obviously explained by an extreme difference in the rate of cultic growth. Specifically, my hypothesis is that the mainland cultic centers were attracting workers by financing their migration and/or training them and locking in their investment returns by requiring the beneficiary workers to be immobilized as slaves.

In discussing the women with eastern Aegean toponymic, Nikoloudis (2008a: 48) notes that they are not called slaves but that "whether the women were captives or refugees, i.e. slaves or free is debatable." In fact, contractual/ voluntary slavery is well known in the ancient Near East and in Rome (Silver 1995a: 117–119). In Pylos, there are also (Aa 807) thirty-two "captive" women *ra-wi-ja-ja/*lawiaiai* (Nosch 2003: 65). That these women—located in Pylos Kereza in Pylos' Hither Province—are explicitly called captives does not mean that the other groups of working women were not slaves. The word *lawiaia* has been related to Homer's (*Iliad* 20.193) *lēiades* 'female war captives', and perhaps this is correct. Olsen (2014: 133 n. 316) observes, "The etymology is plausible but not definitive." Perhaps there is an element of circularity in the meaning of *lawi-aiai* due to linking it with the word *lāwagetās*, which is understood to refer to a *military* leader. Fine, but *lāwagetās* is from *laos* 'people', and its general meaning is "leader of the people." Thus, *ra-wi-ja-ja/*lawiaiai* may not refer to the *form of slavery*—that is, by (self-)sale or by forcible capture—but rather to the *form of*

---

[68]   However, see §5 above for the origin of the *ti-nwa-si-ja*.

service of the slave women—that is, they are owned "by the leader"—meaning they are "public slaves."[69] So, seen more broadly, the *lawagetas* is the manager of the public slaves and, in this capacity, is himself a slave of the people.[70]

There is some evidence that possibly points to the institution of contractual slavery in Mycenaean Pylos. The translated Linear B of Pylos tablet Ae 303 reads: "Pylos. Of the priestess 14 women slaves because of/on account of the sacred gold" (Nafassi 2013: 98 n. 70[71]). My understanding is that the women received temple gold from the priestess in return for becoming temple slaves. Zurbach (2016: 432) agrees that the women received money but thinks they became debt-slaves: "It can be argued that gold is a money (*Hackgold* ...), and in this case the text reveals the role of the temple as money-lender and the use of debt as a source of workforce, which is not a surprise given the widely attested Near Eastern practice." Of course, other interpretations are possible. For any interpretation, a key challenge is why it was recorded—that is, what was the palace's interest in the transaction?

My view is that the scribe's focus was not on the economic transaction itself, in which it had no stake, but on the changed legal status of the fourteen women from free to slave. The new slaves could no longer be taxed or subjected to corvée by the Palace. That there was, in fact, an important change in legal status would explain why the sounds in the entry seem to be repeated in a religious fashion (Tsitsibakou-Vasaloa 1986: 168). Witton (1960: 416) has, indeed, called attention to the practice of recording land ownership, generally, and of Eritha, in verse (cf. Kelder and Poelwijk 2016: 576). The proposed change in linguistic usage is most important and, in my opinion, deserves much more attention than it has received.

---

[69] In the *Iliad*, the "captives" are women of Lyrnessos taken away by Achilles.

[70] Olsen (2014: 63) explains that, like the *wanax*, "the *lawagetas* has personnel assigned to him (designated by the adjective *ra-wa-ke-si-jo*) as well as a *temenos* (also described by *ra-wa-ke-si-jo*). His *temenos* is significantly smaller than that of the *wanax*, but he is the only other human to possess a *temenos* in his own right. He also contributes to cult offerings to Poseidon, but once again on a smaller scale than the *wanax*."

[71] See also Richard Vallance Janko 2014 available at: https://linearbknossosmycenae. com/2014/03/15/translation-of-pylos-tablet-ae-08-on-the-internet-vs-my-own-translation/ (accessed February 12, 2021).

Excursus 1

Purplers as Contractual Slaves

SOMETHING of the background of the migration of contractual slaves from Anatolia to Bronze Age Greece may be found in an earlier noted letter (KUB XI V 3 = AhT 4 = CTH 181) dating from the first half of the thirteenth century BCE from the (unnamed) Hittite king to the (unnamed) "Great King" of the Ahhiyawans (the king of the Mycenaeans in Chap. 12.4). The letter touches on the actions of the "brother" of the Ahhiyawan king named Tawagalawa[1] (represented by the rich-in-tradition Greek name Eteocles[2]) in connection with the movement/ flight of 7,000 Hittite subjects from port cities to the land of Ahhiyawa.

Apparently, Hittite subjects, who are designated in Sumerian as NAM.RA.MES (Hittite *arnuwala*), had negotiated with one Piyamaradu to be relocated elsewhere in Anatolia and then transferred to Ahhiyawa (lines iii. 7–21).[3] I conjecture that those who fled (the Lukka people?) agreed to be sold to merchants who conveyed them to the Greek ownership whether in Anatolia or Greece (Ergin 2007: 274–276). Perhaps the Hittite subjects had fled from royal taxation much to the dismay of the ruler.

Returning to the *nam.ra* people, a Hittite text (Kbo XII 42) composed in epic style tells of a caravan of merchants of Ura (in western Cilicia) that boast of having in their possession ample stocks of various merchandise (cattle, sheep, ... grain) and valuables (gold, silver ...) and "many *nam.ra*-people" (Hoffner 1968: 36, 39). Presumably, the *nam.ra*-people were for sale like the other merchandise; otherwise, their mention in the text would be pointless. This does not mean that they were "ordinary" slaves who were sold/sold themselves as individuals. Historically, there seem to be cases in which groups sold themselves into

---

[1]   Miller (2010) has argued that Tawagalawa had himself been the king of the Ahhiyawa before his unnamed brother. If the kingship refers to Ahhiyawa, then this would imply a rotating or elective limited-term kingship. Taracha (2018: 16) reads the text to mean that Tawagalawa was the "brother" (literal or not) of the king of Ahhiyawa but was also, at the same time, the king of a different Greek land. I cannot judge whether the literal reading of the letter calls for such an interpretation. I do not find it appealing that there were two Mycenaean kingdoms in Anatolia.

[2]   Eteoclēs is a son of Oedipus (West 2001: 296).

[3]   Sources: tr. Beckman 2011; Bryce 2003: 76–78, 85; 2011; and M. L. West 2001: 265.

slavery with a stipulation against sales of individuals outside their territory/ group (e.g. the Mariandyni in northern Anatolia, as discussed by Euphorion and Poseidonius in Athenaeus 6.263c–d). The Mariandyni were called *dōrophoroi* "gift-bearers" which would reflect what they gave but also what they received from their owners.

L. R. Palmer (1963: 90–91) suggests that in the Pylos "Rower Texts" (PY An 610) that the men designated as *me-ta-ki-ti-ta*—a word he renders as "transported people"—are comparable to the Hittite *nam.ra* people. The corresponding alphabetic Greek term *metanastēs* or *metanistēmi* refers to someone who has departed/been removed from his homeland (LSJ s.v.) with the implication of not having rights in his new land.[4]

Homer provides some relevant evidence. In *Iliad* 9.644 ff., Achilles complains that he is being treated as if he were a *metanastēs*. Achilles is plainly saying that he is being treated contemptuously. This does not mean that he is being treated as if he were an immigrant, or even a fugitive immigrant or a "suppliant." It does mean, however, that he is being treated like a slave/freedman who bears "the stain of slavery"—not a slave/freedman who had been transported/removed from his/her homeland by *force*. As Silver (2013) has argued, the feeling of others towards someone made into a slave by force might be indifference or pity; the feeling of contempt was reserved for those who had been stained by *selling themselves* into slavery to better their life prospects. Such an individual, I propose, is a *metanastēs*.[5]

In the Mycenaean example, the betterment for the alien self-seller would be the grant of a plot of land (his becoming a *me-ta-ki-ti-ta*) in return for serving as an *e-re-ta* 'rower' (Nikoloudis 2006: 103ff). It may be reasoned that *ki-ti-ta* refers to "settlers" who received public land for performing public services without first becoming slaves.

I see no reason to doubt that Greek elites, like the Roman, harbored contempt for those who voluntarily surrendered their autonomy for material gain. In addition, it seems that once again Homer reflects Bronze Age institutions.

---

[4] Py An 610 also mentions *ki-ti-ta* 'settlers' and *po-si-ke-te-re* 'immigrants' and *me-ta* 'after' or 'later settlers'. "The term *me-ta-ki-ti-ta* /metaktitas/ has been compared to later Greek *metoikos*. The meaning of '*meta-*' could be either 'accompanying' (as in *metoikos*) or 'substituting' (as in *metanastēs*) The literal translation of *po-si-ke-te-re* is 'to-comers,' composed of *pos + ikō* 'I come' > *pos-hiktēr*, giving *pos-hik-tēres* 'immigrants, newcomers' " (Nikoloudis 2006: 103; references omitted; my transliterations).

[5] Epeios, the builder under Athena of the Trojan Horse, falls under an antiheroic light for reasons that are not entirely clear. M. Robertson (1967: 8) notes: "A story is told later that he was cursed with cowardice because his father was forsworn." It is well to recall Herodotus' (2.49, 58) mention of the "golden fetters" received from Darius by a Greek doctor.

10

The Labyrinth as a Textile Trader

Seeking Commercial Knowledge
from Iconographic Symbols

PART I viewed the Labyrinth as a showplace for marketing fine textiles. This perspective opens opportunities for fortifying our understanding of Bronze Age Aegean commercial practices by analyzing manifestations of the very rich iconographic symbols of the Labyrinth.

Chapters 10 and 11 direct attention to iconographic symbols, such as *spiral, double-headed axe, "horns," sacral knot, figure-eight shield, genius/dog, lion, dragon, and griffin*. This analysis is difficult and sometimes frustrating, but I hold out the promise that patient readers who complete the journey will be rewarded with important insights about commercial life not available by means of studying texts and ruins.

It needs to be added that insights into economic roles will be limited if we are constrained by initial assumptions regarding the possible function of human figures who engage in fantastic activities or who are associated with fantastic creatures. Crowley (2008: 77) is ready to classify such figures as VIPs—that is, they are priestesses or priests, queens or kings, and goddesses or gods. However, this is to assume that ancient ideologists erected a wall between sacred and secular actors. In fact, I think, they saw them as interacting. Thus, the human being who is associated with a fantastic griffin may turn out to be a quite ordinary Syrian merchant bound for Pylos or Knossos. To understand the role of the human figure, we need first to understand why the iconographers have *chosen* to place him/her in the company of the fantastic being.

1. Double-Headed Axe

There are strong empirical reasons for considering the double-headed axe as a prime symbol of the cult/firm known as the Labyrinth. There are also strong ideological reasons for the choice of this emblem.

Scholars have attributed various meanings to the double-headed axe and associated it with various religious/philosophical concepts (Flouda 2015: 44). Silver (2019: 116) has argued that the double-headed axe is "*a Janiform symbol with the intrinsic meaning 'coming-going' or 'circling'/'circuiting'.*" The circuiting interpretation connects the double-headed axe with the cult/firm known as Labyrinth, as the word *laburinthos* with its –*nth* suffix is arguably not merely a "Pre-Greek" word (Beekes s.v.) but a *traveler* from Anatolia.[1] That is, the double-headed axe as a symbol of mobility was selected by its directors to symbolize the Labyrinth because it is a mobile organization.[2]

The double-headed axe cult/firm (the Labyrinth) had headquarters in Knossos but must have operated (or had branches) elsewhere in Crete, in Akrotiri (Thera), on the Greek mainland, and, as will be seen below, in Anatolia (see §7 below on circuiting).

As already argued, Potnia of the Labyrinth was heavily invested in and integral to the display and sale of costly, fashionable textiles. I would propose that the cult/firm not only made and traded textiles on its own behalf but also provided support for individual participants in the textile industry—shepherds to salespersons. Support provided to participants in the textile industry would explain the widely distributed finding of (presumably) votive offerings of double-headed axes in Potnia's cult places (Flouda 2015: 43ff.). Hundreds of double-headed axes, including axes wrought from gold, were discovered in a Bronze Age hoard at Arkalochori in Crete some fifteen to twenty miles from Heraklion. On Mt. Juktas, a few miles from Knossos, a number of double-headed axes were discovered along with a sealing depicting a goddess standing on a mountain between two lions (Karetsou 1981: 145–146, 151; Chaps. 4 and 6.3 above). MacGillivray (2012: 119) adds: "The six small bronze examples [of double-headed axes] from the MH I tumuli at Kastroulia in Messenia are unique in the Greek Peloponnese and may indicate a unique Cretan presence there."

MacGillivray (2012: 118–122) has brought together a good deal of Bronze Age evidence for the double-headed axe and its connection to the sacral knot.

---

[1]   Accordingly, the double-headed axe may have been employed independently of Potnia of the Labyrinth by several deities who periodically moved between cult centers. Presently, I know of no evidence that this kind of duplicative use of the symbol took place, at least during the Bronze Age. In the *Homeric Hymn to Mercury* (526–532), Apollo offers by oath the use of the valuable *kērykeion* symbol to Hermes. It is understood that the latter god cannot benefit from the use of the symbol until making an accommodation with the former god. Note that even gods make oaths and are bound by them! I do not believe that Potnia allowed her "trademark" to be infringed. For Aphrodite's reaction to infringements of her trademarks in Ptolemaic Egypt, see Silver (2019: 61–63).

[2]   The Janiform of the double-headed axe also encourages its deployment as the symbol of the socioeconomic instrument whose prime function is to "go around": coins or, more generally, money and the place in which they rest, the treasury (see Silver 1992: 29–33 and below).

As far as his data supports any specific connection, it serves to connect the double-headed axe symbol with the Minoan palace, gold, and textiles including the sacral knot itself:

[In the Protopalatial Period:] "The double axe is the most frequent sign incised onto blocks when the Minoans, starting in MM IB, build Crete's first great buildings with central courts, known to archaeologists as palaces";

[In the early Neopalatial period:] "The Theran fresco examples from Xeste 4 are two double axes painted to represent gold with incised lines suspended from an elaborate offering stand, ... held by a red haired male in a procession that climbs the building's stairs."; "The earliest firm evidence for metal signet rings with representations of double axes with people, common in LM IB and later, is on a LM IA sealing from Akrotiri in Thera. Here we see a figure, perhaps male, in an elaborate garment holding the emblem on its haft";

[In the Late Neopalatial Period] "Perhaps most striking is the symbol's incorporation of new elements, such as the length of cloth or rope that Evans [1921: 430; see Chap. 10.2] dubbed the 'Sacral Knot' motif in place of the haft (Fig. 5).[3] This Sacral Knot is also reproduced in faience and ivory,[4] which underscores its importance. Evans compared it to the Egyptian *ankh*, symbol for eternal life, but a closer likeness may be found in the Egyptian *tiet*, also known as the Blood of Isis, or the Isis Knot, the length of cloth that secures the gods' garments";

[In the Post Palatial Period:] "Single inhumations in boxes, or larnakes appear in large cemeteries. Vance Watrous [1991: 287-8] believes that the Minoan-Mycenaean larnax is based on the Egyptian linen chests that were buried with their owners."

The discussion of the "Sacral Knot" is continued in the next section.

---

[3] See *CMS* II.5, no. 234 (= Arachne 159977) from Phaistos (Matoušková 2018: 20 n.31). The sacral knot as shaft of the double-headed axe is found also in a vase painting from Gournia, Crete Available at: https://www.penn.museum/sites/journal/469/ (accessed February 12, 2021).

[4] See PM I, 433, Matoušková 2018: 21 Fig. 8.

2. Sacral Knot, Snake Goddesses, and La Parisienne

The combination of the sacral knot and double-headed axe recorded by MacGillivray is reproduced in Figure 13, opposite. Notice how the (top) looped cloth called "sacral knot" by Evans is made into the shaft of the double-headed axe, thus merging the two symbols.[5] The sacral knot is a form of textile (Younger 1988: xiii) and its age and cultic importance is signaled by the fact that a (sometimes hard to see) looped cord is worn on the chest by each of faience figures known as "Snake Goddesses" (HM 63 left and HM 65 right) that were excavated in Knossos' "Temple Repositories" (Plate 10). The sacral knot is depicted in Knossos' "Campstool Fresco" as worn behind the neck on the back of the dress of the elegant "La Parisienne" (see Chap. 11.5 with Plate 16): "She wears an elaborately woven blue and red striped dress, with a blue banded edge attached with red flecked loops. Tied to the back of the dress is a 'sacred knot.'... This is a loop of long cloth tied with another loop at the nape of the neck, leaving a length of the cloth trailing down the back" (German 2018). "La Parisienne's" knot is blue. German (2018) goes on to note that representations of women actually wearing the sacred knot are rare,[6] but it is seen on seals, painted on ceramics, and rendered in ivory and faience.

When the "Snake Goddesses" (Plate 10) were excavated, the taller "Snake Goddess" (Y 63 = HM 63) had two (or more) snakes wound around both arms and her waist. *The spiral symbolism could not be more obvious.* However, the snake is not only a spiral symbol but is a practically chosen symbol for the protectress of an underground treasury. One may identify Athens in this connection (see Chap. 6.2). The smaller of the two "Snake Goddesses" (Y 65 = HM 65) held a short jagged striped stick in her right hand, which has been understood (wrongly, I think) to represent a snake. The checkerboard effect of the skirt worn by HM 65 is paralleled only in the gold filial from Mycenae (Plate 3).

With respect to the jagged striped stick, Miller Bonney (2011: 178) has noted, "Indeed the textured surface of the upper original portion of the 'serpent' seems to reflect the craftsman's intent to depict a twisted object such as a rope or cord." Thus, the jagged stick may be the "crooked thread" or meander/spiral symbol that is associated with the *Labyrinthos* (Chap. 4.2.c). In Greek myth, Ariadne extricates Theseus from the Labyrinth by giving him either a ball of thread (*agathis*) or a spindle wound with thread (Silver 1992: 233). Accepting the spindle version, I would supplement Miller Bonney's hypothesis of a "rope or cord" with the proposition that HM (=Y) 65 holds a spindle or distaff, albeit

---

5   The sacral knot with its top-loop is also depicted in glyptic together with the figure-eight shield (*CMS* II.8, no. 127 = Arachne 160757), and, as will be seen, is a prominent symbol of the Labyrinth.
6   However, see also Matoušková 2018: 22–23.

a distaff shaped like a key,[7] wound with yarn or thread. This conjecture has the advantage of identifying HM (=Y) 65 with Potnia of the Labyrinth and linking the goddess to textile production.

Figure 13. Sacral knot/double axe ivory relief from Palaikastro (PM I, 433 after Evans 1921: Fig. 310d).

Panagiotaki (1999: 96–97 with Figure 210) adds important details about the "Snake Goddesses" connecting them with luxury textiles:

> Whoever they might be intended to be, they exemplify to the full the skill of the Minoan artisan and are among his most elaborate creations in this material. Every detail, not only in their physique, but even the designs of the material of their dresses has been brought out in the most exquisite way. On the taller more complete 'Snake Goddess' (Y 63) the winding of her tall crown is (originally) purple.

Panagiotaki 1999: 54[8]

3. Labyrinth as Textile House

A Minoan sealing image from Knossos called the "Mountain Mother" (Figure 4 in Chap. 6.3) arguably allows us to visualize the outside of the Labyrinth complex. In this sealing, figures—reasonably identified as king and goddess—appear

---

[7]   For actual distaffs with the shape of keys, see Di Giuseppe (2017: 273–274).

[8]   Panagiotaki (1999: 54) adds: "One defect, which it seems the artist was unable to control, was the colour of the skin, which, unlike human skin, is in turquoise." Turquoise is not a characteristic murex color, but it is within the capabilities of properly prepared murex dye (Jensen 1963: 111). Thus, it is possible the "Snake Goddesses" did not make a mistake.

together with a multistoried building/building complex decorated on its roofs/terraces with "horns." In another seal (depicted in Figure 7 in Chap. 6.3), the "horns" are clearly represented as portions of the tops of double-headed axe blades.[9]

Figure 14. Potnia or an agent displays a garment, seal from Knossos
(*CMS* II.3, no. 8 = Arachne 159089).

Thus, Potnia of the Labyrinth is seen as a circuiting goddess that presides in a real multi-storied structure marked out by "horns" that also symbolize the double-headed axe. This structure is her *woikos*, an economically significant term,[10] and it features depictions of and actual elaborate luxury garments arguably for marketing. The next step is to develop iconographic evidence implicating Potnia and her Labyrinth in textile marketing.

The exposition begins with Figure 14, a seal from Knossos which depicts a female—Potnia or her Priestess—who stands in front of an altar with a double-

---

[9] Despite the attractive alternatives, I prefer to interpret the "horns" as a stylized version of a ship.

[10] A Linear B tablet from Thebes (TH Of 36.2) has cloth given to the *woikos* 'house/firm' of Potnia. This is a fitting gift for a textile-marketing cult. It appears that *woikos* refers to a temple-owned "house/firm" and *do-de* to a non-cultic "house/firm" (Lupack 2008a: 106, 109–110). Homer, however, does not reserve the term *oikos* for cultic enterprises. To explain this, we need, I think, to consider why Mycenaeans wished to distinguish between cultic and non-cultic firms. They were not after all sociologists requiring a distinctive terms for each perceived socioeconomic phenomenon. The most obvious explanation is that the Mycenaean palace discriminated in favor of cultic firms—that is, they were, as in the example of Hermes, eligible for land-tax exemptions (Kyriakidis 2001: 127) and also received subsidies (material and human "offerings"/"gifts") not available to privately-owned firms. Sources: Silver 1995a: 28–30; Kyriakidis 2001: 127–128; Weilhartner 2013. The palace (central administration) differentiated linguistically because it differentiated fiscally. Homer pre-dates the palace and discrimination so he applies the term *oikos* to all. It is possible to wonder whether in Linear B, *i-jo*, as opposed to *e-jo* as an ending of possessives (considered by Killen 1983: 84–94), reflects a difference in the tax status of the owner and, thus, designated certain owners (the non-Indo-European form) who were receiving a tax break from the palace.

headed axe suspended behind her, as she looks down as if to display or call attention to an elaborate flounced dress, paneled skirt, or pants floating beside her.[11]

I suggest that the woman is stationary and is not carrying the dress to a deity (Warren 1988 22 Fig. 11b). Neither does she seem to be in the process of offering the dress to a deity, as she is facing front and there is no deity waiting to receive the offering as is typical in presentation scenes. The depicted woman is inside her house (the Labyrinth), and the garment suspended next to her is meant to be *adored* (Warren 1988: 22).[12] I offer, as the most likely interpretation, that the tempted unseen audience are buyers of textiles rather than a deity.[13] Thus, the sealing, like the palatial frescoes featuring luxury textiles, conveys in its own way that the house of the double-headed axe is simultaneously a cult center and a place where textiles are displayed for sale.[14] Of further interest in this depiction is a short object that looks like a snake that physically winds over itself forming an overt spiral symbol and the jagged pair of "snakes" or better "crooked threads" near the woman's feet. The woman holding up the garment is the/a "Snake Goddess" and also "Potnia of the Labyrinth" (see above).

In another "garment adoration scene" from Malia (Figure 15, below), two figures seem to *gaze* at a dress (Boloti 2017: 8 with Figure 1.11). On second thought, the figures *promote* the (hanging?) dress to unseen viewers. However, this scene lacks an explicit Labyrinth symbol with the possible exception of the type of garment itself.

Taking into account the combined testimony of Figure 14 and even more of the frescoes reviewed in Part I—with their emphasis on fashion and quality of design—it becomes reasonable to conclude that the role of the double-headed axe is to serve as the trademark and warranty of the Labyrinth's textile marketing enterprise. Furthermore, the seal depicted is likely the emblem of an *agent* of the showroom or, more generally, the emblem of someone who was

[11] "We may notice that the object is quite similar to the loose end of the sacral knot. However, the loop, which represents the first significant part of the symbol, is entirely missing. Therefore, these objects cannot be interpreted as sacral knots and it is most likely that they represent some kind of female clothing that could have been carried in a ceremonial procession" (Matoušková 2018: 12). Additional sources: Boloti 2017: 6; Haysom 2010: 44 Figure 7; B. Jones 2015: 107–108; cf. the procession in *CMS* II.7, no. 5 (= Arachne 160364) from Zakros; Haycom 2010: 43 Figure 5.

[12] See also, Figure 18 for a garment—one arguably for sale—that floats as if it had a life of its own.

[13] A commercial interpretation of the seal is also noted by Boloti (2018: 94–95). Note Coca Cola advertisements from the 1940s in which a woman holds up a "Coke" to unseen viewers who, it is hoped by her employers, will drink and adore (= buy).

[14] "The evidence of the seals, signets and sealings argues that elaborate clothing is of great importance to the Aegean peoples. The detail of fabric weight and surface texture, of pattern, flounce, fringe and tassel bear witness to many hours in the weaving. The shape and sway of the garments denote production through folding, pinning, tying, piercing, and sewing. Sensitivity to the different qualities of the materials, wool, linen, silk, metal and leather is clear in their careful rendering" (Crowley 2012: 7).

directly involved in marketing as opposed to the production or transportation of garments.[15] Apparently, it did not always need to be depicted the same way to inform and reassure the client or palatial official.

Figure 15. Two agents promote a garment, seal from Malia
(*CMS* II.3, no. 145 = Arachne 159237).

Together with "horns," spiral, and sacral knot, the double-headed axe is a transparent and reliable symbol of Potnia of the Labyrinth and of the Labyrinth's production and marketing of textiles. Reliability questions may be raised by the appearance of such symbols in a *funerary* context—that is, on the entrances and walls of Mycenaean and Minoan tholoi (e.g., the "Treasury of Atreus" and the Kamilaris tholos near Agia Triada) and in chamber tombs and on larnakes.[16] On the other hand, it is not surprising that, as a prime symbol of circuiting, the double-headed axe appears in a funerary context and little danger of commercially interpreting scenes in which a recently deceased armless and shroud-wearing individual participates as is depicted in the Agia Triada sarcophagus. This is perhaps the origin but not the full story of Potnia's funerary connection. The tholoi are much earlier than the palaces and, indeed, they may have been their predecessors as marketplaces.

It was noted earlier (Chap. 4.2.c) that Herodotus 2.148 uses the word *labu-rinthos* to refer to a stone structure—a mortuary temple—in Egypt near Lake Moeris: "It has twelve roofed courts with doors facing each other: six face north and six south, in two continuous lines, all within one outer wall. There are also double sets of chambers, three thousand altogether, fifteen hundred above and

---

[15]   This suggestion anticipates the following section, which explores the connection between the device on a seal and the profession of its owner.

[16]   Sources: Girella 2016: 208; Lefevre-Novaro 2001; Sgouritsa 2011: 742–743, 745, 746, 749; Steinmann 2020.

the same number underground" (2.148.4; tr. Godley *LCL*). The identification of a complex and probably winding structure, albeit a mortuary temple, as a labyrinth is not itself surprising. *What does elicit attention is that several Old Kingdom mortuary temples include wall depictions of very active marketplaces.*

Moreover, the mortuary temple of Amenhotep III, who reigned in the first half of the fourteenth century BCE, hosts inscriptions alluding to overseas trade relations including with Aegean places:

> All of the difficult lands north of Asia. All of the lands of the Phoenicians and Nubia (= the north and the south) are at the feet of this good god ... the great ones of all of the southern and the northern foreign lands, who did not know to come to Egypt since the god's time, come on their knees united in one place, so that the breath of life may be given to them,[17] their tribute on their backs.

> Cline and Stannish 2011: 7

Cline and Stannish (2011: 7) further explain:

> The order in which the toponyms are to be read is crucial.... The two place names to the right should be read first, since they face the same direction as these cartouches; they are *kftiw*, i.e., Keftiu, identified as Crete, and *tny* (*ti-nA-y-w*), i.e., Tanaja (Danaia, the Danaoi-Land), identified as mainland Greece. Both are known from other Egyptian sources from the time of Thutmose III onward, and their identification is accepted by most scholars.... The Aegean List's other toponyms are unique; not one of them appears in any other Egyptian source, either before or after Amenhotep III's reign. All scholars agree that these names denote sites and regions in the Bronze Age Aegean, but their identification is sometimes challenging.

It was noted earlier that between eight and ten plaques of Amenhotep III were found at Mycenae.

Egyptian mortuary temples were labyrinths—complex winding architectural structures—and they were marketplaces. Why this combination? Because they were places visited by relatives bearing offerings for those interred in the vicinity and places in which visitors, including traders, would have enjoyed the

---

[17]   The request for the "breath of life" is an ideological way of saying that foreigners requested the right to engage in trading relations within Egypt (see Chap. 8.6). The request for the "breath of life" is an ideological way of saying that foreigners requested the right to engage in trading relations within Egypt (see Chap. 8.6). It is attractive to assume that those granted "life" received the "ankh" symbol from a temple doorkeeper.

peace of the god—that is, of the dead ruler. In short, Egyptian mortuary temples were places for communing with the dead and with the living. The open question is whether the prominent tholos tombs played a similar role in the Aegean.

There are only hints that communal funerary structures were not reserved for the dead. In this connection, I would mention that the "Hypogaeum" at Knossos—with its beehive vault (Chap. 4.3). Pausanias (9.38.2, 9.36.4)—tells that Minyas built a great tholos at Orchemenos to keep his substantial wealth in. Homer (*Iliad* 9.381–382) speaks of "all the wealth that goes into Orchemenos," making it sound like a regular process rather than a one-off affair. A funerary tholos capped with an omphalos vault might provide a foundation for a commercial center. A funerary tholos at which ancestors were worshipped, as at the main tholos tomb in the Kamilari cemetery, would be a starting point for the emergence of a labyrinth-tholos. Thus, there is smoke, and further probing might uncover the linkage between Aegean tholos and trade.[18]

4. Seal Device and Seal User

My base assumption is that transactors often chose/are assigned seal devices that are related to their transactional duties (see Panagiotopoulos 2010: 305–306 and, for the Near East, 2012: 69–70 with Fig. 8). If so, then the devices on seals are capable of providing important information about the kinds of real-life duties performed at some point in time—that is, the period in which they were chosen/assigned.[19]

A poignant example is provided by Minoan roundels from Chania and Agia Triada, which depicts the exchange of a *butterfly* or a *flying bird* with some quantity of a type of garment (*164). In some Chanian sealings (Figure 16, opposite), there appears in front of the bird "an enigmatic cone-shape object with protruding 'horns'" (Weingarten 2017: 104). Weingarten (2017: 106) explains that the "cone with horns" represents the Linear A (and later Linear B) sign AB 80 for wool or woolen goods. *I suggest that the bird and butterfly signify that the owner of the seal travels/flits from one place to another for business.*

The cone adds that the traveling businessperson specializes in woolens (see Weingarten 2017: 106). There is no clear indication that the Labyrinth employs

---

[18] There is evidence of feasting and celebrations with the dead at tholoi (Soles 2010; Caloi 2015). In classical Athens, a round building called the "Tholos" stood at one end of the Agora. The Pylos palace did business at an "agora" (Chap. 8.4), but its location is not known. It is suggestive that *models* of tholoi with a female deity have been found within later Bronze Age buildings (Yiannouli 2011).

[19] For a similar line of reasoning with some supporting evidence for direct object sealings, see Flouda (2010: 73, 80).

the businessmen/birds[20]—that is unless the connection is to be found in the chosen sign (Ab 90) itself with its "horns." Throughout this study, there are

Figure 16. Woolens seeking bird, seal from Chania
(*CMS* VS.1A, 165 = Arachne 165396).

examples of birds linked to pillars and other cultic symbols, however.[21]

5. Figure-Eight Shield: First Look

A modicum of iconographic evidence links the figure-eight shield with both cloth and the Labyrinth/Palace. For example, in a fresco found in a staircase in the palace at Pylos,[22] the figure-eight shields appear to be of *cloth* (M. Shaw and Chapin 2016a: 128 with Fig. 4, 21; M. Shaw and Laxton 2002: 99). The large spotted figure-eight shield between two goddess-like figures at Mycenae (Immerwahr 1990: 121 with Pls. 62–63) also needs to be considered in this light. Another seal from Mycenae (*CMS* I, no. 132 = Arachne 157353) features figure-eight shields and women wearing elaborate Minoan flounced dresses (Blakolmer 2018: 35

---

[20]   However, in a seal from Prosymna in the Argolid (*CMS* I, no. 206 = 157428), birds fly immediately above flying griffins. It is argued in §5 below that the griffin's palatial duties included the protection of circuiting traders.

[21]   Many seals resemble "weave patterns," and Younger (1995: 332–333) suggests "that the main function of the early stamps was to imprint designs on cloth. Their geometric patterns (rectilinear zig-zags, meanders, diamonds, triangles, cruciforms, and curvilinear spirals and concentric circles) are those that could easily be woven into cloth; and it is quite likely that these stamps were used to imprint these designs as an easy alternative to weaving them." In later times the "weave patterns" were incorporated on seals used for sealings as a way of commemorating the patterns or, more likely, those who had created them. Perhaps they even served to confirm legal control over the pattern.

[22]   A figure-eight shield fresco was also found at Tiryns in the "Inner Forecourt" of the palace and another from the acropolis at Mycenae (M. Shaw and Laxton 2002: 99–100 with Figures 6 and 7).

with Fig. 11). There are also figure-eight shields together with sacral knots (e.g., *CMS* II.8, no. 127 = Arachne 160757). I am informed that no Linear B word for "shield" has been identified.

There may be multiple examples, but discomfort with the linkage arises, however. The reason is that it is not obvious why the cult of Potnia should have chosen the figure-eight shield as one of the symbols of its textile business. There is, however, a logical reason for the connection that is further developed in Chapter 11.4: the figure-eight shield is a prime symbol of *male status* and, hence, is appropriately employed by the cult to symbolize the goddess' *potnia*-status—that is, the fact that, like a male, she has the legal right to own property, form contracts, and participate in lawsuits. This is not a minor consideration for an entrepreneurial cult. Therefore, the figure-eight shield is a valid symbol of Potnia of the Labyrinth.

It is a symbol that must be interpreted with extreme caution because, as a device utilized in life by males, it cannot—like (say) the double-headed axe—be unique to Potnia. Thus, as expected, the shield appears on seals that do not feature garments and have no other evident connection to the Potnia and the Labyrinth/Palace. Indeed, the subject matter may seem very distant from the world of textile marketing. For example, on a seal from Mycenae (*CMS* I, no. 12 = Arachne 157233), the figure-eight shield appears behind a sword-bearing male figure, who elevated, stabs downward at his apparent foe. However, scenes such as this may still be relevant and, indeed, realistic indicators of textile distribution by Potnia.

The *youthful* male figure with the sword might be understood as representing the *security providers* for the Labyrinth's textile outreach. The youth who provides security for the Labyrinth arguably is an *agent* of the genius = dog/merchant (see Chap. 11.2) or, more likely, an agent of the *wanax*, who supervises the griffins' corps of protectors (see Chaps. 6.3 and 11.5-6). Thus, in Figure 11, celebrating the festival of flowers (Chap. 7.6), a small, suspended figure, wearing the figure-eight shield, holds up what appears to be a small sceptron—or is it a "stick, cudgel' (*baklon, baculum*) such as might be carried by a policeman (see above). Certainly, the *wanax* collected taxes and produced public services for taxpayers. We know that he gathered forces to protect the coastline. His role would have certainly included wielding the police power—physical force—against criminals on behalf of palatial and private traders. Moreover, this security role was well understood by Thucydides (1.4; tr. Jowett *Perseus Project*):

> Minos is the first to whom tradition ascribes the possession of a navy. He made himself master of a great part of what is now termed the Hellenic sea; he conquered the Cyclades, and was the first coloniser of most of them, expelling the Carians and appointing his own sons to govern in

them. Lastly, it was he who, from a natural desire to protect his growing revenues, sought, as far as he was able, to clear the sea of pirates.[23]

However, doubts about the security role remain, not least because the figure-eight shield is also apparent *behind the foe of the youth* (see also Rehak 1999a: 234 for a stela in which a chariot drives over someone wearing a figure-eight shield). The security argument is clearer in the "Battle Krater" from Shaft Grave IV at Mycenae, in which the warriors on one side use figure-eight shields and those on the other side hold rectangular shields (see Blakolmer 2012a: 62 with Fig. 9). The warriors are otherwise indistinguishable, however.

The figure-eight shield is a relevant symbol. However, it raises problems of meaning that make it much less reliable than the double-headed axe, the rosette, and the spiral for revealing the presence of Potnia's textile enterprise. One redeeming feature should be noted, however: when the figure-eight shield is turned from the vertical position in which it is worn to a horizontal position, it resembles the blade of the double-headed axe. More will be said about the commercial relevance of the figure-eight shield in Chapter 11.2, in which the shield is seen as worn by the "genius" = "dog" = commercial actor.

6. The "Room 31" Fresco: Iconography of Agency and Legal Status

With respect specifically to commercial agents of the Labyrinth, there is iconographic evidence in Room 31 (the "Room with the Fresco Complex") in the palace at Mycenae (Figure 17, below). Three females are depicted each of whom wears a distinctive garment. One (the "Adorant"), who is about half the size as the other two, holds up mysterious "red, flame-like/leaf-shaped objects," whose upper portion is not preserved. She, interestingly, wears on her wrist a seal-stone bracelet indicating that she is an administrator or executive. The second female (the "Sword Bearer") holds a sword point downward, and the third female (the "Spear Bearer") holds a spear point upward. "The large scale of these [two] figures and their

---

[23] Herodotus (1.171.1–3, 3.122.2) writing about King Minos of Knossos adds: "Harpagus, after subjugating Ionia, made an expedition against the Carians, Caunians, and Lycians, taking Ionians and Aeolians with him. Of these, the Carians have come to the mainland from the islands; for in the past they were islanders, called Leleges and under the rule of Minos, not (as far as I can learn by report) paying tribute, but manning ships for him when he needed them. Since Minos had subjected a good deal of territory for himself and was victorious in war, this made the Carians too at that time by far the most respected of all nations.... For Polycrates was the first of the Greeks whom we know to aim at the mastery of the sea, leaving out of account Minos of Cnossos and any others who before him may have ruled the sea; of what may be called the human race Polycrates was the first, and he had great hope of ruling Ionia and the Islands." (tr. Godley *LCL*)

placement directly over the platform suggest that this portion of the fresco represents Mycenaean deities.... Between them, two small, nude male figures stretch out their arms to the Sword Bearer. Without parallel in Aegean painting their meaning remains uncertain"[24] (Chapin 2016a: 83, 86; cf. Immerwahr 1990: 120–121 with Pl. 60). *That the action is staged in a cult center, probably in a labyrinth, is signaled by the framing of the two major figures between spirally fluted columns and by the griffin that accompanies the "Adorant."* The possible connection of the "Adorant" with textiles is taken up shortly.

Figure 17. Reconstruction drawing of the fresco
from Room 31 of the Fresco Complex at Mycenae.

[24] Depictions including miniature figures are plentiful in the later Aegean world (see Silver 2019 for examples and discussion).

It is argued by Silver (2019: esp. 134–136) that adults rendered as miniature figures are to be understood not as VIPs (*pace* Crowley 2008: 77) but as dependents of full-size figures (cf. *CMS* I, no. 159 = Arachne 157380).[25] Also, Silver (2019: esp. 74) argues that when women (goddesses, priestesses, secular women) are depicted as holding a weapon such as a sword or a bow, or wearing a helmet, armor, or specifically male garment, or controlling a chariot, it means that the female figures are to be understood as potnias—that is, as possessing the legal rights to form contracts typically granted only to males.[26] Such depictions are found in Bronze Age seals: for example, *CMS* II.3, no. 16 (= Arachne 159099) from Minoan Knossos depicts a sword-wielding female whose breasts are made fully visible and who wears a long-patterned skirt; the objects with her are difficult to define, but, as in the case of the youthful warrior in the "Chieftain Cup," she holds a plumed sheath in her left hand (Rehak 1984, 1998 esp. Pl. XLVI f cushion seal from Tiryns).[27]

It is well known that in later Greek times, Athena is depicted as a warrior goddess. Not only in later times. In *Iliad* 5.734ff., Athena "let fall upon her father's floor her soft robe, many-colored (*poikilos*), that herself had wrought and her hands had fashioned, and put on her the tunic of Zeus, the cloud-gatherer, and arrayed her

---

[25] In a depiction of the reconstructed fresco that I found online, one miniature figure is red and the other is black. I cannot really be sure whether they are males or females. The figures are offering trays to "Sword Bearer." I submit that the two miniature "males" should be understood as (foreign?) slaves and possibly as slave-agents (see the discussion of the fresco Py No. 7 below). In a depiction from Mycenae, a woman (apparently) seated on a cushioned throne holds or has presented to her a miniature *woman*, not a child in my opinion (see B. Jones 2009: 318ff. with Fig. 13); the miniature woman is the slave/agent (see Weilhartner 2013: 157 on gift processions).

[26] See above Chap. 5.3. Relevant sources: Brecoulaki et al. 2008: 376–378; Kryzszkowska 2005: 143 with no. 251; similarly no. 250; Rehak 1999c: 708; see also Rehak 1984: 543. For examples of Minoan/Mycenaean cross-dressing, see Brecoulaki et al. 2008: 377. So also the small figure wearing a long robe with a vertical central band in *CMS* I, no. 17 (= Arachne 157238), a gold signet ring from Mycenae. A famous example is the statue of a bearded female from Phylakopi in Melos (Renfrew 1986: 127). In fact, the provision of women (white faces, prominent breasts, and more) is well-known at Mycenae and elsewhere. Thus, a plaster head "found in a room north of the [Mycenae] palace, where it was associated with the Ivory Triad and other precious finds (Fig. 7a-d) [was initially [based on] its pointed chin, considered to be a beard, constituted the main argument in favor of its identification as a male. Since the discovery of new figures and representations in other artistic media, however, we now know that a pointed or painted chin is frequently found on representations of women, either as an artistic convention or for other reasons that are unclear to us. The face, moreover, is painted entirely white, a characteristic typical of depictions of women in Minoan frescoes" (Palaiologou 2015: 100–101 modified). Note the comment of Evans (1935: 23): "This ritual assimilation to the male sex is a make-believe of the same kind as that which led wives of Libyan chiefs to adopt the native *penistasche* of the men or the analogous custom of the Queens of Meroe of asserting their titular kingship by wearing false beards. In such cases it implied a recognition of the fact that government was of rights a male prerogative." See also the burnesha "women (who have chosen) to be men" in Albania (https://www.nytimes.com/2021/08/08/world/europe/sworn-virgins-albania.html; accessed August 9, 2021).

[27] *CMS* II.3, no. 16 = Arachne 159099; *CMS* 11, no. 26 = Arachne 1160054.

in armour for tearful war" (tr. Murray *LCL* modified; emphasis added; cf. Whittaker 2012: 195–196). Athena is depicted as a male because she (her cult) is understood to have the legal powers of a male.[28] Circe is famous for carrying a *rhabdos* (*Odyssey* 10.238) that transformed what she touched with it into her property (Silver 2019: 145). Like the archaic Greek *kouroi* and the unique Minoan Palaikastro Kouros, Athena and Circe are sometimes depicted with left leg striding forward (Silver 2019: 146) as if in the act of taking possession of a property (including of citizenship powers).

Wearing armor or carrying a spear or a bow (*CMS* XI, no. 26 = Arachne 167239; *CMS* XI, no 29 = Arachne 167242) to advertise one's legal status raised no problems for goddesses, but what did mortal women do? It comes to mind that they might have accomplished their goal by replicating male symbols—better, they wore those symbols. We have already mentioned the painting of the chin to suggest a beard (cf. Pliatsola 2012: 615). From frescoes and graves, there is evidence that women possessed and wore necklaces of figure-eight-shaped bead, gold rings with battle scenes, and pendants, such as the one worn by the "Lady of Midea," a Mycenaean terracotta figure, with a vertical eight-shield element on her chest.

> Contrary to the pendants or necklaces of other figures that are suspended from a band around the neck, this piece is sewn (?) or attached (?) just below the neckline of the figure's dress, at the upper end of a central seam (?) line that runs down the torso and joins the diagonal folds (?) of the blouse. If our interpretation is correct, these small artifacts of eight-shield shape make an interesting addition to the attractive assortment of Mycenaean buttons, clips and belt buckles of precious materials, which have recently been identified by experimental replication of 'inconspic-uous' small finds in museum storerooms.
>
> Nikolaidou 2020: 192; cf. Pliatsika 2012: 615–616

My point is that this kind of jewelry and clothing might have been legally functional as well as decorative. In addition, potnias may have worn jewelry plaques depicting male genitals or had them sewn into their garments (for "female satyrs," see Surtees 2014: 282-84). Finally and significantly, I suggest that in a world of bare-chested adult male "citizens" the wearing of a dress with an open bodice identified the female wearer as/with a potnia.

Another seal from Zakros (Figure 18), on the northeastern coast of Crete, depicts "a procession involving two male figures wearing hide skirts: one carries a

---

[28] Born fully armed means that Athena is born with the legal status of a man. Elsewhere, Silver (1992: 26-33) has argued that the "birth" of Athena (or of other gods) from the "*head*" of Zeus (or other gods) is a reference to the financing of her cult—the reference is to seed heads (capital).

double-axe, the other is associated with a floating tassled garment[29] ('sacred knot'?)" (Krzyszkowska 2005: 8). However, the "tassled object" has no loop so it is not a sacred

Figure 18. Procession of male agents of labyrinth, seal from Zakros
(*CMS* II.7, no. 17 = Arachne 160376).

knot. It is a kind of female robe or cuirass/vest (Matoušková 2018: 12–14). The double-headed axe shows that the two men are agents of the goddess of the Labyrinth. Calling the skirts worn by the two males "ceremonial" does not really take us very far. Silver (2019: 73–74) has argued that cross-dressing males are to be understood as agents of a female deity.[30] In this case, the female deity is Potnia of the Labyrinth.

The figures in the processions may be identified as a type of "cult functionary" called *di-pte-ra-po-ro* and interpreted with uncertainty as /dipʰtʰera-pʰoroi/ 'leather-carriers' and/or 'leather-wearers' (discussed by Weilhartner 2013: 159–161). However, as noted by Meißner and Tribulato (2002: 308), they may also be interpreted as '*leather-sellers*' (/dipʰtʰera-pōloi/; alphabetic Greek *diphtherapōlēs* 'leather seller') (see Beekes s.v. *pōleō* 'to offer for sale, sell'). It may be objected that these cultic agents of Potnia only "go to and fro, circuit," wearing/carrying leather (see Beekes s.v. *pōleomai = pelomai*). But why do they do this? Terming peculiar behavior "cultic" does not explain it.[31] There is, of course, a long history of traders who "go around"

---

[29] See Figure 14 for a garment being displayed for sale that floats next to its vendor.

[30] Both men and women appear to wear the hide skirt; see Weilhartner's (2013: 159–161 with n. 63) discussion of the term *di-pte-ra-po-ro*. Sometimes the material is described as "red-colored": "Remains of red-dyed leather were found in a tholos tomb near Kazarma in the Peloponnese" (Weilhartner 2013: 160 with n. 69).

[31] Nikoloudis (2012: 291 n. 34): "Perhaps ... the *di-pte-ra-po-ro* was the figure responsible for transporting ('carrying') and ensuring the safe arrival of the processed hides (*di-pte-ra* properly refers to *treated* hides) from the leather-processing area(s) to the palace, or elsewhere, for distribution or further working. Whether or not this would have constituted a strictly religious role is unknown." Thus, an economic role is proposed but it does not seem to reflect the iconographic message. The

with trade goods (Silver 1992: 131–135; 2020: 75–79). Thus, combining the linguistic interpretation of the *-po-ro* element (carrying or selling) with an iconographic interpretation (wearing, carrying, and displaying) makes it possible to view the *di-pte-ra-po-ro* as one who goes around bearing/wearing and displaying leather in order to sell it.

Returning to the Room 31 fresco, based on her relatively small size and the accompanying griffin, I understand the "Adorant" to be an agent of "Sword Bearer." Furthermore, the mysterious objects held up by the "Adorant" arguably have specifically to do with the fine "golden-colored" fabric sea-silk that is made with the secretion/"beard" of the mollusk *Pinna nobilis*.[32] Burke (2012: 175–176) noting the finds of *Pinna* shells at Mycenae challenges the view that she holds sheaves of grain:

> An alternative source of inspiration for the Mycenaean artists and cult practitioners was the sea. It is possible that the woman in the Room of the Fresco in the Cult Centre at Mycenae is holding *Pinna nobilis* fan shells. The fact that several *Pinna* shells were found in the excavation around the Cult Centre adds some support to this argument.... The reddish color in the fresco for the items held by the woman is characteristic of the *Pinna* fibers. It is my contention that the woman in the lower panel at the Cult Centre at Mycenae is holding *Pinna nobilis* fan shells: it better fits the iconography and the archaeological context than sheaves of grain.[33]

Burke's theory seems reasonable.

In my non-specialist view, what the "Adorant" holds in her hands resembles an element in a textile pattern from Pylos in which a gold fan-shape contains

---

-po-ro element is also found in the word *ka-ra-wi-po-ro* which is clearly /klāwi-pʰoros/ meaning someone who goes about with a key (Meißner and Tribulato 2002: 308).

[32] See https://muschelseide.ch/ (accessed February 17, 2021).

[33] In the excavation of the West Wing in the Knossos Palace, a small room was discovered with two stone chambers called East Temple Repository (ETR) and West Temple Repository (WTR). Among the object found in the Repositories is the "Big Snake Goddess," the "Small Snake Goddess," three (?) plaques of elaborate dresses and girdles decorated with crocus flowers, and numerous (at least 80) specimens of fan-shaped shells (see Stevens and Simandiraki-Grimshaw 2016: Figures 4.1, 4.2) that look to me like cockle shells. This would be of some interest as the Elder Pliny has cockle shell used as bait in the capture of murex: "Purples are taken with a kind of osier kipe of small size, and with large meshes; these are cast into the sea, and in them cockles are put as a bait, that close the shell in an instant, and snap at an object, just as we see mussels do. Though half dead, these animals, as soon as ever they are returned to the sea, come to life again, and open their shells with avidity; upon which the purples seek them, and commence the attack, by protruding their tongues. The cockles, on the other hand, the moment they feel themselves pricked, shut their shells, and hold fast the object that has wounded them: in this way, victims to their greediness, they are drawn up to the surface hanging by the tongue" (*Natural History* 9.61.37; tr. Bostock and Riley, *Perseus Project*).

reddish lines also in a fan shape (M. Shaw 2010: Fig. 10.2 from Lang 1969: Pl. 113). The point being that the shell of the *Pinna nobilis* may well have inspired a textile design. *It has become possible to see the "Adorant" as representing a commercial agent dealing in dyed textiles who operates under the direction of Potnia of the Labyrinth.*

7. Pyxis from Aptera: Iconography of "Colonization"

The overseas mobility of Potnia/the Labyrinth is reflected in Plate 11, a pyxis from Aptera located about eight miles to east of Chania. In the Aptera pyxis, we see double-headed axes bracketed by "horns," but I simultaneously see ships whose sail is in the form of a double-headed axe (such as Potnia Calypso might have helped Odysseus to build in *Odyssey* 5.228–260). The zigzag, or meander patterns, between the ships and above the structure holding the man represent the waves of the sea, but (here and elsewhere) they also represent the twisted thread and the labyrinth itself. As proposed in Chapter 7.5, "horns" are an idealized version of the stern and bow of the ancient vessel. The ships, I propose, are directed to distant destinations by the "prophecies" rehearsed/sung by the holder of the lyre.[34] This lyre holder (ship holder?) prophet in his shrine also holds a branch (of laurel or olive?) in his other hand. He is showing/guiding and, in some sense, accompanying the ships to land/a destination. I am reminded of the seer of the Achaeans, the significantly named Calchas ("Murex Man") who (bearing purple-dyed garments) guided their ships to Troy (*Iliad* 1.69–72, 13.39–45).[35] The Troad is known to be a place that welcomes bearers of murex-dyed textiles

A second, even better, identification for the lyre-player in the structure (a tholos?) is Apollo who is famous for his *lyre* and for his role in "prophecies," colonial foundations, and circuiting.[36] Notice the association of the lyre with birds—a connection that is also manifest in Pylos (see below Chap. 11.5). Most importantly, in the *Homeric Hymn to (Pythian) Apollo* (3.388–440), Apollo is portrayed as guiding the ship of Minos of Knossos that was bound for Pylos for "business and gain" (*prēxin kaichrēmata* 3.397) to various ports and as incorporating the crew into his priesthood (see at length Chap. 11.5).[37]

---

[34]   Cults provided economically valuable geographic information to clients that was framed as "prophecy."

[35]   The same kind of role is played by the Argo's oracular timber (see Parke 1967: 13, 36).

[36]   Sources: Apollo and lyre, *Homeric Hymn to (Pythian) Apollo* 3.184–185; Silver 1992: 264–266 with references; Apollo and colonial foundations/circuiting, Burkert 1985: 84; Silver 1995a: 25–27 with references, Silver 1992: 236–239.

[37]   The god Baal, who presided at Ugarit, a major western Syrian port in the fourteenth to thirteenth centuries BCE, is said to "call a caravan into his house (temple)," or he "calls out a trade route in his house" (Silver 1995a: 4 with references).

In this kind of context of enterprise mobility, the finding of double-headed axes in Anatolian contexts—at Mashat in central Bulgaria and, most importantly, in the northern Pontic region on the Black Sea shore (Harding 1984: 238; Suchowska 2009: 169)—take on added significance. Some of the specimens may have been made in Greece. Even more importantly, as suggested by metal tests, some double-headed axes were manufactured locally. The double-headed axe, as already seen, is neither an exotic souvenir nor a traded commodity. It is one of several symbols of circuiting cults[38] and it is, more specifically, the symbol/trademark of a *cultic enterprise* owned and operated by Potnia of the Labyrinth (§3 above).[39]

The Black Sea finding of a cultic symbol known to be of central importance to Potnia of the Labyrinth reinforces the central proposition of this study: namely that the Minoans/Mycenaeans exported textiles to the Black Sea region and returned with gold.

As noted earlier, Pylos knew a Potnia with Anatolian connections. Pylos (PY Fr 1206) knew a goddess named Potnia *Aswiya*. *Aswiya* has generally been identified as Assuwa in western Anatolia (Morris 2001: 425; more doubtful, Chadwick 1957: 125–126; "Asia" *Iliad* 2.461). Pausanias (3.24.7) places a temple of "Athena Asia" in Colchis on the Black Sea. My suggestion is that Potnia sponsored a quarter or colony of Anatolian artisans and merchants stationed in Pylos.[40] In addition, she would have been positioned to facilitate the movement of Greek goods, artisans, and merchants to Asia generally and, specifically, to the Black Sea. An additional thought is that within Anatolia, the goddess bore a Greek-related epithet and sheltered Greek traders and artisans operating there (see Morris 2001: 429).[41] Thus, in the *Iliad* (6.269–279 and elsewhere), Athena in Troy has the Greek epithet *Ageleiē*, perhaps meaning something like "bringer/gatherer of plunder/property" (*ago* + *lēiē*; Deacy 2000: 288).

As noted earlier, my view is that Potnia Asia and Potnia of the Labyrinth are manifestations/specializations of the same goddess—that is, they are owned by

---

[38] A symbol of the circuiting cult not previously mentioned is the "runner" (see Silver 2019) A notable example can be found on so-called "Runner's Ring" from Kato Syme Crete (Marinatos 2010: 177).

[39] Arguably, the goddess/priestess in Plate 3 should be identified with Potnia and the Labyrinth cult and, in addition, the garland of papyrus stems and flowers she holds signals that she/the cult *goes around*—that is, circuits from one location to another. Moreover, this study proposes that Potnia is a business traveler.

[40] Ergin (2007: 280) notes a tablet from Pylos (PY Ep 705) mentioning *to-ro-ja* 'a Trojan woman' who rents land and is a slave of an unnamed goddess or god (*te-o-jo = thea* may be feminine or masculine) whom, he suggests, may be Asian Potnia: "We do not know whether the Trojan women [woman] also worked in the textile industry ... [but] a new technology, grooved loom weights, appeared in the 13th cent. BC and enabled the weaving of more sophisticated textiles."

[41] Bacchylides, admittedly a much later source, has Theanō granting an Achaean embassy entrance into the Athena temple (see M. Davies 2019: 167–170).

a common cultic management.[42] Whether one or many Pontias, it is clear that there were commercial relations with Anatolia.

8. Vase from Pseira, "5-Priestess Ring," Palm, and Papyrus: Headquarters and Branches of the Labyrinth

Earlier sections presented evidence suggesting that the Labyrinth was a multi-branched textile-marketing enterprise. In this section, the focus is more closely on management structure—that is, were the branch enterprises actually "franchises." In other words, I consider whether they were independent firms with the same "trademark" (primarily the double-headed axe) or were they branches

Figure 19. Lid of vase from Pseira.

operating under the control of a cultic center (in Crete)? The answer provided by additional iconographic evidence confirms that multiple units bearing the double-headed axe remained under the control of the center.

Consider first the cover of a vase from Pseira (Figure 19) depicting four separate double-headed axes, each of which is physically attached by its shaft to a central cultic center.[43] The four outlier cultic units may be understood as fixed in

---

[42]   Also at Pylos, there is a *ne-wo-pe-o po-ti-ni-ja* (PY Cc 666). In 1957, Chadwick (1957: 118) wrote: "The word *ne-wo-pe-o* recurs in the lists of slave-women (PY Aa 786, PY Ab 554) and might be a place-name; but in view of PY Ad 688 *ne-wo-pe-oko-wo* it is perhaps more likely a descriptive term for the women; presumably a two-termination compound adjective in *-os*, since its genitive plural is identical with its nominative plural, and therefore not an ethnic. No conclusions as regards Potnia seem possible here." It does not seem that the meaning of *ne-wo-pe-o* has since become clearer, although it appears to be regarded as a place name.

[43]   It is difficult to be sure, but I see two pillars and perhaps an altar.

Figure 20. "5-priestess ring" (seal ring No. 2),
from grave of "Griffin Warrior" in Pylos.

position, or we may instead see one outlier that rotates continuously on its axis to different locations (Marinatos 2010: 127 Fig. 9.19a). What seems clear from the insistence on a physical connection is that the outlier unit(s) are administered by the cultic center. The Labyrinth is a multi-plant/shop, multi-national enterprise.[44]

Next, consider a gold signet ring (Seal Ring No. 2) with Minoan styled imagery that was recently excavated at Pylos from the early Mycenaean grave of the "Griffin Warrior" (Figure 20). The scene depicted on the seal casts new light on the circuiting of the cult of Potnia of the Labyrinth—possibly from Minoan Crete to Pylos. The depiction on the seal is described at length by Davis and Stocker (2016: 640–642 with Figure 10), and I quote fully:

> Five elaborately dressed female figures flank a shrine. The shrine is located on the shore of an inlet that separates three women on the right from two on the left. All five women stand on an undulating band that separates land from sea and is decorated with small impressed circles arranged in horizontal bands (apparently meant to represent a sandy beach).... All five women face the shrine and the tree. The three women on the right are dressed in flounced skirts and short-sleeved bodices. They wear scarves around their necks that appear as peculiar winglike excrescences, with wreaths also around their necks, and double belts around their waists. The large, central figure is depicted in a frontal pose, her breasts prominent, both hands on her hips, and with small subrounded indentations above

---

[44] In considering whether Pseira itself might host a branch of the Labyrinth, note that the town had about 60 buildings (Rehak and Younger 1998: 101–102).

each arm. Her skirt has nine flounces. Two closely spaced bands mark the edge of each of her sleeves, and she wears a bracelet on each wrist. Her head and facial features lack any definition, as is also the case for the other four figures.... The two women to the left of the inlet wear tall conical hats, skirts decorated with horizontal and vertical lines, aprons, and sleeveless jackets; they hold their left hands to their heads, with their right arms extended behind them.... The two smaller figures in the group of three appear to be represented in profile, with only one arm held on the hip and small subrounded indentations above it. There is no indication of breasts, most likely an indication of their youth. The bodice of the figure on the right side has a vertical row of ovoid impressions to the left. The skirt of the figure on the left has seven flounces, that on the right, six. Neither figure wears a bracelet. If the large figure on the right is the Minoan goddess, as we imagine, then she has joined her worshippers in their ritual.

My responses are as follows:

(1) All five figures are linked in a common cult.

(2) The figures on the right and left are separated by a body of water. They can be understood as standing on the seashore (Tully 2020: 368). The two women on the left are Minoans stationed overseas (or else they are natives), but they have retained (or professed) their central cultic allegiance. The allegiance is indicated by the gesture—a kind of salute—they make with their left hands to their heads and extended right arms. The three figures including the goddess wearing the "traditional" Minoan flounced skirt have circuited and returned to their home base. The latter trio is not idiosyncratic as it is depicted elsewhere on at least one seal (*CMS* I, no. 159 = Arachne 157380) from Mycenae and, more importantly, on a sealing (*CMS* II.6, no. 1= Arachne 160071) from Agia Triada.

(3) The two smaller circuiters, who wear elaborate skirts but are topless, are men not women, which fact explains why they do not have visible breasts. The wearing of a skirt (cross-dressing) indicates that the two men are agents of a female, presumably of the goddess who accompanies them (see §6).

(4) The "peculiar winglike excrescences" worn by the goddess and her two male agents are wings that are indicative of habitual circuiting. It is of special interest that the wings are represented in a way close to the neck, inviting comparison to a double-headed axe, in which the head of the figure serves as the shaft.[45] There is reason to believe that the wings were actually worn.[46]

---

[45] For wings as representations of the double-headed axes, see McGowan (2011: 23 with Figure 6).

[46] Tully (2020: 366) suggests that the "wings" are actually garment components attached close to the neck as in the seal *CMS* I, no. 159 from Mycenae and in the sealing *CMS* II.6, no. 7 from Agia Triada both of which feature "a larger female figure flanked by two smaller ones."

(5) I suggest that the winged/circuiting goddess on the right is Potnia of the Labyrinth.

(6) The original user of the seal was possibly an envoy/messenger linking the two cult centers together.

(7) The garment worn by the two priestesses on detached duty is unfamiliar to me, but their conical hats are familiar; they call to mind the "Agia Triada Sarcophagus" (Chap. 2 above). Specifically, one of the short sides of the Sarcophagus (Λ 396) depicts two women wearing pointed hats who ride in a chariot drawn by a winged griffin (Plate 12).[47] The chariot riders are accompanied above and below with center-dotted rosettes. Chapter 11.5 shows that it was the duty of the griffin to protect and convey overseas traders in the interests of the labyrinth/palace. This duty would include the conveyance and protection of priestesses on detached duty.

(8) The question of the *location* of the palm trees is pursued at some length below.

Soles (2016a: 252) has speculated that priestesses of Potnia were likely "to be resident in every town in Crete and in its colonies overseas, including Thera. They represented Knossos and embodied its powers just as the ritual objects[48] from Knossos found all over Crete encapsulated them." This kind of mobility may be alluded to in CMS II.7, no. 7 (= Arachne 160366) from Zakros, depicted in Figure 18, wherein two male cultic agents walk in a procession, one carrying the double-headed axe and the other a sacred garment. In discussing this seal, Soulioti (2016: 159) finds it

> intriguing that iconography precisely stresses the moment of transportation of the symbol and not the moment of the shafting of the symbol. It can be assumed that this transfer was a highly significant part in the use of the symbol or perhaps that the final setting of placement of the joined symbol was an interior space, the representation of which is generally uncommon in Minoan iconography.

Tully (2020: 369) calls attention to the creation by the Minoan textile industry of net-like fabrics for high-fashion garments and wall hangings. Then, citing the net

---

[47] The (conical) shape of the hats may refer to the shape of the "Asherah Poles." (The Agia Triada Sarcophagus also depicts agrimi drawing a chariot.) Mysterious long conical hats are worn by unfinished male figurines from the Knossos harbor area (Evans 1928: 234–235 with Fig. 132). The form of the hat is meaningful and I venture that the conical hat represents the wearer's connection to the triton/murex.

[48] Among these we should include numerous numerous terracotta throne models characterized by Vetters (2011: 327) to be "tokens of the palace": "They evidence the transfer and acceptance of a religious ideology and new rituals such as the epiphany rituals centered on the throne in the palatial megara to the wider Mycenaean populace."

pattern on the shrine in the "5-Priestess Ring"[49] and the seaside location of the scene, she understands it, reasonably I think, as referring to Minoan seaside occupations:

> [T]he presence of elite women wearing elaborate textile garments at a sea shrine, as depicted on the Griffin Warrior Ring No. 2, may refer to cult focused upon all the aspects of the Minoans' relationship with the sea: from the micro-gestures associated with catching and collection of seafoods and harvesting of fabric dyes and materials to the expansive macro-movements involved in the overseas textile trade.
>
> Tully 2020: 374[50]

I propose, finally, to address problem (8)—that is, the problem of the *location* of the date palm trees in the "5-Priestess Ring." I am not aware that Delos or the Troad region possessed a the comparative advantage in cultivation of this tree. Nevertheless, the palm stands out in classical Greek art concerned with the Trojan War. Palm trees appear in the temple precinct of Athena (and in Apollo's).[51] Might these palms be references to Potnia of Asia/Assuwa (Chaps. 6.2, 9.6, 10.7)? More specifically, might they refer to the prominent palm trees along the Black Sea around Sochi? Possibly, the prominently depicted palm trees in the Knossos throne room (Chap. 4.2) are a reference to the multinational status of the Potnia cult. My more limited response to problem (8) is that the palm trees in the throne chamber and in the "5-Priestess Ring" reference the main branch location in the "land of the palms"—that is, in Phoenicia/Syria. Against these more distant identifications, or at least adding new food for thought, is that the Itanos region in eastern Crete is noted for its palm trees in the forest of Vai and also for the possible production of murex preserved with honey (see above Chaps. 7.2, 5).

Indeed, the same kind of branch location explanation might apply to the *papyrus reeds with flowers* depicted in the Knossos throne room (Chap. 4.2) and

49 The "net pattern on the shrine" brings to my mind the aegis worn by Athena (Chap. 6.2) and also a "fishing net" that is woven, worn, and "conveyed" by sea by the Ugaritic goddess Athirat (Asherah) (Natan-Yulzary 2020: 136-38). For an Egyptian beadnet dress, see https://collections.mfa.org/objects/146531 (accessed September 16, 2021).
50 To Tully's list of the applications of net-like textile patterns we should add for sails (Evans 1928: 243 with Fig. 140). In developing Tully's line of interpretation, note the uncertain origin of one gold transfer to the center recorded in Pylos Jo 438 (Chap. 9.5). The name of the place(s) lying behind a "toponymic adjective" has been interpreted as /Tinwanthos/ or /Thinwanthos/. Janko (2019) notes that the concentration of names ending in –*anthos* is in the Western Peloponnese but he grants that the ending may also be –*anda*, an ending widely attested in the ancient place-names of Western Anatolia.
51 In the temple of Trojan Athena, Malibu, J. Paul Getty Museum 80.AE.154 shows palm trees on both sides of the temple of Athena. Palms in the temple of Apollo at Troy: Two palms in Perugia, Museo Archeologico Nazionale 89 and elsewhere in connection to the death of Troilus. Palms in the temple of Apollo at Delos (*Odyssey* 6.162–170).

elsewhere (see Chap. 11.5). Most importantly, as has been briefly noted, the goddess/priestess in Plate 3, whom I have identified with the smaller "Snake Goddess" from the "Knossos Temple Repositories," prominently holds a garland/wreath formed of three papyrus stems, each with a flower with lily petals at the head. I theorize that the garland symbolizes "going around" with the lily symbolizing home (Crete or mainland Greece), and the papyrus referencing *an Egyptian (Nile Delta) branch of the Labyrinth.* Warren (1985: 201), who so very well describes the garland, finds the scene to be "reminiscent enough of Egyptian plaques." Reinforcement for this locational interpretation of the garland is provided in Knossos' "Fresco of Garlands" which features garlands of papyrus together with (red or white) lilies (Warren 1985: 198).[52] A message of possession of multiple cultic centers is also conveyed by the Minoan "*waz*-lily,"[53] which combines papyrus and lily into a single symbol. A prominent example of the latter theme is, as Warren (1985: 198) points out, the necklace/garland of *waz*-lilies worn by the "Prince of the Lilies."[54] Note the reference to cult circulation in the *waz*-lily symbols on the stern cabin in the West House fresco from Akrotiri (Warren 1985: 199).[55]

The depiction of the palm tree and the papyrus plant in the throne room would have served the same purpose as lettering in the windows of upscale shops that announce "With branches in Madrid, Lisbon, London, Geneva."[56] The goddess is identified with her cult place and, hence, with its symbol—that is, the date palm or the papyrus plant *is* Potnia.[57]

---

[52] Admittedly, there is or would be a difficulty with this line of explanation when/if the garlands included plants/flowers not readily identifiable with any particular geographic location.

[53] *Waz* after the Egyptian goddess Wazet.

[54] Note also a gold necklace with *waz* lily shaped beads from the Mycenaean cemetery of Midea tomb 10, Dendra, Greece (National Archaeological Museum Athens, catalogue number 8748).

[55] I suspect that that the "blades" of the double-headed axes in Figure 19 may also represent the *waz*-lily. The "Loom-weight Basements" at Knossos (Chap. 2.d) included a large pot with a painting of three palm trees or, to judge by lowermost leaves having spiral curves, a combination of palm tree with lily (Kantor 1999: 310; PM I, 253–254, Fig. 190). May we think of Egypt and the Near East as destinations for the textiles?

[56] "In an interview conducted by *Corriere della Sera* 2 (April 27, 2015), Miuccia Prada claimed that *Made in Italy* was made famous all over the world through her creations; but she underlined the importance of being international as well: "'Because if you're just Italian, you are cut off from the world. If you are not international, you don't exist'" (Cited by Salvati and Cosenza 2017: 144).

[57] Thus, in *CMS* II.8, no. 126 (= Arachne 160756) two sacral knots flank what appears to be a palm tree. Again, in "The 'Prince' Seal-Stone" (Naxos Archaeological Museum, inventory number 980): "In the right part of the composition, a male figure wearing headdress (*polos*) and loincloth (*perizoma*) and holding a long spear in his outstretched right arm, stands in front of a low offering table stacked with libation vessels (situla, jug and rhyton) and an inverted sword. In the left part stands a large palm tree. The nature of the depicted objects suggests that this is a scene of preparation for a sacrifice" (Vlachopoulos 2016: 158–159 with Fig. 76). The beneficiary would have been Potnia= the palm tree.

Support for the locational significance of both palm and papyrus is provided by the observation that "Nilotic motifs, waterfowl, papyri, and palms, are especially popular on larnakes [coffins].... This purely Nilotic landscape probably represents a faraway and exotic land" (Watrous 1991: 296–297). Support for the marketing value of cosmopolitanism is provided by the observation that "Toward the end of the 15th century other individual Nilotic motifs, such as papyri and waterfowl, become part of the Palace Style repertory, which also featured Minoan motifs of marine life, flora, and luxurious ornamentation" (Watrous 1991: 297).[58]

Against this reasoning, it is possible to suggest that the date palm was chosen as a distinctive symbol of Crete where it grows all over. I doubt that Potnia would have chosen it on these grounds, however. The argument for the selection of the palm as a symbol becomes stronger, I think, when an account is taken of the palm groves of Vai, in which murex dye was arguably produced with the aid of honey (see Chap. 7.2, 5).

A final reference to cultic circuiting is the Agia Triada "Girl on a Swing." This is a restored[59] clay model in which a woman sits on a swing (*aiora*) suspended between two pillars or (better) "horns" "topped by flying birds."[60] Cucuzza (2013: 175, 178) observes that given the current reconstruction of the pillar base as connecting the two pillars, the entire structure may be understood as a reference to "horns of consecration" or, as proposed in Chapter 7.5, the "horns" refer to the extended bow and stern of some ancient ships.

The "back-and-forth" movement of the swing (*aiora*) has been interpreted in terms of "agricultural fertility" or "atonement" (see Cucuzza 2013: 177–179). To date, I have not yet seen the suggestion of an "initiation ritual." Cucuzza (2013: esp. 198ff.) wonders whether the "swinging figure" may be a "flying figure." However, whether "swinging" or "flying," the figure may be understood as a reference to a cultic "back-and-forth" to overseas destinations.[61]

---

[58] In *CMS* VS.1A, no. 55 (= Arachne 165283), a figure in a ship salutes an accompanying palm tree. Does this mean that the palm is travelling to a new location or that the figure is traveling to the (fixed) location of the palm?

[59] The swinging figure and the pillars were found in two different rooms of a building of disputed function (the so-called "Tomb of Gold"). "The lower part connecting the two pillars has been restored: the figurine and pillars were identified as belonging to the same model on the basis of the clay type, the decoration, and the presence of holes for the passage of the thread" (Cucuzza 2013: 175).

[60] For flying birds as symbols of circuiting, see Chap. 10.4 and elsewhere. Birds, understandably not with opened wings, are depicted on pillars topped by a double-headed axe inside A of the Agia Triada sarcophagus (see e.g. https://www.ancient.eu/image/10613/hagia-triada-sarcophagus/ [accessed February 12, 2021]).

[61] Erigonē known in myth as a wine peddler is celebrated in ritual as a "swinger" in the Athenian *Aiōra* festival (Silver 1992: 134–135). More relevant for the present study is Helle, arguably a "swinger" and a passenger (until she "fell off") with Phrixus aboard the Ram with the Golden Fleece on its journey(s) to the Black Sea (Chap. 16 below; see Tiverios 2014).

11

The Labyrinth as a Textile Trader

Seeking Commercial Knowledge from Iconographic Symbols (Concluded)

1. Roundel from Samothrace: Evidence for Potnia's Participation in Overseas Commerce

ADDITIONAL evidence not only links the presence of the double-headed axe in the eastern Aegean with the Minoans but also documents the Labyrinth's participation in transactions there. This evidence comes from the doorstep of Anatolia in Samothrace and takes the form of a roundel (SA Wc 1) excavated at Mikro Vouni, a settlement site on the beach of the island's SW shore.[1]

The Samothracian roundel has a faint Linear A sign group written in ink on the side whose proposed reading is AB 81. The number of transactions is indicated by six seal impressions, but two have been erased with lumps of clay. One of the four transactional seal impressions consists of the double-headed axe (041) and the sepia (019; calamari/cuttlefish) sign. The signs' meanings have been debated, but, using the sound values of Linear B, the proposed syllabic reading of the double-headed axe is *a-sa-sa-ra*, while the second symbol (an ideogram plus the sign AB 77) has the sense of "fence"/"enclosure" (Matsas 1991: 171–172 with references). Thus, it follows that "*a-sa-sa-ra*'s enclosure" is one of the participants in the recorded transaction. That the effort was made to record the transaction together with the presence in Samothrace of balance weights of the Minoan system suggests that the transaction involved a relatively high-value commodity. Obviously, the roundel refers to a transaction in

---

[1] Altogether five Minoan clay mini documents have been discovered at this site—namely two roundels, two noduli, and a nodule—balance weights of the Minoan system have also been excavated (Matsas 1995: 235, 242; on roundels, Hallager 1987a). The Samothrace materials appear to date as early as the second half of the eighteenth century BCE. For Linear A inscriptions more generally, see Chapter 9.6 above.

which Minoans/Minoan agents participated, and it is reasonable to assume that "*a-sa-sa-ra*'s enclosure" is a Minoan institution or enterprise.

Who is *a-sa-sa-ra*? MacGillivray (2012: 120 with references) has noted a number of Linear A inscriptions on pottery and double-headed axes from the Arkalochori cave that *provisionally* have been read as *a-ra-ra* and understood as the name of a Minoan female deity whose name begins with "a."[2] I conjecture that the Minoan goddess is the Potnia of the Labyrinth found in the Linear B tablets. That is, Potnia[3] is the goddess and her "enclosure" is the Labyrinth. A possible clue to the relationship between the two ideograms may be provided by the design on a pendant seal in the Ashmolean Museum (Figure 21): "Two women are shown adoring a double-axe set on an object resembling one form of the so-called gate hieroglyph" (Brice 1965-1966: 67), or is it an altar?[4]

Figure 21. Two women adore double axe on gate-hieroglyph
(*CMS* VI, no. 282 = Arachne 164413).

---

[2] "The a/ja-sa-sa-ra-AB 13 sign-group remains, in fact, the most durable feature of Cretan writing throughout the second millennium BC. It appears for the first time at the very beginning of writing in Crete on Cretan Hieroglyphic seal inscriptions. It continues with its attestations on Linear A vessel inscriptions (both stone and clay), as well as on a silver pin, but it also closes its historic timeline with the last, probably fossilized attestation of Linear A on a figurine from Poros in Herakleion" (Karnava 2016: 353).

[3] *A-ta-na* 'Athena' is attested in both a Linear B tablet and a Linear A inscription on a Cretan pithos from the House of the Ladies at Akrotiri (Karnava 2016: 351–352).

[4] Note that the figure is actually 4c and that Brice appends the note: "V. E. G. Kenna thinks that C is not genuine." For other examples of objects inscribed *a-sa-sa-ra* or the variant *ja-sa-sa-ra*, see Verduci and Davis (2015: 64). For a possible connection of this name to a Semitic deity "Asherah" and/or to tree-like cultic structures ("Asherah Poles"), see Samson (2021) who notes that double-headed axes cap "Asherah Poles" in the Agia Triada Sarcophagus (Side A). Ackerman (2008) argues that Asherah is the patron goddess of textile production in the West Semitic world and mentions that at Ugarit, Asherah is "The Lady who treads on the sea." It is tempting to identify the "Asherah Pole" with the mast of a merchant ship (Rich 2012) and then the "Horn of Consecration."

What was the Samothrace transaction's concern? Matsas (1991: 173) reasons: "Perhaps our roundel represents a receipt by which the Minoan administration of the Sanctuary(?) acknowledges the delivery of some kind of goods or the fulfillment of a certain service from the part of the site's inhabitant in whose house the object was found." What is the item of some value that the "inhabitant" might have delivered? As a solitary establishment located near the sea, there are various possibilities, but, certainly, purple dye and/or purple-dyed cloth are reasonable ones. Purple production is attested on Samothrace as at neighboring Lemnos.

2. Dog as Commercial Actor, as Genius, and Beyond

In Minoan and Mycenaean iconography, the dog represents a commercial actor. Evidence for "dogs" as commercial actors, especially as commercial agents, is explored at length by Silver (1992: Ch. 7). More recently, our understanding of the dog metaphor has deepened and become generalized by Franco (2014) and then by Silver (2019: 138–141). In Greek literature, the insult "dog" or "doggish" is arguably a reference to an individual's personal dependence on or greed for material possessions, including especially commercial greed.

Perhaps the best example of the dog/commercial greed connection is provided by Homer in *Iliad* 10.502–506, in which Diomedes weighs the costs and benefits to select his most "doggish" course of action. As Graver (1995: 47) explains well,

> The issue that concerns him seems ... to be one of quantities: how much plunder can he get away with? Or how many Thracians can he kill? Notice how both bloodshed and looting are expressed in terms of taking something ... as if the lives of Diomedes' enemies are a commodity whose value can be measured against the more portable property. What is most doggish for him to do seems to be determined by a purely materialistic calculation: the most gain in the shortest time.

In terms of my interpretation of the Minoan iconography, most telling is Helen's reference to herself as "*dog-faced*" *kunōpis* (*Iliad* 3.180; *Odyssey* 4.145). In addition, Hephaestus uses this expression of Hera (*Iliad* 18.396) and Achilles of Agamemnon (*Iliad* 1.159). In each case, as this study shows, there are implications of commercial motivation and/or greed.

In addition, to say that someone is (or similar to) a dog likely means that he/ she is in the personally dependent position of an agent, including a commercial agent. This is because the dog, like the ancient agent, is always answerable with his body to his master/principal for unsatisfactory performance. In Ancient Greece, the agent had slave or slave-like legal status (Silver 2019).[5]

This section interprets the much-discussed "genii"[6] of Minoan/Mycenaean iconography as *dogs* and then considers some implications of this insight. All the physical attributes of a genius, including long, pointed ears, can be found in the dog family as illuminated many years ago by Sansone (1988: 7–8):

> An animal which has paws and which can have long, pointed ears is the dog. But of greater relevance than the actual appearance of dogs is, of course, the practice of Bronze-Age artists when dealing with canine representation. To be sure, there is great variety in the depiction of dogs in Minoan and Mycenaean art. Nor is this surprising considering the diversity of breeds. Indeed, this diversity may account for the variation in the appearance of the demons. But the long, pointed ears are very much in evidence, sometimes pricked up, sometimes laid back along the head. And the faces, some short and square, others long and pointed, bear close resemblances to the faces of many of the demons. These resemblances, along with the pointed ears, paws and variation in the depiction of the face, make it quite likely that the appearance of the demons is intended to be canine. This identification is securely confirmed by two observations. *In the first place, on a number of occasions the demon is represented with what appears to be a collar around its neck, and collars are a regular feature of the portrayal of dogs in Minoan and Mycenaean art. In the second place, the role that the demon frequently assumes is that of the hunter, and in art (as in life) the dog is the companion of its master on the hunt.*[7] (emphasis added)

Dogs with long, pointed ears and various types of faces, including long and pointed, are clearly depicted in the (debated) Benaki Museum golden kylix (inventory number 2108; Papageorgiou 2008: Figs. 1–4).[8] It is difficult to understand

---

5   On numerous occasions, Homer refers to Hermes as *diaktoros*, a word whose meaning is disputed. One theory is that it derives from *diaktonos* "slave" (Beekes s.vv. *diaktoros, diaktonos*; Chittenden 1948: 28–29). If the linkage holds, then Hermes would be "one who serves/slaves as an agent." In the Amarna texts from the second millennium BCE, Egyptian individuals are referred to as "dog" and *ardu* "slave" (Galán 1993: 174–175).

6   Although there are depictions with a single genius, there are also scenes in which there are multiple, and, therefore, the figures do not represent a single actor but a family of actors (Sansone 1988: 3). The genii discussed below appear in glyptic art, but a few fragmentary depictions are present in the "Cult Center at Mycenae," which is linked to the palace by the "Processional Way."

7   In Aegean Bronze Age glyptic art, "dogs can be shown as either companions of their masters or as sole protagonists of the chase" (Marinatos in Marinatos and Morgan 2005: 120).

8   "The kylix inv. no. 2108 is decorated on the body with three repoussé animals, which are depicted running one behind the other going from right to left. Their elongated bodies with the

why Sansone's identification has been ignored, especially since, as we have just seen, the dog family has an ample and well-defined interpretation in the ancient world, both Greek and Near Eastern.[9]

However, this section seeks to do more than interpret the genius of a dog as a commercial actor. As already noted, an individual's skin color and/or clothing may serve as an iconographic signal of his/her legal status. This brings us to the "dorsal appendage" frequently worn by the genius/dog from the top of its head usually to about the middle of the calf or even to the ankle. The basic nature of the appendage is clear enough: as explained by Baurain (1985: 103–110), *it is a shield/garment in the form of a figure-eight shield or, what comes close to the same thing, in the form of a double-headed axe.*[10] The shield/garment is held in place at the neck by a "necklace"—actually a *collar*—and at the waist by a belt (well-illustrated in Baurain 1985: 109 Fig. 13).[11] *Thus, the genius wearing the figure-eight shield made of textile is an agent for the Labyrinth (a "table-dog").* In addition, he

---

long necks, their equally long tails and legs, and the depiction of the ribs leave no doubt that the craftsman intended to depict hunting dogs. It is a different matter when it comes to the heads. Though they are all slightly different, the heads of the three hounds could be those of a wolf or a deer, as the characteristic angularity rendering the projection of the eyebrow arches which, in complete accordance with the natural model, is found in most depictions of dogs in Creto-Mycenaean art, is missing (figs 8-10). The excessively long ears, especially in the middle dog and the one on the left of the handle (figs 8-9, 11), suggest alternatively the depiction of a hare. Consequently, it is not surprising that in the early references to the kylix the animals were identified as hares, despite the fact that this would be ruled out by the elongated, long-haired tail.... It should also be noted that it is not unusual for the depiction of a dog in Minoan or Mycenaean art to be confused with that of a wolf or a lion, though mainly in small-scale creations." (Papageorgiou 2008: 20). I have viewed the wolf as representing an argos-dog (an Autolycus)—that is, as acting alertly/commercially not as an agent but on its own behalf but especially in the sheep market (see Chap. 15.1).

9   Specialized Aegean iconographers have sought to trace the origin of the genius to the Egyptian iconography of Taweret.

10   Recall that when the figure-eight shield is turned from the vertical to the horizontal it resembles the blade of the double-headed axe. In this case, the belt serves as the shaft.

11   It would seem that the figure-eight shield/garment worn on the back of the genius might also be worn in front. There is a description of an image on a Minoan sarcophagus that may suggest this arrangement: "The figure *appears* to be wearing a small round shield in front of the upper body, a central circle indicating the boss.... Though the round shield has not survived in the representations of LH/LM IIIA, it could conceivably have been in use during this time. On the other hand, it may be that the beginning of the curved form in the lower part of the body was the other half of a figure-of-eight shield, the centre curiously waisted and striped like the fabric of a dress. Bizarre though it sounds, this possibility cannot be excluded. The figure, with its large eye and upraised locks, is unique.... The extraordinary figure on the larnax, with its otherworldly head, its body clad half in skirt, half it appears in shield, and its staff or spear in front, is surely not intended to be read as human" (Morgan 1987: 177, 190). Morgan (1987: 190–191) goes on to "offer a tentative interpretation only in the form of a question: is this the so-called 'warrior goddess' suspected from Mycenaean representations?" I would suggest that the bizarre creature is a genius with its dorsal appendage turned to its front.

may be an entrepreneurial dog who invests his own capital and takes a risk like the "collectors" (Chap. 8.2; see also the discussion of Odysseus in Chap. 15 with Figure 42).

A dog without the dorsal appendage depicted together with a genius raises questions. One interpretation is that this dog is a commercial actor who is a dependent of the genius but not the Labyrinth. The second, more likely, interpretation is that he is employed by the Labyrinth but in a lower ranking trader status. He has not yet, so to speak, earned his dorsal appendage.

A more difficult question is whether the *apparent/seeming* differences in the materials used to construct the figure-eight shield worn by a genius reveal anything significant about his/her field of entrepreneurship. One thought is that the dog/genius wearing an animal skin—a figure-eight shield decorated with either globules (tassels?) or with spikes that make it look like some seashells—are overseas traders and that the dog wearing a smooth textile is a domestic commercial actor. I will say now that I have found no support for any hypotheses of this kind.[12]

On a gold signet ring from Tiryns (Figure 22, opposite) and on others elsewhere, there are depicted genii wearing dorsal appendages, each of which holds/presents a libation jug to the seated figure of a god or king or, according to Rehak (1995c: 224) and Marinatos (2010: 27–28), and I agree, to a goddess or priestess who wears a flat cap and greets/welcomes them holding up a chalice. That the scene takes place in the Labyrinth is indicated immediately by the series or sequence of what I understand to be stylized motifs of double-headed axes or half-rosettes in the seal's dado-zone. The "genius" with chalice and dorsal appendage is accompanied by the running spiral on another seal *CMS* XII, no. 212 (= Arachne 167989). The running spiral not only places the scene in the labyrinth but also indicates that the genius is an instrument/the property of the labyrinth (compare Günkel-Maschek 2012: 122–124).

The Tiryns scene reminds me of the well-known practice of foreign traders bringing gifts to Egyptian rulers and officials who, in a text from the fifteenth century BCE, are called or likened to "dogs" who perform the "dog-walk":[13] "(Tuthmosis III) who inspects the foreign lands of the Tjehenu (Libyans) who are bowing down because of his majesty's might, their gifts/goods (*aenew*) on their backs, [approach]ing like dogs (*tjesemew*) do to request for them the breath of Life."[14] The "breath of life" is the grant of trading rights.

---

[12] I recognize the possibility that the differences in materials of the garments may be an artistic illusion but I think the possibility of real differences needs to be explored.

[13] The Greeks were familiar with the "dog-walk," note the verb *kuneō*: "to prostate (oneself at), to kiss the ground, to honor by prostrating (Hom.)" (Beekes s.v.).

[14] Urkunden IV 809 8–11; tr. Galán 1993: 177–178 modified; Silver 1992: 148; cf. Chap 8.6 above.

Figure 22. Genii present libations to Potnia, gold ring from Tiryns
(*CMS* I, no. 179 = Arachne 157400).

There is, however, an obvious objection to interpreting the genii/dogs as commercial agents *of foreign origin* who are offering gifts to the ruler. Unlike the merchants depicted in Egyptian tombs, the genii all bear the same object—a libation jug. Therefore, I see the Tiryns procession in a religious light: the Tiryns genii with the figure-eight shields are traders, who are honoring with libations their controlling deity, who must be Potnia of the Labyrinth. Recall: First (see Chap. 4.1), in the megaron at Pylos, there is a libation installation built into the floor next to the space for the throne. Second, the disagreement among scholars over whether the seated figure is male or female is only to be expected. The figure is wearing the long dress normally worn by men (Brecoulaki et al. 2008: 377; cf. Rehak 1995c 225). The explanation, I propose, is that in her relationship with the traders, Potnia must exhibit that she is a *potnia*—that is, that she has the contractual and other legal powers typically possessed by males (see Chap. 6.3). Third, as already noted, the seated figure in the Tiryns seal is surrounded by several symbols of the Labyrinth. The occupant of the throne is Potnia of the Labyrinth.

In an example from Patras Voundeni, Achaia (Figure 23, below)—a dog/genius wearing a figure-eight garment decorated with globules/tassels, and hence an agent of Potnia—conveys a human on its shoulder. I suggest that this form of carriage signals a mode of conveyance probably aboard a ship. Furthermore, the human is not a corpse but rather a living slave whom the genius offers for sale. Indeed, as slave dealers are wont to do, the genius/dog raises its left arm (pointing to the victim) and has its mouth open to extol his commodity to an unseen audience. Rehak (1995c: 220–221) explains of the "corpse": "[H]is pose, with the left arm crossed over the chest and the right

Figure 23. Genius carries and discusses a living man, seal from Achaia
(*CMS* VS.1B, no. 153 = Arachne 165833).

extended, seems odd. This cannot be a moribund figure." The right arm is not only extended but also in a straight line in what appears to be a formal gesture. I submit that the victim, who is being sold/selling himself into slavery, is taking an oath of allegiance to his new owner.[15] (He is seeking "the breath of life.") I understand the slave dealer as an agent operating overseas on behalf of the Labyrinth. A text attesting to the sale of a slave was cited earlier (in Chap. 8.5).

In another seal (Figure 24, opposite), the two flanking dogs, who do not wear dorsal appendages, form a double-headed axe symbol with the genius, whose upright body represents the shaft of the axe. My interpretation is that the double axe/Labyrinth employs all three dogs, but the genius—the individual wearing the figure-eight shield—is the supervisor of the two dogs that flank him.[16] An additional observation, perhaps not so apparent, is that the genius' legs are in the "kneel-running" (*Knielauf*) position with the sense of being simultaneously stationary and in transit. He is a traveling/circuiting head trader.

In Figure 25 (opposite), a seal from Mycenae, the standing genius—i.e. the anthropomorphic dog who seems to wear a smooth textile dorsal appendage—is flanked by two dogs with bare backs, who look back at him as if for control or feeding. They are the (foreign?) agents of the genius. Only the dorsal appendage of the genius connects this trio with the Labyrinth.

Again, in a sealing (*CMS* II.8, no. 248 = Arachne 160878), a muscular young man with a plumed (= lily?) headgear[17]—who resembles one identified as young man A in the "Chieftain Cup" and also the "Priest King" (Figures 3 and 7 in Chap. 6.3)—holds

---

[15]   In the Abusir temple reliefs of the Fifth Dynasty, unfettered Asiatics arriving in Egypt by boat stand and enthusiastically salute Sahure as *"god of the living"* (Bresciani 1997: 228).

[16]   I do not know how to interpret the devices on the bodies of the two agent-dogs.

[17]   On this headgear compare Marinatos (2007: 272–273).

Figure 24. Genius forms double axe with two dogs
(*CMS* VII, no. 126 = Arachne 164842).

the leashes of two large dogs without dorsal appendages who look up at him. I understand the two dogs as agents (table-dogs) of the young man who is himself an agent of the *wanax* or, in the case of the *wanax* himself (young man B), an agent of Potnia.

Figure 25. Genius with two followers, seal from Mycenae
(*CMS* I, no. 161 = Arachne 157382).

In *CMS* XI, no. 208 (= Arachne 167444), found in a tholos grave in Kakovatos, a genius, seemingly in a textile appendage, is standing behind a warrior, directing him as the warrior wields his sword against an upright lion-like beast. The warrior is an employee/subordinate of the merchant/dog serving the Labyrinth. In *CMS* VII, no. 95 (= Arachne 164809), possibly from Hydra in Greece, a genius seemingly in an animal skin appendage is flanked by two men making identical gestures. I think that the humans are security personnel or employees serving the trader who serves the Labyrinth. This service by the genii/dog may explain *CMS* XI, no. 37 (= Arachne 167250), wherein a genius with, perhaps, a dorsal appendage carries two lions on a *pole*.[18] This might indicate the conveyance of enemy combatants into slavery. I have difficulty thinking of the "lions" as sacrificial victims (*pace* Antognelli Michel 2012: 49).

I agree with Blakolmer (2015b: 33) that the genius in *CMS* VII, no. 95 (= Arachne 164809) is a deity to the extent that the two men are clearly subordinated to it in the same way that the two flanking dogs are in *CMS* I, no. 161.[19]

In a fragmentary fresco from Pylos (40 H ne Lang 1969: Plate C), a genius with a smooth pink colored garment on its back holds a yellow garment in a paw-like hand (Plate 13). Despite the missing head, we can confirm that the figure is a genius using a fresco from the immediate vicinity of the megaron-like "Cult Center" (= "Ramp House") at Mycenae, in which a row of otherwise similar genii/dogs are wearing textile-like figure-eight garments decorated with red and blue and carrying a pole on their shoulders (Plate 14). There is something else that cannot be seen on a seal: the genii from both Pylos and Mycenae are painted *white*, which ordinarily signals they are females (Gill 1970: 404). It is perhaps a problem, however, that the frescoes do not provide the genii with any female bodily characteristics. However, as noted earlier, the figure-eight shield is probably best viewed as a *male symbol* (Chap. 9.3), which would signal that the (white = female) genii have male legal status—that is, they have the right to form contracts.

My conclusion is that the genii are males, as indicated by their body shapes and the wearing of figure-eight shields on their backs,[20] *and also that they are agents of a female as indicated by their painted white (= female) skins.* That the female is Potnia of the Labyrinth is indicated by the seal images reviewed above in which genii/dogs with dorsal appendages are regularly linked to symbols of the Labyrinth,

---

[18]   Lions are discussed in §4 below.

[19]   I think we surely can find a deity in the "immortal" (*athanatos*) gold and silver dogs that guarded/protected (*phulazō*) the palace of Alcinoos in Scheria (*Odyssey* 7.91–94). The golden dogs of Alcinoos find their counterpart in a gold seal from a tomb at Poros Heracleion that depicts a large, barking mastiff in a stepped enclosure (Dimopoulou 2010). It is not clear whether these golden dogs have a connection to the genii. See also Karetsou and Koehl (2014: 333 and Plate CII) for figurines from Mt. Juktas including one of gold: "On the gold dog, the collar is ornamented with diagonal hatch-marks…. Perhaps a gold strip was pressed into the groove for a collar whose ends would have been anchored into the hole (Pl. CIIa, c, d, e, g, i). This figurine also preserves other evidence for drilling, but for different purposes. A hole was drilled on its back for a green chlorite inlay, giving the dog's coat a spotted appearance (Pl. CIIa, c, d, f)." As will be seen at the end of this section, the Linear B tablets offer testimony to the presence of a "Dog God" or "God of Dogs."

[20]   That the shields seem relatively smooth is apparently not relevant or not intended by the artists.

including the double-headed axe and figure-eight shield. Further, in the Pylos fresco, the handling/conveyance of a yellow (saffron-dyed) garment fits a commercial agent textile role. In the Mycenae fresco, the poles are probably used to display garments during processions, as probably in Figure 26.[21] We should, however, recall the "lions" on poles.

Figure 26. Figure with garment on pole, seal
(*CMS* II.6 no. 26 = Arachne 160096).

Moving from pure iconography to commercial practice, there are seal impressions depicting genii on Minoan roundels from Malia that serve to record the transfer of valuables (Hallager in Hallager and Weingarten 1993: 11 with Figures 7 and 8): "It seems most likely that the two Malia roundels were impressed by a single person who acknowledged the receipt of two units of a commodity; perhaps he used two different seals because he represents two different parties, offices or interests." I take it as given that the choice of a genius for a seal device reflects the owner's occupation and concerns.

The Linear B titles of the real-world counterparts of the genii/dogs—the agents and entrepreneurs who affixed their seals to transactions—are unknown. In a list of "collectors," (Knossos B798) there is a man named *ku-ni-ta* (Varias 1998-1999: 359). As pointed out earlier (Chap. 8.2), the "collectors" are risk-taking businesspersons. In addition, a text from Knossos (Da 1396) mentions an individual named Kunēus who owns one hundred sheep.[22] As, it is true, do many shepherds. On the other hand, their names do not include the dog-stem. In the "Men and Dogs" fresco from the Pylos palace, the tunic of the hunter has purple

---

[21] For poles for loom-weights, see Hallgher and Wingarten 1993: 14–15; Sansone 1988: 6; Burke 2010: 47ff..

[22] Palaima, personal correspondence cited by Karetsou and Koehl 2014: 336 n. 22.

details (Brecoulaki 2018: 403, 405 Fig. 18). This color scheme may go beyond fashion to indicate the objective of the "hunters."

Finally, there is confirmation for the "Dog God," or "God of Dogs," found in *CMS* VII, no. 95 (= Arachne 164809). In Mycenae (MY Fu 711), it seems that "offerings" are made to a "dog"—the flour ideogram follows the word "dog" (García Ramón 2011: 230–231). Possible offerings for dogs (and mythical creatures such as "Harpies") are found also in the tablets from Thebes (Godart and Saccioni 1997; 898–899; Rousioti 2001: 307–308).

There will be more to say about genii/dogs below including a seemingly iconographic identification of dog with genius and the receipt of "offerings" by dogs and mythical creatures in Sections 5 and 6 below.

3. Bearers of the Pouch

The previously mentioned "Warrior Krater" (Chap. 2) depicts a file of warriors wearing uniforms, including helmets, studded/beaded tunics, shields, and thin spears, to which is tied a peculiar small reddish sack or pouch (Plate 15). Even the warriors' noses are peculiar—uniformly peculiar. Also depicted in the krater is an incomplete woman who stands sideways and raises her right arm, but whose left side is obscured by the poorly preserved handle. Probably she is raising both arms.

The archaeological context of the Krater is *highly* uncertain, but I assume with Burke (2008) that it comes from a grave. Taking this findspot into account, Burke (2008: 84) interprets the raised arms as a gesture of *lament*. Still, objects found in a grave are not necessarily concerned with death, and the woman may be present because she had a prior relationship with the deceased. Moreover, the raised arm gesture does not, I think, signify grief but is instead a characteristic gesture of welcome or, better, appreciation.[23]

I am not interested in converting the soldiers into commercial agents, but there is at least a hint of nonmilitary aspect to their service. The sacks tied to the spears of the soldiers are obviously too small to contain "supplies" or booty unless they are made of a very elastic material. More obviously, they resemble purses for gold dust or gold fragments. Is the woman in the Krater raising her arms in appreciation of having received valuable gifts from the departing "warriors"?

Support for an interpretation of the sacks as purses is provided by a depiction in the tomb of Rekhmire, an official in Egypt's Eighteenth Dynasty,

---

[23] Such a gesture is appropriate for a goddess presiding over a brothel (see the discussion in Chap. 5 of the caravanserai in Knossos).

wherein two Aegean porters are depicted delivering (admittedly larger) red leather bags as "tribute." Further, men of Punt in the register above the Aegeans carry sacks of the same shape and color. Again, "leather bags lacking straps are loaded aboard Hatshepsut's ship at Punt and also brought by men of Punt in a scene of foreign trade from the tomb of Amenmose, the son of Thutmose I."[24] Luján (2019: 2) reports the speculation that Linear B "sack" (leather cup) came in Homeric times to refer to a ceramic cup in the shape of a sack. However, Luján (2019: 10) cites evidence that early ceramics typically imitate still earlier leather versions.

Wachsmann (1987: 74) ventures that the red color of the bags signifies gold. In the mid-fourteenth century BCE, a Babylonian ruler complained to his Egyptian counterpart about the small amount of gold dust he had received for his chariots, white horses, and artistic seal (Silver 1995a: 49).

Evidence supporting or consistent with the interpretation of the red leather bag as a purse for gold—a money sack—is available in Linear B and in Homeric Epic. In Linear B, the word *a-re-se-si* occurs (for the only time) in a Pylos tablet (PY Ub 1318) wherein it refers to an object to be made by a worker from their pieces of red leather (Luján 2019: 1–2). Luján (2019: 2ff.) relates the Linear B word to Homeric *aleison* meaning "cup." In a number of Homeric examples, the cup is made of gold and used for pouring libations. There is, however, a very different kind of usage. In *Iliad* 24.429–431, Priam seeks to bribe Hermes, who is disguised as a slave agent of Achilles, to guard and guide him to the tent of Achilles. The bribe, declined by the agent/Hermes who professes to be fearful of defrauding Achilles, is an *aleison*. In this case, the "cup" is best seen as being made of leather for holding gold.[25]

Further support for a sack-for-gold interpretation is provided by a sealing from Phaistos (Figure 27, below) that depicts a winged dog-like creature, perhaps a griffin (Morgan 2010: 310; see §5 below), with a long snout and what very much looks like a small pouch fixed to the dog's collar (Krzyszkowska 2005: 106 no. 180).[26] Presumably, the seal was applied (twice) to something valuable in the Phaistos palace. The bag is a purse and, as argued above, the dog/griffin is a commercial agent or courier.

---

24 Wachsmann (1987) thinks the bags were transferred from the Punt scene to the Aegean tribute scene but the Aegeans had gold themselves.

25 One would not think that Priam carried a gold cup with him in his attempt to see Achilles.

26 Morgan (2010: 310–311) considers whether the attachment might be a wattle and cites two other examples (*CMS* I, no. 316 = Arachne 157545 and *CMS* III, no. 372 = Arachne 161955), but decides not to reconstruct the feature. Why a wattle? If the hens find the rooster's wattle sexually attractive, then the money pouch has attractive power among humans.

Figure 27. Griffin with purse from Phaistos
(*CMS* II.5, no. 317 = Arachne 160060).

My suspicion is that the soldiers depicted in the Krater are also assigned a commercial duty.[27] Furthermore, their uniformly peculiar nose (cf. §4 below) leads me to conclude that they are *foreigners*.

4. Wearing the Lion's Skin On Top of One's "Natural" Skin

The palace's control of the lion is clearly indicated by its placement next to the throne in Pylos' megaron and by its presence in Mycenae's entrance relief. Moreover, a most interesting gold signet ring (Figure 28, opposite) from Mycenae(?) depicts two lions looking back at the pillar to which they are leashed from whose cornice sacral knots (textiles) are suspended.[28] Clearly, the pillar represents Potnia of the Labyrinth. Here, we have a signal not only of palatial control of lions but of their service in the textile enterprise. Consistent with this interpretation, note that Heracles who served as the agent of King Eurystheus of Mycenae[29] (and of Queen Omphale) is recognized for wearing the skin of a lion on his "labors."

Most importantly, in Homer, a worried Agamemnon dons the *daphoinos* "very red" lion's skin (*Iliad* 10.23) and Diomedes puts on an *aithōn* "fiery" lion's skin (*Iliad* 10.177–178). It might seem from Diomedes' reaction that each of the *basilēōn* "kings" wore the skin of a lion (*Iliad* 10.165ff.). However, Agamemnon

---

[27] The possible circulation of pots of scrap metal sealed by the cult of Arēs is considered below.

[28] See J. L. Palmer (2004). On two seals from Mycenae a female who holds up "horns" surmounted by a double-headed axe is flanked by standing lions (*CMS* I, no. 144 [=Arachne 157365], 145 [= Arachne 157366]).

[29] Eurystheus and Heracles are discussed at many points below.

Figure 28. Lions adore pillar with sacral knots suspended
(*CMS* VI, no. 364 = Arachne 164496).

and Diomedes were not just kings, they were kings of Mycenae and Argos, and, therefore, both would have been directly involved in the negotiations with Paris and his associates about the transfer of Helen (see Chap. 14.5). In the Glaucus episode (*Iliad* 6.116–240), it is made a point that Diomedes' house had Bellerophon as a guest/friend. Moreover, Agamemnon and Diomedes have in common that they are both "dogs"/"doggish" (*Iliad* 1.159, 10.502–506). The lion, including specifically Diomedes and Agamemnon, may be understood as a specialized agent/dog charged with carrying out military missions for the Labyrinth/Palace.[30]

The hypothesis that the lion/lion skin is a signal of palatial agency is used below to pry open the meaning of a fragmentary fresco from Pylos. Immerwahr (1990: 118) has provided evidence suggesting a foreign presence at Pylos: from a fresco dump on the northwest slope

> came fragments of life size males (Py No. 7), including at least one black ... wearing the early form of Minoan kilt. Strangely, his [at least four] red-skinned companions ... wear lion skins [not shown], and all have peculiar snoodlike caps. Although no offerings are preserved, these men seem to be part of a procession to the left against a background that changes along wavy horizontal bands at waist level, as did the Knossian procession.

---

[30] It is delicious that in *Iliad* 10, the lion-skinned agent Diomedes cuts off the "head" ("capital") of Dolōn "Cunning," the son of Eumēdēs, a man "rich in gold and bronze," who wears the skin of a wolf and, like Odysseus, a cap of dog's skin, and whose head continues to bargain as it drops into a chest (see Silver 1992: 175 n. 1). Here, we find on one side a dog and his lion, and on the other, a dog (table-dog) and wolf (argos-dog) combination.

Blakolmer (2012a: 59) addresses the meaning of the fragmentary Pylos fresco:

> Due to the fact that not only their skin colour varies between red and black but also several of them are clad with the skin of a feline (Fig. 4) and wear a cap reminiscent of the Egyptian Nemes headscarf (Figs. 4–5), it is attractive to view this as the depiction of a row of Egyptians, among them at least two dark-skinned Nubians. Unfortunately, the iconographical context of these figures eludes us, and nothing suggests an interpretation as immigrants ... or reflecting a religious or military content.... There exists at least the possibility that they are approaching a male figure facing to the right. We should not exclude the idea of a procession of Egyptian gift-bearers or virtual 'tribute'-bearers comparable to the 'Keftiu paintings' in Egypt.... Thus, it remains unclear whether these Egyptians were perceived as equal partners or as subordinate exotic foreigners in this context.

I will assume that all the figures are foreigners and that the differences in skin color serve as an indicator of differences in specific foreign origin. The interpretation that all the men wearing a lion's skin and with red skin are foreigners finds support in Lang's (1969: 62) observation that the men also have "singularly unformulaic noses (55, 57 H nws)." The noses can serve to confirm their foreign nationality. On this point, let us pause to recall the "Warrior Krater" from Mycenae which depicts a line of soldiers all with the same peculiar nose (§3 above).

Returning to the Pylian procession, all the participants—black and red—are unified by their (assumed) foreign status but even more by wearing the same peculiar caps, which are yellow with red rays or ripples (Weilhartner 2017: 157; Blakolmer and Weilhartner 2015: 19 with Tafel 2, Abb, 4). I note that the colors of the cap match the colors of the two main textile dyes: saffron and murex. Perhaps more revealing is that the colors of the caps match the colors of wealth: gold and purple.

Thus, I offer the hypothesis that the cap shows that all the men are foreigners who serve the Pylos palace (see §7 below on the "chief of the Keftiu"). More specifically, the lion skins indicate that the wearers—all of those with red skin and the same nose—are overseas agents of the palace whose duty is the conveyance of gold. The (early) form of Mycenaean kilt worn by the black-skinned foreigner would indicate that he has been adopted/incorporated into the commercial service of the Pylos palace. Perhaps his duty was in acquiring purple dye.[31] However, such fine-tuning goes much beyond the evidence.

5. Gala Welcome for Traders: Campstools, Syrians, and Griffins

This section is the most integrated and among the most important in this study. It is also very much a work in progress. The reader joins me in confronting successive problems and following the evolution of proposed imperfect solutions, utilizing evidence from all available sources. Running summaries are provided to prevent us from becoming separated.

The following discussion stands on two previously erected pillars. First, from Chapter 7.6, the flowers presented to the goddess in Minoan/Mycenaean iconography, especially glyptic, represent dyed luxury textiles. The occasion for the presentation is a festival celebrated at the opening of the navigation season to welcome the lavish fashion of foreign traders to palatial textile showrooms and other textile marketing facilities. Second, it supports the suggestion made in Chapter 4.1 that the individuals wearing "Syrian" banded robes (see Marinatos 1995: 127–128) who are being feted on "campstools" at Pylos and Knossos are foreign textile traders celebrating the opening of the navigation season. More will be said about the Latin version of the festival shortly.

Why campstools? The next step is to make what seems to be a minor correction but calls for a major adjustment in our understanding of the role of the campstool in the navigation festival. Rehak (1995a: 107) points out that *in Pylos*, the campstools "are not proper campstools; instead the artist has rendered their sides as solid-painted 'hourglass' shapes, but the inward curve of the sides of these seats is close enough to the campstool shape." *The significance of Rehak's observation is that the portable campstools on which the "Syrians" sit are/can be identified with altar bases.*

In what follows, I will seek to identify the festival depicted in Figure 32 with the Linear B festival named *to-no-e-ke-te-ri-jo* 'carrying of thrones/textiles festival'. In Chapter 7.6, the Mycenaean thrones festival was identified with the Latin *sellisternium*, whose details are examined next.

As analyzed by Ando (2011: 63–65): (1) in referring to the *lectisternium*, Livy (40.59.6–7) mentions the *capita deorum* "heads of gods" that were placed on the couches (*lectus,* m.); (2) Paul the Deacon writing in the second half of the eighth century CE notes that the "heads of gods" are actually "bundles made

---

[31] An alternative view is that the peculiar noses of the red-skinned men indicate a common duty, not a common foreign ethnicity.

from grasses," which are called *struppi*; (3) the second century CE lexicographer
Festus explains that "a *stroppus* is what is called a στρόφιον in Greek, and which
priests wear on their heads as insignia"; (4) thus, the "heads of gods" placed on
the couches are chaplets—that is, something like a crown worn on or around
the head of the god/goddess and/or his/her priest. This analysis fits very nicely
with papyrus or date-palm "heads" placed together with/on campstools in the
Minoan/Mycenaean glyptic (see below).

The presence of Potnia's headdress with the campstool would serve to
identify the festival with the *lectisternium* but instead morphs it into what is—
arguably but somewhat disputed[32]—a female sponsored version known as the
sellisternium, meaning "making/spreading of the chair/stool = *sella*, f.)." The
sella is defined as a chair and may (typically) be of the type lacking a back and
arms.[33] On coins, it seems to be depicted in this way, and it is shown draped
with fringed textiles (called *Babylonica*) over the seat upon which sits a portable
cultic emblem (Taylor 1935: 122; Madigan 2013: Chap. 4 with Figs. 44, 45). The
word *sellisternium*, translated as *sellastrōsis*, is found only in a handful of literary
sources. In Festus, it refers to the Babylonian tapestry with which the chairs
were covered. In the secular games, the deities honored at the festivals are said
to be the goddesses Juno and Diana (Taylor 1935: 123–124).[34]

The final step is that I identify the *to-no-e-ke-te-ri-jo* that involved the
"carrying of flowers = textile thrones" with the Latin *sellisternium*. I see processions carrying "thrones" in the sense of luxury dyed textiles (Chap. 7.6) and
also campstools. Upon arrival at the place of celebration, the campstools were
opened and draped with dyed textiles as cushions, turning them into "thrones"
for the arriving strangers; the *to-no-e-ke-te-ri-jo* is the "*opening/spreading of
thrones.*" A complicating factor, referred to above, is the identification of the
campstools with incurved altar bases.

The strangers' welcome loosely fits Livy's (5.13.5–8) description of Rome's
first *lectisternium*, in which private individuals also prepared lavish couches and
on them entertained even complete strangers:

> The duumvirs in charge of the sacred rites then celebrated the first
> lectisternium ever held in Rome, and for the space of eight days sacri-
> ficed to Apollo, to Latona and Diana, to Hercules, to Mercury and to
> Neptune, spreading three couches for them with all the splendour then

---

[32] The issue is not, I think, whether a male can be placed on the chair or a female on the couch but
whether it is sponsored by a male or a female.
[33] In the depictions I have seen, the legs are not incurved, and since they are front views, it is
difficult to tell whether they are folding stools.
[34] Sextus Pompeius Festus is a grammarian of the later second century CE who specialized on the
meaning of early Latin words and Roman antiquities.

attainable. They also observed the rite in their homes. All through the City, they say, doors stood wide open, all kinds of viands were set out for general consumption, all comers were welcomed, whether known or not, and men even exchanged kind and courteous words with personal enemies; there was a truce to quarrelling and litigation; even prisoners were loosed from their chains for those days, and they scrupled thenceforth to imprison men whom the gods had thus befriended. (tr. Foster *Perseus Project*)

Our vision of the role of traders seated in campstools is sharpened by Homer. Thus, in *Odyssey* 17.483–488, when the suitor Antinous strikes the disguised Odysseus, the others are outraged and one warns the offender, "Antinous, thou didst not well to strike the wretched wanderer. Doomed man that thou art, what if haply he be some god come down from heaven! Aye, and the gods in the guise of strangers from afar put on all manner of shapes, and visit the cities, beholding the violence and the righteousness of men." That is, gods travel to communal celebrations disguised as mortal foreigners and take vengeance if they are not treated as befits a god.

Livy's description of the Roman festivals of *lectisternium/sellisternium*; plus *Odyssey* 17.483–488 on strangers as gods; plus the "carrying of thrones" (= dyed textile cushions) in Chapter 7.6; plus the depiction in Chapter 3.3 of the goddess in Akrotiri's Xeste 3 as seated on a throne of cushions on a platform supported by incurved altar bases;[35] all lead me to form the following understanding: *the strangers (visiting traders) at Knossos and Pylos are seated like attributes of gods (exuviae) on the luxury textile-covered seats of campstools/incurved altar bases.* Much iconographic evidence remains to be reviewed, however.

The first question to be examined is whether the banded robes and their wearers are really Syrian. Scholars such as B. Jones (2015), if I understand correctly, do not accept that the banded garments are "Syrian." In an earlier contribution (B. Jones 2003: 448–449), Jones saw the wearers as members of the elite, and she explained, "This costume seems to conform to the representation of mantles tied at the shoulder with long hanging ends on a LC 1a fresco from Keos, and on a figure holding a bird on a seal said to be from Knossos [on this seal see below and Krzyszkowska 2005: 138 #238]."[36]

---

[35] See Soles 2016a: 250 and Eliopoulos 2013: 212–214 with Fig. 2. About incurved altar-bases, Evans 1928: 607–608.

[36] "The early Semitic inhabitants of Babylonia wore either the loin-cloth or the peculiar Semitic plaided robe, which covered the left shoulder and arm, leaving the right shoulder and the right arm bare and reaching from the left shoulder to the ankles (Illustration No. 112). It was wrapped around the body in parallel bands and the ends seem to have been thrown over the left shoulder.... The bands that were wrapped round the body in parallel lines consisted probably

Blakolmer (2018: 44) has recently returned to the nationality question raised by the garment: the banded robes, he suggests, are indicative of a foreign fashion but not of in-the-flesh foreigners in the Mycenaean world; he refers to the "[n]ew fashion of the flounced skirt, the Syro-Levantine long robe with diagonal bands and other costumes stimulated by the Near East during the Neopalatial period." My question is would any such robes have become fashionable in Knossos and Pylos before they were worn there by in-the-flesh foreigners? I think not. Thus, Blakolmer's hypothesis would not exclude actual foreign guests but implicitly invites their (earlier) presence. An alternative explanation is that native overseas traders returned home wearing the Syrian garment.

Figure 29. Figure on throne in Syrian banded robe, seal from Mochlos (*CMS* VS.1B no. 332 = Arachne 166017).

An Akkadian/Syrian cylinder seal of Minoan times from a grave in Mochlos in Crete (Figure 29) depicts the kind of banded garment we are looking for:

The figure seated on the throne wears the characteristic ankle-long, [only seemingly] flounced robe usually described as a *kaunakēs* [/*gaunakēs,*

---

of differently colored materials. Below this dress the loincloth seems to have been worn. The plaided robe seems to have been worn only by the Semitic kings and priests of Babylonia and by the gods, while the bulk of the people probably wore the sack like garment, of the same type as the plaided robe, which consisted of one piece of material reaching from the neck below the knees, but leaving bare both arms and the right shoulder. Like the plaided robe this garment was ungirded." Pritchard (1951: 41 with 39) describes Garment C, a banded robe, depicted in Theban Tomb paintings: "In the same period, which begins about the last quarter of the 15th century, there appears an entirely new type of dress (C). It seems to consist of a long undergarment reaching in folds almost to the ankles, over which is placed a cape worn loosely over the shoulders. Sometimes the undergarment is represented with long sleeves, but more frequently it is not. Type C continues on figures of Syrians well after the 18th dynasty." Pritchard's C and (banded robe) D do not appear to be fastened at the shoulder.

Assyrian *gunakku*], a thick cloak said by the Greeks to be of Persian or Babylonian make. It is sometimes considered to be woolen and always passes under the right arm-pit leaving the arm with the shoulder bare, the left arm being covered with the left hand held against the lower chest.

Davaras and Soles 1995: 32[37]

In addition, the *stool* ("throne") on which the figure sits may be cushioned. All the figures have pronounced noses as in local fresco and glyptic references to Syrians. The so-called "sun-disk in moon-crescent symbol" depicted between the seated figure and the "worshipper" is reportedly "very common" in Near Eastern glyptic (Davaris and Soles 1995: 36); the symbol has been linked to "Asherah."

The form of the "running spiral" or (more accurately) horizontal guilloche with dots [probably rosettes] in the openings depicted on the center-right is characteristic of Syrian iconography (Davaris and Soles 1995: 32).[38] Hence, despite the presumptive relationship to spiral designs depicted on walls in the Zakros palace and on the Zakros Rhyton's "Peak Sanctuary" (Chap. 4.2.c), it cannot be linked *specifically* to the Minoan/Mycenaean labyrinth. It is my view, however, that the horizontal guilloche connects the ceremonial actions of the Syrians in Figure 29 with a Near Eastern branch or version of the labyrinth or *"house of the sea."* Thus, the banded robe is a garment worn by Syrians and the owners of the seal had arguably come to Mochlos, the findspot

---

[37] As previously noted, the garment was worn by important Near Eastern figures, including kings and deities, but I have no systematic information that the long robe leaving one shoulder uncovered was favored by merchants. However, on several Old Babylonian seals (reconstructed from sealings) belonging, as attested in the inscription, to a damkar "merchant," the "the long-robed worshipper" may, I suspect, be the merchant himself (see Verhulst 2015; Davaras and Soles 1995: 42). In the seal from Mochlos, "The gift-bearing worshipper who approaches the enthroned person is a common figure in glyptic. His costume with long mantle draped in a curve and revealing an undergarment, leaving the right shoulder and right arm uncovered, is typical" (Davaras and Soles 1995: 35). I am not aware of a Minoan/Mycenaean counterpart with the possible exception of "La Parisienne" in Knossos' "Campstool Fresco."

[38] Michele Mitrovich (2021: §38.3) has clarified this matter for me: "The pattern on the Syrian seal from Mochlos, which represents the traditional Guilloché or guilloche pattern characteristic of the Near Eastern iconographic vocabulary, rather than the Aegean spiral motif proposed by Morris Silver. The running spiral motif is formed by interconnected concentric circular elements, while the guilloche pattern is constructed by two undulating lines crossing each other in an alternating fashion." The author had been struggling to understand why a ceremony populated by Syrians should be set in an Aegean labyrinth.

of the seal, to do business. The seated worshipped figure is a Syrian but more likely a trader than a god.[39]

In connection with Syrian traders physically present in Crete, note that the "sun-disk in moon-crescent" symbol appears on a set of three ceramics excavated in the "Zakros Pit Deposit." One of the three objects includes also a "rope-like relief decoration" and, on the other side, the head of an agrimi. The latter animal being a source of wool for making textiles (see Chaps. 4.2.c, 7.5, and 10.2).

The next evidence cited seems to offer further support for the Syrian interpretation, but, at the same time, it raises new questions. A seal from Vatheia in Laconia (Figure 30) depicts a man with exceptionally well-defined facial features who wears a banded robe and carries an axe-like ceremonial object on

Figure 30. Man in Syrian banded robe holds ceremonial object, seal from Vatheia in Laconia (*CMS* I, no. 225 = Arachne 157447).

his shoulder.[40] The individual in the banded robe is evidently a Syrian, but what is the "ceremonial object" and what is its national origin?

---

[39] The difficulties in interpretation, as well as the potential gains from pursuing the theme, are illustrated in a richly themed "Syrian Seal" in which two individuals in Syrian banded robes sit on stools facing one another raising drinking vessels. The "platform" on which they sit is formed by/decorated with a horizontal spiral guilloche with central rosettes. Clearly, they are being honored in a "house of the sea" or labyrinth but is it the Cretan or a Syrian counterpart? For a drawing of the seal, see Kantor (1947: Plate XXIII C).

[40] Several different views of the banded robe are available. The version shown above provides the best view of the ceremonial object but does not clearly show the bare right shoulder. The best view of the bare right shoulder is in *CMS* II.3, no. 198 (= Arachne 159291). See also *CMS* IS, no. 113 (= Arachne 162274). In each example, the nose remains pronounced. (see below *CMS* VS.1B, no. 332 = Arachne 166017). Distinctive noses are associated with foreigners in Chaps. 10.6 and 11.3.

Yasur-Landau (2015) maintains that the object is a "fenestrated axe," and Maran (2015) describes it as a "semicircular axe." Both Yasur-Landau and Maran agree that this form of "axe" is of Syrian or, more generally, of Near Eastern origin (cf. Rehak 1995a; 111). So far so good: a man in a Syrian garment holds a Syrian ceremonial object. In fact, however, all is not well with the object.

Yasur Landau (2015: 140–141 with Fig. 2) points out that the "fenestrated axe" held by the man in the banded robe resembles a unique object from the Vapheio tholos (the "Vapheio Axe"; cf. Nagy 2018: §14A). This does yet prove that either is intended to represent an axe. In fact, there are large differences between the "Vapheio Axe" and examples of fenestrated or crescented axes from various Near Eastern places, as depicted by Yasur-Landau (2015: Figs. 3, 4, 5 and elsewhere).

> Due to its fenestrations and deep, semicircular form, the Vapheio axe-head appears, at first glance, to be a typical Levantine fenestrated axe, but what makes the axe from Laconia special are its three socket loops, since all actual finds of fenestrated axes from Western Asia that are known to me either have a closed socket or shaft-holes connected by a continuous straight butt.
>
> Maran 2015: 246–247

On the other hand, both Aegean objects resemble three-pronged "crescented axes" from Byblos and Egypt (Maran 2015: 267–268 Figs. 4–7). There remains a problem even with the latter examples, however: the three "socket loops" protruding from the alleged blade of the "axe" in the Aegean seal (Maran 2015: 246). Furthermore, with respect to the function of the "axes," none of the drawings presented are clear, with the possible exception of Maran's Figure 8, which shows the god Reshef raising/brandishing a crescentic axe. It is clear that neither Yasur-Landau nor Maran provide an example of a ceremonial use as is the case in the Aegean seal.

My conclusion from the above discussion is that the object in the Aegean seals is not likely to be a functional axe, whether Egyptian or Syrian (or even Aegean) but rather something else—something that is not martial but rather ceremonial/symbolic (Maran 2015: 251). What might that be? *Can our analysis survive the holding by a Syrian of a non-Syrian ceremonial object?*

CMS I, 223 (= Arachne 157445)[41] depicts an individual in a Syrian banded robe who holds a griffin on a leash and wears a seal on this left wrist. This individual does not carry a ceremonial object. Based on his control of the Minoan/

---

[41] See also *CMS* I, no. 128 = Arachne 157349 and below.

Mycenaean griffin and the possession of a seal, it has been suggested that individuals in banded robes are not Syrian traders but rather Minoan/Mycenaean priests or officials (Rehak 1994; Rehak 1995a: 111–112). *The most important objection to this interpretation is its failure to consider and explain why presumably Minoan/Mycenaean priests or officials should wear a Syrian garment.* Moreover, a foreign commercial origin for the wearers of the banded robes is not at all excluded by an association with griffins.[42] The griffin symbolizes not only official (*wanax*) power but also the overseas projection of official power. The duties of the griffin would include the protection and preservation of the lives and property of clients and staff of the labyrinth. Recall, that in Chapter 6.1, this duty of protection—the griffin duty—is specifically reserved *for Alcinoos*, the king of the Phaeacians.[43]

It will be suggested in due course that an individual can be both a foreigner and a domestic official. First, however, we must settle the problem of the ceremonial object held by the Syrian. It will be seen that the object is most probably *a symbol of safe passage.*

Pottery decoration and jewelry provide sources for a meaningful alternative interpretation to a fenestrated axe. This reference is to the "miniature umbrella" motif that has been understood by Furumark (1941: 263) as representing "*an unstemmed derivative of the papyrus motif*" (cf. Maran 2015: 252; emphasis added). Maran (2015) provides an example of this motif from the "Royal Tomb" of Isopata in Figure 1 (cf. his Figures 9 and 10). He (Maran 2015: 252) concludes, "Given the, at best, superficial similarity of the motif to the standard ways of depicting papyrus, this view, however, seems much less persuasive than identifying it as a stylized version of a semicircular axe."

However, there is a version of the papyrus motif that contains a more persuasive identification of the object held by the Syrian than as a fenestrated or semicircular axe. A prism seal (Figure 31), again from the island of Mochlos—a north Cretan harbor that figures also in the discussion of Figure 29—depicts a *papyrus flower* (Matoušková 2020: 176), which, in my opinion, resembles the ceremonial object carried by men in banded robes more than a "fenestrated axe" does.[44] The *stylized papyrus flower* in Figure 31 with its three leaves on a fan-shaped sheath is

---

[42] Maran (2015: 251) is aware of the difficulty.

[43] Recall that in Knossos' Throne Room, griffins bear the familiar rosette decoration on a shoulder (Galanakis, Tsitsa and Günkel-Maschek 2017: esp. 76–77), thus revealing their status as agents of the Labyrinth. Seals featuring griffins come from Thessaly and various palatial centers (Rousioti 2016: 238–240). Their linkage to textiles is importantly illustrated by the presence in Xeste 3 of a griffin with purple wings and leash. Minoan-style griffins with a spiral design on the wings "landed" in the second millennium BCE in Egypt.

[44] In *CMS* IX, no. D2b (= Arachne 163100) and in *CMS* IX, no. 21C (= Arachne 162890) the papyrus flower/sacral knot is accompanied by a branch with thin leaves. *CMS* II.8, no. 126 (= Arachne 160756) has two sacral knots bracketing what appears to be a palm tree.

at home in Crete and may have originated there (Kantor 1999: esp. 454–461). The question naturally arises why a visiting Syrian would carry a Minoan/Mycenaean

Figure 31. Papyrus flower on prism seal from Mochlos
(*CMS* II.2, no. 250a = Arachne 158874).

symbol. Moreover, Matoušková notes that besides resembling a papyrus flower, the object in the Mochlos prism seal may also be recognized as a *sacral knot with a stylized loop* (see Figure 13 and *CMS* VS3, no. 331= Arachne 166660). Again, the sacral knot is an object with a strong Minoan/Mycenaean connection.

Given the papyrus fresco in the Knossos throne room (cf. Figure 1) and following Chapter 10.8, a foreigner identified by holding a stick with a papyrus flower might well be recognized as *under the protection of Potnia* or even as an agent of Potnia.[45] This is even more cogent in the case of the sacral knot, with its resemblance to the Egyptian "ankh," which is actually worn by "La Parisienne" in the "Campstool Fresco" (Plate 16) when she greets participants in banded robes. My conclusion is that the Syrian in Figure 30 carries a Minoan/Mycenaean (or possibly universal) safe passage, either a papyrus flower or a sacral knot or something else that remains to be considered.[46]

---

[45] It is tempting to assume that foreign traders granted "life" by the Egyptian ruler were permitted to carry the "ankh" symbol. The latter symbol is known in the Minoan/Mycenaean world including at Phaistos where a triton shell plaque depicts, in relief, a procession of four upright human-like figures with an animal heads each of whom carries an ankh in one lowered hand (Hogarth 1902: 92, fig. 33).

[46] An alternative safe-conduct symbolism that I find attractive is that the ceremonial object carried by the Syrian belongs to the sea-god Poseidon. Specifically, it is Poseidon's *triaina* 'trident'. Homer uses the word three times—twice for hitting something (*Iliad* 12.27, *Odyssey* 4.506) and in *Odyssey* 5.291 for stirring up the waves when Odysseus departs from Calypso. "Hence, we see that as far as Homer is concerned, we have no literary evidence about the attribute of Poseidon, except as to the purposes for which it was employed. *There is nothing to indicate its shape, except that that it must be more or less of*

Indeed, the finding in Mochlos of the prism seal with the "papyrus emblem"/ or "sacral knot" emblem of protection (Figure 30) is suggestive of the physical presence of foreigners. Only foreigners physically present on Potnia's soil would need to stress having her guarantee of safe passage. Even more to this point is the discovery—in Mochlos' "House A," a relatively well-built house of eight rooms served by a cobbled road—of "Canaanite" amphora fragments of LM III date (Soles, Brogan, and Triantaphyllou 2008). I am not entirely clear on the dating, but it appears that in its earlier LM I phase, "House A" "included a large room with columns in the south-east, where a double axe stand was located, cooking areas in the southwest, and storage and workrooms to the north." (Brogan, Smith, and Soles 2002: 98). Rehak and Younger (1998: 100) note the presence of an LM IB industrial area on the shore of Crete opposite Mochlos. Mochlos, a harbor on Crete's north coast. Mochlos, a harbor on Crete's north coast, is well situated for Syrian trade and archaeological evidence from the site, including engraved and miniature double-headed axes, suggests that it hosted a branch of the Labyrinth (Seager 1912: 25ff.). In addition to the Canaanite pottery, there were finds of imported beads of carnelian and hematite in Tomb 16 (Soles 2016b).

Having argued that Syrian traders bearing an emblem of Potnia's protection were present on Minoan/Mycenaean soil, we may next return to the problem raised by Syrian control of a griffin. Might a Syrian trader also be a Minoan/ Mycenaean official?

There is an interesting and substantive way to reconcile the two vocations. In the *Homeric Hymn to (Pythian) Apollo*[47] (3.388–440), Apollo, who takes the form of a *dolphin* (495), guides a ship of Minos of Knossos that was bound for Pylos for "business and gain" (*prēxin kai chrēmata* 3.397) to various Greek ports and then employs "winged words" to incorporate its crew into his priesthood. Thus, we may understand that the only point of Apollo's intervention is to acquire the services of qualified traveling *foreign* merchants. In the latter capacity, they would have earned their living on rocky Delphi by providing oracles services to visiting traders by—giving

---

tripartite shape; that such a shape does not necessarily imply the three-pronged object familiar to us, I will endeavor to show later" (Walters 1992-1893: 14; emphasis added). As Walters (1892-1893: esp. 17) shows, the "trident" has taken many forms in Greek art including a number that have a floral character (the lotos) and that are rather compact like the object held by the Syrian. Even more promising as a symbol of immunity, universal trust, safe conduct, and wealth generation is Hermes' *tripētelon* 'staff with three branches/with three leaves' (*Homeric Hymn to Mercury* 528–532; called *kērukeion* by Herodotus 9.100.1). The *tripetēlos* seems comparable to the symbolic object carried by "Theseus" in Figure 12 and to an ornament on the prow of ships depicted on the Mochlos "Ship Cup," which has been compared to a fleur-de-lys (Chap. 7.6; cf. Anghelina 2017). Unfortunately, I see little or no resemblance between Hermes' *tripētelon* and the object held by the Syrian.

[47] In Chapter 12.1, I advance linguistic arguments that the Homeric Epic and Hymns are valuable Bronze Age sources. Admittedly, however, the *Homeric Hymn to Apollo* includes several "linguistic innovations" not found in *Iliad* or *Odyssey*. Thus, it *may* be "late."

geographic and commercial guidance. Obviously, the Hymn's message is not that all Cretan overseas merchants became employees/priests of Apollo in Delphi, but that a core of priests (perhaps replenished over time) had previously been independent Cretan traders. Apollo wished to become a god of trade, and he (his cult) succeeded in this objective. This willingness to put one's capital in the hands of foreign traders is a key to understanding a number of problems including the Syrian nationality of the "chief of the Keftiu" (§6 below; cf. §4 and Chap. 9.2 above).

An alternative or rather complementary understanding is that all foreign merchants were regarded as priests of a local god. That god might, as we have just seen, be Apollo at Delphi or "Potnia of Asia/Assuwa" at Pylos (see Chaps. 9.6 and 10.7 above). To become a priest of the local god might—but did not necessarily or usually—mean that the foreign merchant became the god's employee or agent but that he was made sacred to the god. The meaning being that he/she was placed under Apollo's/Potnia's protection. *The general point, and one credibly attributed to the Bronze Age realities, is that gods sponsored institutions that served to attract traders to their domains.*

The implicit model or guide offered by the *Homeric Hymn to Apollo* is that Syrian traders dressed in banded robes were regarded as priests by the Mycenaeans.[48] Most likely, with the cooperation of the Mycenaeans, the Syrians founded a cult for a Near Eastern god whom they identified with a local god. Their banded Syrian robes and Syrian cultic objects signaled to Mycenaeans and others their qualifications for doing business and for giving geographic guidance and commercial backing. A Syrian, signaled by his banded robe, stands holding a bird, (*CMS* VI, no. 318 = Arachne 164449) which arguably informs the viewer that he circuits for business or that he controls traveling businessmen (see Chap. 10.4 on the iconography of the bird).

Some Syrians, as signaled in glyptic by their *leashed* griffin, may actually have traded on behalf of Potnia of the Labyrinth whose throne, as seen earlier, was auspiciously served by the creatures. More generally, the leash symbolized the public warning that the traders were under Potnia's protection. Potnia attracted foreign traders to Pylos and Knossos by making them sacred—that is, by assigning/leashing the griffins to look after their welfare. The foreign traders are distinguished by their wearing of Syrian garments. The key to understanding the celebration, in which I presume all the visiting traders participated—that is, both independent traders and palatial agents[49]—is the campstool.

---

[48]   Again, in glyptic, a *dolphin*, depicted vertically, accompanies the *Syrian* trader in a banded robe who, as usual, holds the cultic symbol (see above) on his shoulder (Marinatos 1993: 128 Figure 88.b). Taken together with the *Hymn*, this depiction signals that the Syrian trader is arriving by sea with the guidance and protection of Apollo.

[49]   See §6 below.

Thus, we are returned to the origin of the discussion. The campstool is a seat with no back and with an X-shaped cross-piece for legs that was perhaps originally intended for temporary outdoors use. Whatever its origin and typical use the campstool also had the advantage of resembling (or having the potential to be made to resemble) an altar base.

A glyptic connection exists among Syrians in banded robes, griffins representing Palace/Labyrinth, and campstools. That connection is made visible in a Bronze Age *cylinder*—or roll-seal (Figure 32)—purchased in Beirut, in which an individual in a banded robe[50] holds a *dotted rosette* and a leash while at the same time a griffin places its front legs on a campstool.[51] The rosette and griffin place the festive scene in the palace/labyrinth (Chaps. 4.1, 4.2, 7.3). Having secured the arrival of the Syrian trader, the griffin is opening the camp-

Figure 32. Griffin opens campstool for Syrian in banded robe, seal
(*CMS* X, no. 268 = Arachne 167127).

stool for him to sit on. The holding of the dotted rosette indicates that the banded figure will be honored as a *stephanos* "garland/chaplet" (Warren 1985: 204–205). At the same time, as a decorative fixture on garments from Minoan to Mycenaean times (M. Shaw 1998: 70), the rosette serves to recall the underlying flower (= fine textile) motive of the festival (Chap. 7.6). I understand the

---

[50] The seal does not make clear that the right shoulder is bared.
[51] Rehak (1994: 81) says: "When the cylinder is rolled out, the animal becomes one of a pair that stands back to back, their forepaws resting on a schematically rendered incurved base bisected by a papyrus stalk." He does not mention a campstool. I see the "incurved base" as a campstool and hints of several others. Photographs of the three views of the cylinder are shown by Arachne: there is (1) a human; (2) one griffin; and (3) two heraldically oriented griffins and the papyrus. I think Rehak equates the campstool with an incurved base (meaning altar).

rosette to refer to the cushion that placed on the campstool seat converts it into a throne—that is, a seat of worship.

The central tall papyrus plant almost seems to emerge from the campstool, which reminds one of the papyrus symbol of safe conduct carried by the Syrian in Figure 30.[52] More, it announces the arrival/presence of Potnia at her ceremony, as does, even more, the date-palm in Figure 33 (see Chap. 10.8 on branch cults of Potnia). The latter figure shows two griffins with their front legs on a campstool. Once again, the griffins have rosettes on their shoulders (as in Knossos' Throne Room) and wings (unlike those in Knossos' Throne Room). The adoring griffins are surmounted by a symbol of the labyrinth in the form of either a stylized double-headed axe or a stylized palm tree.[53] Above this symbol floats the goddess herself with so-called "snake frames" (verified by the sealing *CMS* I, 379 = Arachne 157608); cf. Rehak (1995a: 110)

Figure 33. Griffins, campstool, entrance of Potnia, seal
(*CMS* XIII, no. 39 = Arachne 168162).

and Marinatos (1984: 119–120). Marinatos (1984: 119–120) deserves credit for identifying the protruding objects at either end of the "snake frame" as dates.[54] Marinatos is supported by the depictions of the Assyrian "Tree of Life." Thus the "snake frames"

---

[52] Betts (1978: 68–69 Fig. 15) shows a sealing in which two griffins adore a papyrus plant.

[53] See, I think, similarly *CMS* I, no. 98 = Arachne 157319. The palm should be *identified* with Potnia of the Labyrinth (Antognelli Michel 2016: 46; Chap. 10.8). Based on its importance in the iconography of the Knossos Throne Room we may be certain that the Cretan palm, like the griffin, was a prime possession of the goddess.

[54] For variations, see *CMS* I, no. 144 (= Arachne 157365), *CMS* I, no. 189 (= Arachne 157410), *CMS* II.3, no. 276 (= Arachne 159375), *CMS* XIII, no. 39 (= Arachne 168162), in which lions, griffins, the goddess in a flounced skirt, alternative symbols (I think) of the goddess, and the double-headed axe are all present. Obviously, more remains to be learned. A Janiform scepter from Hall IV in the Malia palace combines the axe on one side and a "leopard" in the kneel-run position on the other. The body of the leopard is covered with incised symbols of Potnia including meanders and spirals. See http://odysseus.culture.gr/h/4/eh430.jsp?obj_id=7886 (accessed April 14, 2021).

are best understood as stylized palm branches. I submit that the papyrus flower and the palm branches both correspond to the "heads of gods" (*struppi*), actually, bundles made from grasses, placed on couches in the Latin festival (see above).

The cylinder seal is the perfect choice for conveying much of my message. I find it very difficult to believe that a forger in the Levant knew enough to

Figure 34. Griffins on bench with incurved legs with symbol,
seal from Routsi (*CMS* I, no. 282 = Arachne 157507).

combine, in one cylinder seal, a man in a banded robe, griffin, rosette, and campstool. I surmise that the real-life individual who owned X 268 functioned in a "Griffin Corps" to smooth the way for visiting merchants and their valuables (see below).[55] Furthermore, on the basis of the preceding analysis, I offer the hypothesis that the "individual wearing Syrian robe" evolved from the meaning Syrian merchant to the meaning "foreign merchant."[56]

A seal from a grave in Routsi (Figure 34) depicts two overlapping griffins reclining on a bench (not a stool) with *incurved* (not crossed) legs. The bench's incurved altar base resembles those depicted in Knossos' megara, including the dado (Galanakis, Tsitsa and Günkel-Maschek 2017: 59, 72 Fig. 27). *In addition, it*

---

[55] Several seals show griffins held by leashes by individuals who are not obviously Syrians (see e.g. Rehak 1994: 81–83 Fig. 4). More interestingly, a figure seated in a chair, of indeterminate sex but possibly wearing a banded robe, holds a female griffin by a leash (*CMS* I, 128 = Arachne 157349; Rehak 1994: 83). This seal is from Mycenae.

[56] The role of the griffin in protecting international traders was adapted in funerary art, wherein winged griffins drew chariots as on the Agia Triada sarcophagus. Also, voyage to exotic places was made into a funerary theme: "Other larnakes make their eschatological vision more explicit by adding a ship to the Nilotic landscape. On a LM IIIB larnax from Gazi (Pl. 90:e) a ship sails over spirally waves, while a bird in the foreground pecks at a papyroid plant and a fish swims near in the water. The Nilotic context indicates that the schematized Minoan vessel is to be understood as the funerary barque-like examples on Egyptian tomb paintings, which will transport the deceased to the Afterworld" (Watrous 1991: 298).

reminds one of the incurved "campstools" (altar bases) used by human banqueters at Pylos. A spiral is visible on the shoulder of the front griffin. Importantly—on the same level with but behind the couchant griffins—there appears a sun-disk or rosette. The Linear B tablets from Thebes suggest the presentation of "offerings" to mythical creatures (Section 2 above) and *CMS* I, no. 282, as well

Figure 35. Griffins on altar base with unfamiliar symbol, seal
(*CMS* I, no. 73 = Arachne 157294).

as others, noted below, may be interpreted in this light. That is, as objects of worship, the griffins are portrayed on an altar base.

In Figure 35, the intertwined griffins (they share one head) place their front legs on an incurved campstool/altar base. The complicating factor is that standing off to the side is a new symbol in the shape of a triangle on an elongated shaft. It is the so-called "impaled triangle" with a short horizontal line at the apex. Two points stand out with respect to this symbol: (1) it very much appears to be the Linear B symbol for "grain" (food/rations?); and (2) although it is uncommon, it commonly accompanies animals (Matoušková 2020: 117–122). Accordingly, I suggest the following interpretation: (1) the campstool indicates that the griffins have safely delivered their Syrian charges to the feast; (2) they deservedly will participate in the feast; and (3) as animals/birds, their reward is to be given "feed."[57] To push this one step further, a seal with this kind of motif would belong to a quartermaster in the Griffin Corps. As mentioned in Section 2 (above), the Linear B tablets from Thebes offer possible support for the provision

---

[57] There are a number of seals depicting lions standing on an incurved altar but without the impaled triangle. I have suggested at various points that lions stand for the security force of the Labyrinth. Presumably, Agamemnon and Diomedes, both of whom donned the lion's skin, would have attended the feast (see §4 above). In *CMS* I, no. 98 (= Arachne 157319) from Mycenae, two griffins have their legs on a campstool on which stands a pillar.

Figure 36. Campstool with pillow and griffins(?),
seal (*CMS* II.7, no. 73 =Arachne 160432).

of "offerings" to mythical creatures. For a "Griffin Corps" note the griffin-headed
women in the "Ring of Nestor" (*CMS* VI, no. 277 = Arachne 1157223.

In Figure 36, we see, I think, the pillow on the "campstool" (extreme
incurved altar base) but not the griffins! Are these creatures wingless griffins,
or are they lions or...? However, in a seal from a tholos in Pylos (Figure 37), there
is a winged griffin—perhaps having just arrived since the wings are open—that
is reclining with no visible cushion on a platform whose dado includes the
Labyrinth motif of stylized double-headed axes and/or half-rosettes: "*The shape*

Figure 37. Winged griffin with half-rosettes,
seal from tholos in Pylos (*CMS* I, no. 293 = Arachne 157519).

of an incurved altar is automatically created by two adjacent half-rosettes" (Eliopoulos 2013: 215; emphasis added).

I turn now from glyptic to fresco evidence. At Pylos, in a fragment from the foyer of this procession, men carry indeterminate objects, one of which is described by Lang (1969: II 64) as "the upright of a rectangular frame which rests on his shoulder cushioned by a large white pillow" (perhaps a stool?), while others depict furniture-like and horn-like objects (cf. the Linear B text KN K(1) 872). Wright (2004: 161–162) fully develops Lang's description by noting that other individuals in the procession carry a variety of items: pyxides or baskets, large shallow bowls, and a lamp stand.

On the wall of the megaron itself is the "Bard at the Banquet" scene[58] that shows a lyre-player (actually lyre-*holder*) seated on rocks(?) who wears a robe with alternating bands of brown and white[59] together with a flying bird, a bull, and two individuals wearing white robes with tan (brown) diagonal bands, who are seated on "campstools" (but with incurved solid legs) on either side of a three-legged table. The upper bodies of the figures in banded robes—my Syrian traders—seated across the table from each other are missing, meaning their genders cannot be determined (Lang 1969: II 64, 80–81, 194–195, nos. 43–44 H6, pls. 27–28, 125–126, col. Pl. A; Wright 2004: 161–162). It is assumed that the figures raise goblets, as in Knossos' "Campstool Fresco."

The lyre symbolizes much more than music. It also has to do with "prophecies," most importantly geographic guidance, circuiting, and colonial foundations (see Chapter 10.7).[60] The flying bird that is associated with the lyre-player (Rasmussen McCallum 1987: 124ff.), especially if it is a dove, emphasizes the connection of the celebrated festival to circuiting (Chap. 10.4 esp. about flying birds on sealings). The (now) faint yellow *spiral* reportedly visible on the white chest of the bird (Lang 1969: 80) is arguably a symbol of circuiting and of the Labyrinth.

That the connection between birds and the lyre is not accidental but is verified by the previously discussed pyxis from Aptera, which likewise connects a lyre-holder in a shrine with a flying bird and ships of the Labyrinth (see Chap. 10.7). The shrine in the pyxis and the rocks in the fresco might represent a

---

[58] See https://www.semanticscholar.org/paper/Nestor%27s-Megaron%3A-Contextualizing-a-Mycenaean-at-Egan/a6413dba50be107452fd3617d6c7bc1fb5d49fb7/figure/163 (accessed February 26, 2021).

[59] On matters of colors in the original frescoes, see Brecoulaki (2018). In particular it is important to note that murex purple was used in the background of both the "Lyre Player and the Bird" and the "Procession in the Vestibule." Moreover, purple is visible on the garments of the "Lyre Player" (thus, arguably he is Calchas/Kalkhas).

[60] Apollo, famous for possession of the lyre, is not mentioned in the Linear B tablets, but we know the god cherishes and collects traders. For this reason alone, this god would merit a permanent position at a festival to celebrate the navigation season,

tholos, which has the right shape and, after all, it is a pile of rocks. An alternative is that both seats signified the seat of Apollo's oracle on the rocky island Delphi.[61]

Returning to Lang's reconstruction, it seems credible that some of the figures in Pylos' Room 5 Procession carry cushions (see Wright 2004: 162 Fig. 12). However, cushions cannot be seen on the campstool-like seats depicted in the "Bard at the Banquet" fresco, including for the seated figures who wear "Syrian" robes (see Wright 2004: 163 Fig. 13).

Knossos' "Campstool Fresco"—found in fragments outside the walls of the palace but believed to have come from an upper hall on the west side—displays a "non-standard" sense of fashion. As reconstructed, the Fresco includes figures, males(?) holding goblets who are sitting on campstools across from one another. As Immerwahr (1990: 95) notes:

> [T]he best known figure of the whole composition, the so-called 'La Parisienne' ... [w]ith her large eye, black curl, retroussé nose, red lips (the red somewhat carelessly applied) ... has been taken as the epitome of Minoan female charm, but the blue [sacral] knot ... behind her neck suggests that she is a priestess. [See Chap. 10.1 and Plate 16]

More specifically, the sacred knot she wears is blue with black and red stripes (Matoušková 2016; 12). Whether priestess or model or model-priestess what is striking is that we can see clearly that this "epitome" wears a (partially diaphanous?) dress that is very different from the "standard" Cretan garment with open-bodice. Much about this fragmentary fresco is uncertain but not the non-standard female dress. A second partially preserved woman "wears a yellow skirt with a multicoloured flounced overskirt" (Lenuzza 2012: 257). There is uncertainty about her presence, however.[62]

By contrast, to the campstool-like seats in Pylos' "Bard at the Banquet" fresco, at Knossos,[63] a real campstool and one campstool cushion are clearly visible in the original (not reconstructed) fresco. In addition, two hand-held goblets—one in blue and the other in yellow—are visible in the original (Hood 2005: 55). The gender of the figure on the cushion cannot be determined from the original fresco remains, but this figure wears a striped or banded garment.

---

[61] Pausanias (5.19.1) says that the "Chest of Kypselos" includes a depiction of a lyre-holding Theseus standing with Ariadne.

[62] Rehak (1995a: 106–107 with Plate XXXIXe) mentions the find at Knossos of a sealing depicting a woman (the individual wears a flounced skirt) who sits on a campstool and bends at the waist to take something from a bowl.

[63] See https://commons.wikimedia.org/wiki/File:Camp-stool_Fresco,_Minoan,_from_Knossos,_ AMH,_145371.jpg (accessed February 26, 2021).

However, in the unreconstructed version, another seated figure, whose garment is not visible, clearly has red skin, which indicates the male gender (see Chaps. 6.3, 11.4). The one visible seat cushion is white. However, in this connection, it is well to note Lang's (1969) references to a number of *Pylos* processions (e.g. 53 H nws) in which female participants carry bouquets of red and white flowers and Rehak's (1995a: 107–108) mention of a griffin on a gold cushion.

At this point, our initial objectives have been realized. Despite the difficulties and remaining uncertainties, it can be appreciated that Potnia provided Syrian traders—depicted in banded robes with emblems, possibly papyrus flower, and/ or sacral knot— safe passage and dispatched her Griffin Corps to escort them to Pylos and Knossos for the opening of the navigation season. Once there, Potnia showed her appreciation by having them seated on campstools/incurved altar bases, making them godlike. Our view of the *theoxenia/lectisternium* or, more accurately, the *sellisternium* is sufficiently detailed that we see the "thrones" (campstools, incurved altar bases) opened for the traders by the personnel of the Labyrinth (textile showroom) and sense their warm welcome by Potnia and leading members of the cultic firm, such as "La Parisienne." However, there are hints but we do not clearly see the dyed cushions that should be spread on the campstools for the foreign traders.

Add to this progress recent findings at Pylos that include a fresco from Hall 64 in the Southwest Building depicting three seagoing oared ships (possibly six oars per ship and possibly with sails as well) traversing a sea loaded with fish. My source, Brecoulaki et al. (2015: 281–282), adds that the hull of the lead ship is decorated by a vertical zigzag motif that among other possibilities, such as speed, suggests the idea of textiles.[64] Another ship has a row of argonauts (actually octopuses) on the hull: "Indeed, the primary function of the shell of a female octopus is to allow the animal to ascend from and descend into the ocean by using trapped air to regulate its position, just as a deep-sea diver would do" (Brecoulaki et al. 2015: 282).

Most importantly, the sea on which the ships sail is a *purple sea rendered with murex purple*. In this way, the festival of trade begins. I much appreciate that readers took this journey with me.

---

[64] "At Pylos, the zigzag motif was often used to recall the labyrinth and textiles, as indicated by the use of the pattern in a large-scale skirt depicted on a fragment of a wall painting from the plaster dump immediately northwest of the Palace of Nestor, and in a number of painted floor squares in the palace's megaron (Fig. 20)" (Brecoulaki et al. 2015: 281).

6. More Dogs and Dragons

I do not wish to leave the impression that everything is fully under control. In pursuing the main theme of §5, some unexpected challenges were encountered. Most importantly, the seeming intrusion of *genii*/dogs into the campstool theme.

Figure 38. Genius, goddess, campstool and palm, or papyrus flower, seal from Knossos (*CMS* II.8, no. 262 = Arachne 160892).

Thus, a noteworthy seal from Knossos is either anomalous or suggests that "Syrians" held a similarly themed festival for visiting Minoan/Mycenaean traders. In Figure 38, a goddess seems to invite a human with dog-like features—a trader—to sit on a campstool. I will refer to the creature as a "genius" because it does not wear a dorsal appendage (the figure-eight shield) and, hence, cannot confidently be associated with Potnia of the Labyrinth. The goddess(?) with a prominent nose *may* be standing or seated on a couchant lion, a stance well attested in Syrian iconography (Blakolmer 2017b: esp. 4). An explanation might be that the "genius" figure represents a Minoan/Mycenaean trader, and the amply-nosed goddess is a Syrian goddess who acts as his patron in Syria. This is as far as I can take the interpretative problem raised by this seal at this time.[65]

---

[65] Elsewhere, we find a pair of explicit dog-like humans (*CMS* II.6, no. 74 = Arachne 160144) and a pair of explicit dogs (*CMS* II.8, no. 326 = Arachne 160956): the former pose with their arms on a "campstool"; the latter pose with their front legs on a "campstool." *It is, thus, indicated that the*

Figure 39. "Object" from Ithaca.

Even more interesting is an inscribed scene on an "object," possibly a clay tablet that was excavated at the waterlogged tholos at the "School of Homer" in Ithaca in 2001 (Figure 39). A large ship with a number of rowers and a mast is depicted, and then, off to the right on the shore, a dog-like creature (no dorsal appendage is visible) poses standing with its knee on a campstool. Slightly to the right of the dog is a sign the authors interpret as Linear A AB 09, which has the syllabic sound value SE in Linear B (Kontorli-Papadopolou et al. 2005). It very much looks like Poseidon's trident symbol. I think of the dog as a trader honored perhaps at Ithaca. Of course, Odysseus is the most famous dog connected with Ithaca and he was Poseidon's agent (Chap. 15.1, 4 below).[66] There is no familiar symbol of Potnia in the depiction.

---

iconography places genii and dogs in the same ideological universe. Above the dogs floats a circular "sun-disk in moon-crescent" symbol.

[66] The object was found in an area of the Mycenaean acropolis at the "School of Homer" in Ithaca. Writing in 2017, one of the archaeologists, T. J. Papadopoulos (2017:424), noted: "One further impressive prehistoric (?) monument deserves brief discussion, and that is the so-called *kykloteres* or *tholos* ... It lies further to the East of the underground spring and it was badly destroyed and looted. It produced, however, many interesting finds, among which the most important were one clay tablet bearing incised figures of a ship and *a man tied on its mast* accompanied by mythical creatures and symbol(s) of Linear B (?) (AB09 "SE") ... , pottery sherds and a great number of animal bones. It is worthy of special note that among these bones the most important were two *bucrania* (oxen crania) ... which may be related with bull sacrifices and bones of *Bos primigenius*" (emphasis added). Odysseus tied to the mast of his ship at the instructions of Circe is described in *Odyssey* 12.36-60, 153-190.

Attention will now be directed to some difficult glyptic material bearing on the international movements of traders. On a cylinder seal dated to LM III from a grave at Agia Pelagia Crete (Figure 40, opposite), a man together with a griffin follows a woman(?) who rides sidesaddle on a "dragon" (*drakōn*), a mysterious doglike creature.[67] The dragon appears to convey his seated passenger through foreign territory as indicated by a grove of fan-topped "papyrus-reed" plants (Kenna 1968: 331; Antognelli-Michel 2020: 251ff.).[68] Taken literally, the path traversed is an aquatic one (Palaiologou 1995: 198). It seems that the man carries the griffin on his shoulder,[69] but the meaning is more likely that the man holds on to the griffin as it flies over the aquatic terrain as its wings are spread, not drooping.[70] The griffin is again playing a supportive/protective role, but the supported individual is not depicted as a Syrian. Possibly, he is the Minoan/Mycenaean master/director the "Griffin Corps."[71] Perhaps the griffin and his passenger/controller are together protecting/supporting the passenger on the dragon. It seems indeterminate whether man holds griffin or griffin holds man and, as cited, there are examples of interactions between griffins and humans.

[67] Depictions of dragons are not common in Minoan/Mycenaean iconography. A pair of couchant dragons from a chamber tomb at Mycenae are depicted clearly in VS1B no. 76 = Arachne 165753; their faces are doglike and they seem to be floating in water. In addition, a pair of dragons are depicted with papyrus plants in a sealing from Agia Triada (Levi 1945: 271 Fig. 1B).

[68] It is, of course, tempting to pursue a connection between the papyrus plants in *CMS* VI, no. 321 and the vital one, in *CMS* X, no. 268 (above). This is as far as I can take this problem of the papyrus for the present.

[69] Immerwahr (1990: 121 with Pl 63) notes a fresco found infill in the Fresco Cult Center at Mycenae wherein a woman (white-skinned) wearing a boars'-tusk helmet carries a small griffin that looks back at her.

[70] On the other hand, the griffin's legs are drooping. It seems difficult to tell whether human supports griffin or griffin supports human. Hence, it may be ventured that the difficulty is intentional, and they are identical—the human/griffin is a griffin/human (similarly the Tiyrns seal of a woman(?) holding a large griffin *CMS* VS1B, nol 429 = Arachne 166120; Rehak 1995a: 109). Ideologically the griffin is flying, but, in practice, it is traveling overland. The problem is that the land is water.

[71] In a broken sealing (*CMS* I, no. 324 = Arachne 157553), men interact with griffins and one man seems to hold a weapon and to direct the action (see Morgan 2010: 314). In Middle Kingdom Egypt the griffin sometimes has a human head instead of the head of a falcon (Morgan 2010: 304). The so-called "Ring of Nestor" (*CMS* VI, no. 277 = Arachne 164408) depicts a griffin which sits on a stool and interacts with other "griffin women"—individuals with female bodies and griffin heads (Evans 1930: 154). (The Griffin "Branch" of the Minoan organizational "Tree"?) In *CMS* VI, no. 321 (above) is it possible to think of the human carrying the griffin as a human with the head of a griffin? Further with respect to the reality of a human "Griffin Corps," note that the running spiral, a key symbol of the labyrinth, is often associated with "martial objects" including soldiers, helmets, swords, and spears (Hiller 2005). "The symbolic spiral motif thus characterises objects of utility used by men in contexts of combat, parade, and ostentation of social prestige, and pictorial environments of activities in which men performed or appeared as main actors" (Günkel-Maschek 2012: 123). Griffins are depicted on Mycenean/Minoan gold (Zouzoula 2007: 207-8) and in numerous later sources they are viewed "keepers"/"guardians" of gold (Zouzoula 2007: 42). Herodotus (4.13.1) places the gold guarded by griffins in the Black Sea region.

Figure 40. Dragon and griffin with passengers, seal from grave in Crete
(*CMS* VI, no. 321 = Arachne 164452).

A new study provides additional evidence that a mundane corps of humans stands inside the fantastic griffins. Franković and Matić (2020) observe that *some* Aegeans who are depicted as gift-bearers in Egyptian tombs (Franković and Matić 2020: Figures 1-3) have spiral-shaped fringes and/or locks ["curls"] similar to those seen on the heads of Aegean-type griffins in Egypt and on the heads of *some* humans in contemporary Aegean iconography. This evidence needs to be more fully evaluated, however.

I am not convinced, however, that the dragon's passenger is a woman.[72] I see the sidesaddle stance (discussed by Levi 1945: 274–275) but no female breasts and no long hair. Furthermore, it seems quite possible that the seated individual is wearing a Syrian garment, specifically a *kaunakēs*—that is, the (discussed earlier) Syrian banded robe that passes under the right shoulder leaving it bare and then is tied above the

---

[72] I have not seen a specific argument on the question of gender. Levi (1945: 275–278) says the rider wears a kaunakes, is "undoubtedly a feminine figure," and is (probably?) not seated on a bull (like Europa). There are, indeed, depictions in which the passenger on the dragon is undoubtedly a woman. For example, in *CMS* I, 167 = Arachne 157388 from Mycenae, an undoubtedly female individual rides sidesaddle on a dragon. Her breasts are clear and uncovered, and she wears a skirt. Also, on a gold seal ring from Mochlos (Crete), an individual whose female breasts are very visible sits sidesaddle on the deck of a ship bearing the head of a dragon at the end of its stern; her garment is not very clear (*CMS* II.3, no. 252 = Arachne 159350). It would appear that the stool standing under a tree is her vacated throne (Evans 1928: 250).

left shoulder. Therefore, I leave open that the dragon's passenger represents, as in our other examples, a *male* Syrian merchant who is sailing under protection from Egypt to Crete (or from Crete to Egypt).[73] Then, by parallelism, the man carried over the water by the griffin is most likely a protected Minoan/Mycenaean trader.

I venture that the doglike dragon transporting the Syrian merchant is a Near Eastern symbol and represents a Syrian maritime enterprise. I consider this also to be true of the *Kētos*—the creature that Heracles battled for control over the entrance to the Black Sea at Troy (see Chap. 14.3.e). A creature of this kind is featured in Figure 41. In the present context, the dragon is best viewed as a *kētos*, meaning a *Phoenician ship* (Kaizer 2011: 330).

Figure 41. Dragon = *Kētos*(?), seal (*CMS* II.8, no. 234 = Arachne 160864).

However, I do not wish with talk of mysterious dragons to distract attention from the much better documented role of the griffin. The detailed discussion of the Aegean navigation festival in this section and the preceding one has highlighted the role of the Aegean griffin in supporting palatial trade by offering protection to traders and their valuables.[74] The creature owes popularity to the international movement of artists but most of all, I submit, its fame results from the real-life contribution of the Griffin Corps to the international movement of textiles and gold.

---

[73] Voyatzis (1992: 267) makes an important observation concerning Near Eastern iconographic traditions: "The Eastern riders seated side-saddle also differ from the Aegean ones in that *they usually do not sit directly on the animal's back but on thrones or cushions* (FIG. 9). There was a long history in the Near East of depicting deities or important personages seated sidesaddle in this manner. *The human figures were male or female, the quadrupeds either dragons or actual animals. It appears that the side-saddle pose in itself served to distinguish the status of the rider, and that the dragons generally transported deities.*" (emphasis added). At Akrotiri in Xeste 3, as has been noted, the goddess gathering crocus stamens sits sidesaddle on a throne of textiles.

[74] For diffusion of griffin iconography, see Morgan (2010).

7. The Syrian "Chief of the Keftiu"

Chapter 8.6 noted that we see textiles depicted as gifts/tribute from Keftiu (Aegeans) in the tomb of the "Prophet of Amun" Mencheperresonb (second half of the fifteenth century BCE). A much debated iconographical and historical problem is raised by a scene in Mencheperresonb's tomb (Theban Tomb 86).

The problem is framed by Hussein (2007: 33, 35):

> In the Theban tomb of Menkheperreseneb, High Priest of Amun during the reign of Thutmose III, there is a tribute procession shown in two registers. The upper register of this scene is famous for its depiction of Cretan bearers, identifiable by their typical Minoan dress and hairstyles.... However, the figure of the "Chief of the Keftiu" is very different from the tribute bearers. He has short hair and a beard and is wearing a plainer kilt with a fringe or border. These attributes all appear elsewhere in this composition and others on Syrian or Asiatic figures. The "Asiatic" appearance of this figure, labeled as a "Keftiu" alongside Cretan or Keftiu bearers has puzzled scholars.... Why did the artist of Menkheperreseneb's tomb use a "Syrian" type as the Chief of the Keftiu, when any type could be inserted into this standard composition? The artist took care to give individuals different cultural characteristics, unlike in the tomb of Amenemhat, and the images of Minoans are very accurate, indeed, when compared to images of young men in Minoan art. Why then would the "Chief" figure be inaccurate? If he is "Chief of the Keftiu," why not depict him like the Aegean types which the artist used elsewhere in the tomb?

Rehak (1996: 47) solves the problem in a way—artist confusion—which casts doubt on the documentary value of the Egyptian tomb paintings. However, as he develops his argument, he hints at a more realistic and more useful explanation:

> It is also clear from the paintings that sometimes the Egyptian artists confused Keftiu with Syrians. Thus, men in long robes typical of the Levant often carry Aegean-looking rhyta. In the procession of Syrians from the tomb of Menkheperresoneb, one man wearing Keftiu shoes and a kilt decorated with running spirals has a distinctly Syrian hairstyle, prompting us to wonder whether this is an Aegean native, a Syrian, or perhaps the representative of a mixture of two or more populations that we might expect to find in some of the cosmopolitan port towns of Syria-Palestine or the Nile Delta in the Late Bronze Age.

The answer to the problem of the distinctly non-Aegean appearance of the leader of the trade mission (and of some of the participants) is suggested by the behavior of Apollo as described in the *Homeric Hymn to Apollo* (§5 above). The "Chief of the Aegeans" was, in reality, an experienced Syrian who had been recruited by the palace and put in charge of (a mixed ethnic group of) Minoan traders (see also §4 and Chap. 9.2 above, but compare Matić 2019: 654–655).

The running spirals on the kilt of one of the Keftiu reveal his connection and that of his colleagues to the Labyrinth.[75] It should be noted that even the designation as "Keftiu" of a trade mission composed entirely of obvious Syrians would not change the point. The designation of nationality is determined by who is sending the gifts to Pharaoh, not by the ethnicity of his/her gift-bearers. This needs to be taken into account by scholars when they try to pry historical data from Egyptian tomb paintings.

The "Purpled Economy" was an international economy with respect to textile products but also to the contributing productive human inputs. Despite the barriers posed by communications in the ancient world, labor power still managed to flow to its most productive uses.

---

[75] For Aegean spirals in Egyptian tomb scenes, see Barber (2016: 215–217).

PART III

ACHAEANS, AHHIYAWANS, AND MYCENAEAN TEXTILE TRADE IN ANATOLIA

Foreword to Part III

PART III accepts the scholarly consensus that identifies the "Achaeans" in Homer's epics with the "Ahhiyawans," referred to in numerous letters written to and from Hittite kings beginning in the sixteenth century BCE. The obvious implication of this identification is that one or more Mycenaean rulers established a state that operated within Bronze Age Anatolia. As the scholarly discussion now stands, the question begs how and when such a significant Mycenaean penetration took place. Scholars accepting the identification of Ahhiyawans with Achaeans more or less take as a given the existence of a Mycenaean state operating in Anatolia and mostly seek to locate its home base in Greece. Those who refuse to accept the commonsensical Ahhiyawan = Achaean identification defend their position by calling attention to a totally unexplained (allegedly) "Achaean" state in Anatolia.

Part III lays a foundation for the view that the Ahhiyawan state resulted from the Achaean victory in a historical Trojan War. A finding of more general importance is that the Homeric epics constitute an invaluable source about textile economy in the Aegean Bronze Age.

In Part IV, the Homeric epics are mined for evidence about the Mycenaean textile trade with the Black Sea region. It is perhaps not possible to create a serious history from folklore and fantasy, but it is certainly possible to extract real history from fictionalized history, especially when its author strives to make this possible.[1]

The first step, however, is to confirm the Bronze Age provenance of the Homeric Epics. This step is taken in Chapter 12 and then refined in Chapter 13.

---

[1] In some ways, it is easier to distill serious history from Homer than from self-serving Pharaonic inscriptions concerning barbarians defeated.

12

Homer's Epics

Dating and Value as Historical Evidence

GENERATIONS of scholars have sought to employ features of the Homeric Epics—society, religion, politics, geography, technology, and economics—to place them in a historical setting. "Homeric Greece" has been placed in one or another period *after* the demise of the Mycenaean palaces. None of the often brilliantly engineered proposed datings has won general approval and, as will be emphasized below, none has earned it.[1] The current literature abounds with references to Homeric society being "conventionally dated" to... For a social scientist whose vocation is testing hypotheses, a conventional date is of little or no use.

Strangely, the period that seems to have been ignored by scholars is one *before* the erection of the Mycenaean palaces in roughly 1400 BCE or, more importantly, before the use of Linear B Greek in roughly 1450–1400 BCE.[2] Yet, the proposition that Homer predates the Mycenaean palaces is the only dating that is supported by linguistic evidence (see below) that is ideologically neutral and objective.

Beyond this, the earlier period fits the material features scholars have extracted from the Epics as well or better than later periods.[3] Further, an earlier period best copes with such challenges as why Homer does not seem to be aware of the Hittites or of the "collapse" of the Mycenaean palaces resulting in a "Dark

---

[1] I have not compiled the vast bibliography although many of the most important dating arguments are cited at appropriate points in my discussion in Chap. 12.2–3.

[2] The reader is advised that the absolute dates vary widely among qualified scholars.

[3] Most of the material objects mentioned in Homer do not require dating in the pre-palatial period but, as noted by Benzi (2002: 345–346), for some objects an early dating is very reasonable: "[T]here is no doubt that the silver-studded swords and the large body-shields widely documented in the *Iliad* are scarcely attested in Mycenaean contexts after LHIIIA:1. Similar is the case of Meriones' boar's tusk helmet described in the Doloneia. Though a few such helmets come from late Mycenaean contexts in relatively peripheral areas such as Achaia, Aitolia, Phokis, and Miletus, and fragments of boar's tusk possibly belonging to an heirloom helmet have come to light in the Subminoan Tomb 201 (ca. 1050) at Knossos, there is no doubt that the heyday of this most characteristic of all Mycenaean weapons was the Early Mycenaean period."

Age."[4] Most importantly, known historical and archaeological phenomena—the operation of a Mycenaean state (Ahhiyawa) in Anatolia and that Hisalrik (Troy) was not destroyed—concerning which other datings of the Epics are silent may be regarded as "predictions" of the pre-Palatial hypothesis. Indeed, the rise of the Mycenaean palaces would owe much to an Achaean victory in the War. We will see in the next Chapter that Homer is very much concerned with *purple dye* and *purple dyed garments*.

1. Homer's Language

Homeric Epic is written in an ancient poetic form known as dactylic hexameter. Homer's Greek like the Greek of Mycenaean Linear B has the "w" sound (*digamma*). The "w" sound was lost by the time the epic was written in alphabetic Greek sometime in the earlier first millennium BCE. However, it was written down in terms of the metrics *as if* it still had the lost "w" (compare the formulation of Latacz 2004: 163–164). This commonality with Linear B shows that Homeric Greek is "early"; its origin may "lie at any point in the whole period in which the spoken language possessed the 'w'." (Latacz 2004: 162).[5]

The sharing of the *digamma* (and other extinct Greek language features) between the language of the Mycenaean palaces and of the Homeric Epics brings them closer together temporally and, in so doing, increases the likelihood that the Epics accurately pass down facts of Bronze Age life to the first millennium BCE. Even so, the usefulness of the Homeric Epics as a historical source would be less if they had been composed *de novo* only in the late second/early first millennium BCE. Some history would presumably have been forgotten or misunderstood by that time. *There is strong reason to believe that the composition of the Homeric Greek Epic does not lag behind, even slightly, Mycenaean Greek but predates it.* This kind of dating would increase the historical reliability of the Epics.

The late M. L West (1988: 156ff.) used linguistic evidence to take the language of the Homeric Epics not just temporally close to but prior to the Greek of the Mycenaean palaces. The details of his analysis are beyond the scope of the present study. Suffice it to say with West: "*The significant thing is that certain features of the epic language appear to belong to an earlier stage of Greek than the language of the Linear B tablets*" (M. L. West 1988: 156; emphasis added). This

---

4   In Homer, little scope is given to the bureaucracy and bureaucratic record keeping so evident in the palatial Linear B tablets. Obviously, this lack of emphasis fits the period after the demise of the palaces, but it also fits the period prior to their formation.

5   Note similarly, the disappearance of the *-oio* genitive ending for words ending in *-os* in alphabetic Greek: thus, in the written alphabetic Greek version of Homer there is no *Ilioio*, only *Ilioo* (before about 1050 BCE) and then *Iliō* (spelled /ou/ in classical Greek) (Latacz 2004: 268–271; Pulleyn 2006: 48).

conclusion is based on a scientific consideration of certain words, phrases, and the "phantom consonant" found in the tablets but not necessarily before.

West (1992) defended his central arguments for an early Mycenaean epic—one that predates the Mycenaean tablets—against Chadwick (1990) and Wyatt (1992). Chadwick (1990: 178) suggests:

> These metrical games [played by West], which might be discussed at far greater length, are ingenious and amusing; but do they really tell us anything about the pre-Homeric tradition of epic poetry? West does not mention the problem of the origin of the hexameter.... If we had a complete picture of the evolution of the Greek language from early Mycenaean times down to the time of Homer, we might be able to trace the origin of each locution. Unfortunately, apart from the Mycenaean of the administrative records, almost nothing is known of the dialects before 700 BC, and thereafter we have only fragmentary information on certain dialects, so that anything approaching a complete picture does not emerge before the fourth century. It is therefore very dangerous to look for parallels to Homeric forms in later material and infer that these point to the origin of the Homeric usage.

Chadwick (1990: 177) ends his critique with a call for caution. However, he does not anywhere argue that West's analysis of dating is incorrect. Nor does Wyatt challenge West's arguments about an early Mycenaean epic. For his part, West makes no linguistic concession of any kind to Chadwick and Wyatt.

Other scholars have voiced full or hesitant support for West's linguistically based conclusions concerning the dating of the Homeric Epics. Thus, Pulleyn (2006: 47–48) agrees that: "Certain metrical anomalies, too, can only be explained on the assumption that they reflect the state of the Greek language before the date of the Linear B tablets," and he describes an additional linguistic support: "Another example is the phenomenon of tmesis (the separation of a preverb from its verb), as at *Iliad* 1.25... : in Homer, this must constitute the retention of an archaic linguistic feature of great antiquity. The separation of preverb from verb is found in other Indo-European (Vedic and Hittite) texts, but it is absent from our earliest attested Greek, the Linear B texts of around 1200 BC"[6] (cf. Horrocks 1980: 4).[7] J. Bennet (2007b: 15) agrees; "The fact that it [tmesis] was retained in the Homeric poetic dialect suggests that the origins of

---

[6]   Horrocks (1980:4) provides the following example. In Homer one can say: "He chopped down the tree" or "He chopped the tree down." In Mycenaean and Classical Greek, one can say only: "He chopped down the tree."

[7]   The absence of tmesis may be due to the brevity of the phrases in the Linear B sources. The fact is that it is absent.

this special dialect pre-date the language as attested in the Linear B tablets," and he adds that "certain Homeric forms preserved in formulae—even occasional whole lines—can be scanned more consistently by using reconstructed Mycenaean forms in place of those preserved in the texts as we have them."

Again, there are important linguistic features of the Homeric epics that are not present in and cannot be explained by features of the Mycenaean Greek dialect or by features of the Ionian Greek dialect in which they were written down. Homer is a poet of the earlier Bronze Age. The best (only?) available explanation is that these features were conveyed directly into alphabetic Greek by Bronze Age poetry.

Wiener (2007b: 9 with sources) suggests, "One further argument favors an origin for certain aspects of the [Homeric] poems in periods prior to Mycenaean palatial civilization. Evolving knowledge of Linear B has led to the widespread belief that both the hexameter of the epics and the roots or origins of a number of word forms employed predate the Greek of the Linear B tablets of the palatial period." Wiener (2007b: 10) raises some problems concerning the persistence of older forms of speech in certain outlying areas (e.g. Boeotia) but he concedes: "The recent trend of philological debate has tended toward acceptance of the proposition that pre-Linear B forms can be discerned beneath certain otherwise inexplicable usages in Homer."

Most generally, West's conclusions are supported by Ruijgh (2011: 257–258):

Thanks to the discovery of the Mycenaean dialect linguists can now dispose of synchronic data for the stage reached by Greek in the period 1400-1200, at least for the Proto-Achaean dialect. This enables them to establish which changes—sound changes, analogical formations, borrowings—had already occurred in that period and which changes are of Post-Mycenaean date. A few Homeric formulae contain irregularities which only disappear when they are transposed into a stage of the Greek language which is anterior to the time of the preserved Linear B texts.... Thus we must conclude that the Greek epic tradition had already started in the Proto-Mycenaean period, that is, to say during the initial phase of Mycenaean civilization. At that time the Greeks of Mycenae borrowed several elements from the Minoan civilization of Crete: techniques for producing works of art and use of the syllabic script. It is tempting to suppose that at the same time the dactylic hexameter was taken over from the Minoans as a vehicle for heroic poetry.

The analysis by language scholars *proves* as much as there can be proof about such things that the Homeric Epics were composed *or* began to be composed at some point prior to the foundation of the Mycenaean palaces with their Linear B Greek covering roughly the fifteenth to twelfth century BCE. "Began to be composed" is sufficient for present purposes because, as explained below, there would be no Epic to convey without the Trojan War.

Moreover, the "proof" is by means of rigorous, ideologically neutral analysis not by debatable, sometimes ideologically driven grand theories of societal development, anecdotes, and, most dangerous of all, "What was possible at that time." The argument that the Homeric Epics are earlier than the Linear B tablets is not perfect, but the point is that it is much closer to being perfect than any of the arguments to the contrary.

The discovery that the Epics originated in and therefore very likely preserve features of the pre-palatial period opens up new vistas for a data-driven study of a hitherto unseen or barely seen Aegean world of the first half of the second millennium BCE. Even if the characters and their deeds in the Epics are fictional, the Epics cannot avoid revealing to us a great deal about the times in which they were composed. After all, even today's science fiction works, despite their other-worldly or futuristic intentions, reveal much about the current physical environment, technology, nomenclature, economic and political institutions, religion, demography, mores, and individual relationships and aspirations.[8]

After comparing the names of persons in the Linear B texts with names in the Homeric Epics, Palaima (2004b: 452) finds it "significant that approximately seventy human names in the tablets are also found in the Homeric texts, famous ones like Hector and Achilles among them. Given that these names were not given by parents to their children in the historical period, the Linear B evidence alone demonstrates that the Homeric tradition was not 'coining' names but was freely drawing from the repertory of names borne by real human beings in the Bronze Age, but not the historical period." Thus, *at a minimum*, Homer knew the names of real human beings from the Bronze Age. Presumably, he chose these names of real human beings because he wished to set his Epics in the Bronze Age, an objective that implies that others also knew the origin of the names. The Bronze Age names in Homer, however, do not belong to ordinary or real individuals but to the likes of kings and their followers. Thus, I see two additional (alternative) implications: (1) Homer's names and the Bronze Age names are contemporaries and Bronze Age parents later chose them for their

---

[8]   I understand that scholars have identified some objects in the Epics as belonging in much later times. Perhaps this is correct. That is, these objects were mistakenly introduced by later writers writing in the original tradition. On the other hand, their appearance in a work whose essence (the Trojan War) dates in the earlier second millennium BCE would give an object some claim to authenticity.

children; or else (2) Homer "coined" the names[9] and perfectly ordinary Bronze Age parents later chose them to make their children extraordinary. In the Linear B tablets, it is not uncommon for ordinary individuals to bear high-status names such as "Warrior" (García Ramón 2011: 228–229). *I suggest that "Homer" knew the names of his cast of characters before Linear B did.*[10] That is, Homer composed the names and conveyed them to later writers. Alternatively, the names were available to the later writers in an "archive."

Who is "Homer"? This is an endless scholarly speculation.[11] For me, "Homer" means the genius composer(s) of the Epics, not the individual(s) who, at some uncertain but much later time, wrote them out in alphabetic Greek. This Homer, as will be seen, was mainly interested in the poetic art and in human relationships. Additionally, he had a strong interest in history and made sure that his audience understood the background of the struggle he artfully depicted. Epic may require a war but why with a city controlling the entrance to the Black Sea? Latacz (2004: 170) cautions, we may expect to find clues to the larger context but not details such as individual personal names or topography. In combination with Hittite and Anatolian studies, Linear B, and archaeology/iconography the Homeric epics, as Latacz (2004: 168) puts it, "may now be exploited—for the first time in good scientific conscience."

Integration of the Epics with other data of the Aegean Bronze Age has become not only possible but also required for scholars dealing with the Aegean Bronze Age. The Sections that follow immediately deal with some challenges to using data from the Homeric Epics as a tool for reconstructing the economic, political, and cultic structures of the Aegean Bronze Age. After that, the integration process begins in earnest. Readers should expect no compromise on Bronze Age dating and stability of themes related to the Trojan War.[12]

---

[9]   Thus, "Agamemnon" likely means "much enduring (in battle)/steadfast" (see Kanavou 2015: 44). This name, like many others, would fit a part he is given to play by Homer or an earlier poet.

[10]   That the name Achilles is found at Pylos (Fn 06) and Knossos (Vc 106) does not mean, as G. Holland (1993: 19) maintains, "the name was not invented for the Homeric hero."

[11]   Again, I have not compiled the extensive (endless?) bibliography, but major exemplars are discussed in Chap. 12.2–3.

[12]   M. L. West (2015: 108–109) states: "So long as epic remained purely oral their contents were in flux, continuously evolving" but "flux" seems somehow stronger than "variation." West (2015: 109) adds immediately, "but each established theme had an identity that persisted through the changing performances." Thus, persistence of themes is viewed as consistent with "purely oral" contents. What West is really claiming is not clear to me. The theme of the Trojan War was present in the beginning and it remained at the end. There is no theory that predicts that the basic elements had to be lost over time. Indeed, one can assume with confidence that guilds of bards prided themselves on the stability of their oral presentations of inherited materials. Moreover, they were presumably rewarded according to the accuracy of their memory.

The Homeric Hymns, I think, raise more difficult dating questions but they are in the same epic meter (dactylic hexameter) as the Epics. In addition, they included the digamma and are similar to epic in terms of formulae and dialect. Despite a number of "late features"—mostly linguistic deviations from Homer[13]—I still find it tenable to view the Hymns as valuable sources for the Bronze Age. After reviewing a number of technical issues beyond the scope of the present study, Bonnell (2019: 45) concludes that "the hymnists share with Homer a fundamental part of their technique, but also … they are creative artists in a living tradition" (cf. Brandtly Jones 2010). However, with the exception of the *Homeric Hymn to (Pythian) Apollo* in Chapter 11.5 (above), the Hymns are not relied on as intensively as the *Iliad* and the *Odyssey*.

The poems of the *Trojan Cycle*, including the *Cypria*, like Homer's *Iliad* and *Odyssey, are composed in dactylic hexameter*. Hence, as explained, they have a strong claim to having been created and recited (as opposed to being written in alphabetic Greek) in the Bronze Age.[14] The problem is that, unlike the *Iliad* and the *Odyssey*, the poems of the Trojan Cycle survive only in fragments and in Proclus' extended prose summaries.[15] This raises the danger that the surviving records have been corrupted by the insertion of non-Bronze Age materials until they were written down in classical times. That is, they are important Bronze Age sources, but their reliability is subject to much question. The works of the Trojan Cycle are employed below to *supplement* Homer, as in the example of the "elopement" of Helen.[16]

---

[13] "Yet the loss of most early hexameter poetry, in which parallels would no doubt be found, constrains the method [for dating] somewhat. While the size of the Homeric corpus makes it the best guide to the 'tradition', non-Homeric language is not necessarily chronologically later" (Bonnell 2019: 41 with references).

[14] I see no need to decide whether these poems, or some of them, were earlier or later than Homer's. For me, the important point is that a corpus of Bronze Age *data* was available to poets. No one poet, including Homer, incorporated into his poems all the available evidence about the Trojan War. Kullmann (2015: 108) begins his essay with the following words: "The Homeric *Iliad* narrates only a specific episode of the Trojan War but, as becomes clear from numerous allusions, nonetheless takes for granted its audience's familiarity with the *legend* of the whole war. It is impossible to understand the *Iliad* without knowledge of its *mythical* background" (emphasis added). Homer, the Cyclical poets, and their first audiences arguably belonged to the Bronze Age and they understood that data/facts were being creatively coded into mythical poetry. Later audiences knew the clues for reverse engineering the received body of myths into original facts.

[15] Proclus is dated to the fifth century CE.

[16] Burgess (2001: 49) remarks: "One can still argue that the Homeric testimony for the "Cyclic" story of the Trojan War only occurred in a later manifestation of the Homeric poems that incorporated myth not known to an earlier, supposedly more authentic manifestation. But how do we identify the 'later' myth that is so radically different that it contaminates portions of the poems, making them somehow inauthentic? Most scholars now take a unitarian approach to the Homeric poems, even if they posit a relatively long and complicated process of composition.

2. Questions of Rulership and Global Politics

Such words in Epic as *temenos* and *anax* are also prominent in the Mycenaean Linear B tablets. Excavations of Bronze Age palaces suggest, however, that Homeric kings are very different from the later in time Mycenaean kings. It seems that Mycenaean palace culture recalls historically attested ancient Near Eastern monarchies. However, the heroes in the Epics who are under great pressure to prove their excellence and status recall the aristocrats in archaic Greek poetry (Stein-Hölkeskamp 1989).

On the other hand, this perspective seems highly subjective. One wonders why even the oldest fashion king cannot wish to win fame as a hero in addition to power. May we think in this connection of Sargon of Akkad or Gilgamesh, both established rulers whose careers are the subject of adventure stories? Moreover, how much do we really know social relations in either the Mycenaean palace period (about 1400 to 1200 BCE) or in the archaic period? Not a great deal.

Homer portrays the leadership of the forces besieging Troy, mainly called Achaeans, Danaans, and Argives, as a collegium of kings. So perhaps each represents or is drawn from a distinct geographic, legal, or socioeconomic community.[17] Palaima (2007a: 140) believes: "*Epos* is an important source for our knowledge of the past. The prevailing communal spirit in the kingdom of Pylos in the Mycenaean period may have been very much like how Homer depicts the kingdom of Pylos under King Nestor in the *Odyssey*." Further, all the Achaean kings owe allegiance to one great king: Agamemnon. However, I cannot perceive a "communal spirit" from the Linear B tablets from Pylos and from the other Mycenaean palatial centers. Undoubtedly, qualified scholars can read between these lines. However, I am more inclined to follow popular opinion since Schliemann[18] and identify Homer's kings (and Hesiod's "race of heroes") with the Mycenaean elites who wished to be buried with rich grave goods including the spectacular gold masks found in the Shaft Graves (see Chap. 9.5). The Shaft Graves at Mycenae date, however, not to Archaic Greece or to the Mycenaean palaces of Linear B times but to *very much earlier in the 17th-16th centuries BCE*.

Emanuel (1997: 5–6) chooses to place the Homeric Epics in the disturbed period after the collapse of the Mycenaean palaces. To do this he notes, among other things, "Homer's lack of awareness of the Hittites" and "Odysseus' declaration that

---

[17] The role of the kings is discussed below with reference to the role of Helen. I return to this problem in Chapter 14.6.

[18] More recently, see the discovery of the rich-in-gold "Griffin Warrior" in a large stone-built shaft grave of Late Helladic IIA date near Tholos Tomb IV in the renewed excavations at the Palace of Nestor in Pylos; the "Griffin Warrior" is regarded by Stocker and Davis as having "laid the foundations of Mycenaean civilization" (http://www.griffinwarrior.org/griffin-warrior-tomb [accessed February 12, 2021]).

he led nine successful maritime raids prior to the Trojan War" (*Odyssey* 14.229–233). These are fair points. Based on its wealth from control of the entrance to the Black Sea, Troy/Hisarlik was, it will be argued, a major regional power. Further, "awareness" of the Hittites would not be expected if the Trojan War took place during a period (say in the earlier second millennium BCE) in which the Hittites were not yet a dominant power in the Troad and Black Sea region.[19] After all, the Hittites had to get it together before they could fall apart around 1200–1800 BCE.[20] It might also be said that Homer seems unaware that his Trojan War is set in an unusually disturbed period. With respect to raiding, Emanuel (1997: 30) elsewhere cites "documentary evidence from the prosperous 14th and 13th centuries BCE, which clearly demonstrates the significant seaborne threat to coastal polities at this time. Egyptian inscriptions, letters from the Amarna archive, and Hittite documents refer to maritime marauders carrying out coastal raids, conducting blockades, and intercepting ships at sea (for the latter in Homer see, for example, *Odyssey* iv 660–674)." Hence, the raids carried out by Odysseus (and Achilles) do not indicate that Hittite power had already collapsed. As Emanuel (2017: 32) well notes: "After all, piracy is naturally most successful when coastal settlements and trade routes are present, regular, and prosperous." It is not clear that the raids mentioned in Homer are excessive historically speaking.

Another supposed resemblance of Epic society to archaic Greek times in the earlier first millennium BCE[21] is the prominence of the polis. The towns described in the *Iliad* and the *Odyssey* "may not be fully developed poleis, as for example … Gschnitzer (1981: 42) believes, but they are already 'spatially institutionalised' and the assemblies of the heroes mark the first step toward political

[19]   In Hittite texts, the Zalpuwa region or Zalpa is generally assumed to be situated on or near the Black Sea. Based on these texts, Rutherford (2019: 394–395 with n. 8, 401) concludes that Zalpa "seems to have been under full Hittite control only in the sixteenth century BCE and the [early] thirteenth century BCE," when Hattusili III recaptured Nerik, a city lying far beyond the Hittite core territory ("Hatti"). The political connection between Kaska Nerik and Zalpa is not clear to me, however. Rutherford (2019: 395 n. 8) adds: "Understanding Zalpa/Zaluwa is beset with difficulties, not least because Hittite and Assyrian texts know up to four places with that name, the other ones in various parts of southeastern Anatolia and northern Syria." Was Zalpa itself an international (commercial) power? It is not clear to me how or why Homer should have shown awareness of the Hittites. Did the Hittites control every nation and did they intervene whenever a nation in western Anatolia was invaded? If so, did the Ahhiyawans obtain and maintain a foothold in Anatolia by defeating the Hittites? As far as we know, the Hittites did not become a continental power before the earlier 15th century BCE.

[20]   Placing the Trojan War before the Hittites became important does not make it "mythical." Further, as to the possible relevance of the Hittites: the *Cypria* may have included that Paris and Helen were somewhere hosted by one Motylos, founder of Samylia in Caria (Stephanus of Byzantion). Perhaps, Motylos refers to Muwatalla "Mighty" an epithet of the Hittite "Storm God." Perhaps the early Hittites benefited from the Helen enterprise in Troy (M. L. West 2013: 93).

[21]   If the Homeric Epics were composed in the earlier first millennium BCE it is rather surprising that they exhibit no memory of the "collapse" of the palaces in ca. 1200 BCE.

institutionalization" (Grethlein 2009: 127). I agree with Grethlein. This resemblance need not be limited to earlier first millennium BCE Greece. Structural conditions tend to be repetitive with the result that history repeats itself with both predictable and random differences. Thus, for example, "city-states" governed by assemblies were prominent in third millennium BCE Sumer *before* being transformed into city and territorial "monarchies." My point is that it is not possible to know that the towns and assemblies in Homer would have found their political institutionalization in the archaic polis rather than in the Mycenaean palace.

Despite the linguistic evidence, considerations of the above kind together with a "hard-headed, realistic historical frame of mind" are often used to date the Epics to the earlier first millennium when they were written down. Thus, important religious/political Epic words such as *temenos* and *anax* are taken to be somewhat ill-fitting survivals from the Mycenaean world. It is ignored that conditions similar to those that led from archaic to classical Greek society may earlier have guided the transition from Epic times to palatial society. Decentralization and small scale of institutions are not conditions unique to archaic Greece. Palatial society and classical Greece are very different but each inherited certain terminology and institutions from predecessor societies. The point is that perceived similarities between Epic society and archaic society do not require that they were close in time. History, I insist, does not travel a straight line but tends to repeat itself.

Thus, Homer's term *basileus*, which relates to a regional/subordinate king seems to have evolved in palatial times into a *qa-si-re-u* (*g*ʷ*asileus*) meaning a local official of the palace charged with the responsibility for such tasks as allocating metals to local smiths (Palaima 1995: 124). Presumably, this happened because of an increase in centralization and bureaucratization. Although traces of more prestigious applications of the term remain, the evolution was from Homer's usage to the palace's, not from the palace's to Homer's as usually is assumed (Blackwell 2018: 515). Note Palaima's (1995: 124 with references) observation: "It is thought to be clear that the *qa-si-re-u* in the Mycenaean period lacks the lofty aristocratic associations of the term in the Homeric epics. This is true in relative terms, when one compares Mycenaean usage with Homeric and later usage."[22] That is, with the rise of a relatively centralized palatial society the *basileus* lost his lofty

---

[22] Palaima (1995: 123): "The Homeric poems use two terms to refer to the heroes who lead contingents from the various natural geographic districts of Greece. The main term is ... *basileus*. The second is used more sparingly: ... *anax* or *wanax*.... Zeus, for example, is given an epithet 'ruler of gods and men' which uses *wanax*. The term *wanax* occurs almost always in the singular in Homer (271 of 276 instances). It therefore seems to denote overarching 'monarchical power' as opposed to *basileus* which is applied to all the single heroes and in the plural to a number of such leaders even within one community (*e.g.*, Ithaka, Phaiakia)." Traces of the Homeric usage are found in Pylos PY 40 (Ventris and Chadwick 1973: 172–173).

sociopolitical position but retained a localized authority. The common factor in Homeric and palatial times is very probably that *basileūs* is an appointed position.

The citations of supposed differences in the centralization of rule, of achievement motivation, and in the development of the polis are not rigorous enough to justify placing the scenery of Epic in the first millennium BCE. All the arguments based on these factors leave room for much doubt. The same applies, of course, to the palatial period. With the strong support of the Shaft Graves the way is open to consider that Homeric Epic is at home in the pre-palatial Aegean.

3. Questions of Geography

Dickinson (2007: 233–237) argues strongly that the *Iliad* does not reflect the geography of the Mycenaean world:

> [T]he Catalogue of Ships [*Iliad* 2.494–759] is *not* a good picture of the world of the Mycenaean palaces, nor is that which is given in the Homeric poems generally. I will concede that the epic tradition clearly incorporates some memories from the Mycenaean age, particularly that places like Mycenae, Pylos and Troy, insignificant in the eighth century B.C., had once been centres of power.... The Trojan War tradition shows no knowledge of the Hittites *at all*.... Troy is presented in the *Iliad* as acknowledging no superior.... It is surely obvious to Delphi, given its old name Pytho [*Il.* 9.405; *Od.* 8.80] as a wealthy shrine of Apollo, the seat of an oracle, reflect a situation that is certainly not Mycenaean and it is difficult to place before the eighth century.... It [the Catalogue] has many peculiar features ... and was surely composed from materials of different ages and origins.

The presence of Apollo in Epic but not in Linear B tablet (considered later) is a disparity in Dickinson's favor. He does not, I think, recognize that his comments on the inaccuracy of the "Catalogue of Ships," even if correct,[23] are consistent with Epic being *earlier* rather than much later than the palaces as he believes. Dickinson concedes that Mycenae and Pylos are important centers in Homer and in the Bronze Age but not in the eighth century. Again, *if* the Hittites controlled Troy in palatial times, it does not follow that they did so in still earlier times and, consequently, there is no reason for Homer to refer to it.

---

[23]   Chapin and Hitchcock (2007: 262): "The unfortunate conclusion of a comparative review of Homeric topography and recent archaeological investigations is that the evidence supporting the identification of sites named in the Catalogue of Ships remains woefully weak, even if it is assumed that our ancient sources preserve prehistoric truths. Yet neither can it be proven that Homer's Catalogue of Ships is a complete fiction."

However, Homer's geography in the Catalogue of Ships deserves more credit for its Bronze Age realism than is granted by Dickinson or even by Chapin and Hitchcock (2007). Thus, Latacz (2004: 244–247) compares the mention in the Theban section of the Catalogue (*Iliad* 2.500–502) of two *unknown* Boeotian towns, Eutresis and Eleon, with their apparent Bronze Age counterparts, *e-u-te-re-u* and *e-re-o-ni*, mentioned in a Theban Linear B tablet (TH Ft 140) listing towns contributing oil and grain.[24] Bachvarova (2016: 152–156), on whose transliterations I rely, finds Latacz's comparison to be "particularly cogent" in demonstrating that Homer includes some "accurate reminiscences from the Bronze Age." Bachvarova does not explain why the two extinct towns should have been *remembered* by Homer.

Bachvarova tends, against Latacz (2004), not to believe that Homer recalls a "real conflict." I find her objections inconclusive in that they play off one political unknown against another. One of Bachvarova's more concrete objections to a real Trojan War involves a geographical problem—the status of Lesbos. Homer is, however, realistic or at least consistent on this point: Lesbos belonged to Priam of Troy until it was seized from him by the Achaeans (*Iliad* 9.129–130, 664–665). What happened to Lesbos, if Lazpa is really Lesbos, many years later during Hittite/Ahhiyawan times is not part of Homer's focus. One more point, the *Mycenaeans* were interested in defeating Troy not because of their affairs in *southwestern Anatolia* (so Bachvarova 2016: 354), a concern that would completely miss the point, but because of their profitable or potentially profitable affairs in the Troad and Black Sea region.

In short, what is known about the geography does not justify placing Homer long after the Aegean Bronze Age.

4. Questions about the Historicity of the Achaeans and Troy

Homer, a pre-palatial source, tells that a Greek population group he calls "Achaeans" were active in the Troad during the Bronze Age. They were active in besieging a place called "Troy"/"Illios." The Hittite texts testify "Ahhiyawans"

---

[24]   A tantalizing clue from Eleon's Tomb 9 (SEA1a), became visible at the end of the 2017 season: "With the removal of two blue covering stones that slightly overlapped each other, initial excavation revealed a single young adult with the head oriented to the northwest and the body turned toward the west. The single grave good was a murex seashell placed northeast of the individual" (Burke et al. 2020: 458). The "Blue Stone Structures" are dated by the excavators to the Early Mycenaean times (the "Shaft Grave Period" in Middle Helladic I). Burial with only the shell of a murex testifies strongly to the commitment of the deceased with the dyeing of cloth and perhaps would also attest its importance in the community. Remarkably, Burke et al. (2020: 458 with Fig. 15) also report finding the remains of a (simple weave) textile in Tomb 10 (SWA1b).

were active in Anatolia during the Bronze Age. The Hittite texts also mention a place called "Wilusa." In what follows, we will examine the relationships among these places and groups.

First, is the Troy besieged by the Achaeans a fictional place? This would be highly improbable as a unique place in the Troad very well fits Homer's description of Troy. Latacz (2004: 75, 85ff., 96ff.) has noted: "The ruins of an ancient and unique citadel, called Hisarlik by the Turks, are positioned, like Homer's Troy/Ilios, in the Troad close to the Dardanelles—that is, near the narrow strait giving access to the Black Sea from the Mediterranean. Excavations at the site have disclosed the presence of an extensive Bronze Age city" and, Latacz continues, "Hittite texts mention a region called *Wilusa*, commensurate with the Troad, within which is an area called *Taruwisa* (or *Tru(ui)isa*). Phonetic and sound change arguments make possible the identification of Hittite Wilusa with Homer's Ilios. Argument by geographic proximity makes possible the identification of Homer's Troia with Hittite Taruwisa."

Thus, not only is it credible that the Troad knew a Troy/Ilios pre-dating the Mycenaean palaces but also that this ancient Troy/Ilios is best placed in Hisarlik or, perhaps better, in its excavation level "Troy VI." Homer's Troy is a historical reality and it lay in north-west Asia Minor where Homer located it.

However, the identification of Troy/Ilios with Hittite "Wilusa"/"Wilios" remains more controversial.[25] Latacz (2004: 101) maintains: "Moreover, in the 'land of Wilusa', at the end of the fifteenth century BC, the Hittites knew an area called *Taruwisa* or *Tru(ui)isa* which can scarcely be distinguished from the Greek *Troia*." Nevertheless, *geographic* evidence for the identity is not available. On the other hand, Steiner (2007: 603) concedes that the Troad, which includes Wilusa and Taruwisa, was apparently outside the sphere of the Hittites. He seeks to counter a possible Mycenaean presence there by noting the absence of written documents or writing generally which is significant but not a decisive consideration.

Support from considerations of the likeness of sounds or of geography for the identification of Troy/Ilios with Wilusa/Wilios is provided by a Hittite Treaty (AhT 6 + CTH 183) of the mid-thirteenth century (tr. Beckman 2011). This identifies the ruler of Wilusa to be Alaksandu, a name that may be understood to be Greek but unlikely to be of Hittite or Luvian origin (Güterbock 1986: 33–34). Alexander, of course, is the alternate name of Paris, a non-Greek name, in the *Iliad* (e.g. 24.25–30). In addition, in the *Iliad*, Ilios is six times referred to as "steep (*aipeinē*) Ilios" (e.g. 13.773) but a Luwian song begins with the line "When they came from steep (*alati*) Wilusa" (Watkins 1986: 59–62). This is an additional clue

---

[25] Ilios is found numerous times in the *Iliad* together with Troy for the scene of the Trojan War. Recall that in later alphabetic Greek the initial *w* had disappeared.

that the two places, both famous, Wilusa and Troy, both "steep," are in fact the same place. Thus, while the identification of Troy with Wilusa lacks a proven foundation in geography and philology it has found support in a number of less rigorous considerations.

Second, are Homer's Achaeans a fictional creation albeit by a poet of the Bronze Age? Presumably, Homer as a participant in Bronze Age society was working from a stock of Bronze Age materials ("backstories") rather than inventing them from whole cloth (A. Porter 2014). Beyond such common sense considerations some evidence is available in the Mycenaean Linear B tablets: "We should, however, take note of the possible place-name *a-ka-wi-ja-de* Achaiwia, which appears on one of the Linear B tablets from Knossos (C 2 914).[26] While the specific reference is somewhat problematical in this case, it at least provides evidence of an authentic Bronze Age pedigree for the name Achaia, though the name may well have had a much more restricted application in its Bronze Age context than is suggested by Homeric tradition" (Bryce 1989: 4). Hajnal (2016) does not seem to find the Linear B reference to Achaeans in C 914.B to be problematical. He suggests that it refers to sacrificial animals (fifty he-goats) with an indication of direction—*a-ka-wi-ja-de* "for the *Akhaiwiande*"—the reference would apply to a commemorative feast. Similarly, Killen (1994) suggests that this term may not refer to a place in Crete but rather to a festival (the "Achaia"). Thus, "Achaean" may refer not to a little-known place in Crete but to Greeks from/in various locations who celebrated a common festival at that place. Perhaps, the festival celebrated the foundation by mainland Greeks of their first self-governing polis in Crete. *Alternatively, the festival celebrated the victory of the Achaeans over the Trojans.*

In any event, the indication is that Homer is the earlier source of the term "Achaean." *Odyssey* 19.172–181 wherein the disguised Odysseus tells Penelope about conditions in Crete is of special interest: "There is a land called Crete, in the midst of the wine-dark sea, a fair, rich land, begirt with water, and therein are many men, past counting, and ninety cities. They have not all the same speech, but their tongues are mixed. There dwell Achaeans, there great-hearted native Cretans, there Cydonians, and Dorians of waving plumes, and goodly Pelasgians. Among their cities is the great city Cnosus, where Minos reigned when nine years old, he that held converse with great Zeus, and was father of my father, great-hearted Deucalion. Now Deucalion begat me and prince Idomeneus" (tr. Murray *LCL*). Hooker (1969: 70–71) notes the absence of "a reference to the Achaeans as a dominant power in Crete or to an Achaean invasion. Our Homer knows nothing

---

[26] Thebes Of 27 mentions the word *(a)-ka-i-je-ja* that might be understood as the adjective "Achaean." The obstacle is the absence of the digamma, but it has been noted that the digamma is sometimes dropped in Mycenaean times (Kelder and Poelwijk 2016: 575).

of this, and indeed, he has virtually nothing to say of Minoan-mainland relations."[27] There is additional support for Homer as nonfiction. The Hittite letter called "The Indictment of Madduwatta" (AhT 3) dating to the early fourteenth century BCE mentions one "Attarasiya/Attarrissiya, the man of Ahhiya" who had been raiding Alasiya (probably Cyprus) (tr. Beckman 2011; Bryce 2011: 97–100). In 1924, the Swiss Hittitologist Forrer (1924), while admitting the philological problems, proposed to identify this "man of Ahhiya" with Atreus the name of the "father" of Agamemnon and of Menelaus in Homer (e.g. *Iliad* 1.5). Of course, Forrer's identification of the name remains disputed and is not mentioned by Bryce (2011: 97–100) in his recent discussion of the text. However, no less a philologist than M. L. West (2001: 266) sees reason, together with several other scholars, "to suspect that behind the patronymic 'Atreidēs' [my transliteration] lies a Mycenaean name such as *Atrehion or *Atrehias, with Atreh from older *Atres-.... The name of the early fourteenth century freebooter commemorated in the Indictment of Madduwatta may very well be interpreted as Atresias or Atersias (or Atarsias < *A-tr̥s-ias)." West, however, sees no identity of this name with the name of the father of the Atreidai (cf. Steiner 2007: 592). With respect to the various coincidences I am tempted to say, "in for a penny, in for a pound."

"The Indictment of Madduwata" also provides evidence of an early connection between Greeks and Anatolians within Anatolia in the mention of the name "Muksu" (§33.75), probably an Achaean leader (Yakubovich 2008: 194). Individuals with this name are known from later Greek sources, but not in Homer. Examples include Mopsos the seer, Mopsos the Argonaut, and Mopsos who was born to Manto after she migrated from Thebes to the Ionian coast of Asia Minor before the Trojan War.[28] However, the name Mopsos (*mo-qo-so*) is found in Linear B tablets from Pylos (PY Sa 774) and Knossos (KN De 1381.B). So the name Mopsos is found in both Anatolia and Greece but where did it originate? López-Ruiz (2009: 492) provides the answer: "The mention of Muxas in this Hittite source is, furthermore, associated precisely with Ahhiyawa. Moreover, the linguistic evidence supports the Greek origin of the name, which would have arrived in Anatolia as a foreign word Muksu-/Muksa-, according to the form attested in the Hittite and Luwian texts. As Öttinger has pointed out, if the name was Anatolian (say, Hittite), it would have been rendered differently, e. g., Mu-ku-ssu/Mu-ku-ssa-, not

---

[27] He (Hooker 1969: 71) finds a suggestion of late interpolation in the mention of "Dorians" (unique in Homer) but, as Hooker noted earlier, "The mere mention of Achaeans in Crete is, of course, not surprising; it would be strange if they had been omitted, for no doubt settlers from the mainland had been coming to Crete throughout the LM III period" (Hooker 1969: 70). However, if Crete was a major commercial and cultural center that attracted settlers from the mainland it would be strange if Dorian merchants had no representation there.

[28] Sources for Mopsos: Strabo 14.4.3, 14.5.16; Pausanias 9.33.2; Burkert 1992: 52–53; Finkelberg 2005: 150–152, 153, 158.

Muksu/Muksa."[29] So according to accepted philological rules "Mopsus" moved from West to East, just as Greek literature maintains. This is not to say, however, that the name has a Greek etymology (Bachvarova 2016: 318–319).

Third, and most importantly, should the Hittites' "Ahhiyawans" be identified with Homer's "Achaeans"? The short answer is that philological rules do not permit identification of the two names. The philological obstacle to the identification is that there is no reflection in the Hittite of the second *a* (Beekes s.v. *Akhaioi*; but see Finkelberg 1988). The philological problem may be a mutation due to a chain of translations of the names from one language to another or from "independent adaptations" (Palaima 2007b: 202) or it may arise from difficulties in implementing the poetic metrics. The more important consideration, as has been argued, is that it is not a case of trying to identify a fictional name "Achaean" with a historically attested name—that is, of employing the Hittite's Ahhiyawans to demonstrate the reality of Homer's Achaeans but rather of making two historical sources reinforce one another. Both groups are real and the identity of their names in terms of sounds or letters is too strong to dismiss as the basis for a least a working hypothesis. Add to this, that the name Ahhiya, the shorter and older form of Ahhiyawa which appears in two Hittite texts (AhT 3 = CTH 147 and AhT 22 – Kbo 16.97) even more resembles the name Achaean.

De Fideo (2008: 1, 100 with n. 37) concludes: "That *Ahhiyawa* is the Hittite form of the Greek *Akhaiw(i)a*, the land of the *Akhaioi* (another, more frequent collective name for the Greeks in Homer), despite residual resistance on the part of certain scholars, no longer seems to be seriously at issue" (but compare Steiner 2007: 605). I agree with de Fideo that Ahhiyawa is the land of the Achaioi but I regard her conclusion as only a strong working hypothesis as the identity of Achaean and Ahhiyawan has not been proven geographically (Steiner 2007: 592–594). The hypothesis allows scholars to move forward with reasonable confidence to determine whether it "predicts" other known phenomena and opens up new problems for historical research.

De Fideo (2008: 1, 100 with n. 38) regards it as "certain" that the kingdom of Ahhiyawa is not located in Anatolia but in Mycenae, or Rhodes, or Thebes. As reasoned well by Niemeier (2005: 18): "Further evidence for the location of Ahhiyawa outside western Asia Minor is formed by the fact that Hittite troops never entered it and by the unique role of Ahhiyawa in the Hittite texts.... Ahhiyawa is constantly active in connection with the states in western Asia Minor, but, in contrast to these, any information about the geography of Ahhiyawa (except the mention of the islands belonging to Ahhiyawa) and any mention of its political and social structure (except for the reference to the

---

[29] López-Ruiz cites Öttinger 2008 65, esp. points 5–6; cf. Finkelberg 2005: 152 n. 36.

king) is missing. To the Hittites Ahhiyawa was a distant and rather unknown country, apparently situated overseas."

Nevertheless, I have strong reservations about locating Ahhiyawa, the land of the Achaioi, outside Anatolia. There are cogent arguments and evidence for the presence of the Ahhiyawan kingdom *inside* Anatolia (see Steiner 2007: 597–601). The most decisive consideration has been overlooked, I think. It is whether the Hittites would have taken so seriously the Anatolian machinations of Ahhiyawa had that kingdom's territorial base been located overseas. This is possible as witnessed by the reaction of the United States to the U.S.S.R.'s positioning of missiles in Cuba in the early 1960s. The situation would certainly have been much different if Ahhiyawa was based in the Troad and controlled the sea-entrance to the Black Sea. In that event, Ahhiyawa would have been wealthy and geographically positioned to deploy significant forces including expensive chariots and thousands of foot soldiers within regions of interest to the Hittites. Its characterization in Hittite texts would *appropriately* have been that of recognized great power, not that of occasional nuisance (Kelder 2004–2005). At the same time, so long as their textiles moved unopposed from Greece to the Black Sea the Mycenaeans in Greece would have had little need to know anything about the Hittites. It seems most reasonable to understand Ahhiyawa as an ethnic Greek maritime power based in the Troad. For reasons that will become clear below, I regard the Ahhiyawan state to be the direct descendant of the Achaeans who invaded Troy.

Further, as developed more fully below, I do not believe Homer's statement that the Argives sailed home after the sacking (*Iliad* 12.16). That is, if that statement means that the Achaeans completely deserted a *ruined* Troy. At least some Mycenaeans remained behind or perhaps replacements were sent. Rather than leaving the great city fallow some Mycenaeans stayed on in order to benefit from its strategic position or to prevent others from doing so. In short, my suggestion is that the historical Ahhiyawa refers to the Greek "bridgehead" in the Troad formed in the aftermath, as Homer tells it, of the Achaean victory in the Trojan War. The point remains that the Ahhiyawans were Mycenaeans and that Ahhiyawa was a Mycenaean kingdom that may have maintained its connection with/allegiance to the Mycenaean kingdom(s) in the Aegean islands and Greek mainland.

To sum up, there are reasonable grounds for identifying Homer's Achaeans with the Hittites' Ahhiyawans. There are much stronger grounds for identifying Homer's Troy with (Turkish) Hisarlik in the Troad. There are weaker but reasonable grounds, including as one of several factors the likeness of sounds and the openness of the Troad, for identifying Homer's "Troy/Ilios" with the Hittite's "Wilusa"/"Wilios."

The likeness of sounds between a small but key set of names of places/ groups in Homer and those in Hittite documents constitutes *prima facie* evidence of familiarity with those places/groups in real time. Instead of inventing the names (as in a work of fiction), Homer made the effort to recreate the alien sounds of the actual names. The temporal trends that constitute philological rules for the pronunciation of foreign names could not apply to poetry composed for recital before those empirical regularities had asserted themselves. Devotion to art and history does not require authors to bear the costs of anticipating the factors underlying philological regularities and so informed to advance from likeness to exactitude. Moreover, this is not yet to mention the identification of numerous names in Homer with names in the Linear B tablets. This identity cannot be explained as coincidence.

Let us turn again, briefly, to some largely unsettled questions about Homer's "Achaeans." It also appears that the term refers to a kind of an association rather than strictly to an ethnic group. This interpretation finds support in Nestor's reference to "compacts" and "oaths" among the fighters (*Iliad* 2.339) and the fact that *Achaioi* does not have a recognized Greek etymology. Beekes (s.v.) says the word is "no doubt Pre-Greek."[30] Indeed, if one considers Beekes' related discussion of possible connection between Greek *achos* and the name *Achilleus*,[31] it is clear that we are dealing with hotly disputed matters. I will not pursue this path, but I will note, following Nagy (1979: Chap. 5), that *achos* is the root of *Achaioi*. *Achos* is translated by LSJ as "pain, distress" but it has a wider range of meanings. In Homer, Cook (2003: 165 n. 2) explains: "The first type of *akhos* is caused by extrinsic loss, most commonly of *philoi* 'family and friends' who may be dead or simply absent. Responses to such loss vary from yearning to lamentation and even flight for home. The second type of *akhos* is caused by loss of *time* ("honor and status") either by an individual or the group to which he belongs. Those who experience it often respond by retaliating or continuing to fight." At a number of points, Cook cites "indignation" as an expression of *achos* (Cook 2003: see esp. 166, 185, 194) and he notes the "thematic identity of both Akhilleus and the Akhaioi in Homer." Accordingly, *achos* applies to *anger* or, more specifically, to the feeling of "*righteous indignation.*"

In Chapter 14, I argue that the Trojans and "Argives" formed a trading contract involving the transfer of the "Helen enterprise" from Greece to Troy. The Trojans/Paris violated this contract. "Achaeans" refers to the indignant/

---

[30] One question is whether Homer's Achaeans refers to all inhabitants of Greece. This is answered in the negative when the disguised Odysseus remarks that the Cretan population includes Achaeans in addition to Pelasgians, Kydonians, and Eteocretans (*Odyssey* 19.172–177). The Achaeans are distinct from other population groups. Odysseus makes Achaean sound like a term that applies to all Greeks. On the other hand, the reference may refer to the time when members of an association of some Greeks—the Achaeans—made itself into a political presence on Crete. This would have been followed by the Trojan expedition of the Achaeans. My view is that Achaeans are at this time only a subset of Greeks.

[31] Sources: Holland 1993; Nagy 1994; Kanavou 2015: 29–36.

dishonored Greeks who vowed to invade Troy and punish the Trojans for their betrayal of trust. I consider it possible that the avenging Greeks called their association "Achaeans." I consider it possible that "Achaeans" is Homer's name for the association. I do not know whether the original authority for the designation made a difference to either Greeks or Hittites in later times. With the passage of time, a fictional term can become a historical term.[32] I will return to this interpretation in Chapter 14.

I do not have the impression from Homer that Achaeans from Greece were joined in the siege of Troy by a significant body of Anatolian Greeks.[33] The besieging forces are often referred to as Danaans who may find an echo in the (later) Anatolian Danuniyim (López-Ruiz 2009: 497–498).[34] It is certainly clear that the supreme leader was Agamemnon of Mycenae. Without Homer, the Hittite texts tell us little or nothing about Greece. The Hittite texts mainly reveal that after the Trojan War numbers of Achaeans remained in Anatolia or migrated there from Greece (see e.g. López-Ruiz 2009: esp. 494–496).

We might apply to the Homeric Epics a version of the Hollywood film disclaimer: "This is a work of fiction based on real events." Obviously, some changes must have been introduced in the epics over the course of time both inadvertently and by choice. However, the essential theme in Homer is always the Trojan War. Without this theme, the original Bronze Age epic crumbles into nothingness. Further, it would be perverse to doubt the historical reality of Homer's Achaeans and of their siege of his Troy. Homer's Achaeans are an association formed from among Greeks originating on the mainland and on Crete with the objective of breaking the hold of the Trojans over the entrance to the Black Sea. I propose that the military victory of this Achaean association is attested on the Greek mainland in at least two visible ways. First, there is the

---

[32]   Similarly, it probably made no difference to Mycenaean parents whether Achilles was a real person of Homer's creation.

[33]   Book 6.116–240 of the *Iliad* tells of the declaration of Glaucus, a Lycian fighting on the Trojan side that he descends from Bellerophon of Argos who, it turns out, had been a guest-friend of the house of Diomedes, the Argive warrior. In this way, Homer attests the longstanding relationship between Greece, specifically Argos, and Anatolia. Yakubovich (2008: 173) comments: "In fact, the Lycian ethnicity of the Homeric Lycians has better philological support than the putative Luvian ethnicity of the Homeric Trojans." I consider it possible/probable that ethnic Greeks and ethnic Anatolians fought on both sides in the War.

[34]   In one important speech to rally his troops, Agamemnon refers to them in a single sentence as Argives and Danaans (*Iliad* 8.229–230). The mysterious Homeric *Danaoi* have been connected with the Egyptian geographical term "Tanaja" ("Danaya") which is used in the first half of the second millennium BCE in an inscription at Amenhotep III's mortuary temple to refer to mainland Greece namely parts of the Peloponnese and Kythera (Bachvarova 2016: 317–318 with references). This finding would reinforce the already powerful argument that Homer predates the Mycenaean palaces. However, I do not believe this solves the mystery. I will have some further thoughts in Chapter 14.6.

precipitous increase in wealth manifested in Mycenae's Grave Circle A (taking as the wealth-base the older and more modest Grave Circle B). Second, as Heitz (2008: 21) emphasizes, there is a sharpening of the military factor: "The items [tomb deposits] belonging to the warrior set become more numerous and precious, and further elements were added: the toilet articles were used further (tweezers, combs, razors, mirrors), helmets made of boar tusks were now equipped with ornaments, breast plates occur, and many of the swords and daggers are now decorated not only with precious pommels, but with hilts of precious material and high craftsmanship." Scholars refer to this emergent warlike and wealthy society as "Mycenaean." A third attestation of the Achaean victory is that "Ahhiyawa," a Mycenaean kingdom, emerges as a major power in Anatolia. Thus, the Achaeans and their textile marketing palaces find their place in Bronze Age economic history.

5. Trojan Problems

There remains to be considered the unsettled problem of the language/ethnicity of the Trojans/Wilusans. Yakubovich (2008: 151) notes, "none of the proper names associated with Wilusa has a clear Luvian etymology." In Homer, there is only Priam, a name sometimes associated with Luwian *Pariyamuwas*. Even in this case a Greek reading is preferable as the very similar form *pi-ri-ja-mi-ja*, perhaps to be read **Priamias*, occurs in a Linear B tablet PY An 39 from Pylos (Kanavou 2015: 83). Later Greeks associated the name Priam (also Podarces, see below) with Greek *priasthai* 'buy'.[35] This association is most appealing not least because Homer famously has Priam purchase the body of his son Hector (also a Greek name).[36] Hence, it can be that Homer and the Hittite sources agree that the Greeks were not fighting Luwians.

In Homer, a number of Trojans have Greek names but in the Hittite documents there is only *Alaksandu,* a name associated with the Greek Alexander (*Alexandros*). Perhaps it should be held against the historical value of the *Iliad* that there are too many Greek-named Trojans. Perhaps Homer chose Greek names for some Anatolians to make them, or their behavior, more understandable to his Greek audience. However, the bearing of a double name (*epiklesis* 'name of invocation') is well attested for elites in Bronze Age Anatolia (Bachvarova 2016: 151–152). For good reason: the bearing of a name specific to an ethnic/geographic group served in antiquity as a kind of passport for hospitable treatment in that group. The point is well illustrated in Genesis 32 when Jacob, after a long sojourn with his

---

[35] Sources: Lycophron *Alexandra* 37–39 with Hornblower 2016: 192–193; LSJ s.v.; compare Kanavou 2015: 77–78.

[36] The name "Hektor" appears in a Linear B text from Pylos (En 74) as a slave of the goddess and a landholder (Palaima 2004b: 453). His son is named Astyanax "ruler of the city" (Greek) but Hector calls him "Skamandrios" (Anatolian? Pre-Greek?).

kinsman Laban in Haran in Aram, arrived to meet his brother Esau in Seir in Edom bringing along his "acquired cattle, asses, sheep, and male and female slaves" (v.5), his name is miraculously changed to "Israel" (v.29). The name "Israel" was owned by Seir and its possession certified that "Jacob" should be treated there as a kinsman. Note that Paris/Alexander and Hector had commercial connections with Greece (Silver 2018: 169; on *nom de commerce* 'commercial names' see Watkins 1986: 49). I would suggest that Hector and other Greek named Trojans, including Priam's father Laomedon (*Iliad* 15.4, 19–21, 525–543) and the Dardanian Antēnōr,[37] were understood as having prior dealings with Greeks but also bore Anatolian names that Homer does not choose to mention (Watkins 1986: 51; 1998: 206–211).[38]

Individuals bearing dual ethnic names are characteristic of a polyethnic society, but this does not necessarily of even commonly signify they have a (biologically) mixed ethnic heritage. An ethnic group may gift or sell one of its stock of names to an ethnic stranger. I suspect that the names "Jacob" and "Israel" belonged to different ethnic groups. For a discussion of the formation of "name-capital" and the market in names, see Silver 1995a: 42–45.

Also, as Yakubovich (2008: 160 n. 23) admits: "An additional ethnic group that represents a possible candidate for the Bronze Age population of Wilusa is the Tyrrhenians (Tyrsenoi). Herodotus (1:94) narrates a story of the famine-driven resettlement of Tyrrhenians from northwestern Anatolia to Italy. This story finds confirmation in the similarity of the Etruscan language and the language of an inscription found on Lemnos in 1884. Strabo (5.2.4) and Thucydides (4.109) both place Tyrsenoi in Lemnos. Beekes [2003], author of the latest comprehensive attempt to defend the Anatolian homeland of Tyrrhenians/Etruscans, suggests that their migration may be relevant to the origin of the legend about the flight of a group of Trojans to Italy, which is best known from Virgil's *Aeneid*. Nevertheless, the author wisely abstains from advocating a direct equation between the Trojans and the Tyrrhenians, which would have no linguistic support whatsoever."[39] Obviously, the fact that Aeneas (*Aineias*), a "Dardanian" fighting for Troy along with "Antēnōr's two sons, Archelochus and Acamas" (*Iliad* 2.819–820) has a name of unknown origin

---

[37] Antēnōr appears to be a good Greek compound name (Kanavou 2015: 143).

[38] For prior dealings, see the discussion in Chap. 14.5 of the transfer of the Helen enterprise. Idomeneus, the leader of the Cretan Achaeans, kills three warriors whose names indicate Cretan connections: "These warriors are Phaistos (*Il.* 5.43–44) and Asios Hyrtakides (*Il.* 13.383–93)—the names and patronymics of whom respectively recall the names of two Cretan cities (Phaistos and Hyrtakina)—and also Othryoneus (*Il.* 13.363–372), whose name is etymologically related to the word 'mountain' in the Cretan dialect (Hesychius, s.v. Ὄθρυν)" (Kotsonas 2018b: 22–23). In Lycophron (*Alexandra* 337–339), Priam has the Greek name Podarkes 'Swift-Foot' (Kanavou 2015: 77–78).

[39] Kloekhorst (2012: 50) suggests that the root of Troy in Hittite, *trū-*, and in Greek, *trō*, appears to be the same as the root in the name of the Etruscans, *tru-*.

does not mean he is of Tyrrhenian origin. A non-linguist may be pardoned for wondering about the ethnic status of the non-Luwian proper names associated with Wilusa in the Hittite texts. Did any have a clear etymology? Bachvarova (2016: 362 with n. 59) responds: "However, besides Alaksandu, who has a Greek name, we know the names of only two other second millennium Wilusan rulers, Kukkunni and Walmu, the latter having a name possibly related to Hitt. *Walwa-* "lion," and the former having a shape like other Anatolian names. Neither has a secure etymology."

Finally, Yakubovich may have underestimated the linguistic interaction between Greek and Luwian. Dale (2015: 432) argues:

> The phonology, semantics, and geographical distribution of Greek ethnics in *-ēnos* all point to the seemingly inescapable conclusion that Greek speakers appropriated this item of derivational morphology from the inhabitants of the very lands where the forms are attested. That the geographical distribution of ethnics in *-enos* should be in essence coterminous with the areas of Asia Minor and Syria already identified as Luwian serves to bolster the argument for deriving *-ēnos* from *-wann(i)*, which in turn would corroborate the view ... that western Asia Minor contained a significant Luwian element in its population, and that there was extensive contact between Greek and Luwian speakers from a very early period, and quite possibly before the end of the Bronze Age.

6. Was Hisarlik/Troy Destroyed and Deserted?

As noted above there are strong grounds for identifying Hisarlik with Homer's Troy. Archaeologists have found no specific evidence that (Hisarlik =) Troy VIh (very probably the Homeric Troy) suffered man-made destruction (Korfmann 1986a: 95; Mac Sweeney 2019: 51). Neither is there evidence to speak of a military destruction of Troy VII (Korfmann 1986a: 95–60).[40]

---

[40] Compare Kirk (1990: 40) who "finds it extremely improbable that either what remained of Troy's perhaps legendary treasure, or its strategic and economic potential once captured, would have made the expedition economically worthwhile. [I]f Troy-Hisarlik did escape major damage and social collapse from armed attack towards the end of the Bronze Age, then it would have been the *only* great fortified centre in the eastern Mediterranean to have done so." Kirk underestimates the economic value of Troy's position and he is mistaken in putting its defeat near the end of the Bronze Age. The important point is that Troy was too valuable to destroy, and the available facts tell that it was not destroyed.

In this connection, note how quickly another valuable property, Akrotiri on Thera, was rebuilt after a powerful earthquake. Indeed, it appears that Troy VI was destroyed or severely damaged by an earthquake and then followed by Troy VII. Troy was indeed rebuilt and redesigned and indications are that the citadel behind its fortification walls hosted a larger population than before the earthquake (Rose 2013: 30; Mac Sweeney 2018: 56).

The evidence does not indicate that Troy (= Hisarlik) was deserted. Production of pottery continued in LH III, well after the dating of the defeat of Troy and archaeology also reveals continuity in occupation of the city into the Iron Age (Bachvarova 2016: 362–364). Consistently with the archaeology, Strabo (13.1.40) reports: "The present Ilians further tell us that the city was, in fact, not completely wiped out at its capture by the Achaeans and that it was never even deserted" (tr. Jones *LCL*).

Of first importance is that, as Hiller (1991: 207 with n. 3) points out, "[A] considerable quantity of Mycenaean pottery was found in the ruins of Troy VI, and Mycenaean vases were still imitated by potteries of Troy VII." Korfmann (1986a: 27) has written: "If it were not for the name Troy and the epic *Iliad*, Hisarlik would doubtless have been pronounced a Mycenaean trading colony, on the basis of the substantial amount of Mycenaean pottery recovered there." There are also a number of double-headed axes associated with the Minoan/Mycenaean cult of Potnia. There will be more to say about the double-headed axes below.

There are additional details indicating that Troy (= Hisarlik) was taken over by the Achaeans, not destroyed. Guzowska and Becks (2005: 279) observe that at the beginning of Troy VI there are multiple changes in architecture and pottery, but they call attention to a "unique phenomenon" not shared with other sites in Anatolia. The reference is to new loom-weights that replaced those previously used at Troy: some [new] weights are characterized by a shallow groove marking on the edge rather than directly above the perforation. "This feature of the implements is alien to Anatolia and characteristic of the Aegean cultural mileau" (Guzowska and Becks 2005: 279). Later on, it appears that weights without grooves were reintroduced and used together with grooved weights possibly for distinct types of product. There is much that is mysterious to me here, but it is possible to wonder whether at the beginning of the Troy VI period the Trojan weavers were replaced by newcomers from the west Aegean world and from elsewhere in Anatolia.

Simple political economy and archaeology join forces to tell us that Troy was not destroyed and that it fell under the control or influence of the Achaeans. A final signal of this truth is that, as noted in Chap. 10.7, a Linear B tablet (PY Ep 705) dating to long after the presumed destruction of Troy refers to the *to-ro-ja*

'Trojan or Tlojan[41] woman' and the woman is a slave of a goddess who is renting land in Pylos (Ergin 2007: 279–280). Homeric evidence bearing on the fate of Troy is analyzed in Chaps. 12.5 and 14.7.

To conclude, the Hittite references to the troublesome Ahhiyawans and their lack of surprise at their presence in Anatolia testify to the historicity of the Trojan War and the victory therein of Homer's Achaeans. Further, the victory of the Achaeans and the consequent opening of the Black Sea trade in luxury textiles helps to explain the rise of the Mycenaean palaces. How the victory was accomplished (including its finance) are discussed in Chapter 14.

---

[41]   *Tlōs* possibly being a later Anatolian toponym. For discussion of the "Trojan" question, see Palaima (2007b: 202–203).

13

Interest of the Ahhiyawans/Mycenaeans in Trade

1. The Hittite Embargo

THERE is indeed evidence from the thirteenth century BCE of a Hittite embargo against the Ahhiyawans (Mycenaeans) intended to prevent their ships/cargo from participating in trade with Assyria (AhT 2 = CTH 105; tr. Beckman 2011; Bryce 2011: 68).

The Hittite ruler in calling for a trade embargo against his enemy Assyria instructs his vassal on the coast to prevent *merchants* from other states from traveling inland to the Assyrians. The letter (as restored) specifically instructs the vassal not to permit "any *ship* [of Ahh]iyawa to go to him" (tr. Beckman 2011; Bryce 2011: 68 with n. 94). Presumably, the ships would have unloaded cargoes of expensive textiles on the coast for transshipment to the Assyrians in the interior. Shipment by land would not have prohibitively raised the cost at the destination.[1]

However, as noted by Kolb (2004: 589), "the possible Ahhijawa *passus* is separated from this reference [to merchants] by a *passus* in which the Hittite king calls upon the king of Amurru to get ready for war against the Assyrians. This is followed by the Ahhijawa *passus* in which merchants and trade do not appear." Thus, an alternative interpretation of the letter is that the trade embargo applied to merchants of all states with the exception of Ahhiyawan/ Mycenaean merchants. However, there was no real exception because there were no Ahhiyawan/Mycenaean merchants selling goods to Assyrians. There

---

[1] Larsen (1977: 136) estimated that in the earlier second millennium BCE when fine woolen textiles were regularly shipped by donkey caravan some 700 miles from Assur in Assyria to Kanesh (later Hittite Nesa) in Anatolia, this raised the cost of the textiles by no more than 25 percent. Indeed, Silver (1995a: 85) who used the entire difference between average sale and purchase prices to estimate transport cost found that the shipment of tin from Assur to Kanesh raised its cost by no more than 93 percent. In general, there is a tendency to underestimate the potentialities of overland trade in the ancient world (see Silver 1995a: Chap. 4.A).

were only Ahhiyawan/Mycenaean individuals who sought to sell themselves to the Assyrians as mercenaries. Presumably, the practice was for Mycenaean (passenger?) ships to sail away leaving the mercenaries behind to make their way to the interior.

Kolb's interpretation makes itself *possible* by subtracting Ahhiyawan merchants from the unqualified meaning of the first sentence. It seeks *credibility* by accepting without discussion or even acknowledgment the swashbuckling image of the Mycenaeans as swordsmen who sought wealth by fighting but never by trading.[2] Even Assyrian/Mycenaean "gift-trade" seems to be excluded. This is an anachronistic perspective. During the Bronze Age the trader was able to defend himself from thieves and other aggressors; the soldier or diplomat had a keen idea for opportunities to acquire wealth.[3] All had to be ready to use force.

My understanding is that the Hittite king wrote this letter to prevent trade with the Assyrians. Thus, in his first sentence he called for an embargo against merchants trading with the Assyrians. The prohibition already included merchants of Ahhiyawa. Then he alluded to literal combat with the Assyrians and then, one sentence later, he returned to the theme of trade embargo but emphasizing the mandated compliance of Ahhiyawans whom, as other letters make clear, Hittite rulers had much difficulty controlling.

My interpretation, like Kolb's, is *possible* but it gains in *credibility* by means of an appeal to the Linear B tablets and other Hittite letters. Why did the Mycenaean palaces in fact put so much effort into making textiles if they were interested in war but not trade? Chapter 11.5 presents strong iconographic

---

[2]   But the Hittite ruler does *not* say "Do not permit any *man* of the Ahhiyawans to go to him"; the Hittite ruler says "Do not let any *ship* to go to him." "Ships" are associated mainly with trade and cargoes, not with mercenary warriors. Kramer-Hajos (2016: 146), citing Cline's (1994: 277) catalogue, notes that foreign objects found at Pylos are few, only five as compared to Mycenae (85), Tiryns (35), and Thebes (41), and she goes on to suggest that the more frequent ship iconography at Pylos indicates that Pylos is less motivated by foreign trade than the other palatial centers. This is counterintuitive, however. If anything, more frequent ship iconography indicates a greater, not a lesser, interest in trade and while Pylos is lacking in exotic foreign objects, as seen earlier, they are not laggards in references to ships and ship-building (see Chap. 17) and to gold and references to gold.

[3]   The dual role is not exceptional and it may well be illustrated in a burial in Lefkandi (Euboea), albeit in the ninth century BCE, in which the deceased is accompanied by sword, spearhead, arrowheads and other objects but also with weights and a cylinder seal (Pooham and Lemos 1995). Palaima (1999a: 374) notes that the Linear B texts from Knossos provide the personal names of 26 "collectors" and of these we find four "named respectively 'man-slayer', 'far-slayer', 'army-slayer' and 'poison-slayer' must say something significant about the sphere of activity through which ultimately they or their families attained their economic prominence." Perhaps, but I find it more likely that the four were named by their wealthy families who, indeed, were indeed concerned with warrior prowess.

evidence that Syrian merchants were visiting Mycenaean palaces at Knossos and Pylos. If the Ahhiyawans did not practice trade but only war we need to understand why a Hittite letter, discussed in the next Section, mentions the [Ah]hiyawan as tarrying in Lukka seeking metal ingots? Why did they "tarry, wait" instead of seizing ingots by force if not in Lukka then somewhere else?

More directly, did the Assyrians have a specific trade-good that the Ahhiyawans/Mycenaeans valued enough to annoy the Hittite ruler? The answer, I think, is yes and the product is the cylinder seal especially seals made of the regularly imported very rare mineral called lapis lazuli (Younger 1979). My evidence is primarily the finding at Thebes of a workshop (at Oedipus St. 14) in proximity to a Palace "Treasure Room" holding a hoard of more than 42 seals, mostly Babylonian, of which 34 were of lapis lazuli (Porada 1981/1982; Kopanias 2008: 55, 2012). The seals were probably destined to be reworked for use by Theban officials or recycled into jewelry (Cline 1994: 25–26; Kopanias 2008: 56). In return for the elegant seals the Thebans and, more generally, Mycenaeans could have offered textiles or gold in which, as Porada (1981/1982: 68–69) and this study have noticed, they were rich. I am proposing that the Ahhiyawan vessels referenced in the Hittite letter carried textiles and/or gold earned from the Black Sea trade which they intended to exchange for seals that expert Assyrian craftsmen had fashioned from lapis lazuli imported from Afghanistan.[4]

2. Copper Trade

There is, as just noted, a Hittite letter that reinforces the view that the Ahhiyawans/Mycenaeans were motivated to trade. In AhT 27A (§7) the Hittite ruler reports that he has heard that the [Ah]hiywans are lingering in the Lukka lands (southwestern Anatolia) to obtain [copper] ingots. He goes on to direct ships to carry ingots to them (cf. AhT 27B (§6)). There is no indication that the Ahhiyawans are motivated to use force to obtain the copper they want. They are waiting like ordinary buyers for a seller or, possibly, for a lower market price. There is a market interface and I would propose that the Ahhiyawans were offering textiles or gold previously acquired by the sale of textiles. Ingots of copper (348 weighing ten tons) and tin (120 weighing one ton) were main items in the cargo of the Ulu Burun ship that was wrecked off the southern coast of Turkey in the later fourteenth century. The ship also carried a gold chalice, a gold ring ingot, scrap gold, cut gold jewelry, and pieces of gold ingots for use in

---

[4]   It is not necessary for the purposes of this argument to follow Porada (1981/1982) in identifying Ahhiyawa specifically with Thebes and assuming that the seals had been sent to Thebes by
Tukulti-Ninurta I as a gift/invitation to trade. Note that the Ulu Burun merchant ship carried a
number of seals, about which Collon (2005: 47).

making payments (Pulak 2010). I would add that the Hittite king himself sounds very much like someone in close touch with traders.

3. Lazpa and Trade in Purple Garments

In another Hittite text (KUB 19.5 + KBo 19.79 = AhT 7 = CTH 182) dating to the early 13th century BCE a vassal ruler, Manapa-Tarhunta, complains to the Hittite king that Piyamaradu (and the new vassal Atpa) attacked *Lazpa* leading to the defection of three groups of craftsmen (*šaripitu*), one group belonging (literally, I believe) to Manapa-Tarhunta, a second group belonging to the Hittite king, and a third belonging to the Storm God.

I. Singer (2008: 22), citing Lackenbacher (2002: 95–96 with n. 276), has pointed out that the *šaripitu* are specifically "*purple dyers.*" This interpretation is supported by Teffeteller (2013: 569–570) and by Hoffner (2009). I am not aware of any scholarly objections.

I have chosen to rely on Hoffner's translation of the Hittite vassal's complaint because it responds more openly to I. Singer's brilliant analysis of the text. However, Beckman's translation is cited for additional clarification.

> When Piyamaradu had humiliated me, set up Atpā over? me and attacked (the country of) Lazpa, all of the purple-dyers without exception who were mine joined with him. And all of the purple-dyers of His Majesty without exception joined with him. And x-x-ḫuḫa, the domestic and table man, who had been put in charge? of the purple-dyers, x-x- ḫuḫa made those to meet (with him). However, ...-ḫuḫa (and) the purple-dyers addressed a petition to Atpā in the following words: 'We are purple-dyers [to the Hittite king?] and we came across the sea. Let us present (our) purple-dyed stuffs! [Beckman: *'We are persons subject to tribute, [and] we have come across the sea. We want [to deliver] our tribute.'*] Šiggauna rebelled, but we did nothing whatsoever!' And when they had made their purple-dyed stuffs (the subject of) a petition, Atpā did not carry them off. He would have let them go home, but Piyama-radu dispatched Šiggauna to him and spoke to him in this manner: 'The Storm God presented to you a boon, why should you (now) give them back?' When Atpā in his turn heard the word of Piyama-radu, he did not return them to me. But now, when Kaššū arrived here, Kupanta-LAMMA sent a message to Atpā: 'The purple dyers of His Majesty who are there (with you), let them go home!' And he (Atpā) let the purple-dyers who belong to the gods (i.e., to the temple[s]), and who belong to His Majesty all (of them) without exception go home. And

Kupanta-LAMMA wrote to me as follows: "We did what you said to me, 'Write to Atpā about the purple-dyers!' To Atpā I did write about the purple-dyers!" . . . he shall/did . ... the basket-weavers. To Kupanta-LAMMA . . . my lord . . . I raided again (or: I undertook a counter-raid). (tr. Hoffner 2009: 294–296)

A problem in interpretation arises, highlighted in the translation, because Hittite *arkammaš* (line 15) means both "tribute"/"income" and "purple-dyed stuffs" (I. Singer 2008: 22–23). I. Singer (2008: 29) is of the opinion that *arkammaš* refers to "purple-dyed stuff" and that the mission of the "purple-dyers" was "the dedication of purple-dyed *anathemata* to some important deity of Lazpa." I do not believe that three groups of purple dyers would have the same objective. Instead, I suggest that the purple dyers were sent to Lazpa to produce and/or market purple-dyed textiles. Now they wished to return home and to share the proceeds from their work with their principals.

It is unlikely that if the purple dyers were free men that a point would be made of their defecting. Free persons do not defect—they change employers. They were slaves permitted to live away from their owners and share earnings with them (Silver 2014, 2015a). Forcibly enslaved persons would not be granted this kind of life-style freedom (Silver 2016b). Thus, they were likely autonomous contractual slaves.

The question: "Where is Lazpa?" is dealt with in the next Section together with the fate of the purple-dyers. *However, the main point is that the importance placed by Hittite elites on purple dyers and their products.* Given the participation of a Hittite ruler and his vassal it is reasonable to assume that some, perhaps most, of the garments were sold to Anatolians. This finding is supportive of the thrust of the present study.

4. Lazpa: Lesbos or Anatolia?

Mason (2008) notes that most scholars have identified Lazpa with Lesbos which was under Hittite control at the time the text (KUB 19.5 + KBo 19.79 = AhT 7 = CTH 182) was written. There are problems with this identification. Mason (2008: 57) points out: "Classicists have described 'Lazpa' as an Anatolian spelling of Greek Lesbos ... but the Anatolian form is attested four centuries before the Greek," and he adds that it "conforms to the familiar correspondence of second millennium Luwian /a/ to first millennium Greek /e/, found, for example in *Apasa/Ephesos* and *Parha/Perge*." On the other hand, there are reasons to believe that Lazpa is a place somewhere in Anatolia.

Let us next examine these problems in more detail. First, there is Lesbos a (later) Greek translation of Lazpa. Mason (2008: 57–58) points out: "[W]ords ending in βα, βη, and βος, including place-names, are not very common in Greek; besides the Boeotian *Thebai* and *Thisbe* we should note, significantly, *Arisba/Arisbe*, the name of cities in Lesbos and the Troad (Hdt. 1.151; Homer, *Il.* 2.836)." A minimum question is why when the Greeks translated Lazpa into Lesbos they did not do the same for Arisbe. It very much sounds to me as if Arisbe is an Anatolian foundation in Greek Lesbos. Further, "Lesbos" is in fact mentioned by Homer in *Iliad* 9.1129 and 24.544 and Homer predates the Hittite texts mentioning Lazpa.[5]

Noting that the Hittite text (quoted in the previous Section) has purple-dyers travelling over the sea to Lazpa, Mason (2008: 57) concludes that Lazpa is an island, like Lesbos. This conclusion does not follow logically as the text does not tell from which shore the dyers travelled to Lazpa and neither does it reveal the ethnicity of the dyers.

In fact, it is reasonable to assume that purple-dyers were active in Lesbos long before the Hittite texts. Homer notes the presence of skilled weavers there in a passage where Agamemnon tries to win over Achilles:

> Not without booty were a man, nor unpossessed of precious gold, whoso had wealth as great as the prizes my single-hooved steeds have won me. And I will give seven women skilled in goodly handiwork, women of Lesbos, whom on the day when himself took well-built Lesbos I chose me from out the spoil, and that in beauty surpass all women folk. These will I give him, and amid them shall be she that then I took away, the daughter of Briseus; and I will furthermore swear a great oath that never went I up into her bed neither had dalliance with her as is the appointed way of mankind, even of men and women.

Iliad 9.125–134; tr. Murray *LCL*[6]

Were the sea-traveling purple-dyers of the Hittite text perhaps reinforcements needed for a newly growing textile industry in Lesbos? Or, instead, did the

---

[5] The *Iliad* has the Trojans controlling Lesbos and much more. Thus, in the words of Achilles: "And of thee [Priam], old sire, we hear that of old thou wast blest; how of all that toward the sea Lesbos, the seat of Macar, encloseth, and Phrygia in the upland, and the boundless Hellespont, over all these folk, men say, thou, old sire, wast preeminent by reason of thy wealth and thy sons. Howbeit from the time when the heavenly gods brought upon thee this bane, ever around thy city are battles and slayings of men" (*Iliad* 24.543–545; tr. Murray *LCL*).

[6] Achilles raided Lesbos in *Iliad* 9.129 and 664 and in *Iliad* 24.544–545 he refers to Lesbos as the "seat of Makar." Thus, the Achaeans took control of Lesbos from the Trojans and after defeating Troy some stopped in Lesbos (*Iliad* 3.169). Later on, they may have lost control to the Hittites.

purple dyers travel overseas *from* places stocked with purple-dyers such as the islands of Lesbos, Lemnos, Crete, and the Greek mainland *to* Anatolia?

Indeed, it seems possible to be more specific about an Anatolian destination for the sea-traveling specialists. Mason (2008: 57) comments: "*Lazpa* incorporates the highly productive Anatolian place-name suffix –*pa/ba*, and finds an exact phonetic match in *Gazpa*, a variant spelling of Kazapa, a city on the northern border with Kaska." Using *purpurissum* or fresh dye preserved with honey it is possible for dyers to serve garment producers far from the sea deep inside Anatolia. Or possibly they marketed purple dyed garments there. What is clear is that placing Lazpa near Kaska in the northeast brings us closer to the shores of the Black Sea.[7]

5. Conclusions

Homeric epic originated before the Mycenaean palaces and Linear B. West's linguistic arguments on this score are rigorous and have not been refuted. The main objection, it seems to me, is that West's "news" does not "fit" comfortably into current discussions of oral transmission. However, it may be stipulated that the epic we possess is not entirely the Bronze Age version—it has undergone revision. However, the Bronze Age original was not abstract; it had a narrative content, which was preserved: the Trojan War. The Trojan War is so central that without it there is no epic at all. Later poets or bards may inadvertently or deliberately have changed some of the details in the epic they received from their predecessors but they did not invent and insert the story of the Trojan War. The Trojan War is the Bronze Age content. This does not yet mean that there was *really* a Trojan War but it does mean that the received story of the War is largely the version recited/written in the Bronze Age.

I find myself in rare agreement with Kirk's (1990: 44) comments on historical distortion in oral epics:

> The degree of error [in oral traditions] varies enormously according to subject matter, local conditions and, especially, the tightness in expressive or retentive terms, of the particular narrative tradition. Neither of these epics [*Chanson de Roland* and *Nibelungenlied*] had anything like the disciplined form of the Homeric poetry, and therefore the potential for relatively accurate preservation of details over several generations.[8]

---

[7] Yakar (2008). Herodotus (4.145) says that descendants of the Argo's crew were driven from Lemnos to Lakeidaimon.

[8] Questions raised by generations of scholars about the mode of presentation and the processes of preservation, reception, and revision of the epic are challenging and significant (see e.g.,

This *Part* of the study has strongly reinforced the linguistic and logical arguments for a Bronze Age epic by other kinds of evidence including facts that justify the identification of the Troad's Hisarlik, a citadel and city controlling the entrance to the Black Sea, with Homer's Troy and facts that justify the identification of the Hittite's Ahhiyawa with Homer's Achaeans who besieged Troy and then stayed on.[9] As a result of this examination Homer's Trojan War almost makes good its escape from fiction into history. "Almost" because the motivation for the War offered by Homer, or more accurately the motivation focused on by scholars and others, is not convincing.

In what follows it will be made clear that the motivations for the War offered by Homer are convincing. I develop the position that Homer knew the historical facts of a Trojan War. Second, Homer placed great value on history so that even when fulfilling other poetic/artistic goals he found ways to preserve history for his audience. Sometimes he practiced misdirection or omission but he did not subvert the facts. However, in the interest of his art, Homer sometimes chose to place crucial historical facts in contexts that might easily be overlooked by audiences, including contemporary ones, seeking entertainment or cultural elevation rather than dismal economics.

In order to recover Homer's hidden history of the Trojan War and its cause Part IV will mine a number of episodes that have for long been considered puzzling or even ignored by scholars. It will be seen that the story of the Trojan War is not only a very old story but also the story of a real war fought for commercial reasons. Specifically, relying on Homer it will be demonstrated that at its base the Trojan War was a war fought for control over the trade in luxury textiles in the Black Sea region.

Bachvarova 2016: Chapter 15) but they do not need to be answered by the present study.

[9]   Ahhiyawa is the name given by the Hittites to the state founded in the Troad by an association of Greeks that called themselves Achaeans.

PART IV

THE HOMERIC EPICS AND
BRONZE AGE AEGEAN TEXTILE TRADE

14

The Commercial Origin of the Trojan War

1. Setting Homer in the Prepalatial Mycenaean Period

M. L WEST (1988: 159–160) observed: "However, it seems strange that in a poetic tradition inherited from early Mycenaean times the sack of Troy should play such a prominent part, while the catastrophic destructions of so many major Greek palaces in the thirteenth and twelfth centuries, Thebes, Mycenae, Tiryns, Pylos, Iolkos, have scarcely left an echo." This is a good observation but also a puzzling one. Puzzling because the linguistic evidence West has himself provided indicates Homer's poetry is not an early Mycenaean "tradition" but rather an early Mycenaean epic. That is, it is a work written before the Linear B tablets and the destruction of the palaces. The defeat of Troy is not an insertion in the later Mycenaean period or even later but is a central feature of the earlier Mycenaean period.[1] *The defeat unleashed the Mycenaean economy and so provided impetus for the development of the palaces.*

In attempting to place Homer in a historical context, Crielaard (2000: 53) reviews some of salient economic facts:

> The fifty female slaves who are occupied with the production of textiles in Odysseus' palace (*Od.* XXII 421–3) are in sharp contrast to the more than one thousand female labourers who, according to the tablets, are employed by the palace of Pylos. Odysseus—who is reputed exceptionally rich—owns several flocks of pigs, goats, sheep and cattle; together these numbered in hundreds or thousands of animals. Despite the fact that epic poetry tends to exaggerate the scale of things, Odysseus' flocks are still considerably smaller than the flock of 100,000 sheep the palace of Knossos had at its disposal. All this makes it clear the poet had

---

[1] Kirk (1990: 39) maintains that the "Catalogue of Trojan Allies" (*Iliad* Book 2) is suppressing much of the central Anatolian coast: "[E]ven Miletus is described as Carian, despite its long Mycenaean history, to avoid the appearance of anachronism." Suppressed by whom and for what reason?

no clue of the socio-economic conditions prevalent in the Mycenaean era.

Hence, it *appears* that some palaces in some regions were much larger in the time of the Mycenaean palaces. To begin with, however, Crielaard had no strong reason for placing the poet in the "Late Bronze Age." Certainly, questions may be raised about whether Odysseus' palace might be *too large* for this period! Homer does not, and should not, know the Mycenaean palaces but he does know that the Achaeans won the Trojan War, a victory that, as just noted, set the stage for the much larger enterprises of later times.

2. Gods Take Sides in the Trojan War

The god familiar in later times mentioned in Linear B tablets include Zeus, Hera,[2] Artemis, Poseidon, Dionysus, Hermes, Arēs, Hephaestus (once indirectly), Athena (once with some doubt as already noted), and possibly Demeter. Aphrodite and Apollo (a possible reading on one tablet) are not found in palatial tablets (Hiller 2008: II 183–185).

In Homer's Trojan War, Aphrodite and Apollo are supporters of Troy, while Hera supports the Greeks. Athena, despite her temple in Troy, strongly supports the Achaeans, as in *Iliad* 4.339. Why are gods portrayed as caring enough about the War to take sides? An obvious answer is that they—that is, their cults—had a material interest in the War.

Hera, the strongest advocate of the Greek cause (see e.g. *Iliad* 1.518–521), at the very least had, as will be suggested below, a most powerful *reputational motive* for her advocacy. It was she who summoned the various Greek groups to participate in the crusade against Troy (*Iliad* 4.26–28) and later, as will be seen, she rallied the Achaean defense when the Trojans had breached the Achaean Wall.

Poseidon had a material interest in the conduct of the Trojan War. First, he had built (with Apollo) the Trojan Wall and the War was depriving him of his expected returns/honors from ownership. Poseidon also had links with the Achaean textile trade as is clearly demonstrated by his dispatch of Odysseus on missions involving sheep (Chap. 15.4; cf. Chap. 6.3). Most important is Poseidon's connection with Calchas, the seer of the Achaeans. "Calchas son of Thestor, far the best of bird-diviners, who knew the things that were, and that were to be, and that had been before, and *who had guided the ships of the Achaeans to Ilios* by

---

[2]   Hera *e-ra* as deity is attested only on the Greek mainland (Pylos Tn 316 v.8 and Thebes TH Of 28.2). There is no reference in the Linear B texts to a temple of Hera although *e-ra* is included in personal names and often in place names at Knossos.

his own prophetic powers which Phoebus Apollo had bestowed upon him" (*Iliad* 1.68–72; tr Murray *LCL*). Calchas, who guided the Achaean ships to Troy is said to have an original connection with Apollo. Currently—that is, during the War—he is an instrument of Poseidon. In *Iliad* 13.39–45 Poseidon acts through Calchas to rally the Achaeans—that is, Calchas is the *eidōlon* 'image' = 'agent' of Poseidon.

There are strong reasons to understand the name "Kalkhas" as being related to the word *kalkhē* (Chantraine 1968–1980 s.v.; Beekes s.v.; LSJ s.v.). It is a word of unknown origin with the meaning "murex, purple flower" (cf. *kalkhaino* whose meanings include "make purple"; Chap. 7.3). In Calchas we find Homer's first revelation of the commercial foundation of the Achaean expedition to Troy: Calchas is the authority who knows where the Achaeans should take their "purple flowers/purpled textiles." The name chosen for the seer is not mere coincidence and the message it conveys is amplified in the episode of "Agamemnon's Purple Portent of War" (§4 below).

Perhaps, Aphrodite and Apollo supported the Trojans because their main cultic bases are in Anatolia and the Near East. More specifically, these gods sought to protect their investments in the Trojan side. In Proclus' "Summary of the *Cypria*"[3] Aphrodite is clearly a sponsor of the Trojan enterprise: Aphrodite advises the building of ships to take Paris' mission to Sparta and she calls on her "son" the Trojan Aeneas to accompany Paris.

With respect to the materialistic depth of Apollo's Trojan connections much depends on whether the god's epithet *lukēgenēs* (*Iliad* 4.109, 119) means "wolf-born"/"wolf-created"[4] or, the newer interpretation, "Lycia-born" (Beekes s.v.). In any event, it is clear that Apollo was drawing significant wealth from the Trojan Wall he had constructed together with Poseidon. The Achaean attackers by disrupting normal commercial life were threatening the wealth of Apollo's cult. This review may seem cursory, but I have spread the net and found little that might possibly explain why Apollo took the Trojan side in the War.

As previously noted, Aphrodite is unmentioned in the Linear B tablets but, consistently, Homer also does not assign her a cult place in either mainland Greece or Crete. On the other hand, Homer places an Apollo cult in mainland Greece: in *Odyssey* 8.80f. Agamemnon consults the oracle of Apollo at Pytho (Delphi). Therefore, it is disturbing that the god is not mentioned in the Linear B texts.

---

[3] The *Cypria* is one of six poems forming the "Trojan Cycle"; the title means "The Epic of Cyprus" (or possibly the epic of Aphrodite = "the *Cyprian*") and has been dated (the writing-down, at least) by scholars to the seventh or sixth century BCE.

[4] For the commercial role of "wolves," see esp. Chap. 11.2 and Chap.15.1.

On the other hand, *Iliad* 1.33 mentions the "Sminthean god" referring to Apollo (the Olympian)[5] and the name *si-mi-te-u* "Smintheus" is mentioned in Linear B texts from Knossos (KN Am 827, KN As 1516; see Palaima 2004b: 453). In addition, a text from Knossos mentions *pa-ja-wo-ne* "Paiawonei" (dative) (Beekes s.v. *paian*) in a list of gods. Paiawon may be an alternative name for Apollo or a distinct god as Homer's Paieon seems to be in *Iliad* 5.401 and 5.900 and in *Odyssey* 4.231–232 (cf. Huxley 1975: 121–122). There is some reason to conclude that Homer uses two names for the same god. Thus, In *Iliad* 1.472–473, it is *Apollo*, not Paieon, who is associated with the Greek *paean-song*[6] and, again, in *Odyssey* 8.80 Apollo is associated with Delphi's *theoxenia* festival (see Chap. 11.5), a festival finding a reflection in Linear B, not "Paieon." So conceivably Homer's references to Apollo are not anachronistic but, instead, Knossos' "Paiawonei" conceals Apollo. Otherwise, I cannot offer a specific explanation of the absence of Apollo in Linear B.[7] It is important to keep in mind that the Linear B records deal not with everything in the society but with matters of concern to the palace. The cult of Apollo at Pytho may have been a "private" cult operating outside the purview of any one palace but offering "prophecies" including geographic guidance to all.[8]

There is another path of approach to the possible presence of Apollo in palatial Mycenaean society. First, as developed further below, a Hittite Treaty (AhT 6 + CTH 183) of the mid-thirteenth century identifies the ruler of Wilusa/Troy to be Alaksandu. How did an Anatolian ruler acquire a name so closely identified with the Greek *Alexandros*? As is well known, Alexander, is also the alternate name of the Trojan Paris, a non-Greek name (e.g. *Iliad* 24.25–30) who, in pre-palatial times, voyaged to Greece where he negotiated for possession of Helen. It is reasonable that the Greeks gave to Paris the "international name" Alexander as a gesture of

---

[5] The Sminthean Apollo unleashed a plague, probably bubonic plague, on the Achaeans encamped before Troy. The plague was inflicted at the behest of the priest Chryses who served Apollo in the Troad.

[6] Beekes (s.v. *paian*) says, "In origin, the word may well be Pre-Greek" (cf. Huxley 1975).

[7] Rachele Pierini has called my attention to the term *po-to-a2-ja-de* in Thebes tablets (Av 104) and noted that in the *editio princeps* of the Thebes tablets it is explained as an allative "to the festivals on the Ptoion," a mount hosting a shrine to Apollo in later times. Thus, there is another possible clue to the presence of Apollo in the Linear B world. All the same, I do not think that Apollo is absent from Bronze Age iconography. As discussed earlier, I believe that in the "Pyxis from Aptera" the lyre-playing (better lyre-holding) figure in the shrine who is associated with flying birds and guides ships of the Labyrinth on their journey is Apollo. Further, the lyre-player (again better lyre-holder) depicted with a flying bird in Pylos' "Bard at the Banquet" fresco and who appears to sponsor a celebration for foreign traders/priests perhaps represents Apollo.

[8] I am reminded that Dionysus was found only by good luck when KN Gg 5 was reexamined. For other evidence of Euripides (Alexander Fr. 42d) suggests Paris was given the second (Greek) name because he had a reputation as a sheepman: "he drove off brigands and protected the flocks" (tr. Collard and Cropp LCL). gods with sanctuaries outside palatial centers, see Palaima (2009: 527).

trust and welcome.[9] Watkins (1998: 207–208) goes further and suggests that in this process Alexander adopted/was adopted by the Greek god Apollo whom he returned to Troy/Wilusa under the name ᴰᴼᴺᴳᴵᴿ]Appliunaš whom, he notes, is the first god of Wilusa named in the treaty with the Hittite ruler. This would make Apollo a historical Greek god and, if I understand correctly, Beekes (s.v. *Apollōn*) sees the Hittite name as "Pre-Greek." Apollo's origin remains disputed, and the appearance of a King Alaksandu in the thirteenth century is puzzling.

The Trojans thought they might win the support of Athena with gifts of precious textiles made by Paris' skilled Sidonian women, but they failed (*Iliad* 6.284ff.). Athena's motivations are not made clear by Homer with the exception that the Trojans felt fine textiles could influence her. At Knossos (KN V 52) there is a reference to *a-ta-na-po-ti-ni-ja* which might be read as Potnia Athena or as Potnia At(h)ana, conceivably Athens. My position, as stated earlier, is that Athena the goddess is not only a Potnia but also *the* Potnia of the Labyrinth, a goddess based in Crete. Athena's absence in Linear B would be a major discrepancy given her importance in Epic. She is not absent, however.

The case of Arēs (Linear B *a-re*) is perhaps the most challenging and certainly the most interesting. Arēs supports the Greeks in *Iliad* 4.12 wherein Menelaus is termed *arēiphilos* "dear to Arēs" but he also supports Hector on the Trojan side (*Iliad* 5.830–834, 21.410–414). Menelaus is obviously Greek and linked to "Helen of Troy" but also "Hector" is a Greek name and, as will be seen shortly, he is linked with Greek commerce in later sources. Significantly, on the other hand, Arēs rallies the multilingual Trojan allies in *Iliad* 4. 435-40.

In a Linear B tablet from Knossos (KN Le 641) one *a-re-i-jo* takes delivery of various textiles from six named places. The name *a-re-i-jo* possibly means "*son* of Arēs" (Burke 2010: 91; emphasis added). The textiles delivered from five of the places are probably made there by female workers, but the sixth delivery is from Knossos' *tepe*-making women, a word possibly suggesting alphabetic Greek *tapēs* "tapestry, thick bedding, rug" (Burke 2010: 92). Thus, it very much seems that a "son" = "agent of Arēs" is not a military figure but rather a participant in the Mycenaean textile industry.

Arēs is a misunderstood deity. He is usually termed a "god of war" but Bailey (1959: 93) has pointed out that the Indo-Iranian base *ar-* meaning both "get" and "cause to get" is found in Hittite (*char-* "hold"; *ark-*, *arg-* "share/share out") and is reflected in Greek *arnumai* "win, gain take," in *mistharnos* "wage-earner" and in *aros* "use, profit."[10] Chantraine is difficult (for me) to follow but in meaning

---

[9] Euripides (Alexander Fr. 42d) suggests Paris was given the second (Greek) name because he had a reputation as a sheepman: "he drove off brigands and protected the flocks" (tr. Collard and Cropp LCL).

[10] To the best of my knowledge Bailey is not cited by later writers considering the etymology of *Arēs* (see, for example Willi 2014).

(2) he relates the name Arēs to *aros* "profit," "gain," "help" to *ophelos* "further-ance," "advantage," "help" and to *epikouria* "succoring" (LSJ s.vv.). Thus, in etymological terms, a case can be made that Arēs is a god who seeks material gain and/or inspires/helps others who seek material gain.[11] The others would surely include Arēs' beloved Menelaus and Hector.

The Chorus in Aeschylus' *Agamemnon* (437–455) provides insight into Arēs as a god of war for profit:

> Ares barters the bodies of men for gold; he holds his balance in the contest of the spear; and back from Ilium to their loved ones he sends a heavy dust passed through his burning, a dust cried over with plen-teous tears, in place of men sending well made urns with ashes. So they lament, praising now this one: "How skilled in battle!" now that one: "Fallen nobly in the carnage,"—"for another's wife"—some mutter in secret, and grief charged with resentment spreads stealthily against the sons of Atreus, champions in the strife. But there far from home, around the city's walls, those in their beauty's bloom have graves in Ilium—the enemy's soil has covered its conquerors. (tr. Weir Smyth *LCL*)

Arēs is portrayed, especially in the Greek, as literally a war profiteer seeking and returning *gold-dust* from the Trojan War. Where is the origin of the gold? Agamemnon, it will be seen shortly, is also a seeker of gold.

The etymologically predicted relationship of Arēs to striving for material gain finds support not only in his "son's" receipt of textiles but also in a Linear B tablet from Pylos wherein the epithet *a-re-ja* is borne by Hermes (*e-ma-a$_2$*), who is well known in later times for his connections with commercial life.[12] Thus, Palaima (1999b: 454) comments: "Hermes in Tn 316 v. 7 has the epithet *Areias* which places Hermes here in the sphere of war and martial prowess" (cf. Gulizio 2001: 35–36; but compare Macedo 2016). This is curious combination, but not impossible as even specialized gods may have started their careers as multidimensional figures. On the other hand, it is equally legitimate to place Arēs in the sphere of commerce together with Hermes. In TN 316 Hermes is a business agent of several goddesses and (the ending of) the epithet *a-re-ja* not only links Hermes to "Arēs" but also

---

[11]   Why is Arēs so reviled? Not because he is a god of war.

[12]   In Homer, Hermes is referred to twenty-seven times as *argeiphontēs* which is typically under-stood to mean "Slayer of Argos." The story of the slaying of the giant Argos is not told by Homer making it strange that *argeiphontēs* is used as an alternate name (Chittenden 1948: 25–26). There is, however, an Argos in Homer. Argos is the name of Odysseus' dog, a dog that fends for himself—that is, he is not a table-dog. Silver (1992: 171–172) follows Cunliffe (1963 s.v.) in under-standing *argeiphontēs* as *argos* + *phainō* with the meaning "creator of Argos" meaning something like "creator/sponsor of entrepreneurs."

feminizes him—that is, it feminizes (the activity of) seeking profit (= Arēs).[13] To simply classify Arēs as a "god of war" will not do.[14] Arēs and his followers strive for profit/gain as does his "sister" (*kasignētē*/'colleague' (*hetaira*) the goddess Eris who "throws evil strife" alike among Trojans and Achaeans (*Iliad* 4.440–441). Eris is important because the literature offers clues to the form of the "evil strife" instigated by the goddess. Suffice it to say that Eris' role was to finance strife.[15]

The next Section considers the role of Poseidon in detail.

3. Poseidon and the Achaean Wall

This Section examines an important clue left by Homer that the aims of the Greeks in the Trojan War were much more materialistic than is suggested by the motif of returning a stolen woman named Helen to her legal husband Menelaus.[16]

[13] In Pylos Tn 316 *Hermāhās* (Hermes) "*Areias*" shares three different cult-places with the *female* deities: *Pe-re-*82*, *Iphimedeia*, and *Diwija* and with *di-ri-mi-jo di-wo i-je-we Drimios* a male god. Gulizio (2000: 115) notes the Pylos Of series and other evidence of Hermes' "clustering around other female deities." *One might reason that he acts as a business agent for these deities.* As the male agent of females he would be given female attributes (Silver 2018: 72–74) as is attested in Tn 316 by his feminine epithet *A-re-ja* (Duev 2006: 53–55; cf. 2012: 200 n. 35). Hermes' feminine status is also attested in Knossos D 411 (Killen 2000: 116). Gulizio (2001: 35) reads *A-re-ja* as a masculine long –a- stem. In later times, the epithet is attested for Zeus as *Areios* (masculine) and for Athena, and Aphrodite as *Areia* (feminine) (Burkert 1985: 169). Macedo (2016 with references) seems to focus on the meaning of the epithet although he mentions the gender problem (70 n. 14). With respect to the meaning, if I understand Guilleux (2012: 471) correctly, *Areias* is a compound (**Arēi(-)arŏgos* meaning "He who helps/serves Arēs") but taking into account the feminine ending and the meaning of "Arēs," I would propose "She who serves (female) seekers of profit"/"capital." A Linear B specialist cautions me that assigning gender status is "tricky" and he doubts that a masculine a-stem should be viewed as feminine simply because the bulk of Greek nouns of the a-declension are feminine. On the other hand, the gender status interpretation of names seems valid also in the ancient Near East (see Stokl 2013: 74).

[14] It is well to keep in mind that ancient wars were often (typically?) fought precisely to acquire (or keep) wealth. Note this line of meaning in the *Iliad*. "She found Helen in the hall, where she was weaving a great purple web of double fold, and thereon was broidering many battles [*athlous* 'efforts, labors, contests' LSJ s.v.] of the horse-taming Trojans and the brazen-coated Achaeans, that for her sake they had endured at the hands of Arēs" (*Iliad* 3.125–128; tr. Murray *LCL*).

[15] Proclus' Summary of the Cypria tells that "Eris instigated a quarrel about beauty (*kallous*) between Athena, Hera, and Aphrodite" (tr. M. Davies 2019:51–52). Apollodorus (*Epitome* 3.2) expands on this theme: "Strife threw (*emballō*) an apple (*mēlon*) as [a prize] for beauty (*kallous*) to be contended for by Hera, Athena, and Aphrodite; and Zeus commanded Hermes to lead them to Alexander on Ida in order to be judged by him" (tr. Frazer LCL modified). The "apple" offered/advanced ("thrown") as prize to the contestants is capital—that is, flocks (sheep) and/or gold ingots/apples (perhaps inscribed with a reference to gold). Sources for "(golden) apples" and inscribed "apples": Silver 1992: 62–64, 108; 2018: 122–123; and B. Foster 1899: 50–51.

[16] Fighting the Trojans for Helen would be understandable had Helen been the property of Menelaus. As shown below, Helen was legally married to Paris and this was the result of a negotiation between Achaeans and Trojans. There was no theft that Menelaus had to avenge to recover his *timē*. The case of Odysseus fighting and killing the suitors is different as the wealth they consumed in courting Penelope belonged to Odysseus not to Penelope (see further Silver 2018: Ch. 18).

a. Building a second Troy

In *Iliad* 7.442ff. and 12.1–35 we learn that the Achaeans constructed a very formidable wall somewhere near Troy (hereafter the Achaean Wall). This was an elaborate and strong wall with turrets and wide gates. Indeed, there are indications that this Achaean Wall has seven gates like the great city of Thebes in Boeotia.[17] In this way, Singor (1992: 403) observes: The Achaean camp is made into a city comparable to Thebes and Troy; its gate keepers are called "holy" like those guarding Troy's gates; the new Achaean city rivals Troy not just militarily but in civic terms; and quite possibly the implicit reference to Thebes is meant to recall the tradition of that cities "double foundation."[18] The meaning of all of this is that the Achaean Wall sheltered a second Troy.[19]

Sometimes the descriptions suggest that the Achaean Wall was weak and flimsy. Thus, "At times, a mere human can topple it, as Sarpedon does with such alarming ease when he tears off battlements with his bare hands (12.397–399) or as Hector does when he breaches the wall at 13.679–844. On the other hand, or rather viewed in another light, the wall appears more like a city than a defensive structure, given its size and architectural details—indeed, like a virtual copy of Troy.[20] It is equipped with lofty towers, possibly seven in all" (J. Porter 2011: 3–4).

---

[17]   "A minority opinion [among scholiasts] stated that the gates must have been seven in number and that the epithet of the gates: *pulas eu araruias* (H 339; 439) actually should be read as *pulas (...) epi araruias.* (Schol. A ad H 339 [Erbse]; Eustathius 689 ad *Il.* 438 [Van der Valk]). Yet the anonymous scholars who had deduced a total of seven gates were undoubtedly right—as can be demonstrated easily. In book I of the '*Iliad*' Agamemnon appoints commanders charged with guarding the gates in the Achaean Wall: seven names are mentioned, followed by the words: *epi esan ēgemones phulachōn* (I 80-8). Each of these seven commanded a hundred men. Later, in book K the guards are inspected during the night. They appear to be posted in front of the gates (K 55–59; 97–99; 126–127), in other words in the open space before the wall (K 180–189), and Nestor can speak to them before crossing the moat (K 190–194). The seven guard-posts correspond clearly with seven gates in the wall. Consequently the Achaean Wall should be imagined as a wall with seven gates" (Singor 1992: 402–403; my transliterations).

[18]   The seven-gated Thebes is explicitly mentioned in *Iliad* 4.405–407 and in *Odyssey* 11.462–463. "Homeric epic already includes traces of both foundation stories. We can find confirmation of the importance of Cadmus at Thebes in the *Iliad*'s name for the Thebans (Καδμεῖοι) and in the presence of Ino-Leucothea, the daughter of Cadmus, in the *Odyssey* where the Theban heroine is presented as a goddess, while the Amphion narrative is privileged in both the *Iliad* and *Odyssey* as the foundation story of the city of Thebes, implicitly placing the story of Cadmus later." (Pache 2016: 279).

[19]   As pointed out by Quinlan (2009: 107–108), the Achaean "camp" has been fitted with the main elements of a polis including an agora with temples of twelve gods.

[20]   It has been remarked that, in addition to other seemingly Homeric themes in the West House at Akrotiri on Thera, a fresco on the right half of the north wall depicts a wall with triangular projections that is built along the shoreline of a besieged walled city (Laffineur 2007: 81). We cannot be sure whether the fresco, dated roughly to the mid-second millennium BCE, is meant to depict a standard Bronze Age theme or whether it is meant to depict a scene from a still earlier Homeric epic.

So perhaps there was more than one wall, or perhaps Homer wished to gloss over the reality of the Achaean Wall, or something else entirely.

b. Poseidon's outrage

However, that it was a real wall and formidable is proven not only by the elaborate details of its construction but also even more by the explicit reaction of Poseidon to it. Upon seeing it, Poseidon recalls the wall that he and Apollo previously built for Laomedon, then ruler of Troy and father of Priam the current ruler. The god complains bitterly that the status (honor) of his Trojan Wall is being undermined by the new Achaean Wall being built by the Greek intruders and so it was.

> Thus were they toiling, the long-haired Achaeans; and the gods, as they sat by the side of Zeus, the lord of the lightning, marvelled at the great work of the brazen-coated Achaeans. And among them Poseidon, the Shaker of Earth, was first to speak: "Father Zeus, is there now anyone of mortals on the face of the boundless earth, that will any more declare to the immortals his mind and counsel? Seest thou not that now again the long-haired Achaeans have builded them a wall to defend their ships, and about it have drawn a trench, but gave not glorious hecatombs to the gods? Of a surety shall the fame thereof reach as far as the dawn spreadeth, and men will forget the wall that I and Phoebus Apollo[21] built with toil for the warrior Laomedon." Then greatly troubled, Zeus, the cloud-gatherer, spake to him: "Ah me, thou Shaker of Earth, wide of sway, what a thing thou hast said! Another of the gods might haply fear this device, whoso was feebler far than thou in hand and might; whereas thy fame shall of a surety reach as far as the dawn spreadeth. Go to now, when once the long-haired Achaeans have gone with their ships to their dear native land,] then do thou burst apart the wall and sweep it all into the sea, and cover the great beach again with sand, that so the great wall of the Achaeans may be brought to naught of thee." (*Iliad* 7.442–464; tr. Murray *LCL*)

Understandably, J. Porter (2011: 3) expresses disbelief: "The Achaeans came to attack a wall, not to build one, let alone to defend one (oddly reversing roles with the Trojans). Why are they seemingly duplicating Troy on a smaller scale—creating their own 'great wall,' as Zeus himself observes (7.46)." The most basic

---

[21] Homer does not consider Apollo's reaction to the building of the Achaean wall. There is a hint that Poseidon had earlier displaced Apollo from his due rewards from the Trojans by claiming he built the walls alone while Apollo only served Laomedon as a herder (*Iliad* 21.445–455). Bertany (2018: 17–25) interprets the angry reaction of Artemis (*Iliad* 21.472–477) in this light.

answer to Porter's objections is that conventional ideas about why Homer has the Achaeans coming to Troy are incorrect or at least incomplete. Clearly, critics need to be more subtle about the motives of the Achaeans and about why it was the very wise and experienced Nestor of Pylos who advocated construction of the Wall (*Iliad* 7.336–343). *By erecting the Achaean Wall, the invaders displaced or sought to displace Troy as controllers of the entrance to the Black Sea. Just as obviously, the Trojans did not appreciate this threat to their livelihood.*

Why is Poseidon so concerned about the Achaean Wall? It seems a trivial concern, especially for no less a god than the brother of Zeus. Still it is not a trivial matter. To understand why one must keep in mind that in the ancient Greek world terms such as "fate," "glory," and "honor" were not solely ideological but also had an important dimension of material wealth.[22] To diminish or fail to consider the material wealth of a deity was to diminish his "fame" (*timē*) among humans and among fellow deities (Adkins 1972: 6). *For the ancients, or at least for Homer, a god is a special form of life produced and sustained by a cultic enterprise. The god is the ideological superstructure of the enterprise and the cult is its material base; if base withers and dies so dies superstructure.*[23]

The Achaeans built a wall themselves and hence felt no need to offer glorious rewards to sustain Poseidon. This seems fair enough. Poseidon sees a problem, however. The problem likely takes the form of a zero-sum game—that is, behind their walls the Trojans were positioned to collect tolls from travelers and to reap commercial gains. Now the Trojans were trapped behind their walls and the Achaeans behind their own wall collected the tolls and the commercial profits. The Trojan Wall had enabled the Trojans to accumulate wealth, which they properly shared with Poseidon. The Achaean Wall damaged this process. The bypassing of the Trojan wall meant that Trojans would no longer be able (or obligated) to repay Poseidon in the accustomed fashion. Poseidon completely understands that the Greeks were threatening his livelihood by *founding*[24] an alternative city on the doorstep of Troy.

Note that Poseidon's materialistic motivations surface even in his description of building Troy's wall. The god complains that Laomedon refused to pay him and Apollo for their work:

---

[22]   Adkins (1972). Note in support of a materialist understanding that in line 86 of the *Homeric Hymn to Demeter* 2 we learn that for "honor," he (Hades) got one-third at the world's first division (cf. *Iliad* 15.187–193). In Aeschylus' *Eumenides* (890) Athena offers to honor the Erinyes with landed estates.

[23]   A god is an enterprise, for example the Poseidon enterprise.

[24]   Wall building is an act of foundation. As noted by Pache (2014: 280): "The same connection between walls and city founding is also found in Poseidon's description of how he and Apollo built the Trojan wall and thus made Troy into a *polis* (πολίσσαμεν, [*polissamen*] *Il.* 7.453)." As noted earlier, Athena built the walls of Troy (of Laomedon).

"Neither rememberest thou all the woes that we twain alone of all the gods endured at Ilios, what time we came at the bidding of Zeus and served the lordly Laomedon for a year's space at a fixed wage ["promised payment"], and he was our taskmaster and laid on us his commands. I verily built for the Trojans round about their city a wall, wide and exceeding fair, that the city might never be broken; and thou, Phoebus, didst herd the sleek kine of shambling gait amid the spurs of wooded Ida, the many-ridged. But when at length the glad seasons were bringing to its end the term of our hire, then did dread Laomedon defraud us twain of all hire, and send us away with a threatening word." (*Iliad* 21.441–445; tr. Murray *LCL*; cf. *Iliad* 7.451–453).=

It is significant in understanding Achaean motivations that, as in the case of payment for building the Trojan Wall, the Trojans had also defrauded Heracles of the horses he had earned for serving them (*Iliad* 5.640–641, 650f., 20.144–148). Laomedon (the Trojans) had a reputation for sharp business practices.

However, there is no trace in Poseidon's current complaint about the Achaean Wall that he had not received his treasured hecatombs (sacrifices of cattle = material rewards) from the Trojans. Needless to add the honors received by Poseidon were shared with his cult—that is, his priests and priestesses.[25] J. Porter (2011: 15–16, 19–20) sympathizes with the view that Poseidon's worried reaction is "misplaced" or "irrational" or "illogical." However, Poseidon's reaction is that of a selfish human but not at all of someone irrational.

c. Arrival of traders from Lemnos

Poseidon's reaction to the Achaean Wall leaves no room to doubt its importance. Moreover, Homer is determined to leave no doubt in the minds of this audience and so immediately reports the arrival of Lemnian traders.

Homer makes the materialist motivation of the Achaeans manifest by reporting on extensive trade with Lemnians behind the Wall. Even the Trojans appear to participate[26]—but all of this happens without compensation for Poseidon!

On this wise spake they, one to the other, and the sun set, and the work of the Achaeans was accomplished; and they slaughtered oxen throughout the huts and took supper. And ships full many were at hand

---

[25] For offerings to Poseidon and his cult in Mycenaean Pylos, see Lupack 2011. Montecchi (2016b: 122–123) finds it "quite safe to assume that there was a sanctuary of Poseidon at *pa-ki-ja-ne*, and that a festival dedicated to this god was celebrated there," and further that the name of the place "would mean something like 'the place of the slaughter officers, sacrificers'." A Linear B specialist informs me that a forthcoming article will dispute this meaning.

[26] Thus, a "Peace of the Gods" was proclaimed for this event.

from Lemnos, bearing wine, sent forth by Jason's son, Euneus,[27] whom
Hypsipyle bare to Jason, shepherd of the host. And for themselves alone
unto the sons of Atreus, Agamemnon and Menelaus, had Euneos given
wine to be brought them, even a thousand measures. From these ships
the long-haired Achaeans bought them wine, some for bronze, some
for gleaming iron, some for hides, some for whole cattle, and some for
slaves; and they made them a rich feast. So the whole night through
the long-haired Achaeans feasted, and the Trojans likewise in the city,
and their allies; and all night long Zeus, the counsellor, devised them
evil, thundering in terrible wise. Then pale fear got hold of them, and
they let the wine flow from their cups upon the ground, neither durst
any man drink until he had made a drink-offering to the son of Cronos,
supreme in might. Then they laid them down, and took the gift of sleep.
(*Iliad* 7.465ff.; tr. Murray *LCL*)

The traders reward Zeus with drink offerings, not Poseidon.

d. Fate of the walls

Zeus assures Poseidon that when the Achaeans depart, he will destroy totally
the Achaean Wall (cf. *Iliad* 12.1–35). Maitland (1999: 10) believes that after the
War Poseidon also destroyed the walls of Troy. Why would Poseidon agree to do
this? He would not. The clear implication of Zeus' promise to Poseidon that he
will be permitted to destroy the Achaean Wall is that the Achaeans intend to take
ownership of Troy, not to destroy it. Otherwise, the destruction of the Achaean
Wall would be an irrational act by a rational god. The point is that the Trojan
Walls will remain, and Poseidon will be made whole—that is, his cult will once
again share in the profits earned by Troy's new Achaean owners (see further
below). This is what Zeus promises to Poseidon. These considerations support
Eustathius' claim that the Achaean Wall is "more renowned" than the "Trojan"
(cited by J. Porter 2011: 20). Homer omitted the destruction of Troy's Wall from
his account because it, unlike the Achaean Wall, was never demolished. This
reasoning once again confirms the validity of subjecting the Epics to materialist
scrutiny. This scrutiny is in fact encouraged and facilitated by Homer.

    The Achaean Wall and, more specifically the reaction of the cult of Poseidon
to its presence and to the coming of the Lemnians is a strong element of realism.
*There is no reason for the inclusion of the Achaean Wall theme unless there was really
a Trojan War and an Achaean Wall.* The Wall is enough to signal the reality of a
face-to-face conflict between Trojans and Achaeans. As noted earlier, there is

---

[27]   The name Eunēos is attested in Linear B in KN As 1520, B 799 and Dv 206.

also the question of whether victory in the War represents an important step in establishing an Achaean kingdom in Anatolia. We do know from a Hittite treaty that in later times (about 1275 BCE)—that is, after the Trojan War was won by the Greeks—the ruler of Wilusa had the Greek name *Alaksandu*. This problem is dealt with more fully later.

e. Achaean strategy

There are additional questions that need to be addressed. First, at what point during the Trojan Wars was the Achaean Wall constructed? Maitland (1999: 2), citing earlier discussion of Thucycides' remarks, seems to understand that the Achaean Wall was built on the arrival of the Greeks but, as we have it, in *Iliad* 7.327–343, the wall was built in the tenth year of the war.[28] Thucydides approached the problem of dating as follows:

> The cause of the inferiority was not so much the want of men as the want of money; the invading army was limited, by the difficulty of obtaining supplies, to such a number as might be expected to live on the country in which they were to fight. After their arrival at Troy, when they had won a battle (as they clearly did, for otherwise they could not have fortified their camp), even then they appear not to have used the whole of their force, but to have been driven by want of provisions to the cultivation of the Chersonese and to pillage. And in consequence of this dispersion of their forces, the Trojans were enabled to hold out against them during the whole ten years, being always a match for those who remained on the spot. Whereas if the besieging army had brought abundant supplies, and, instead of betaking themselves to agriculture or pillage, had carried on the war persistently with all their forces, they would easily have been masters of the field and have taken the city; since, even divided as they were, and with only a part of their army available at any one time, they held their ground. Or, again, they might have regularly invested Troy, and the place would have been captured in less time and with less trouble. Poverty was the real reason why the achievements of former ages were insignificant, and why the

---

[28]   "Needless to say, scholars have wondered why the fortifications were not built earlier, rather than in the tenth year of the war. Some have suggested that the incident is a later interpolation. It should be pointed out, however, that this is one of several incidents in the *Iliad* that are out of place chronologically (for example, Priam's asking Helen to identify the key Greek warriors, who have been on Trojan soil for ten years [3.162–242]). Whoever authored this scene, whether Homer or a later hand, was obviously unconcerned about the chronological niceties" (Roisman 2005: 19, n. 11).

Trojan War, the most celebrated of them all, when brought to the test of facts, falls short of its fame and of the prevailing traditions to which the poets have given authority. (Thucydides *History* 1.11.1–2; tr. Jowett *Perseus Project*)

Thucydides reasons that the Achaeans built the Wall virtually upon arrival at Troy. Then, having done this, they chose to occupy themselves with commerce and pillage instead to conquering Troy. He does not recognize the possibility that the "peripheral" activities were the real reason for which the Achaeans came to the Troad. That is, their objective was not to immediately storm Troy and capture the city but to make the Trojans withdraw behind their walls and then take over their source of wealth. *This is a repeat of the strategy reportedly employed by the seaborne kētos against Troy: the kētos forced Heracles to retreat from the seashore and then to take shelter behind a wall in the plain erected for him by the Trojans and Pallas Athena (Iliad 20.144–148).*[29]

That this was the Achaean strategy from the very beginning is supported by Thucydides line of reasoning (compare Davison 1965: 7) and in Proclus' "Summary of the *Cypria*" where it is told that even before landing in Troy the Achaeans "send an embassy to the Trojans, demanding back Helen and her possessions. When the Trojans pay no heed, they build a defensive wall" (tr. M. Davies 2019: 164). The point is made most strongly in Herodotus 2.118, as translated by Finkelberg (2002: 154–155):

After the rape of Helen, a vast army of Greeks, assisting Menelaus, went to set sail into the Teucrian territory; having disembarked, *and having settled with their camp (kai idrutheisan tēn stratiēn ktl.),* they sent ambassadors to Ilium, and Menelaus himself went. They then went within the walls, and demanded back both Helen and the riches which Alexander gone off with. ... (modified; my transliteration).

---

[29] A most peculiar story. I find it difficult to place the wall behind which Heracles retreated unless it was a wall of Troy—a wall built by Athena and the Trojans. In any event, Heracles defeated the *kētos* but he was not helping the Trojans against the intruding Achaeans! See also, *Iliad* 7.451–453, 21.442–457; Apollodorus *Library* 2.5.9. In *Odyssey* 11.520–521, Odysseus reveals that Eurypylus and his associates (*hetairai*), the *Kēteioi*, who were seeking "gifts for a woman" were killed in battle by Neoptolemus. For the *kētos* as a canine entrepreneurial unit attached to a multi-unit enterprise called the "Scylla" by Silver (2019: esp. 171; cf, *Odyssey* 12.90, the Scylla has six heads). *Kētos*, *Kēteioi*, and Skylla are mythologized (coded) references to real institutions. Thus, the "woman" may be Scylla and the *Kēteioi* are surely more likely Phoenicians than Hittites (Silver 2019: 171). There is much in common, I think, between the *kētos* and the well-financed (many-headed) Hydra defeated by Heracles at Lerna (see Chaps. 9.6 and 11.5; for "head" as "capital" Silver 1992: Chap. 1 and 67–68). Both creatures are dog-like (Chap. 11.2, 5, 7).

However, the important point is that the "defensive wall" served to separate the Trojans from the sea and permitted the Achaeans to *replace* Troy.

If the Trojans could not disrupt the Achaean plan, say by destroying their ships, they would eventually have to surrender. Thus, Hector ridiculed the Achaean Wall but knew that he had to destroy it and then the Achaean ships: "Fools they are, that contrived forsooth these walls, weak and of none account; these shall not withhold our might, and our horses shall lightly leap over the digged ditch. But when I be at length come amid the hollow ships, then see ye that consuming fire be not forgotten, that with fire I may burn the ships and furthermore slay the men, even the Argives beside their ships, distraught by reason of the smoke" (*Iliad* 8.177ff.; tr. Murray *LCL*). Meanwhile, Hector "caged behind walls" lamented the continuous expenditure of Troy's *keimēlia* 'fine treasures' (*Iliad* 18.287-92). The Trojans, not the Achaeans, had a difficult problem of supply.

With respect to the Achaean alternative (to the Trojan) economy it is quite possible that the Achaeans were sending their ships back to Greece for newly produced luxury textiles and then taking them to the Black Sea region. "The distance of Troy from Greece is often much exaggerated by both ancient and modern writers; it was in fact, in favourable conditions, about 4-5 days' sail from Mycenae (or Aulis), slightly closer than Rhodes" (Andrews 1965: 34).

That Achaean ships and traders were active during the siege of Troy is revealed by Nestor's admonitions to Agamemnon in *Iliad* 9.71–72: "Full are thy huts of wine that the ships of the Achaeans bring thee each day from Thrace, over the wide sea; all manner of entertainment hast thou at hand, seeing thou art king over many" (tr. Murray *LCL*). What did the Achaeans offer to the Thracians for the wine they regularly brought to Troy? Recall also that in the earlier second millennium BCE Assyrian merchants stationed their houses permanently in Kanesh (in Anatolia) and wrote home to Assur about the kinds of textiles that were in demand and, therefore, should be produced and sent to them by overland donkey caravan.

But it also seems possible that the Achaeans were producing textiles in their "camp"/"city" and then carrying them to the Black Sea. We are told that in the earlier stages of the Trojan War Achilles and others were raiding various cities and taking spoils. For example, Nestor tells Telemachus: "My friend, since thou hast recalled to my mind the sorrow which we endured in that land, we sons of the Achaeans, unrestrained in daring, — all that we endured on shipboard, as we roamed after booty (*lēis*) over the misty deep whithersoever Achilles led; and all our fightings around the great city of king Priam; —lo, there all our best were slain." (*Odyssey* 3.102ff.). The word *lēis* (*leia*) is usually rendered as "plunder"/"booty" but it also mean "flocks and herds" (LSJ s.v.). Of course, the Achaeans besieging Troy needed food, but they may have taken enough animals as booty to use in producing textiles. They also took human captives some of whom had textile-making skills. Thus, Agamemnon refuses Calchas' offer to ransom his daughter Chruseis in the following terms: "Let me not find you, old man, by the hollow ships, either tarrying now or coming back later, lest your staff and the wreath of the god not protect you. Her I will not set free. Sooner shall old age come upon her in our house, in Argos, far from her native land, as she walks to and fro before the loom and serves my bed" (*Iliad* 1.10 ff.; tr. Murray *LCL*). Still, Argos was years in the future and Chruseis may have served his bed and loom in the Achaean camp.

There is another clue that the initial aim of the Achaeans invaders was to form an alternative textile economy in the Troad. I have in mind the diversion of part of their forces to Lemnos:

> And they that dwelt in Methone and Thaumacia, and that held Meliboea and rugged Olizon, these with their seven ships were led by Philoctetes, well-skilled in archery, and on each ship embarked fifty oarsmen well skilled to fight amain with the bow. But Philoctetes lay suffering grievous pains in an island, even in sacred Lemnos, where the sons of the Achaeans had left him in anguish with an evil wound from a deadly water-snake. There he lay suffering; yet full soon were the Argives beside their ships to bethink them of king Philoctetes. Howbeit neither were these men leaderless, though they longed for their leader; but Medon marshalled them, the bastard son of Oïleus, whom Rhene bare to Oïleus, sacker of cities. (*Iliad* 2.716–725; tr. Murray *LCL*)

Homer mentions only Lemnos and the bite of a water snake. Proclus' summary of the *Cypria* (¶32–¶33) says that Philoctetes was bitten by a water snake at a feast on Tenedos and abandoned in Lemnos because of the bad smell. M. Davies (2019: 154) infers that the bad spell is "of his wound." Lemnos, however, with its extensive purple dye-making facilities had the capacity to be malodorous. Moreover, Philoctetes hailed from Thessaly like Jason, recognized by Homer as an earlier sojourner on smelly Lemnos.

Strabo's (1.2.28) comments, which I quote in part only, are informative: "For Demetrius [of Scepsis] says that Achilles sacked Lesbos and other places, but spared Lemnos and the islands adjacent thereto on account of his kinship with Jason and with Jason's son Euneos who at that time possessed the island of Lemnos. Now how comes it that the poet knew this, namely, that Achilles and Jason were kinsmen or fellow-countrymen, or neighbours, or friends in some way or other (a relationship that could not be due to any other fact than that both men were Thessalians, and that one was born in Iolcus and the other in Achaean Phthiotis" (tr. H.L. Jones *LCL*).[30]

It is commercially significant, I think, that the Thessalian Philoctetes, whose name means "gain-seeker"/"gain-lover," remained behind in Lemnos. Moreover, Philoctetes being "bitten" by a "snake" is a play on a commercial transaction. Being "bitten" has the sense of taking a loan with interest deducted in advance or even of being distrained for failure to repay in time. More directly relevant to the present theme is that the "snake" is the frightening guardian of the underground temple vault of the nymph Chryse "Golden" (Silver 1992: 157–158). Further, for the "snake" links of Philoctetes to Potnia of the Labyrinth and Athena and textile trade (see Chaps. 6.2 and 7.6 and discussion of Figure 14 and Plates 9 and 10). I suggest that "Philoctetes" represents those Achaeans stationed at Lemnos to keep the forces trading behind the Achaean Wall supplied with luxury garments. This "desertion of Philoctetes" is the occasion for a feast on Lemnos at which Agamemnon boasts of the coming victory over the Trojans (*Iliad* 8.229-35).

The suggestion that the Achaean's war strategy was to trade in textiles behind their Achaean Wall is tenuous, but it is much more credible than that the Myceneans bore the cost of assembling an army from all over the Greek world and invading the Troad with more than one thousand ships and then confined themselves to fighting beneath Troy's wall for ten years.

f. Location of Achaean wall

Next, let us address the question of the location of the Greek ships and hence of the Achaean Wall. This problem has been discussed as some length by Korfmann (1986a: 10–15) who concludes: "This brings us to the central point of my paper, that Homer's geographical description, despite meter and poetic license, not only conveys a remarkably accurate impression of the Troad in general, but also provides a concrete description of Besika Bay as the harbor and encampment of the Greek troops" (Korfmann 1986a: 12–13). The point being that the Achaeans positioned themselves opposite the island of Tenedos in the harbor of Hisarlik on the Aegean (termed "on the Hellespont") where they displaced the Trojans in controlling "the commerce from the Black Sea and that from the Aegean and the Mediterranean" (Korfmann 1986a: 15).

On the other hand, none of the (Troy VI or VIIa) objects found can be verified as having come from the Black Sea region. Although mention should be

[30] Both Jason (Pindar *Pythian Ode* 4.10ff.) and Achilles (*Iliad* 11.832) had been educated by Cheiron the Magnesian centaur. The latter being understood as half-man and half-horse, man above and horse below. It is difficult to imagine the curriculum except that the mountain-dwelling centaur taught about sheepherding and wool. It was Cheiron who assigned him the name Iasōn "purpled" (Pindar *Pyhian Ode* 4.119). Achilles brings purple-dyed textiles with him to Troy (*Iliad* 9.200, 24.644–645).

made of "3 very tiny gold objects" from Besika Bay and, from the cemetery at Troy itself, 2 objects of electron or gold and 3 disks of embossed gold sheet (cited by Kolb 2004: 590–591). Of course, this is not the only gold found in Troy.

Korfmann (1986a: 15) goes beyond arguments in terms of geography and historical terminology to consider the finds in the local cemetery: "There can be no doubt that the Mycenaeans were familiar with our settlement near the straits, the substantial amount of Mycenaean pottery found here (many times more than any other location so far to the north) attest it" (conceded by Kolb 2004: 591). The findings in the cemetery also included 5 Mycenaean seals about which Kolb (2004: 591) counters that "since Mycenaean seals were widely diffused in the Eastern Mediterranean and Western Anatolia, their use was not necessarily limited to Mycenaean traders." "Not necessarily," but it is certainly arguable that Mycenaean traders or officials were buried in this cemetery.[31] Korfmann is certainly justified in concluding that the area was of special interest to the Mycenaeans.

That the Achaean camp was at Besika Bay, a little over four miles from Troy, is strongly argued for by Kirk (1990: 47–50) who concludes that the shoreline of the Bay on the west side of the citadel had receded a mile or so in the years between Troy I to Troy VI[32] leaving the western part of the wall the least well defended in which connection he cites Andromache's cautions to Hector in *Iliad* 6.434. Kirk (1990: 49) also takes note of the excavation of the large cemetery on the northern end of Besika Bay adding: "The search for the corresponding habitation-site, which must have been more than a mere hamlet, is still in progress."

Homer testifies that the Achaeans built a formidable wall and that Poseidon made known his bitter resentment about this to the assembled gods. There is nothing romantic or awe-inspiring about these details and Homer's only motive in revealing them is his commitment to historical truth. The Achaeans really invaded the Troad and they did this with the intention of taking for themselves the profit from controlling the entrance to the Black Sea and its lucrative textile trade. There really was a Troy and the only war worth fighting over it is a trade war. In mentioning the Achaean Wall and in other ways discussed immediately below Homer is telling, better insisting, that his Trojan War is about trade. Homer provides brackets for his history: in the beginning Paris brought the textile firm to Troy; in the end Menelaus returned it to Sparta.

---

[31] Karytinos (1998: 85) explains: "They [the seal stones] were probably owned by people of higher status, and possibly played an active role as symbols of this status…. Additionally they kept this role after their owner's death, for of nearly a thousand pre-palatial seals known up to now, the vast majority come from cemeteries, tholos and house tombs." Presumably, the Mycenaean seal bearers had Trojan and other counterparts.

[32] For a more scientifically rigorous discussion of these issues, see Kraft, Rapp, Kayan, and Luce (2003).

If The Trojan War is being "rationalized," the rationalizer is Homer himself.

4. Agamemnon's and Zeus' Purple Portent of War

The Achaean cause is going badly when Agamemnon acts in a most peculiar way:

> Hera put it in Agamemnon's mind himself to bestir him, and speedily rouse on the Achaeans. So he went his way along the huts and ships of the Achaeans, *bearing his great purple cloak in his stout hand*, and took his stand by *Odysseus' black ship*, huge of hull [*koilos* 'hollow'], that was in the midst so that a shout could reach to either end, both to the huts of Aias, son of Telamon, and to those of Achilles; for these had drawn up their shapely ships at the furthermost ends, trusting in their valour and in the strength of their hands. There uttered he a piercing shout, calling aloud to the Danaans: "Fie, ye Argives, base things of shame fair in semblance only. Whither are gone our boastings, when forsooth we declared that we were bravest, the boasts that when ye were in Lemnos ye uttered vaingloriously as ye ate abundant flesh of straight-horned kine and drank bowls brim full of wine, saying that each man would stand to face in battle an hundred, aye, two hundred Trojans! whereas now can we match not even one, this Hector, that soon will burn our ships with blazing fire. (*Iliad* 8.219–236; tr. Murray *LCL*; emphasis added)

Hector is about to burn the ships of the Achaeans. Why does Agamemnon, at the instigation of Hera, hold a purple cloak and why in particular does he choose the ship of Odysseus?

By his behavior, Agamemnon is saying, "Look! This is what we came to Troy on our ships about! Will you give up now?" Purple cloth represents/commands wealth and more specifically wealth in gold.[33]

Kirk's (1990: 317) remarks on the passage are most informative: "[In *Iliad* 11.5–9...] Eris similarly shouts to the Achaeans, moreover she holds in her hands a 'portent of war' *polemoio teras*, at 11.4, rather like Agamemnon with his red *pharos* confirming the connexion between the two passages." The parallel, I submit, is that Agamemnon, like Eris, represents strife and that his *purple cloak is to be understood as a (the) portent of war.* Then the war would be a war fought

---

[33]   By holding the purple cloth in front of the ships Agamemnon might be referring to the fact that the ships were used for carrying purple cloth to the Black Sea or that the ships were loaded with purple cloth or to the gold stored in the ships from marketing purple cloth or to some combination of these references.

over wealth and even, taking into account that the provocation is the burning of the ships, a war over trade. Without ships, the Achaeans will no longer be able to send their luxury textiles to the Black Sea for gold.

There is more direct evidence that the purple cloak is a portent of war = something well worth fighting for. In *Iliad* 17.543–552 Zeus and Athena join forces to rally the Achaeans:

> Then again over Patroclus was strained taut the mighty conflict, dread and fraught with tears, and Athene roused the strife, being come down from heaven; for Zeus, whose voice is borne afar, had sent her to urge on the Danaans, for lo, his mind was turned. As Zeus stretcheth forth for mortals *a purple [porphureus] rainbow* from out of heaven to be a portent whether of war or of chill storm that maketh men to cease from their work upon the face of the earth, and vexeth [*kēdei*] the flocks; even so Athene, enwrapping herself in *a purple [porphureus] cloud*, entered the throng of the Danaans, and urged on each man. (tr. Murray *LCL* modified; emphasis added)

This passage is loaded with references to murex-dye. Athena, the sky itself, clearly possesses the vivid purple glow that defines murex-dye. This epiphany which probably recalls her purple peplos (Nagy 2010: 281–284) not only reminds the Achaeans of their purpose in coming to Troy but also associates Athena with the Labyrinth (see Chap. 6.2).

Zeus' purple *rainbow* is clearly a reference to the empirically known transition of shades and colors characteristic of textiles bathed and boiled—the boiling is the storm—with murex-dye (Grand-Clément 2016: 125–126; cf. Eickhoff n.d.). Many animals are "vexed" by a storm but hardly by a rainbow, which appears *after* a storm, so the reference to "sheep" is fairly regarded to be deliberate and significant reference to the wool dyeing process. Moreover, the primary verb is *kēdomai* 'to care, be cared for' (Beekes s.v. *kēdos*). Thus, I think the meaning could also be that the purple cares for/services the sheep. That is, their wool is cared for/treated with purple dye. However, precisely, this is interpreted the large reference is to the seemingly magical transition in the colors of woolens undergoing the dyeing process.

Why does Agamemnon, like Eris in Book 11 and explicitly in Book 8, choose the ship of Odysseus in particular to rally the Achaeans? The reason, I propose, is that Odysseus and his ships are participants in the trade in purple-dyed textiles. To begin with, recall that Naiads weave purple wraps (*phare*) in

Odysseus' home harbor at Ithaca (*Odyssey* 13.107–108).[34] Next note three additional connections with purple dye: (1) Odysseus is an agent of Poseidon (see Chap. 15.4) and, probably to indicate the latter status, Odysseus, like Nestor and Thoas, wears a purple-dyed cloak to the War (see Chap. 15); (2) Odysseus' ship mentioned as "huge of hull"/"hollow" may have been specially designed (by Poseidon) for the trade with the Black Sea[35]; and (3) Odysseus' twelve ships are, unlike the others ships, stated to be *miltoparēas* 'red cheeked' (*Iliad* 2.637) and as *phoinikoparēos* 'purple-cheeked' (*Odyssey* 11.124, 23.271).

Obviously, the red/purple "cheeks" could symbolize purple dye, but the connection is debatable. In the *Odyssey* 9.125–130 we learn: "For the Cyclopes have at hand no ships with vermilion [cinnebar] cheeks, nor are there shipwrights in their land who might build them well-benched ships, which should perform all their wants, passing to the cities of other folk, as men often cross the sea in ships to visit one another" (tr. Murray *LCL*). This passage is typically taken to mean that the Cyclopes had *no ships*, which would mean that ships were typically "red-cheeked." Indeed, Emanuel's (2017: 145–146) analysis of the Gurob ship-cart model revealed a base layer of white paint "over which a stripe of red paint just below the caprail and above the oarports, and a coating of black asphalt covering the bottom half of the hull were added." The latter sealant would explain the description of the Achaean ships, including Odysseus', as *melas* 'black.' So also the red stripe, whatever its function (see below) might be a common feature of the Achaean ships. On the other hand, as Emanuel (2017: 246) points out, *only* Odysseus' ships are described as "red-" or as "purple-cheeked." Thus, the Cyclopes reference might mean that despite the excellent wool of their sheep (see Chap. 15.3), the backward Cyclopes possessed no ships of their own that were specifically designed or designated for the luxury textile trade.

Katsaros (2008) has dealt with the "red-cheeks" and identified *miltoparea* as referring to the covering of the "front area and the whole of the bottom area of the vessel" with *mitsos* (*miltos*) meaning a paint made of a lead-rich red earth available from Kea Island. This coating served as a superior protection and sealant of the wood from seawater. Katsaros theorizes that this kind of coating was relatively expensive to apply. If so, it may have been used only for ships carrying expensive and vulnerable cargoes such as purple-dyed textiles. This reasoning may explain the finding of a painted "red stripe" on the Gurob ship-cart model. The lower hull of the model was treated with

---

34 Ithaca is strategically located for trade relations since it had east-west contacts through the Corinthian Gulf plus north-south contacts along the coast of Ionia (Agourides 1997).

35 The expression "hollow" focuses attention on the "unrealized potentiality" to be filled with wealth (Ward 2019).

asphalt and Odysseus' ships are black. The implication being that the special paint was not utilized on the lower hull. There is much here that is not fully understood. In any event, the "red" and "purple" cheeks of Odysseus' ships, whether symbolic or functional or both serve to link Odysseus with the trade in purple-dyed textiles.[36]

Agamemnon's holding of the purple cloak and the specifically Odyssean considerations credibly configure the Trojan War as a war over trade in luxury textiles. There are additional references to murex purple in the Epic. Helen incorporates the pattern of a battle scene into the purple-colored diplax she is weaving on her loom (*Iliad* 3.125–127; Wagner-Hasel 2002: 23; see the Front Cover Image). It is also significant that in the Homeric epics, *porphureos thanatos* 'purple-colored death' (e.g. *Iliad* 5.8) refers to "the glorious death that occurs on the battlefield" (Brecolaki 2014: 10).

Agamemnon's behavior in holding the purple cloak before the Achaean ships calls to mind his words in the famous "Carpet Scene" which he plays with Clytemnestra on his return to Argos in Aeschylus *Agamemnon* 945ff.; Agamemnon: "Well, if you will have your way, quick, let someone loose my sandals, which, slave-like, serve the treading of my foot! As I walk upon these purple vestments may I not be struck from afar by any glance of the gods' jealous eye. A terrible shame it is for one's foot to mar the resources of the house by wasting wealth and costly [*argurōnētous*; also 'bought with silver'/'acquired/disposed of in the market'] woven work" (tr. Weir Smyth *LCL*; LSJ s.v.). Flintoff's (1987: 126) analysis is insightful and compact:

> In order to mount her astonishing reception Clytemnestra has had to do something which in many houses would have imperiled the finan-cial—and sacral—well-being of the house itself. That is the point of her words at 958f. where she makes, I think, two separate but connected assertions, that this particular house at least has an abundance of such wealth and that so long as no one tampers with the source of supply there is no danger that the wealth cannot be replaced. Now doubtless there is something even in this. And for a moment or two it does seem possible that the Chorus will accept what Clytemnestra has done and said at its face value. For wealth—and in particular the stupendous wealth that has accrued to Argos as a consequence of its long war—has been one, indeed perhaps the main one, of the concerns of the Chorus throughout the play (see for example 374ff., 437ff. 750ff., 770ff.). In view of this there may be something to be said for such a voluntary diminution of wealth.

---

[36] Admittedly, the connection with murex would have been made stronger had Homer used *porphyra* for the color of cheeks on Odysseus' ship.

Aeschylus' Agamemnon is clearly in the purple-dyed textile business and his wife, as she describes herself, is "dog (*kuna*) of the house."[37]

Kolb (2004: 588) insists (inexplicably) that Homer knows nothing about trade wars and that "Troy is not brought into connection with ships and trade." He sees the idea of a Bronze Age trade war over access to the Black Sea to be "anachronistic" considering that trade wars arise under specific economic conditions including *"extensive trade of essential goods for daily consumption and the existence of largely autonomous cities"* (Kolb 2004: 589; emphasis added). Again, Bronze Age states did not have wars aimed at "protecting or fostering 'national' trade or 'free trade' for merchants of different states" (Kolb 2004: 589). However, despite the diversionary tactics about the definition of "trade war," Kolb (2004: 589) is forced by the Hittite Ahhiyawa correspondence discussed earlier (AhT 2 [§13] = CTH 105) to grant that "Near Eastern powers sometimes led wars for economic purposes, trying to control trade routes and ports of trade." But such wars are not "trade wars" and, more importantly, nothing of the sort could have happened at the Dardanelles because Troy was economically unimportant. Once again, Kolb does not recognize as a motivating force the profit to be gained by those who participated in the production and export of valuable textiles.[38] It is possible to view the Trojan War as a war and as being important even if the reported annual number of participants/casualties was small by later standards.

---

[37] In the *Iliad* 11.15–30 we hear of a great gift from Cinyras to Agamemnon: "But the son of Atreus shouted aloud, and bade the Argives array them for battle, and himself amid them did on the gleaming bronze. The greaves first he set about his legs; beautiful they were, and fitted with silver ankle-pieces; next he did on about his chest the corselet that on a time Cinyras had given him for a guest-gift. For he heard afar in Cyprus the great rumour that the Achaeans were about to sail forth to Troy in their ships, wherefore he gave him the breastplate to do pleasure to the king. Thereon verily were ten bands of dark cyanus, and twelve of gold, and twenty of tin; and serpents of cyanus writhed up toward the neck, three on either side, like rainbows that the son of Cronos hath set in the clouds, a portent for mortal men." (tr. Murray *LCL*). That Athena's "rainbow" refers to the magical transition in colors in the murex-dyeing process has already been discussed. Why did Cinyras in Cyprus send such a purpled portent to Agamemnon on the eve of the expedition to Troy? I see the gift as a reminder of his interest, a kind of investment intended to smooth Cinyras' access to the Black Sea and the gains therefrom. The name *ki-nu-ra* probably Kinyras appears in a Linear B tablet at Pylos (PY Qa 1301) and for a shipbuilder (*na-u-do-mo*) in Vn 865.7 (Nakassis 2013: 139–140).

[38] I do not mean to suggest that Kolb is alone in his view that an interpretation of Troy as a commercial center and of the Trojan War as a war fought over trade is anachronistic (see e.g. Bintliff 2002: esp. 155). Here and elsewhere, Kolb states such views the most openly and makes few concessions to "modernistic" conceptions.

5. Helen as a Greek-Trojan Wife and as a Greek-Trojan Textile Enterprise

a. Helen and her two husbands

Homer leaves no doubt that Helen is legally the wife of both Menelaus and Paris.[39] In Troy, Helen is the wife of Paris/Alexander but prior to her departure and again when she returns to Sparta, she is the wife of Menelaus. "As Helen well knows, she is the wife of the one who happens to have her in his possession. As her appellatives and the words for 'wife' that are used of her show, Helen's fundamental identity at Troy is that of wife.... When she returns to Sparta she becomes again the wife (*alochos*) of Menelaus" (Edmunds 2019: 25).

It seems clear that the travels of Paris and Helen correspond to something in the Trojan/Greek cultic calendar, which, in turn, probably corresponds to something in the navigational calendar. Woolsey (1917: 124) suggested that Menelaus was the summer-husband of Helen (in Laconia) and Paris her winter-husband (in Troy).[40] That Helen has a recognized legal status in Troy is sufficient to demonstrate that she was *sent* to Troy by those in Sparta who had legal rights to her services. That is, Helen went to Troy as the result of an agreement between her Greek owners and Paris. It follows from her shared wife status that the issue of the Trojan War is not the elopement of Helen with Paris but rather his (the Trojan's) decision not to return her at an appointed time.[41] Note that Helen had "earlier" been abducted from Sparta by Theseus who took her to to his "mother" Aithra (see §5.c below) in Aphidna, an Attic deme, but she was later returned to the Dioskouroi.[42]

Helen's status as wife by location finds a legal parallel or model, obviously not an *inspiration*, in classical Athens in the famous case of Neaira whom two men, Stephanus and Phrynion, claimed as their wife. After heated disputes and legal eviction actions a solution:

[39] Other sources are explicit: "And sailing away to Troy (Paris) celebrated his marriage (*gamos*) to Helen" (Proclus *Chrestomathia*/"Summary of the *Cypria*"; tr. M. Davies 2019: 108); a wedding of Paris and Helen is also referred to in Aeschylus *Agamemnon* 699–703 (discussed by M. Davies 2019: 108).

[40] The Dioskouroi alternated daily in immortality (*Odyssey* 11.302–304). More to the point, it is well known in Greek and Near Eastern history that men who expected to be away from home for extended periods legally took "secondary" wives at their away-from-home residences. Theseus and Ariadne are famous practitioners of this institution (Silver 2018: 13–17). What is novel is that an arrangement of this kind was available for women as well.

[41] A scholion of Hellanikos has Menelaus and Paris going to Delos and "receiving an incomprehensible response to their inquiries about children/a wife respectively" (Fowler 2000: II, 530). Based on Hesiod Fragment 96 we may understand that Apollo who generally facilitated trade encouraged Menelaus and Paris to agree to share Helen.

[42] Sources: *Cypria* Fragment #11, Scholiast on *Iliad* 3.242; Plutarch *Theseus* 3-7, 31-4; and Edmunds 2016: 70–76.

These men came together in the temple, and after hearing the facts from both parties and from the woman (Neaira) herself gave their decision, and these men acceded to it. The terms were: that the woman should be *free (eleutheron) and her own master (autē hautēs kuria)* but that she should give back to Phrynion all that she had taken with her from his house except the clothing and the jewels and the maid-servants; for these had been bought for the use of the woman herself; and that she should live with each of the men on alternate days, and if they should mutually agree upon any other arrangement, that arrangement should be binding; that she should be maintained by the one who for the time had her in his keeping; and that for the future the men should be friends with one another and bear no malice (Demosthenes 59.46; tr. DeWitt and DeWitt *LCL* modified; emphasis added).

There is no reason to assume that the legal status *autē hautēs kuria* was created *de novo* for Neaira by a temple arbitration panel; evidently she was placed within a long-existing, legal and marital status (Silver 2018: 81). I will return to Neaira later in considering the *demand for Helen's return* (in §e below).

Helen is a legally transferred wife—that is, she was transferred with the consent of her owner(s) in Greece. I will try below to suggest that the transfer was the result of a negotiation and, further, that Helen is simultaneously a transferred enterprise. To put it more bluntly: Helen the transferred mortal wife is the mythologized version of the goddess Helen who controls an enterprise.

b. Formation of the Helen enterprise

Homer and the *Cypria* provide clues that a Trojan group led by Paris negotiated in the Argolid with an Achaean group to form a textile enterprise—the "Helen enterprise"—to operate in the Troad. Perhaps the postulated enterprise was to be incorporated in the Zeus cult and to operate under the auspices of an existing goddess named "Helen." In the *Iliad* (three times in Book 3) and the *Odyssey* (three times in Book 4 and once in Book 24) we are told in various formulations that Helen was *Zeus' daughter*. Alternatively, the name "Helen" was given to a deity newly born to Zeus (or to an *eidōlon* 'representative') at the time when the wife Helen/the Helen enterprise was shared with Paris and his group, as in Euripides *Helen* 31–35.

Proclus' "Summary of the *Cypria*" tells that Zeus, with the assistance of Hermes, organized on Mt. Ida a "Beauty Contest" known also as the "Judgment of Paris"; for choosing Aphrodite as winner rather than Athena or Hera, the Trojan *shepherd* Alexander/Paris is rewarded with Helen by Aphrodite and/or by Zeus).[43] Homer seems to allude to the "Judgment of Paris"/"Beauty Contest" in Book 24 of the *Iliad*. Most importantly, he places the encounter with the three goddesses in Paris' *mesaulos* 'inner courtyard' for keeping animals (*Iliad* 24.29). As the winner, Paris will receive the world's most beautiful woman who is also exceptionally skilled in textile work. However, at the same time by placing the contest in his *mesaulos* on Mt. Ida, Homer calls attention to what Paris has to offer in return, namely Anatolian wool (*Iliad* 11.4–6, 20.90–93, 188–194; *Homeric Hymn to Aphrodite* 53–55, 68–80).

The commercial significance of the gathering on Mt. Ida is signaled by the participation of Hermes rather than of Iris "who regularly appears in the *Iliad* as the messenger of the gods (and of Zeus in particular) and as such she is despatched to both mortals and divinities" (M. Davies 2019: 121). This prior contact sets the stage for the voyage of Paris and his colleagues to Greece (see §6 below). The commercial aspect is underlined by the notice in the *Cypria* (Athenaeus 15.682 D–E) that Aphrodite presented herself for judgment to Paris in in "garments which the Graces and the Seasons had made and dyed (*ebapsan*) in the flowers of spring-time, garments such as the Seasons wear, dyed in crocus and hyacinth [see §5.d] and in the blooming violet and in the fair flower of the rose, sweet and fragrant, and in ambrosial flowers of the narcissus and the lily." such as are made and worn by the Graces and the Seasons (tr. M. Davies 2019: 59, 63–64). *Thus, serving as models, Aphrodite (and her associated fashion models) exhibited to Paris the dyed and perfumed fashions that the new firm (Helen) would be capable of bringing to the market.* It is not entirely clear to me whether Aphrodite's fashion show should be identified with the "Judgment of Paris" at Ida (M. Davies 2019: 59–60, with 68) or as a separate festival celebrated upon Paris' arrival in Greece.

I see a reference to a prior negotiation for Helen when during the War, Hector complains to Paris: "Were you such a one when in sea-faring ships you sailed over the sea, having gathered your trusty comrades [*hetairos*], and mingling [*michtheis*] with foreigners, brought back a beautiful woman from a distant land, the sister-in-law of warriors" (*Iliad* 3.46ff.; tr. Edmunds 2019: 23; Murray's translation is not useful). Admittedly, Hector does not specifically say that Paris' objective was to bring back Helen but, on the other hand, *Iliad* 24 proves that acquiring Helen is not merely incidental to the motive for a journey in sea-faring ships.

---

[43]   The prize is noted in only few words in the *Cypria* and expansively in Apollodorus *Epitome* 3.1–2; cf. Euripides *Trojan Women* 9. Sources: *Cypria* Fragment #11, Scholiast on *Iliad* 3.242; Plutarch *Theseus* 3–7, 31–34; Edmunds 2016: 70–76). The role of Eris and her golden apple was mentioned previously and interpreted in terms of finance. In evaluating this radical hypothesis is is well to consider that the goddess Nemesis ("Distributer"), like Eris, a deified personification, is known from later times for witnessing oaths and for making interest-bearing loans at her temple in Rhamnous (Silver 1995: 15 with references). Like Aphrodite, the Rhamnousian Nemesis is linked with the apple (Foster 1899: 40–41).

Note that *hetairai* does not have the sense of only servants/retainers or of a mere collection of individuals. Indeed, it can have the sense of membership in a formal association: a business association. Paris' purpose was not tourism although he and his associates may often have traveled to discover business opportunities. Most likely, the associates knew of Aphrodite's offer when they journeyed to Greece.[44] That "Paris" was successful in dealing with the Greeks is attested by his possession of the Greek *epiklesis* "Alexandros," which may have been awarded to him by his Greek trading partners in the present or a previous occasion. That this name remained in elite circulation is demonstrated by a Hittite treaty in which the ruler of Wilusa has the name Alaksandu. It may even be suggested that Paris took with him back to Troy the cult of the Greek god Apollo (see Watkins 1998: 207–208).

With several possible exceptions, Paris' business associates are not named. The first exception is Phereklos. At the moment of his death in battle at Troy at the hands of the Cretan Meriones, Homer reveals that "He [Phereklos] it was that had also built for Alexander [Paris] the shapely ships, source of ills, that were made the bane of all the Trojans and of his own self, seeing he knew not in any wise the oracles of the gods" (*Iliad* 5.61ff.; tr. Murray *LCL*). Further, we learn that Phereklos is the son of Tektōn "Carpenter, Joiner" who is himself the son of Harmonidēs "Joiner." All three names are Greek, indicating that as many as three generations of craftsmen had previously left Greece and set up shop in Anatolia.[45] Add that Phereklos need not have been a laborer but rather the owner of a shipbuilding enterprise.[46]

[44] I would say the same about the "godlike companions" (*antitheois hetaroisi*) in the "Cretan version" of Odysseus' *nostos*. Therein, an Aeotolian tells the swineherd Eumaeus in Ithaca that he "had seen Odysseus among the Cretans at the house of Idomeneus, mending his ships which storms had shattered. And he said that he would come either by summer or by harvest-time, *bringing much treasure along with his godlike comrades.*" (*Odyssey* 14.379–385; tr. Murray *LCL*; emphasis added). Odysseus went to Crete from Troy and he will return to Ithaca even richer together with a group of rich associates.

[45] See Gregory Nagy (2016) "A Sampling of Comment on Rhapsody 5." Available at: https://chs.harvard.edu/CHS/article/display/6556.rhapsody-5 (accessed February 12, 2021). Surely, the primary meaning of Phere-klos is 'fame-bringer'.

[46] A second possible Trojan associate in Paris' enterprise is Deiphobos. According to Proclus' "Summary of the *Little Iliad*" (page 106, lines 28–29), Deiphobos, one of Priam's sons, took control of Helen after the death of Paris (cf. Servius on Virgil *Aeneid* 2). Perhaps this was legally required. On the other hand, as Gantz (1993: 639) explains, this takeover was known to Homer as, "the story of Helen's attempt to reveal the secret of the Wooden Horse includes the fact that Deiphobos accompanied her there, although Menelaus does not call him her husband, and when the Achaeans emerge from the Horse Odysseus and Menelaus proceed to Deiphobos' house (*Odyssey* 4.274-76, 8.517-20)." Thus, we may take it as possible that Deiphobos was a leading colleague of Paris in controlling the Helen enterprise. Also, I think Hector played a role based on his Greek name, explicit wearing of a purple cloak, the symbolism of the burial of his bones in a golden coffin covered by purple garments (*Iliad* 24.795-796) and the reference to him as a "dog"

A second candidate for membership in Paris' syndicate is Aeneas but he is named not by Homer but in Proclus' "Summary of the *Cypria*" wherein Aeneas advises the building of ships and in that source we learn also that "Aphrodite tells Aeneas to sail with him [Paris]."[47] In the *Homeric Hymn to Aphrodite*, Aeneas is the son fathered on Aphrodite by Anchises on Mt. Ida. Thus, the cult of Aphrodite maintains its involvement in Paris' journey/enterprise. We understand that as Aphrodite's "son," Aeneas would use his good offices to smooth Paris' path to the acquisition of Helen.

More, why in the first place is Homer's audience told that Paris used new ships and who built them? This information is not required by the introduction of Aphrodite nor does it serve to make Paris' alleged elopement with Helen more romantic or less dishonorable. The special construction of ocean-going vessels only serves to make the theme of a business venture involving Helen more credible. Were sea-going ships unavailable in Troy?[48] Why did Paris need new ships to travel to Greece? Homer is somewhat ambiguous on these kinds of questions but Proclus' "Summary of the *Cypria*" (page 102, line 19) makes clear that Aphrodite advised Paris to build ships for traveling *to* Greece. Perhaps the ships that carried Paris to Troy and returned with Helen to Troy also carried a valuable cargo of Greek-made luxury textiles belonging to Paris' Greek trading partners and/or to Helen herself. In this case Paris' new ships would have been spacious, secure, and embodied the new technology for dealing with the winds and currents at the entrance to the Black Sea. An entrepreneurial role is easily predicted for the Greek shipbuilder who apparently had come to Troy in search of new commercial opportunities. New ships were not required, however, simply to transport Helen and her personal property.

Significantly, Homer has Paris and his associates "mingle" (*mignumi*) with their Greek counterparts. "Mingle" is the kind of word that serves myth-making very well.[49] For mingling in the meaning of *commercial intercourse*, note Latin *misceo* 'mingle': "to unite or attach as allies or associates, to combine (resources etc.) in a single enterprise or common cause, to cement (a relationship), to give

---

by Achilles (*Iliad* 22.337ff) and by Diomedes (*Iliad* 11.360f.) with reference to his status as Apollo's agent (Silver 2019: 169).

[47] Translated by Gregory Nagy and revised by Eugenia Lao. Available for download at: https://chs.harvard.edu/CHS/article/display/5288 (accessed 12, 2021).

[48] A scholion on *Iliad* 5.64 (Hellanikos fragment 142) refers to an oracle that the Trojans should avoid seafaring and devote themselves to agriculture. Probably this is a reference to Zeus' plan to destroy men who strive for gain (see below). Pherekydes fragment 138 says Alexander/Paris sailed to Greece with nine ships. (Source: Fowler 2000: II, 529–530).

[49] In the epic literature *mignumi* = *meignumi* 'mingle' has the meaning "hold intercourse [in guest friendship]" (LSJ s.v. *meignumi* B). *Mixis* 'mixing, mingling' means "intercourse (with others), especially sexual intercourse or commerce" (LSJ s.v. *mixis* II). Thus the range of meanings of "mingling, mixing" would include virtually any form of interaction, including trade relations.

and take, exchange" (*OLD* s.v. 5, 10). Add that commercial applications of terms meaning "mingling" are well attested in the ancient Near East from the later second to the earlier first millennium BCE.[50] Given the proximity of Hector's reference to a "beautiful woman" (in *Iliad* 3.46ff.) it is reasonable to understand that Helen was obtained legally through standard commercial means by Paris and his *hetairai*.

With respect to possible negotiating partners on the Greek side, mainly both outside Homer and the Trojan Cycle, there are references to the "Oath of Tyndareus": Tyndareus, king of Sparta, made each of Helen's diverse and numerous "marriage suitors" swear to come to the aid of the chosen "husband" should he be attacked with respect to the marriage.[51] Thus, again, we have evidence of a syndicate or consortium but now on the Greek side. In return, Tyndareus helped Odysseus to acquire Penelope. One implication is that Odysseus, even if only at one remove from Helen's suitors, belonged to the consortium of investors. More importantly, the reported oath makes sense only in defense of a business plan calling for Menelaus to transmit Helen to a third party. All the beneficiaries of the contract were bound to assist Menelaus if the third party violated the agreement on terms of use.

Continuing on the theme of negotiations, according to Proclus' "Summary of the *Cypria*" (¶8–¶9), Paris was first hosted in Greece by the "sons of Tyndareus" (Castor and Polydeuces, the Dioskouroi) and then he went to Menelaus in Sparta and there Paris gave gifts to Helen.[52] These details are realistic and deserve mention.

---

[50]   In the "Synchronistic History," an Assyrian chronicle dating from the late second to early first millennium BCE, there is the phrase "the people of Assyria and the people of Babylonia mingled (*ibballu*)" (CAD *balalu* 7 "to mix"). Brinkman (1990: 88) explains: "[T]hough we are as yet unable to appreciate all the connotations of this pregnant expression ... No matter where one turns in the text, one is confronted with statements that Assyrians and Babylonians made compacts together, swore oaths together, established comprehensive peace agreements together, and of course mingled together." The commercial point of "mingling" is made explicit in an inscription of the Assyrian ruler Sargon II (721–705) who boasts that he opened Egypt's sealed *karu* 'embankment, harbor district, trading station' (CAD s.v. *karu* A) adding "Assyrians and Egyptians I mingled together and I made them trade" (Elat 1978: 27).

[51]   Sources: Scholium [D] Homer *Iliad* 2.339 = Stesichorus Fragment 87 Finglass; Hesiod *Catalogue of Women* Fragments 204.78-85; Euripides' *Iphigenia at Aulis* 51-65; Apollodorus 3.10.9; cf. Glantz 1993: 564-567. Note that in *Iliad* 2.339, Nestor refers to oaths taken by the combatants. The latter myth might be an "explanation" perhaps after the fact, of why Menelaus was able to claim so many allies in his attempt to recover his wife Helen. However, I suspect that there is real substance—that is, explanatory value hidden in the later myths. Specifically, it reflects the formation of a trading consortium on the Greek side. That the "suitors" are the "investors" in the Helen enterprise finds support in the correspondence of their names with those in the "Catalogue of Ships" in Book 2 of the *Iliad*.

[52]   The visit of Paris and his colleagues to the Dioskouroi would hardly be the first contact between the Greek and Trojan parties but one of their final contacts. It may have been intended to solicit

Now let us return to Proclus' report of gifts given by Paris to Helen. We may understand that Paris *purchased* Helen/the Helen cult from herself—that is, the cult is visualized as a *woman in her own hands* who engages in an act of "auto-*ekdosis*" (Silver 2018: 35–38). In Euripides *Iphigenia at Aulis* 65–70, Helen *chose* Menelaus in marriage from among her suitors. We learn elsewhere that this choice was determined by monetary considerations: Helen married Menelaus because he outbid her other suitors (Hesiodic *Catalogue of Women* Fragments 154, 155; Most *LCL*). The auto-*ekdosis* interpretation of her marriages first to Menelaus and then to Paris finds support in the etymologizing of the name "Helen" as "She Chooses for Herself" (Silver 2019: 54 with references). Note also Smoot's (2016) "Etymology 5 (*Selenā*), 'seize', 'abduct' cognate with Greek *helein*, English *sell*." "Helen" might then be rendered something like "The Transferred/Sold One." However, Helen willingly participated in the sales to both Menelaus and Paris. Helen's self-sale to Paris was legal because Menelaus, the original husband/owner *divorced* Helen/freed the Helen cult. Then Paris purchased Helen in marriage/took ownership of the Helen cult and carried her/it to the Troad. When the appointed time came, Paris refused to divorce his wife/transfer the Helen cult back to Menelaus. Accordingly, the "Oath of Tyndareus" came into force.

That the agreement called for the return of Helen fits the logic of Helen's marriages to both Menelaus and Paris, the existence of an "Oath of Tyndareus," and the embassy of Odysseus and Menelaus to reclaim Helen in Proclus' "Summary of the *Cypria*" and in *Iliad* 3.205–208. The "Oath of Tyndareus" would have been made known to Paris and his associates at the time when Helen was transferred to them. That Paris chose to disregard the promised consequences of his decision not to return Helen does not mean that the "Oath" lacked any deterrent value.

---

good auspices and/or navigational information for the forthcoming return voyage to Troy. In later times, the Dioskouroi bore the epithet *sōtēr*, meaning they were protectors of both persons and their wealth, especially on the seas (Silver 1992: 103). I suspect a deeper motive for the visit. Specifically, that the Dioskouroi audited the transactions of Paris' group and cleared them for departure from Sparta. Silver (1992: 102) has noted that the Dioskouroi were called *aphetērioi* at Sparta (as cited by Pausanias 3.14.7), a title having the sense of "senders-off" or "dischargers." The Argonauts began their voyage at a port in Magnesia called Aphetai (fragment of Hesiod cited by Huxley 1969: 107 with references). Lindsay (1965: 88) explains that "*Aphetai* was the ritual name given to animals set free for consecration to a god, or to men liberated by the gods for certain earthly servitudes or as a result of carrying out their wills" (for the passive use, see LSJ s.v. *aphetos*; cf. Dominique Thillaud, AEGEANET, September 26, 1998). Also, Huxley (1969: 107) has noted that the related term *aphetai* has the meaning "place of quittance" (cf. LSJ s.v. *aphetos*; Beekes s.v. *aphētōr*, an epithet of Apollo derived from *aphiēmi* 'who sends off' [with "prophecies" = navigational guidance]). The Dioskouroi (their cult) qualified to play this kind of role because they were merchants (*empolē*) or rather they were gods of merchants (Silver 1992: 103, citing Pollux and Aristophanes *Heroes* fragment 310). It cannot be shown, however, that the Dioskouroi played a commercial role in the Bronze Age.

c. Character of Helen as enterprise

It is most difficult to believe that Paris acquired ships built with Greek expertise and journeyed to the Argolid with a group of associates solely to acquire a beautiful woman for his bed. *The new ships, attested in both Homer and the Cypria, testify that Paris' visit to Greece had a commercial dimension.*[53] The problem remains that the sources do not reveal what Paris planned to carry back to Troy in his ships. Did he intend to load his ships with purchased Greek-made textiles? With textiles consigned to him? Hector's formulation of Paris' journey (quoted earlier) suggests to me that the acquisition of Helen was not incidental to, but rather intrinsic to, his business plan.[54] That is, in our sources "Helen" is both a marital and a commercial acquisition.[55]

Bearing on the possible nature of Helen as an enterprise, Homer tells that in addition to Helen, Paris took with him to Troy an *"old woman."* Not an "old woman" who did Helen's hair or bathed her but rather the one who carded her wool in Sparta (*Iliad* 3.385f.; cf. Franklin 2016b). Homer considers this fact to be worth mentioning.[56]

In Greek and Roman comedy the person called "old woman" is often a *promnēstria* (or *proxenetria*) or (Latin) *nutrix* 'go-between' or 'matchmaker' and, in fact, an agent (Silver 2019: 51–52).[57] In *Iliad* 6.87, *geraiai* "old women" are specifically called upon by Hector to accompany the queen, the priestess Theanō and others for the purpose of presenting an especially valuable textile (and sacrifices) to Athena so that the goddess (in return) would agree to spare Troy.

---

[53] The alternative view is that Paris' deed was premeditated. That is, he planned to steal Helen and Menelaus' wealth and therefore built ships to store it.

[54] The reasons why the negotiations for Helen took place in the Argolid specifically are explored in §6 below.

[55] The distinction between the two forms of enterprise is not as profound as might appear at first glance. The terminology of taking of a 'wife' (*alochos*) can be applied to the formation of an organization/enterprise in that it lays a foundation for/prepares a bed for future dividends/offspring (*tokos*). A key question is what Homer meant by his phrase *alochos mnēstē* 'wooed bedmate' as applied to Penelope (*Odyssey* 11.177) and Clytemnestra (*Odyssey* 1.36) and, implicitly, to Helen. *Mnēstē* is rendered 'wooer'/'suitor' but the word also has to do with 'memory'/'remembrance'. (Linguistic sources consulted: Beekes; LSJ). Another question for future research is the role of the "husband" of Helen in the enterprise: Menelaus and Paris are the husbands but also Agamemnon and Priam are the "kings.".

[56] Homer does not at this point mention the name of Helen's "old woman." However, *Iliad* 3.143–144 mentions that one of Helen's close helpers/counselors is "Aithra, daughter of Pittheus." (A second companion is "Clymene," a name borne by nymphs.) Sources name an "Aithra, daughter of Pittheus" as the mother of Theseus with whom the latter lodged Helen when he abducted her (see §5.a). Versions differ about this Aithra's arrival in Troy. In one, it was Hector who brought her to Troy from Greece. A (white-haired) old woman named Aithra is rescued from the captured Troy (Pausanias 10.25.7–8; British Museum 1842,0822.1; Glantz 1993: 288–291).

[57] In Statius' *Thebaid* 5.105ff. the speaker who incites the Lemnian women to kill their men is an old woman named Polyxo.

Perhaps the "old women" were needed because of their expertise in making bargains. The specialized occupation of "old women" is perhaps to market (or at least display) finished textiles to clients including the "guests"/"foreigners."

At the same time, and quite reasonably, "old woman" may simply mean "experienced woman." In fact, this meaning emerges in a Linear B tablet from Knossos (KN Ap 694). As discussed by Burke (2016: 640), the first line deals with women making a special kind of cloth (*pawea koura*); the second line mentions women who are *ka-ra-we* which is understood to mean "old women"[58] and the third line mentions *a-ze-ti-ri-ja* women who are typically understood to be "seamstresses" or else "decorators/finishers." However, the latter term has also been related to alphabetic Greek *askein* 'to work with skill' an interpretation lending itself to the view that, aside from their specific specialty, the *a-ze-ti-ri-ja* are apprentices (Lejeune 1971: 105). That is, they are learning to be skilled at an occupation or task. If this is so, then the role of the "old women" becomes understandable: they are mentioned in the text because they are training the *a-ze-ti-ri-ja* women (Nosch 2001). Generalizing from this finding, Helen's "old woman" would have trained her employees, even already skilled ones, to make special textiles. Perhaps, they were to be trained in making textiles with elaborate pictorial themes (see Chap. 3).

On the voyage back to Troy, Paris went to Sidon and acquired skilled textile workers. These women produced the special textiles presented to Athena in an attempt to convince her to spare Troy (*Iliad* 6.289–292). Thus, Homer makes his audience understand that Paris acquired together with Helen and her "old woman" the personnel for a textile enterprise whose most important participant was Helen, herself a superbly skilled textile worker.

Paris is portrayed as an entrepreneur and indeed as a wealthy entrepreneur for he afforded to build his own palace: "Hector went his way to the palace of Alexander, the fair palace that himself had builded with the men that were in that day the best builders in deep-soiled Troy; these had made him a chamber and hall and court hard by the palaces of Priam and Hector in the citadel" (*Iliad* 6.313ff.; tr. Murray *LCL*). Paris is much more powerful than Homer admits. In addition, Menelaus, Helen's Spartan husband has a reputation for great wealth. Thus, (outside Homer) he won the bidding for Helen and, as Homer reveals, Menelaus returned with Helen to Sparta a very wealthy man even though the wealth is attributed to his wanderings.

Now as he [Telemachus] spoke fair-haired Menelaus heard him, and he spoke and addressed them with winged words: "Dear children, with

---

[58] *Ka-ra-we* is interpreted by Chadwick [Ventris and Chadwick *Docs. 2* 176] as *grāwes* 'old women' (cf. Baumbach 1986: 273–274).

Zeus verily no mortal man could vie, for everlasting are his halls and his possessions; but of men another might vie with me in wealth or haply might not. For of a truth after many woes and wide wanderings I brought my wealth home in my ships and came in the eighth year. Over Cyprus and Phoenicia I wandered, and Egypt, and I came to the Ethiopians and the Sidonians and the Erembi, and to Libya, where the lambs are horned from their birth. For there the ewes bear their young thrice within the full course of the year; there neither master nor shepherd has any lack of cheese or of meat or of sweet milk, but the flocks ever yield milk to the milking the year through. While I wandered in those lands gathering much livelihood, meanwhile another slew my brother by stealth and at unawares, by the guile of his accursed wife. Thus, thou mayest see, I have no joy in being lord of this wealth; and you may well have heard of this from your fathers, whosoever they may be, for full much did I suffer, and let fall into ruin a stately house and one stored with much goodly treasure. Would that I dwelt in my halls with but a third part of this wealth, and that those men were safe who then perished in the broad land of Troy far from horse-pasturing Argos." (*Odyssey* 4.75–99; tr. Murray *LCL*).=

Apparently, Menelaus exemplifies that wealth attracts wealth. Homer tells that Helen continued working her luxury textiles even using a *golden spindle laden with precious black violet woolen yarn* (*Odyssey* 4.133–136).

The implication of the reference to Helen's post-War wealth-generating textile production on the return journey and in Sparta is reinforced by a crucial reference to her weaving *in Troy*. At the precise time of being called to witness the duel for her possession between Paris and Menelaus, Helen was "in the hall, where she was weaving a great purple web of double fold, and thereon was broidering many battles [*athlous* 'efforts, labors, contests' LSJ s.v.] of the horse-taming Trojans and the brazen-coated Achaeans, that for her sake they had endured at the hands of Arēs" (*Iliad* 3.125–128; tr. Murray *LCL*). *Homer had no need to set the duel for beautiful Helen and Helen's innovative weaving in such close proximity unless he wished the two events to be understood as one: it is also Helen the weaver of purpled textiles whom Paris refuses to return.*

Further, it is precisely when Helen is doing textile work that she is called *numphē* 'nymph'. The reference cannot be to her marital status, she is explicitly married, but rather to her profession—that is, to her devotion to weaving valuable textiles. She is placed on the same footing in this respect as the nymphs in *Odyssey* 12 (shepherds of Helios) and those in *Odyssey* 13 (makers of purple-dyed cloth on Ithaca). Homer uses the same mode of communication in *Iliad*

6.321–324: "He (Hector) found Paris in his chamber busied with his beauteous arms, his shield and his corselet, and handling his curved bow; and Argive Helen sat amid her serving-women and appointed to them their glorious handiwork" (tr. Murray *LCL*). Paris is cast as *Wanax* and Helen as Potnia of the Labyrinth.

Helen is of value because of her personal beauty and because of the beauty of the weaving of her crew. Helen is *not* portrayed by Homer at her bath or dressing table where her physical beauty would be emphasized[59] but rather at her weaving where her diligence and skill are emphasized. Hence, I am willing to venture that Helen as beautiful woman is a mythologized reference to Helen as beautiful textile enterprise.

Homer also has Helen demonstrate awareness of her commercial role: by referring to herself as a *dog* (*Iliad* 3.180, 6.344, 356). "Dog," as already explained, (in Chap. 11.2) has the sense of acquisitiveness including commercial acquisitiveness. Helen's connection with dogs and purple persisted into later times. Palaephatus (4th century BCE?), in his *On Unbelievable Tales* 62, says that while Helen was walking on the beach her dog chewed on a shell with the result that his snout had a beautiful purple color; consequently, Helen demanded that each suitor provide a dress dyed with murex-purple.[60] It is quite possible that the entrepreneurial dog is Helen herself and her cult continued to be noted for the production of purple-dyed garments.[61]

d. Helen, Heleneia, and Hyacinth

Historically, Helen's periodic returns to Sparta were apparently celebrated in Therapne's Menelaion with a festival called "Heleneia" about which little is known. Skutch (1987: 189) comments: "We have no definite evidence as to the time of the Heleneia, except that Theocritus [18] says in line 2 that the [celebrant] girls are wearing blooms of hyacinth in their hair so spring seems certain."[62] Thus, that a link is formed between Helen's return and the opening of the navigation season seems assured.

---

[59] The bystanders on the Trojan Wall remark on Helen's "goddess-like" beauty but that is all (*Iliad* 3.154ff.).

[60] A similar story is told about Heracles by lexicographer Pollux *Onomasticon* 1.45–49.

[61] "[P]ossible post-Homeric puns on the name include a fragment of Sosibius (*FGrH* 59 5F 20), of ca. 200 BC, which suggests an image of Helen as the 'corposant' hostile to ships; on the other hand, Euripides (*Or.* 1637) introduces a Helen who is benevolent to sailors" (Kanavou 2015: 72).

[62] The flower worn by the maidens may not have been the one that is called "hyacinth" today (Garlick 19211; Irwin 1990: 214). "Thanks to Sappho we know that the ancient hyacinth has a *porphureon anthos* (105C Lobel-Page, Voigt, *apud* Ath. 15.677F, Meleager 46.3–4 [4237–8 Gow-Page *HE*])" (Griffith 2005: 332; my transliteration). Actually what was worn by the celebrants might not have been a "flower" at all but a purple-dyed headband (Boedeker 1984: 93 citing Petegorsky 1982).

Even more importantly, the hyacinth worn by celebrants links the return of Helen with *purple-dye* (see Chap. 7.6 on the Minoan/Mycenaean festival of flowers = dyed textiles and §5.c above). Note that the Greek adjectives *huakinthos* and compounds in *huakinth-* usually described a color produced by dye that is specifically said to be a purple with more blue content than *porphureus*. (Irwin 1990: 206–207).

Admittedly, this evidence is not from the Linear B tablets or from Homer[63] but it still adds to the body of evidence supporting the hypothesis that Helen's circuits involved the production of purple-dyed textiles.[64]

e. Demand for Helen's return

What was the material content of the Achaean demand for the "return of Helen"? In order to audit this wealth we begin with the terms of the duel between Menelaus and Paris over the return of Helen:

> Rise, thou son of Laomedon, the chieftains of the horse-taming Trojans, and of the brazen-coated Achaeans, summon thee to go down into the plain, that ye may swear oaths of faith with sacrifice. But Alexander and Menelaus, dear to Arēs, will do battle with long spears for the woman's sake; and whichsoever of the twain shall conquer, *him let woman and treasure* (*ktēma*) follow; and we others, swearing friendship and oaths of faith with sacrifice, should then dwell in deep-soiled Troy, but they will depart to Argos, pastureland of horses, and Achaea, the land of fair women. (*Iliad* 3.250ff; tr. Murray *LCL*; emphasis added)

It is clear from these terms that Paris had carried to Troy Helen *and* wealth.

However, neither Homer nor the *Cypria* say that the wealth represents "stolen goods." At no point in the *Iliad* does anyone, including Menelaus, say that Paris took property belonging to him from the palace of Menelaus without his permission. Even Herodotus (2.114.2), although accusing Paris of fraud, does not say that Helen took Menelaus' property with her: "A stranger has come, a Trojan, who has committed an impiety in Hellas. After defrauding his guest-friend, he

---

[63]   In the *Odyssey* when Odysseus arrived naked in Phaeacia Athena made his wooly (*oulos*) hair hyacinth colored.

[64]   It would take us too far afield to discuss the Hyakinthia festival. However, note in this connection report that a "tomb" of Apollo Hyakinthos was located to the south of the port of Taras (Tarentum) in southern Italy (Polybius 8.30). Mycenaean remains have been found just to the east of Taras at Satyrium and the region received Spartan settlers in the eighth century. Taras (Tarentum) was noted in antiquity for its rich murex beds and dye-factories. Source: Silver 1992: 250–254. Cultic circuits and wool are linked in the Agia Triada Sarcophagus by the depiction in Side D of a chariot that is drawn not by horses but by wild goats judging by traces of long horns (Nauert 1965: 92–93). Nauert (1965: 93 with n. 16) considers that chariots drawn by griffin (Side B) and agrimia qualify as the "kannathra" utilized in the Hyacinthia Festival at Amyklai.

has come bringing the man's wife and a very great deal of wealth, driven to your country by the wind. Are we to let him sail away untouched, or are we to take away what he has come with?" (tr. Godley *LCL*). Instead, it is strongly implied that the wealth is Helen's.[65]

Alternatively, perhaps it belonged jointly to Menelaus and Helen. Paris declares:

> "Howbeit I will speak amid the gathering of horse-taming Trojans and declare outright: my wife will I not give back; *but the treasure that I brought from Argos to our (ēmeteros) home*, all this am I minded to give, and to add thereto from mine own store."... At dawn Idaeus [the Herald] went his way to the hollow ships. There he found in the place of gathering the Danaans, squires of Arēs, beside the stern of Agamemnon's ship; and the loud-voiced herald took his stand in the midst and spake among them: "Son of Atreus, and ye other princes of the hosts of Achaea, Priam and the other lordly Trojans bade me declare to you—if haply it be your wish and your good pleasure—the saying of Alexander, for whose sake strife hath been set afoot. The treasure that Alexander brought to Troy in his hollow ships—would that he had perished first!— all this he is minded to give, and to add thereto from his own store; but the wedded wife of glorious Menelaus, he declares he will not give; though verily the Trojans bid him do it." (*Iliad* 7.362–364, 392–394; tr. Murray *LCL*; emphasis added)

A revealing aspect of this report is that Paris says that the wealth was brought from Menelaus' house to "*our (ēmeteros) home.*" Ordinarily the property ascribed to a Greek *oikos* belonged to the husband not jointly by husband and wife. Helen in Troy certainly had wealth of her own and in this wealth we are entitled to include the marriage/partnership "gifts" that Helen received from Menelaus and from Paris.

To move beyond this we must I think recall the status of Neaira cited in part *a* of this Section: My understanding is that under the terms of the arbitration Neaira *regained* the legal status of woman "in her own hands" (*autē hautēs kuria*). The property Neaira agreed to return to Phrynion's must have been her

---

[65] In the *Iliad*: "Helen and all her possessions" (3.70; 3.90f, 255f. "woman and treasure"; cf. 3.82 3.458); 22.114–115: "Helen, and with her all the store of treasure that Alexander brought in his hollow ships to Troy"; 13.626–627, Menelaus accuses the Trojans: "For ye bare forth wantonly over sea my wedded wife and therewithal much treasure, when it was with her that ye had found entertainment" (tr. Murray *LCL*; cf. *Iliad* 7.350, 362ff., 368ff.). According to the summary of the *Cypria* by Proclus, Helen took much property (*ktēma*) with her when she left Sparta and accompanied Paris to Sidon and then Troy.

peculium from him.[66] Paris offered to return Helen's *peculium* from Menelaus. The gifts he gave to Helen prior to departing from Sparta constituted Paris' *peculium*. I interpret the additional wealth Paris offered as the Greek syndicate's share of the current earnings of the Helen enterprise. Paris refused to return Helen the wife/Helen the enterprise who had produced the additional wealth. That is, Paris intended to retain Helen's future earnings, not share with the Achaeans.

The mystery of what was in the holds of Paris' newly constructed ships remains. I think that there is value in my materialist interpretation but I am not yet satisfied with my analysis of a Helen enterprise. There is much evidence for a Helen textile enterprise but also there are important missing clues. Part of the problem is that we have been given only the Achaean side of a business dispute.

6. Helen, Hera, and the Argives: A Speculative Interpretation

But what in all of the negotiation and strife between Trojans and Achaeans is the relevance of "Argos"/"Argive"? In Homer, the most frequent epithet of Helen is "the Argive" (9x *Iliad*; 4x *Odyssey*). This designation is used despite her coming from Sparta which would make her "Laconian" (Edmunds 2019: 40). Also, the Greeks besieging Troy are sometimes designated as "Argives" or as leaving from Argos are from/departed from all over the Greek mainland and Crete.

Edmunds (2019: 42) thinks "Argive" is a matter of nomenclature: "In the *Odyssey*, however, the significance of 'Argive' has changed." Because the Achaeans are no longer assembled in a single place and working together toward a common end, there is no longer a need for a single word to describe the many peoples of Greece and distinguish them from a foreign enemy. 'Argive' is used only to recall the Achaeans at Troy." The geography of "Argos" is very confusing, but it is most doubtful that Homer's "Argive" is strictly a geographic designation.

My view, deduced in part from the epithet "Argive" and in part from her extreme pro-Achaean behavior is that the negotiation and contractual oaths sworn by Paris and his colleagues and their Greek counterparts: (a) took place in (Achaean) Argos; and (b) took place under Hera's auspices.

That international businesspersons would meet in Argos makes logistical sense as the Gulf of Argos and the route to Anatolia are easily accessible from

---

[66] Although, the term *peculium* is Latin, it is clear that heroic and classical Greece knew slaves with significant personal assets. Take for example, Eumaeus, the purchased swineherd in *Odyssey* 4.115, 14.452. In classical Greece, the best attested example is, of course, Neaira (Demosthenes 59.30–31, 45–46, 49). Fragment 142 of Euripides's *Andromeda* explicitly refers to a wealthy slave (Silver 2018: 128 modified).

the Argive plain (Tomlinson 1972: 7ff.).[67] The Lydian warrior Glaucus gives his golden armor in exchange (*ameibō*) for the bronze armor worn by King Diomedes of Argos (*Iliad* 6.116–240). Homer (the narrator) thinks that Glaucus lost his senses in making this "unbalanced" exchange. However, the name Glaucus offers testimony to the economic importance of Argos and to Glaucus' possible motivation. *Glaukos* means "(with no color) Bright" but also "(of the sea) Bluish Green or Gray" (Beekes s.v.). The name "Bright" (in the sense of "Alert") suggests an entrepreneurial capacity but also there is an interest in the sea (perhaps to the depths inhabited by murex snails). My interpretation is that the overpayment by Glaucus was intended to place Diomedes "Zeus-counselled" (LSJ) in moral debt to him at a time when a properly sponsored visit to Argos might earn the visitor immense economic returns.[68] Glaucus did not lose his senses except perhaps in the sense that he overestimated what Diomedes could do for him.[69]

However, there may be a more specific reason having to do with textiles for the importance of Argos and for a Helen enterprise in particular. As already noted in Chapter 3, by reasoning from pictorial themes on exported Mycenaean pottery in Rhodes and elsewhere, Barber (2016: 229) has theorized that Mycenaean weaving sought to depict real objects and scenes "rather than merely trying to cover the cloth with a pleasing pattern." Barber (2016: 229–230) adds:

> Technical analyses have demonstrated that all the Mycenaean-looking pottery on Rhodes in the LH IIIA and IIIB periods was in fact imported from the mainland, and specifically from the Argolid, and that in Cyprus at least the chariot kraters, along with much else, were imports from there too. So if we are looking to Rhodes and Cyprus for such fancy textiles as may have inspired this pottery, we will need to look

---

[67] Of course, Pelasgian Argos, mentioned in *Iliad*, 2.681, which refers to Thessaly is also a very good candidate in respect to positioning for trade with Anatolia. I leave aside the question of why "Argos" (Achaean or Pelasgian) is named "Argos" but see Bailey (1959: 93) on the significance of the *ar*-stem.

[68] In the background of the exchange of armor between Glaucus and Diomedes is an exchange between Glaucus' ancestor Bellerophon, an Argive who wandered to Lycia, and his Argive host Oeneus, the father of Diomedes: Oeneus gave a *purple-dyed belt* and received a *gold cup* from Bellerophon (*Iliad* 6.215–221).

[69] Wagner-Hasel (2020: 104) explains the unbalanced exchange in terms of status inversion: "The arms-exchange inverts the principles of status and achievement, and the final comment on its inequality shows that this inversion is established knowingly by the poet. The genealogically inferior man [Diomedes], who is thus also subordinate in terms of the unity between status and success in battle, receives the gold armour. The genealogically superior man [Glaucus], who is also the stronger in battle, makes do with the bronze armour." I do not believe this is an *explanation*.

right back to the mainland, to the Argolid, where we thought all the textiles were plain.

This reasoning suggests that, as revealed by its pottery (Demakopoulou and J. Crouwel 1992; Steel 1998), the *Argolid*, including the Argive Heraion, was the dynamic center for the production of new textiles featuring representational art. Moreover, as Homer (*Iliad* 3.125–128) reveals, *Helen* excelled in precisely this kind of weaving. Barber's theory provides good reason why Paris went to the Argolid and negotiated for Helen.

With respect to Hera, my hypothesis is that the negotiations for the transfer of Helen took place in an Argive Heraion[70] under the auspices of Argive Hera (*Iliad* 4.8 = 5.908). *Thus, the Achaeans besieging Troy would be "Argives" in the sense that they came to Troy on behalf of an agreement negotiated and sworn before in Argos before Hera.* Similarly, Helen is the "Argive" in the sense that she came to Troy under the terms of an agreement negotiated before Argive Hera.[71]

That Hera would have been relied upon by diverse Achaean groupings to perform a sensitive international role finds support in Hera's profession: "Verily have I three cities that are far dearest in my sight, Argos and Sparta and broad-wayed Mycenae" (*Iliad* 4.50–52; tr. Murray *LCL*). Greek gods did not love mortals who did not love them. That Hera was very early worshipped in Anatolia is confirmed by the credit given her for aiding the Argo to penetrate to the Black Sea (*Odyssey* 12.70–72). Hera in the Argive Heraion was trusted by all the negotiators.

When Paris reneges on the return of Helen, Hera, in my hypothesis the sponsor of the agreement, is on the verge of becoming a useless goddess—one who could neither bind nor punish those (the Trojan negotiators) who had falsified their oaths taken before her. Argive Hera protected Argos, Sparta, and Mycenae but, more importantly, she protected herself.[72] It is Hera, desperate to preserve her status, who issues the call for the Greeks expedition to Troy; she

---

[70] The temple would have been located in or near Prosymna, a site with prominent remains from the Bronze Age (Antonaccio 1992).

[71] Support for my acquisition of capital or even shareholder interpretation of Helen's negotiated transfer to Paris is provided by the fact that the (previously discussed) possessions Helen took with her to Troy "are twice connected with her Argive identity (*Iliad* 3.458, 7.350)" (Edmunds 2019: 40). With respect to Hera's sponsorship of an Achaean-Trojan commercial venture, note also that in Hesiod (*Theogony* 313–318) Hera is said to have "nourished" the Hydra, see serpent, whom Heracles defeated at Lerna in the coastal Argolid (see Chap. 9.6).

[72] Perhaps as a "potnia" (Chap. 6.2) "Hera of the Golden Throne" (*Iliad* 14.153) was also legally liable under the terms of the contract.

who multiple times risks the wrath of Zeus to protect the Achaean expeditionaries, and she who rallies the Achaeans when their spirits wane:[73]

> Then would the Argives have accomplished their return even beyond
> what was ordained, had not *Hera* spoken a word to Athena, saying:
> "Out upon it, child of Zeus that beareth the aegis, unwearied one! Is it
> thus indeed that the Argives are to flee to their dear native land over
> the broad back of the sea? Aye, and they would leave to *Priam and the
> Trojans their boast*, even Argive Helen, for whose sake many an Achaean
> hath perished in Troy, far from his dear native land. But go thou now
> throughout the host of the brazen-coated Achaeans; with thy gentle
> words seek thou to restrain every man, neither suffer them to draw into
> the sea their curved ships." (*Iliad* 2.155–165; tr. Murray *LCL*; emphasis
> added)

Here, it seems to Hera that the Trojan ruling class, not just Paris, was determined to keep Helen and merited punishment.

My hypothesis, namely that the previous negotiations had been sanctified
by Hera, would be sufficient to explain her leading role in the opposition to
Troy. That is, Hera's hostility to Troy is explained without resort to her being

---

[73] Agamemnon fears that his wounded brother will die, causing the Achaeans to abandon Troy
and "Argive Helen" (*Iliad* 4.174). Edmunds (2019: 42) notes that this may mean that Helen
belongs only to Menelaus, which would indeed fit the usual interpretation that has Helen and
the property as belonging only to Menelaus. However, Edmunds (2019: 42 n. 9) explains: "But
the passages discussed here can also be taken to mean that the Achaeans have a national claim
to Helen. For the accusative form of the formula here and at 2.161 = 177 as a 'pendant runover'
see Tsagalis (2008: 45–46)." Again, the point is that the Achaeans are involved precisely because
they have a joint interest in the project of recovering Helen. They have a joint interest because
they invested as a group in Helen's textile enterprise with Paris. This conclusion seems to find
support in a study by Oikonomaki (2018: 37–38): "Achaioi is statistically the predominant term in
the Homeric epics and seems to be the most general unmarked term as it corresponds to many
different categories, for example the warriors in the Trojan War and the inhabitants of specific
regions of the Greek world. Argeioi and Danaoi symbolize mostly the warriors of Troy and in the
Odyssey are linked with the heroic past of the Odyssean heroes. Even though sometimes these
terms are mutually interchangeable, as they cannot be distinguished from one another, I hope
to have shown that the poet often intends to apply them in a distinctive manner in particular
contexts to produce meaning and that the criterion of their differentiation is not mainly their
ethnic determined characteristics, for he probably does not have in his mind a coherent perception of the historical background. Many times in the *Iliad* and the *Odyssey* the epic poet ascribes
to every ethnic group different qualities, which are contextually determined, in order to draw
attention and produce meaning. Even though sometimes each term overlaps the other, they are
not always used haphazardly, but they have a functional role in the poems, sometimes distinct
in the *Iliad* and the *Odyssey*. In this textual world carefully constructed by the epic poet these
names are associated with certain characteristics of the heroic world and, finally, shed light on
a character, a fact, or an action. This conclusion reassesses the significance of the three names,
but of course more remain to be explored in the light of contextual and metrical analysis."

mortified by not being chosen by Paris in a "Beauty Contest" on Mt. Ida.[74] As suggested earlier, the "Gathering of Gods" on Mt. Ida explored the feasibility of a commercial project involving the Helen enterprise. Hera hated Paris (and the Trojans) because when he violated his oath to her (and Athena) he inflicted ἄτη (*Iliad* 24.28; cf. 6.356); a word that can be rendered as "damage (the reputation)"[75] (Beekes s.v) that includes also the reaction to being damaged (Wyatt 1982: 247 who cites the verb *aaō* 'to damage').

I realize that many scholars will regard my hypothesis to be redundant, but my explanation has the advantage of incorporating the evidence provided in Homer and the *Cypria* of a *negotiation* for possession of Helen including Aphrodite's role as a sponsor of Paris' mission. In addition, it offers an explanation for the centrality of "Argive." The "Beauty Contest," it will be recalled, was held on Mt. Ida not in Argos.[76]

The indignation of the "damaged" Hera and her resulting wrath is fully understandable if we accept that Hera was a *participant* in the agreement to send Helen to Troy. In the prologue of Euripides' *Helen* (31–36) we find: "But Hera, indignant at not defeating the goddesses, made an airy nothing of my [Helen's] marriage with Paris [created out of the wind]; she gave to the son of king Priam not me, but an image (*eidōlon*), alive and breathing, that she fashioned out of the sky and made to look like me; and he thinks he has me—an idle fancy, for he doesn't have me" (tr. Coleridge *Perseus Project*). Hera is a direct participant in

---

[74] Homer (*Iliad* 24.25–30): "And the thing was pleasing unto all the rest, yet not unto Hera or Poseidon or the flashing-eyed maiden, but they continued even as when at the first sacred Ilios became hateful in their eyes and Priam and his folk, by reason of the sin of Alexander, for that he put reproach upon those goddesses when they came to his steading, and gave precedence to her who furthered his fatal lustfulness" (tr. Murray *LCL*). The translation of 29–30 raises problems. Proclus' "Summary of the *Cypria*" refers to the "Judgment" as follows: "Paris judges Aphrodite to be the prize-winner, excited at the prospect of union with Helen" (tr. M. Davies 2019: 73). No one can second-guess a goddess, but Hera's reaction is disproportionate to Paris' crime. The crime is not in choosing Helen but in not returning her, as he must have promised. My hypothesis does not, however, explain the opposition of Athena to Troy. I have suggested that Athena should be identified with Potnia of the Labyrinth. If correct, then Athena would naturally have been drawn to Argos as a textile-export center. The only trace of this interest is the otherwise unexplained, but very pronounced, special interest of Athena and the "dog-minded" Diomedes and his father Tydeus. For example, in *Iliad* 4.389–390; 5.1–2, 8, 114–121, 122, 123–133, 792–834, 855–859; 10.482–522, 552–553, 570–579.

[75] This sense is clear in the damage done by Agamemnon to Achilles in seizing the prize awarded to him by the Achaeans. The word has the secondary sense of legal damage including a fine as in the Gortyn Law Code (e.g., 11.34).

[76] See §5.b above. The "Judgment of Paris" "explains" the mortification and hostility of Hera and Athena but not that of Poseidon (*Iliad* 24.25–30). Is the latter god still angry at Laomedon's for his refusal to pay him for building the Trojan Wall or is it Priam/Paris whose refusal to return Helen ultimately cost him his hecatombs? Apparently, Apollo had gotten over his anger at Laomedon for cheating him.

the negotiations to send the Helen enterprise to Troy with Paris. The meaning is that Hera invested in the enterprise by sending a unit of the Helen cult headed by one of her cult statues.[77] Of course, Helen (the audience) knows very well that her parent cult guarantees that one Helen is as beautiful as the next. The "Beauty Contest" framework is trivialized[78] by making it the vehicle for a humorous reference to a standard cultic practice—the possession of multiple images of the deity.[79] However, the deeper implication is that Hera, not Zeus (see above), had administrative control over the cult of Helen. Sending an "image"/"likeness" of Helen means that Hera sent her *agent* to Troy. The best supporting evidence for this interpretation comes from the early second millennium Old Assyrian trade with Cappadocia. In this context, the expression "*sha kīma (PN)*," 'representative of PN' but literally means "likeness of PN" (*CAD* s.v. *kīma*). Obviously, Hera would be indignant if Paris refused to return her agent. In addition, that Hera was a participant and, indeed, sponsor of the negotiations might better explain Hera's zeal to punish the Trojans but also how the Achaeans acquired the capital to launch so ambitious a campaign against the Trojans.

By way of postscript, Homer and the *Cypria* provide reason to believe that there was a negotiation over Helen resulting in her legal transfer to the Trojans group for a *limited duration*. Helen was to focus on production of luxury textiles for the benefit of the Trojan and Argive syndicate operating from Troy. It is also made obvious that Menelaus was enabled to become even wealthier by retaking Helen from the Trojans and having her with him on the return journey. Otherwise, many questions about Helen remain unanswered. What is answered

---

[77]   Note Smoot's (2012) observation that "the peploi Helen wears, which Alexandros brought back from Phoenicia, sets her in the same typology as the peplos worn by statues, images of goddesses." Note also Smoot's (2012) observation that in the *Iliad* "the Achaeans and the Trojans fight over a fake double of Aineias fashioned by Apollo (*Iliad* 5.445–454)." Euripides' obscure references to "wind" and "breath" may be references to the animation of a cult statue.

[78]   The "Beauty Contest" was actually a "Gathering of Gods" (Aphrodite, Athena, Hera, Hermes, and Zeus) for determining the feasibility of an important commercial project. The commercial aspect is signaled by the participation of Hermes rather than Iris.

[79]   For the use of multiple cultic images, see Silver (2019: 112 n. 69). The innovation that "not Helen but an *eidōlon*" accompanied Paris to Troy is often attributed to Stesichorus (*Papyrus Oxyrhynchus* 2506, 26 col. I = Stesichorus fragment 193 Davies/Page). As Smoot (2012 modified) observes: "A fifth reason for not thinking that Stesichorus invented the story of Helen's double is simply the fact that he was reportedly not the first author to mention it: according to the scholiast on Lycophron 822, Hesiod was the first to introduce Helen's *eidōlon*.... Merkelbach and West assign this to Hesiod's *Fragmenta Dubia* (358), but their grounds for skepticism are shaky in light of the aforementioned four reasons. Moreover, as Gregory Nagy [1992: 36ff.] has argued one may construe the Hesiodic label (and the alternative Homeric label as well) not so much as reflecting a historical author as the crystallization and canonization of oral epic traditions that either seek or have attained Panhellenic prestige. Thus, the scholiast's assertion that Hesiod was the first to introduce Helen's double may simply mean that this story had once been widespread in early archaic Greece." I respectfully disagree with this understanding.

by what we know about Helen and, much more, about the Achaean Wall, and about "Agamemnon's Purple Portent" is that Homer's Trojan War is a commercial war. This explanation stands out among the many unexplained and perhaps unexplainable features of the Epics.

7. Aftermath of a Commercial War: From Achaean to Ahhiyawan

In Part III the fate of Troy was considered mainly in the perspective of archaeological evidence. In this Section, reliance is placed on evidence from Homeric Epic.

In previously unappreciated passages, the *Iliad* strongly testifies to the historical reality of the Trojan War and to its underlying commercial causation.[80] First, that the Achaeans had a prior relationship with the Trojans is signaled by the cultic circuit of Helen between Greece and Troy, the completion of which apparently involved a transfer of wealth that had been kept under Helen's auspices. The War was not fought simply to return a very beautiful woman but also a very wealthy woman. The themes of the building of the Achaean Wall and of Agamemnon's holding of a purple cloak reveal the economic underpinnings of the War. There would have been no need to insert such crass themes into a fictional poetic account of a war fought by great heroes.

Homer shows us great heroes but also subtly that they are motivated by glory and fame in the form of material wealth. The same motive probably applies to all Homer's gods and certainly to Arēs, Aphrodite, and Poseidon. We

---

[80]   The Trojan War is not Greece's sole Bronze Age commercial war. Hesiod (*Works & Days*) alludes to a still earlier fight for material gain: "Demi-gods, the race before our own, throughout the boundless earth. Grim war and dread battle destroyed a part of them, *some in the land of Cadmus at seven-gated Thebes when they fought for the flocks of Oedipus*, and some, when it had brought them in ships over the great sea gulf to Troy for rich-haired Helen's sake: there death's end enshrouded a part of them" (lines 160–165; tr. Evelyn-White; emphasis added). Fighting for possession of "beautiful Helen" and fighting for possession of the "flocks" ("gold") may be seen as comparable activities/objectives for the "race of heroes." Helen is the *mēla* that Eris instigated the heroes to strive for (Apollodorus *Epitome* 3.2; M. Davies 2019: 48–57). What a pity that no ancient author provided details about this struggle "for the flocks of Oedipus" (but see Cingano 1992: esp. 7–8). Reflecting ancient Near Eastern sources, the *Cypria* and post-Homeric sources attribute to Zeus a plan to destroy an *asebeia* 'impious' heroic race. This theme can be understood as a reference to prosperous populations which disturb a god with their "noisy" striving to make themselves immortal—that is, to become wealthy/rich in gold like gods (see Silver 1995b: 181–182). Alternatively, the growth in population that weighed so heavily on Earth [*Cypria* (F 1)] resulted from economic growth due to the striving for wealth. Consistently with this line of interpretation, Hesiod (*Fragment* 96) links the Trojan War to seafaring for gain (West 1961: 133–134; M. Davies 2019: esp. 22–24; Scodel 1982). *Homer was certainly aware that his heroes are materialistically motivated. Helen is precisely such a symbol.* In the context of their building the wealth-motivated Achaean Wall, he refers to the Achaeans as *ēmitheoi* (*Iliad* 12.23)—humans that are like gods. A new element is that the Hesiod Fragment portrays Apollo, who misunderstood Zeus' plan, as an enlightened champion of trade as a benefit to humanity.

are explicitly shown the gains resulting from trade relationships conducted under the protection of the Achaean Wall by the arrival of the fleet of Jason's "son" Euneos and by the gifts rendered to Agamemnon by Achaean traders. Agamemnon's holding[81] the purple cloak in front of Odysseus' capacious ship testifies directly that the Achaean expedition was motivated by the sale of purple-dyed textiles for gold. The centrality of the Black Sea region and trade in luxury textiles is made clear by the centrality in the Epic of Troy itself but also in other ways such as the otherwise unnecessary references of the epic voyage of the Argonauts to the Black Sea.

The building of the formidable "Achaean Wall" arguably signals that the Greeks were preparing for a long and profitable stay in the Troad. Therefore, we should not look for destruction and desertion of Troy by the Achaean victors. Had they as victors left the city destroyed and deserted, they would have foregone the profit available from taking control over access for themselves. Troy was simply too valuable a property to be left to lie fallow; *someone* would have rebuilt it to the dismay of the Mycenaeans.

However, Homer (*Iliad* 12.14, 16) reveals in a "flash forward"[82] that after the sack (*perthō*) of Troy but before the Achaean Wall was destroyed (*amalounō*), "the Argives had gone back in their ships to their dear native land." However, since I accept: (1) the Trojan War was a commercial war; (2) the strategic and tactical savvy of the Achaeans; (3) the archaeological identification of Hisarlik in the Troad with Troy; and (4) the identification of Ahhiyawa (probably) in the Troad as a Mycenaean kingdom, I cannot accept Homer's statement at face value. Moreover, Homer's statement raises problems of internal consistency. Specifically, as promised by Zeus, Poseidon destroys the Achaean Wall that had so undermined his "fame" as builder (with Apollo) of Troy's walls (see above). This act of destruction is pointless if Troy's walls were destroyed much earlier when the Achaeans departed.[83] At no point does Poseidon agree to the loss of the "hecatombs"—that is, the loss of material goods due him as builder of Troy's walls. No, the Achaean Wall is certain to be destroyed because the victorious Achaeans will move into Troy and Poseidon will again receive his due and, more importantly, keep his access to the Black Sea cloth trade.

While being entertained in Phaeacia Odysseus requests the bard Demodocus to sing about the fall of Troy:

---

[81]   Agamemnon is not said to be "waving" or even "raising" the purple cloak, but the entire point of his action would be lost unless it was made quite clear to all what he was "holding."

[82]   Pache (2016: 294) notes a remarkable fact: "The conversation between Poseidon and Zeus takes place as the wall is in the process of being finished, and so the audience learns of its future destruction before its completion in the narrative."

[83]   In *Iliad* 12.10–12 there is a fluctuation in timing: the Wall will be destroyed not when the city is taken and sacked but *ten years* after the Achaeans departed.

So he spoke, and the minstrel, moved by the god, began, and let his song be heard, taking up the tale where the Argives had embarked on their benched ships and were sailing away, after casting fire on their huts, while those others led by glorious Odysseus were now sitting in the place of assembly of the Trojans, hidden in the horse; for the Trojans had themselves dragged it to the citadel. So there it stood, while the people talked long as they sat about it, and could form no resolve. Nay, in three ways did counsel find favour in their minds: either to cleave the hollow timber with the pitiless bronze, or to drag it to the height and cast it down the rocks, or to let it stand as a great offering to propitiate the gods, *even as in the end it was to be brought to pass; for it was their fate to perish when their city should enclose the great horse of wood*, wherein were sitting all the best of the Argives, bearing to the Trojans death and fate. (*Odyssey* 8.499–514; tr. Murray *LCL*; emphasis added)

I understand Demodocus' song to mean that Troy was not destroyed in the immediate aftermath of its conquest by the Greeks. Instead, the Great Wooden Horse was exhibited in the continuing city as a monument with destruction to take place subsequently if and when the Horse was enclosed/covered. In the worship of the Horse one may see the presence of the Poseidon cult.[84] Poseidon granted a conditional reprieve to Troy.

However, the Achaeans could have continued to control Troy only if they had sent in replacements for their departed warriors. According to Proclus' "Summary of the *Little Iliad*" (*Ilias parua* page 107, lines 12–14, 22–31), after the success of the Trojan Horse, the leading Trojans were purged and replaced by

---

[84] Segal (1962: 32) makes an important supplementary observation concerning some terminology in the Song of Demodocus: "[T]he verb *amphikaluptein* is used four times in close succession of the 'covering over' of the Phaeacian island by a mountain (13.152, 158, 177, 183; also 8.569), but it is employed also, somewhat strangely, in Demodocus' song of the fate of Troy" (my transliteration). Covering with a mountain sounds like natural destruction which is consistent with the archaeological evidence considered in Part III. There is more. In the prophecy of Phaeacian destruction it is Poseidon who will cover the Phaeacians with the mountain because of their aid in transporting all comers without his permission (see below). Is the point that Poseidon *Hippeos* will destroy Troy for covering Poseidon the Horse? Hippios "Horse" is not an epithet of Poseidon in Homer, but in *Iliad* 13.11–16 the god resorts to his palace beneath the sea where he harnesses his horses to a chariot and drives across the sea. Poseidon is, however, described as *kuanochaita* in *Iliad* 20.144 and *Odyssey* 9.536 and the same term is applied to a horse in *Iliad* 20.224: hence, Poseidon is "black-maned" (Maitland 1999: 1) but better (and more significantly) "*blue-maned*" (Griffith 2005). Also, in the *Iliad*, the Trojans are collectively identified as *hippodamoi* typically rendered as "tamers of horses" (e.g. 3.127). In Homer, Poseidon is referred to as *Enosichthōn* "Earthshaker" (and similar terms) including in *Iliad* 7.445 where he complains to Zeus about the construction of the Achaean Wall (Maitland 1999: 1 with n. 3). Consequently, there is ample evidence of Homer linking Poseidon with horses and earthquakes and Troy with Poseidon.

the Achaeans who escorted the Horse and, more importantly, by a contingent under Sinon who sailed to Troy from Tenedos.[85] Also, perhaps the account of the belated arrival in Troy of Philoctetes, who had been left behind by the Achaeans at Lemnos, is meant to tell us about a step in the formation of an Achaean state based in Troy. "There [in Lemnos] he lay suffering; yet full soon were the Argives beside their ships to bethink them of king Philoctetes" (*Iliad* 2.720–721; tr. Murray *LCL*). In *Iliad* 2.719–720, Philoctetes and his forces are specifically described as skilled archers (cf. *Odyssey* 8.219–220). The bow had been the weapon of choice for the Trojans because they are typically stationed on walls at arrow loops or on either side of gates (see Mackie 2009: 6). With the victory, it became, even if only temporarily, the weapon of choice for the troops of the Achaeans—that is, of Philoctetes' troops. "Temporarily" because Nestor (in *Odyssey* 3.190) says that Philoctetes arrived safely home after the War.

There are still deeper currents, however. Proclus' "Summary of the *Little Iliad*" (page 107, lines 12–14, 22–31) explains that the Trojans destroyed part of their wall to let the Horse inside and then celebrated a festival. The theme of destruction of Troy's wall to accommodate the Horse and celebration of a festival bring to mind the (previously discussed) song of the bard Demodocus. Further, according to several later mythographers, Aeneas (or Aeneas and the Dardanian Antēnōr) rebelled successfully against Priam and Paris. Specifically, in the fourth century BCE, Menecrates of Xanthus[86] claimed that Aeneas rebelled and "become one of the Achaioi"[87] (tr. Cary *LCL*; discussion Fowler 2013, II: 563). An internal uprising in Troy would explain the destruction of the Wall and the festival in honor of the triumphant Horse = Poseidon. That something like a revolt or a coup occurred is confirmed in the *Iliad* (20.290) when Poseidon first saves Aeneas from death at the hands of Achilles and follows immediately with a striking prophecy: "For at length hath the son of Cronos come to hate the race of Priam; and now verily shall the mighty Aeneas be *king among the Trojans*, and his sons' sons that shall be born in days to come" (20.307–308 tr. Murray *LCL*). Homer does not explicitly say that Aeneas will rule the Trojans

---

[85] However, in Proclus' "Summary of the *Ilou Persis*" it seems that all the Achaeans depart after the victory. There is perhaps a problem in that Proclus' "Summary of the *Nostoi*" begins with an argument between Agamemnon and Menelaus about the voyage home from Troy. There is no explicit statement that thereafter all the Greeks left but this seems possible.

[86] Quoted by Dionysius of Halicarnassus *Roman Antiquities* 1.48.3 = *Fragments of Greek History* 769 Fragment 3.

[87] An interesting formulation in that, as mentioned earlier, *a-ka-wi-ja-de* 'for the Achaiwia' (KN C 2 914) arguably refers to a celebration held by an *association*, not necessarily a single ethnic group (see further below). The greatest archer among the Achaeans at Troy is the *nothos* 'bastard' half-brother of the greater Ajax (8.284) whose Greek name, Teukros/Teucer, means "the Trojan" (Andrews 1965: 33, 36–37). The "Trojan" was an Achaean.

within Troy as well as in the Troad. This understanding of "leader/king" *anaxes* 'among the Trojans' is reasonable given that "Trojans" certainly refers to the residents of Troy and, further, that as a *Dardanian*, not as Trojan, Aeneas' house was already established in the Troad. Thus, Homer does not make him leader of the Dardanians, which would be redundant but leader of Troy, which was not. Aeneas not only survived the Achaean victory but also he was promoted to the position that had been held by Priam (called "Dardanides")!

The *Iliad* would not portray Poseidon as a false prophet especially with regard to matter of such importance.[88] Thus, our primary source believes and testifies that (the new) Achaean Aeneas ruled Troy/the Troad after the Trojan War. Further Aphrodite makes the same prophecy in the *Homeric Hymn to Aphrodite* (5.193–202): "Then Aphrodite the daughter of Zeus answered him: 'Anchises, most glorious of mortal men, take courage and be not too fearful in your heart. You need fear no harm from me nor from the other blessed ones, for you are dear to the gods: and you shall have a dear son who shall reign among the Trojans, and children's children after him, springing up continually. His name shall be Aeneas [*Iliad* 2.819, 20.209], because I felt awful grief in that I laid me in the bed of a mortal man: yet are those of your race always the most like to gods of all mortal men in beauty and in stature'" (tr. Evelyn-White *LCL*).

Thus, in the Iliad Troy is not destroyed by Agamemnon. Instead, Aeneas, the leader of the Dardanians, rules it as an Achaean. There would be no reason for the poet to insert matter-of-fact information of this sort if the Trojan War was completely fictional. That Proclus' "Summary of the *Little Iliad*" has Aeneas and his followers escaping or being exiled from Troy may be regarded as a minor difficulty. The more interesting problem is how the Aphrodite and Poseidon cults maneuvered these waters.

I understand that Homer's ending in the *Iliad* is an ending that not only provides closure but also readies the stage for the *nostoi*. So perhaps Homer employed some misdirection. The Great Wooden Horse remained behind with Achaeans inside when the Achaeans sailed away for home and the Achaean Wall was (at some point) demolished. Troy, however, remained intact and arguably formed the base for the Ahhiyawan kingdom. A Troy surviving into the palatial period is supported by references in Linear B tablets. Palaima (2010: 72) notes *to-ro-wo* "Troy" in three palatial centers Thebes, Knossos, and Pylos: (TH Gp 164, KN Ag 89, PY An 129, Vn 130) and the personal name *Trōs*, *Trōwos* "the Trojan" or *Tlōs*.

---

[88] In *Iliad* 13.458–461 Aeneas hangs back from the battle because, as the narrator explains, he is not honored by Priam. Thus, Poseidon's prophecy is not completely isolated in the original Homeric account (Scafoglio 2013).

The time has come to return to issues raised earlier concerning the *denominations* of the Greek forces besieging Troy in the *Iliad*. The latter terms, Achaeans, Argives, and Danaans (Chaps. 12.2, 4), perhaps represent different ways of looking at the origin or motivation of the Greeks. Most obviously, "Argives" refers to the Greek invaders in terms of the place Argos (or the Argive Heraion) where they negotiated and swore to abide by a commercial agreement conveying the "Helen enterprise" from Laconia to Troy. *The "Argives" are the Greek contractors.* "Achaeans" refers to the Greek invaders in terms of their vow to avenge the violation of the commercial agreement by the Trojans. *The "Achaeans" from achos are the indignant Greek contractors.* The best I can offer for "Danaans" is that it refers to the subset of Achaeans/Argives with elite status—they are the leading warriors and traders (*Odyssey* 11.559, 24.81; *Iliad* 1.90–91).[89]

8. Postscript

With the exception of the possible desertion of Troy the findings developed above are those predicted by a materialist interpretation of a real war fought to control commercial access to the Black Sea. This brings us face-to-face with a challenge raised by Kirk (1990: 36–37):

> The *Iliad* after all, is more than anything else a great drama, concerned with people and feelings rather than concrete environmental or historical background as such. Some critics even resent attention being paid to the material aspects of the poem, or expect them to be excluded from ordinary commentaries and confined to archaeological handbooks. That is absurd, if only because human affairs are affected by external circumstances and the concrete controls on behavior; moreover both singers and early audiences clearly devoted careful attention to these matters. But, leaving that aside, can it really be said that historical accuracy affects literary quality in any serious way?

I agree with Kirk with the exception that I do think historical accuracy affects literary quality. My view is that it is a much greater achievement to create a great drama while maintaining basic historical accuracy than to create a work of complete fiction. I think Homer was aware of this difference and proud of his achievement. That is why the poet exerted himself to provide clues, or better to leave many "words for the wise." He reminds the audience that his tragic Achilles was even greater for having to fit into a historical framework.

---

[89] For a more conventional discussion of the three denominations, see Oikonomaki (2018).

15

Homeric Heroes and Gods as Participants in the Cloth Trade

1. Odysseus: Predicting His Role from His Name and Genealogy

THE name *Odysseus*, or *Olysseus*, bears the "stamp of antiquity" (West 1992: 159, cf. 2014: 6). Although not the name itself, the ending *-eus* is found in the Linear B tablets. West (2014: 7 with n. 7) notes that the divergence of the *d* and *l* forms of the name are not explained by any normal dialect development and he finds credible the view that the name is not only old but also pre-Greek. Some recent scholars have pointed to evidence of variation between *d* and *l* in Anatolian languages.

Kanavou (2015: 98) has discussed the spelling problem at some length:

> There are different spellings of the name, some of which have λ instead of δ: 'Ολισεύς, the standard spelling of the Korinthian form, appears on vase inscriptions since the late seventh century BC, and there follow the Attic form 'Ολυτ(τ)εύς in the early sixth century, and the Boeotian 'Ολυσεύς in the late sixth century. The 'standard' form 'Οδυσ(σ)εύς is not epigraphically attested until the mid-sixth century, but it certainly was dominant by the mid-fifth, when the form with λ became extinct in Greek (it was preferred in Etruscan and then in Latin).

Kanavou (2015: 99) agrees with West about a pre-Hellenic origin of the λ form of the name:

> As far as 'scientific' etymology is concerned, the forms with λ suggest a strong case for a pre-Hellenic origin of the name. 'Ολυ- (Olympos, Olynthos) and σσ- are thought to be pre-Greek elements. Linguistic evidence reinforces the possibility of a proto-name for Odysseus, which suits the hero's alleged great antiquity. As Odysseus clearly had

an already long history behind him when he became part of the epic stories, it is not impossible that the alternative dialectal forms of the name are traces of different stages in the development of the figure. It is probably fair to say that the exact etymological meaning of the name 'is lost in antiquity'.

Perhaps the meaning of the name is not completely lost.

Autolycus, the name of Odysseus' grandfather (*Odyssey* 24.334), contains the λ element and has the meaning "self-wolf"/"one's own wolf" or perhaps "ideal/ perfect-wolf." *A wolf is a kind of dog that acquires food for itself outside the house of a master.* In terms of personality, wolves are frequently contrasted with the sheep that they prey on. Various sources tell that the canine (wolf) Autolycus was a trader—an Argonaut—and a leather tanner, as well as an accomplished thief and liar (Silver 1992: 173 with n. 1). However, Autolycus is *also* a "*son* of Hermes"— meaning not (or not only) a biological son (or likeness/duplicate) but an "*agent* of Hermes," who acquires for his principal Hermes. The distinction between the two types of dogs/business persons is made clear in *Odyssey* 17.308–309 when Odysseus asks whether his dog Argos has "speed" or is just a "table-dog" (*trapezēes kunos*). "Speed" means Argos acts for itself and/or is quick to grasp opportunities for satisfaction (see Chap. 11.2).

I think table-dogs are represented iconographically in Minoan Knossos by seals in which a young god is flanked by two dogs whom he holds by leashes as they look up at him as if expecting to be fed or led (Marinatos 1993: 189 with Fig 159). The young god can be Hermes, who appears in the "guise of a young man" (= agent = slave) in *Odyssey* 10.275–306 (cf. Chittenden 1948: 28). Perhaps the most appealing example (Figure 42) is from a clay vessel from Syros. Betancourt (2007: 17) sees a "hedgehog," but I see a dog pleading to be fed.

Figure 42. Table-dog, clay vessel from Syros.

The distinction between acting as an agent and acting on one's own behalf is apparent, but, without reference to canines, in *Odyssey* 1.407–409, Penelope's suitor Eurymachus asks Telemachus about the identity of his guest Mentes/disguised Athena: "Does he bring some tidings of thy father's coming, or came he hither in furtherance of some matter (*chreos*) of his own?" (tr. Murray *LCL*). That is, "Does he bring someone else's message or does he bring his own proposition?"

Chreos is often translated as "business" or "debt," but Frazer (1973) translates it as *"prophecy,"* which I think is revealing as to what the ancients meant by the latter term: "If you do this for me, then I will do that for you" is both a (business) proposition and a prophecy, as the contractor who proposes/prophesizes "I will do that for you" becomes a "debtor." Thus, in *Odyssey* 3.367, Mentor/Athena excuses himself/herself by saying, "I will go to the great-hearted Cauconians, where a debt (*chreios*) is owing to me, in no wise new or small" (tr. Murray *LCL*). [1]

But agent status for Autolycus contradicts entrepreneur or "self wolf" status, so we would have to understand that he is *both* an argos-dog (entrepreneur) who acquires for himself and takes the associated risks and a table-dog (agent) who acquires for another who bears the risk. A dual role of this kind is familiar in economic history[2] and, moreover, it is famously played by Heracles in Greek myth, who, in addition to *aethloi* 'labors'/'commissions' for others, performs *praxeis* 'deeds' and *parerga* 'incidentals' for himself (Silver 1992: 118–120).

In the *Odyssey* 19.405f., Autolycus names his grandson "Odysseus." However, Carpenter (1946: 131) explains that in classical Greece, grandfathers named the oldest grandson after themselves and, in line with this practice, Carpenter goes on to suggest that Odysseus' original name should have been *Olykios* or *Olixes*, both of which he sees as connected to "wolf." Thus, Odysseus is predictably someone actively concerned with the acquisition of property on his own behalf. In Sophocles' *Ajax*, Athena applies dog terms, including the dog-stem, to Odysseus (5–8) and she abets him in his *kunagia* "(dog's) hunt" (37). In *Odyssey* 14.203–206, wherein Odysseus tells a tale about his wealthy Cretan father Castor, he also credits his fictional father with the patronymic Hylakides, thus making him "son of Barker" (Floyd 1989: 347 n. 25). This would make Castor and

---

[1]   Athena also assumes the identity of another old friend of Odysseus named "Mentes, the Taphian trader." The two—Mentor and Mentes—are, as Belmont (1969: 111; cf. Frame 2009: 25–28) explains, almost certainly doublets. More specifically, Mentes is a sea-traveller/sea-dweller (*Odyssey* 1.180). Thus, in choosing Mentor/Mentes, Athena has made herself into a character very much like the strongly *motivated* Odysseus himself (Beekes s.v. *menos*).

[2]   Individuals who combined the two roles of independent merchant and agent merchant are well-attested in the texts of the ancient Near East (Silver 1995a: 167–171).

Odysseus—his fictional son—into dogs. There are other canine connections (see Silver 1992: 173–77),

Kanavou (2015: 105) provides additional evidence for Odysseus' qualifications as an entrepreneur, including a common epithet with Hermes, a god of commercial life:

> Another adjective, πολύτροπος 'of many ways', 'resourceful', is also strongly associated with Odysseus; significantly, it is otherwise only used for Hermes (*h.Merc.* 13 and 43.9 [*Homeric Hymn to Mercury/Hermes*]), a god characterised by guile, and with whom Odysseus' grandfather Autolykos seems to have had a connection; the adjective is thus an integral part of Odysseus' trickster identity. Polytropos has a prominent place in the proem, where the hero's name (first mentioned at 1.21) is notably absent. The adjectival nature of *polytropos* is not very strong, as it is only used twice (*Od.* 1.1, 10.330), and only in connection with Odysseus; the adjective is used alongside Odysseus' name at 10.330, but not in the proem, where it may have been interpreted almost as an alternative name by some among the audience.

Odysseus' entrepreneurial status is also signaled by his *uniform*: when he left Ithaca to participate in the Trojan War, he a wore purple cloak and a "brooch upon it was fashioned of gold with double clasps, and on the front it was curiously wrought: a hound [*kuōn* 'dog'] held in his fore paws a dappled fawn" (*Odyssey* 19.225–227; tr. Murray *LCL*). *This dog fed itself.* Furthermore, he had to be persuaded to go to Troy by Agamemnon and Menelaus (*Odyssey* 24.115–119).

Is there any indication of the kind of business that Odysseus might have favored? *There is reason to believe that "wolf" refers to a specialized entrepreneur dealing in sheep and/or wool.* Herodotus (4.145) explains that the descendants of the Argonauts (called Minyae[3]) were driven from Lemnos and settled at Lacedaemon in Laconia. Later on, Theras, of the family of Cadmus, decided to take some of the Minyae with him to Thera:

> But as Theras' son would not sail with him, his father said that he would leave him behind as a sheep among wolves (*oin en lukoisi*); after which saying the boy got the nickname of Oeolycus "sheep-wolf," and it so

---

[3] The Minyae are mysterious and referring to them as originally a "tribe" in Boeotia near Orchemonos (cf. *Iliad* 2.511; *Odyssey* 11.284) does not help, as that term is also mysterious. The meaning of Minyae might be functional rather than ethnic. Perhaps it refers to guild of sheep men in both Iolcus and Orchemonos.

happened that this became his customary name. He had a son, Aegeus, from whom the Aegidae, a great Spartan clan, take their name.

Herodotus 4.149.1; tr. Godley LCL

Oeolycus, the "sheep-wolf"—that is, the "son" of Theras—is a sheep/wool-merchant trading with the Minyae (Silver 1992: 151). I understand that he carried on his commercial duties in an inland area, not on the Mediterranean Sea. *Odysseus/Olysseus is predictably an Oeolycus.*

2. Odysseus As Sheep and Textile Entrepreneur in Ithaca

We know that Odysseus owns large flocks on the mainland, in Epirus, Aetolia, Elis, and Arcadia, as well as locally in Ithaca, as the swineherd Eumaeus informs the disguised Odysseus:

> Verily his substance was great past telling, so much has no lord either on the dark mainland or in Ithaca itself; nay, not twenty men together have wealth so great. Lo, I will tell thee the tale thereof; twelve herds of kine has he on the mainland; as many flocks of sheep; as many droves of swine; as many packed herds of goats do herdsmen, both foreigners and of his own people, pasture. And here too graze roving herds of goats on the borders of the island, eleven in all, and over them trusty men keep watch. And each man of these ever drives up day by day one of his flock for the wooers, even that one of the fatted goats which seems to him the best. But as for me, I guard and keep these swine, and choose out with care and send them the best of the boars.

Odyssey 14.95–108; tr. Murray LCL; cf. 20.185–187

Ithaca itself had little grazing land (*Odyssey* 4.600–608; cf. Malkin 1998: 130–131). Presumably, then, Odysseus' herding activities on the mainland would have taken him inland away from the sea.

In *Odyssey* 22.421–423, we find slaves being taught cloth-making skills in Odysseus' *oikos*: "Fifty women servants (*dmōai*) hast thou in the halls, women that we have taught (*didaxamen*) to do their work, to card the wool and bear the lot of slaves (*doulosunēn*)."[4] Indeed, Odysseus' wife Penelope is famed for her spinning prowess, and the suitors, eager to own her services, shower Penelope with valuable gifts (*dōra*) (*Odyssey* 18.285–304; tr. Murray *LCL*). Odysseus'

---

4   In Linear B tablets from Knossos, children of women workers, probably slaves, are referenced (by abbreviations) as *di-da-ka-r* 'being taught' (Ak 614 and Ak 781).

wealthy household has purple-dyed furnishings (*Odyssey* 4.115, 154; 20.250–252). However, although fifty trained textile workers is not a huge number, it is a large enough number to assume a production "surplus" beyond household needs.

The *Odyssey* also shows us an Ithaca that is a center for the production of luxury textiles in the hands of *nymphs*. *Odyssey* (13.95ff.; tr. Murray *LCL*) tells,

> There is in the land of Ithaca a certain harbor of Phorcys, the old man of the sea, and at its mouth two projecting headlands sheer to seaward, but sloping down on the side toward the harbor. These keep back the great waves raised by heavy winds without, but within the benched ships lie unmoored when they have reached the point of anchorage. At the head of the harbor is a long-leafed olive tree, and near it a pleasant, shadowy cave sacred to the nymphs that are called Naiads. Therein are mixing bowls and jars of stone, and there too the bees store honey. And in the cave are long looms of stone, at which the nymphs weave webs of purple dye, a wonder to behold; and therein are also ever-flowing springs.

It is no accident that in Homer, as Malkin (2001: 11) notes, "Nymphs seem to mediate between the traveler's debarkation and actual 'arrival'" (quoted from Silver 2018: 155–156). Visits of traders are attested to in the *Odyssey* (13.113f.) by the mention that the Phaeacians were familiar with the location: "Here they rowed in, knowing the place of old; and the ship ran full half her length on the shore in her swift course, at such pace was she driven by the arms of the rowers" (tr. Murray *LCL*). That the "cave" (*antron, speos*), in which the nymphs produced textiles and stored "honey," is a temple (even a palace) is confirmed by its neat double-entrance system—one for gods and the other for mortals (*Odyssey* 13.109–110)—and by Athena's advice to Odysseus (*Odyssey* 13. 360ff.) that he should "set his goods [the treasure given to him by the Phaeacians] in the innermost recess (*muchō* also meaning "store chamber") of the wondrous cave, where they may abide for you in safety" (tr. Murray *LCL*; but compare *Odyssey* 5.194–225).

Odysseus looked like a merchant to other merchants. In Phaeacia:

> Euryalus made answer and taunted him [Odysseus] to his face: "Nay verily, stranger, for I do not liken thee to a man that is skilled in contests, such as abound among men, but to one who, faring to and fro with his benched ship, is a captain of sailors who are merchantmen (*prēktēres*), one who is mindful of his freight, and has charge of a home-borne cargo, and the gains of his greed. Thou dost not look like an athlete."

> *Odyssey* 8.158–165; tr. Murray *LCL*

We can expect that the Phaeacians knew what a merchant looked like for they were used to visiting the cave of the Naiads in Ithaca—perhaps they came with "honey" to exchange for textiles. One look at his legs should have been sufficient to identify him as a merchant, as Odysseus admits to being a merchant when he refers to a problem with his legs: "In the foot race alone I fear that someone of the Phaeacians may out strip me, for cruelly have I been broken amid the many waves, since there was in my ship no lasting store of provisions; therefore my limbs are loosened" (*Odyssey* 8.230ff; tr. Murray *LCL*; 17.196), and elsewhere Odysseus walks with the aid of a staff. *Lameness is a standard attribute of the commercial circuiter* (Silver 1992: 135–144).

Why did Odysseus go to fight in the Trojan War? Perhaps he had to because he was a "king" (*basilēus*) in Ithaca. Although the term indicates a *local authority* and might be a kind of transferable property yielding wealth and prestige,[5] the greater king who made the local kings might expect services in return. Putting aside the question of how Odysseus became a subordinate king, we learn that there were many others in Ithaca, including among the suitors. Perhaps some of the other kings returned earlier from Troy, but we do not hear of other kings from Ithaca in the Catalogue of Ships. Furthermore, Agamemnon in Hades reminds Amphimedon that when he and Menelaus went to Ithaca to recruit Odysseus for the War, they stayed in the house of his father, Melaneus, but there is no reference to either man serving in the Trojan War (*Odyssey* 24.115–119).

Apparently, service in the War was not universal, but, if not, what was the criterion of selection? I see a hint from Homer that participation in textile manufacturing was a motivating factor for military service. The hint is Penelope's concern, even obsession, with what Odysseus wore when he left Ithaca and went off to the War. She asks the disguised Odysseus,

> "Now verily, stranger, am I minded to put thee to the test, whether or no thou didst in very truth entertain there in thy halls my husband with his godlike comrades, even as thou sayest. Tell me what manner of raiment he wore about his body, and what manner of man he was himself; and tell me of the comrades who followed him." Then Odysseus of many wiles answered her, and said: "Lady, hard is it for one that has been so long afar to tell thee this, for it is now the twentieth year since he went thence and departed from my country. But I will tell thee as my mind

---

[5]   Telemachus tells the suitor Antinous, "Nay, it is no bad thing to be a king. Straightway one's house grows rich and oneself is held in greater honor. However, there are other kings of the Achaeans full many in seagirt Ithaca, both young and old. One of these haply may have this place, since goodly Odysseus is dead. But I will be lord of our own house and of the slaves that goodly Odysseus won for me" (*Odyssey* 1.394 ff.; tr. Murray *LCL*).

pictures him. A fleecy cloak of purple did goodly Odysseus wear, a cloak of double fold [or a cloak that was double woven, see Chap. 3], but the brooch upon it was fashioned of gold with double clasps, and on the front it was curiously wrought: a hound (*kuōn*) held in his fore paws a dappled fawn, and pinned it in his jaws as it writhed. And at this all men marvelled, how, though they were of gold, the hound was pinning the fawn and strangling it, and the fawn was writhing with its feet and striving to flee. And I noted the tunic about his body, all shining as is the sheen upon the skin of a dried onion, so soft it was; and it glistened like the sun."

Odyssey 19.215–235; tr. Murray *LCL*

Levaniouk's (2011: 110) more literal translation catches one's attention: "Odysseus had a woolen purple cloak, a two-fold one, and in it was a pin of gold."

It may be noted that Odysseus' "uniform" combines the Mycenaean export—a purple-dyed cloak—with the Mycenaean import—gold; in itself, it symbolizes the Black Sea textile trade. Moreover, the gold bears the image of an argos-dog. We already know that Odysseus participated in the textile economy at Ithaca. What I am suggesting is that Homer dressed Odysseus in a purple cloak and shining tunic because he went to Troy in furtherance of/in the interest of his profession.[6] That is, he, like others who went off to fight, had a vested interest in the luxury textile trade.[7]

Homer mentions only a few Achaean expeditionaries having purple cloaks. There is Agamemnon—the doggish king of Mycenae—who "held" his purple cloak to rally the Achaeans. There is Thoas, one of the suitors of Helen[8] who led the Aetolians (*Iliad* 2.638–644; *Odyssey* 14.500); Aetolia being a region in which the dog Odysseus, another suitor, kept flocks.[9] Also, the wily Nestor from Pylos, "mother of flocks" (*Odyssey* 15.226), whose outfit resembles the one worn by Odysseus: "Around him buckled a purple cloak (*chlaina*) of double fold and wide,

---

[6]   The double-folded or double-woven (*diploos*) cloak (*chlaina*) worn by Odysseus and several other Achaeans (see below) may have embodied a very significant innovation in textile weaving that was discussed in Chapter 3.

[7]   Priam thinks that Odysseus looks like a ram: "And next the old man [Priam] saw Odysseus, and asked: 'Come now, tell me also of yonder man, dear child, who he is. Shorter is he by a head than Agamemnon, son of Atreus, but broader of shoulder and of chest to look upon. His battle-gear lieth upon the bounteous earth, but himself he rangeth like the bell-wether of a herd through the ranks of warriors. Like a ram he seemeth to me, a ram of thick fleece, that paceth through a great flock of white ewes.' To him made answer Helen, sprung from Zeus: 'This again is Laertes' son, Odysseus of many wiles, that was reared in the land of Ithaca, rugged though it be, and he knoweth all manner of craft and cunning devices'" (*Iliad* 3.191–203; tr. Murray LCL).

[8]   Named in the *Ehoiai/Catalogue of Women* (Glantz 1993: 565).

[9]   Textiles, including purple-dyed textiles, have been discovered in a cemetery in Stamna, Aeotolia; the findings are dated to 1100–800 BCE (Kolonas et al. 2017: 535–536).

whereon the down was thick" but his pin (*perone*) is not mentioned to be of gold (*Iliad* 10. 133–134; tr. Murray *LCL*; discussed by Bortwick 1976: 1; cf. Zanker 2016: 303). It was the wise Nestor whose idea it was to build the Achaean Wall (*Iliad* 7.336–343). Perhaps, there were others, but Homer does not single them out. Clearly, however, Agamemnon, Odysseus, Thoas, and Nestor of Pylos[10] are leading figures in the textile trade.

On the Trojan side, Homer mentions Hector as wearing a purple cloak (*Iliad* 8.220f.). Significantly, for his true role in the Helen enterprise, Hector's bones were buried in a *golden chest covered with soft purple robes* (*Iliad* 24.795–796).[11] In addition, Andromache, the wife of Hector, is described as "weaving a web [*peplos* 'cloak'] in the innermost part of the lofty house, a purple web of double fold, and therein was broidering flowers of varied hue" (*Iliad* 22.441–442; tr. Murray *LCL*). It is quite clear that Hector (actually his cult) had a long-lasting reputation for participation in profitable trade between Troy and Boeotian Thebes.[12]

According to Apollodorus (*Library* 1.9.16), Laertes, the father of Odysseus, participated in the expedition of the Argonauts. M. L. West (2014: 23) thinks that having Laertes as his father "perhaps does not go back to his earliest phase of celebrity." I disagree. The connection of Odysseus' father with the Black Sea and the Golden Fleece, as well as his residence at textile-producing Ithaca, serve to strengthen Odysseus' connection to the luxury textile trade. Homer makes sure to mention the mission of Jason to the Black Sea as a kind of preamble to that

[10] Pylos, as already noted, is a major center of cloth production and of the Poseidon cult. Also, in Homer, wherein Poseidon is the god of Nestor's house and Nestor is "tamer of horses" (*Odyssey* 3.15f.). It becomes difficult to tell where Nestor ends and Poseidon begins. Frame (2009: 28–29) proposes that the verbal root of "the name *Néstōr* ... is the root **nes* of the verb *néomai*, 'return home,' and of the related noun *nóstos*." Nestor's name does not have the intransitive sense 'he who returns' that would correspond to the meaning of the middle verb *néomai*: the name *Néstōr* has a transitive sense, *'he who brings back'*" (Kanavou 2015: 63–66; emphasis added). Frame (2009: 47–48 and elsewhere) understands "*brings back from death*." What did Homer understand by "death"? He did not mean by it to cease to exist. I think her refers to exit from a cultic structure known as "Hades."

[11] *Hektōr* is from the root *hekhō* (1) verb 'to possess, retain, have,' aorist 'to take (into posses- sion)'. Thus, Hector might be understood as "he/one who takes things into property," or from *hekhō* (1) 'to transport' or 'be carried on a vehicle, boat'. In this case, Hector is himself the prop- erty. (Beekes s.vv.; Frame 2009: 24 takes *hekhes* to mean "protect" [rather than "keep, hold"]). Interestingly, at Pylos, "Hektōr is a servant [slave] of the god and is listed as a landholder in multiple texts" (Nakassis 2013: 246).

[12] Perhaps the most significant testimony is provided in Pausanias 9.18.5: "There is also at Thebes the grave of Hector, the son of Priam. It is near the spring called the Fountain of Oedipus, and the Thebans say that they brought Hector's bones from Troy because of the following oracle:—"Ye Thebans who dwell in the city of Cadmus, If you wish blameless wealth (*ploutos*) for the country in which you live, Bring to your homes the bones of Hector, Priam's son, from Asia, and rever- ence him as a hero, according to the bidding of Zeus" (tr. Jones and Ormerod *LCL*; cf. Lycophron *Alexandra* 1189–1283; cf. scholia on *Iliad* 13.1).

of the Achaeans at Troy. If this was only later "attached" to Odysseus, it fits him very well.

It is sometimes noted that Odysseus' importance in Homeric Epic is not proportionate to the number of ships he leads to Troy in the Catalogue of Ships: he brings twelve ships (*Iliad* 2.637), as compared to Agamemnon's one-hundred, Nestor's eighty, and Menelaus' sixty. Perhaps this discrepancy is a matter of quality vs. quantity. Recall that Agamemnon holds the purple cloak to rally the Achaeans while standing by Odysseus' ship, which is described "huge of hull" (Chap. 14.4).

3. From Flocks to Textiles: The *Nostos* of Odysseus

On his "return to life" journey, Odysseus makes five encounters between Troy and Circe: first are the Ciconians and last the Laestrygonians; the second and fourth are the Lotus-eaters and winds of Aeolus, and the Cyclopes are the third. So far as I can see, flocks play no role in the cases of the Lotus-eaters (*Odyssey* 9.82–105) or in the wind-wallets of Aeolus (*Odyssey* 10.1–80). However, sheep play a featured role in the other three stories.

The story of the Cyclops Polyphemus—a Greek name meaning "much fame" (M. L. West 2014: 13)—prominently features sheep and wool. M. L. West (2014: 13) dismisses the story as a standard "folktale," but then he did not count the sheep! Neither did West take into account that Polyphemus, the sheepherder, is a "son"/agent of Poseidon (*Odyssey* 9.529).

To begin with, Polyphemus' "cave" is surrounded by sheep:

> But when we had reached the place, which lay close at hand, there on the land's edge hard by the sea we saw a high cave, roofed over with laurels, and there many flocks, sheep and goats alike, were wont to sleep. Round about it a high court was built with stones set deep in the earth, and with tall pines and high-crested oaks. There a monstrous man was wont to sleep, who shepherded his flocks alone and afar, and mingled not with others, but lived apart, with his heart set on lawlessness. For he was fashioned a wondrous monster, and was not like a man that lives by bread, but like a wooded peak of lofty mountains, which stands out to view alone, apart from the rest.

> *Odyssey* 9.180–192; tr. Murray *LCL*

Second, Odysseus famously uses sheep to make good his escape from Polyphemus' cave:

Nay, do thou pray to our father, the lord Poseidon. So they spoke and went their way; and my heart laughed within me that my name and cunning device had so beguiled. But the Cyclops, groaning and travailing in anguish, groped with his hands and took away the stone from the door, and himself sat in the doorway with arms outstretched in the hope of catching anyone who sought to go forth with the sheep— so witless, forsooth, he thought in his heart to find me.... Rams there were, well-fed and thick of fleece, fine beasts and large, *with wool dark as the violet*. These I silently bound together with twisted withes on which the Cyclops, that monster with his heart set on lawlessness, was wont to sleep. Three at a time I took. The one in the middle in each case bore a man, and the other two went, one on either side, saving my comrades. Thus every three sheep bore a man. But as for me—there was a ram, far the best of all the flock; him I grasped by the back, and curled beneath his shaggy belly, lay there face upwards with steadfast heart, clinging fast with my hands to his *wondrous fleece*. So then, with wailing, we waited for the bright dawn. As soon as early Dawn appeared, the rosy-fingered, then the males of the flock hastened forth to pasture and the females bleated unmilked about the pens, for their udders were bursting. And their master, distressed with grievous pains, felt along the backs of all the sheep as they stood up before him, but in his folly he marked not this, that my men were bound beneath the breasts of his fleecy sheep. Last of all the flock the ram went forth.

Odyssey 9.410–450; tr. Murray *LCL*; emphasis added

Notice the attention given to the quality of the fleece: "Rams there were, well-fed and thick of fleece, fine beasts and large, *with wool dark as the violet*."

Then, after escaping:

Speedily then we drove off those long-shanked sheep, rich with fat, turning full often to look about until we came to the ship. And welcome to our dear comrades was the sight of us who had escaped death, but for the others they wept and wailed; yet I would not suffer them to weep, but with a frown forbade each man. Rather I bade them to fling on board with speed the many sheep of goodly fleece, and sail over the salt water.

Odyssey 9.464–474; tr. Murray *LCL*

The sheep might have been intended for eating on the journey, but the emphasis is not on their potential as meals but rather on the quality of their fleece and, hence, potential as textiles.

Odysseus loads many of Polyphemus'—that is, Poseidon's—best sheep onto his ship. Thus, the tale of the Cyclops, whether of foreign origin or not, makes numerous important points. First, Odysseus will do whatever it takes to acquire fine sheep. Second, Poseidon, Polyphemus' father, kept sheep through an agent even in a place so remote from civilization that hosts cherished their visitors only by devouring them! Third, Polyphemus' mother is the nymph Thoōsa, daughter of Phorkys the Old Man of the Sea (*Odyssey* 1.71ff.), which connects Polyphemus with the distant(?) cave of the textile-producing nymphs in Ithaca, the home of Odysseus. Finally, unless we assume that Poseidon ignored his "son," we are entitled to suspect that beneath the folkloristic theme of isolation, there is regular trade between the Cyclopes, Odysseus, and other agents of Poseidon. With respect to the textile-related activities of Ithaca's nymphs, recall also that the "isolated" Phaeacians who had learned the craft of sailing from Poseidon were very familiar with the nymph's cave in Ithaca.

Odysseus' comments on the undeveloped island next to the land of the Cyclopes are noteworthy:

> For the isle is nowise poor, but would bear all things in season. In it are meadows by the shores of the grey sea, well-watered meadows and soft, where vines would never fail, and in it level ploughland, whence they might reap from season to season harvests exceeding deep, so rich is the soil beneath; and in it, too, is a harbor giving safe anchorage, where there is no need of moorings, either to throw out anchor-stones or to make fast stern cables, but one may beach one's ship and wait until the sailors' minds bid them put out, and the breezes blow fair. Now at the head of the harbor a spring of bright water flows forth from beneath a cave, and round about it poplars grow.
>
> *Odyssey* 9.130–140; tr. Murray *LCL*

As Faraone (2019: 55) observes, these words do not reflect the perspective of a pirate. Rather, they reflect the perspective of a dog—that is, an entrepreneur who sees the potential for economic development.

And while the Cyclopes might be limited economically because they lack ships—actually, no "red-cheeked" ships, or shipbuilders themselves (*Odyssey* 9.125f.)—they had become familiar with visiting ships and traders as is proven by Polyphemus' asking Odysseus, who possessed a "red-cheeked" ship, pointed questions, such as, "Strangers, who are ye? Whence do ye sail over the watery ways? Is it on some business (*prēxin*), or do ye wander at random over the sea, even as pirates, who wander, hazarding their lives and bringing evil to men of other lands?" and "But tell me where thou didst moor thy well-wrought ship on thy coming. Was it haply at a remote part of the land, or close by? I fain would know" (*Odyssey* 9.252–255, 279–280; tr. Murray *LCL*; Burgess 2011: 275). What was it that induced ships to visit the land of the Cyclopes? Homer makes sure to narrow the choice to the fine sheep bred there.

It is not difficult to see beneath the stale surface of Homer's Cyclops folk-tale that it is a vehicle for the theme of Poseidon-sponsored sheep breeding and, ultimately, textile trade. The only discordant note that I see is that the Phaeacians had once lived in Hypereia near the Cyclopes but moved far away because the latter had mistreated them (*Odyssey* 6.4–8).

In the episode of the Ciconians—Odysseus' first adventure after leaving Troy—he and his crew sack the city and would have escaped unscathed but for the fact that they stopped to slaughter and feast on sheep (*Odyssey* 9.44ff.). The Laestrygonians were next:

> So for six days we sailed, night and day alike, and on the seventh we came to the lofty citadel of Lamus, even to Telepylus of the Laestrygonians, where herdsman calls to herdsman as he drives in his flock, and the other answers as he drives his forth. There a man who never slept could have earned a double wage, one by herding cattle, and one by pasturing white sheep; for the out goings of the night and of the day are close together. When we had come thither into the goodly harbor, about which on both sides a sheer cliff runs continuously, and projecting headlands opposite to one another stretch out at the mouth, and the entrance is narrow, then all the rest steered their curved ships in, and the ships were moored within the hollow harbor close together; for therein no wave ever swelled, great or small, but all about was a bright calm. But I alone moored my black ship outside.

> *Odyssey* 10.80–95.; tr. Murray *LCL*

Obviously, what is being described is a specialized livestock breeding center with a busy labor force in a great harbor that served merchants of wool and other livestock products. But why does this matter to Homer?

In *Calypso's* first appearance, there is mention of her weaving (*Odyssey* 5.59–62). Even earlier (*Odyssey* 1.14) and soon afterward (*Odyssey* 5.149), she is termed "Potnia." Calypso gives Odysseus a double-headed axe (*pelekus*) to build a ship (*Odyssey* 5.234). For other textile connections, we must rely on non-Homeric sources. Kanovou (2015: 114) summarizes:

Her name is mentioned in several books of the Odyssey, but primarily in 5. Outside the Homeric epic, it belongs to a known tradition of names for the Oceanids, as suggested in Hesiod's *Theogony* (358). A Kalypso is said to be the daughter of Okeanos in Hesiod (*Th.* 36 2, cf. *h.Dem.* 4 23), and the daughter of Atlas in the *Odyssey* (1.52, 7. 24 5; in Apollod. 1.12.2 a Nereid—this may suggest that the name was shared by different nymphs). The name is from the verb καλύπτω and is clearly significant. It is similar to feminine names inspired by the veil worn as head-cover by women, e. g. Καλύπτρη (AP 9. 240). The *Theogony* passage includes the epithet κροκόπεπλος "with yellow dress," used for one of the Oceanids (though not for Kalypso herself), while *Od.* 5. 23 2 (κεφαλῇ δ᾽ ἐφύπερθε καλύ πτρην "and on her head she placed a veil"), which refers to Kalypso, was perhaps meant as a pun on the name. A meaning such as 'the veiled one' may be encouraged by the similarities between Kalypso and the divine alewife Shiduri of the epic of Gilgamesh, who is introduced as 'veiled with a veil'.

The important point is that Calypso is a nymph (*Odyssey* 5.14f.) who resides in a "cave" (*Odyssey* 1.10–15), and in this role, as at Ithaca, she may be linked to the production of luxury textiles and, as will be seen shortly, with the shepherding of Helios' extensive flocks.

Calypso tells the story:

Him (Odysseus) I saved when he was bestriding the keel and all alone, for Zeus had smitten his swift ship with his bright thunder-bolt, and had shattered it in the midst of the wine-dark sea. There all the rest of his goodly comrades perished, but as for him, the wind and the wave, as they bore him, brought him hither. Him I welcomed kindly and gave him food, and said that I would make him immortal and ageless all his days. But since it is in no wise possible for any other god to evade or make void the will of Zeus who bears the aegis, let him go his way, if Zeus thus orders and commands, over the unresting sea. But it is not I that shall give him convoy, for I have at hand no ships with oars and no men to send him on his way over the broad back of the sea. But with a ready heart will I give him counsel, and will hide naught, that all unscathed he may return to his native land.

Odyssey 5.130ff.; tr. Murray *LCL*

It is clear that by saving Odysseus from the sea, Calypso made him her slave. That Calypso had reduced him to bondage is recognized by Athena when she says that Odysseus is held by *ananggkē* 'compulsion'/'force' (*Odyssey* 5.14–15; LSJ s.v.; Rankine 2011: 40–41). It is even possible that the episode with Ino (= Calypso?) really refers to before—not after—she made him her slave. When Odysseus had served out his term of service to Calypso, as divinely ordained by Zeus, he was released. Ultimately, Odysseus chose "life" rather than the "immortality" Calypso offered to him.

After departing from Calypso on a raft, Odysseus is saved at sea by Ino-Leucothea, daughter of *Cadmus* (*Odyssey* 5.333), a most significant figure. From non-Homeric sources, we learn that Ino is the second wife of the Minyan Athamas in Boeotia. The Argonauts who departed from Thessaly are also Minyans, and Ino herself has connections with Corinth and is the stepmother of Phrixus and Helle, who journeyed to the Black Sea aboard the ram with the Golden Fleece. Ino seemingly appears out of nowhere and then instructs Odysseus to wear her veil (*krēdemon*; *Odyssey* 5.333ff). She tells Odysseus, "But when with thy hands thou hast laid hold of the land, loose it from thee, and cast it into the wine-dark sea far from the land, and thyself turn away" (*Odyssey* 5.348–350; tr. Murray *LCL*). Two points need to be made. First, that Odysseus wears the garment of a woman. Silver (2019: esp. 73–74) has argued that not only did Greek iconography portray agents as youths, but, in addition, when a male served as a woman's agent, this cross-gender service was signaled by providing the male with elements of a female identity. Thus, Heracles wore women's clothes when he was the slave-agent of Omphale. Therefore, we see that Odysseus is the slave-agent of Ino, but the latter probably is the same as Calypso. Second, the instruction to "turn away" means that Odysseus is no longer Ino's slave, and his nakedness signals his freedom and, consequent, readiness for new enterprises either as an agent or on his own behalf.

Putting Circe herself aside for the moment, let us review her words about Helios who has sheep, lots of them, in Thrinacia. Helios' "thick-fleeced sheep" are noted also in the *Homeric Hymn to Apollo* (3.411ff). Circe, who is the daughter (= agent) of Helios (*Odyssey* 10.138), prophesies to Odysseus:

> And thou wilt come to the isle Thrinacia. There in great numbers feed the kine of Helios and his goodly flocks, seven herds of kine and as many fair flocks of sheep, and fifty in each.[13] These bear no young, nor do they ever die, *and goddesses are their shepherds, fair-tressed nymphs, Phaethusa and Lampetie*, whom beautiful Neaera bore to Helios Hyperion. These their honored mother, when she had borne and reared them, *sent to the isle Thrinacia to dwell afar, and keep the flocks of their father* and his

---

[13] A specialist informs me that flocks are reported in units of fifty in the Linear B tablets.

sleek kine. If thou leavest these unharmed and heedest thy homeward way, verily ye may yet reach Ithaca, though in evil plight. But if thou harmest them, then I foretell ruin for thy ship and for thy comrades, and even if thou shalt thyself escape, late shalt thou come home and in evil case, after losing all thy comrades.

Odyssey 12.127–142; tr. Murray *LCL*; emphasis added

Note that nymphs are teams of agents posted by their principals to distant places to care for flocks.

Not only are sheep tended by nymphs the center of attention but also, beyond any astronomical connection, Homer references the standard shepherding contract: (1) shepherds must replace dead animals—hence, the sheep are deathless—which is a duty illustrated in Herodotus 9.92.2–95, wherein Euēnius, the shepherd of Helios' sheep, buys replacements for animals killed by wolves. (2) To prevent disputes over ownership, there is a contractual stipulation that all newly born sheep belong legally to the shepherd. Hence, the flocks bear no young. This provision also incentivized the shepherd.[14] As noted earlier, there are hints of this contract in the Linear B documents mentioning missing sheep.[15] What did the nymphs do with the wool of the sheep they shepherded? Based on the weaving connections of nymphs in Homer and elsewhere,[16] I suggest that they made fine textiles.

Similarly to Calypso, Circe is termed "Potnia" (e.g. *Odyssey* 8.448, 10.394) and concerns herself with weaving: "So they stood in the gateway of the fair-tressed goddess, and within they heard Circe singing with sweet voice, as she went to and fro before a great imperishable web, such as is the handiwork of goddesses, finely-woven and beautiful, and glorious" (*Odyssey* 10.220ff.; tr. Murray *LCL*). I do

[14] Herdsmen in the ancient Near East typically received a share of the newborn animals as payment. A Babylonian contract of the early second millennium calls for the shepherd to keep twenty percent of the increase (Finkelstein 1968: 33). For herding Laban's flock, Jacob was to receive the newly born "brown" sheep and variegated color goats (Genesis 30: 32–33). Jacob explained that under this innovative arrangement, when Laban came to look over his herd, "every one that is not speckled and spotted among the goats, and dark among the sheep ... shall be counted as stolen."

[15] Kazansky (2009: 120) has commented on linguistic features of the Helios passage: "The archaic forms of words and some coincidences in use with the Mycenaean documents are striking. It seems to me probable that the archaic in many respects Homeric passage on the herds of Helios may go back to the Mycenaean antiquity." The problem is that Kazansky *assumes* that the Homeric material originated in the Archaic period and does not consider that the terminology is *earlier* than Linear B.

[16] Note especially the naiad Creusa in Pindar (*Pythian Ode* 9:15 ff.): "She loved not the path walked to and fro before the looms, nor the pleasures of dining with her *oikoriai hetairai* [female housemates]" (tr. Kennedy 2015: 65).

not mean to say, however, that the occupation of weaving was Circe's primary occupation.

Concerning the weaving of Calypso and Circe, it might be objected that for women, including, goddesses, weaving was a standard activity. However, Circe has Argonautic associations. She mentions the "Clashing Rocks" and is the sister of Aeetes, the king of Colchis: "The epithet *Aiaiē* applied to her island and to herself derives, like Aites' name from Aia, the traditional name of the land to which the Argonauts sailed in quest of the Fleece" (M. L. West 2014: 119; my transliteration). As noted earlier, "Aia" appears in a Linear B text from Pylos. Again, we see the fleece/cloth connection.

But more concretely with respect to entrepreneurial motivation, more than once Odysseus shows himself willing to make current sacrifices to secure large future rewards. He is, as Redfield (2009: 286) explains, the "economic man." Thus, the disguised Odysseus tells Penelope,

> So they [his crew] all perished in the surging sea, but he on the keel of his ship was cast forth by the wave on the shore, on the land of the Phaeacians, who are near of kin to the gods.[17] These heartily showed him all honor, as if he were a god, and gave him many gifts, and were fain themselves to send him home unscathed. *Yea, and Odysseus would long since have been here, only it seemed to his mind more profitable to gather wealth by roaming over the wide earth*; so truly does Odysseus beyond all mortal men know many gainful ways, nor could any mortal beside vie with him. Thus Pheidon, king of the Thesprotians, told me the tale.
>
> *Odyssey* 19.277–287; tr. Murray *LCL*; emphasis added

The nature of the profits sought by Odysseus in Thesprotia is unstated, but we may assume, from *Odyssey* 16.424–427, that they regularly sent ships to Ithaca (Malkin 1998: 130); *the truth about Odysseus' role is most apparent in his lies* (cf. Malkin 1998: 131–132). More importantly, it is known from the report of the swineherd to (disguised) Odysseus that Odysseus had flocks in the region (*Odyssey* 14.95–108).[18]

---

[17] The economic connections of the Phaeacians will be considered shortly.

[18] Mentes (Athena) tells that Odysseus was searching at Ephyra for *pharmaka* (*Odyssey* 1.255–264). Wagner-Hasel (2020: 301) suggests that the *pharmaka* he sought might be purple dye.

4. Odysseus: Agent of Poseidon

With respect to Odysseus' role as agent, it should be noted that "Six times in the *Odyssey*[19] the life-experience of Odysseus is defined by the word *aethlos*. Both in Homer and in Greek in general the word (*athlos* after Homer) and its cognates have two meanings: of 'athletic contest' and of 'labor', the latter being best exemplified by the labors of Heracles" (Finkelberg 1995: 2). The "labors" of Heracles were performed as an agent required by his (Heracles') owner. Furthermore,

> in Odyssey 4 the term *aethlos* extends over Odysseus' experience during the war itself, both generally, as in 4.170 … and particularly, in Helen's reminiscence of how Odysseus penetrated Troy disguised as a beggar (4.241). *Thus, all of Odysseus' experience, from his fighting at Troy to his return to Ithaca, is consistently described in the poem as falling into the sphere of aethloi.*
>
> Finkelberg 1995: 8; emphasis added

It is not made clear whether this is a metaphor or a concrete legal agency. Recall, however, his "uniform" and that he had to be persuaded to fight in Troy.

To judge whether Heracles' "labors" served a mercantile/commercial motivation, we must, in the first instance, study the motives of his legal principal. In most cases, the motives are clouded in myth and folktale.[20] However, I will argue below that Odysseus labored for Poseidon as a commercial agent ("table-dog"), in addition to acting on his own behalf as an "argos-dog." In this respect, of course, the "*godlike*" Odysseus resembles Heracles.[21]

In describing Odysseus and Menelaus' embassy to the Trojans to reclaim Helen, Antēnōr, who hosted the two, refers to Odysseus as "godlike" and to Menelaus as "dear to Arēs" (*Iliad* 3.205–206). Antēnōr goes on to explain that in his home, he learned the *mēdea pukna* "cunning/well-conceived plans" of both men (*Iliad* 3.208; cf. 11.140). Readers of this study will not be surprised by my suspicion that fulfillment of their plans is in addition to their duty to reclaim Helen on behalf of Arēs (Menelaus) and in the service of an unnamed deity (Odysseus). My inclination to see both delegates as planning to do Trojan business on their own behalf finds support in Antēnōr's following report that the two men "gathered" (*ageirō*) and "mingled" (*mignumi*) with Trojans, albeit that Menelaus towered over his Trojan counterparts (*Iliad* 3.209–210). What

---

[19] *Odyssey* 1.18; 4.170, 241; 23.248, 261, 350.
[20] See, however, §5 below for a clear business law example. For a wider discussion, see Silver (1992: esp. 116–120).
[21] For "likeness" and "image" as metaphors for agent, see §5 below.

kind of "side business" was Odysseus involved in? Antēnōr's revelation about the Odysseus' plans immediately follows Priam's characterization of Odysseus: "His battle-gear lieth upon the bounteous earth, but himself he rangeth like the bellwether of a herd through the ranks of warriors. Like a ram he seemeth to me, a ram of thick fleece, that paceth through a great flock of white ewes" (*Iliad* 3.196–198; tr. Murray *LCL*). Odysseus is so consumed by sheep and wool that in the mind of Antēnōr, he seemed to be a ram.

In one of his lies, Odysseus says he refused to serve Idomeneus of Crete[22] as *therapōn* [the position of Meriones in the *Iliad*] and instead commanded his own men.[23] So perhaps the "real" Odysseus did "labor" for Idomeneus while fighting in Troy. His service to Idomeneus finds support in the report of an Aeotolian to Eumaeus the swineherd: he saw Odysseus repairing ships with Idomeneus and the Cretans in Crete (*Odyssey* 14.382–383; Haft 1984: 291–294; cf. *Odyssey* 14. 235–239, 19.180–184). As a slave, Odysseus could still have commanded his own men (*hetairōn*).

We may speculate that Odysseus journeyed to the Underworld as Circe's agent—he followed her prophecy to go and, more importantly, to return to her—where he learned about the sheep of Helios and the prophecy of Teiresias (*Teiresiēs*) (*Odyssey* 10.537–540; Frame 1978: 38ff.), the latter describing his service as Poseidon's agent. There is reason to believe that Odysseus agreed to be her agent-slave in return for being sent home. Odysseus addresses Circe as follows: "Circe, fulfill for me the promise which thou gavest to send me home; for my spirit is now eager to be gone, and the spirit of my comrades, who make my heart to pine, as they sit about me mourning, whensoever thou haply art not at hand" (*Odyssey* 10.483–485; tr. Murray *LCL*). Circe had promised to send him home; what promise did he give her in return? Her response might be understood to mean, "I will but first you have to go to Hades on a final labor (the *Nekyia*) for me."[24]

Odysseus' role as an agent becomes fully visible only in *Odyssey* 11.119–134, when Teiresias says that after killing the suitors, Odysseus would leave Ithaca to journey to people who did not know the sea and make sacrifices to Poseidon.

---

[22]   Having returned to Ithaca in disguise, Odysseus tells the disguised Athena that he fled from Crete after having "slain the dear son of Idomeneus, Orsilochus.... Now he would have robbed me of all that booty of Troy, for which I had borne grief of heart, passing through wars of men and the grievous waves, for that I would not shew favour to his father, and serve as his squire in the land of the Trojans, but commanded other men of my own" (*Odyssey* 13, 262–266; tr. Murray *LCL*).

[23]   A leader may have *therapontes*, and a *therapōn* may have *therapontes* (Aitken 1982).

[24]   Faraone (2019) notes the similarity of Circe's direction to Odysseus to a colonization oracle.

Odysseus then is/becomes Poseidon's agent.[25] This status is confirmed by Odysseus himself:

> And Odysseus of many wiles answered her [Penelope], and said: "Strange lady! Why dost thou now so urgently bid me tell thee? Yet I will declare it, and will hide nothing. Verily thy heart shall have no joy of it, even as I myself have none; for Teiresias bade me go forth to full many cities of men, bearing a shapely oar in my hands, till I should come to men that know naught of the sea, and eat not of food mingled with salt; aye, and they know naught of ships with purple cheeks, or of shapely oars that serve as wings to ships. And he told me this sign, right manifest; nor will I hide it from thee. When another wayfarer, on meeting me, should say that I had a winnowing fan on my stout shoulder, then he bade me fix my oar in the earth, and make goodly offerings to lord Poseidon—a ram and a bull and a boar, that mates with sows—and depart for my home, and offer sacred hecatombs to the immortal gods, who hold broad heaven, to each one in due order. *And death shall come to me myself far from the sea, a death so gentle, that shall lay me low, when I am overcome with sleek old age, and my people shall dwell in prosperity around me. All this, he said, should I see fulfilled.*"

> *Odyssey* 23.263–284; tr. Murray *LCL*; emphasis added

One might object that Odysseus' role was to placate Poseidon by serving as his missionary. Still, Odysseus' *nostos* had already taken him to out-of-the-way places, including sheep places. Recall the tale of Polyphemus "son of Poseidon," wherein Odysseus found very special sheep with "black violet" wool in a place without ships or builders of ships but which knew ships and traders. And Odysseus had to spend time in the cave of the nymph Calypso, producer of textiles. Calypso lives in Ogygia in the "midst of the sea," but she has no ships and, as noted by Dimock (1956: 57), her very name suggests concealment/hiding (*kalyptei*) or being in the middle of nowhere (cf. Segal 1962: 21). Recall, also, that Odysseus kept flocks in Aetolia, whose contingent in the Trojan War was led by Thoas, who had a special relationship with Poseidon in that the deity addresses him personally and at some length (*Iliad* 13.92, 215–218).

M. L. West (2014: 5) believes that perhaps, unlike some other figures, Odysseus "has a role in the story [of the Trojan War] as far back as we can see." Moreover, he has important roles including devising the Trojan horse. Unlike West (2014: 9), I do not accept that Odysseus' adoption by inland places is a

---

[25]   As noted in Chap. 6.3, Poseidon shared Sphagianes, the district in which the king of Pylos is chosen, with Potnia the main sponsor of luxury textiles.

matter of communities late to enter pan-Hellenic culture seeking to gain status by claiming they were founded by an ancient hero. There is neither evidence nor reason to assume that Odysseus' repeated connections with inland sites are a late and artificial insertion in Homer. Indeed, in an alternative version, the agent role of Odysseus may have been more openly depicted. Thus, as summarized by Burgess (2017: 32–33), in the *Telegony* of the Trojan Cycle, which is (conventionally) dated to the sixth century BCE,

> The summary by Proclus reports two journeys on the mainland after the slaughter of the suitors. First Odysseus visits Elis to see after livestock. After the Elis sojourn, Odysseus returns to Ithaca—note the back-and-forth sea and land interconnectivity at play here—before returning to the mainland for another journey. Odysseus now travels to Thesprotia, which becomes an alternative homeland when he stays with the queen and produces a child. In some respects Odysseus' mainland journey seems like a real-world version of the inland journey. Correspondence between the "inland journey" and the Thesprotian journey is implicitly implied in Apollodorus (*Epitome* 7.34), where it is specified that Odysseus in Thesprotia performs sacrifices enjoined by Tiresias in order to propitiate Poseidon.

However, in the *Odyssey* (14.95–108, 19.277–287), Elis and Thesprotia are regions where Odysseus had flocks of sheep, and Odysseus (in his lie) sought wealth in Thesprotia instead of returning directly home to Ithaca from Phaeacia. Proclus' abstract adds that before leaving Ithaca for Elis, Odysseus sacrificed to the (textile-producing and marketing) nymphs. Poseidon's (and Odysseus') concern with sheep, wool, and textiles is obvious in the labors after the killing of the suitors.

Odysseus represents a combination of a commercial agent and an entrepreneur, specifically in the production and marketing of textiles. These duties required him to participate in the Trojan War. They also explain his wanderings after the War to obscure sheep and textile country—his final "labor" (*Odyssey* 23.248–250): Teiresias, the seer, knew that Poseidon, the Bronze Age god, wanted wool and sheep for breeding and he also knew that Odysseus, the Bronze Age man, was professionally well-qualified to obtain it. This is the nature, I submit, of Odysseus' service to Poseidon. Moreover, of course, for the places of service to be of service, they could not be very far from the sea.

The agent in antiquity had to be the slave of his principal, so we must assume that Odysseus was the slave of the god Poseidon. However, we may understand that Odysseus agreed to serve in this capacity because he was promised great rewards. Perhaps it was Poseidon who elevated Odysseus to kingship in Ithaca in the first place.[26] The final reward, as can be seen, is that he would not only be freed from his labors (achieve *psuchē* 'life'), but, like Heracles, become immortal.[27] Whether his death and worship come when he is "apart/away from the sea"—that is, in one of the inland regions he was assigned to develop—or "from the sea" while in Ithaca remains ambiguous (discussed by W. Hansen 1977). The meaning "away from the sea" would predict inland shrines to Odysseus.

Admittedly, I have not taken into account Poseidon's wrath against Odysseus for blinding his agent Polyphemus. However, Odysseus had performed many textile-related services before blinding Polyphemus, including traveling to his rich-in-sheep homeland. Moreover, as Murgatroyd (2015: 444) notes, "But the only specified manifestation of that anger is the storm roused by the sea-god after Odysseus leaves Calypso in Book 5, in the tenth year after Polyphemus' prayer to his father for revenge." *Odyssey* 1.20–21, 1.68–75 may be read, I submit, to mean that Poseidon, as a hard and demanding taskmaster, drove Odysseus from one labor to another before he consented to let him return to Ithaca. What does stand out without argument is that Poseidon, and only Poseidon, controlled Odysseus, as is exemplified in *Odyssey* 1.19-20: "And all the gods pitied him save Poseidon; but he continued to rage unceasingly against godlike Odysseus until at length he reached his own land" (tr. Murray *LCL*). I understand "godlike" *antitheos* in the sense "acted for"/"represented" a god. The god represented by Odysseus can only be Poseidon.

5. Wealthy Phaeacia and the Wrath of Poseidon

Upon being washed up in Scheria, Odysseus is attended to by Athena, who, among other enhancing features, *colors his wooly (oulos) hair hyacinth/purplish-blue* (*Odyssey* 6.243–244; Griffith 2005: 331–332; Chapter 15.5.e above). This transformation not only attests to his great value but also links Odysseus' mission in Phaeacia with purple-dyed textiles.

Then, Odysseus receives a prophecy from the nymph-like Nausicaa:

---

[26]   As Telemachus tells one of the suitors: "Nay, it is no bad thing to be a king. Straightway one's house grows rich and oneself is held in greater honor" (*Odyssey* 3.394; tr. Murray *LCL*). Homer does not explain how Odysseus became a king in Ithaca: "Throughout most of the *Odyssey* Laertes is portrayed as a simple, helpless old man whose responsibilities have long since passed to Odysseus, and hence to Telemachus and Eumaeus; Arceisius [his paternal grandfather] is no more than a name (4.755; 16.118; 24.270, 517), and entirely without mention in the *Iliad*" (Haft 1984: 293 n. 13).

[27]   Calypso offered immortality to her slave Odysseus, but he rejected it. Homer says nothing about the labors Odysseus carried out during his seven years as Calypso's slave.

But turn not thine eyes upon any man nor question any, for the men here endure not stranger-folk, nor do they give kindly welcome to him who comes from another land. They, indeed, trusting in the speed of their swift ships, cross over the great gulf of the sea, for this the Earth-shaker [Poseidon] has granted them; and their ships are swift as a bird on the wing or as a thought.

Odyssey 7.31–35; tr. Murray *LCL*

The Phaeacians' personal names are saturated with connections to the sea, as is explained by Kanavou (2015: 121–122), who notes that such naming is "appropriate for the Phaeacians as descendants of Poseidon and mostly seamen ... and allude to one or other aspect of seamanship: the ability to sail, the ships and the building of ships, and the sea itself." The Phaeacian women have not been overlooked. They are highly skilled in the craft of textile production, and this is their gift from Athena: "For as the Phaeacian men are skilled above all others in speeding a swift ship upon the sea, so are the women cunning workers at the loom, for Athena has given to them above all others skill in fair handiwork, and an understanding heart" (*Odyssey* 7.107ff; tr. Murray *LCL*).[28]

In fact, Queen Arētē leans against a pillar as she and her "slaves" (*dmōai*) (*Odyssey* 6.306) spin purple cloth that is a "wonder to behold," utilizing weaving skill given to them by Athena (*Odyssey* 7.71, 7.111). And the Queen's slaves are numerous and productive: "And fifty slave-women he had in the house, of whom some grind the yellow grain on the millstone, and others weave webs, or, as they sit, twirl the yarn, like unto the leaves of a tall poplar tree; and from the closely-woven linen the soft olive oil drips down" (*Odyssey* 7,144–146; Murray *LCL*). The women are making sheer linen.

Nothing more is heard about the relationship between Athena and the Phaeacian women with the possible exception of Athena's advice to Odysseus that he should first seek help from Queen Arētē, not from King Alcinoos (*Odyssey* 7.50ff.). Perhaps the point is that Athena has, because of her gifts, a special relationship with the Phaeacian women.

More certainly, there is irony in Homer's report (*Odyssey* 6.8) that the Phaeacians had founded their city far from the *alphēstaōn*—that is, far from "men who eat grain" or "men of enterprise" (LSJ s.v. *alphēstai*; Beekes s.v.

---

[28] Through the words of Nausicaa, Homer (*Odyssey* 6.291ff.) makes clear that the grove (*alsos*) of Athena is located next to the land (*temenos*) of King Alcinoos. We are free to wonder whether a grateful Alcinoos carved out Athena's land from his own or whether she bestowed hers to him (L. R. Palmer 1963: 83–84).

alphēstēs).[29] Are we to understand that the Phaeacian production of cloth and their seaborne travels were personal leisure activities? Sherratt (1996: 91) writes, "For the Phaeacians, seafaring is desirable only for the sake of competitive sportsmanship—a kind of physical exercise to keep them fit rather than as a means of grasping profit sought by such maritime traders as the Phoenicians or as the *Hymn of Apollo*'s [458] Cretans." Perhaps the Phoenicians and Cretans also enjoyed thinking of themselves in terms of this ideology that eschews effort but not the enjoyment of its fruits (see Sherratt 1996: 92).

Nevertheless, the Phaeacians have become wealthy—very wealthy, as it is easy to see. Most obviously, they are viewed as *agchitheio* "godlike"/"close to the gods" (*Odyssey* 19.279; LSJ s.v) and as *philoi athanatoisin*, or "loved by the immortals." "Godlike" means that the Phaeacians had gold and purple like the gods in their temples; "loved by the immortals" means more generally that they were wealthy.[30] That the Phaeacians were not fortuitously wealthy but actively sought wealth is proven by the report that before retiring for the night, it was their practice to offer a toast to Hermes, the god of commerce (*Odyssey* 7.136–138). Not only did they seek wealth but it also came to them every day and, indeed, they even dreamed of it! Homer has a very good sense of humor.

The Cyclops is an explicit agent of Poseidon. There are reasons to believe that the Phaeacians are his agents as well. They are called *antitheoioi* 'godlike Phaeacians' (*Odyssey* 6.242), which, I think, can be understood as "acting for"/"representing" gods, as in the instance of Odysseus. Their agent status is firmly indicated by Poseidon's complaint that the Phaeacians are acting on their own behalf without his permission. Thus, Alcinoos, the king of the Phaeacians, informs Odysseus:

> And tell me thy country, thy people, and thy city, that our ships may convey thee thither, discerning the course by their wits. For the Phaeacians have no pilots, nor steering-oars such as other ships have, but their ships of themselves understand the thoughts and minds of men, and they know the cities and rich fields of all peoples, and most swiftly do they cross over the gulf of the sea, hidden in mist and cloud, nor ever have they fear of harm or ruin. Yet this story I once heard thus told by my father Nausithous, who was wont to say that *Poseidon*

---

[29]   They did not live far from the settlements of grain-eaters. Is the joke that the "godlike" Phaeacians were far from the "grain-eaters" in the sense of enjoying a more luxurious diet? See below.

[30]   Coating the statue of a god with gold makes it "immortal and unaging" and the "application of gold leaf provides sparkling surfaces not only by reflexion, but also from 'inner light', associating it directly with the divine sphere" (Brecoulaki 2014: 32).

was wroth with us because we give safe convoy to all men.[31] He said that someday, as a well-built ship of the Phaeacians was returning from a convoy over the misty deep, Poseidon would smite her and would fling a great mountain about our city. So that old man spoke, and these things the god will haply bring to pass, or will leave unfulfilled, as may be his good pleasure.

Odyssey 8.555–570; tr. Murray *LCL*; emphasis added

The same point is made directly by Poseidon to Zeus:

"Father Zeus, no longer shall I, even I, be held in honor among the immortal gods, seeing that mortals honor me not a whit—even the Phaeacians, who, thou knowest, are of my own lineage (*genethlē*). For I but now declared that Odysseus should suffer many woes ere he reached his home, though I did not wholly rob him of his return when once thou hadst promised it and confirmed it with thy nod; yet in his sleep these men have borne him in a swift ship over the sea and set him down in Ithaca, and have given him gifts past telling, stores of bronze and gold and woven raiment, more than Odysseus would ever have won for himself from Troy, if he had returned unscathed with his due share of the spoil."

Odyssey 13.125–138; tr. Murray *LCL*

Poseidon asserts that the Phaeacian men who convoy—that is, work for all comers—without having received his permission (cf. *Odyssey* 8.570f.) are his *genethlē* "offspring." This status is confirmed by the report that *Arētē* descends from Poseidon and that Poseidon is the grandfather of Alcinoos, King of Phaeacia (*Odyssey* 7.56ff). The Phaeacians are Poseidon's children, meaning his agents, but they are disobedient and self-interested agents.

In the fabulous tale of the high-living Phaeacians, Homer has embedded a reference to a real-life legal dispute between agent and principal. Legally speaking, Poseidon's complaint is that his agents, the Phaeacian men, are doing business on their own without their principal Poseidon's permission. The diversion of their personal effort (labor) damages Poseidon's interests, and they damage them even more if they do side business using Poseidon's capital—his ships, for example. To judge by their speed, the ships are probably state of the art oared galleys: "Here (Ithaca) they (the Phaeacians) rowed in, knowing

---

[31] Had the Phaeacians really lived far from men who live by work there would have been little occasion for Poseidon to complain about such behavior. Yet Alcinoos speaks as if such conveyance was normal or even frequent (*Odyssey* 8.31–33).

the place of old; and the ship ran full half her length on the shore in her swift course, at such pace was she driven by the arms of the rowers" (*Odyssey* 13.113f. tr. Murray *LCL*).

An interesting example of illicit "side business" is found in the penalization of Heracles in his commission to remove the dung from the cattle yard of Augeius. As explained by Silver (1992: 119):

> A legal dispute arose because Heracles, despite his status as Eurystheos' agent, made a side-deal with Augeios for a tenth (*dekatēn*) of the cattle. When Augeios learned of Herakles' *athlos* for Eurystheos, he refused to pay the promised tenth. For his part, Eurytheos refused to credit Herakles with a fulfilled commission because his activity 'had been performed for hire' (*misthō peprachhthai*) (Apollodorus *Library* 2.5.5).

Silver goes on to illustrate Eurystheus' complaint by citing Babylonian long-distance trading contracts.

Alcinoos belatedly responds to Poseidon's threats by ordering the Phaeacians to cease giving escort to all comers (*Odyssey* 13.180–181). Until then, as Burgess (2011: 283) suggests, the Phaeacians have made isolated Scheria into a "travel hub."

In the light of Poseidon's demands on the Phaeacians, it might be suggested that Odysseus received hostile treatment from Poseidon not because he blinded Polyphemus—admittedly an agent of Poseidon[32]—but rather because he was inclined to go off and do business on his own behalf: for example, instead of returning to Ithaca, he sought wealth in Thesprotia.

---

[32] In fact, Odysseus insinuates to Polyphemus that it was Poseidon's will that he come to his primitive land (*Odyssey* 9.283).

Excursus 2

Speculative Remarks on Currency in Homer

1. Hermes Rescues Arēs from the Pot

IT IS well to preface the following remarks with more realistic ones concerning contemporary ancient economies. From Bronze Age sources, including the Amarna letters, and somewhat earlier Babylonian sources, comes evidence that fragments of precious metals were placed into *sealed* sacks and pots and used to make payments—that is, they circulated as currency (G. Singer 2013; Silver 2006b; Chap. 11.3).

That the two gods Hermes and Arēs enjoyed cooperative relations in Pylos is suggested in *Iliad* 5.385–391, wherein Hermes rescues Arēs,[1] who had been bound/restrained in a "bronze pot" (*chalkeō en keramō dedeto*; LSJ s.v. *keramos*). Homer's text explains that Arēs, as *atos polemoio* "insatiate of war," would otherwise have perished from his confinement (tr. Murray *LCL*). However, If we understand the meaning of *polemoio* to include not only "formal war" (the engagement of troops representing different states) but "strife"/"contest"/"battle," we may understand that the god was insatiate not solely for physical violence but also for the rivalrous process of acquisition—that is, Arēs had to be free to move about to conquer/accumulate.[2]

At this point, it becomes possible to detect a theme of commercial cooperation, or at least complementary cooperation, between Hermes and Arēs. That is, in telling the tale of the rescue, Homer had in mind pots of precious metal bearing the validation stamp of Arēs (Silver 1992: 68–69). Thus, Hermes would have freed the pot from the temple vault and allowed Arēs to circulate in accordance with his true nature as *business capital*.[3]

---

[1]   Recall the earlier discussion of the etymology of Arēs in the context of Aeschylus' *Agamemnon*.

[2]   "The Hittite word, *lahha-* denoted a military campaign and a commercial trip (CHD L-N 4f.). Only the context can show which is intended in any given occurrence." (Hoffner 2002; cf. Nikoloudis 2008b: 591–592).

[3]   Homer's choice of *chalkeō* may offer an additional clue. Beekes explains (s.v. *chalkos*): "The prehistory of Greek *chalkos* is obscure. An IE term is improbable, as a word with an aspirate and

2. The Double-Headed Axes of Iron
as an Archery Prize

In the *Iliad*, there is an archery contest sponsored by Achilles, "son of Pelius," in which the prizes are made of *ioenta sidēron*, or "dark/violet colored iron"; the first prize is ten *pelekus*, and the second prize is ten *ēmipelakka*. *Pelekus* means "double-axe" (Beekes s.v.) and *ēmipelekkon* might then be rendered as "half (of a double-headed) axe." Meriones wins the first prize, and Teucer the second, and then they take the prizes to their ships (*Iliad* 23.851, 882).

Do these prizes have the physical form of iron double-headed axes? That this is the case is supported by another archery contest won by Odysseus (*Odyssey* 21.421–423), in which double-headed axes are themselves the target: Odysseus wins by (obscurely) threading twelve double-axes (Fraser 1932). S. Morris (1997: 623 with Fig. 1) cites a sealing from Beth Shean in which Ramses II (thirteenth century BCE) shoots arrows through the body of a double-headed axe. Once again, Homer is credibly linked to Bronze Age material.

A further point is that Achilles would not have offered multiple double-axes as prizes unless they were valuable—that is, the double-axes are not simply souvenirs or of only symbolic value. That the double-axes are *counted* indicates that they are somehow standardized. That is, one would not think of a prize comprised of double-axes of varying sizes or weights. Neither I think would prizes of standard shape and weight be expected to vary much in metal quality. What I am getting at is that, in addition to any utilitarian value of the axes or the metal itself, the prizes were qualified to serve as money in exchange transactions.

Finally, why a double-headed axe? As noted earlier, the Janiform symbol with its implication of "coming-going" makes it a fitting symbol for money. At the same time, the double-axe is the prime symbol of the Labyrinth. Hence, I propose that the iron double-axes were produced under the auspices of Potnia to serve as a medium of exchange. On the latter score, there is Hittite evidence that is conveniently summarized by Siegelova and Tsumoto (2011: 281, 296–297):

> In Hittite sources of the 17th-16th centuries (Old Hittite period) iron still appears as an extraordinary material, restricted to the production of royal insignia and weapons such as lances and sceptres, which were at the same time used in ritual and magical contexts. In texts of the Middle Hittite period (15th-beginning of the 14th century BC), the repertoire

---

a voiceless stop is not tolerated. The similarity with the word for 'purple' *kalchē* also *chalkē*, and *chalchē* is hardly accidental. It would point to an original meaning 'red metal' for *chalkos* ... which is conceivable" (my transliterations).

of iron objects grew and now included ceremonial objects such as various axes and the *lituus* as well as jewellery, which was distributed to cult functionaries. Under the Hittite empire (14th-13th centuries BC), the attestations for iron objects rise considerably. Again, the repertoire broadens: in addition to royal insignia, it was used for cultic objects, such as idols in anthropomorphic or zoomorphic shape, which testifies to the high appreciation of iron. Simultaneously, however, larger numbers of knives, daggers, and/or swords or spearheads appear in Hittite texts of this time. On the other hand, iron jewellery becomes rarer. That iron was more widely used during the Empire period is also corroborated by the fact that communities delivered their taxes in iron and that it was now weighed in *minas*. "Black iron," which is mentioned in written documents, has sometimes been interpreted as meteoric iron. The archaeological finds do not allow any conclusions to be drawn about the nature or origin of this material. However, judging from its quantities mentioned in written texts, it is hard to conclude that it was indeed of meteoric origin.

Unfortunately, I cannot summon any direct evidence for the use of iron double-headed axes as money in the Bronze Age Aegean. The *Iliad* (7.466ff. 475) describes a trade festival in the shelter of the newly completed Achaean Wall, in which Euneos, the son of Jason, unloads wine from his ships and exchanges it with the Achaeans (and Trojans) for hides, bronze, whole cattle, slaves, and "gleaming/fiery iron."

However, the iron is not said to be in the form of the double-headed axe and is surrounded by barter transactions (in hides, and cattle). On other hand, I can cite some suggestive Hittite evidence. First, the reference to the use of iron in the second millennium Anatolia is not anachronistic. Specifically, the Hittites produced "various axes" and probably produced "black iron" (AN.BAR GE$_6$) and "good iron" (SIG$_5$), probably meaning "purified iron." Furthermore, the Hittites used metal ingots as means of payment and as prizes in festivals (I. Singer 2006: esp. 254). In one intriguing case (KUB 42.21), a chest holding assorted metallic objects "includes the item 6 PAD *TA-YA-AR-TU* (obv. 10). The basic meaning of *tayyartut(m)* is 'return, repetition' (CDA, 402), which may perhaps refer to a crescent-shaped ingot" (I. Singer 2006: 254). Instead, it may refer to a double-headed ingot; the metallic content of the ingot is not stated.

To state the obvious: much more evidence is required not only about the use of metal ingots but also about the role of Achilles, the son of Peleus by the nymph Thetis.

PART V

QUESTIONS OF AEGEAN TEXTILE TRADE
BEFORE THE TROJAN WAR
AND AFTER THE MYCENAEAN PALACES

16

Thoughts on the Golden Fleece and Textile Trade

HOMER mentions a voyage of the Argo to somewhere in the Pontic area,[1] and it is easily inferred that the Argonauts were led by Jason.[2] The voyage is fixed in relative time: it took place before the events that Homer is concerned with—that is, before the Trojan War. There are other clues that narrow the timing: for example, the voyage of the Argo became famous ("well known to all" *Odyssey* 12.70), a fact that in a world of slow communications would mean it took place some years before. I disagree with Lordkipanidze (2001: 8) and Strabo 1.2.40 that the fame of the voyage necessarily implies that it must have passed through "well-known and populous regions," although this would have hastened its notoriety.

Lemnos, as has already been seen, has a special place in the *Iliad*. It is not only sacked but also trades with the Achaeans. Although he knows Lemnos and the Hellespont and Aeetes (*Odyssey* 10.137–150), Homer is rather vague about the geographic coordinates of the Argo's destination. This does not necessarily mean that the coordinates were unknown at the time of the voyage or in Homer's time (Endsjø 1997 is instructive but overly critical). Further, as noted by Homer (*Odyssey* 10.135–139) "… and we came to the isle of Aeaea, where dwelt fair-tressed Circe, a dread goddess of human speech, own sister to Aeetes of baneful mind; and both are sprung from Helius, who gives light to mortals, and from Perse, their mother, whom Oceanus begot." Bremmer (2007: 21 with references) adds that Aietes, the son of Helios, "clearly derived his name, 'the man from Aia', from the island of Aia, where Helios rises each day. This connection of

---

[1]   "All the Pontic features related to the voyage of the Argonauts were used by Homer particularly in his description of the Ocean, and in this, he probably followed his source. The ship of the Argonauts is also directly mentioned in the *Odyssey* (12.70) in the oceanic context, which implies that the Argonauts must have sailed over the Ocean. Thus, in Homeric time, the voyage of the Argonauts was localized in Ocean and in the Black Sea at the same time, which also confirms the hypothesis that one was identical with the other" (Ivantchik 2017: 14)

[2]   The name "Jason" is mentioned in a Linear B tablet from Pylos (PY Cn 655).

Aia with the sun must be a Hittite heritage, as Aia is the name of the wife of the Sun in Hittite and Mesopotamian religion."

So, Homer knows of the voyage of the Argonauts to the Black Sea. He also knows, as is reflected in later sources, that Lemnos played a role in the voyage. Moreover, Euneos (Eunēus)—the king of Lemnos and son of Jason—appears in both Homer and the Linear B tablets at Knossos, in the latter as *e-u-na-wo* (KN As 1520, B 799 and Dv 206). In addition, some of the places and participants mentioned in later sources appear to be attested to in the Linear B tablets. Thus, Hiller (1991: 214) has proposed that *i-wa-so* in a Pylos tablet (PY Cn 655.6) refers to the name *Jason*. However, Palaima (2007b: 200 n. 21) notes, with respect to *i-wa-so*, that the consensus of scholarly opinion favors an identification with *Iwasos*—Homeric *Iasos*. As noted earlier, there is an ambiguity problem here, as in alphabetic Greek, the *w* disappears, and Linear B omits final consonants—that is, both Iason and Uasis are possible.[3]

Even without "Iason," the mention in the Linear B tablets of a number of additional names associated with the voyage of the Argonauts suggests that the Mycenaeans had Black Sea connections (Palaima 2007b: 200). C. Thomas (2005: 72–73) has called attention to a related point, namely the appearance of names ending in -*eus* among Homer's heroes (some fifty names including Odysseus and Achilleus), among the Argonauts (at least six names including Oileus, Orpheus, and Peleus), and among legendary heroes generally (e.g., Aegeus, Theseus, Eurystheus). This is a striking naming practice because, in classical Greece, such names are virtually non-existent. For example, in classical Athens, names ending in –*eus* amount to a mere 0.38% among all named individuals (A. Davis 2000: 35–36). Did later writers *choose* these names for ancient heroes precisely because they were no longer current? If so, the names are very ancient because, in Mycenaean time, there were among living individuals, some 130 different –*eus* names out of 1,800 names or 7.26%. A. Davis (2000: 35) notes that "the onomastics of epic language matches to a certain extent that of Mycenaean but the later language is different." C. Thomas (2005: 73) suggests that the Argonauts, together with such companions as Heracles, "belong to an earlier heroic generation than the heroes associated with the Trojan War," (cf. Chap. 12.1) to which we might add, earlier also than the Mycenaeans of Linear B times.

The reference to a famous voyage may be fictional, but it is not in itself a myth. Homer's vague reference to the voyage's destination may be mythical, however. I mean that "Ocean" may be a coded reference to Colchis—that is, the

---

[3]   In the Pylos An series oxen tablets, *i-wa-so* functions as a descriptive term, perhaps an ethnic term, and the same is thought to apply to the mentioned occurrence in Cn 655.6. A descriptive term might fit very well as I view Jason to mean something like "purpled" (see below). In the *Odyssey* 18.246 there is a reference to "Iasian Argos."

place ruled by Aeetes, whom the Hittites knew as the son of Helios, the sun. On the other hand, perhaps, Homer's vagueness is merely intended to convey that the Argo's voyage was in some sense pioneering and, therefore, deserving of an aura of mystery and suspense. An aura of mystery is appropriate not only for the first voyage from the Greek mainland to the Black Sea but to a resumption of contact after a lengthy hiatus. Thus, the Minyan Jason reportedly voyaged from *Thessaly* to the Black Sea (Colchis), but an earlier and much more mysterious contact is indicated by the report that Phrixus, also a Minyan, flew on a golden-fleeced ram or, much better, swam—that is, traveled on a ship with the head of a ram[4]—from *Boeotia* to the Black Sea. Interestingly, Phrixus' ram had a golden fleece *before* it arrived in the Black Sea region and, therefore, did not have to be made golden by being used as the liner of a sluice-box for catching gold in a stream.[5] Phrixus was welcomed in Colchis by Aeetes, who had earlier migrated from *Corinth* to Colchis.[6]

Aeetes appears to be the first Greek colonist in the Black Sea region. Phrixus, who had to flee Boeotia, may also be understood to be a Greek colonist (Braund 1994: 21–22). However, why is Phrixus made to bring a golden fleece with him to the Black Sea region? More than a colonist, Phrixus resembles the figure of the trader who settles down in a distant port and takes a local woman as his secondary wife. Phrixus did not intend to sever his ties to Boeotia, but, due to unforeseen circumstances, he did not make his way back to his homeland. However, the "sons of Phrixus" wished to return to Greece, and, in some versions, they returned before the Argo sailed (Matthews 1977: 204–205).

Why did Jason take the Argo to distant shores little trodden by natives of the Greek mainland? When asked by a reporter why he wanted to climb Mt. Everest, George Mallory, who died on the mountain in 1924, answered, "Because it's there." Perhaps we should understand that Jason went to "Aia"

---

4   See Robertson 1940: 3–4. Several Bronze Age clay "sauceboats" from mainland Greece (Zygouries, Corinth, and Tiryns) have ram's heads (Weinberg 1969). One can imagine that the originals were of gold. Some context for the head of a ram on a vessel's bow is provided by the depiction of moths on the masts and prows of ships depicted in frescoes in the West House at Akrotiri. The building, which contained loom-weights, may have participated in the (wild) silk industry (Panagiotakopulu 2000: 585–588), a theory supported by the finding of a *Pachypasa otus* cocoon at Akrotiri.

5   No real explanation is offered for the return of the fleece to Iolcus. In Pindar (*Pythian Ode* 4.160ff.), Peleas asks Jason to "bring back" Phrixus' "soul" (*psuchē) and* the fleece that saved him from the sea. Why bring it back? I surmise that the reference is to a *cult installation* for Phrixus that includes a statue/image of a fleece or ram.

6   Aeetes must be viewed as a merchant who set up a trading station in Colchis on the Black Sea region. At least, I see no other explanation for his departure wherein he entrusted Corinth to Bounos, who was the "son of Hermes and Alkidameia." Sources: Eumelus *Corinthiaca* Fragments 3.88, 19 2.3.10; Pausanias 1.115.15–16, 2.3.10.

(Aiaiēn = Circe's Island) because its very presence challenged his heroic nature. It is another thing to say that those gods and mortals, whom we are told by the sources contributed significant resources for his voyage, were similarly challenged. The alternative understanding to a search for adventure is that Jason and/or his backers—Athena, Hera, and King Pelias, by whom he was assigned the "labor" (commission) to bring back the *chruseion kōas* 'Golden Fleece'—were mainly motivated by the acquisition of wealth.[7] Homer couples Pelias with Neleus (king of Pylos): both are servants of Zeus; and "Pelias dwelt in spacious Iolcus, and was *rich in flocks*, and the other dwelt in sandy Pylos" (*Odyssey* 11.256–257; tr. Murray *LCL*; emphasis added). Thessaly generally was rich in flocks: *Iliad* 2.696, 2.705–706, 2.711–715 and, in *Iliad* 2.795, the port town Pyrasos is "flowery," meaning, I propose, rich in dyed textiles (see Chap.7.6).

The wealth motivation was certainly recognized by Hesiod (*Works and Days* 681ff.): "For my part I do not praise it, for my heart does not like it. Such a sailing is snatched, and you will hardly avoid mischief. Yet in their ignorance men do even this, for wealth means life to poor mortals; but it is fearful to die among the waves" (tr. Evelyn-White *LCL*). Indeed, a merchant-adventurer who returned to his home port with a purse full of gold might well be regarded as a hero! Certainly, the acquisition of wealth would have very much enhanced interest in the voyage of the Argo to the point it became known to all. Add to this that Euneos "*Ship-Man*" sought gain when, as Homer tells it, he traded with the Greeks and others (Chap. 14.3.c). Like father, like son?

In some versions of the myth, the Argonauts are a kind of organized criminal enterprise commissioned to *steal* the Golden Fleece. Raiders are always more interesting than traders! Still, would the Argonauts have earned undying fame for a single criminal caper? I think not, especially when the Golden Fleece they stole is, as we are told, the same one that Greeks had previously given as a goodwill gift to the Colchians. For such unheroic (and pointless) behavior, they more likely would have earned infamy rather than *kleos*. Moreover, the question remains what it was that the Argonauts stole. That is, what is a "golden fleece" (*chryseion kōas*), and does it differ from gold? More generally, a major problem with a theft interpretation is the emphasis placed on fleeces in the myth. Thus, Apollonius Rhodius makes it a point to tell that aboard the Argo, Jason slept in "soft woolen fleeces" (*Argonautica.* 1.1088f.; tr. Race *LCL*). Indeed, we find Jason himself represented as a purple-dyed fleece and, indeed, not only does he often

---

[7]   Pindar (*Pythian Ode* 4.41) has Argonauts take slave-agents (*therapontes*) with them and in Apollonius Rhodius *Argonautica* 1.305, Jason mentions his slaves (*dmōes*). Braswell (1988: 121) understands they are all going on the expedition. Thus, what is portrayed is a major undertaking of not only fifty-five "heroes."

wear a purple cloak (a gift of Athena, a gift of Hypsipyle of Lemnos[8]) but also even his very ancient name arguably means *"purpled."*[9] The process by which Jason is "purpled" is visible in later Greek iconography.[10] The opening up of a long-lasting, lucrative trade network, in which woolen fleeces were exchanged for gold, would be celebrated by the participants. Diverse communities would find a reason to advertise that Jason, the great adventurer, "slept here"!

Homer leaves clues to a commercial motivation, including the names of such figures as Philoctetes "gain-lover"/"gain-seeker." The malodorous Philoctetes left behind on Lemnos recalls the malodorous Lemnian women, who Silver (1991: 248–252) surmised purple-dyed the fleeces brought to Lemnos aboard the Argo.[11] Of course, although Silver did not know this when he wrote in 1991, there is ample evidence in Bronze Age Lemnos not only of a purple-extraction industry but of connections to Thessaly from whence the Argo originated. The bad odor is not intrinsic to the Lemnian Women[12] or Philoctetes; it is from something done on Lemnos.[13]

---

[8] The source for the gifts of purple-dyed garments is Apollonius Rhodius *Argonautica*: gift from Athena (1.721ff,); from Hypsipyle (3.1205–1206); also, from a Lemnian woman to Polydeuces (2.30–31); in Colchis, Medea wears a purple robe (4.1659–1663). Garments as prizes in the Lemnian games are noted by Pindar *Pythian Ode* 4.253.

[9] Iasōn from the verb *iaomai* 'to heal' is cognate to the goddess of healing Iasō (Braswell 1988: 370). However, in no version of the Argonaut myth does Jason heal anything (compare Swanson1974: 273; and Mackie 2001. This is not a decisive objection in terms of etymology, but Ustinova (2004: 509), citing various ancient authorities, and LSJ s.v. *iaomai* notes the meaning *"to be a violet color."* This meaning actually fits the evidence.

[10] In London, British Museum E163, we see a ram emerging from/being submerged into a boiling cauldron. I quote the description: "A woman ministers (Medea?) and a man with white-hair looks on (interpreted as Jason but he was young). In the centre is a large lebes on a tripod stand, over a blazing fire indicated by *purple flames* rising from an irregular mass of fuel on the ground; out of the *lebes* appears the fore part of a ram springing to the left towards Medea, who sprinkles over it some medicaments." Available at: https://www.britishmuseum.org/research/collec-tion_online/collection_object_details.aspx?objectId=399141&partId=1. In reviewing the appear-ance of Jason, Medea uses the term verb *porphureō* (Apollonius Rhodius 3.456), which includes the meanings "to become purple or red." "In this context, it is very difficult not to associate the etymology of the verb with the importance of red for the erotics of gaze" (Kampakoglou 2018: 130). It is even more difficult not to associate the verb with the purple-dyeing of cloth. Apollonius Rhodius and Simonides provide numerous clues for identifying Jason with a purple-dyed cloak.

[11] Zissos (2017: 208) explains that "one of the most persistent traditions about Lemnos in pre-Apollonian sources is that the Argonauts competed in athletic games there, judged by Hypsipyle," with clothing as prizes (Pindar *Olympian Ode* 4.17–27, *Pythian Ode* 4.251–254; Simonides PMG 547).

[12] But the *dysosmia* of the Lemnian women does not appear in all versions of the myth. It is mentioned by two post-Myrsilan authors, Apollodorus *Library* 1.9.17 and Hyginus *Fabulae* 15 (Jackson 1990: 79).

[13] Strabo 16.2.23: "The city [Tyre] was also unfortunate when it was taken by siege by Alexander; but it overcame such misfortunes and restored itself both by means of the seamanship of its

There are many other clues left by the mythmakers suggesting a commercial motivation, including the name "Argo."[14] The iconography, for example, includes an apparent identification of Jason with the ram and, indeed, with a purple-dyed cloak. In addition, in one version, we find Greeks freely giving the Golden Fleece to the Colchians, who in turn financed the activities of the Greek givers. Did the Greeks give a Golden Fleece, or did they give a Purple Fleece[15] that was transformed into gold by being sacrificed/traded? Alternatively, did they sacrifice/trade a Purple Fleece and receive a sheepskin sack filled with gold (like the Hittite *kurshas*)? Alternatively, did they sacrifice/trade a Purple Fleece and receive an ingot of gold in the form of an "oxhide" (copper) ingot? Alternatively, did they sacrifice/trade an ordinary sheepskin and receive one that was impregnated with gold by being used as the lining of a sluice-box?[16] *It is*

---

people, in which the Phoenicians in general have been superior to all peoples of all times, and by means of their dye-houses for purple; for the Tyrian purple has proved itself by far the most beautiful of all; and the shell-fish are caught near the coast; and the other things requisite for dyeing are easily got; and although the great number of dye-works makes the city unpleasant to live in, yet it makes the city rich through the superior skill of its inhabitants" (tr. Jones *LCL*). In other words, the city stunk but it was worth it!

[14] "Argo," the name of the ship, is from Argus its builder, or from *argus* meaning: "(of dogs) swift" (LSJ s.v.). The two sources may come to the same thing as the builder may not mean shipwright but capitalist, and "swift" may not refer to speed in an mph sense but to quickness/mental alertness in grasping opportunities—*entrepreneurial capacity*.

[15] In some of the oldest versions, the fleece is "purple" (Simonides *PMG* 576; Acusilaus [of Argos 6th BCE]); *FGrH* 2 F 37 = 37 Fowler "The Fleece [*chrōma* "skin"] was not golden, but dyed purple by the sea." Apparently, its brilliance can be expressed in terms of both gold and red." (Kampakoglou 2018: 130). Bachhuber (2016: 357) provides a novel twist on the golden fleece as gold on a background of purpled cloth: "At the same time, I am struck by the use of red in the presentation of EBA Anatolian metal finery in both museum displays and books. A casual stroll through the Museum of Anatolian Civilizations in Ankara, or a flip through the *Gold of Troy* volume [Tolstikov and Treister 1996] ... shows a regular tendency to display metal objects from sites like Alacahöyük and Troy against felts of red. The greens in copper-based objects, the yellows in gold and the blues in silver illuminate in brilliant contrast against a red cloth" Bachhuber (2016: 358) cites Anatolian examples of gold beads sewn to woolen textiles or the use of gold thread to sew on faience beads, and he "proposes that this effect was enhanced by dyed textiles, particularly when the colour is red, and when the red interacts with the yellows, blues and greens glinting from decorative metal objects."

[16] The Hittite's *kursha* is a fleecy hunting bag/pouch made of goat skin or sheep skin. It is depicted hanging on a wall near the *eya*-tree symbolizing prosperity (Watkins 2000: 2–3 with Figure 1). This is as close as we have come to the sluice-box model of gold stuck in carpet(bag). It is "merely" a receptacle for valuables and normally kept in the "house of the hunting bags." It was periodically replaced the way that carpet for sluice bag would be. Texts say that it contained "sheep fat" and other good things and might be kept in the house of the "war god." Sources: Bremmer 2007: 23; McMahon 1991: 143–188, 250–254; Bachvarova 2016: 103–104, 246 Fig. 8, 425 n.21. There is little doubt that golden basket-shaped earrings from Troy (Tolstikov and Treister 1996: 116 cat. 125 and 126) are modeled after the Hittite *kurshas*. Some 22 examples of such earrings have been found at Troy, in the Troad, and at Poliochni in Lemnos (Treister 1996: 200).

well to keep firmly in mind that however the Colchians obtained their gold and whatever its physical form, this fact would not explain how the Argonauts obtained the gold they returned with to Thessaly.[17] There is no free Golden Fleece.

Another very basic question is why Homer mentions the Argo's voyage at all. It does not seem to be required to solve any problem raised by his plot. Or perhaps it is. We are left with the thought that the mention of the voyage is a clue for understanding the motivation for the Trojan War itself. This intuition is amplified by the emphasis Homer places on the dress of Odysseus at the time he departs for the war: a double-fold, purple-dyed cloak with a gold pin stuck in it. That is, a purple-dyed fleece able to draw to itself the gold or *ambrosia* that Homer's "doves" carried away from the Black Sea region.[18]

Finally, there is the central role played by Iolkos in Thessaly as the origin of the Argo's voyage to the Black Sea: Iolkos was a Mycenaean center and as the most northernmost center, it was at the same time the most convenient Greek point of departure for such a voyage (Hiller 1991: 213–214), Moreover, many names featured in the story of the Argonauts can be transliterated so as to have counterparts in the Linear B texts from Pylos. These include but are not limited to Aiaia, Aiates, Jason, and Mopsos (Hiller 1991: 214 and see above).

---

[17] Apollonius Rhodius *Argonautica* 2.1143–1145 says that Phrixus was riding a ram that "Hermes had turned into gold" (tr. Race *LCL*). This is strong testimony to a belief in the role of trade in transforming fleeces into wealth.

[18] Homer (*Odyssey* 2.62–63) has doves carrying ambrosia to Zeus. Is this Zeus who imports ambrosia located in the Pontic area or on the Greek mainland? That is, are the doves entering the Black Sea area or leaving it? In *Odyssey* 12.70, Circe unquestionably has Jason go through the Planctae *after* leaving Aia (Hopman 2012: 12). Thus, it seems reasonable to assume that the doves followed in Jason's wake carrying ambrosia. As Seaton (1887: 436) reasons, "but birds do not try to fly between them, but by them." Homer's point is not about the doves but about the ambrosia! What is ambrosia? Athena's sandals are *ambrosia chruseia* 'immortal gold', and as S. West (1988: 77) points out, "there is a clear semantic connection between these two adjectives; gold being imperishable [*aphthitos*], is symbolic of immortality, and the gods' possessions are characteristically of gold or silver, however inconvenient or impractical this may seem." Perhaps also the gods themselves are made of/with gold. The gods are "immortal and unaging" and, significantly, as noted by Clay (1981-1982: 117), "The formula to describe this state occurs in Homer without immediate reference to the gods: to describe the deathless and unaging golden dogs who guard the palace of Alcinoos" (*Odyssey* 7.94). The gods most closely resemble these beautiful imitations of nature, the art, the divine art of Hephaestus.

17

The Mycenaean Palaces
Collapse or Disintegration?

1. The Demise of the Mycenaean Palaces

AROUND 1200-1700 BCE (Late Helladic IIIB – IIIC:1), the Mycenaean palaces with their production facilities and elaborate showrooms for luxury textiles ceased to function: for example, "At Pylos, all of the texts (with a small number of exceptions) date to the year of the final destruction of the palace, ca. 1200bc, and cover a five to seven-month period" (Nakassis 2013: 22). The demise of the palatial system of textile production is commonly referred to as a "collapse." Substantial literature—theoretical and empirical—has developed around the problem of why this happened (Knapp and Manning 2016).[1]

Without attempting to review the various causal explanations, it is clear that there is a common theme with respect to the result: a centuries-long deterioration, if not a "dark age," in the economic life not only of Greece but of other centers in the ancient Near East. None of the proposed explanations have received general support. Perhaps this is because the theorists have looked only for things that went wrong instead of for things that went right![2] The present chapter aims to explore a new theory in which the palatial system of textile production collapses to make way for an economically superior organization of textile production.[3]

The currently favored causes of "collapse" include the destruction of the palaces—whether by natural or political causes—and their abandonment. There are, of course, problems of evidence to support this theory: "But destructions, whether by earthquake or by war or in the interest of reconstruction

---

[1] There is also a view that the "Dark Ages" were perhaps not so dark in the sense of a loss of generalized prosperity in areas such as Achaea and Italy that were less integrated than in the palatial economy (Hitchcock 2019).

[2] Palaima (2007a) provides a realistic discussion of the many things that went right, but he agrees that the system "collapsed."

[3] Some scholars may prefer other values than general living standards.

and abandonments of palatial centers are difficult to date by means of pottery styles. The easiest pots to date are painted pots and these are relatively rare at Pylos" (Middleton 2019: 13). This is a minor issue as compared to the theoretical issue. The destruction and even abandonment of palatial centers do not necessarily signal the collapse of international markets for luxury textiles or of the development of more local markets for cheaper colored textiles. In economic life, "bygones are bygones," meaning that if palaces remained optimal textile producers (in terms of profitability), they would eventually have been rebuilt, if not at the original sites then elsewhere. This difficulty is not taken into account by Wiener (2007b: 19–21), but it is recognized by Middleton (2010: 33). *Why did this restoration not take place?*

Was there an exogenous change in international markets, technology, or living standards calling for a radical decline in luxury textile production? It is easy enough to imagine such events but there is no evidence beyond the "palatial collapse" itself to suggest that anything like this actually happened. On the other hand, as will be seen, much evidence suggests that the Mycenaean society not only survived but also increased or maintained its participation in international trade.

That those destroyed palaces were not rebuilt and/or that functional palaces were abandoned might just as well signal not an economic collapse of the textile industry, to which the palaces had been devoted, but rather that the luxury textile industry had grown for long enough to enter a new phase of its lifecycle. Specifically, it is proposed that what scholars have referred to as a "collapse" is the culmination of an inevitable process in which a handful of *large vertically integrated* textile producers were displaced by numerous *small, vertically disintegrated* textile producers. This was a process in which a few generalists were defeated in the marketplace by numerous specialists. My theory is that the palaces did not "collapse"—they "disintegrated."

As I anticipate that many readers of this book will not be familiar with the economics of vertical integration and disintegration, I have included an Appendix that addresses the essentials of this analysis.

2. Vertical Structure in Minoan and Mycenaean Palaces

Were the Minoan palaces vertically integrated? Unfortunately, the Linear A tablets, which could tell us about their industrial structure, remain undeciphered. Militello (2007: 43; emphasis added) summarizes the available information:

[A] contrasting picture seems to emerge from the collected data. The long tradition and the high quality of Cretan craftsmanship make the elaborated ceremonial dresses a typical prestige item of palatial display. Moreover, an interest in this kind of production by the central authority is demonstrated, *at least for the First Palaces,* by seal impressions and marks. The great variety and specialization of Minoan cloth manufacture is also demonstrated by the compound signs for different kinds of clothes in Linear A. Two of these ligatures (TELA+*TE*, TELA+*ZO*) will be also found in the Mycenaean period, together with the ideogram for wool, showing the strength of Minoan tradition.[4] On the other hand, the spatial distribution of archaeological evidence does not hint at a centralized production. On the contrary, workshops and ateliers are often very far from the centers of power. The lack of strong central control is also evident in hieroglyphic and Linear A archives. This apparent contradiction can be solved if we consider the Minoan Palaces as a place of cloth consumption, not of textile production. The palace was not interested in the basic stages of the textile chain of production (breeding and cultivation) but only in the final stages (weaving and manufacture), in order to fulfill its needs.

Militello seems to be suggesting that Minoan textile production was perhaps at one time vertically integrated but that it (later) became vertically disintegrated. The latter outcome is implicit in his remarks about the decentralization of textile production and in his remarks elsewhere (Militello 2014: 277):

> As far as textiles are concerned, therefore, I suggested that Minoan court centered buildings and, in LM 1, Minoan villas, functioned differently from Mycenaean palaces, and were only interested in the later stages of the cycle of production, the weaving of special fabrics and the manufacture of beautiful cloth. This would imply that the major part of production cycle for wool occurred outside the scope of the major centres, probably at household level, as a consequence disappearing from the evidence in our possession of the Proto- and Neo-palatial periods.

The texts and tools of textile production seem to be concentrated in certain houses, villas, and smaller palaces, but, according to Burke and Chapin (2016: 36), the larger palaces (Knossos and Phaistos) offer no evidence at all for weaving in the Neopalatial Period.

---

[4]   See Chap. 7.3.

The point about relative decentralization in Minoan Crete finds support in a comparison with the distribution of sealed documents:

> All together 1,160 sealed documents are known from the Linear B administration [in Knossos]. When the distribution map of Linear B sealed documents [sealings that had been attached to documents] is compared with that of the [Minoan] Linear A sealed documents, a difference between the two systems springs to the eye. In the Linear B system the sealed documents—with two exceptions ... are found only in the palaces. This contrasts with the Linear A system where sealed documents were found all over the island and not only in palaces or palatial buildings.
>
> Hallager 2015: 147

Clearly, the Linear A sealed documents (and the packet sealings) are decentralized as compared to the Linear B.

However, decentralization is not the same as vertical disintegration. Geographically dispersed production units may be controlled from a single center. However, the point remains that geographic dispersion is economically antagonistic to central control because it raises the costs of detailed control by a central administration. *Other things remaining equal*, in order to lower control costs, vertically integrated firms would also tend to be relatively more geographically concentrated. That they are not, as in the case of the Linear A sealed documents, is a sign (but far from a sure sign) that the dispersed centers were not, or at least less than the later Mycenaean, under unified control.[5]

Wiener (2016: 371–372) had noted clear differences between Minoan and Mycenaean administrative procedures:

> To begin, ... Linear B tablets are much larger and more crowded with the text often continuing on the back of the tablet, whereas in Linear A, the subjects on the front and back of tablets are often different. Mycenaean Linear B tablets thus often contain far more information than Minoan Linear A tablets. Moreover, Linear B tablets are much more neatly composed, suggesting that they represent a more finished form of the information recorded. Minoan administration, however, made far greater use of seals, which sometimes show evidence of attachment to

---

[5] Militello's final point about palaces as centers of consumption is not consistent with the evidence, especially the significant investment in displaying them to best advantage. The Minoan palaces—integrated or disintegrated—were focused on marketing textiles not consuming them.

leather/parchment so far unattested on the mainland.... Furthermore, the proportion of the populace using seals in Neopalatial Crete seems higher than in later Mycenaean Greece, if the imposing number of seal stones found at Minoan sites is any indication.

These observations are qualitative or even subjective, but they suggest, especially in the widespread use of seals, that, *at the moment of observation*, the Minoan economy was less, not more, centralized than the Mycenaean. By comparison, the Minoan enterprises were relatively smaller with more face-to-face contacts, and there were *more nodes of authority*. Perhaps we need to take seriously that, in later Minoan times, the textile industry was already in the hands of independent producers.

Based on the above observations, it may be tentatively suggested that during their latest period, the Minoan palaces were already well into the predicted phase of transformation from vertical integration to vertical disintegration. In the final phase of this transformation, they would "collapse" and be replaced by small independent textile firms. Indeed, perhaps the rebuilding or repurposing of *Mycenaean* palace buildings was already underway in the later thirteenth century—that is, before the dramatic destruction and/or abandonment of palaces. Thus, industrial installations were built close to the palace, even blocking a ceremonial entrance (Shelmerdine 1985). The question for my theory is whether these installations were run by the palace or by independent entrepreneurs.[6]

The remainder of this discussion is focused on the Mycenaean Era, for which we have not only the deciphered Linear B tablets but also much archaeological evidence. Burke and Chapin (2016: 37) make an important evaluation:

> But unlike the Minoan system, the Linear B tablets of the Mycenaean palaces show strong administrative interest in all phases of textile production, from sheep and flax field to finished cloth. Linear B texts document the numbers of sheep in various flocks and record amounts of the raw materials (wool and flax) collected from the towns and villages under the administration of the palaces. Once cloth was woven, palace scribes used a variety of ideograms and terms to make distinctions between different types of cloth, usually indicating the heaviness and amounts of wool used. The documents also provide information related to the textile personnel, including the allocation of food rations for dependent workers involved in the industry. All indications are that

---

[6] Dickinson (2006: 75) notes that in the Postpalatial Period, there was growth in the production of finely decorated stirrup jars of the type used to hold liquids like perfumed oil.

the craftsmen and craftswomen listed were highly specialized, as the tablets record specific occupations such as spinners, weavers, fullers, and finishers.

Note that the palatial ownership of sheep is not arbitrary and fits into a new-products-for-new-markets theoretical framework. The reason is that not all wool is wool! That is, for one thing, wool from different breeds of sheep and goats receives dye differently (Melena 1975b: 105–106; Palaima 1991: 277). The choice of sheep breed depends on the entrepreneur's insight into the color preferences of the overseas consumers. In this connection, Palaima (1991: 277) notes the processing of "Cypriot wool" in Linear B tablets from Crete.

There is little direct evidence of textile production inside the palatial centers, but, as noted earlier, there are suitable spaces in the palaces and also deposits of textile records. Palaces may then have employed specialists to finish cloth obtained from impendent producers through the *ta-ra-si-ja*, or the putting-out-wool system. Most of all, it is clear that the palaces went downstream from production to marketing textiles by displaying them for sale in their *megaron-*showrooms (the Labyrinths).

That the Pylos palace had ships of its own may be indicated in PY Na 568 by the tax abatement granted to the shipbuilders: "Thus at Pylos, personnel and ships were co-opted by the palace, whether to form state fleets or to work as private contractors in the service of the state contractors." (Tartaron 2013: 124).

The Linear B texts from Pylos provide compelling textual evidence for palatial oversight of building, finding crews for, and sailing ships at least in Messenia…. The personnel drafted for these tasks are listed or named. Shipbuilders (*na-a-do-mo*) are mentioned on two tablets at Pylos. On Vm 865 *na-u-do-mo* is the heading of a list of 12 names, each followed by the numeral 1, probably one ship each. On Na 568, a group of men with this title is recorded with a single place name and an exemption [from dues/taxes] of 50 units of flax while they are supervising construction.

Tartaron 2013: 130–131

Thus, the raw material was in place for private ownership and operation of the Mycenaean trading vessels, although Kramer-Hajos (2016: 137) notes that Linear B evidence for ships is confined to Pylos.

In understanding the extent of vertical integration, it is also necessary to take *diseconomies of scale* into account, along with the entrepreneurial problems posed by new products for new markets. The co-existence of a number of independently owned and managed vertically integrated palatial centers—Pylos, Mycenae, Tiryns, Thebes, Orchomenos, Argos (with more than one?), and Crete, Knossos, and Agios Vasilios—would attest that, beyond some point, costs rose with output due to diseconomies of scale. Otherwise, why not have only one vertically integrated palace?

On the other hand, concerning this assumption regarding the independent palatial centers, Postgate (2001: 160) has raised an *unanswered* challenge:

> My question is prompted by the assurances by the Linear B experts that in their paleography and documentary format the tablets from the different sites are virtually indistinguishable.... If in the Near East a number of contemporary administrative archives displaying such similarities were excavated in different cities, the obvious assumption would be that they fell under the same government, the uniformity of scribal practice resulting from, and tacitly proclaiming the strength of central control.

Following Postgate, we would understand the Mycenaean "palatial" centers as separate "plants" of a single firm along lines very familiar in economic history. Accordingly, there is some reason to think that the various palatial centers were currently under a unified control or perhaps had been *in the not-so-distant past.*[7] To conclude, I would not wish to minimize the difficulties with the evidence, but it does seem that, even near the end of the system, the Mycenaean palaces remained, in many dimensions, vertically integrated. This is the assumption on which my analysis proceeds.

What is really interesting is that many of the palatial features pointed out by Sherratt (2001 214) as looking "like the kind of cultural features which, once established ought to be able to maintain some sort of continued existence regardless of the fortunes of particular political or economic systems" are precisely the features that will not be able to maintain a continued existence in the normal course of events. That is, the palatial system of production collapsed not because the palaces were imposters but because they were the real thing.

The entrepreneurial replacements for the palaces would be drawn, at least initially, from specialists, including slaves, directly employed by the palace's textile enterprises (Nosch and Perna 2001) and, most obviously, by the private

---

[7] That all the palaces collapsed, at least roughly, simultaneously at the end of the thirteenth century BCE is also suggestive of (but does not prove) single management. Another indicator is the attestation of "collectors"—that is, independent contractors who serviced more than one palace. At least several contractors with the same name appear in this role at more than one site, including the mysterious *ma-ri-ne-ti* who appears at Knossos in Crete and on the mainland in Thebes (Olivier 2001: 150, 156; Bendall 2007: 89–91).

contractors referred to as "collectors" (Chapters 8.2, 4–5, 9.2). Thus, as previously noted, at Pylos, a "collector" ("businessman") named Amphimēdēs (Linear B *a-pi-me-de*) had three *do-e-ro* 'slaves', who are described as *hekʷesioi* "of the mobilizing agent" (*Ed 847*). This Amphimēdēs managed a flock of 190 sheep (*Cn 655*), but also was a landholder of a type designated as *etōnion* (*Eb 473*/*Ep 539*), meaning perhaps that he did not have to pay taxes (Lejeune 1966; Nakassis 2013: 13 n, 98,164 n. 29, 171).

At the same time, experience transformed members of maritime communities into galley owners (Wedde 2005: 33–36), who became the instruments for implementing the business plans of small, vertically disintegrated producers of luxury textiles. The latter rented cargo space, or, more likely, they sold their textiles to independent merchants who arranged for shipping the textiles. Thus, Tartaron (2013: 69) considers the possibility that the oared galley served to foster the rise of "alternative power centers [that] materialized at coastal nodes in the periphery of the palaces."

The palatial period groomed many individuals to become entrepreneurs serving an international market. Some would have learned the potentialities of the market while serving the palace; others learned by observing from the outside. Some individuals would have founded businesses within the boundaries of the (former) palaces; others in virgin territories. Thus, while my theory predicts *global* growth of the market (vertical disintegration) and the decline in central planning (vertical integration), it does not pick from among the potential progressive regions. Presumably, the territories of the former palaces retained certain advantages relative to other areas.

However, my model predicts the emergence of new urban centers near coastlines. These new centers owed their status mainly to the presence of specialized marketers of textiles. The latter marketers were relieved of the responsibility of managing flocks and, perhaps, textile production. Having also become a specialist activity, stock management would have retreated to the rural interior. That is, stock management would have predictably returned to the kinds of remote areas from which it had earlier retreated (some peak sanctuaries) when the palaces were first formed.

Originally, palaces were positioned in "compromise" or hybrid locations better suited to a combination of herding, producing wool, weaving cloth, and marketing textiles (Papadimitriou 2009: 101). This kind of compromise location was necessary to reduce control costs in vertically integrated palaces. The compromise was no longer viable or necessary in a vertically disintegrated textile economy.

On the other hand, the post-palatial period lasted from 150 to 200 years, and during such a lengthy period, regional advantages might have changed a great deal. Thus, the focus must be on whether the collapse of the palace corresponded to a severe decline in aggregate participation in the international textile market or whether aggregate participation was maintained or increased while changing its form.

My prediction is that a handful of palatial executives were replaced by many nobodies who made their own business plans. This replacement was not the "eventual" result of the collapse, *it was* the collapse (compare Deger-Jalkotzy 1996). Both the aggregate production of the textile industry and the number of producing firms increased. However, individually, these new firms were very far from having "palatial" status. It was sufficient for each producer to have its own showroom. No longer was it efficient to build/maintain large showrooms, not to mention structures that housed a *wanax* and police force. Furthermore, although the new entrepreneurs earned more than under the palace, they did not necessarily, or even typically, become wealthy enough to afford/desire villas with beautiful art. Nostalgia for a past way of life is understandable, but in the sweep of economic history, there have always been innovations leading to the emergence of grand vertically integrated firms and, ultimately, their replacement by hard-working nobodies.[8]

3. Evidence for the Post-Palatial Period (LH IIIC)

The archaeological picture, as summarized, for example, by Tartaron (2013: 18–19) offers general support for my interpretation of collapse in terms of vertical disintegration: "[T]here was no immediate 'dark age' and the culture that followed the collapse was Mycenaean" (cf. Middleton 2010: 11).

a. Developments on the Ground[9]

In the Peloponnese, sites were abandoned and Messenia and Laconia may have experienced significant depopulation. Other areas including, as will be noted below, the coast of Attica and the northwestern part of the Peloponnese peninsula (Achaea) demonstrate growth.

To judge by the reoccupation of the Citadels and the expansion of the Lower Town, at Tiryns, the population increased (Maran 2016: 2; Middleton 2010:

---

[8] The geographic decentralization of commercial and industrial life would, of course, be accompanied by some decentralization in political structures. Where only one state (government) had provided public goods for the residents, there might now several or even none. There are obvious advantages and disadvantages to large governments (palaces?) relative to small governments. However, history shows that both versions are capable of serving their communities. If a community remains prosperous, it will be able to provide needed public goods via the payment of taxes to its government or by joint action in face-to-face stateless societies. The key question remains whether the disappearance of the palaces was accompanied by a notable disappearance of commerce and manufacturing.

[9] Much of what follows relies on Tartaron (2013).

97–99). The Tiryns megaron was rebuilt using materials from its pre-collapse predecessor (Building T; Mazarakis Ainian 1997: 159–161). It is, of course, true that the megaron recalls the Mycenaean ruler's dwelling and, as noted by Yasur-Landau (2010: 68), "[t]he Tiryns treasure, a collection of bronze vessels as well as a rich array of jewelry … supports a similar claim of palatial ancestry." The "treasure" has been dated to the post-collapse period. On the other hand, the megaron recalls the display and sale of textiles to visitors and the "treasure" may be understood in the light of this practical usage. That is, we might say the treasure has a "commercial ancestry."

The "large and well-built structures that were constructed outside the walls of the [Tiryns] acropolis, suggest the fragmentation of power in LHIIIC" (Yasur-Landau 2010: 68). However, the new buildings incorporate "megaron like structures" with "painted stucco and stone pillar bases" (Yasur-Landau 2010: 69). Thus, the building of new structures outside the former walls of Tiryns suggests the "fragmentation of commercial power" as predicted by the disintegration hypothesis.

The possible emergence of numerous small textile centers at Tiryns finds support in the observation that with the passage of time, the buildings there became smaller and courtyards became more frequent. These and other evolutionary changes "give the sense that more activities were organized and undertaken by individual household units rather than members of a social hierarchy" (Lantzas 2016: 467).

Much of the settlement within the walls of Mycenae was rebuilt and occupied at a diminished level throughout the twelfth century (Middleton 2010: 99–100) before it disappeared. Significantly, a fresco depicting a life-sized seated woman dressed in a (double axe-shaped?) "flounced kilt" (B.R. Jones 2009: 321) found near the "Southwest House" at Mycenae has been dated to LH IIIC based on the accompanying pottery fragments. There is, in addition, evidence of continuity at Midea, a third regional Mycenaean center. A large megaron located on the lower terraces was damaged in an earthquake and was "repaired and remodeled in LHIIIC when a row of three columns replaced the four columns that had stood around the central hearth of the LHIIIB phases" (Yasur-Landau 2010: 71 with Figure 3-13). However, it also was eventually abandoned. No socioeconomic catastrophe is evident.

For the Argolid generally, Lantzas (2016: 471) notes, "While the number of cumulative inhumations contexts decreased, the number of individual mortuary contexts increased." Furthermore, the evidence provided by an analysis of ceramic material and metal objects demonstrates that patterns of consumption and production remained relatively unchanged" (Lantzas 2016: 474). One may dispute this or that point, but it is difficult to argue that the Argolid experienced a severe material retrogression in living standards after Late Helladic IIIB (about 1200 BCE).

For the region of Thebes in Boeotia: "Most of the postpalatial material published so far belongs to the LH IIIC pottery phase, which demonstrates close links with the sites in Euboea and other areas in Central Greece, both at the end of the Bronze and the beginning of Early Iron Ages" (Aravantinos 2019: 192–193). Of course, the pottery may be of lower quality than in LH IIIB but the linkages to other places suggests that the Thebes area did not fall into a "Dark Age" of economic isolation.

Although Achaea (northwestern Peloponnese) had not previously known a palace, there is evidence of growth there as well (see further below). There was a building and population increase at Aigeira and in other places, such as Grotta on Naxos and Metropolis during LHIIIC (Yasur-Landau 2010: 71–77 with references). In particular, "In Grotta, north of the Mitropolis area, a large megaroid (megaronlike) structure, Building F" (Yasur-Landau 2010: 75). Thus, again, the standard of living escalator may be going down, but not with a crash. Indeed, the continuing interest in megaronlike structures is consistent with a continuing interest in textile sales.

Actually, there is quite a lot more to say about trends in Achaea. Eder (2007: 43) agrees that palatial period evidence from the chamber tombs in Achaea (and the Ionian Islands) "is characterised by rather low and medium levels of wealth." Eder (2007: 43) goes on to note that examination of burials from later times "has revealed numerous and richly furnished burials ... and bears witness to a period of prosperity for these parts of western Greece in the period after the fall of the Mycenaean palaces. The range of grave goods gave not only larger quantities, but also valuable items such as armour and weapons, documenting at the same time a clear increase in the number of Italian imports." Thus, for Achaea (and the Ionian islands) there appears to be evidence for an improvement in economic conditions in LH IIIC and it appears to be linked to foreign trade.

Turning to Cephalonia, the burial evidence for LH IIIC indicates population growth and generalized prosperity, not despair. Moreover, Moschos (2009: 362–363) concludes: "On a regional level, the island's maritime role seems to have been promoted during this [post palatial] period. It is not only passing ships that bring wealth, but the fleet of the Cephallenes themselves, which follows the trends and advantages of the new era. This is also reflected by the presence of the exotic amber whose quantity during this period (LH IIIC) is larger than the amber that has been found in the rest of the Mycenaean world." Here we have evidence not only of LH IIIC participation in international trade but of increased participation. This kind of evidence can hardly be dismissed as being due to the remnants of the crumbling IIIB infrastructure. For Thessaly the picture is cloudy with some regions seeming to fall and others to rise after the collapse (Eder 2007: 42-3).

Continuing the survey, Mitrou in East Locris does not return to its pre-palatial urban status but with rebuilding it is continuously occupied and not a disaster area (Van de Moortel 2007: 249–250). The Kynos findings are more impressive: the excavated LH IIIC buildings have kilns for metals and ceramics and storerooms and there are over 1500 bronze objects from the Elateia-Alonaki cemetery (Lemos 2011-2012: 21; Deger-Jalkotzy 2014: 43). Also "flourishing" [in addition to Mitrou and the area of Livanates in East Locris] are LH IIIC Kalapodi and Perati (on the coast of Attica) (Van de Moortel 2007: 252). "Flourishing" is of course a term that covers much ground, however. On the other hand, the word provides no comfort for the view that the economy and infrastructure had collapsed together.

Lemos (2011-2012: 22) concludes:"Lefkandi [in Euboea] was a prosperous LHIIIC site and it became especially prosperous in the LHIIIC Middle Period after destruction of LHIIIC Early." Rutter (2014: 203) notes the prevalence in LH IIIC Lefkandi of kraters with decorative themes depicting relations between parents and children, including griffins, and makes the intriguing suggestion that they were intended for a different group than those who consumed late Mycenaean kraters. If only we knew more about the market for this new pottery. In discussing finds on the promontory called Xeropolis, Lemos (2011-2012: 22–23) points especially to a continuously occupied LH IIIC building which has been named "Megaron" based on its size, architectural plan, and proximity to the eastern harbor. Here the commercial potentialities are evident.

The trend in post palatial economies in Crete seems at least mildly positive in that large buildings were apparently constructed after the palatial collapse (J. Bennet 1988: 34 with archaeological references Yasur-Landau 2010: 79). Furthermore, "Although frequently considered as part of the systematic collapse of the Mycenaean mainland ... the picture in the Cyclades is one of development rather than of continuity, at least until LH IIIC Middle" (Yasur-Landau 2010: 81). It seems that a new Mycenaean settlement appears at Emporio in Chios in the post-palatial period (Yasur-Landau 2010: 156).

There is no clear on-the ground evidence of a break in Greek relations with Lemnos, the gateway to Troy and the Black Sea.

The [Mycenaean] pottery from Myrina is very important and confirms the existence of a settlement during LBA that will continue without a gap into the historical times. The absence of Mycenaean pottery of LH III A2 at Poliochni and Koukonisi is very significant in terms of settlement distribution and it can be interpreted as an abandonment of the traditional site in favour of other places located in promontories commanding a fine harbour. These new sites,

Hephaestia and Myrina, became the most important settlements in the historical times, showing a long continuity in occupation since the LBA (Cultraro 2005: 243, 244).

So it seems possible that the East Aegean trade with Anatolia may have been dislodged and then resumed in new Lemnian quarters.

The above survey makes no claim to being either systematic or complete. It is, however, objective. The survey reveals little or no on-the-ground evidence for a generalized post-palatial societal collapse. The palaces no longer functioned, but apparently the surrounding societies did and sometimes nicely. The griffin who arguably protects international traders continues to be depicted in LH IIIC but perhaps it has been domesticated.

The main conclusion of recent archaeological research is that "In general ... areas on the edge of the former Mycenaean world with good access to the sea prospered in the postpalatial period: the Ionian Islands, the coastal northwestern Peloponnese, the east coast of Attica, and certain of the Aegean islands flourished" (Middleton 2010: 90). Second, and more controversially, Middleton (2010: 101) sees a reduction in the number of sites, and he suggests, "The areas that did best in postpalatial Greece seem largely to have been those that were not part of the palatial states, or at least not directly integrated in them." The (alleged) degree of integration is not easily measured, however. Third, with respect to foreign contacts, Dickinson (2006: 72, 203) proposes, "The quantities of foreign items found in Postpalatial contexts, which are more conspicuous than in the Third Palatial Period, might reasonably be taken to suggest that traders were still visiting the Aegean, especially from the Near East" and "the overwhelming impression given by the material culture is of the continuance of past traditions in a whole range of features, house plans and fittings, ordinary pottery and artifacts for domestic use, burial customs and religion, as identified by the ritual use of figurines." These reflections on post palatial Mycenaean society, by independent scholars, is consistent with (indeed supportive of) my hypothesis that vertically integrated textile producers (the palaces) were replaced by relatively cost effective vertically disintegrated firms. This displacement would have been economically progressive.

b. Indicators of Continued Textile Exports

"In the post-palatial period, there is clearly an increase in the depiction of ship scenes and the clothing of men. Specifically, representations of Mycenaean [oared] galleys increase dramatically in LH IIIC" (Tartaron 2013: 66, 69), and the depictions reveal no hints of deterioration in shipbuilding skills (Middleton 2010: 71–72 with references). Kramer-Hajos (2016: 161) notes post-palatial depictions of ships at Kynos with sailors fighting on deck, but also three terra-cotta ship models—one with wheels from slightly later IIIC—show no signs of fighting, and two Lefkandi LH IIIC Middle krater sherds depict ships with human figures, one of which shows two figures "holding their oars with both hands" that are lacking in any hint of military dress—that is, helmets, shields, or iden-tifiable corselets.

With respect to clothing: "On LHIIIA and LH IIB pottery, status differentia-tion is indicated by the depiction of clothing. There is much contrast between naked figures carrying chairs, parasols, or spears or walking in front of char-iots and figures clad in spotted robes carrying swords or riding in chariots" (Yasur-Landau 2010: 89). In a Kynos scene from LH IIIC, the main figures wear fringed garments (Yasur-Landau 2010: 89 Figure 3.34). I have not found pictorial evidence for women.

There is also evidence of textile production in the rising post-palatial centers throughout Greece. Yasur-Landau (2010: 132–133 with Figures 5.28–5.30) calls attention to "large numbers of unbaked or poorly fired clay spools, either cylindrical or hourglass shaped," and he cites evidence for their use as loom-weights. These objects are prevalent in Kynos, Lefkandi, and Asine in mainland Greece and, in Crete, at Halasmenos and Chania. Outside Greece, the purported loom-weights have been found at Cyprus, Beth Shean, and Ashkelon in Israel, and in Anatolia in Troy VIIa (Yasur-Landau 2010: 132–133). The peculiar form of the loom-weights is unexplained.

Eleon, in Boeotia (Chap. 12.3)—with ties to both Thebes and to the coast—survived almost to the Early Iron Age. Its survival and even strength seems attributable to textile production. Evidence for textile production at Eleon in post-palatial times begins with "two types of loom weight; a spool loom weight that is probably of foreign origin, and a heavy loom weight possibly used in the specialized production of very thick textiles like rugs" (Van Damme 2017: iii). Van Damme (2017: 431) finds, "At least three households show evidence for textile production on a scale that superseded household needs, and was likely intended for trade. Abundant storage in these same complexes could have provisioned the labor necessary for weaving." Obviously, this is only rough evidence for textile exports. However, at Eleon, it is accompanied by evidence for interactions with the outside world: "Ceramic evidence also suggests foreign influence and perhaps even a foreign potting community at Eleon. This includes the appearance of foreign shapes such as the carinated cup and handmade burnished ware. There are also close stylistic ties with the site of Xeropolis (Lefkandi)" (Van Damme 2017: iii).

Finally, textiles, including purple-dyed textiles, have been discovered in a cemetery in Stamna Aeotolia; the findings are dated to 1100-800 BCE (Kolonas et al. 2017: 535–536). Aeotolia and King Thoas are implicated with Odysseus in wool production and in the Trojan War (see Chap. 15.2).

c. Quantitative Implications of Vertical Disintegration

My model predicts an increase in participation in the textile industry and a decrease in the production cost per garment (better in the marginal cost of garments). The result would be an increase in the export of garments—a consequence of a downward and to the right shift of the positively sloped supply curve of garments—and, given the constancy of the negatively sloped foreign demand curve, a decrease in price. The direction of the change in the proceeds of the garment sellers at the putative lower price would depend on the elasticity of the foreign demand curve. That is, on whether the percentage increase in the number of garments sold was (numerically) greater than (demand elastic), (numerically) equal to (unitary elasticity of demand) or (numerically) less than (demand inelastic) the percentage decrease in price. *Thus, the theory does not generate a prediction in terms of total receipts (gold earned).*

S. C. Murray (2018a) has provided estimates of total imports of objects (Mainland + Crete) before (LH IIIB, 1300-1125) and after the collapse (LH IIIC/SM, 1175-1050). Using Table 2.9 (traditional chronology), the total number of imported objects (228) per year equal to 2.0 declined to a total of 136 imported objects equal to 0.9 per year. On the basis of the earlier figure of 2.0, this amounts to a 55% decline in imported objects per year. The decline in imports varies according to the chronological boundaries selected between the Greek mainland and Crete, but the pattern is consistent: there is a large relative decline in imports.

Putting aside the caveats about the number of imported objects[10] and chronology (carefully enumerated by Murray), I will take the decline in imported objects as representing a decline in gold imports. In terms of my model, this decline means only that foreign demand is inelastic, not that there was a significant collapse in the volume of textile exports and in the post-Mycenaean economy. My initial intuition is that, as a luxury product, the post-Mycenaean textiles would have had an elastic demand—meaning that receipts/imported objects would increase—but this is intuition and not necessarily the case (see S. C. Murray 2017: 85).

---

[10] For example, faience and glass beads are numerous (in the many thousands) in the LBA but they are not usually counted as imports, although they might be imported, as demonstrated by the Ulu Burun wreck (S. C. Murray 2018a: 75–76). The inclusion of beads would dominate and perhaps reverse the direction of change in imported objects.

Additional evidence is to be found in a vast and exclusively post-palatial (LH IIIC) twelfth-century cemetery Perati in east Attica. In S. C. Murray (2017: Table 2.2 p. 88), under the heading "Single-import tombs from Perati," are listed ten tombs, and of these, six had gold in various forms: earrings, a ring, an amulet, beads and wire, and "gold." Again, for Perati, S. C. Murray (2018b: Tables 1 and 2) lists together twenty-two tombs, and of these, ten contained gold objects in various forms (listed under "Nonimported Tomb Contents") with a total number of twenty-eight gold objects. For the later phase of the Perati cemetery alone, there are eight tombs with four gold objects for a total of ten gold objects.[11] The cemetery is entirely post-palatial, so there can be no before- and after-collapse comparison. However, the fact that ten out of twenty-two tombs with imported exotica (45%) had gold objects seems appreciable for an (allegedly) destabilized/collapsed economy. Thus, it is at least credible that the gold at Perati came from current commercial activity including from Greek textile exports to the Black Sea region.

The indications of an *increase* in production and exports of textiles would include the geographic spread of the industry, especially to ports, an increase in the number of participants in the industry, and a rise in living standards. S. C. Murray (2018: 86–87), if I understand correctly, senses an increased dispersal of industrial production after the palatial collapse. However, she interprets the increased dispersal as signaling a *decline* in industrial production and in exports. My model of vertical disintegration would predict that the increased production and the export of textiles and would be accompanied by the increased geographic dispersion of the textile industry. Certainly, no decline in dispersion would be anticipated.

In assessing production trends, S. C. Murray (2018a: 83) has observed, without providing numbers, that spindle whorls and loom-weights are widely distributed at most sites. It seems reasonable that this observation would refer more to LH IIIC than to the preceding palatial period. *In fact, the finding is that the proportion of all sites with evidence of spinning and weaving increases from LH IIIB to IIIC.* Professor Murray interprets the wider distribution to mean that cloth was produced for local use. This is possible. However, increased dispersion would be expected if participation in the textile export economy became more widespread/less centralized after the collapse.[12]

---

[11] Note that only tombs with at least one exotic imported object are considered in the tables. This means that tombs with only locally produced exotic objects are not listed in the table, no matter how much gold they may have contained.

[12] I suspect that the underlying problem is that without the vertical integration/disintegration model, it is difficult to imagine that the production rose in the post-collapse period. My thanks to Professor Murray for her assistance in this matter.

Post-collapse textile-producing firms would be relatively *small* because the Bronze Age textile industry, with the possible exception of dyeing installations, did not know important economies of scale. The emerging independent firms would also be relatively specialized—that is, *disintegrated*—because experience with trade had, at last, taught ordinary individuals, artisans, nautical personnel, farmers, and others that it was profitable to participate in the production of luxury textiles for the international market. The small, specialized producers would be cost-effective not least because they could be minimally literate—that is, they would have little need to employ and pay scribes for keeping elaborate written records.

To conclude, I see little or no evidence that must be interpreted in terms of a post-palatial collapse in textile production, textile exports, and general living standards. I see some evidence that can be interpreted in terms of an increase in textile exports, textile production, and living standards. Based on the currently mostly qualitative evidence available, my tentative conclusion is disintegration better characterizes the IIIC Mycenaean economy than collapse. More refined tests are, of course, required to adequately test this position. We may never be able to find evidence directly concerning the fate of high style. Probably our only chance is to carefully track the gold that would have been received in payment.

PLATES

Plate 1. Young "Priestess," from West House at Akrotiri.

Plate 2. Processioner at Tiryns Palace (restored).

Plate 3. Gold finial on silver pin, from shaft grave III at Mycenae.

Plate 4. Faience plaque depicting crocus-decorated garment, from Knossos, East Temple Repositories.

Plate 5. "Chieftain Cup" from Agia Triada.

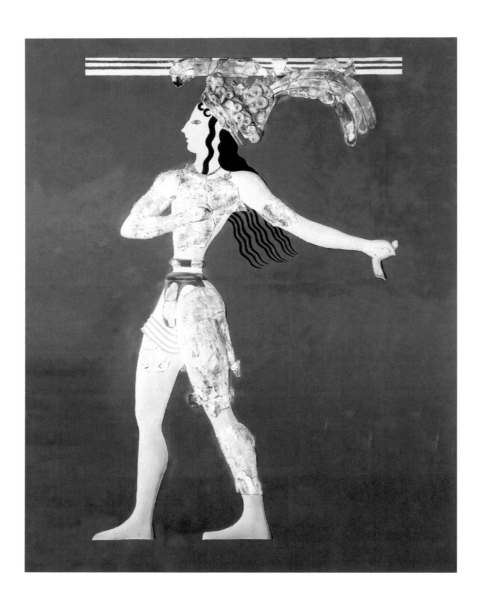

Plate 6. "Priest King," from Knossos "Corridor of Processions."

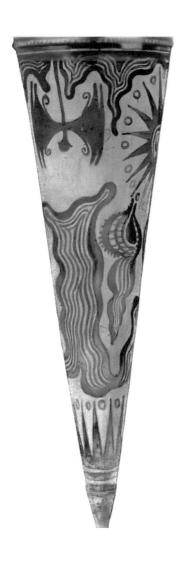

Plate 7. Rhyton from Palaikastro.

Plate 8. Terracotta cup with murex decoration.

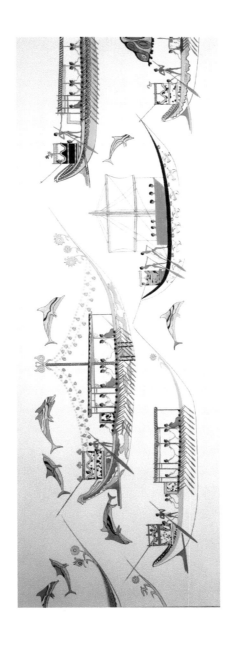

Plate 9. "Ship Fresco" from Room 5, West House, Akrotiri.

a.

b.

Plate 10. Snake Goddesses, from Knossos temple
repositories (as restored).

Plate 11. Pyxis, from Aptera.

Plate 12. Griffin drawing chariot with "Priestess" riders. One of the narrow sides of the Agia Triada sarcophagus.

Plate 13. Headless Genius with garment.

Plate 14. Row of Genii with pole, from Mycenae.

Plate 15. Warrior Krater, from Mycenae.

Plate 16. "La Parisienne," from the Knossos "Campstool Fresco."

Appendix
The Basics of Vertical Industrial Structure

WHEN the producer of a specific product/process takes on the production of upstream and/or downstream products/processes by means of a nonmarket interface—that is, he produces them in his own firm—economists refer to that enterprise as *vertically integrated*. Thus, for example, a merchant wishing to market wine might produce the wine in his own vineyard and then transport it to the market in his own ship (*backward integration*) and, finally, carry out his objective of selling the wine. Alternatively, an entrepreneur of ceramic pots might first extract clay (backward integration) and then sell the pots he produces in his own shop (*forward integration*).

On the other hand, entrepreneurs might sometimes perform/produce only a single product/process: for example, the wine merchant purchases wine from the vintner and then sells it to the consumer; the pot-manufacturer purchases clay from the digger and then sells his pots to itinerant merchants. When the producer of a product/service integrates with upstream and/or downstream operations/processes by means of a market interface, economists say that the enterprise is *vertically disintegrated*.

It should be noted, however, that enterprises are rarely, if ever, *completely* vertically integrated or disintegrated. The important question is why firms/ entrepreneurs *choose* a particular point along the vertical structure spectrum and, more specifically, what causes *changes* in the point selected.

It is sometimes (mistakenly) claimed that vertical integration is the most cost-effective form of industrial organization. This mistaken view was championed for modern economies by Alfred D. Chandler Jr. (1977) in his *The Visible Hand* and is accepted, probably independently of Chandler, by some Roman economy scholars and many Marxists. The point to understand is that vertical integration is itself a natural response to the emergence of new markets and/or products (Silver 1984, 2009b, 2009c, 2013b, 2014a).

An entrepreneur sees the potential of an emerging opportunity but productively qualified producers do not, and they are unwilling to invest their own resources in the innovation process. Thus, to take a textile-making example, if the production of a new type of garment requires using a different type of loom, the weaver would have to spend significant time learning new bodily movements and unlearning the original ones (Cutler 2012: 149). The artisan may decline to make this investment because he has no strong reason to believe the new garment will be a market success and, so, reward his effort. Thus, if the entrepreneur wishes to implement his vision, he is likely to find that he must first purchase control over the productive resources of the qualified producers, including land, livestock, labor power and/or even the laborer himself, and invest in occupational training. He/she who directly controls the production process accepts most of the risk of failure in the market.[1]

However, vertical integration is not typically, nor ideally, the most efficient (cost-effective) structure for carrying out the entrepreneur's end vision. The vertically integrated producer must participate in several activities, for which he typically lacks the appropriate skill set. He is a textile merchant, not a weaver. Alternatively, she is a weaver, not a merchant. The entrepreneur must use (actually "waste") his scarce time controlling activities for which he lacks a comparative advantage. *This controlling comes at the expense of devoting his limited time and energy to matters specific to the innovation.*

This state of affairs is rarely permanent. Once qualified producers become accustomed to the new market or product—that is, they see that it is a success—then they cease to resist and become willing to invest their own time and resources. The original entrepreneur learns that he can now lower his production cost/increase and free up his own time by divesting himself of those activities in which he lacks a comparative advantage and can devote himself more fully to those in which he does.[2] Sometimes, the proven success of the new product or market makes irrelevant the original firm created by the

---

[1] Entrepreneurs who have opened new markets include kings. Alternatively, perhaps we should say that successful entrepreneurs might become kings! "In Sumerian legend we find two early rulers, Enmerkar and Gilgamesh pictured as traders who opened new markets" (Silver 2006: 7 with references and discussion).

[2] The basic idea is easily illustrated. Sometimes a specialized producer operating independently can perform an activity—say weaving a garment—at a lower total cost than the vertically integrated firm. In this case, the specialized producer has an absolute advantage over the vertically integrated firm. Sometimes, however, the entrepreneur can perform the activity at a lower total cost than the specialized producer can—that is, he/she has an absolute advantage. Nevertheless, despite his lower production cost, the entrepreneur might prefer to divest himself of this activity. Consider the classic example of Billy Rose, the Broadway impresario who flourished in the first half of the twentieth century. Rose ranked among the world's fastest typists, but, still, he hired typists. He did this in order to free up his finite time for doing what he excelled at: producing shows. By spending a few extra dollars on typing services, Rose gained the opportunity to make thousands of dollars producing more shows. The hired worker had a *comparative advantage* in typing but Rose had a *comparative advantage* in producing shows. Rose had an absolute advantage in both activities.

entrepreneur—that is, it ceases to have any special advantage over newcomers, except perhaps that of being the first.[3] Consequently, the original firm may be totally or largely replaced by specialized, often small, firms including some led by former employees and contractors. Thus, in the life cycle of an industry, vertical integration is typically followed by vertical disintegration. In the limiting case of vertical disintegration, each step in the creation of textiles is the province of a specialized firm: one firm produces wool, a second markets the wool to producers, a third produces the textiles, and a fourth markets textiles to consumers. In a mostly economically unchanging world, most firms would be mostly vertically disintegrated.

The point is that in a market economy, there is a major innovation in product/technology/market that is typically implemented by means of vertically integrated firms, but, eventually, the innovation becomes the routine practice, and the vertically integrated enterprise is replaced by much more specialized, vertically disintegrated firms. This does not mean that the industry has "collapsed"—far from it. Actually, it becomes even larger and more cost-efficient.

Vertical integration is only a phase in the lifecycle of a product or industry, and vertical disintegration is the norm in both modern and ancient businesses.[4] The problem in recognizing the pervasiveness of *The Invisible Hand* in economic life is that firms producing new products for new markets are typically vertically integrated. The pioneers in new enterprises catch the eye. Everyone noticed Dell when it produced its PCs from the ground up, but the later Dell, who relied on sub-contractors for all kinds of parts, was only one participant in an industry no longer on the cutting edge. Dell was on the way to becoming the baker who purchases flour on the market and sells bread to a retailer. Who cares? As this is being written, Intel—the silicon in "Silicon Valley"—in the face of costly failures, is on the verge of exiting from the manufacturing of chips called central processing units (CPUs) in order to devote itself to their design.[5]

---

[3] By this time, the entrepreneur may have lost his edge, retired, or gone on to new challenges, leaving his firm in the hands of not particularly inspired, able, or motivated offspring and/or professional managers. In real life, business is conducted for better or worse by real people. The economist's model of the profit-maximizing firm is most useful in a changeless world and least useful during and immediately after periods of intense change.

[4] It is sometimes asserted that only states are capable of amassing great/valuable quantities of commodities for trading purposes. This view is expressed by scholars living out their lives in market economies, in which this view is disproven by any random glance. One unnamed scholar wonders what interest Near Eastern traders would have in coming to Greece during the Postpalatial Period, "where no state organization capable of assembling large quantities of commodities like staple agricultural goods or textiles now existed." It might well be pondered that the sum of a large number of small things need not be small.

[5] "A Silicon Valley Identity Crises," *Wall Street Journal*, Saturday/Sunday November 7-8, 2020, Section B, B1-B6.

References

List of Abbreviations

AA = Archäologischer Anzeiger

AAA = Archaiologika analekta ex Athenon. Athens Annals of Archaeology

AegArch = Aegean Archaeology

AF = Altorientalische Forschungen

AfO = Archiv für Orientforschungen

Ä&L = Ägypten und Levante. Egypt and the Levant (E&L). Internationale Zeitschrift für ägyptische Archäologie und deren Nachbargebiete

AHB = Ancient History Bulletin

AION(archeol) = Annali di archeologia e storia antica. Napoli: Istituto Universitario Orientale di Napoli, Dipartimento di Studi del Mondo Classico e del Mediterraneo Antico

AJA = American Journal of Archaeology

AJP = American Journal of Philology

AncSoc = Ancient Society

Anodos = Anodos: Studies of the Ancient World

AntK = Antike Kunst

Arachne = Arachne. Occasional Publication for the History of Costume and Textiles in the Aegean and Eastern Mediterranean

ArchaeolRep = Archaeological Reports

ArcheoSciences = ArcheoSciences, revue d'Archéométrie

ArchEph = Archaiologike Ephemeris

ArchNews = Archaeological News

ATR = Archaeological Textiles Review

AS = Anatolian Studies: Journal of the British Institute of Archaeology at Ankara

ASAtene = Annuario della Scuola Archeologica di Atene e delle Missioni Italiane in Oriente

ASDIWAL = ASDIWAL. Revue genevoise d'anthropologie et d'histoire des religions

AuOr = Aula Orientalis (Barcelona)

AWE = Ancient West & East

BaBesch = BaBesch Annual Papers on Mediterranean Archaeology

BASOR = Bulletin of the American Schools of Oriental Research

BCH = Bulletin de Correspondance Hellénique

References

BCHSupp = Bulletin de Correspondance Hellénique Supplément

BICS = Bulletin of the Institute of Classical Studies, University of London

BiOr = Bibliotheca Orientalis

BMCR = Bryn Mawr Classical Review

BPS = Baltic-Pontic Studies

BRL = Bulletin of the John Rylands University Library of Manchester, Manchester

BSA = Annual of the British School at Athens

BSAStud. = British School at Athens Studies

BSASupp. = British School at Athens Supplements

Camb.Archaeol.J = Cambridge Archaeological Journal

CArchJ = Cambridge Archaeological Journal

CCJ = Cambridge Classical Journal

CJ = Classical Journal

ClAnt = Classical Antiquity

CP = Classical Philology

CQ = Classical Quarterly

CR = Classical Review

CRAI = Comptes rendus de l'Académie des Inscriptions et Belles-Lettres

CretAnt = Creta Antica: Rivista annuale di studi archeologici, storici ed epigrafici

CW = Classical World

DialHistAnc = Dialogues d'histoire ancienne

DocPraehist = Documenta Praehistorica

EchCl = Echos du monde classique. Classical Views

ElectronAnt = Electronic Antiquity

ELR = Legal Roots, The International Journal of Roman Law, Legal History and Comparative Law

Eras = Eras: the Journal of Monash University's School of Philosophical, Historical and International Studies

Glotta = Glotta: Zeitschrift für griechische und lateinische Sprache. Göttingen: Vandenhoeck und Ruprecht

GM = Gottinger Miszellen

G&R = Greece and Rome

GRBS = Greek, Roman and Byzantine Studies

Hermathena = A Trinity College Dublin Review

Hesperia = Hesperia: The Journal of the American School of Classical Studies at Athens

HesperiaSupp = Hesperia Supplements

Historia = Historia. Zeitschrift für alte Geschichte

HR = History of Religions

HSPh = Harvard Studies in Classical Philology

ICS = Illinois Classical Studies

IGForsch = Indogermanische Forschungen
IJNA = International Journal of Nautical Archaeology
IncidAntico = Incidenza dellAntico, Dialoghi di Storia greca
IndogermF = Indogermanische Forshungen
JAEI = Journal of Ancient Egyptian Interconnections
Jahrb.f.cl.Philol. = Jahrbuch für classische Philologie
JANEH = Journal of Ancient Near Eastern History
JANER = Journal of Ancient Near Eastern Religions
JAOS = Journal of the American Oriental Society
JArchaeolSciRep = Journal of Archaeological Science: Reports
JCS = Journal of Cuneiform Studies
JEH = Journal of Economic History
JEMAHS = Journal of Eastern Mediterranean Archaeology & Heritage Studies
JESHO = Journal of the Economic and Social History of the Orient
JHS = Journal of Hellenic Studies
JLL = Journal of Latin Linguistics
JMA = Journal of Mediterranean Archaeology
JNES = Journal of Near Eastern Studies
JPR = Journal of Prehistoric Religion
JRS = Journal of Roman Studies
Kadmos = Zeitschrift für vor- und frühgriechische Epigraphik
Kaskal = Kaskal: Rivista di Storia, ambiente e culture del Vicino Oriente Antico
Kernos = Kernos: Revue internationale et pluridisciplinaire de religion grècque antique
MAA = Mediterranean Archaeology and Archaeometry
MBAH = Marburger Beiträge zur Antiken Handels-, Wirtschafts- und Sozialgeschichte
    (Formerly Münstersche Beiträge zur Antiken Handelsgeschichte)
MDAI = Mitteilungen des DeutschenArchäologischen Instiuts, Athenische Abteilung
Minos = Minos: Revista de filología egea
MusHelv = Museum Helveticum
NEASB = Near East Archaeological Society Bulletin
OJA = Oxford Journal of Archaeology
OpAth = Opuscula Atheniensia: Annual of the Swedish Institute at Athens
Pasiphae = Pasiphae: Rivista di Filogia e Antichchita Egee
PCPS = Proceedings of the Cambridge Philological Society
Quat.Int. = Quatenary International
QUCC = Quaderni Urbanati di cultura classica, Rome
RA = Revue Archéologique
RheinMusPhilol = Rheinisches Museum für Philologie. Frankfurt am Main: Sauerländer.
RivStudiOrien = Rivista degli Studi Orientali

References

SMEA = *Studi micenei ed egeo-anatolici. Roma: CNR, Istituto per gli Studi Micenei ed Egeo-Anatolici.*

ST = *Studia Troica. Aegeus Society*

Stud.Hercnyia = *Studia Hercynia*

SyllClass = *Syllecta Classica*

SymbOslo = *Symbolae Osloenses*

Talanta = *Τάλαντα: Proceedings of the Dutch Archaeological and Historical Society.*

TAPA = *Transactions of the American Philological Association*

TC = *Trends in Classics*

TransPhilolSoc = *Transactions of the Philological Society*

UF = *Ugarit Forshungen*

WorldArchaeol. = *World Archaeology*

Živa antika = *Ziva antika: Antiquité vivante*

References

Ackerman, Susan. 2008. "Asherah, the West Semitic Goddess of Spinning and Weaving?" *JNES* 67: 1–30.

Adams, Ellen. 2017. *Cultural Identity in Minoan Crete: Social Dynamics in the Neopalatial Period.* Cambridge.

Adkins, A. W. H. 1972. "Homeric Gods and the Values of Homeric Society." *JHS* 92: 1–19.

Adrimi-Sistani, Vassiliki, Maria Filomena Guerra, and Philippe Walter. 2009. "La tombe mycénienne de Kazanaki (Volos) et le mythe de la toison d'or." *ArchéoSciences* 33: 673–686.

Agourides, Christos. 1997. "Sea Routes and Navigation in the Third Millennium Aegean." *OJA* 16: 1–24.

Aitken, Ellen Bradshaw. 1982. ὀπάων *and* ὀπάζω: *A Study in the Epic Treatment of Heroic Relationships.* Available at https://chs.harvard.edu/book/opaon-and-opazo-a-study-in-the-epic-treatment-of-heroic-relationships/.

Alberti, Benjamin. 2001. "Faience Goddesses and Ivory Bull-Leapers: The Aesthetics of Sexual Difference at Late Bronze Age Knossos." *WorldArchaeol* 33: 189–205.

Alberti, Maria Emmanuella. 2007. "The Minoan Textile Industry and the Territory from Neopalatial to Mycenaean Times: Some First Thoughts." *CretAnt* 8: 243–262.

Alberti, Maria Emmanuela. 2008. "Murex Shells as Raw Materials: The Purple-Dye Industry and Its By-products; Interpreting the Archaeological Evidence." *Kaskal* 5: 73–90.

Alfaro, C. 2016. "Colchis, Wool and the Spinning Fates in Catullus *Carmen* 64." In Fanfani, Harlow, and Nosch, eds., *Spinning Fates and the Song of the Loom*, 271–284.

Alfen, Peter G. van. 1996-1997 [1998]. "The Linear B Inscribed Stirrup Jars as Links in an Administrative Chain." *Minos*: 31–32, 251–274.

Allen, Archibald. 1993. *The Fragments of Mimnermus: Text and Commentary*. Stuttgart.

Alram-Stern, Eva, Fritz Blakolmer, Sigrid Deger-Jalkotzy, Robert Laffineur, and Jörg Weilhartner 2016, eds. 2016. *Metaphysis: Ritual, Myth and Symbolism in the Aegean Bronze Age. Proceedings of the 15th International Aegean Conference, Vienna, Institute for Oriental and European Archaeology, Aegean and Anatolia Department, Austrian Academy of Sciences and Institute of Classical Archaeology, University of Vienna, 22-25 April 2014*. Leuven.

Andersson Strand, Eva and Marie-Louise Nosch, eds. 2015. *Tools, Textiles and Contexts: Investigating Textile Production in the Aegean and Eastern Mediterranean Bronze Age*. Ancient Textiles Series Vol. 21. Oxford.

Ando, Clifford. 2011. "Praesentia numinis. Part 2: Objects in Roman cult." *ASDIWAL* 6: 57–69.

Andolfi, Ilaria. 2019. *Acusilaus of Argos' Rhapsody of Prose: Introduction, Text, Commentary*. Berlin.

Andrews. P. B. S. 1965. "The Falls of Troy in Greek Tradition." *G&R* 12: 28–37.

Anghelina, Catalin. 2017. "Rhabdos Tripetēlos." *CP* 112: 219–227.

Antognelli Michel, Nicoletta. 2012. "Palms and Papyruses in the Late Minoan/ Helladic III: The Exotic World, the Fantastic World and the Afterworld." In Stampolides, Kanta, and Giannikoure, eds., *Athanasia*, 41–52.

Antognelli Michel, Nicoletta. (2020). "Wingless Griffins among Papyrus Plants from Neopalatial Knossos? A Reconstruction Proposal of the Seal Impression *CMS* II.8, no. 321." *BSA* 115: 247–268.

Antonaccio, Carla M. 1992. "Terraces, Tombs, and the Early Argive Heraion." *Hesperia* 62: 83–105.

Apostolakou, Stavroula, Philip Betancourt, Thomas Brogan, and Dimitra Mylona. 2016. "Chryssi and Pefka: The Production and Use of Purple Dye on Crete in the Middle and Late Bronze Age." In Jónatan Ortiz Garcia, Carmen Alfaro Giner, Luis Turell and Maria Julia Martínez Garcia, eds., *Textiles, Basketry and Dyes in the Ancient Mediterranean World. Proceedings of the Vth International Symposium on Textiles and Dyes in the Ancient Mediterranean World (Montserrat, 19-22 March, 2014) Purpurea vestes*, 251–274. València.

Apostolakou, Vili, Thomas M. Brogan, and Philip P. Betancourt, eds. 2020. *Alatzomouri-Pefka: A Middle Minoan IIB Workshop Making Organic Dyes*. Prehistory Monographs 62. Philadelphia.

References

Aravantinos, Vasileios (Vassilis). 1990. "The Mycenaean Inscribed Sealings from Thebes: Problems of Content and Function." In Thomas G. Palaima, ed., *Aegean Seals, Sealings and Administration. Proceedings of the NEH-Dickson Conference of the Program in Aegean Scripts and Prehistory of the Department of Classics, University of Texas at Austin, January 11-13, 1989*, 149–174. Liège.

———. 2010. "Mycenaean Thebes: Old Questions, New Answers." In Isabelle Boehm and Sylvie Müller, eds., *Espace civil, espace religieux en Égée durant la période mycénienne: approches épigraphique, linguistique et archéologique*, 51–70. Lyon.

———. 2015. "The Palatial Administration of Thebes Updated." In Weilhartner and Ruppenstein, eds., *Tradition and Innovation in the Mycenaean Palatial Polities*, 21–49.

———. 2019. "Old Memories versus New Trends in Postpalatial Thebes." In Brogna et al., eds., *MNHMH/MNEME*, 187–197.

Aruz, Joan. 2003. "Art and Interconnections in the Third Millennium B.C." In Joan Aruz and Ronald Wallenfels, eds., *Art of the First Cities: The Third Millennium B.C. from the Mediterranean to the Indus*, 239–250. New York.

Aslan, Rüstem, Stephan Blum, Gabrielle Kastl, Frank Schweizer, and Diane Thumm, eds. 2002. *Mauerschau: Festschrift für Manfred Korfmann*. Remshalden-Grunbach.

Aston, Emma. 2009. "Thetis and Cheiron in Thessaly." *Kernos* 22: 83–107.

Auburt, Jean-Jacques. 1994. *Business Managers in Ancient Rome: A Social and Economic Study of Institores, 200 B.C.–A.D. 250*. Leiden.

Avramidou, Amalia, and Denise Demetriou, eds. 2014. *Approaching the Ancient Artifact: Representation, Narrative, and Function. A Festschrift in Honor of H. Alan Shapiro*. Berlin.

Bachhuber, Christoph. 2003. "Aspects of Late Helladic Sea Trade." Unpublished MA thesis. Texas A&M University, College Station, TX.

———. 2009. "The Treasure Deposits of Troy: Rethinking Crisis and Agency on the Early Bronze Age Citadel." *AS* 59: 1–18.

———. 2016. "The Industry and Display of Textiles in Early Bronze Age Western Anatolia." In Ernst Pernicka, Sinan Ünlüsoy, and Stephan W. E. Blum, eds., *Early Bronze Age Troy: Chronology, Cultural Development and Interregional Contacts: Proceedings of an International Conference held at the University of Tübingen*, 339–363. Bonn.

Bachvarova, Mary R. 2016. *From Hittite to Homer: The Anatolian Background of Ancient Greek Epic*. Cambridge.

Bailey, H. W. 1959. "Iranian *Arya-* and *Daha-*." *TransPhilolSoc* 58: 71–115.

Bakola, Emmanuela. 2016. "Textile Symbolism and the 'Wealth of the Earth': Creation, Production and Destruction in the 'Tapestry Scene' of Aeschylus'

Oresteia (*Ag.* 905–978)." In Fanfani, Harlow and Nosch, eds., *Spinning Fates and the Song of the Loom*, 115–136. Oxford.

Banou, Emilia. 2008. "Minoan 'Horns of Consecration' Revisited: A Symbol of Sun Worship in Palatial and Post-Palatial Crete?" *MAA* 8: 27–47.

Barber, Elizabeth J. W. 1991. *Prehistoric Textiles: The Development of Cloth in the Neolithic and Bronze Ages with Special Reference to the Aegean.* Princeton.

———. 1994. *Women's Work: The First 20,000 Years; Women, Cloth, and Society in Early Times.* New York.

———. 2016. "Minoans, Mycenaeans, and Keftiu." In Shaw and Chapin, eds., *Woven Threads*, 205–237.

Baumbach, Lydia. 1986. "The Personal Names on the Knossos ApTablets." In Etter, ed., *O-o-pe-ro-si*, 273–278.

———. 1987. "Mycenaean *tu-ru-pte-ri-ja* and Herodotus II. 180." In Petar Hr. Ilievski and Ljiljana Crepajac, eds., *Tractata Mycenaea Proceedings of the Eighth International Colloquium on Mycenaean Studies*, 49–54. Skopjie.

Baurain, Claude. 1985. "Pour une autre interprétation des génies minoens." *BCHSupp.* 11: 95–118.

Bazzanella, Marta, Anna Mayr, Luisa Moser, and Antoinette Rast-Eicher, eds. 2003. *Textiles: intrecci e tessuti dalla preistoria europea.* Trento.

Beckman, Gary. 2011. "The Ahhiyawa Texts: Translation." In Beckman, Bryce, and Cline, eds., *The Ahhiyawa Texts.*

Beckman, Gary, Trevor Bryce, and Eric Cline, eds. 2011. *The Ahhiyawa Texts.* Atlanta.

Beekes, Robert. S. P. 2003. *The Origin of the Etruscans.* Amsterdam.

———. 2010. *Etymological Dictionary of Greek.* Leiden Indo-European Etymological Dictionary Series 10/1–2, 2 vols. Leiden.

Belgiorno, Maria Rosaria. 2008. "Ancient Perfumes and Textiles at Pyrgos-Mavroraki." *Cyprus Today* 46: 4–13.

Belleli, Vincenzo. 2002–2003. "Gli Argonauti all'imbarco." *AION(archeol)*, 9–10, 79–90.

Belmont, David E. 1969. "Athena and Telemachus." *CJ* 65: 109–116.

Bendall, Lisa Maria. 1998–1999. "A Time for Offerings: Dedications of Perfumed Oil at Pylian Festivals." In Bennet and Driessen, eds., *A-na-qu-ta*, 1–9.

———. 2003. "A Reconsideration of the Northeastern Building at Pylos: Evidence for a Mycenaean Redistributive Center." *AJA* 107: 181–231.

———. 2007. *Economics of Religion in the Mycenaean World: Resources Dedicated to Religion in the Mycenaean Palatial Economy.* Oxford.

Benecke, Norbert, Frank Fecht, and Jan Lichardus. 2000. *Forschungen in der Mikroregion von Drama (Südostbulgarien): Zusammenfassung der*

References

Hauptergebnisse der bulgarisch-deutschen Grabungen in den Jahren 1983-1999. Bonn.

Bennett, Emmet L. 1958. *The Olive Oil Tablets of Pylos. Texts of Inscriptions Found in 1955.* Suplementos a *Minos 2.* Salamanca.

Bennet, John. 1988. "'Outside in the Distance': Problems in Understanding the Economic Geography of Mycenaean Palatial Territory." In Jean-Pierre Olivier and Thomas G. Palaima, eds., *Texts, Tablets and Scribes: Studies in Mycenaean Epigraphy and Economy Offered to Emmett L. Bennet, Jr.,* 19–41. Salamanca.

———. 2007a. "The Aegean Bronze Age." In Walter Scheidel, Ian Morris, and Richard Saller, eds., *The Cambridge Economic History of the Greco-Roman World,* 175–210. Cambridge.

———. 2007b. "Representations of Power in Mycenaean Pylos: Script, Orality, Iconography." In Lang, Reinholdt, and Weilhartner, eds., *Stephanos Aristeios,* 11–22.

Bennet, John, and Jan Drissen, eds. 1998–1999. *A-na-qo-ta: Studies Presented to J. T. Killen* (= *Minos* 33–34). Salamanca.

Bennet, John, and Paul Halstead. 2014. "O-no! Writing and Righting Redistribution." In Nakassis, Gulizio, and James, eds. *KE-RA-ME-JA,* 271–282.

Benton, Sylvia. 1934/1935. "The Evolution of the Tripod-Lebes." *BSA* 35: 74–130.

Benzi, Mario. 2002. "Anatolia and the Eastern Aegean at the Time of the Trojan War." In Franco Montanari and Paola Ascheri, eds., *Omero tremila anni dopo,* 343–385. Rome.

Bertany, Edward M. 2018. "The Best of the Olympians: The Character of Apollo in the Homeric Epics and Hymns." Unpublished Ph.D. dissertation. University of Washington, Seattle.

Betancourt, Philip P. 2007. *Introduction to Aegean Art.* Philadelphia.

Betancourt, Philip P., Michael C. Nelson, and Hector Williams, eds. 2007. *Krinoi kai Limenes: Studies in Honor of Joseph and Maria Shaw.* Prehistory Monographs 22. Philadelphia.

Betancourt, Philip P., Thomas M. Brogan, and Vili Apostolakou. 2020. "Discussion and Conclusions." In Apostolakou, Brogan, and Betancourt, eds., *Alatzomouri-Pefka,* 129–136.

Betts, John H. 1968. "Trees in the Wind on Cretan Sealings." *AJA* 72: 149–150.

———. 1978. "More Aegean Papyrus: Some Glyptic Evidence." *AAA* 11: 61–74.

Bierl, Anton, Menelaos Christopoulos, and Athina Papachrysostomou, eds. 2017. *Time and Space in Ancient Myth, Religion and Culture.* Berlin.

Bietak, Manfred. 2000. "The Mode of Representation in Egyptian Art in Comparison to Aegean Bronze Age Art." In Susan Sherratt, ed., *The Wall Paintings of Thera*, Volume I, 209–246. Athens.

Billigmeier, Jon-Christian. and Judy A. Turner. 1981. "The Socio-Economic Roles of Women in Mycenaean Greece: A Brief Survey from Evidence of the Linear B Tablets." In Helene P. Foley, ed., *Reflections on Women in Antiquity*, 1–18. New York.

Bintliff, John L. 2002. "Rethinking Early Mediterranean Urbanism." In Aslan, Blum, Kastl, Schweizer, and Thumm, eds., *Mauerschau*, 153–177.

Blackwell, Nicholas G. 2018. "Contextualizing Mycenaean Hoards: Metal Control on the Greek Mainland at the End of the Bronze Age." *AJA* 122: 509–539.

Blakely, Sandra. 2007. "Kadmos, Jason, and the Great Gods of Samothrace: Initiation as Mediation in a Northern Aegean Context." *ElectronAnt* 11: 67–95.

Blakolmer, Fritz. 2008. "Processions in Aegean Iconography II: Who are the Participants?" In Hitchcock, Laffineur, and Crowley, eds., *Dais*, 257–268.

———. 2010a. "A Pantheon without Attributes? Goddesses and Gods in Minoan and Mycenaean Iconography." In Jannis Mylonopoulos, ed., *Divine Images and Human Imaginations in Ancient Greece and Rome*, 21–61. Leiden.

———. 2010b. "Small is Beautiful. The Significance of Aegean Glyptic for the Study of Wall Paintings, Relief Frescoesand Minor Relief Arts." In Müller, ed., *Die Bedeutung der mykenischen und mykenischen Siegelglyptik VI*, 91–108.

———. 2012a. "The Missing 'Barbarians': Some Thoughts on Ethnicity and Identity in Aegean Bronze Age Iconography." *Talanta* 44: 53–77.

———. 2012b. "Image and Architecture: Reflections of Mural Iconography in Seal Images and Other Art Forms of Minoan Crete." In Panagiotopoulos and Günkel Maschek, eds., *Minoan Realities*, 83–114.

———. 2015a. "The Many-Faced Minoan 'Genius' and His Iconographical Prototype Taweret. On the Character of Near Eastern Religious Motifs in Neopalatial Crete." In Jana Mynářová, Pavel Onderka, and Peter Pavúk, eds., *There and Back Again—the Crossroads II. Proceedings of an International Conference Held in Prague, September 15-18, 2014 Charles University*, 197–219. Prague.

———. 2015b. "Was the 'Minoan Genius' a God? An Essay on Near Eastern Deities and Demons in Aegean Bronze Age Iconography." *JAEI* 7: 29–40.

———. 2017a. "Spirals in Malta and 'Ropes and Pulley' from the Eurasian Steppe? On the Origin of Some Ornaments of the Aegean Bronze Age." In Fotiadis, Laffineur, Lólos, and Vlachopoulos, eds., *Hesperos*, 105–114.

———. 2017b. "Deities above Animals: On the Transformation of Eastern Iconography in Minoan Crete." In *Proceedings of the 12th International Congress of Cretan Studies* (Heraklion 21–25. 2016), 1–12. Heraklion.

———. 2018. "A 'Special Procession' in Minoan Seal Images: Observations on Ritual Images in Minoan Crete." In Pavúk, Klontza-Jaklová, and Harding, eds., *Eudaimōn*, 31–48.

———. 2019a. "The Language of Colour and Material: Were Architectural Façades in the Aegean Bronze Age Brightly Painted?" In Shiyanthi Thavapalan and David Alan Warburton, eds., *The Value of Colour. Material and Economic Aspects in the Ancient World* (Berlin Studies of the Ancient World), 255–282. Berlin.

———. 2019b. "No Kings, No Inscriptions, No Historical Events? Some Thoughts on the Iconography of Rulership in Mycenaean Greece." In Jorrit M. Kelder and Willemijn J. I. Waal, eds., *From 'LUGAL.GAL' TO 'Wanax': Kingship and Political Organisation in the Late Bronze Age Aegean*, 49–94. Leiden.

———, ed. 2020. *Current Approaches and New Perspectives in Aegean Iconography (Aegis 18)*. Louvain.

Blakolmer, Fritz, and Jörg Weilhartner. 2015. "Eberzahnhelmträger und ke-se-nu-wo: Die Aussage der Bildkunst und der Linear B-Texte zu Identität und Fremdenbild in der ägäischen Frühzeit." In Andreas Pülz and Elisaabeth Trinkl, eds., *Das Eigene und das Fremde: Akten der 4. Tagung des Zentrums Archäologie und Altertumswissenschaften an der Österreichischen Akademie der Wissenschaften, 26.-27. März 2012*, 9–31. Vienna.

Blegen, Charles W., John L. Caskey, Marion Rawson, Jerome Sperling, and Cedric G. Boulter. 1950. *Troy: The First and Second Settlements*. Princeton.

Blegen, Charles W., and Marion Rawson. 1973. *The Palace of Nestor at Pylos in Western Messenia*. Princeton.

Boardman, John. 2014. "Homer and the Legacy of the Age of Heroes." In Joan Aruz, Sarah B. Graff, and Yelena Rakic, eds., *Assyria to Iberia: At the Dawn of the Classical Age*, 24–32. New York.

Bobokhyan, A. 2009. "Trading Implements in Early Troy." *AS* 59: 19–50.

Boedeker, Deborah Dickmann. 1984. *Descent from Heaven: Images of Dew in Greek Poetry and Religion*. Chico.

Boëlle, Cécile. 2004. *Po-ti-ni-ja: l'élément féminin dans la religion mycénienne, d'après les archives en linéaire B*. Paris.

Boertien, Jeannette Hannah. (2013). "Unravelling the Fabric: Textile Production in Iron Age Transjordan." Unpublished Ph.D. dissertation. University of Groningen, Groningen.

Boloti, Tina. 2014. "*E-ri-ta*'s Dress.: Contribution to the Study of Mycenaean Priestesses' Attire." In Harlow and Nosch, eds., *Prehistoric, Ancient Near Eastern and Aegean Textiles and Dress*, 245–270.

———. 2016. "A 'Knot'-Bearing (?) Minoan Genius from Pylos. Contribution to the Cloth/Clothing Offering Imagery of the Aegean Bronze Age." In Alram-Stern, Blakolmer, Deger-Jalkotzy, Laffineur, and Weilhartner, eds., *Metaphysis*, 505–510.

———. 2017. "Offering of Cloth and/or Clothing to the Sanctuaries: A Case of Ritual Continuity from the 2nd to the 1st Millennium BCE in the Aegean?" In Cecilie Brøns and Marie-Louise Nosch, eds., *Textiles and Cult in the Ancient Mediterranean*, 3–16. Oxford.

———. 2018. "Offering of Cloth/Clothing and Wool to Divinities: The Linear B Data." *Arachne* 5: 88–99.

Bonfante, Giuliano, and Larissa Bonfante. 2002. *The Etruscan Language: An Introduction*, rev. ed. Manchester.

Bonfante, Larissa. 2016. "Innovations: Myth, Inscriptions, and Meanings." In Nancy Thomson de Grummond and Lisa C. Pieraccini, eds., *Caere*, 61–71. Austin.

Bonnell, Kyle. 2019. "*Homeric Hymn to Apollo*: Introduction and Commentary on Lines 1–178." Unpublished Ph.D. dissertation. Oxford University, Oxford, UK.

Borgna, Elisabetta. 2012. "Remarks on Female Attire of Minoan and Mycenaean Clay Figures." In Nosch and Laffineur, eds., *Kosmos*, 335–342.

Borgna, Elizabetta, and Paola Cassola Guida, eds. 2009. *From the Aegean to the Adriatic: Social Organisations, Modes of Exchange, and Interaction in Postpalatial Times (12th – 11th B.C.)*. Rome.

Borgna, Elisabetta, Ilaria Caloi, Filippo Carinci, and Robert Laffineur, eds. 2019. *MNHMH/MNEME: Past and Memory in the Aegean Bronze Age: Proceedings of the 17th International Aegean Conference, University of Udine, Department of Humanities and Cultural Heritage, Ca' Foscari University of Venice, Department of Humanities, 17-21 April 2018*. Leuven.

Borthwick, E .K. 1976. "The 'Flower of the Argives' and a Neglected Meaning of *Anthos*." *JHS* 96: 1–7.

Bosanquet, Robert C. 1904. "Some 'Late Minoan' Vases Found in Greece." *JHS* 24: 317–329.

Bosanquet, Robert C., and Richard A. Dawkins. 1923. "The Unpublished Objects from the Palaikastro Excavations, 1902–1906." *BSASupp* I: i-xii, 1–160.

Bossert, Helmuth Th. 1942. *Altanatolien: Kunst und Handwerk in Kleinasien von den Anfängen bis zum Völligen Aufgehen in der Griechischen Kultur*. Berlin.

Boulotis, Christos. 2009. "Koukonisi on Lemnos: Reflections on the Minoan and Minoanizing Evidence." In Erik Hallager, Colin F Macdonald, and Wolf-Dietrich Niemeier, eds., *Minoans in the Central, Eastern and Northern Aegean: New Evidence*. Acts of a Minoan Seminar 22-23 January 2005 in Collaboration with the Danish Institute at Athens and the German Archaeological Institute at Athens, 175–218. Athens.

———. 2012. "Archaeological Site of Poliochni at Kaminia Area." Available for download at http://odysseus.culture.gr/h/3/eh351.jsp?obj_id=2534.

Bouzek, Jan. 2007. "The Amber Route, Apollo, and the Hyerboreans." In Galanaki, Tomas, Galanakis, and Laffineur, eds., *Between the Aegean and Baltic Seas*, 357–361.

Boyd, Michael J. 2016. "Distributed Practice and Cultural Identities in the 'Mycenaean' Period." In Molloy, ed., *Of Odysseys and Oddities*, 385–409.

Branigan, Keith. 1974. *Aegean Metalwork of the Early Middle Bronze Age*. Oxford.

Braswell, Bruce Karl. 1988. *A Commentary on the Fourth Pythian Ode of Pindar*. Berlin.

Braund, David, and G. R. Tsetskhladze. 1989. "The Export of Slaves from Colchis." *CQ* 39: 114–125.

Braund, David. 1994. *Georgia in Antiquity: A History of Colchis and Transcaucasian Iberia 550 BC – AD 562*. Oxford.

Brecoulaki, Hariclia. 2014. "'Precious Colours' in Ancient Greek Polychromy and Painting: Material Aspects and Symbolic Values." *RA*, Fasc. 1: 3–35.

———. 2018. "Does Colour make a Difference? The Aesthetics and Contexts of Wall-painting in the "Palace of Nestor" at Pylos." In Vlachopoulous, ed., *Paintbrushes*, 391–405.

Brecoulaki, Hariclia, Caroline Zaitoun, Sharon R. Stocker, Jack L. Davis, Andreas G. Karydas, Maria Perla Colombini, and Ugo Bartolucci. 2008. "An Archer from the Palace of Nestor: A New Wall Painting Fragment in the Chora Museum." *Hesperia* 77: 363–397.

Brecoulaki, Hariclia, Jack L. Davis, and Sharon R. Stocker, eds. 2015. *Mycenaean Wall Painting in Context: New Discoveries, Old Finds Reconsidered*. Athens.

Brecoulaki, Hariclia, Sharon R. Stocker, Jack L. Davis, and Emily C. Egan. 2015. "An Unprecedented Naval Scene from Pylos: First Considerations." In Brecoulaki, Davis, and Stocker, eds., *Mycenaean Wall Painting in Context*, 257–287.

Bremmer, Jan. N. 2007. "The Myth of the Golden Fleece." *JANER* 6: 9–38.

Breniquet, Catherine, and Cécile Michel, eds. 2014. *Wool Economy in the Ancient Near East and the Aegean: From the Beginning of Sheep Husbandry to Institutional Textile Industry*. Oxford.

Bresciani, Edda. 1997. "Foreigners." In Sergio Donadoni, ed., *The Egyptians*, 221–253. Chicago.

Briault, Camilla. 2007. "Making Mountains Out of Molehills in the Bronze Age Aegean: Visibility, Ritual Kits, and the Idea of a Peak Sanctuary." *WorldArchaeol.* 39:122–41.

Brice, William C. 1965–1966. "The Minoan 'Libation Formula." *BRL* 48: 56–68.

Brodie, Neil, ed. 2008. *Horizon: A Colloquium on the Prehistory of the Cyclades.* Cambridge.

Brogan, T. M, R. A. K. Smith, and J. S. Soles. 2002. "Mycenaeans at Mochlos? Exploring Culture and Identity in the Late Minoan IB to IIIA1 Transition." *AegArch* 6: 89–118.

Briault, Camilla. 2007. "Making Mountains Out of Molehills in the Bronze Age Aegean: Visibility, Ritual Kits, and the Idea of a Peak Sanctuary." *WorldArchaeol.* 39: 122–141.

Brinkman, John A. 1990. "Political Covenants, Treaties, and Loyalty Oaths in Babylonia and Between Assyria and Babylonia." In Luciano Canfora, Mario Liverani, and Carlo Zaccagnini, eds., *I Trattati Nel Mondo Antico Forma Ideologica Funzione*, 81–111. Rome.

Bruins, Frans. 1970. "Royal Purple and the Dye Industry of the Mycenaens and Phoenicians." In Michel Mollat, ed., *Sociétés et compagnies de commerce en Orient et dans l'océan Indien; actes du huitième Colloque international d'histoire maritime (Beyrouth, 5-10 septembre 1966)*, 73–90. Paris.

Bryce, Trevor R. 1989. "The Nature of Mycenaean Involvement in Western Anatolia." *Historia* 38: 1–21.

———. 2003. "History." In H. Craig Melcher, ed., *The Luwians*, 27–127. Handbook of Oriental Studies 68. Leiden.

———. 2011. "The Ahhiyawa Texts: Commentary." In Beckman, Bryce, and Cline, eds., *The Ahhiyawa Texts.*

———. 2015. "The Land of *Hiyawa* (*Que*) Revisited." *AS* 66: 67–79.

Budin, Stephanie Lynn, and Jean MacIntosh Turfa, eds. 2016. *Women in Antiquity: Real Women across the Ancient World.* London.

Burgess, Jonathan S. 2001. *The Traditon of the Trojan War in Homer and the Epic Cycle.* Baltimore.

———. 2011. "Belatedness in the Travels of Odysseus." In Franco Montanari, Antonios Rengakos, and Christos Tsagalis, eds., *Homeric Contexts: Neoanalysis and the Interpretation of Oral Poetry*, 269–290. Berlin.

———. 2017. "Land and Sea in the *Odyssey* and the *Telegony*." In Bierl, Christopoulos, and Papachrysostomou, eds., *Time and Space in Ancient Myth, Religion and Culture*, 27–40.

References

Burke, Brendan. 1997. "The Organization of Textile Production on Bronze Age Crete." In Laffineur and Betancourt, eds., *TEXNH*, Vol. II, 413–422.

———. 2002. "Anatolian Origins of the Gordion Knot Legend." *GRBS* 42: 255–261.

———. 2005. "Materialization of Mycenaean Ideology and the Ayia Triada Sarcophagus." *AJA* 109: 403–422.

———. 2006. "Textile Production at Petras: The Evidence from House II." In E. A. Kaloutsakis and E. Tampakaki, eds., *Πεπραγμένα Θ' Διεθνούς Κρητολογικού Συνεδρίου, Ελούντα, 1-6 Οκτωβρίου 2001. Α1: Προϊστορική Περίοδος, Ανασκαφικά Δεδομένα*, Ηράκλειο, [*Pepragmena Th' Diethnous Krētologikou Synedriou: Elounta, 1-6 Oktōvriou 2001*, 279–295. Hērakleio.

———. 2008. "Male Lament in Greek Tragedy." In Anne Suter, ed., *Lament: Studies in the Ancient Mediterranean and Beyond*, 70–92. Oxford.

———. 2010. *From Minos to Midas: Ancient Cloth Production in the Aegean and in Anatolia*. Oxford.

———. 2012. "Looking for Sea-Silk in the Bronze Age Aegean." In Nosch and Laffineuir, eds., *Kosmos*, 171–177.

———. 2016. "Beyond Penelope: Women and the Role of Textiles in Early Greece." In Budin and Turfa, eds., *Women in Antiquity*, 635–645.

Burke, Brendan, Bryan Burns, Alexandra Charami, Trevor van Damme, Nicholas Herrmann and Bartłomiej Lis. 2020. "Fieldwork at Ancient Eleon in Boeotia, 2011–2018." *AJA* 124: 441–476.

Burke, Brendan, and Anne C. Chapin. 2016. "Bronze Age Aegean Cloth Production: A Cottage Industry No More." In Shaw and Chapin, eds., *Woven Threads*, 17–42.

Burke, Brendan, Bryan Burns, Alexandra Charami, Trevor van Damme, Nicholas Herrmann and Bartłomiej Lis. 2020. "Fieldwork at Ancient Eleon in Boeotia, 2011–2018." *AJA* 124:441-76.

Burkert, Walter. 1985. *Greek Religion*. Cambridge, MA.

———. 1987. *Ancient Mystery Cults*. Cambridge, MA.

———. 1992. *The Orientalizing Revolution: Near Eastern Influence on Greek Culture in the Early Archaic Period*. Cambridge, MA.

Buttman, Phillip Karl. 1840. *Lexilogus: A Critical Examination of the Meaning and Etymology of Numerous Greek Words and Passages, Intended Principally for Homer and Hesiod*. 2nd. ed. rev. London.

Buxton, Richard. 2010. "How Medea Moves: Versions of a Myth in Apollonius and Elsewhere." In Heike Bartel and Anne Simon, eds., *Unbinding Medea: Interdisciplinary Approaches to a Classical Myth from Antiquity to the 21st Century*, 25–38. London.

Çakırlar, Canan, and Ralf Becks. 2009. "'Murex' Dye Production at Troia: Assessment of Archaeomalacological Data from Old and New Excavations." *ST* 18: 87–103.

Cameron, Mark A. S. 1970. "New Restorations of Minoan Frescoes from Knossos." *BICS* 17: 163–166.

———. 1971. "The Lady in Red: A Complementary Figure to the Ladies in Blue." *Archaeology* 24: 35–43.

Campbell, Leanne Michelle. 2013. "Bronze Age Adyta: Exploring Lustral Basins as Representations of Natural Spaces and Places." *Eras* 14: 1–32.

Carless Unwin, Naomi. 2017. *Caria and Crete in Antiquity: Cultural Interaction between Anatolia and the Aegean*. Cambridge.

Caloi, Ilaria. 2015. "Recreating the Past: Using Tholos Tombs in Protopalatial Mesara." In Sarah Cappel, Ute Günkel-Maschek, and Diamantis Panagiotopoulos, eds., *Minoan Archaeology: Perspectives for the 21st Century*, 255–266. Louvain.

Carannante, Alfredo. 2011. "Purple-Dye Industry Shell Waste Recycling in the Bronze Age Aegean? Stoves and Murex Shells at Minoan Monastiraki (Crete, Greece)." In Canan Çakırlar, ed., *Archaeomalacology Revisited: Non-dietary Use of Molluscs in Archaeological Settings*. Proceedings of the Archaeomalacology Sessions at the 10th ICAZ Conference, Mexico City, 2006, 9–18. Oxford.

Carlier, Pierre, ed. 2010. *Études mycéniennes 2010: actes du XIIIe Colloque international sur les textes égéens: Sèvres, Paris, Nanterre, 20-23 septembre 2010*. Pisa.

Carpenter, Rhys. 1946. *Folk Tale, Fiction, and Saga in the Homeric Epics*. Berkeley.

Cavanagh, William. 2001. "Empty Space? Courts and Squares in Mycenaean Towns." In Keith Branigan, ed., *Urbanism in the Aegean Bronze Age*, 119–134. London.

Chadwick, John. 1957. "Potnia." *Minos* 5: 117–129.

———. 1990. "The Descent of the Greek Epic." *JHS* 110: 174–177.

———. 1998. "Pylian Gold and Local Administration PY Jo 438." In Bennet and Driessen, eds., *A-na-qo-ta*, 31–37.

Chandler, Albert D. 1977. *The Visible Hand: The Managerial Revolution in American Business*. Cambridge, MA.

Chantraine, Pierre. 1968–1980. *Dictionnaire Étymologique de la langue grecque: Histoire des Mots*. Paris.

Chapin, Anne. P. 1997. "A Re-Examination of the Floral Fresco from the Unexplored Mansion at Knossos." *BSA* 92: 1–24.

———. 2008. "The Lady of the Landscape: An Investigation of Aegean Costuming and the Xeste 3 Frescoes." In Cynthia S. Colburn and Maura K. Heyn, eds.,

Reading a Dynamic Canvas: Adornment in the Ancient Mediterranean World, 48–83. Newcastle.

———. 2010. "Frescoes." In Eric H. Cline, ed., *The Oxford Handbook of the Bronze Age Aegean,* 223–236. New York.

———. 2016a. "The Performative Body and Social Identity in the Room of the Fresco at Mycenae." In Mina, Triantaphyllou, and Papadatos, eds., *An Archaeology of Prehistoric Bodies and Embodied Identities in the Eastern Mediterranean,* 81–88.

———. 2016b. "Mycenaean Mythologies in the Making: The Frescoes of Pylos Hall 64 and the Mycenae Megaron." In Alram-Stern, Blakolmer, Deger-Jalkotzy, Laffineur, and Weilhartner, eds., *Metaphysis,* 459–466.

Chapin, Anne P., and Louise A. Hitchcock. 2007. "Homer and Laconian Topography: This is What the Book Says, and This is What the Land Tells Us." In Morris and Laffineur, eds., *Epos,* 255–282.

Chapin, Anne P., and Maria C. Shaw. 2006. "The Frescoes from the House of the Frescoes at Knossos: A Reconsideration of Their Architectural Context and a New Reconstruction of the Crocus Panel." *BSA* 101: 57–88.

Chittenden, Jacqueline. 1948. "Diaktoros Argeiphontes." *AJA* 52: 24–33.

Cingano, Ettore. 1992. "The Death of Oedipus in the Epic Tradition." *Phoenix* 46: 1–11.

Clay, Jenny Strauss. 1981–1982. "Immortal and Ageless Forever." *CJ* 77: 112–117.

Cline, Eric H. 1994. *Sailing the Wine-Dark Sea: International Trade and the Late Bronze Age.* Oxford.

———. 2007. "Rethinking Mycenaean International Trade with Egypt and the Near East." In Galaty and Parkinson, eds., *Rethinking Mycenaean Palaces II,* 190–200.

———. 2010. *The Oxford Handbook of the Bronze Age Aegean (ca. 3000 - 1000 BC).* Oxford.

Cline, Eric H., and Diane Harris Cline, eds. 1998. *The Aegean and the Orient in the Second Millennium. Proceedings of the 50th Anniversary Symposium, Cincinnati, 18-20 April 1997.* Liège.

Cline, Eric. H., and Steven M. Stannish. 2011. "Sailing the Great Sea: Amenhotep III's 'Aegean List' from Kom el-Hetan, Once More." *JAEI* 3: 6–16.

Collins, Billie Jean, Mary R. Bachvarova, and Ian Rutherford, eds., *Anatolian Interfaces: Hittites, Greeks, and Their Neighbours: Proceedings of an International Conference on Cross-Cultural Interaction, September 17-19, 2004, Emory University, Atlanta, GA.* Oxford.

Collon, Dominique. 2005. "Aspects of Bronze Age Trade." In Villing, ed., *The Greeks in the East,* 47–51.

Constantinidou, Soteroula. 1989. "*Xenia* and *Lekhestroterion*: Two Mycenaean Festivals." *Dodoni* 18: 9–26.

Cook, Erwin F. 2003. "Agamemnon's Test of the Army in *Iliad* Book 2 and the Function of Homeric *Akhos*." *AJP* 124: 165–198.

Craik, Elizabeth Mary. 2010. "The Myth of Philoktetes." *Collection of Western Classics* 22: 14–22. Available for download at http://hdl.handle.net/2433/108539.

Crawford, Janice L. 2012. "Prestige Clothing in the Bronze Age Aegean." In Nosch and Laffineuir, eds., *Kosmos*, 231–239.

Crielaard, Jan Paul. 2000. "Homeric and Mycenaean Long-Distance Contacts: Discrepancies in the Evidence." *BaBesch* 75: 51–63.

Crooks, Sam, Caroline Tully, and Louise Hitchcock. 2005. "Numinous Tree and Stone: Re-animating the Minoan Landscape." In Alram-Stern, Blakolmer, Deger-Jalkotzy, Laffineur, and Weilhartner, eds., *Metaphysis*, 157–164.

Crowley, Janice. L. 2008. "In Honour of the Gods—But Which Gods? Identifying Deities in Aegean Glyptic." In Hitchcock, Laffineur, and Crowley, eds., *Dais*, 75–87.

Cultraro, Massimo. 2005. "Aegeans in Smoke-Shrouded Lemnos: A Re-Assessment of the Mycenaean Evidence from Poliochni and Other Sites." In Laffineur and Greco, eds., *Emporia*, 237–246.

Cunliffe, Richard John. 1963. *A Lexicon of the Homeric Dialect*. Norman.

Cutler, Joanne. 2012. "Ariadne's Thread: The Adoption of Cretan Weaving Technology in the Wider Southern Aegean in the Mid-Second Millennium BC." In Nosch and Laffineur, eds., *Kosmos*, 145–154.

———. 2016. "Fashioning Identity: Weaving Technology, Dress, and Cultural Change in the Middle and Late Bronze Age Southern Aegean." In Evi Gorogianni, Peter Pavuk, and Luca Girella, eds., *Beyond Thalassocracies: Understanding Processes of Minoanisation and Mycenaeanisation in the Aegean*, 172–186. Oxford.

Cucuzza, Nicola. 2013. "Minoan Nativity Scenes? The Ayia Triada Swing Model and the Three-Dimensional Representation of Divine Epiphany." *ASAtene* 91, Series III, 13: 175–207.

D'Agata, Anna Lucia, and Sara De Angelis. 2014. "Minoan Beehives: Reconstructing the Practice of Beekeeping in Bronze Age Crete." In Touchais, Laffineur, and Rougemont, eds., *Physis*, 349–357.

Dakouri-Hild, Anastasia, and Sue Sherratt, eds. 2005. *Autochthon: Papers Presented to O. T. P. K. Dickinson on the Occasion of His Retirement*. Oxford.

Dale, Alexander. 2015. "Greek Ethnics in *ēnos* and the Name of Mytilene." In Nicholas Chr. Stampolides, Çiğdem Maner, and Konstantinos Kapanias, eds., *Nostoi: Indigenous Culture, Migration + Integration in the Aegean Islands + Western Anatolia during the Late Bronze + Early Iron Ages*, 421–444. Istanbul.

Dakouri-Hild, Anastasia, and Sue Sherratt, eds. 2005. *Autochthon: Papers Presented to O. T. P. K. Dickinson on the Occasion of his Retirement*. Oxford.

D'Alessio, Giovan Battista. 2005. "The *Megalai Ehoiai*: A Survey of the Fragments." In Richard Hunter, ed., *The Hesiodic Catalogue of Women: Constructions and Reconstructions*, 176–216. Cambridge.

Dalley, Stephanie. 1984. *Mari and Karana: Two Old Babylonian Cities*. London.

Davaris, Costis. 1976. *Guide to Cretan Antiques*. Park Ridge, NJ.

———. 2004. "The Mochlos Ship Cup." In Jeffrey S. Soles, ed., *Mochlos IC: Period III, Neopalatial Settlement on the Coast; The Artisans' Quarter and the Farmhouse at Chalinomour; The Small Finds*, 3–15. Philadelphia.

Davaris, Costis, and Jeffrey Soles. 1995. "A New Oriental Cylinder Seal from Mochlos." *ArchEph* 134: 29–66.

Davies, Anna Morpurgo. 2000. "Personal Names and Linguistic Continuity." In Simon Hornblower and Elaine Matthews, eds., *Greek Personal Names: Their Value as Evidence. Proceedings of the British Academy, vol. 104*, 15–39. Oxford.

Davies, Macolm. 2019. *The Cypria*. Cambridge, MA.

Davies, Percival Vaughan. 1969. *Macrobius: The Saturnalia*. New York.

Davis, Brent, and Robert Laffineur, eds. 2020. *Neôteros: Studies in Bronze Age Aegean Art and Archaeology in Honor of Professor John G. Younger on the Occasion of His Retirement. Aegeaum 44*. Liège.

Davis, Jack L., and Sharon R. Stocker. 2007. "Summary of Research at the Palace of Nestor between September 2006 and October 2007." Available at https://classics.uc.edu/prap/reports/HARP2007.html.

———. 2016. "The Lord of the Gold Rings: The Griffin Warrior of Pylos." *Hesperia* 85: 627–655.

Davison, J. A. 1965. "Thucydides, Homer, and the 'Achaean Wall'." *GRBS* 6: 5–28.

Day, Jo. 2011a. "Counting Threads: Saffron in Aegean Bronze Age Writing and Society." *OJA* 30: 369–391.

———. 2011b. "Crocuses in Context: A Diachronic Survey of the Crocus Motif in the Aegean Bronze Age." *Hesperia* 80: 337–379.

Deacy, Susan. 2000. "Athena and Ares: War, Violence, and Warlike Deities." In Hans van Wees, ed., *War and Violence in Ancient Greece*, 247–295, 357–359. Swansea.

Deacy, Susan, and Alexandra Villing. 2009. "What Was the Color of Athena's Aegis?" *JHS* 129: 111–129.

De Boer, Jan. G. 2006–2007. "Phantom Mycenaeans in the Black Sea." *Talanta*, 38–39, 277–302.

De Fidio, Pia. 2008. "Mycenaean History." In Duhoux and Davies, eds., *A Companion to Linear B*, I, 81–114.

Deger-Jalkotzy, Sigrid. 1972. "The Women of Py An 507." *Minos* 13: 137–160.

———. 1996. "On the Negative Aspects of the Mycenaean Palatial System." In Ernesto De Miro, Louis Godart, and Anna Sacconi, eds., *Atti e memorie del secondo Congresso internazionale di micenologia: Roma-Napoli, 14-20 ottobre 1991*, 715–728. Rome.

———. 2014. "A Very Underestimated Period: The Submycenaean Phase of Early Greek Culture." In Nakassis, Gulizio, and James, eds., *KE-RA-ME-JA*, 41–52.

Deger-Jalkotzy, Sigrid, and Irene S. Lemos, eds. 2006. *Ancient Greece: From the Mycenaean Palaces to the Age of Homer.* Edinburgh.

Del Freo, Maurizio, Marie-Louise Nosch, and Françoise Rougemont. 2013. "The Terminology of Textiles in the Linear B Tablets, including Some Considerations on Linear A Logograms and Abbreviations." In Michel and Nosch, eds., *Textile Terminologies*, 338–373.

Del Valle Muñoyerro, Maria. "Troy and Ilios in Homer: Region and City." *Glotta* 74: 213–226.

Demakopoulou, K., and J. H. Crouwel. 1992. "Mycenaean Pictorial Pottery from the Argive Heraion." *Hesperia* 61: 491–500.

Dewan, Rachel. 2015. "Bronze Age Flower Power: The Minoan Use and Social Significance of Saffron and Crocus Flowers." *Chronica* 5: 42–55.

Dickinson, Oliver. 2006. *The Aegean from Bronze Age to Iron Age.* New York.

———. 2007. "Aspects of Homeric Geography." In Morris and Laffineur, eds., *Epos*, 233–238.

———. 2009. "Social Development in the Postpalatial Period in the Aegean." In Borgna and Guida, eds., *From the Aegean to the Adriatic*, 11–19.

Di Giuseppe, Helga. 2017. "The Female *Pensum* in the Archaic and Hellenistic Periods. The *Epinetron*, the Spindle, and the Distaff." *Origini* 40: 259–276.

Dimock, G. E., Jr. 1956. "The Name of Odysseus." *Hudson Review* 9: 52–69.

Dimopoulou, Nota. 2010. "A Gold Discoid from Poros, Herakleion: The Guard Dog and the Garden." *BSA* 18: 89–100.

Doumas, Christos. 1992. *The Wall-Paintings of Thera.* 2nd. ed. Athens.

Driessen, Jan. 2002. "'The King Must Die': Some Observations on the Use of Minoan Court Compounds." In Driessen, Schoep, and Laffineur, eds., *Monuments of Minos*, 1–14.

Driessen, Jan, ed. 2016. *RA-PI-NE-U: Studies on the Mycenaean World Offered to Robert Laffineur for his 70th Birthday.* Louvain.

Driessen, Jan, Ilse Schoep, and Robert Laffineur, eds. 2002. *Monuments of Minos:Rethinking the Minoan Palaces: Proceedings of the Inernational Workshop "Crete of the Hundred Palaces?" Held at the Université Catholique de Louvain, Louvain-la-Neuve, 14-15 December 2001.* Liège.

References

Dubcová, Veronika. 2020. "Bird-demons in the Aegean Bronze Age: their Nature and Relationship to Egypt and the Near East." In Blakolmer, ed., *Current Approaches and New Perspectives in Aegean Iconography (Aegis 18)*, 205–222.

Duev, Ratko. 2006. "Hermaphroditus: The Other face of Hermes?" *Sobria ebrietas. u spomen na Mirona Flašara, Zbornik Filozofskog fakulteta, serija A: Istorijske nauke, knjiga XX*, 47–58. Beograd.

———. 2007. "Zeus and Dionysus in the Light of Linear B Records." *Pasiphae*, I, 223–230.

———. 2012. "*di-wi-ja* and *e-ra* in the Linear B Texts." In Carlier, et al., eds., *Études mycéniennes 2010*, 195–205.

Duhoux, Yves. 2011. "La fonction des vases a etrier inscrits en lineaire B." *Kadmos* 49: 47–92.

Duhoux, Yves, and Anna Morpurgo Davies, eds. 2008. *A Companion to Linear B: Mycenaean Greek Texts and their World*. 2 Volumes. Louvain.

Earle, Jason W. 2012. "Cosmetics and Cult Practices in the Bronze Age Aegean? A Case Study of Women with Red Ears." In Nosch and Laffineur, eds., *Kosmos*, 771-777.

Easton, D. F., J. D. Hawkins, A. G. Sherratt, and E. S. Sherratt. 2002. "Troy in Recent Perspective." *AS* 52: 75–109.

Eaverly, Mary Ann. 2013. *Tan Men/Pale Women: Color and Gender in Archaic Greece and Egypt, a Comparative Approach*. Ann Arbor.

Eder, Birgitta. 2006. "The World of Telemachus: Western Greece 1200-700 BC." In Deger-Jalkotzy and Lemos, eds., *Ancient Greece*, 549–580.

———. 2007. "The Power of Seals: Palaces, Peripheries and Territorial Control in the Mycenaean World." In Galanaki, Tomas, Galanakis, and Laffineur, eds., *Between the Aegean and Baltic Seas*, 35–44. .

Edmunds, Lowell. 2016. *Stealing Helen: The Myth of the Abducted Wife in Comparative Perspective*. Princeton.

———. 2019. *Toward the Characterization of Helen in Homer: Appellatives, Perphrastic Denominations, and Noun-Epithet Formulae*. Berlin.

Edwards, Ruth B. 1979. *Kadmos the Phoenician: A Study of Greek Legends and the Mycenaean Age*. Amsterdam.

Efkleidou, Kalliopi. 2002–2003. "The Status of 'Outsiders' within Mycenaean Pylos: Issues of Ethnic Identity, Incorporation, and Marginality." *Minos* 37–38: 269–291.

Egan, Emily Catherine. 2012. "Cut from the Same Cloth: The Textile Connection between Palace Style Jars and Knossian Wall Paintngs." In Nosch and Laffineur, eds., *Kosmos*, 317-324.

————. 2015. "Nestor's Megaron: Contextualizing a Mycenaean Institution at Pylos." Unpublished Ph.D. dissertation. University of Cincinnati, Cincinnati, OH.

Egan, Emily C., and Hariclia Brecoulaki. 2015. "Marine Iconography at the Palace of Nestor and the Emblematic Use of the Argonaut." In Brecoulaki, Davis, and Stocker, eds., *Mycenaean Wall Painting in Context*, 289–309.

Eickhoff, Erica. n.d. "A Colorful Quandary: An Exploration of Color Terms in Homeric Poetry." Unpublished paper available online.

Eiring, Jonas. 2004. "The 'Knossos Hunt' and Wild Goats in Ancient Crete." *BSAStud* 12: 443–450.

Elat, Moshe. 1978. "The Economic Relations of the Neo-Assyrian Empire with Egypt." *JAOS* 98: 20–34.

Eliopoulos, Theodore. 2013. "Some Observations on the Iconography of the 'Ring of Nestor'." *ASAtene*, serie III, 13: 209–222.

Elmer, David, Douglas Frame, Leonard Muellner, and Victor Bers. 2012. *Donum natalicium digitaliter confectum Gregorio Nagy septuagenario a discipulis collegis familiaribus oblatum: A Virtual Birthday Gift: Presented to Gregory Nagy on Turning Seventy by His Students, Colleagues, and Friends.* Washington, DC. Available at: https://chs.harvard.edu/book/donum-natalicium-digi-taliter-confectum-gregorio-nagy-septuagenario-a-discipulis-collegis-familiaribus-oblatum/.

Emanuel, Jeffrey P. 2014. "Odysseus' Boat? New Mycenaean Evidence from the Egyptian New Kingdom." In *Discovery of the Classical World: An Interdisciplinary Workshop on Ancient Societies, a Lecture Series Presented by the Department of The Classics at Harvard University, Cambridge, MA.* Available at https://dash.harvard.edu/handle/1/24013723.

————. 2017. *Black Ships and Sea Raiders: The Late Bronze and Early Iron Age Context of Odysseus' Second Cretan Lie.* Lanham, MD.

Endsjø, Dag Øistein. 1997. "Placing the Unplaceable: The Making of Apollonius's Argonautic Geography." *GRBS* 38: 373–385.

Enegren, Hedvig Landenius, and Francesco Meo, eds., *Treasures from the Sea: Purple Dye and Sea Silk.* Oxford

Ergin, Gürkan. 2007. "Anatolian Women in Linear B Texts: A General Review of the Evidence." In Meltem Dogan-Alparslan, Metin Alparslan, and Hasan Peker, eds., *Belkis Dinçol ve Ali Dinçol'a armagan = Vita Festschrift in Honor of Belkis Dinçol and Ali Dinçol*, 269–283. Istanbul.

Etter, Annemarie, ed. 1986. *o-o-pe-ro-si: Festschrift für Ernst Risch zum 75. Geburtstag.* Berlin.

Evans, Arthur J. 1901. "Mycenaean Tree and Pillar Cult and Its Mediterranean Relations." *JHS* 21: 99–204.

References

———. 1964 [1921–1935]. *The Palace of Minos*. 4 Vols. New York.

Evely, Doniert. 2010. "Materials and Industries." In Cline, ed., *The Oxford Handbook of the Aegean Bronze Age*, 387–404.

Evely, Doniert, Irene S. Lemos, and Susan Sherratt, eds. 1996. *Minotaur and Centaur: Studies in the Archaeology of Crete and Euboea Presented to Mervyn Popham*. Oxford.

Fanfani, Giovanni, Mary Harlow, and Marie-Louise Nosch, eds., *Spinning Fates and the Song of the Loom: The Use of Textiles, Clothing and Cloth Production as Metaphor, Symbol and Narrative Device in Greek and Latin Literature*. Oxford.

Fantuzzi, Marco, and Christos Tsagalis, eds. 2015. *The Greek Epic Cycle and Its Ancient Reception: A Companion*. Cambridge.

Faraone, Christopher A. 2019. "Circe's Instructions to Odysseus (*Od.* 10.507-40) as an Early Sibylline Oracle." *JHS* 139: 49–66.

Farinetti, Emeri. 2003. "Boeotian Orchomenos. A Progressive Creation of a *Polis* Identity." In Hero Hokwerda, ed., *Constructions of Greek Past: Identity and Historical Consciousness from Antiquity to the Present*, 1–10. Gronigen.

Farmer, Jarrett L., and Michael F. Lane. 2016. "The Ins and Outs of the Great Megaron: Symbol, Performance, and Elite Identities around and between Mycenaean Palaces." *SMEA* 2 (new series): 41–79.

Farnell, Lewis Richard. 1961. *Critical Commentary on the Works of Pindar*. Amsterdam.

Finkelberg, Margalit. 1988. "From Ahhiyawa to Ἀχαιοί." *Glotta* 66: 127–134.

———. 1995. "Odysseus and the Genus 'Hero'." *G&R* 42: 1–14.

———. 1998. "Bronze Age Writing: Contacts between East and West." In Cline and Harris Cline, eds., *The Aegean and the Orient in the Second Millennium*, 265–272.

———. 2002. "The Sources of *Iliad* 7." *Colby Quarterly* 38: 151–161.

———. 2005. *Greeks and Pre-Greeks: Aegean Prehistory and Greek Heroic Tradition*. Cambridge.

———. 2016. "Out of the Mainstream: Some Thoughts Concerning the Submersion Process of the Poems of the Trojan Cycle." In Andreas Ercolani, ed., *Submerged Literature in Ancient Greek Culture: [Volume 3], The Comparative Perspective*, 33–42. Berlin.

Finkelstein, Jacob J. 1968. "An Old Babylonian Herding Contract and Genesis 31.38f." *JAOS* 88: 30–36.

Finley, Moses. 1952. *Studies in Land and Credit in Ancient Athens 500-200 B.C.* New Brunswick, NJ.

———. 1981. *Economy and Society in Ancient Greece*. Ed. Brent D. Shaw and Richard P. Saller. New York.

Firth, Richard. 2007. "Re-considering Alum on the Linear B Tablets." In Gillis and Nosch, eds., *Ancient Textiles*, 130–137.

———. 2012. "An Interpretation of the Specification of the Textiles on Ln 1568." In Carlier, De Lamberterie, Egetmeyer, Guilleux, Rougemont and Zurbach, eds., *Études mycéniennes*, 229–241.

Flintoff, Everard. 1987. "The Treading of the Cloth." *QUCC* 25: 119–130.

Flouda, Georgia. 2010. "Agency Matters: Seal Users in Pylian Administration." *OJA* 29: 57–88.

———. 2015. "Materiality and Script: Constructing a Narrative on the Minoan Inscribed Axe from the Arkalochori Cave." *SMEA* 1 (new series), 43–56.

Floyd, Edwin D. 1989. "Homer and the Life-Producing Earth." *CW* 82: 337–349.

Forrer, Emil. 1924. "Vorhomerische Griechen in den Keilschrifttexten von Boghazköi." *Mitteilungen der Deutschen Orient-Gesellschaft zu Berlin* 83: 1–22.

Foster, Benjamin Oliver. 1899. "Notes on the Symbolism of the Apple in Classical Antiquity." *HSCP* 10: 39–55.

Foster, Ellen D. 1974. "The Manufacture and Trade of Mycenaean Perfumed Oil." Unpublished PhD dissertation. Duke University, Durham, NC.

———. 1977. "*Po-ni-ki-jo* in the Knossos Tablets Reconsidered." *Minos* 16: 52–66.

Fotiadis, Michael, Robert Laffineur, Yannos Lólos, and Andreas G. Vlachopoulos, eds. 2017. *Esperos = Hesperos: The Aegean Seen from the West: Proceedings of the 16th International Aegean Conference, University of Ioannina, Department of History and Archaeology, Unit of Archaeology and Art History, 18-21 May 2016.* Leuven.

Fowler, Robert I. 2000. *Early Greek Mythography.* 2 Vols. Oxford.

Frame, Douglas. 1978. *The Myth of Return in Early Greek Epic.* New Haven, CT.

———. 2009. *Hippota Nestor.* Hellenic Studies 37. Washington, DC.

———. 2012. "New Light on the Homeric Question: The Phaeacians Unmasked." In Elmer, Frame, Muellner, and Bers, eds., *Donum natalicium digitaliter confectum Gregorio Nagy septuagenario a discipulis collegis familiaribus oblatum: A Virtual Birthday Gift Presented to Gregory Nagy on Turning Seventy by his Students, Colleagues, and Friends.* http://nrs.harvard.edu/urn-3:hul. ebook:CHS_Bers_etal_eds.Donum_Natalicium_Gregorio_Nagy.2012.

———. 2020. "Athena among the Phaeacians." Lecture sponsored by the Center for Odyssean Studies, dated November 3, 2020. Available at: https://chs.harvard.edu/curated-article/douglas-frame-athena-among-the-phaeacians/.

Francis, Jane. 1992. "The Three Graces: Composition and Meaning in a Roman Context." *G&R* 49: 180–198.

Franco, Christiana. 2014. *Shameless: The Canine and the Feminine in Ancient Greece.* Oakland.

References

Franković, Filip, and Heitz, Christian. 2008. "Burying the Palaces? Ideologies in the Shaft Grave Period." Available for download at: http://archiv.ub.uni-heidelberg.de/propylaeumdok/volltexte/2008/89. Accessed September 10, 2021.

Franković, Filip, and Matić, Uroš. 2020. "The Lion, the Weapon and the Warlord: Historical Evaluation of the Early Late Bronze Age Aegean Iconography." *Ä&L* 30: 343–375.

Frangipane, Marcella, Eva Andersson Strand, Romina Laurito, Susan Möller-Wiering, Marie-Louise Nosch, Antoinette Rast-Eicher, and Agnete Wisti Lassen. 2009. "Arslantepe, Malatya (Turkey): Textiles, Tools and Imprints of Fabrics from the 4th to the 2nd Millennium BCE." *Paléorient* 35: 5–29.

Franklin, John Curtis. 2016a. *Kinyras: The Divine Lyre*. Hellenic Studies 70. Washington, DC. Available at: http://nrs.harvard.edu/urn-3:hul.ebook:CHS_FranklinJ.Kinyras.2016.

———. 2016b. "Lady Come Down: The Eastern Wandering of Helen, Paris, and Menelaus." Available at https://classical-inquiries.chs.harvard.edu/lady-come-down-the-eastern-wandering-of-helen-paris-and-menelaus/.

Fraser, A. D. 1932. "The Suitors' Competition in Archery." *Classical Weekly* 26: 25–29.

Frazer, R. M. 1973. "Eurymachus' Question at *Odyssey* 1. 409." *CP* 68: 259–267.

Frontisi-Ducroux, Françoise. 1975. *Dédale: mythologie de l'artisan en Grèce ancienne*. Paris.

Furumark, Arne. 1941. *The Mycenaean Pottery: Analysis and Classification*. Stockholm.

———. 1960. "Gods of Ancient Crete." *OpAth* 6: 85–98.

Galán, José M. 1993. "What is He, the Dog?" *UF* 25: 173–180.

Galanaki, Ioanna, Helena Tomas, Yannis Galanakis, and Robert Laffineur, eds. 2007. *Between the Aegean and Baltic Seas: Prehistory Across Borders: Proceedings of the International Conference Bronze and Early Iron Age Interconnections and Contemporary Developments between the Aegean and the Regions of the Balkan Peninsula, Central and Northern Europe, University of Zagreb, 11-14 April 2005*. Liège.

Galanakis, Yannis, Efi Tsitsa, and Ute Günkel-Maschek. 2017. "The Power of Images: Reexamining the Wall Paintings from the Throne Room at Knossos." *BSA* 112: 47–98.

Galanakis, Yannis, Toby Wilkinson, and John Bennet, eds. 2014. *Athyrmata: Critical Essays on the Archaeology of the Eastern Mediterranean in Honour of E. Susan Sherratt*. Oxford.

Galaty, Michael L. and William A. Parkinson, eds. 2007. *Rethinking Mycenaean Palaces II: Revised and Expanded Second Edition*. Los Angeles.

Gantz, Timothy. 1993. *Early Greek Myth: A Guide to Literary and Artistic Sources.* Baltimore.

García Ramón, J. L. 2011. "Mycenaean Onomastics." In Duhoux and Davies, eds., *A Companion to Linear B*, II, 213–251.

Garlick, Constance. 1921. "What Was the Greek Hyacinth?" *CR* 35: 146–147.

Gates, Charles. 2004. "The Adoption of Pictorial Imagery in Minoan Wall Painting: A Comparativist Perspective." *Hesperia Supplements* 33 (*Charis: Essays in Honor of Sara A. Immerwahr*), 27–46.

German, Senta. 2018. "Minoan Woman or Goddess from the Palace of Knossos ('La Parisienne')." *Smarthistory*, August 14, 2018. Available at https://smarthistory.org/la-parisienne/

Gill, Margaret A. V. 1965. "Some Observations on Representations of Marine Animals in Minoan Art, and their Identification." *BCHSupp.* 11: 63–81.

———. 1970. "Apropos the Minoan 'Genius'." *AJA* 74: 404–406.

Gillis, Carole. 2010. "Purple Dye." In Fanni Faegersten, Jenny Wallensten and Ida Östenberg, eds., *Tankemönste: en festskrift till Eva Rystedt*, 84–91. Lund.

Gillis, Carole, and Marie-Louise Nosch, eds. 2007. *Ancient Textiles: Production, Crafts and Society.* Oxford.

Girella, Luca. 2016. "Aspects of Ritual and Changes in Funerary Practices Between MM II and LM I on Crete." In Alram-Stern, Blakolmer, Deger-Jalkotzy, Laffineur, and Weilhartner, eds., *Metaphysis*, 201–212.

Godart, Louis and Anna Sacconi. 1997. "Les archives de Thèbes et le monde mycénien." *CRAI* 141–143: 889–906.

Grand-Clément, Adeline. 2016. "Gold and Purple: Brilliance, Materiality, and Agency of Color in Ancient Greece." In Rachael B. Goldman, ed., *Essays in Global Color History: Interpreting the Ancient Spectrum*, 123–157. Piscataway.

Graver, Margaret. 1995. "Dog-Helen and Homeric Insult." *ClAnt* 14: 41–61.

Graves, David E. 2017. "What is the Madder with Lydia's Purple? A Reexamination of the *Purpurarii* in Thyatira and Phillipi." *NEASB* 62: 3–28.

Greco, Alessandro. 2012. "The Background of Mycenaean Fashion: a Comparison between Near Eastern and Knossos Documents on Sheep Husbandry." In Nosch and Laffineur, eds., *Kosmos*, 271–278.

Gregersen [Nosch], Mari Louise Bech. 1997. "Pylian Craftsmen: Payment in Kind/Rations or Land?" In Laffineur and Betancourt, eds., *TEXNH* Vol. II, 397–403.

Grethlein, Jonas. 2009. "From 'Imperishable Glory' to History: The *Iliad* and the Trojan War." In David Konstan, and Kurt A. Raaflaub, eds., *Epic and History*, 122–144. Malden.

Grethlein, Jonas, and Antonios Rengakos. 2009. *Narratology and Interpretation: The Content of Narrative Forms in Ancient Literature.* Berlin.

Griffith, R. Drew. 2005. "Gods' Blue Hair in Homer and in Eighteenth-Dynasty Egypt." *CQ* 55: 329–334.

Gschnitzer, Fritz. 1981. *Griechische Sozialgeschichte von der mykenischen bis zum Ausgang der klassischen Zeit.* Wiesbaden.

Guilleux, Nicole. 2012. "L'Hermes Areias des sources myceniennes et les malheurs d'Ares avec les Aloades." In Carlier, De Lamberterie, Egetmeyer, Guilleux, Rougemont, and Zurbach, eds., *Études mycéniennes 2010*, 455–473.

Gulizio, Joann. 2001. "*A-re* in the Linear B Texts and the Continuity of the Cult of Ares in the Historical Period." *JPR* 15: 32–38.

Gulizio, Joann. 2011. "Mycenaean Religion at Knossos." Unpublished Ph.D. dissertation. University of Texas, Austin, TX.

Günkel-Maschek, Ute. 2012a. "Spirals, Bulls, and Sacred Landscapes: The Meaningful Appearance of Pictorial Objects within their Spatial and Social Contexts." In Panagiotopoulos and Günkel Maschek, eds., *Minoan Realities*, 115–138.

———. 2012b. "Reflections on the Symbolic Meaning of the Olive Branch as Head-Ornament in the Wall Paintings of Building Xeste 3, Akrotiri." In Nosch and Laffineur, eds., *Kosmos*, 361–367.

———. 2016. "Establishing the Minoan 'Enthroned Goddess' in the Neopalatial Period: Images, Architecture, and Elitist Ambition." In Alram-Stern, Blakolmer, Deger-Jalkotzy, Laffineur, and Weilhartner, eds., *Metaphysis*, 255–262.

———. 2020. *Minoische Bild-Räume: Neue Untersuchungen zu den Wandbildern des spätbronzezeitlichen Palastes von Knossos.* Heidelberg.

Güterbock, Hans G. 1986. "Troy in Hittite Texts: Wilusa, Ahhiyawa, and Hittite History." In Mellink, ed., *Troy and the Trojan War*, 33–44.

Guzowska, Marta, and Assaf Yasur-Landau. 1999. "Before the Aeolians: Prolegomena to the Study of Interactions with the North-East Aegean Islands in the 13th and 12th Centuries BC." In Kyparissi-Apostolika and Papakonstantinou, eds., *The Periphery of the Mycenaean World*, 471–481.

Guzowska, Marta, and Ralf Becks. 2005. "Who Was Weaving at Troia? On the Aegean Style Loomweights in Troia VI and VIIA." In Laffineur and Greco, eds., *Emporia*, 279–285.

Haft, Adele J. 1984. "Odysseus, Idomeneus and Meriones: The Cretan Lies of *Odyssey*: 13-19." *CJ* 79: 289–306.

Hägg, Robin. 1985. "Pictorial Programmes in the Minoan Palaces and Villas?" *BCHSupp.* 11: 209–217.

Hägg, Robin, and Nanno Marinatos, eds. 1981. *Sanctuaries and Cults in the Aegean Bronze Age.* Stockholm.

Hajnal, Ivo. 1998. *Mykenisches und homerisches Lexikon: Übereinstimmungen, Divergenzen und der versuch einer Typologie (Innsbrucker Beiträge zur Sprachwissenschaft).* Vorträge und Kleinere Schriften 69. Innsbruck.

———. 2018. "Graeco-Anatolian Contacts in the Mycenaean Period." In Jared Kilein, Brian Joseph, and Matthias Fritz, eds., *Handbook of Comparative and Historical Indo-European Linguistics.* Vol. 3, 2037–2055. Berlin.

Hallager, Eric. 1987a. "The Knossos Roundels." *BSA* 82: 55.

———. 1987b. "Sealing Without Seals: An Explanation." Working Paper no. 99-01, Centre for Cultural Research, University of Aarhus (November 26, 2001). Available at https://www.scribd.com/document/437722118/Sealing-Without-Seals-Vip.

———. 2015. "Mycenaean Administrative Sealing Practice: A World of its Own?" In Weilhartner and Ruppenstein, eds., *Tradition and Innovation in the Mycenaean Palatial Polities,* 141–153.

Hallager, Eric, and Judith Weingarten. 1993. "The Five Roundels from Malia, with a Note on Two New Minoan Genii." *BCH* 117: 1–18.

Halstead, Paul. 1999/2007. "Toward a Model of Mycenaean Palatial Mobilization." In Galaty and Parkinson, eds., *Rethinking Mycenaean Palaces II,* 66–73.

———. 2001. "Mycenaean Wheat, Flax and Sheep: Palatial Intervention in Farming and its Implications for Rural Society." In Voutsaki and Killen, eds., *Economy and Politics in the Mycenaean Palace States,* 38–50.

Hankey, Vronwy. 1980. "The Aegean Interest in El Amarna." *JMA* 1: 38–49.

Hansen, Solvejg. 2015. "Using Textiles to Propose: A New Identity for the So-called Goddess of Xeste 3." In Jane Fejfer, Mette Moltesen, and Annete Rathje, eds., *Tradition: Transmission of Culture in the Ancient World,* 117–130. Copenhagen.

Hansen, Wm. F. 1977. "Odysseus' Last Journey." *QUCC* 24: 27–48.

Hard, Robin. 2004. "Jason and the Argonauts." In Robin Hard, ed., *The Routledge Handbook of Greek Mythology,* 377–400. London.

Harder, Annette. 2012. *Callimachus Aitia: Introduction, Text, Translation, and Commentary.* Volume 2. Commentary. Oxford.

Harding, A. F. 1984. *The Mycenaeans and Europe.* London.

Harrell, Kate. 2014. "Man/Woman, Warrior/Maiden: The Lefkandi Toumba Female Burial Reconsidered." In Galanakis, Wilkinson, and Bennet, eds., *Athrymata,* 99–104.

Haskell, Halford W. 2004. "*Wanax* to *Wanax*: Regional Trade Patterns in Mycenaean Crete." *Hesperia Supplements* 33, (*Charis: Essays in Honor of Sara A. Immerwahr*), 151–160.

——. 2011. "Trade." In Halford W. Haskell, Richard E. Jones, and Peter M. Day, *Transport Stirrup Jars of the Bronze Age Aegean and East Mediterranean*, 125–131. Philadelphia.

Hatzaki, Eleni. 2009. "Structured Deposition as Ritual Action at Knossos." *HesperiaSupp* 42: 19–30.

Hauptmann, Andreas, and Sabine Klein. 2009. "Bronze Age Gold in Southern Georgia." *ArcheoScience* 33: 75–82.

Haysom, Matthew. 2010. "The Double-Axe: A Contextual Approach to the Understanding of a Cretan Symbol in the Neopalatial Period." *OJA* 29: 39–55.

Heath (Wiencke), Martha C. 1958. "Early Helladic Clay Sealings from the House of the Tiles at Lerna." *Hesperia* 27: 81–121.

Heitz, Christian. 2008. "Burying the Palaces? Ideologies in the Shaft Grave Period." Available for download at: http://archiv.ub.uni-heidelberg.de/propylaeumdok/volltexte/2008/89. Accessed September 10, 2021.

Hiller, Stefan. 1975. "*ra-mi-ni-ja*: Mykenische-kleinasiatische Beziehungen und die Linear B-Texte." *Živa antika* 25: 388–412.

——. 1991. "The Mycenaeans and the Black Sea." In Laffineur and Basch, eds., *Thalassa*, 207–216.

——. 1998–1999. "KU-NA-KE-TA." In Bennet and Driessen, eds., *A-na-qo-ta*, 191–196.

——. 2005. "The Spiral as a Symbol of Sovereignty and Power." In Dakouri-Hild and Sherratt, eds., *Autochthon*, 259–270.

——. 2006. "Some Minor Observations Concerning the New Thebes Texts." In Sigrid Deger-Jalkotzy, Oswald Panagl, and Thomas Lindner, eds., *Die neuen Linear B-Texte aus Theben: ihr Aufschlusswert für die mykenische Sprache und Kultur: Akten des internationalen Forschungskolloquiums an der Österreichischen Akademie der Wissenschaften, 5.-6. Dezember 2002*, 71–75. Vienna.

——. 2008. "Mycenaean Religion and Cult." In Duhoux and Davies, eds., *A Companion to Linear B*, II, 169–211.

Hirsch, Ethel S. 1980. "Another Look at Minoan and Mycenaean Interrelationships in Floor Decoration." *AJA* 84: 453–462.

Hitchcock, Jocelyn McKenzie Claire. 2019. "Crisis Averted: How the Collapse of the Palatial Centers Provided the Perfect Storm for Prosperity and Growth in the 12th/11th Centuries BCE in the Central Mediterranean." Unpublished MA thesis. National and Kapodistrian University of Athens, School of Philosophy, Athens.

Hitchcock, Louise, Robert Laffineur, and Janice L Crowley, eds. 2008. *Dais: the Aegean Feast: Proceedings of the 12th International Aegean Conference,12e*

Rencontre égéenne internationale, University of Melbourne, Centre for Classics and Archaeology, 25-29 March 2008. Liège.

Hoffmann, Axel. 1982. *Prähistorische Goldfunde aus Europa: Spektralanalytische Untersuchung und deren Auswertung*. Volume 2. Berlin.

Hoffner, Harry A. Jr. 1968. "A Hittite Text in Epic-Style about Merchants." *JCS* 22: 34–45

———. 2002. "Some Thoughts on Merchants and Trade in the Hittite Kingdom." In Thomas Richter, Doris Prechel and Jörg Klinger (eds.), *Kulturgeschichten. Altorientalistische Studien für Volkert Haas Zum 65. Geburtstag*. Saarbrücken: Saarbrücker Druckerei und Verlag, 179-89.

———. 2009. *Letters from the Hittite Kingdom*. Atlanta.

Hoffner, Harry A. Jr., trans. and Gary M. Beckman, ed. 1998. *Hittite Myths*. 2nd ed. Atlanta.

Hogarth, D. G. 1902. "The Zakro Sealings." *JHS* 22: 76–93.

Holland, Gary B. 1993. "The Name of Achilles: A Revised Etymology." *Glotta* 71: 17–27.

Holland, Leicester B. 1929. "Mycenaean Plumes." *AJA* 33: 173–205.

Hollinshead, Mary B. 1985. "Against Iphigeneia's Adyton in Three Mainland Temples." *AJA* 89: 419–440.

Hood, Sinclair. 2005. "Dating the Knossos Frescoes." In Morgan, ed., *Aegean Wall Painting*, 45–81.

Hooker, J. T. 1967. "The Mycenae Siege Rhyton and the Question of Egyptian Influence." *AJA* 71: 269–281.

———. 1969. "Homer and Late Minoan Crete." *JHS* 89: 60–71.

———. 1995. "Linear B as a Source of Social History." In Anton Powell, ed., *The Greek World*, 22–41. London.

Hopkins, Clark. 1968. "The Megaron of the Mycenaean Palace." *SMEA* 6: 45–53.

Hopman, Marianne. 2012. "Narrative and Rhetoric in Odysseus' Tales to the Phaeacians." *AJP* 133: 1–30.

Hornblower, Simon. 2015. *Lykophron, Alexandra: Greek Text, Translation, Commentary, and Introduction*. Oxford.

Horrocks, G. C. 1980. "The Antiquity of the Greek Epic Tradition: Some New Evidence." *PCPS* 26: 1–11.

Hruby, Julie. 2013. "The Palace of Nestor, Craft Production, and Mechanisms for the Transfer of Goods." *AJA* 117: 423–427.

Hussein, Angela Murock. 2007. "The Chief of the Keftiu." *GM* 214: 33–38.

Hutton, William F. 1990-1991. "The Meaning of *QE-TE-O* in Linear B." *Minos*, 25–26, 105–131.

Huxley, George. 1969. *Greek Epic Poetry: From Eumelos to Panyassis*. Cambridge, MA.

———. 1975. "Cretan *Paiawones*." *GRBS* 16: 119–124.

Immerwahr, Sara A. 1990. *Aegean Painting in the Bronze Age*. University Park, PA.

Irwin, Eleanor M. 1990. "Odysseus' 'Hyacinthine Hair' in *Odyssey* 6.231." *Phoenix* 44: 205–218.

Ivantchik, Askold. 2017. "The Greeks and the Black Sea: The Earliest Ideas about the Region and the Beginning of Colonization." In Valeriya Kozlovskaya, ed., *The Northern Black Sea in Antiquity: Networks, Connectivity and Cultural Interactions*, 7–25. Cambridge.

Jackson, Steven. 1990. "Myrsilus of Methymna and the Dreadful Smell of the Lemnian Women." *ICS* 15: 77–83.

Jacobson, Howard. 1974. *Ovid's Heroides*. Princeton.

James, Matthew A., Nicole Reifarth, Anna J. Mukherjee, et al. 2009. "High Prestige Royal Purple Dyed Textiles from the Bronze Age Royal Tombs at Qatna, Syria." *Antiquity* 83: 1109–1118.

James, Matthew A., Nicole Reifarth, and Richard P. Evershed. 2011. "Chemical Identification of Ancient Dyestuffs from Mineralised Textile Fragments from the Royal Tomb." In Peter Pfälzner, ed., *Interdisziplinäre Studien zur Königsgruft von Qaṭna*, 449–469. Wiesbaden.

Janko, Richard. 2019. "Amber Inscribed in Linear B from Bernstorf in Bavaria: New Light on the Mycenaean Kingdom of Pylos." Available at https://www.bavarian-studies.org/amber-inscribed-in-linear-b-from-bernstorf-in-bavaria/.

Jansen, Anton. 1997. "Bronze Age Highways at Mycenae." *EchCl* 26: 1–16.

Jensen, Lloyd B. 1963. "Royal Purple of Tyre." *JNES* 22: 104–118.

Jimenez Delgado, José Miguel. 2015. "The Etymology of Myc. *ku-na-ke-ta-i*, Ion.-Att. κυνηγέτης, and Myc. *ra-wake-ta*, Dor. γᾱγέτᾱς." *Glotta* 91: 116–128.

Jones, Bernice R. 2001. "The Minoan Snake Goddess, New Interpretations of Her Costume and Identity." In Laffineur and Hägg, eds., *Potnia*, 259–269.

———. 2003. "Veils and Mantles: An Investigation of the Construction and Function of the Costumes of the Veiled Dancer from Thera and the Camp Stool Banqueter from Knossos." In Polinger Foster and Laffineur, eds., *Metron*, 441–450.

———. 2005. "The Clothes-Line: Imports and Exports of Aegean Cloth(es) and Iconography." In Laffineur and Greco, eds., *Emporia*, 707–715.

———. 2009. "New Reconstructions of the 'Mykenaia' and a Seated Woman from Mycenae." *AJA* 113: 309–337.

———. 2015. *Ariadne's Threads: The Construction and Significance of Clothes in the Aegean Bronze Age*. Aegaeum (Annales d'archéologie égéenne de l'Université de Liège et UT-PASP 38). Leuven.

———. 2016a. "The Three Minoan 'Snake Goddesses'." In Koehl, ed., *Studies in Aegean Art and Culture*, 93–112.

———. 2016b. "A New Reading of the Fresco Program and the Ritual in Xeste 3, Thera." In Alram-Stern, Blakolmer, Deger-Jalkotzy, Laffineur, and Weilhartner, eds., *Metaphysis*, 365–373

———. 2018. "Costumes of Beauty." In María Lagogiánni-Georgakarákou, ed., *The Countless Aspects of Beauty in Ancient Art. Exhibition Catalog May 25th - June 17th 2018*, 177–190. Athens.

Jones, Brandtly. 2010. "Relative Chronology within (an) Oral Tradition." *CJ* 105: 289–318.

Judas, Beth Ann. 2015. "Keftiu and Griffins: An Exploration of the Liminal in the Egyptian World." In Massimiliano S. Pinarello, Justin Yoo, Jason Lundock, and Carl Walsh, eds., *Current Research in Egyptology 2014: Proceedings of the Fifteenth Annual Symposium*, 123–134. Oxford.

Judson, Anna P. 2013. "The Linear B Inscribed Stirrup Jars." *Kadmos* 52: 69–110.

———. 2017. "The Mystery of the Mycenaean 'Labyrinth': The Value of Linear B pu_2 and Related Signs." *SMEA*, NS 3: 53–72.

Kaizer, Ted. 2011. "Interpretations of the Myth of Andromeda at Iope." *Syria* 88: 323–339.

Kampakoglou, Alexandros. 2018. "Gazing at Heroes in Apollonius' *Argonautica*." In Alexandros Kampakoglou and Anna Novokhatko, eds., *Gaze, Vision, and Visuality in Ancient Greek Literature*, 113–139. Berlin.

Kanavou, Nikolatta. 2015. *The Names of Homeric Heroes: Problems and Interpretations*. Berlin.

Kanold, Inge Boesken. 2017. "Dyeing Wool and Sea Silk with Purple Pigment from *Hexaplex trunculus*." In Enegren and Meo, eds., *Treasures from the Sea*, 67–72.

Kantor, Helene J. 1947. "The Aegean and the Orient in the Second Millennium B. C." *AJA* 51: 1–15, 17–103.

———. 1999. *Plant Ornament in the Ancient Near East*. Chicago.

Karetsou, Alexandra. 1981. "The Peak Sanctuary of Mt. Juktas." In Hägg and Marinatos, eds., *Sanctuaries and Cults in the Aegean Bronze Age*, 137–153.

Karetsou, Alexandra, and Robert B. Koehl. 2011. "An Enigmatic Piece of Gold-Work from the Juktas Peak sanctuary." In F. Carinci, N. Cucuzza, P. Militello and O. Palio, eds., Κρήτης Μινωίδος [*Krētēs Minōdos*]: *Tradizione e identità minoica tra produzione artigianale, pratiche cerimoniali e memoria del passato. Studi offerti a Vincenzo La Rosa per il suo 70° compleano. Studi di Archeologia Cretese 10*, 207–223. Padova.

———. 2014. "The Minoan Mastiffs of Juktas." In Touchais, Laffineur, and Rougemont, eds., *Physis*, 333–339.

Karnava, Artemis. 2005. "The Tel Haror Inscription and Crete: A Further Look." In Laffineur and Greco, eds., *Emporia*, 838–843.

———. 2008. "Written and Stamped Records in the Late Bronze Age Cyclades: The Sea Journeys of an Administration." In Brodie, ed., *Horizon*, 377–386.

———. 2010. "The LM IA Cretan Sealings from Akrotiri: Chronological and Historical Implications." *Pasiphae* 4: 87–92.

———. 2016. "On Sacred Vocabulary and Religious Dedications: The Minoan 'Libation Formula'." In Alram-Stern, Blakolmer, Deger-Jalkotzy, Laffineur, and Weilhartner, eds., *Metaphysis*, 345–355.

Karytinos, Alexios. 1998. "Sealstones in Cemeteries: A Display of Social Status?" In Keith Branigan, ed., *Cemetery and Society in the Aegean Bronze Age*, 78–85. Sheffield.

Katsaros, Thomas Th. 2008. "The Redness of Ulysses' Ships." In S. A. Paipetis, ed., *Science and Technology in Homeric Epics*, 385–389. New York.

Kazansky, Nikolai N. 2009. "The Description of Helios Herds (*Od.* 12, 127-136): A Mycenaean Commentary." *Pasiphae* 3: 117–120.

Kefalidou, Eurydice. 2008. "The Argonauts Krater in the Archaeological Museum of Thessaloniki." *AJA* 112: 617–624.

Kelder, Jorritt. 2004-2005. "The Chariots of Ahhiyawa." *Dacia* 48–49: 151–160.

Kelder, Jorritt, and Marco Poelwijk. 2016. "The Wanassa and the Damokoro: A New Interpretation of a Linear B Text from Pylos." *GRBS* 56: 572–584.

Kenna, V. E. G. 1968. "Ancient Crete and the Use of the Cylinder Seal." *BICS* 72: 321–336.

Killen, John T. 1964. "The Wool Industry of Crete in the Late Bronze Age." *BSA* 59: 1–15.

———. 1979. "The Knossos Ld(1) Tablets." In Ernst Risch and Hugo Mühlestein, eds., *Colloquium Mycenaeaum. The Sixth International Congress on the Aegean and Mycenaean Texts at Chaumont sur Neuchâtel, September 7-13*, 151–181. Neuchâtel.

———. 1983. "Mycenaean Possessive Adjectives in *-e-jo*." *TransPhilolSoc* 81: 66–99.

———. 1984. "The Textile Industry at Pylos and Knossos." In Cynthia W. Shelmerdine and Thomas G. Palaima, eds., *Pylos Comes Alive: Industry + Administration in a Mycenaean Palace: Papers of a Symposium*, 49–64. New York.

———. 1985. "The Linear B Tablets and the Mycenaean Economy." In Anna Morpurgo Davies and Yves Duhoux, eds., *Linear B: A 1984 Survey. Proceedings of the Mycenaean Colloquium of the VIIlth Congress of the International Federation of the Societies of Classical Studies*, 241–305. Louvain-La-Neuve.

———. 1986. "Two Mycenaean Words." In Etter, ed., *o-o-pe-ro-si*, 279–284.

———. 1994. "Thebes Sealings, Knossos Tablets and Mycenaean State Banquets." *BICS* 39: 67–84.

———. 1995. "Some Further Thoughts on 'Collectors'." In Laffineur and Niemeier, eds., *Politeia*, 213–226.

———. 1999/2007. "Critique: A View from the Tablets." In Galaty and Parkinson, eds., *Rethinking Mycenaean Palaces II*, 114–117.

———. 2000. "Discussion of J. Gulizio." *Živa Antika* 50: 116.

———. 2001. "Some Thoughts on *TA-RA-SI-JA*. In Voutsaki and Killen, eds., *Economy and Politics in the Mycenaean Palace States*, 161–180.

King, Cynthia. 1983. "Who Is That Cloaked Man? Observations on Early Fifth Century B. C. Pictures of the Golden Fleece." *AJA* 87: 385–387.

Kirk, G. S. 1990. *The Iliad: A Commentary*. Cambridge.

Kirschenbaum, Aaron. 1987. *Sons, Slaves and Freedmen in Roman Commerce*. Jerusalem

Kloekhorst, Alwin. 2012. "The Language of Troy." In Jorrit M. Kelder, Günay Uslu, and Ömer Faruk Serifoglu, eds., *Troy: City, Homer, Turkey*, 46–50. Amsterdam.

Knapp, A. Bernard, and Sturt W. Manning. 2016. "Crisis in Context: The End of the Late Bronze Age in the Eastern Mediterranean." *AJA* 120: 99–149.

Koehl, Robert B. 1986. "The Chieftain Cup and a Minoan Rite of Passage." *JHS* 106: 99–110.

———. 2006. *Aegean Bronze Age Rhyta*. Philadelphia.

———, ed. 2016. *Studies in Aegean Art and Culture: A New York Aegean Bronze Age Colloquium in Memory of Ellen N. Davis*. Philadelphia.

Kokiasmenou, Eleni, Claudia Caliri, Vasiliki Kantarelou, et al. 2020. "Macroscopic XRF Imaging in Unravelling Polychromy on Mycenaean Wallpaintings from the Palace of Nestor at Pylos." *JArchaeolSciRep* 29: 1–12.

Kolb, Frank. 2004. "Troy VI: A Trading Center and Commercial City?" *AJA* 108: 577–613.

Kolonas, Lazaros, Kalliope Sarri, Christina Margareti, Ina Vanden Berghe, Irene Skals, and Marie-Louise Nosch. 2017. "Heirs from the Loom? Funerary textiles from Stamna (Aitolia, Greece). A Preliminary Analysis." In Fotiadis, Laffineur, Lólos, and Vlachopoulos, eds., *Esperos = Hesperos*, 533–542.

Konstantinidi-Syvridi, Eleni. 2015. "Buttons, Clips and Belts... 'Inconspicuous' Dress Accessories from the Burial Context of the Mycenaean Period (16th-12th cent. BC)." In Mary Harlow, Cécile Michel, and Marie-Louise Nosch, eds., *Prehistoric, Ancient Near Eastern and Aegean Textiles and Dress: An Interdisciplinary Anthology*, 143–157. Oxford.

Kontorli-Papadopolou, L., Th. Papadopoulos, and G. Owens. 2005. "A Possible Linear Sign from Ithaki (AB09 'SE')?" *Kadmos* 44: 183–186.

Kopaka, Katerina. 2001. "A Day in Potnia's Life: Aspects of Potnia and Reflected 'Mistress Activities in the Aegean Bronze Age." In Laffineur and Hägg, eds., *Potnia*, 15–27.

Kopanias, Konstantinos. 2008. "The Late Bronze Age Near Eastern Cylinder Seals from Thebes (Greece) and their Historical Implications (64 Abbildungen)." *MDAI* 123: 39–96.

———. 2012. "Raw Material, Exotic Jewellery or Magic Objects? The Use of Imported Near Eastern." In Nosch and Laffineur, eds., *Kosmos*, 397–406.

———. 2015. "From the Mythical Atreus to the Ruler Attarissiya." In Panagiotopoulos, Kaiser, and Kouka, eds., *Ein Minoer im Exil*, 211–222.

Kopcke, Günter. 2016. "For Ellen Davis: Transylvanian Gold." In Robert B. Koehl, ed., *Studies in Aegean Art and Culture: A New York Aegean Bronze Age Colloquium in Memory of Ellen N. Davis*, 27–34. Philadelphia.

Korfmann, Manfred. 1986a. "Beşik Tepe: New Evidence from the Period of the Trojan Sixth and Seventh Settlements." In Mellink, ed., *Troy and the Trojan War*, 17–28.

———. 1986b. "Troy: Topography and Navigation." In Mellink, ed., *Troy and the Trojan War*, 1–16.

Kosma, Maria. 2012. "The Lady of Lefkandi." In Nikolaos Chr. Stampolides, ed., *"Princesses" of the Mediterranean at the Dawn of History*, 57–69. Athens.

Kotsonas, Antonis. 2018a. "A Cultural History of the Cretan Labyrinth: Monument and Memory from Prehistory to the Present." *AJA* 122: 367–396.

———. 2018b. "Homer, the Archaeology of Crete and the 'Tomb of Meriones' at Knossos." *JHS* 138: 1–35.

Kouremenos, Theokritos. 1996. "Herakles, Jason and 'Programmatic' Similes in Apollonius Rhodius' 'Argonautica'." *RheinMusPhilol* 139: 233–250.

Kraft, John C., George (Rip) Rapp, Ilhan Kayan, and John V. Luce. 2003. "Harbor Areas at Ancient Troy: Sedimentology and Geomorphology Complement Homer's *Iliad*." *Geology* 31: 163–166.

Kramer, Samuel Noah, and John R. Maier. 1985. *Myths of Enki, the Crafty God*. New York.

Kramer-Hajos, Margaretha. 2016. *Mycenaean Greece and the Aegean World: Palace and Province in the Late Bronze Age*. New York.

Kremer, Christoph. 2017. "The Spread of Purple Dyeing in the Eastern Mediterranean: A Transfer of Technological Knowledge?" Enegren and Meo, eds., *Treasures from the Sea*, 141–157.

Krevans, Nita. 2002/2003. "Dido, Hypsipyle, and the Bedclothes." *Hermathena* 173/174: 175–183.

Krzyszkowska, Olga. 2005. *Aegean Seals: An Introduction*. London.

Kullmann, Wolfgang. 2015. "Motif and Source Research: Neoanalysis, Homer, and Cyclic Epic." In Fantuzzi and Tsagalsi, eds., *The Greek Epic Cycle and Its Ancient Reception*, 108–125.

Kyparissi-Apostolika, Nina, and Mani Papakonstantinou, eds. 2003. *The Periphery of the Mycenaean World: 2nd International Interdisciplinary Colloquium*. Athens.

Kyriakidis, Evangelos. 1997. "Nudity in Late Minoan I Seal Iconography." *Kadmos* 36: 119–126.

———. 2001. "The Economics of Potnia: Storage in 'Temples' of Prehistoric Greece." In Laffineur and Hägg, eds., *Potnia*, 123–129.

———. 2005. "Unidentified Floating Objects on Minoan Seals." *AJA* 109: 137–54.

———. 2008. "Who's Who: The Shepherds in the Cn Series at Pylos." *Pasiphae* 2: 449–459.

———. 2010. "'Collectors' as Stakeholders in Mycenaean Governance: Property and the Relations between the Ruling Class and the State." *CCJ* 56: 140–177.

Labaree, Benjamin W. 1957. "How the Greeks Sailed into the Black Sea." *AJA* 61: 29–33.

Lackenbacher, Sylvie. 2002. *Textes akkadiens d'Ugarit: textes provenant des vingt-cinq premières campagnes*. Paris.

Laffineur, Robert, ed. 1999. *POLEMOS. Le contexte guerrier en Égée a l'Âge du Bronze. Actes de la 7è Rencontre égéenne international (Liège, 14-17 avril 1998) (Aegaeum 19)*. Liège.

———. 2007. "Homeric Similes: A Bronze Age Background?" In Morris and Laffineur, eds., *Epos*, 79–85.

———. 2010. "Jewelry." In Cline, ed., *The Oxford Handbook of the Bronze Age Aegean*, 443–454.

Laffineur, Robert, and Lucien Basch, eds. 1991. *Thalassa, l'Egée prehistorique et la mer: actes de la troisième rencontre égéenne internationale de l'Université de Liège, Station de recherches sous-marines et océanographiques (StaReSO), Calvi, Corse (23-25 avril 1990)*. Liège.

Laffineur, Robert, and Philip J. Betancourt, eds. 1997. *TEXNH: Craftsmen, Craftswomen and Craftsmanship in the Aegean Bronze Age*. (Aegaeum 16). Liège.

Laffineur, Robert, and Emanuele Greco, eds. 2005. *Emporia: Aegeans in the Central and Eastern Mediterranean. Proceedings of the 10th International Aegean Conference/10th Recontre égéinternationale. Athens, Italian School of Archaeology, 14-18 April 2004*. 2 vols. Liège.

Laffineur, Robert, and Robin Hägg, eds. 2001. *Potnia: Deities and Religion in the Aegean Bronze Age*. Liège.

Laffineur, Robert, and Wolf-Dietrich Niemeier, eds. 1995. *Politeia: Society and State in the Aegean Bronze Age (Aegaeum 12)*. 2 Vols. Liège.

References

Lane, Michael Franklin. 2016. "Returning to Sender: PY Tn 316, Linear B i-je-to, Pregnant Locatives, *perH3-, and Passing between Mycenaean Palaces." *Pasiphae* 10: 39–90.

Lang, Felix, Claus Reinholdt, and Jörg Weilhartner, eds. 2007. *Stephanos Aristeios. Archäologische Forschungen zwischen Nil und Istros: Festschrift für Stefan Hiller zum 65. Geburtstag*. Vienna.

Lang, Mabel. L. 1969. *The Palace of Nestor in Western Messenia II: The Frescoes*. Princeton.

Lantzas, Katie. 2016. "Reconsidering Collapse: Identity, Ideology, and Postcollapse Settlement in the Argolid." In Ronald K. Faulseit, ed., *Beyond Collapse: Archaeological Perspectives on Resilience, Revitalization, and Transformation in Complex Societies*, 459–485. Carbondale.

Larsen, Mogens Trolle. 1976. *The Old Assyrian City-State and Its Colonies*. Copenhagen.

———. 1977. "Partnerships in Old Assyrian Trade." *Iraq* 39: 119–145.

Latacz, Joachim. 2004. *Troy and Homer: Towards a Solution of an Old Mystery*. Oxford.

Laurence, Ray. 1999. *The Roads of Roman Italy: Mobility and Cultural Change*. London.

Lefevre-Novaro, Daniela. 2001. "Un nouvel examen des modeles reduits trouves dans la grande tombe de Kamilari." In Laffineur and Hägg, eds., *Potnia*, 89–98.

Legarra, Herro Borja. 2019. "Gold, Conspicuous Consumption and Prestige—ARelationship in Need of Review. The Case of Early and Middle Bronze Age Crete." In Xosé-Lois Armada, Mercedes Murillo-Barroso and Mike Charlton, eds., *Metals, Minds and Mobility: Integrating Scientific Data with Archaeological Theory*, 107–119. Oxford.

Lejeune, M. 1966. "Le récapitulatif du cadastre Ep du Pylos." In L. R. Palmer and John Chadwick, eds., *Proceedings of the Cambridge Colloquium on Mycenaean Studies*, 260–264. Cambridge.

———. 1971. "Les sifflantes fortes du Mycénien." In M. Lejeune, ed., *Mémoires de Philologie Mycénienne (Deuxième Série 1958-1963)*, 97–139. Rome.

Lemos, Irene S. 2011–2012. "Euboea and Central Greece in the Post-Palatial and Early Greek Periods." *ArchaeolRep* 58: 19–27.

Lemos, Irene S., and Antonis Kotsonas, eds. 2020. *A Companion to the Archaeology of Early Greece and the Mediterranean*. 2 Vols. Hoboken.

Lenuzza, Valeria. 2012. "Dressing Priestly Shoulders: Suggestions from the Campstool Fresci." In Nosch and Laffineur, eds., *Kosmos*, 255–264.

Levaniouk, Olga. 2011. *Eve of the Festival: Making Myth in Odyssey 19*. Hellenic Studies 46. Washington, DC.

Levi, Doro. 1945. "Gleanings from Crete." *AJA* 49: 270–329.

Lewy, Hildegard. 1964. "The Assload, the Sack, and Other Measures of Capacity." *RivStudiOrien* 39: 181–197.

Littauer, M. A., and J. H. Crouwel. 1986. "The Earliest Known Three-dimensional Evidence for Spoked Wheels." *AJA* 90: 395–398.

López-Ruiz, Carolina. 2009. "Mopsos and Cultural Exchange Between Greeks and Locals in Cilicia." In Ueli Dill and Christine Walde, eds., *Antike Mythen: Medien, Transformationen und Konstruktionen*, 487–501. Berlin.

Lordkipanidze, Otar. 2001. "The Golden Fleece: Myth, Euhemeristic Explanation, and Archaeology." *OJA* 20: 1–38.

Luján, Eugenio R. 1996–1997. "El léxico micénico de las telas." *Minos* 31–32: 335–369

———. 2010. "Payment and Trade Terminology on Linear B Tablets." In Maria Paz Garcia-Bellido, Laurent Callegarin, and Alicia Jiménez-Díaz, eds., *Barter, Money and Coinage in the Ancient Medierranean (10th-1st Centuries BC)*, 25–32. Madrid.

———. 2013. "Mycenaean Textile Terminology at Work: The KN Lc(1) Tablets and the Occupational Nouns of the Textile Industry." In Michel and Nosch, eds., *Textile Terminologies*, 374–387.

———. 2019. "Mycenaean *a-re-se-si* and Homeric ἄλεισον Revisited." *GRBS* 59: 1–14.

Lupack, Susan M. 1999/2007. "Palaces, Sanctuaries, and Workshops: The Role of the Religious Sector in Mycenaean Economics." In Galaty and Parkinson, eds., *Rethinking Mycenaean Palaces* II, 54–65.

———. 2006a. *The Role of the Religious Sector in the Economy of Late Bronze Age Mycenaean Greece*. Oxford.

———. 2006b. "Deities and Religious Personnel as Collectors." In Massimo Perna, ed., *Fiscality in Mycenaean and Near Eastern Archives: Proceedings of the Conference held at Soprintendenza archivistica per la Campania, Naples, 21-23 October 2004*, 89–108. Paris.

———. 2011. "Redistribution in Aegean Palatial Societies: A Viewpoint from Outside the Palace; The Sanctuary and the *Damos* in Mycenaean Economy and Society." *AJA* 115: 207–217.

———. 2017. "Assessing Religious Hierarchies: Their Economic Influence in Mycenaean Society." *Pasiphae* 11: 189–202.

Lutz, Henry F. 1923. *Textiles and Costumes among the Peoples of the Ancient Near East*. Leipzig.

Luyster, Robert. 1965. "Symbolic Elements in the Cult of Athena." *HR* 5: 133–163.

Macedo, Jose Marcos. 2016. "Hermes *a-re-ja* (PY Tn 316): A New Interpretation." *Kadmos* 55: 67–82.

MacGillivray, J. Alexander. 2012. "The Minoan Double Axe Goddess and Her Astral Realm." In Stampolides, Kanta, and Giannikoure, eds., *Athanasia*, 117–128.

MacKendrick, Paul. 1981. *The Greek Stones Speak: The Story of Archaeology in Greek Lands.* 2nd ed. New York.

Mackie, C. J. 2001. "The Earliest Jason. What's in a Name?" *G&R* 48: 1–17.

———. 2009. "The Earliest Philoctetes." *Scholia* 18: 2–16.

Mackil, Emily, and Dimitri Nakassis. 2019. "Review of Zurbach." *BMCR* 2018.08.06.

Mac Sweeney, Naoise. 2018. *Troy: Myth, City, Icon.* London.

Madigan, Brian. 2013. *The Ceremonial Sculptures of the Roman Gods.* Leiden.

Maggidis, Christofilis. 2019. "The Palace Throne of Mycenae: Constructing Collective Historical Memory and Power Ideology." In Borgna, Caloi, Carinci, and Laffineur, eds., *MNHMH/MNEME*, 165–172.

Maitland, Judith. 1999. "Poseidon, Walls, and Narrative Complexity in the Homeric *Iliad*." *CQ* 49: 1–13.

Malkin, Irad. 1998. *The Returns of Odysseus: Colonization and Ethnicity.* Berkeley.

———. 2001. "The *Odyssey* and the Nymphs." *Gaia* 5: 11–27.

Mantzourani, Eleni. 1995. "Notes on the Depictions of Various Vases and Vessels in Aegean Wall Painting." *BICS* 40: 123–141.

Mantzourani, Eleni, and Philip P. Betancourt, eds. 2012. *PHILISTOR: Studies in Honor of Costis Davaras.* Prehistory Monographs 36. Philadelphia.

Maran, Joseph. 2005. "Late Minoan Coarse ware Stirrup jars on the Greek Mainland: A Postpalatial Perspective." In Anna Lucia D'Agata and Jennifer Alice Moody, eds., *Ariadne's Threads. Connections between Crete and the Greek Mainland in Late Minoan III (LMIIIA2 to LM IIIC). Proceedings of the International Workshop held at Athens Scuola Archeologica Italiana, 5-6 April 2003*, 415–432. Athens.

———. 2006. "Coming to Terms with the Past: Ideology and Power in the Late Helladic IIIC." In Deger-Jalkotzy and Lemos, eds., *Ancient Greece*, 123–150.

———. 2009. "Mycenaean Citadels as Performative Space." In Joseph Maran, Carsten Juwig, Hermann Schwengel, and Ulrich Thaler, eds., *Constructing Power: Architecture, Ideology and Social Practice*, 75–88. Berlin.

———. 2015. "Near Eastern Semicircular Axes in the Late Bronze Age Aegean as Entangled Objects." In Panagiotopoulos, Kaiser and Kouka, eds., *Ein Minoer im Exil*, 243–270.

———. 2016. "Against the Currents of History: The Early 12th c. BCE Resurgence of Tiryns." In Driessen, ed., *RA-PI-NE-U*, 201–220.

Maran, Joseph, and Eftychia Stavrianopoulou. 2007. "*Potnios Anēr*: Reflections on the Ideology of Mycenaean Kingship." In Eva Alram-Stern and Georg Nightingale, eds., *Keimelion: Elitenbildung und elitärer Konsum von der mykenischen Palastzeit bis zur Homerischen Epoche : Akten des internation-alen Kongresses vom 3. bis 5. Februar 2005 in Salzburg = The formation of elites and elitist lifestyles from Mycenaen palatial times to the Homeric period*. Wien: Österreichische Akademie der Wissenschaften, 285–297. Vienna.

Maran, Joseph, and James C. Wright. 2020. "Mycenaean Culture and Palatial Administration." In Lemos and Kotsonas, eds., *A Companion to the Archaeology of Early Greece and the Mediterranean*, 99–132.

Maran, Joseph, and Ulrich Thaler. 2017. "Adding (More Than) Colour: Wall-Paintings in the Palace of Tiryns." In Maria Lagogianni-Georgakarakos, ed., *Odysseys*, 79–82. Athens.

Marcar, Ariane. 2004. "Aegean Costume and the Dating of the Knossian Frescoes." *BSAStud* 12: 225–238.

Marcos, José Macedo. 2016. "Hermes *a-re-ja* (PY Tn 316): A New Interpretation." *Kadmos* 55: 67–82.

Marin-Aguilera, Beatriz, Francesco Iacono, and Margarita Gleba. 2018. "Colouring the Mediterranean: Production and Consumption of Purple-dyed Textiles in Pre-Roman Times." *JMA* 31: 127–154.

Marinatos, Nanno. 1984. "The Date-Palm in Minoan Iconography and Religion." *OpAth* 15: 115–122.

———. 1985. "The Function and Interpretation of the Theran Frescoes." *BCHSupp* 11: 219–230.

———. 1988. "The Fresco from Room 31 at Mycenae: Problems of Method and Interpretation." In E. B. French and K. A. Wardle, eds., *Problems in Greek Prehistory: Papers Presented at the Centenary Conference of the British School of Archaeology at Athens, Manchester April 1986*, 245–251. Bristol.

———. 1989. "The Minoan Harem: The Role of Eminent Women and the Knossos Frescoes." *DialHistAnc* 15: 33–62.

———. 1995. *Minoan Religion: Ritual, Image, and Symbol*. Columbia, SC.

———. 2007. "The Lily Crown and Sacred Kingship in Minoan Crete." In Betancourt, Nelson, and Williams, eds., *Krinoi kai Limenes*, 271–276.

———. 2010. *Minoan Kingship and the Solar Goddess: A Near Eastern Koine*. Urbana.

Marinatos, Nanno, and Lyvia Morgan. 2005. "The Dog Pursuit Scenes from Tell el Dabᶜa and Kea." *BSA* 13: 119–122.

Marinatos, Spyridon, and Max Hirmer. 1960. *Crete and Mycenae*. New York.

Martelli, Isabelle. 2016. "'*The Tomb of a Rich Athenian Lady, ca. 850 B.C.*': Honey and Purple for a Textile Interpretation Attempt." *Pasiphae* 10: 117–144.

Maslow, Abraham H. 1970. *Motivation and Personality*. 2nd ed. New York.

Mason, Hugh J. 2008. "Hittite Lesbos?" In Collins, Bachvarova, and Rutherford, eds., *Anatolian Interfaces*, 57–62.

Matić, Uroš. 2019. "Memories into Images: Aegean and Aegean-like Objects in New Kingdom Egyptian Theban Tombs." *CArchJ* 29: 653–669.

———. 2020. "Looking Like Griffins: Spiral-Shaped Fringes and Locks in the Coiffure of Aegean Emissaries Represented in Aegean Eighhteenth Dynasty Theban Tombs." *JAEI* 9: 37–46.

Matić, Uroš, and Filip Franković. 2017. "Out of Date, Out of Fashion—The Changing of Dress of Aegean Figures in the Theban Tombs of the Egyptian 18th Dynasty in the Light of Aegean Bronze Age Costume." *SMEA*, Nuova Serie 3: 105–130.

Matoušková, Monika. 2018. "The Sacral Knot and Its Iconographic Use." *Stud. Hercynia* 22: 9–31.

———. 2020. "The Use of Symbols in Minoan and Mycenaean Iconography." Unpublished MA Thesis. Charles University, Prague.

Matsas, Dimitris. 1991. "Samothrace and the Northeastern Aegean: The Minoan Connection." *ST* 1: 159–179.

———. 1995. "Minoan Long-Distance Trade: A View from the Northern Aegean." In Laffineur and Niemeier, eds., *Politeia*, 235–246.

Matthews, Victor J. 1977. "Naupaktia and Argonautika." *Phoenix* 31: 189–207.

Mazarakis Ainian, Alexander. 1997. *From Rulers' Dwellings to Temples: Architecture, Religion and Society in Early Iron Age Greece (1100-700 B.C.)*. Jonsered.

Mazow, Laura B. 2017. "A Weaving Sword at Miletus? Combat or Weaving Sword and the Complexities of Gender Construction." *ATR* 59: 3–16.

McCabe, Donald F. 1985. *Dydima Inscriptions: Texts and List*. Princeton.

McEnroe, John C. 2010. *Minoan Crete: Constructing Identity in the Aegean Bronze Age*. Austin.

McGowan, Erin. 2011. *Ambiguity and Minoan Neopalatial Seal Imagery*. Uppsala.

McMahon, Gregory. 1991. *The Hittite State Cult of the Tutelary Deities*. Chicago.

McPhee, Brian D. 2017. "Numbers and Acrostics: Two Notes on Jason's Prayer at Pagasae in Apollonius' *Argonautica*." *Akropolis* 1: 111–120.

Mee, Christopher. 2010. "Death and Burial." In Cline, ed., *The Oxford Handbook of the Bronze Age Aegean*, 277–290.

Meißner, Torsten. 2004. "Two Mycenaean Problems." In J. H. W. Penney, ed., *Indo-European Perspectives: Studies in Honour of Anna Morpurgo Davies*, 258–265. Oxford.

———. 2019. "Greek or Minoan? Names and Naming Habits in the Aegean Bronze Age." In Robert Parker, ed., *Changing Names: Tradition and Innovation in Ancient Greek Onomastics*, 21–46. Oxford.

Meißner, Torsten and Olga Tribulato. 2002. "Nominal Composition in Mycenaean Greek." *TransPhilolSoc* 100: 289–330.

Melena, José L. 1975a. "*PO-NI-KI-JO* in the Knossos Ga Tablets." *Minos* 14: 77–84.

———. 1975b. *Studies on Some Mycenaean Inscriptions from Knossos Dealing with Textiles*. Salamanca.

Mellink, Machteld J., ed. 1986. *Troy and the Trojan War: A Symposium at Bryn Mawr College, October 1984*. Bryn Mawr.

Mersereau, Rebecca. 1993. "Cretan Cylindrical Models." *AJA* 97: 1–47.

Michailidou, Anna. 1999. "Systems of Weight and Social Relations of 'Private' Production in the Late Bronze Aegean." In Angelos Chaniotis, ed., *From Minoan Farmers to Roman Traders: Sidelights on the Economy of Ancient Crete*, 87–113. Stuttgart.

Michel, Cécile. 2001. *Correspondance des marchands de Kaniš au début du IIe millénaire av. J.-C.* Paris.

Michel, Cécile, and Marie-Louise D. Nosch, eds. 2013. *Textile Terminologies in the Ancient Near East and Mediterranean from the Third to the First Millennia BC*. Oxford.

Middleton, Guy D. 2010. *The Collapse of Palatial Society in LBA Greece and the Postpalatial Period*. (BAR S2110). Oxford.

Militello, Pietro. 2007. "Textile Industry and Minoan Palaces." In Gillis and Nosch, eds., *Ancient Textiles*, 36–44.

———. 2014. "Wool Economy in Minoan Crete before Linear B: A Minimalist Position." In Breniquet and Michel, eds., *Wool Economy in the Ancient Near East and the Aegean*, 264–282.

Miller, J. L. 2010. "Some Disputed Passages in the Tawagalawa Letter." In Itamar Singer, ed., *Ipamati kistamati pari tumatimis: Luwian and Hittite Studies Presented to J. David Hawkins on the Occasion of His 70th Birthday*, 158–169. Tel Aviv.

Miller Bonney, Emily. 2011. "Disarming the Snake Goddess: A Reconsideration of the Faience Figurines from the Temple Repositories at Knossos." *JMA* 24: 171–190.

Mina, Maria, Sevi Triantaphyllou, and Yiannis Papadatos, eds. 2016. *An Archaeology of Prehistoric Bodies and Embodied Identities in the Eastern Mediterranean*. Oxford.

Mitrovich, Michele. 2021. "Discussion following Silver's presentation." MASt@ CHS—Spring Seminar 2021 (Friday, April 16): Summaries of Presentations and Discussion. Available for download at: https://classical-inquiries.chs.harvard.edu/mastchs-spring-seminar-2021-friday-april-16-summaries-of-presentations-and-discussion/.

Molloy, Barry P. C., ed. 2016. *Of Odysseys and Oddities: Scales and Modes of Interaction between Prehistoric Aegean Societies and their Neighbours*. Oxford.

Montecchi, Barbara. 2016a. "The Labyrinth: Building, Myth, and Symbol." In Alram-Stern, Blakolmer, Deger-Jalkotzy, Laffineur, and Weilhartner, eds., *Metaphysis*, 165–174.

———. 2016b. "*Pu-Ro, Pa-Ki-Ja-Nai-Ne*, and the Sanctuary of Poseidon." *SMEA* 2: 119–136.

———. 2017. "Classification, Use, and Function of Hanging Nodules in the Neopalatial Administrative Practices (Minoan Crete)." *AA* 1: 1–18.

Morgan, Lyvia. 1985. "Idea, Idiom and Iconography." *BCH Suppl* 11: 5–19.

———. 1987. "A Minoan Larnax from Knossos." *BSA* 82: 171–200.

———. 1988. *The Miniature Wall Paintings of Thera: A Study in Aegean Culture and Iconography.* Cambridge.

———. 2000. "Form and Meaning in Figurative Painting." In Susan Sherratt, ed., *The Wall Paintings of Thera: Proceedings of the First International Symposium, Petros M. Nomikos Conference Center, Thera, Hellas, 30 August - 4 September 1997*, 925–944. Vol. II. Piraeus.

———. 2005. "New Discoveries and New Ideas in Aegean Wall Painting." In Morgan, ed., *Aegean Wall Painting*, 21–44.

———, ed. 2005. *Aegean Wall Painting: A Tribute to Mark Cameron.* London.

———. 2010. "An Aegean Griffin in Egypt: The Hunt Frieze at Tell el Dabᶜa." *ÄgLev* 20: 303–323.

Morris, Sarah P. 1997. "Homer and the Near East." In Ian Morris and Barry B. Powell, eds., *A New Companion to Homer*, 599–623. Leiden.

———. 2001. "Potnia Aswiya: Anatolian Contributions to Greek Religion." In Laffineur and Hägg, eds., *Potnia*, 423–432.

———. 2014. "Helen Re-Claimed, Troy Re-Visited: Scenes of Troy in Archaic Greek Art." In Avramidou and Demetriou, eds., *Approaching the Ancient Artifact*, 3–14.

Morris, Sarah P., and Robert Laffineur, eds. 2007. *Epos: Reconsidering Greek Epic and Aegean Bronze Age Archaeology. Proceedings of the 11th International Conference, Los Angeles, UCL A- The J. Paul Getty Villa, 20-23 April 2006.* Liège.

Moschos, Ioannis. 2009. "Evidence of Social Life, Reorganization and Reconstruction in Late Helladic IIIC Achaea and Modes of Contacts and Exchange via the Ionian and Adriatic Seas." In Borgna and Guida, eds., *From the Aegean to the Adriatic*, 345–414.

Moss, Marina. 2010. "The 'Mountain Mother' Seal from Knossos—A Reevaluation." *Prudentia* 32: 1–24.

Muellner, Leonard. 1976. *The Meaning of Homeric EYXOMAI through Its Formulas.* Innsbruck.

Muhly, James D. 1983. "Gold Analysis and Sources of Gold in the Bronze Age," In *Temple University Aegean Symposium 8, 1983: A Symposium Sponsored by the*

Department of Art History, Temple University, Philadelphia, PA, with the Theme "Gold in the Aegean Bronze Age," on March 25, 1983, 1–14. Philadelphia.

Müller, Walter, ed. 2010. *Die Bedeutung der mykenischen und mykenischen Siegelglyptik. VI. Internationales Siegelsymposium, 9.-12. Oktober 2008*. Mainz am Rhein.

Murgatroyd, P. 2015. "The Wrath of Poseidon." *CQ* 65: 444–448.

Murray, Caroline, and Peter Warren. 1976. "*Po-ni-ki-jo* Among the Dye-Plants of Minoan Crete." *Kadmos* 15: 40–60.

Murray, Sarah C. 2013. "Trade, Imports, and Society in Early Greece: 1300-900 BCE." Unpublished Ph.D. disseration. Stanford University, Stanford, CA.

———. 2017. *The Collapse of the Mycenaean Economy: Imports, Trade and Institutions 1300-700 BCE*. New York.

———. 2018a. "Imported Objects as Proxy Data for Change in Greek Trade after the Mycenaean Collapse: A Multi-Variate Quantitative Analysis." In Pavúk, Klontza-Jaklová, and Harding, eds., *Eudaimōn*, 71–91.

———. 2018b. "Imported Exotica and Mortuary Ritual at Perati in Late Helladic IIIC East Attica." *AJA* 122: 33–64.

Murray, Susan Peterson. 2014. "Reconsidering the Room of the Ladies at Akrotiri." Hesperia Supplements 33 (*Charis: Essays in Honor of Sara A. Immerwahr*), 101–130.

———. 2016. "Patterned Textiles as Costume in Aegean Art." In Shaw and Chapin, eds., *Woven Threads*, 43–103.

Nagy, Gregory. 1979. *The Best of the Achaeans: Concepts of the Hero in Archaic Greek Poetry*. Baltimore.

———. 1992. *Greek Mythology and Poetics*. Ithaca.

———. 1994. "The Name of Achilles: Question of Etymology and 'Folk-Etymology'." *ICS* 19: 3–9.

———. 2003. *Homeric Responses*. Austin.

———. 2010. *Homer the Preclassic*. Berkeley.

———. 2015a. *Masterpieces of Metonymy: From Ancient Greek Times to Now*. Hellenic Studies Series 72. Washington, DC. Available at https://chs.harvard.edu/book/nagy-gregory-masterpieces-of-metonymy-from-ancient-greek-times-to-now/.

———. 2015b. "From Athens to Crete and Back." *Classical Inquiries*, 2015.09.10. Available at https://classical-inquiries.chs.harvard.edu/from-athens-to-crete-and-back/.

———. 2018. "A Plane Tree in Nafplio: Decorating a Reader for Travel-study in Greece, March 2018." Available for download at: https://classical-inquiries.chs.harvard.edu/a-plane-tree-in-nafplio-decorating-a-reader-for-travel-study-in-greece-march-2018/.

———. 2020a. "Minoan-Mycenaean Signatures Observed by Pausanias at a Sacred Space Dominated by Athena." *Classical Inquiries*, 2020.05.15. Available at https://classical-inquiries.chs.harvard.edu/minoan-myce-naean-signatures-observed-by-pausanias-at-a-sacred-space-dominated-by-athena/.

———. 2020b. "More about Minoan-Mycenaean Signatures Observed by Pausanias at Sacred Spaces Dominated by Athena." *Classical Inquiries* 2020.05.22, rewritten 2020.05.23. Available at: https://classical-inquiries. chs.harvard.edu/more-about-minoan-mycenaean-signatures-observed-by-pausanias-at-sacred-spaces-dominated-by-athena/.

———. 2020c. "About some kind of an Epiphany as Pictured in Minoan Glyptic Art, and about its Relevance to a Myth as Retold by Pausanias." *Critical Inquiries* 2020.05.29. Available at https://classical-inquiries.chs.harvard. edu/about-some-kind-of-an-epiphany-as-pictured-in-minoan-glyptic-art-and-about-its-relevance-to-a-myth-as-retold-by-pausanias/.

———. 2021. "How the First Word in Song 1 of Sappho is Relevant to her Reception in the Ancient World—and to Various Different Ways of Thinking about the Greek Word *hetairā*." *Classical Inquiries* 2021.01.15. Available at https://classical-inquiries.chs.harvard.edu/how-the-first-word-in-song-1-of-sappho-is-relevant-to-her-reception-in-the-ancient-world/.

Nakassis, Dimitri. 2010. "Reevaluating Staple and Wealth Finance at Mycenean Pylos." In Daniel J. Pullen, ed., *Political Economies of the Aegean Bronze Age*, 127–148. Oxford.

———. 2012. "Prestige and Interest: Feasting and the King at Mycenaean Pylos." *Hesperia* 81: 1–30.

———. 2013. *Individuals and Society in Mycenaean Pylos*. Leiden.

Nakassis, Dimitri, Hoann Gulizio, and Sarah A. James, eds. 2014. *KE-RA-ME-JA: Studies Presented to Cynthia W. Shelmeridine*. Philadelphia.

Natan-Yulzary, Shirly. 2020. "Lady Athirat of the Sea—A New Look at KTU 1.4 ii 3-11." *AuOr* 38: 131—146.

Nauert, Jean Porter. 1965. "The Hagia Triada Sarcophagus: An Iconographic Study." *AntK* 9: 91–98.

Neils, Jenifer. 1994. "Reflections of Immortality: The Myth of Jason on Etruscan Mirrors." In Richard Daniel De Puma and Jocelyn Penny Small, eds., *Murlo and the Etruscans: Art and Society in Ancient Etruria*, 190–195. Madison.

Nelis, Damien P. 1991. "Iphias: Apollonius Rhodius, *Argonautica* 1.311-16." *CQ* 41: 96–105.

Niemeier, Wolf-Dietrich. 1991. "Minoan Artisans Travelling Overseas: The Alalakh Frescoes and the Painted Plaster Floor at Tel Kabri (Western Galilee)." In Laffineur and Basch, eds., *Thalassa*, 189–201.

———. 2005. "Minoans, Mycenaeans, Hittites and Ionians in Western Asia Minor: New Excavations in Bronze Age Miletus-Millawanda." In Villing, ed., *The Greeks in the East*, 1–36.

Niesiolowski-Spanò, Lukasz and Marek Węcowski, eds. 2018. *Change, Continuity, and Connectivity: North-Eastern Mediterranean at the Turn of the Bronze Age and in the Early Iron Age*. Wiesbaden.

Nikolaidou, Marianna. 2016. "Materialised Myth and Ritualised Realities: Religious Symbolism on Minoan Pottery." In Alram-Stern, Blakolmer, Deger-Jalkotzy, Laffineur, and Weilhartner, eds., *Metaphysis*, 97–108.

———. 2020. "Blessed (?) Charms: The Shield in the Aegean Arts of Personal Adornment." In Davis and Laffineur, eds., *Neôteros*, 181–192.

Nikoloudis, Stavroula. 2006. "The *ra-wa-ke-ta*, Ministerial Authority and Mycenaean Cultural Identity." Unpublished Ph.D. dissertation. University of Texas, Austin, TX.

———. 2008a. "Multiculturalism in the Mycenaean World." In Collins, Bashvarova, and Rutherford, eds., *Anatolian Interfaces*, 45–56.

———. 2008b. "The Role of the *ra-wa-ke-ta*. Insights from PY Un 718." *Pasiphae* 2: 587–594.

———. 2012. "Thoughts on a Possible Link between the PY Ea Series and a Mycenaean Tanning Operation." In Carlier et al., eds., *Études mycéniennes 2010*, 285–302.

Nilsson, Martin P. 1971. *The Minoan-Mycenaean Religion and its Survival in Greek Religion*. 2nd rev. ed. New York.

Nosch, Marie Louise B. 2000a. "The Organization of the Mycenaean Textile Industry." Unpublished Ph.D. dissertation. Universität Salzburg, Salzburg.

———. 2000b. "Acquisition and Distribution: *ta-ra-si-ja* in the Mycenaean Textile Industry." In Carole Gillis, Christian Risberg, and Birgitta Sjöberg, eds., *Trade and Production in Premonetary Greece: Acquisition and Distribution of Raw Materials and Finished Products*, 43–61. Jonsered.

———. 2000c. "Schafherden unter dem Namenspatronat von Potnia und Hermes in Knossos." In Fritz Blakolmer, ed., *Österreichische Forschungen zur ägäischen Bronzezeit 1998: Akten der Tagung am Institut für Klassische Archäologie der Universität Wien, 2.-3. Mai 1998*, 211–215. Vienna.

———. 2001. "The Textile Industry at Thebes in the Light of the Textile Industries at Pylos and Knossos." In I. Radova, ed., *Festschrift in honour of A. Bartonek* (Studia Minora Facultatis Philosophica Universitatis Brunensis 6), 177–189. Brno.

———. 2003a. "Center and Periphery in the Linear B Archives." In Kyparissi-Apostolika and Papakonstantinou, eds., *The Periphery of the Mycenaean World*, 63–68.

———. 2003b. "The Women at Work in the Linear B Tablets." In L. L. Loven and A. Stromberg, eds., *Gender, Cult, and Culture in the Ancient World from Mycenae to Byzantium: Proceedings of the Second Nordic Symposium on Gender and Women's History in Antiquity, Helsinki, 20-22 October 2000 (SIMA-166, PB)*, 12–26. Savedalen.

———. 2004. "Red Colored Textiles in the Linear B Inscriptions." In Liza Cleland and Karen Stears, eds., *Colour in the Ancient Mediterranean World*, 32–39. Oxford.

———. 2011. "The Mycenaean Administration of Textile Production in the Palace of Knossos: Observations on the Lc(1) Textile Targets." *AJA* 115: 495–505.

———. 2012. "The Textile Logograms in the Linear B Tablets. Les idéogrammes archéologiques des textiles." In Pierre Carlier, ed., *Études mycéniennes 2010: actes du XIIIe Colloque international sur les textes égéens: Sèvres, Paris, Nanterre, 20-23 septembre 2010*, 305–306. Pisa.

———. 2014a. "The Aegean Wool Economies of the Bronze Age." In *Textile Society of America 2014 Biennial Symposium Proceedings: New Directions: Examining the Past, Creating the Future, Los Angeles, California, 1-September 10-14, 2014*, 1-14. Available at https://digitalcommons.unl.edu/tsaconf/900/.

———. 2014b. "Mycenaean Wool Economies in the Latter Part of the 2nd Millennium BC Aegean." In Breniquet and Michel, eds., *Wool Economy in the Ancient Near East and the Aegean*, 371–400.

———. 2014c. "Linen Textiles and Flax in Classical Greece: Provenance and Trade." In Kerstin Droß-Krüpe, ed., *Textile Trade and Distribution in Antiquity*, 17–42. Wiesbaden.

———. 2015. "The Wool Age: Traditions and Innovations in Textile Production, Consumption and Administration in the Late Bronze Age Aegean." In Weilhartner and Ruppenstein, eds., *Tradition and Innovation in the Mycenaean Palatial Polities*, 167–201.

———. 2016. "Spinning Gold and Casting Textiles." In Driessen, ed., *RA-PI-NE-U*, 221–232.

———. 2017. "Mycenaean Textile Crops and Textile Workers." In Oller, Pàmias, and Varias, eds., *Tierra, territorio y población en la Grecia antigua*, I, 3–38.

Nosch, Marie-Louise B., and Agata Ulanowska. 2021. "The Materiality of the Cretan Hieroglyphic Script: Textile Production-Related Referents to Hieroglyphic Signs on Seals and Sealings from Middle Bronze Age Crete."

In Philippa Steele, Philip Boyes, and Natalia Elvira Astoreca, eds., *The Social and Cultural Contexts of Historic Writing Practices*, 73–100. Oxford.

Nosch, Marie-Louise B., and Massimo Perna. 2001. "Cloth in the Cult." In Laffineur and Hägg, eds., *Potnia*, 471–477.

Nosch, Marie-Louise B., and Robert Laffineur, eds. 2012. *Kosmos: Jewellry, Adornment and Textiles in the Aegean Bronze Age. Proceedings of the 13th International Aegean Conference/13e Rencontre égéenne internationale, University of Copenhagen, Danish National Research Foundation's Centre for Textile Research, 21-26 April 2010*. Leuven.

Nugent, S. Georgia. 1996. "Statius' Hypsipyle: Following in the Footsteps of the *Aeneid*." *Scholia* 5: 46–71.

Oikonomaki, Androniki. 2018. "Ἀχαιοί, Ἀργεῖοι, Δαναοί: Revisiting the System of Denomination of the Greeks in the Homeric Epics." Unpublished paper available at https://research-bulletin.chs.harvard.edu/2018/05/23/report-denominations-homeric-poetry/.

Okrostsvaridze, Avtandil V., David I. Bluashvili, and Nona E. Gagnidze. 2014. "Field investigation of the Mythical 'Gold Sands; of the Ancient Colchis Kingdom and Modern Discussion on the Argonauts' Expedition." *Episodes* 37: 1–8.

Okrostsvaridze, Avtandil V., N. Gagnidze and K. Akimidze. 2016. "A Modern Field Investigation of the Mythical 'Gold Sands' of the Ancient Colchis Kingdom and 'Golden Fleece' Phenomena." *Quat.Int.* 409: 61–69.

Olivier, Jean-Pierre. 1986. "Cretan Writing in the Second Millennium B.C." *WorldArcheol* 17: 377–389.

———. 1987. "Des extraits de contrats de vente d'esclaves dans les tablettes de Knossos." In John T. Killen, José L Melena, and Jean Pierre Olivier, eds., *Studies in Mycenaean and Classical Greek Presented to John Chadwick* (*Minos 20-22*), 479–498. Salamanca.

———. 2001. "Les 'collecteurs': leur distribution spatiale et temporelle." In Voutsaki and Killen, eds., *Economy and Politics in the Mycenaean Palace States*, 139–159.

Oller, Marta, Jordi Pàmias, and Carlos Varias, eds. 2017. *Tierra, territorio y población en la Grecia antigua: aspectos institutcionales y miticos*. 2 vols. Mering.

Olsen, Barbara A. 2014. *Women in Mycenaean Greece: The Linear B Tablets from Pylos and Knossos*. London.

Öttinger, Norbert. 2008. "The Seer Mopsos (Muksa) as a Historical Figure." In Collins, Bachvarova, and Rutherford, eds. *Anatolian Interfaces*, 63–66.

Özgüç, Nimet. 1966. "Excavations at Acemhöyük." *Anadolu/Anatolia* 10: 2–52.

Pache, Corinne. 2014. "Theban Walls in Homeric Epic." *TC* 6: 278–296.

Palaiologou, Heleni. 1995. "'Minoan Dragons' on a Sealstone from Mycenae." In Christine Morris, ed., *Klados: Essasys in Honour of J. N. Coldstream*, 195–199. London.

Palaiologou, Heleni. 2015. "A Female Painted Plaster Figure from Mycenae." In Brecoulaki, Davis, and Stocker, eds., *Mycenaean Wall Painting in Context*, 95–125.

Palaima, Thomas G. 1991. "Maritime Matters in the Linear B Tablets." In Laffineur and Basch, eds., *Thalassa*, 273–310.

———. 1995. "The Nature of the Mycenaean *Wanax*: Non-Indo-European Origins and Priestly Functions." In Rehak, ed., *The Role of the Ruler in the Prehistoric Aegean*, 119–139.

———. 1997. "The Potter and the Fuller: The Royal Craftsmen." In Laffineur and Betancourt, eds., *TEXNH*, Vol. II, 407–412.

———. 1999a. "Mycenaean Militarism from a Textual Perspective, Onomastics in Context: *lāwos*, *dāmos*, and *klewos*." In Laffineur, ed., *POLEMOS*, 367–378.

———. 1999b. "Kn 02 – Tn 316." In Sigrid Deger-Jalkotzy; Stefan Hiller and Oswald Panagl, eds., *Floreant studia Mycenaea: Akten des X. Internationalen Mykenologischen Colloquiums in Salzburg vom 1.-5. Mai 1995*, 437–461. Vienna.

———. 2000. "*Themis* in the Mycenaean Lexicon and the Etymology of the Place-Name **ti-mi-to a-ko*." *Faventia* 22: 7–19.

———. 2004a. "Sacrificial Feasting in the Linear B Documents." *Hesperia* 73: 217–246.

———. 2004b. "Appendix One: Linear B Sources." In Stephen M. Trzaskoma, R. Scott Smith, and Stephen Bruner, eds., *Anthology of Classical Myth: Primary Sources in Translation*, 439–454. Indianapolis, IN.

———. 2007a. "Mycenaean Society and Kingship: *Cui Bono*? A Counter-Speculative View." In Morris and Laffineur, eds., *Epos*, 129–140.

———. 2007b. "Ilios, Tros and Tlos: Continuing Problems with *to-ro*, *to-ro-o*, *to-ro-wo*, *to-ro-ja*, *wi-ro* and *a-si-wi-ja/a-si-wi-jo*." In Lang, ed., *Stephanos Aristeios*, 197–204.

———. 2006. "*Wanaks* and Related Power Terms in Mycenaean and Later Greek." In Deger-Jalkotzy and Lemos, eds., *Ancient Greece*, 53–71.

———. 2009. "Continuity from the Mycenaean Period in an Historical Boeotian Cult of Poseidon (and Erinys)." In Despoina Danielidou, ed., *Doron: Timetikos Tomos gia ton Kathegete Spyro Iakobide*, 527–536. Athens.

———. 2011. "Euboea, Athens, Thebes and Kadmos: The Implications of the Linear B References." In David W. Rupp and Jonathan E. Tomlinson, eds., *Euboea and Athens Colloquium in Memory of Malcolm B. Wallace: Proceedings of a Colloquium in Memory of Malcolm B. Wallace. Athens 26-27 June 2009*, 53–75. Athens.

———. 2015. "The Mycenaean Mobilization of Labor in Agriculture and Building Projects: Institutions, Individuals, Compensation and Status in the Linear B Tablets." In Piotr Steinkeller and Michael Hudson, eds., *Labor in the Ancient World*, 617–648. Dresden.

———. 2016. "The Ideology of the Ruler in Mycenaean Prehistory: Twenty Years after the Missing Ruler." In Koehl, ed., *Studies in Aegean Art and Culture*, 133–158.

———. 2020a. "Problems in Minoan and Mycenaean Writing Style and Practice: The Strange Case of *33 ra3 on Pylos Tablet Aa 61." In Davis and Laffineur, eds., *Neôteros*, 3–14.

———. 2020b. "'*Porphureion*' and '*Kalkhion*' and Minoan-Mycenaean Murex Dye Manufacture and Use." In Apostolakou, Brogan, and Betancourt, eds., *Alatzomouri-Pefka*, 123–128.

Palmer, Jennifer Linda. 2014. "An Analysis of Late Bronze Age Glyptic Motifs of a Religious Nature." Unpublished Ph.D. dissertation. University of Birmingham, Birmingham, UK.

Palmer, Leonard R. 1963. *The Interpretation of Mycenaean Greek Texts*. Oxford.

Palmer, Ruth. 1994. *Wine in the Mycenaean Palace Economy*. Liège.

———. 1995. "Wine and Viticulture in the Linear A and B Texts of the Bronze Age Aegean." In Patrick E. McGovern, Stuart J. Fleming and Solomon H. Katz, eds., *The Origins and Ancient History of Wine*, 269–285. Amsterdam.

Palyvou, Clairy. 2002. "Central Courts: The Supremacy of the Void." In Driessen, Schoep, and Laffineur, eds., *Monuments of Minos*, 107–177.

———. 2005. *Akrotiri, Thera: An Architecture of Affluence 3,500 Years Old*. Philadelphia.

———. 2018. *Daidalos at Work: A Phenomenological Approach to Minoan Architecture*. Philadelphia.

Panagiotaki, Marina. 1999. "The Central Palace Sanctuary at Knossos." *BSASupp* 31: 1–300.

Panagiotakopoulou, Eva. 2000. *Archaeology and Entomology in the Eastern Mediterranean: Research into the History of Insect Synanthropy in Greece and Egypt*. Oxford.

———. 2010. "A Systemic Approach to Mycenaean Sealing Practices." In W. Müller, ed., *Die Bedeutung der mykenischen und mykenischen Siegelglyptik. VI. Internationales Siegelsymposium, 9.-12. Oktober 2008*, 259–269. Berlin.

Panagiotopoulos, Diamantis. 2006. "Foreigners in Egypt in the Time of Hatshepsut and Thutmose III." In Eric H. Cline and David B. O'Connor, eds., *Thutmose III: A New Biography*, 369–412. Ann Arbor.

———. 2010. "A Systemic Approach to Mycenaean Sealing Practices." In Müller, ed., *Die Bedeutung der mykenischen und mykenischen Siegelglyptik VI*, 259–269.

———. 2012. "Aegean Imagery and the Syntax of Viewing." In Panagiotopoulos and Günkel Maschek, eds., *Minoan Realities*, 63–82.

Panagiotopoulos, Diamantis, Ivonne Kaiser and Ourania Kouka, eds., 2015. *Ein Minoer im Exil: Festschrift für Wolf-Dietrich Niemeier.* Bonn.

Panagiotopoulos, Diamantis, and Ute Günkel-Maschek. 2012. "Introduction: The Power of Images and Architecture." In Panagiotopoulos and Günkel Maschek, eds., *Minoan Realities*, 1–8.

———, eds. 2012. *Minoan Realities: Approaches to Images, Architecture, and Society in the Aegean Bronze Age.* Louvain.

Pantazis, Thanos, et al. 2003. "X-Ray Fluorescence Analysis of a Gold Ibex and Other Artifacts from Akrotiri." In Polinger Foster and Laffineur, eds., *Metron*, 155–165.

Papadatos, Yiannis. 2012. "An Early Minoan Boat Model from Kephala Petras, Siteia." In Mantzourani and Betancourt, eds., *PHILISTOR*, 155–159.

Papadimitriou, Alkestis, Ulrich Thaler, and Joseph Maran. 2015. "Bearing the Pomegranate Bearer: A New Wall-Painting from Tiryns." In Brecoulaki, Davis, and Stocker, eds., *Mycenaean Wall Painting in Context*, 173–211.

Papadimitriou, Nikolas. 2008. "Both Centre and Periphery? Thessaly in the Mycenaean Period." In Περιφέρεια Θεσσαλίας [Perifereia Thessalias]. 1ο Διεθνές Συνεδρίο Ιστορίας και Πολιτισμού της Θεσσαλίας. Πρακτικά Συνεδρίου, 9-11 Νοεμβρίου 2006, 98–113. Thessaloniki.

Papadopoulos, Thanasis J. 2017. "Mycenaean Citadels of Western Greece: Architecture, Purpose and their Intricate Role in the Local Communities and their Relations with the West." In Fotiadis, Laffineur, Lólos, and Vlachopoulos, eds., *Esperos = Hesperos*, 419–429.

Papageorgiou, Irini. 2008. "The Mycenaean Golden Kylix of the Benaki Museum: A *dubitandum?*" *Mouseio Benaki* 8: 9–37.

———. 2014. "The Practice of Bird Hunting in the Aegean of the Second Millennium: An Investigation." *BSA* 109: 111–128, 438–440.

Pareja, Marie Nicole, Philip P. Betancourt, Vili Apostolakou, et al. 2016. "Aegean Dyes: Unearthing the Colours of Ancient Minoan Textiles." *Expedition* 58: 21–27.

Parke, H. W. 1967. *The Oracles of Zeus: Dodona, Olympia, Amon.* Oxford.

Paskiewic, T. M. 1988. "Aitia in the Second Book of Apollonius' *Argonautica.*" *ICS* 13: 57–61.

Pavúk, Peter. 2002. "The City on the Slope: Some Observations on Two-Dimensional Representations of Architecture in Aegean Art." In Aslan, Blum, Kastl, Schweizer, and Thumm, eds., *Mauerschau*, 567–583.

Pavúk, Peter, Věra Klontza-Jaklová, and Anthony Harding, eds. 2018. *Eudaimōn: Essays in Honour of Jan Bouzek.* Prague.

Paylock, Barbara. 1990. *Eros, Imitation, and the Epic Tradition.* Ithaca, NY.

Payton, Robert. 1991. "The Ulu Burun Writing-Board Set." *AS* 41: 99–106.

Peatfield, Alan Alfred Demetrius. 1989. *The Peak Sanctuaries of Minoan Crete.* Unpublished PhD thesis, University of London, London, UK.

———. 1990. "Minoan Peak Sanctuaries: History and Society." *Opuseula Atheniensia* 18: 117–131.

———. 1992. "Rural Ritual in Bronze Age Crete: The Sanctuary at Atsiphades." *Camb.Archaeol.J* 2: 80–81.

Phillips, Jacke, and Eric Cline. (2005). "Amenhotep III and Mycenae: New Evidence." In Dakouri-Hild and Sherratt: 317–328.

Rackham, Oliver, and Jennifer Moody. 1996. *The Making of the Cretan Landscape.* Manchester.

Pendlebury, J. D. L. 1933. *A Handbook to the Palace of Minos at Knossos, with its Dependencies.* Cambridge.

Peperaki, Olympia. 2004. "The House of the Tiles at Lerna: Dimensions of 'Social Complexity'." In John C. Barrett and Paul Halstead, eds., *The Emergence of Civilisation Revisited*, 214–231. Oxford.

———. 2016. "The Value of Sharing: Seal Use, Food Politics, and the Negotiation of Labor in Early Bronze II Mainland Greece." *AJA* 120: 3–25.

Perna, Massimo. 1994. "The Roundel in Linear A from Zakro Wc 3 (HM 84)." *Kadmos* 33: 29–37.

———. 2004. *Recherches sur la fiscalité mycénienne.* Études Anciennes 28. Nancy.

Petegorsky, Dan. 1982. "Context and Evocation: Studies in Early Greek and Sanskrit Poetry." Unpublished Ph.D. dissertation. University of California at Berkeley, Berkeley, CA.

Petrakis, Vassilis P. 2002–2003. "*TO-NO-E-KE-TE-RI-JO* Reconsidered." *Minos*, 37–38, 293-316.

———. 2010. "Localising Pylian Religion: Thoughts on the Geographic References in the Fr Tablets Provoked by a New Quasi-Join." *Pasiphae* 4: 199–215.

———. 2011. "Politics of the Sea in the Late Bronze Age II-III Aegean: Iconographic Preferences and Textual Perspectives." In Giorgos Vavouranakis, ed., *The Seascape in Aegean Prehistory*, 185–234. Athens.

———. 2012. "'Minoan' to 'Mycenaean': Thoughts on the Emergence of the Knossian Textile Industry." In Nosch and Laffineur, eds., *Kosmos*, 77–86.

———. 2014. "Appendix I: The Inscribed Stirrup Jar (El Z 1)." In Michael B. Cosmopoulos, *The Sanctuary of Demeter at Eleusis: The Bronze Age II*, 177–216. Athens.

———. 2016. "Writing the *wanax*: Spelling Peculiarities of Linear B *wa-na-ka* and their Possible Implications." *Minos* 19: 61–158.

References

———. 2020. "Topic 1: Some Thoughts on the Significance of the Occurrence of the Adjective /*wanakteros*/ on Late Minoan III Inscribed Transport Stirrup Jars." Available at https://classical-inquiries.chs.harvard.edu/mast-chs-friday-november-6-2020-summaries-of-presentations-and-discussion/.

Phillips, Jacke, and Eric Cline. 2005. "Amenhotep III and Mycenae: New Evidence." In Dakouri-Hild and Sherratt, eds., *Autochthon*, 317–328.

Pierini, Rachele. 2018. "AB 54+04, Mycenaean te-pa, Alphabetic Greek τήβεννα, Latin Toga: Semantic Remarks and Possible Near East Parallels." *JLL* 17: 111–119.

Peirini, Rachele, and Tom [Thomas G.] Palaima. 2021. "MASt@CHS—Winter Seminar 2021 (Friday, February 5): Summaries of Presentations and Discussion." In *Classical Inquiries* March 21, 2021. https://classical-inquiries.chs.harvard.edu/mastchs-winter-2021-seminar/.

Pini, Ingo. 2004. "Seals as an Indicator of Trade." In Laffineur and Greco, eds., *Emporia*, 777–783.

Platon, Lefteris. 2015. "Sacred Prostitution in Minoan Crete: A New Interpretation of Some Old Archaeological Findings." *JAEI* 7: 76–90.

Platon, Nikolaos. 1985. *Zakros: The Discovery of a Lost Palace of Ancient Crete*. Amsterdam.

———. 2010. "On the Dating and Character of the 'Zakros Pits Deposit'." *BSAStud* 18: 243–257.

Pliatsika, Vassiliki. 2012. "Simply Divine: the Jewellery, Dress and Body Adornment of the Mycenaean Clay Female Figures in Light of New Evidence from Mycenae." In Nosch and Laffineur, eds., *Kosmos*, 609–625.

Polinger Foster, Karen, and Robert Laffineur, eds. 2003. *Metron: Measuring the Aegean Bronze Age: Proceedings of the 9th International Aegean Conference = 9e Rencontre égéenne internationale, New Haven, Yale University, 18-21 April 2002*. Liegé.

Popham, Mervyn R,. and Irene Lemos. 1995. "A Euboean Warrior Trader." *OJA* 14: 151–157.

Porada, Edith. 1981/1982. "The Cylinder Seals at Thebes in Boeotia." *AfO* 28: 1–70.

Porter, Andrew. 2014. "Reconstructing Laomedon's Reign in Homer: *Olympiomachia*, Poseidon's Wall, and the Earlier Trojan War." *GRBS* 51: 507–526.

Porter, James I. 2011. "Making and Unmaking: The Achaean Wall and the Limits of Fictionality in Homeric Criticism." *TAPA* 141: 1–36.

Postgate, J. N. 2001. "Question." In Voutsaki and Killen, eds., *Economy and Politics in the Mycenaean Palace States*, 160.

Preston, Laura. 2004. "A Mortuary Perspective on Political Changes in Late Minoan II-IIIB Crete." *AJA* 108: 321–348.

Pritchard, James B. 1951. "Syrians as Pictured in the Paintings of the Theban Tombs." *BASOR* 122: 36–41.

Privitera, Santo. 2005. "Hephaestia on Lemnos and the Mycenaean Presence in the Islands of the Northeastern Aegean." In Laffineur and Greco, eds., *Emporia*, 227–235.

Pulak, Cemal. 2001. "The Cargo of the Ulu Burun Ship and Evidence for Trade in the Aegean and Beyond." In Larissa Bonfante and Vassos Karageorghis, eds., *Italy and Cyprus in Antiquity: 1500-450 BC: proceedings of an International Symposium held at the Italian Academy for Advanced Studies in America at Columbia University, November 16-18, 2000*, 13–60. Nicosia.

———. 2010. "Ulu Burun Shipwreck." In Cline, ed., *The Oxford Handbook of the Bronze Age Aegean*, 862–876.

Pulleyn, Simon. 2006. "Homer's Religion: Philological Perspectives from Indo-European and Semitic." In Michael Clarke, Bruno Currie, and R. O. A. M. Lyne, eds., *Epic Interactions: Perspectives on Homer, Virgil, and the Epic Tradition: Presented to Jasper Griffin by Former Pupils*, 47–73. Oxford.

Quinlan, Stephen B. 2009. "The *Iliad*, the Athlete and the Ancient Greek Polis: A Descriptive Study of Homer's *Iliad* as Hero Myth." Unpublished Ph.D. dissertation, University of Ottawa, Canada.

Raman, Rahim A. 1975. "Homeric *aotos* and Pindaric *aotos*: A Semantic Problem." *Glotta* 53: 195–207.

Rankine, Patrice. 2011. "Odysseus as Slave: The Ritual of Domination and Social Death in Homeric Society." In Richard Alston, Edith Hall, and Laura Proffitt, eds., *Reading Ancient Slavery*, 34–50. London.

Rasmussen McCallum, Linda. 1987. "Decorative Program in the Mycenaean Palace at Pylos: The Megaron Frescoes." Unpublished Ph.D. dissertation. Univeristy of Pennsylvania, Philadelphia, PA.

Redfield, James M. 2009 (1983). "The Economic Man." In Lillian E. Doherty, ed., *Oxford Readings in Classical Studies: Homer's Odyssey*, 265–287. Oxford.

Reese, David S. 1987. "Palaikastro Shells and Bronze Age Purple-Dye Production in the Mediterranean Basin." *BSA* 82: 201–206.

———. 1990. "Triton Shells from East Mediterraean Sanctuaries and Graves." *JPR* 3: 7–14.

Rehak, Paul. 1984. "New Observations on the Mycenaean 'Warrior Goddess'." *AA* (1984): 535–545.

———. 1992. "Minoan Vessels with Figure-Eight Shields." *OpAth* 19: 115–124.

———. 1994. "The Aegean Priest on *CMS.I.223*." *Kadmos* 33: 76–84.

References

———. 1995a. "Enthroned Figures in Aegean Art and the Function of the Mycenaean Megaron." In Rehak, ed., *The Role of the Ruler in the Prehistoric Aegean*, 95–118.

———, ed. 1995b. *The Role of the Ruler in the Prehistoric Aegean: Proceedings of a Panel Discussion Presented at the Annual Meeting of the Archaeological Institute of America, New Orleans, Louisiana, 28 December 1992, with Additions*, 119–139. Liège.

———. 1995c. "The 'Genius' in Late Bronze Age Glyptic: The Later Evolution of an Aegean Cult Figure." In Walter Müiller, ed., *Sceaux minoens et mycéniens: IVe symposium international 10-12 septembre 1992, Clermont-Ferrand (Beiheft V. Corpus der minoischen und mykenischen Siegel)*, 215–231. Berlin.

———. 1996. "Aegean Breechcloths, Kilts, and the Keftiu Paintings." *AJA* 100: 35–51.

———. 1997. "The Role of Religious Painting in the Function of the Minoan Villa: The Case of Ayia Triadha." In Robin Hägg, ed., *The Function of the "Minoan Villa": Proceedings of the Eighth International Symposium at the Swedish Institute at Athens, 6-8 June 1992*, 163–174. Stockholm.

———. 1998. "Aegean Natives in the Theban Tomb Paintings: The Keftiu Revisited." In Cline and Harris Cline, eds., *The Aegean and the Orient in the Second Millennium*, 39–50.

———. 1999a. "The Mycenaean Warrior Goddess Revisited." In Laffineur, ed., *POLEMOS*, 227–239.

———. 1999b. "The Aegean Landscape and the Body: A New Interpretation of the Thera Frescoes." In Nancy L. Wicker and Bettina Arnold, eds., *From the Ground Up: Beyond Gender in Theory in Archaeology: Proceedings of the Fifth Gender and Archaeology Conference, University of Wisconsin-Milwaukee, October 1998*, 11–22. Oxford.

———. 1999c. "The Monkey Frieze from Xeste 3, Room 4: Reconstruction and Interpretation." In Philip P Betancourt, ed., *Meletemata: Studies in Aegean Archaeology Presented to Malcolm H. Wiener as He Enters His 65th Year*, 705–709. Liège.

———. 2004. "Crocus Costumes in Aegean Art." *Hesperia Supplements* 33 (*Charis: Essays in Honor of Sara A. Immerwahr*), 85–100.

———. 2006. "Aegean Breechcloths, Kilts, and the Keftiu Paintings." *AJA* 100: 35–51.

———. 2007. "Children's Work: Girls as Acolytes in Aegean Ritual and Cult." In Ada Cohen and Jeremy B. Rutter, eds., *Constructions of Childhood in Ancient Greece and Italy*, 205–225. Princeton.

———. 2008. "Aegean Natives in the Theban Tomb Paintings: the Keftiu Revisited." In E. H. Cline and D. Harris Cline, eds., *The Aegean and the Orient in the Second Millennium* (Aegaeum 18), 39–50. Liège.

Rehak, Paul and John G. Younger. 1998. "Review of Aegean PrehistoryVII: Neopalatial, Final Palatial, and Postpalatial Crete." *AJA* 102: 91–173.

Reinholdt, Claus. 2008. *Der frühbronzezeitliche Schmuckhortfund von Kap Kolonna: Ägina und die Ägäis im Goldzeitalter des 3. Jahrtausends v. Chr.* Vienna.

Renfrew, Colin. 1986. "The Prehistoric Maltese Achievement and Its Interpretation." In Anthony Bonnano, ed., *Archaeology and Fertility Cult in the Ancient Mediterranean*, 118–130. Amsterdam.

Rethemiotakis, Giorgos. 2020. "Tylissians and Knossians: An Interactive Relationship; New Evidence on the Miniature Wall Paintings from Tylissos." In Blakolmer, ed., *Current Approaches and New Perspectives in Aegean Iconography (Aegis 18)*, 117–142.

Reusch, H. 1956. *Rekonstruktion des Frauenfrieses von Theben.* Berlin.

Rizzo, Maria Antonietta, and Marina Martelli. 1988/89. "Un incunabolo del mito greco in Etruria." *ASAtene* 66/67: 7–56.

Robbins, Emmet. 1975. "Jason and Cheiron: The Myth of Pindar's Fourth Pythian." *Phoenix* 29: 205–213.

Robertson, D. S. 1940. "The Flight of Phrixus." *CR* 54: 1–8.

Robertson, Martin. 1967. "Conjectures in Polygnotus' Troy." *BSA* 62: 5–12.

Robkin, A. L. H. 1981. "The Endogram *WE* on Mycenaean Textiles *146 and *166 + *WE*: A Proposed Identification." *AJA* 85: 213.

Rodenwaldt, Gerhart. 1912. *Tiryns II, DieFresken des Palastes.* Athens.

Roisman, Hannah. M. 2005. "Nestor the Good Counsellor." *CQ* 55: 17–38.

Rose, Charles Brian. 2003. *The Archaeology of Greek and Roman Troy.* Cambridge.

Ross, Charles Stanley. 2004. *Publius Papinius Statius: The Thebaid and Seven Against Thebes.* Baltimore.

Rougemont, Françoise. 2009. *Contrôle économique et administration à l'époque des palais mycéniens (fin du IIe millénaire av. J.-C.).* Athens.

———. 2014. "Sheep Rearing, Wool Production and Management in Mycenaean Written Documents." In Breniquet and Michel, eds., *Wool Economy in the Ancient Near East and the Aegean*, 340–370.

Rousioti, Dimitra. 2016. "Sharing Images, Shaping Power in the Periphery: The Influence of the Mycenaean Palatial System in the Iconography of the Late Bronze Age Thessaly." *Anodos* 12: 233–242.

Ruijgh, C. J. 1998-1999. "The Social Status of Persons Indicated by Possessive Adjectives in *-E-Jo*, with Some Linguistic Observations." In Bennet and Driesen, eds., *A-na-qo-ta*, 251–272.

References

————. 2011. "Mycenaean and Homeric Language." In Yves Duhoux and Anna Morpurgo Davies, eds., *A Companion to Linear B: Mycenaean Greek Texts and their World*, 255–298. Louvain-la Neuve.

Ruscillo, Deborah. 2005a. "Faunal Remains and Murex Dye Production." In Joseph W. Shaw and Maria C. Shaw, eds., *Kommos V: The Monumental Minoan Buildings at Kommos*, 776–844. Princeton.

————. 2005b. "Reconstructing Murex Royal Purple and Biblical Blue in the Aegean." In Daniella E. Bar-Yosef Mayer, ed., *Archaeomalacology: Molluscs in Former Environments of Human Behaviour*, 99–106. Oxford.

Rutherford, Ian. 2013. "Mycenaean Religion." In Michele Renee Salzman, ed., *The Cambridge History of Religions in the Ancient World*, 256–279. Cambridge

————. 2019. "From Zalpuwa to Brauron: Hittite-Greek Religious Convergence on the Black Sea." In Sandra Blakely and Billie Jean Collins, eds., *Religious Convergence in the Ancient Mediterranean*, 391–410. Atlanta.

Rutter, Jeremy B. 2014. "Reading Post-Palatial Mycenaean Iconography: Some Lessons from Lefkandi." In Galanakis, Wilkinson, and Bennet, eds., *Athyrmata*, 197–205.

Säflund, Gösta. 1981. "Cretan and Theran Questions." In Hägg and Marinatos, eds., *Sanctuaries and Cults in the Aegean Bronze Age*, 189–208.

Şahoğlu, Vasif. 2005. "The Anatolian Trade Network and the Izmir Region during the Early Bronze Age." *OJA* 24: 339–361.

Salvati, Luisa, and Luana Costenza. 2017. "Creativity and Business: The Localization of *Made in Italy*." In Giovanna Motta and Antonello Biagini, eds., *Fashion Through History: Costumes, Symbols, Communication (Volume II)*, 144–153. Cambridge.

Samson, A. Olivier. 2021. "Multiple Sequence Alignment of Libation Formulae Suggest Linear A is Minoan-Greek." Available for download at SSRN: https://ssrn.com/abstract=3907913 or http://dx.doi.org/10.2139/ssrn.3907913. Accessed September 9, 2021.

Sansone, David. 1988. "The Survival of the Bronze-Age Demon." *ICS* 13: 1–17.

Scafoglio, Giampiero. 2013. "The Betrayal of Aeneas." *GRBS* 53: 1–14.

Schoep, Ilse. 2004. "Assessing the Role of Architecture in Conspicuous Consumption in the Middle Minoan I-II Periods." *OJA* 23: 243–269.

Schoep, Ilse, Peter Tomkins, and Jan Driessen, eds. 2012. *Back to the Beginning: Reassessing Social and Political Complexity on Crete during the Early and Middle Bronze Age*. Oxford.

Schofield, Elizabeth. 1996. "Wash and Brush Up at the 'Travellers' Rest': The Caravanserai Reconsidered." In Evely, Lemos, and Sherratt, eds., *Minotaur and Centaur*, 27–33.

Schweizer, Beat. 2006. *Griechen und Phöniker am Tyrrhenischen Meer: Repräsentationen kultureller Interaktion im 8. und 7. Jh. v. Chr. in Etrurien, Latium und Kampanien.* Münster.

Scodel, Ruth. 1982. "The Achaean Wall and the Myth of Destruction." *HSPh* 86: 33–50.

Scott, John A. 1913. "Paris and Hector in Tradition and in Homer." *CP* 8: 160–171.

Seager, Richard B. 1912. *Explorations in the Island of Mochlos.* Boston.

Seaton, R. C. 1887. "The Symplegades and the Planctae." *AJP* 8: 433–440.

Segal, Charles Paul. 1962. "The Phaeacians and the Symbolism of Odysseus' Return." *Arion* 1: 17–64.

Selden, Daniel L. 1998. "Alibis." *ClAnt* 17n2: 289–412.

Sgouritsa, Naya. 2011. "Remarks on the Use of Plaster in Tholos Tombs at Mycenae. Hypotheses on the Origin of the Painted Decoration of Tombs in Mainland Greece." In Helen Cavanagh, William Cavanagh, and James Roy, eds., *Honouring the Dead in the Peloponnese: Proceedings of the Conference Held at Sparta 23-25 April 2009*, 737–754. CSPS Online Publication 2. Nottingham. https://www.nottingham.ac.uk/csps/documents/honoringthedead/sgouritsa.pdf.

Shank, Elizabeth B. 2007. "Throne Room Griffins from Pylos and Knossos." In Betancourt, Nelson, and Williams, eds., *Krinoi kai Limenes*, 159–165.

———. 2012. "The Jewelry Worn by the Mature Women in Xeste 3, Akrotiri." In Nosch and Laffineur, eds., *Kosmos*, 559–565.

Shaw, Joseph W. 1978. "Evidence for the Minoan Tripartite Shrine." *AJA* 82: 429–448.

Shaw, Maria C. 1996. "The Bull-Leaping Fresco from below the Ramp House at Mycenae: A Study in Iconography and Artistic Transmission." *BSA* 91: 167–190.

———. 1998. "The Painted Plaster Reliefs from Pseira." In Philip P. Betancourt and Costas Davaras, eds., *Pseira II: Building AC (the "Shrine") and Other Buildings in Area A*, 55–76. Philadelphia.

———. 2004. "The 'Priest-King' Fresco from Knossos: Man, Woman, Priest, King, or Someone Else?" *Hesperia Supplements* 33 (*Charis: Essays in Honor of Sara A. Immerwahr*), 65–84.

———. 2010. "A Fresco of a Textile Pattern at Pylos: The Importation of a Minoan Artistic Technique." In Olga Krzyszkowska, ed., *Cretan Offerings: Studies in Honour of Peter Warren*, 315–320. London.

Shaw, Maria C., and Anne P. Chapin. 2016a. "Palace and Household Textiles in Aegean Bronze Age Art." In Shaw and Chapin, eds., *Woven Threads*, 105–131.

References

————. 2016b. "Sailing the Shining Sea: Maritime Textiles of the Bronze Age Aegean." In Shaw and Chapin, eds., *Woven Threads*, 149–181.

————, eds. 2016c. *Woven Threads: Patterned Textiles of the Aegean Bronze Age.* Oxford.

Shaw, Maria C., and Kessa Laxton. 2002. "Minoan and Mycenaean Wall Hangings: New Light from a Wall Painting at Ayia Triada." *CretAnt* 3: 93–104.

Shelmerdine, Cynthia W. 1985. *The Perfume Industry of Mycenaean Pylos.* Göteborg.

————. 1995. "Shining and Fragrant Cloth in Homeric Epic." In Jane B. Carter and Sarah P. Miles, eds., *The Ages of Homer: A Tribute to Emily Townsend Vermeule*, 99–107. Austin.

————. 1998. "Where Do We Go from Here? And How Do the Linear B Tablets Help Us to Get There?" In Cline and Harris Cline, eds., *The Aegean and the Orient in the Second Millennium*, 291–299.

————. 2007. "Administration in the Mycenaean Palaces: Where's the Chief?" In Galaty and Parkinson, eds., *Rethinking Mycenaean Palaces II*, 40–46.

————. 2011. "The Individual and the State in Mycenaean Greece." *BICS* 54: 19–28.

————. 2016. "Women in the Mycenean Economy." In Budin and Turfa, eds., *Women in Antiquity*, 617–634.

Shelton, Kim S. 2002–2003. "A New Linear B Tablet from Petsas House, Mycenae." *Minos*, 37–38, 387–396.

Sherratt, Susan. 1996. "With Us but Not of Us: The Role of Crete in Homeric Epic." In Evely, Lemos, and Sherrat, eds., *Minotaur and Centaur*, 87–99.

————. 2001. "Potemkin Palaces and Route-Based Economics." In Voutsaki and Killen, eds., *Economy and Politics in the Mycenaean Palace States*, 214–254.

Shoep, Ilse. 2011. "The Minoan 'Palace-Temple' Reconsidered: A Critical Assessment of the Spatial Concentration of Political, Religious and Economic Power in Bronze Age Crete." *JMA* (2010) 23n2: 219–44.

Siegelova, Jana, and Hidetoshi Tsumoto. 2011. "Metals and Metallurgy in Hittite Anatolia." In Hermann Genz and Dirk Paul Mielke, eds., *Insights Into Hittite History and Archaeology*, 275–300. Leuven.

Silver, Morris. 1983. *Prophets and Markets: The Political Economy of Ancient Israel.* Boston.

————. 1984. *Enterprise and the Scope of the Firm: The Role of Vertical Integration.* Oxford.

————. 1991. "The Commodity Composition of Trade in the Argonaut Myth." In Morris Silver, ed., *Ancient Economy in Mythology: East and West*, 241–282. Savage, MD.

————. 1992. *Taking Ancient Mythology Economically.* Leiden.

————. 1995a. *Economic Structures of Antiquity.* Westport, CT.

———. 1995b. "Prophets and Markets Revisited." In K. D. Irani and Morris Silver, eds., *Social Justice in the Ancient World*, 179–198. Westport, CT.

———. 2006a. "Public, Palace, and Profit in the Ancient Near East." *Akkadica* 127: 6–12.

———. 2006b. "'Coinage Before Coins?': A Further Response to Raz Kletter." *Levant* 38: 193–195.

———. 2007. "Review of *The Cambridge Economic History of the Greco-Roman World*." Edited by Walter Scheidel, Ian Morris, and Richard Saller. *JEH* 71: 260–267.

———. 2009a. "Must Frequently Performed Economic Services Have Distinctive Names? A Probe of Finley's Hypothesis." *Historia* 58: 246–256.

———. 2009b. "The Role of International Trade in the Transformation of Attica's Agricultural Organization: From Solon to Socrates." *MBAH* 27: 95–162.

———. 2009c. "Glimpses of Vertical Integration/Disintegration in Ancient Rome." *AncSoc* 39: 171–184.

———. 2011a. "Transaction/Administrative Costs in Greco-Roman Antiquity, With Special Reference to the Implications of Atheism/Naturalism in Classical Athens." *MBAH* 29: 49–92.

———. 2011b. "Contractual Slavery in the Roman Economy." *AHB* 25: 73–132.

———. 2013a. "*Macula Servitutis*: The Selective Stain of Roman Slavery." *Hephaistos* 30: 53–61.

———. 2013b. "Vertical Integration/Disintegration in the Roman Economy: A Reply to Wim Broekaert." *AncSoc* 43: 309–315.

———. 2014a. "Vertical Integration Again: Another Reply to Wim Broekaert." *AncSoc* 44: 347–349.

———. 2014b. "Autonomous Slaves in Greco-Roman Legal and Economic History." *ELR* 3: 231–266.

———. 2014c. "The Market for Uncertainty Bearing in Roman Egypt." *BICS* 57: 39–48.

———. 2015a. "'Living Apart,' Apeleutheroi and Paramone-Clause: A Response to Canevaro and Lewis." *IncidAntico* 13: 139–161.

———. 2015b. "Imperialism in the Emergence of Roman Gaul: Pouring Ancient Wine into Discarded Bottles." *MBAH* 33: 33–55.

———. 2016a. "Public Slaves in the Roman Army: An Exploratory Study." *AncSoc* 46: 203–240.

———. 2016b. "At the Base of Rome's Peculium Economy." *Fundamina* 22: 67–93.

———. 2018. *Slave-Wives, Single Women and 'Bastards' in the Ancient Greek World: Law and Economics Perspectives*. Oxford.

———. 2019. *Sacred Prostitution in the Ancient Greek World: From Aphrodite to Baubo to Cassandra and Beyond*. Münster.

Simon, Erika. 1976. *Die griechischen Vasen*. Munich.

References

Simon, Zsolt. 2018. "Anatolian Influences on Greek." In Niesiolowski-Spanò and Węcowski, eds., *Change, Continuity, and Connectivity*, 76–418.

Singer, Graciela Gestoso. 2013. "The Gold and Silver Hoard from Tell El-Amarna." *AuOr* 31: 249–259.

Singer, Itamar. 2006. "Ships Bound for Lukka: A New Interpretation of the Companion Letters RS 94.2530 and RS 94.2523." *AF* 33: 244–262.

———. 2008. "Purple-Dyers in Lazpa." In Collins, Bachvarova, and Rutherford, eds., *Anatolian Interfaces*, 21–43.

Singor, H. W. 1992. "The Achaean Wall and the Seven Gates of Thebes." *Hermes* 120: 401–411.

Sist, Evina. 2013. "Mapping Counterfactuality in Apollonius' *Argonautica*." In Marios Skempis, and Ioannis Ziogas, eds., *Geography, Topography, Landscape: Configurations of Space in Greek and Roman Epic*, 161–180. Berlin.

Skelton, Christina. 2011. "A Look at Early Mycenean Textile Administration in the Pylos Megaron Tablets." *Kadmos* 50: 101–121.

Skempis, Marios, and Ioannis Ziogas. 2009. "Arētē's Words: Etymology, *Ehoie*-Poetry and Gendered Narrative in the Odyssey." In Grethlein and Rengakos, eds., *Narratology and Interpretation*, 213–240.

Skutch, Otto. 1987. "Helen, Her Name and Nature." *JHS* 107: 188–193.

Smith, C.J. 1999. "Medea in Italy: Barter and Exchange in the Archaic Mediterranean." In Gocha R. Tsetskhladze, ed., *Ancient Greeks, East and West*, 179–206. Leiden.

Smith, Joanna S. and Iris Tzachili. 2012. "Cloth in Crete and Cyprus." In Gerald Cadogan et al., eds., *Parallel Lives: Ancient Island Societies in Crete and Cyprus*, 141–155. London.

Smoot, Guy. 2012. "Did the Helen of the Homeric Odyssey ever go to Troy?" Available at: https://chs.harvard.edu/ guy-smoot-did-the-helen-of-the-homeric-odyssey-ever-go-to-troy/

———. 2016. "Helenos and the Polyphyletic Etymologies of Helen." Available at https://classical-inquiries.chs.harvard.edu/helenos-and-the-polyphyletic-etymologies-of-helen/.

Soetens, Steven, Apostolos Sarris, and Sofia Topouzi. 2001. "Peak Sanctuaries in the Minoan Cultural Landscape." In Alexes Kalokairinos, ed., *9th International Congress of Cretan Studies: Elounda, 1-6 October 2001*, 2–12. Herakleio.

Soles, Jeffrey S., Thomas M. Brogan, and Sevi Triantaphyllou. 2008. *Mochlos IIA: Period IV, The Mycenaean Settlement and Cemetery: The Sites*. Prehistory Monographs 23. Philadelphia.

———. 2010. "Evidence for Ancestor Worship in Minoan Crete: New Finds from Mochlos." *BSAStud* 18: 331–338.

―――. 2012. "Mochlos Boats." In Mantzourani and Betancourt, eds., *PHILISTOR*, 187–199.

―――. 2016a. "Hero, Goddess, Priestess: New Evidence for Minoan Religion and Social Organization." In Alram-Stern, Blakolmer, Deger-Jalkotzy, Laffineur, and Weilhartner, eds., *Metaphysis*, 247–253.

―――. 2016b. "The Symbolism of Certain Minoan/Mycenaean Beads from Mochlos." In Alram-Stern, Blakolmer, Deger-Jalkotzy, Laffineur, and Weilhartner, eds., *Metaphysis*, 457–461.

Sotiropoulou, Sophia, et al. 2021. "Review and New Evidence on the Molluscan Purple Pigment Used in the Early Late Bronze Age Aegean Wall Paintings." *Heritage* 4: 171–187.

Soulioti, Eleni. 2016. "The Social Role of Minoan Symbols." Unpublished Ph.D dissertation. Durham University, Durham, UK.

Spantidaki, Youlie, and Christophe Moulherat. 2012. "Greece." In Margarita Gleba and Olla Mannering, eds., *Textiles and Textile Production from Prehistory to AD 400*, 185–200. Oxford.

Speidel, Michael P. 1993. "The *Fustis* as a Soldier's Weapon." *AntAfr* 39:137–149.

Spyropoulos, Theodoros G. and John Chadwick. 1975. *The Thebes Tablets II*. Salamanca.

Stampolides, Nikolaos Chr., Athanasia Kanta, and Angeliki Giannikoure, eds. 2012. *Athanasia: The Earthly, the Celestial and the Underworld in the Mediterranean from the Late Bronze and the Early Iron Age*. International Archeological Conference, Rhodes 28-31 May, 2009. Herakleion.

Starr, Chester G. 1984. "Minoan Flower Lovers." In Robin Hägg and Nanno Marinatos, eds., *The Minoan Thalassocracy: Myth and Reality*, 9–12. Stockholm.

Steel, Louise. 1994. "Representations of a Shrine on a Mycenaean Chariot Krater from Kalavasos-Ayios Dhimitrios, Cyprus." *BSA* 89: 201–211.

―――. 1998. "The Social Impact of Mycenaean Imported Pottery in Cyprus." *BSA* 93: 285–296.

―――. 2020. " 'Little Women': Gender, Performance, and Gesture in Mycenaean Female Figurines." *JAnthropolArchaeol.* 58: 1–15.

Steele, Phillippa M. 2020. "Literacy in Mycenaean Greece." In Lemos and Kotsonas, eds., *A Companion to the Archaeology of Early Greece and the Mediterranean*, 248–269.

Stein-Hölkeskamp, Elke. 1989. *Adelskultur und Polisgesellschaft: Studien zum griechischen Adel in archaischer und klassischer Zeit*. Stuttgart.

Steiner, Gerd. 2007. "The Case of Wilusa and Ahhiyawa." *BiOr* 64: 590–611.

Steinmann, Bernhard F. 2020. "The Chamber Tombs at Prosymna: A New Social and Political Interpretation for a Group of Tombs." *Hesperia* 89: 379–412.

Stevens, Fay, and Anna Simanddiraki-Grimshaw. 2016. "Composite, Partial, Created and Floating Bodies: A Re-Assessment of the Knossos Temple Repositories." In Mina, Triantaphyllou, and Papadatos, eds., *An Archaeology of Prehistoric Bodies and Embodied Identities in the Eastern Mediterranean*, 25–31.

Stocker, Sharon R., and Jack L. Davis. 2020. "An Early Mycenaean Wanax at Pylos? On Genii and Sun-Disks from the Grave of the Griffin Warrior." In Blakolmer, ed., *Current Approaches and New Perspectives in Aegean Iconography (Aegis 18)*, 293–298.

Stokl, Jonathan. 2013. "Gender Ambiguity in Ancient Near Eastern Prophecy? A Re-Assessment of the Data Behind a Popular Theory." In Corinne L. Carvalho and Jonathan Stökl, eds., *Prophets Male and Female: Gender and Prophecy in the Hebrew Bible, the Eastern Mediterranean, and the Ancient Near East*, 59–79. Atlanta.

Stöllner, Thomas, and Irina Gambashidze. 2011. "Gold in Georgia II: The Oldest Gold Mine in the World." In Ünsal Yalçın, ed., *Anatolian Metal V*, 187–199. Bochum.

Strand, Eva Andersson, and Marie-Louise Nosch. 2015a. "Summary of Results and Conclusion." In *Tools, Textiles and Contexts*, 351–383.

———, eds. 2015b. *Tools, Textiles and Contexts: Investigating Textile Production in the Aegean and Eastern Mediterranean Bronze Age*. Oxford.

Suchowska, Paulina. 2009. "Communication Space of the Northern Pontic Area as Viewed by Aegeans." *BPS* 14: 156–175.

Sukenik, Naama, Alexander Varvak, Zohar Amar, and David Iluz. 2015. "Chemical Analysis of Murex-dyed Textiles from Wadi Murabba'at, Israel." *JArchaeolSciRep* 3: 565–570.

Surtees, Allison. 2014. "Satyrs as Women and Maenads as Men: Transvestites and Transgression in Dionysian Worship." In Avramidou and Demetriou, 281–93.

Susmann, Natalie M. 2015. "Preliminary Approaches for the Identification and Classification of Mediterranean Murex Dye Production Sites." *ATR* 57: 89–103.

Swanson, Roy Arthur. 1974. *Pindar's Odes*. Indianapolis.

Tamvaki, Angela. 1974. "The Seals and Sealings from the Citadel House Area: A Study in Mycenaean Glyptic and Iconography." *BSA* 69: 259–293.

Taracha, Piotr. 2018. "Approaches to Mycenaean-Hittite Interconnections in the Late Bronze Age." In Niesiolowski-Spanò and Wecowski, eds., *Change, Continuity, and Connectivity*, 8–22

Tartaron, Thomas F. 2013. *Maritime Networks in the Mycenaean World*. New York.

Taylor, Lilly Ross. 1935. "The *Sellisternium* and the Theatrical *Pompa*." *CP* 30: 122–130.

Teffeteller, Annette. 2013. "Singers of Lazpa: Reconstructing Identities on Bronze Age Lesbos." In Alice Mouton, Ian Rutherford, and Ilya S. Yakubovich, eds., *Luwian Identities: Culture, Language and Religion between Anatolia and the Aegean*, 567–589. Leiden.

Thavapalan, Shiyanthi. 2018. "Purple Fabrics and Garments in Akkadian Documents." *JANEH* 3: 1–27 [online publication].

Thomas, Carol G. 2005. *Finding People in Early Greece*. Columbia, MO.

Thomas, Carol G., and Michael Wedde. 2001. "Desperately Seeking Potnia." In Laffineur and Hägg, eds., *Potnia*, 3–14.

Thomas, Nancy R. 2004. "The Early Mycenaean Lion Up to Date." *Hesperia Supplements* 33 (*Charis: Essays in Honor of Sara A. Immerwahr*), 161–206.

Thomas, Richard F. 1982. "Catullus and the Polemics of Poetic Reference (Poem 64.1-18)." *AJP* 103: 144–164.

Tiverios, Michalis. 2014. "Phrixos' Self-sacrifice and his 'Euphemia'." In Avramidou and Demetriou, 105–116.

Tournavitou, Iphiyenia, Eva Andersson Strand, Marie-Louise Nosch, and Joanne Cutler. 2015. "Textile Production at Mycenae, Mainland Greece." In Andersson Strand and Nosch, eds., *Tools, Textiles and Contexts*, 253–265.

Treister, Michail Yu. 1996. "The Trojan Treasures: Description, Chronology. Historical Context." In Tolstikov and Treister, *The Gold of Troy*, 197–232.

Tolstikov, Vladimir, and Michail Yu Treister. 1996. *The Gold of Troy: Searching for Homer's Fabled City*. New York.

Tomkins, Peter, and Ilse Schoep. 2010. "Crete." In Cline, ed., *The Oxford Handbook of the Bronze Age Aegean*, 66–82.

Tomlinson, R. A. 1972. *Argos and the Argolid: From the End of the Bronze Age to the Roman Occupation*. London.

Touchais, Gilles, Robert Laffineur, and Françoise Rougemont, eds. 2014. *Physis: l'environnement naturel et la relation homme-milieu dans le monde égéen proto-historique: actes de la 14e Rencontre égéenne internationale, Paris, Institut National d'Histoire de l'Art (INHA), 11-14 décembre 2012*. Leuven.

Tournavitou, Iphiyenia. 2017. *The Wall Paintings of the West House at Mycenae*. Philadelphia.

Trnka, Edith. 2007. "Similarities and Distinctions of Minoan and Mycenaean Textiles." In Gillis and Nosch, eds., *Ancient Textiles*, 127–129.

Tsagalis, Christos. 2008. *The Oral Palimpsest: Exploring Intertextuality in the Homeric Epics*. Hellenic Studies Series 29. Washington, DC.

———. 2017. *Early Greek Epic Fragments I: Antiquarian and Genealogical Epic*. Berlin.

Tsagrakis, Aggelos. 2012. "Furniture, Precious Items and Materials Recorded in the Linear B Archives." *SMEA* 54: 323–341.

Tsipopoulou, Metaxia. 2016. "Potter's Marks." In Metaxia Tsipopoulou, ed., *Petras, Siteia I: A Minoan Palatial Settlement in Eastern Crete. Excavation of Houses I.1 and I.2*, 138–160. Philadelphia PA.

Tsitsibakou-Vasalos, Evanthia. 1986. "Two Homeric Formulae in the P. Lille Poem." *Glotta* 64: 165–184.

Tully, Caroline. 2020. "Cockles, Mussels, Fishing Nets, and Finery: The Relationship between Cult, Textiles, and the Sea Depicted on a Minoan-Style Gold Ring from Pylos." *JEMAHS*, 3–4, 365–378.

Tully, Caroline, and Sam Crooks. 2020. "Enthroned Upon Mountains: Constructions of Power in the Aegean Bronze Age." In Liat Naeh and Dana Brostowsky Gilboa, eds., *The Ancient Throne: The Mediterranean, Near East, and Beyond, from the 3rd Millennium BCE to the 14th Century CE. Proceedings of the Workshop Held at the 10th ICAANE in Vienna, April 2016*, 37–57. Vienna.

Turfa, J. Macintosh, and A. G. Steinmayer Jr. 1999. "The Earliest Foresail, on another Etruscan Vase." *IJNA* 28: 292–296.

Tzachili, Iris. 1990. "All Important Yet Elusive: Looking for Evidence of Cloth-Making at Akrotire." In D. A. Hardy, ed., *Thera and the Aegean World III. I, Archaeology*, 380–387. London.

Tzachili, Iris, Stella Spantidaki, Eva Andersson Strand, Marie-Louise Nosch, and Joanne Cutler. 2015. "Textile Tools from Akrotiri, Thera, Greece." In Andersson Strand and Nosch, eds., *Tools, Textiles and Contexts*, 243–246

Tzagrakis, Angelos. 2016. "The *wa-na-ka – (F)anaxs- anax*." *Pasiphae* 10: 201–216.

Uchitel, Alexander. 1984. "Women at Work." *Historia* 33: 257–282.

Ulanowska, Agata. 2017. "Textile Technology and Minoan Glyptic Representations of Loom Weights on Middle Minoan Prismatic Seals." In Katarzyna Żebrowska, Agata Ulanowska, and Kazimierz Lewartowski, eds., *Symposium Egeiskie: Papers in Aegean Archaeology*, I, 57–65 + Plates. Warsaw.

———. 2018. "But How Were They Made? More about Patterned Textiles in the Aegean Bronze Age." In Jerzy Maik and Piotr Strrzyż, eds., *Dynamics and Organisation of Textile Production in Past Societies in Europe and the Mediterranean*. FASCICULI ARCHAEOLOGIAE HISTORICAE FASC. XXXI, Lodz: Instytut Archeologii i Etnologii PAN, Warszawa and Polska Akademia Nauk, Oddział w Łodzi, 39–54.

Ulanowska, Agata, and Malgorzata Siennicka. 2018. "The Economics of Textiles in Bronze Age Greece." In Maria Stella Busana, Margarita Gleba, Francesco Meo and Anna Rosa Tricomi, eds., *Textiles and Dyes in the Mediterranean Economy and Society. PURPUREAE VESTES VI Textiles and Dyes in Antiquity*,

39–48. Proceedings of the VIth International Symposium on Textiles and Dyes in the Ancient Mediterranean World. Zaragoza.

Ustinova, Yulia. 2004. "Jason the Shaman." In Jörg Gebauer, Eva Grabow, Frank Jünger, and Dieter Metzler, eds., *Bildergeschichte: Festschrift Klaus Stähler*, 507–514. Möhnesee.

Van Damme, Trevor Matthew. 2017. "Life after the Palaces: A Household Archaeology Approach to Mainland Greece during Late Helladic IIIC." Unpublished PhD dissertation. University of California, Los Angeles, Los Angeles, CA.

Van de Moortel, Aleydis. 2007. "The Site of Mitrouand East Lokris in 'Homeric Times'." In Morris and Laffineur, eds., *Epos*, 243–254.

Van der Meer, L. Bouke. 2011. *Etrusco Ritu: Case Studies in Etruscan Ritual Behavior*. Louvain.

Varias, Garcia Carlos. 1998–1999. "The Personal Names from the Knossos B-Tablets and the Mycenae Tablets." In Bennet and Driessen, eds., *A-na-qo-ta*, 349–370.

———. 2012. "The Word for 'Honey' and Connected Terms in Mycenaean Greek." In Carlier, ed, *Études mycéniennes*, 403–418.

———. 2017. "Mycenaean Terms with the Ttem /*XENWOS*/: 'Foreigner, Guest, Host'." In Marie-Louise Nosch and Hedvig Landenius Enegren, eds., *Aegean Scripts: Proceedings of the 14th International Colloquium on Mycenaean Studies, Copenhagen, 2-5 September 2015*, 417–427. Rome.

Veenhof, Klaas R. 1972. *Aspects of Old Assyrian Trade and Its Terminology*. Leiden.

———. 2010. "Ancient Assur: The City, Its Traders, and Its Commercial Network." *JESHO* 53: 39–82.

Ventris, Michael, and John Chadwick. 1973. *Documents in Mycenaean Greek III: Additional Commentary*. Cambridge.

Verduci, Josephine, and Brent Davis. 2015. "Adornment, Ritual, and Identify: Inscribed Minoan Jewellery." *BSA* 110: 51–70.

Verhulst, Astrid. 2015. "An Old Babylonian Seal from Sippar with Trading Owners." *JNES* 74: 255–265.

Vetters, Melissa. 2011. "Seats of Power? Making the Most of Miniatures—The Role of Terracotta Throne Models in Disseminating Mycenaean Religious Ideology." In Walter Gauß, Michael Lindblom, R. Angus K. Smith, and James C. Wright, eds., *Our Cups Are Full: Pottery and Society in the Aegean Bronze Age Papers Presented to Jeremy B. Rutter on the Occasion of his 65th Birthday*, 319–330. Oxford.

———. 2016. "All the Same Yet Not Identical? Mycenaean Terracotta Figurines in Context." In Alram-Stern, Blakolmer, Deger-Jalkotzy, Laffineur, and Weilhartner, eds., *Metaphysis*, 37–48.

References

Villing, Alexandra, ed. 2005. *The Greeks in the East*. London.

Vlachopoulos, Andreas G. 2007. "*Mythos, Logos* and *Eikon*: Motifs of Early Greek Poetry in the Wall Paintings of Xeste 3 at Akrotiri, Thera." In Morris and Laffineur, eds., *Epos*, 107–118.

———. 2016. "Purple Rosettes/Πορφυροί ρόδακες: New Data on Polychromy and Perception in the Thera Wall Paintings." In Koehl, ed., *Studies in Aegean Art and Culture*, 59–76.

———, ed. 2018. *Paintbrushes: Wall-Painting and Vase-Painting of the Second Millennium BC in Dialogue. Proceedings of the International Conferenceo n Aegean Iconography Held at Akrotiri, Thera, 24-26 May 2013*. Athens.

———. 2019. "Naxos in the Mycenaean Age." In Anastasia Angelopoulou (Scientific Advisor), *From Homer's World: Tenos and the Cyclades in the Mycenaean Age. Tenos, Museum of Marble Crafts, 12/7 - 14/10/2019*, 135–146. Athens.

Voutsaki, Sofia, and John T. Killen, eds. 2001. *Economy and Politics in the Mycenaean Palace States*. Cambridge.

Voyatzis, Mary. 1992. "Votive Riders Seated Side-Saddle at Early Greek Sanctuaries." *BSA* 87: 259–279.

Wachsmann, Shelley. 1987. *Aegeans in the Theban Tombs*. Leuven.

Wagner-Hasel, Beate. 2002. "The Graces and Colour Weaving." In Lloyd Llewellyn-Jones, ed., *Women's Dress in the Ancient Greek World*, 17–32. London.

———. 2020. *The Fabric of Gifts: Culture and Politics of Giving and Exchange in Archaic Greece*. Lincoln, NE.

Walters, H. B. 1892–1893. "Poseidon's Trident." *JHS* 13: 13–20.

Ward, Matthew. 2019. "Glory of *Nostos*: The Ship-Epithet *Koilos* in the *Iliad*." *CQ* 69: 23–34.

Warren, Peter. 1985. "The Fresco of the Garlands from Knossos." *BCHSupp* 11: 187–208.

———. 1988. *Minoan Religion as Ritual Action*. Gothenburg.

———. 1989. *The Aegean Civilizations*. 2nd ed. New York.

Watkins, Calvert. 1986. "The Language of the Trojans." In Mellink, ed., *Troy and the Trojan War*, 45–62.

———. 1998. "Homer and Hittite Revisited." In Peter Knox and Clive Foss, eds., *Style and Tradition: Essays in Honor of Wendell Clausen*, 201–211. Stuttgart.

———. 2000. "A Distant Anatolian Echo in Pindar: The Origin of the Aegis Again." *HSPh* 100: 1–14.

Watrous, Vance. 1991. "The Origin and Iconography of the Late Minoan Painted Larnax. *Hesperia* 60: 285–307.

Wedde, Michael. 2005. "The Mycenaean Galley in Context: From Fact to *Idée Fixe*." In Laffineur and Greco, eds., *Emporia*, 29–37.

van Wees, Hans. 2005. "Clothes, Class and Gender in Homer." In Douglas Cairns, ed., *Body Language in the Greek and Roman Worlds*, 1–36. Swansea.

Weinberg, Saul S. 1968. "A Gold Sauceboat in the Israel Museum." *AntK* 12: 3–8.

Weilhartner, Jörg. 2012. "Religious Offerings in the Linear B Tablets: An Attempt at Their Classification and Some Thoughts about their Possible Purpose." In Carlos Varias García, ed., *Actas del Simposio Internacional: 55 Años de Micenología (1952-2007)*, 207–231. Bellaterra.

———. 2013. "Textual Evidence for Aegean Late Bronze Age Ritual Processions." *Opuscula* 6: 151–173.

———. 2017. "The Interrelationship between Mycenaeans and Foreigners." In Oller, Pàmias, and Varias, eds., *Tierra, territorio y población en la Grecia antigua*, I 151–168.

———. 2019. "'The Use of 'Heirlooms' in Mycenaean Sealing Practices." In Borgna, Caloi, Carinci, and Laffineur, eds., *MNHMH/MNEME*, 497–505.

Weilhartner, Jörg, and Florian Ruppenstein, eds. 2015. *Tradition and Innovation in the Mycenaean Palatial Polities: Proceedings of an International Symposium Held at the Austrian Academy of Sciences, Institute for Oriental and European Archaeology, Aegean and Anatolia Department, Vienna, 1-2 March, 2013.* Vienna.

Weingarten, Judith. 1989a. "Old and New Elements in the Seals and Sealings of the Temple Repository, Knossos." In Robert Laffineur, ed., *Transition: le monde égéen du Bronze moyen au Bronze récent: actes de la deuxième Rencontre égéenne internationale de l'Université de Liège (18-20 avril 1988)*, 39–47. Liège.

———. 1989b. "Formulaic Implications of Some Late Bronze Age Three-Sided Prisms." In Ingo Pini, ed., *Fragen und Probleme der bronzezeitlichen agaischen Glyptik: Beiträge zum 3. Internationalen Marburger Siegel-Symposium 5.-7. September 1985*, 299–313. Heidelberg.

———. 1997. "Another Look at Lerna: An EH IIB Trading Post?" *OJA* 16: 147–166.

———. 2010. "Minoan Seals and Sealing." In Cline, ed., *The Oxford Handbook of the Bronze Age Aegean*, 317–328.

———. 2017. "When One Equals One: The Minoan Roundel." In Jasing, Anna Margherita, Judith Weingarten, and Silvia Ferrara, eds., *Non-scribal Communication Media in the Bronze Age Aegean and Surrounding Areas: The Semantics of A-literate and Proto-literate Media (Seals, Potmarks, Mason's Marks, Seal-impressed Pottery, Ideograms and Logograms, and Related Systems)*, 100–108. Florence.

Weingarten, Judith, J. H. Crouwel, M. Prent, and G. Vogelsang-Eastwood. 1999. "Early Helladic Sealings from Geraki in Lakonia, Greece." *OJA* 18: 357–376.

Weingarten, Judith, S. Macveagh Thorne, M. Prent, and J. H. Couwel. 2011. "More Early Helladic Sealings from Geraki in Lakonia, Greece." *OJA* 30: 131–163.

Werner, Kjell. 1993. *The Megaron during the Aegean and Anatolian Bronze Age: A Study of Occurrence, Shape, Architectural Adaptation, and Function.* Jonsered.

West, Martin L. 1961. "Hesiodea." *CQ* 11: 130–145.

———. 1988. "The Rise of the Greek Epic." *JHS* 108: 151–172.

———. 1992. "The Descent of the Greek Epic: A Reply." *JHS* 112: 173–175.

———. 2001. "Atreus and Attarissiyas." *Glotta* 77: 262–266.

———. 2002. "'Eumelos': A Corinthian Epic Cycle." *JHS* 122: 109–133.

———. 2007. "Phasis and Aia." *MusHelv* 64: 193–198.

———. 2013. *The Epic Cycle: A Commentary on the Lost Troy Epics.* Oxford.

———. 2014. *The Making of the Odyssey.* Oxford.

———. 2015. "The Formation of the Epic Cycle." In Fantuzzi and Tsagalis, eds., *The Greek Epic Cycle and Its Ancient Reception*, 96–107

West, Stephanie. 1988. "Books I-IV." In Alfred Heubeck et al., *A Commentary on Homer's Odyssey I: Introduction and Books I-VIII*, 51–255. Oxford.

Whitelaw, Todd. 2012. "The Urbanisation of Prehistoric Crete: Settlement Perspectives on State Formation." In Schoep, Tomkins, and Driessen, eds., *Back to the Beginning*, 14–76.

Whittaker, Helene. 1999. "The Status of Arētē in the Phaeacian Episode of the *Odyssey*." *SymbOslo* 74: 140–150.

———. 2006. "Religious Symbolism and the Use of Gold in Burial Contexts in the Late Middle Helladic and the Early Mycenaean Periods." *SMEA* 48: 283–289.

———. 2012. "Some Reflections on the Use and Meaning of Colour in Dress and Adornment In the Aegean Bronze Age." In Nosch and Laffineur, eds., *Kosmos*, 193–198.

Wiener, Malcolm H. 2007a. "Palatial Potters in Mycenaean Greece." In Lang, Reinholdt, and Weilhartner, eds., *Stephanos Aristeios*, 271–277.

———. 2007b. "Homer and History: Old Questions, New Evidence." In Morris and Laffineur, eds., *Epos*, 3–33.

———. 2016. "Beyond the Versailles Effect: Mycenaean Greece and Minoan Crete." In Driessen, ed., *RA-PI-NE-U*, 365–378.

Willi, Andreas. 2014. "Ares the Ripper: From Stang's Law to Long-diphthong Roots." *IndogermF* 119: 207–225.

Willms, Lothar. 2010. "On the IE Etymology of Greek (w)anax." *Glotta* 86: 232–271.

Witczak, Krzysztof Tomasz. 2011. "Dioscuri in the Mycenaean Times." *Do-so-mo* 9: 55–66.

Witton, Walter F. 1960. "The Priestess, Eritha." *AJP* 81: 415–421.

Woolsey, John M. 1917. *Symbolic Mythology and Translation of a Lost and Forgotten Language*. New York.

Woudhuizen, Fred C. 2009. "Minoan and Mycenaean Oversea's Contacts: The Epigraphic Evidence." *Dacia* 53: 5–11.

Wright, James C. 2004. "A Survey of Evidence for Feasting in Mycenaean Society." *Hesperia* 73: 133–178.

Wyatt, William F. Jr. 1992. "Homer's Linguistic Forebears." *JHS* 112: 167–173.

Xenake-Sakellariu, Agne, Friedrich Matz, Margaret A. V. Gill, and Ingo Pini, eds. 1964. *Corpus der minoischen und mykenischen Siegel: 1 Die minoischen und mykenischen Siegel des Nationalmuseums in Athen*. Berlin.

Yakar, Jak. 2008. "The Archaeology of the Kaska." *SMEA* 50: 817–826.

Yakubovich, Ilyas. 2002. "Labyrinth for Tyrants." *Studia Linguarum* 3: 93–116.

———. 2008. "Sociolinguistics of the Luvian Language." Unpublished Ph.D. dissertation. University of Chicago, Chicago, IL.

Yasur-Landau, Assaf. 2010. *The Philistines and Aegean Migration at the End of the Late Bronze Age*. Cambridge.

———. 2015. "From Byblos to Vapheio: Fenestrated Axes between the Aegean and the Levant." *BASOR* 373: 139–150.

Yiannouli, Evyenia. 2009. "The Emergence and Development of a Round Building Tradition in the Aegean and Crete." *MAA* 9: 89–113.

———. 2011. "O-pi e-de-i: On Round Building as an Archetypical Form of Sacred Space in the Aegean." *DocPraehist* 38: 221–230.

Younger, John. G. 1979. "Semi-Precious Stones to the Aegean." *ArchNews* 8: 40–44.

———. 1988. *The Iconography of Late Minoan and Mycenaean Sealstones and Finger Rings*. Bristol.

———. 1995. "Interactions between Aegean Seals and Other Minoan-Mycenaean Art Forms." In Ingo Pini and Walter Müller, eds., *Corpus der minoischen und mykenischen Siegel, Beiheft 5*, 331–348. Berlin.

———. 2009. "Tree Tugging and Omphalos Hugging on Minoan Gold Rings." In Anna Lucia D'Agata and Aleydis Van de Moortel, eds., *Archaeologies of Cult: Essays on Ritual and Cult in Honor of Geraldine G. Gesell* (*Hesperia Supplement* 42), 43–49. Athens.

———. 2016a. "Minoan Women." In Budin and Turfa, *Women in Antiquity*, 573–594.

———. 2016b. "Identifying Myth in Minoan Art." In Alram-Stern, Blakolmer, Deger-Jalkotzy, Laffineur, and Weilhartner, eds., *Metaphysis*, 433–438.

Zanker, Andreas T. 2016. "Vergil's Sheep and Simonides *PMG* 576." *Mnemosyne* 69: 301–306.

Zeman, Piotr. 2019. "Strategies of Pottery Acquisition in the Mycenaean Palace at Pylos." *Stud.Hercynia* 22: 31–55.

References

Zervos, Christian. 1956. *L'art de la Crète néolithique et minoenne.* Paris.

Zissos, Andrew. 2017. "Generic Attire: Hypsipyle's Cloaks in Valerius Flaccus and Apollonius Rhodius." In Federica Bessone and Marco Fucecchi, eds., *The Literary Genres in the Flavian Age: Canons, Transformations, Reception,* 201–227. Berlin.

Zouzoula, Evgenia. 2007. "The Fantastic Creatures of Bronze Age Crete." Unublished Ph.D. dissertation. University of Nottingham, Nottingham, UK.

Zurbach, Julien. 2016. "Aegean Economies from Bronze Age to Iron Age: Some Lines of Development, 13th–7th centuries BC." In Juan Carlos Moreno Garcia, ed., *Dynamics of Production in the Ancient Near East,* 426–438. Oxford.

Index